Feminist Approaches to Theory and Methodology

An Interdisciplinary Reader

Edited
by

SHARLENE HESSE-BIBER
Boston College

CHRISTINA GILMARTIN
Northeastern University

ROBIN LYDENBERG
Boston College

The Graduate Consortium in Women's Studies at Radcliffe

New York • Oxford
Oxford University Press
1999

Oxford University Press

Oxford   New York
Athens   Auckland   Bangkok   Bogotá   Buenos Aires   Calcutta
Cape Town   Chennai   Dar es Salaam   Delhi Florence   Hong Kong   Istanbul
Karachi   Kuala Lumpur   Madrid Melbourne   Mexico City   Mumbai
Nairobi   Paris   São Paulo   Singapore   Taipei   Tokyo   Toronto   Warsaw

and associated companies in
Berlin   Ibadan

Copyright©1999 by Oxford University Press

Published by Oxford University Press, Inc.,
198 Madison Avenue, New York, New York 10016
http://www.oup-usa.org

Library of Congress Cataloging-in-Publication Data
Feminist approaches to theory and methodology : an interdisciplinary
reader / edited by Sharlene Hesse-Biber, Christina Gilmartin, Robin Lydenberg,
p. cm.
Includes bibliographical references and index.
ISBN 0-19-512521-5 (cloth : alk. paper). — ISBN 0-19-512522-3
(pbk. : alk. paper)
1. Women's studies—Methodology. 2. Feminism—Research-
-Methodology. 3. Social sciences—Research—Methodology.
4. Feminist theory. I. Hesse-Biber, Sharlene
II. Gilmartin, Christina III. Lydenberg, Robin,
HQ1180.F43   1999
305.42'01—dc21   98-35110
                                                      CIP

9 8 7 6 5 4 3 2
Printed in the United States of America
on acid-free paper

CONTENTS

IV. Power and Resistance

V. Representations of the Body

VI. Social Policy and Female Agency

FOREWORD

From time to time in academia, shared need, individual talent, strong commitment, valued resources, and venturesome leadership align to transcend organizational and disciplinary boundaries. When they do, powerful collaborations can take hold. Fields of scholarship can gain momentum and intellectual lives can flourish. So it happened in Boston when the Graduate Consortium in Women's Studies at Radcliffe College began in 1993.

A group of brilliant feminist thinkers working in several research universities in the Boston area shared a growing concern about the paucity of opportunities for graduate-level education in women's studies. They felt keenly their own isolation in separate disciplines and institutions and longed for deeper interdisciplinary collaboration to advance their own work and women's studies scholarship. The working relationship among these faculty members turned into a friendship and this friendship generated the trust and mutual commitment necessary to risk exploration across intellectual and institutional boundaries. Together they envisioned a new institutional model that would simultaneously address the following problems in graduate education that they had identified.

For graduate students in their own institutions, as in most academic institutions, opportunities for graduate-level study in women's studies were nonexistent or limited to independent study with already overcommitted faculty members. Further, most graduate-level work was highly focused within disciplines, creating specialists ignorant of the concepts, issues, and methodologies of other disciplines and unable to see or mine the connections nascent and necessary in women's studies scholarship. The pedagogy in their institutional environments ignored the importance of combining academic knowledge with experiential knowledge to advance women's studies scholarship.

Acutely aware of early feminism's neglect of the interactions among gender, race, class, age, sexuality, and ethnicity, these scholars also sought to embed in their work a deep commitment to addressing the full range of these lenses of experience. Impatient with the pace of progress on the educational and social frontier of women's advancement, these feminist leaders recognized the importance of linking theory, policy, and practice. They also knew that their own careers, and those of junior faculty members, would depend on opportunities for development to deepen their understanding, broaden their intellectual networks, and produce new work, both in teaching and in scholarship.

The genius of this group of faculty members was their design of a consortium of scholars and teachers in which all these needs could be addressed simultaneously. What they lacked was an institutional home, financial and physical resources, and an encouraging and compatible environment. They also needed organizational expertise to negotiate with their home institutions and to help them realize their objectives in ways that would give them a firm foundation while providing academic freedom and flexibility to explore.

These faculty leaders approached Radcliffe College, a longstanding leader in women's education and research with unique resources for women's scholarship, especially in women's studies, as a possible home for this new consortium. My recent statements, as the newly installed president of Radcliffe, about my commitment to explore collaborative approaches to advance society by advancing women through education, research, and policy had caught their attention. They were also aware of my previous experiences in fostering and overseeing graduate education, interdisciplinary research, and interinstitutional collaboration in major university settings. An exciting collaborative exploration began.

As the president of Radcliffe College, I collaborated with the faculty organizers to design an organizational framework to protect institutional prerogatives and to give a faculty board authority over academic policy within a carefully articulated set of principles. Radcliffe agreed to offer credit for the completion of courses; committed space, staff, and budget; and negotiated a Memorandum of Understanding with leaders of the participating institutions.

Together the founding faculty members, from Boston College, Brandeis University, Harvard University, Massachusetts Institute of Technology, Northeastern University, and Tufts University, refined their ideas about organization, scholarship, and pedagogy and engaged their colleagues and graduate students in identifying topics and themes of greatest interest and import to serve as the basis for the development of new graduate courses. They designed the Consortium to offer exclusively new, team-taught, interdisciplinary courses at the graduate level as electives to students matriculating in graduate programs in these institutions. Committed to deep collaboration across disciplinary boundaries, the founders decided that each course would be led, not serially, but throughout the course, by two or three faculty members from different disciplines and different institutions. All courses would consider gender, race, age, class, sexuality, and ethnicity as variables and all would address the links among theory, policy and practice.

A pilot course, "Feminist Perspectives in Research: Interdisciplinary Practice in the Study of Gender," began the Consortium's offerings and came to serve as a continuing core course that evolved each year as different faculty collaborated to lead it. Additional course proposals would continue to emerge from workshops convened around interdisciplinary themes in which faculty and graduate students shared the directions and issues in their research and found collaborators to advance their scholarship and teaching in ways that penetrated disciplinary boundaries and enlarged concepts and methodological expertise.

In 1998 the Graduate Consortium in Women's Studies (GCWS) at Radcliffe College celebrated its fifth anniversary and its splendid success in bringing together Boston-area feminist scholars and teachers to advance graduate teaching and interdisciplinary scholarship in women's studies. The courses not only examine existing feminist scholarship, but they also open paths to the creation of new knowledge. They provide crucial intellectual support for students pursuing feminist work within the framework of traditional disciplines while at the same time advancing feminist pedagogy and fostering valuable faculty development.

High-quality teaching and scholarship have been hallmarks of this enterprise from the beginning. All course proposals are extensively reviewed and improved through discussion with the faculty members who comprise the Consortium Board of Directors. All courses are evaluated at their conclusion. A Visiting Committee composed of distinguished scholars from Harvard, Yale, and Princeton recently reviewed the Graduate Consortium and gave it high praise as an outstanding enterprise and a truly unique interinstitutional experiment. They called it "one of the few utopian models that have been put successfully into practice." Faculty and students alike report each semester that their work in GCWS is one of their most intellectually exciting and rewarding academic experiences.

We have reveled in the intellectual exchange and the opportunity to work together to achieve multiple goals simultaneously and well. It has been my great privilege as president of Radcliffe College to help bring this ambitious experiment to fruition and to support its continuing development. Given the success of this pioneering endeavor, Radcliffe College and the faculty who lead the GCWS have sought ways to share this valuable work more broadly. Course syllabi have been shared; workshops have been offered; and the rotating membership of the Board of Directors and changing interdisciplinary teams of faculty who teach Consortium courses bring a continuing flow of new perspectives and disseminate the work in their home institutions.

Now, with the publication of this collection of interdisciplinary essays, the first scholarly edited volume of GCWS has been produced. Prepared by Consortium faculty, this important work that is based on the "Feminist Perspectives" core course provides further testimony to the unique intellectual experiment that has occurred within our Consortium. I am especially pleased that this superbly crafted anthology will extend the international reach of the work and ideas of the Consortium and share the benefits of the commitment of the participating faculty members and their institutions, both past and present.

Linda S. Wilson
President
Radcliffe College

ACKNOWLEDGMENTS

We appreciate the help of a number of people who supported the work toward this anthology endeavor. We are indebted to the Graduate Consortium in Women's Studies (GCWS) at Radcliffe College for providing the forum for us to develop the course, "Feminist Perspectives in Research: Interdisciplinary Practice in the Study of Gender," on which this anthology is based. For their early encouragement and support of the project, we want to thank all the Board members of the GCWS as well as the faculty "Feminist Perspectives" members who have taught the course including Laura Frader, Mary Loeffelholz, and Shulamit Reinharz who created the first syllabus for the course. We are also grateful to all our students who inspired us to think and teach from an interdisciplinary perspective. For her thoughtful contributions to all stages of this project we are grateful to Laura Frader. Thanks to Alexandra Chasin, Christine Gailey, Carol Hurd Green, Jenny Sharpe, Sarah Shoenfeld, and Christopher Wilson for their research consultation and bibliographic advice. We also wish to thank Michael Black, Debra Johnston, Elena Manzelli, and Kristen McMahon for their skillful work in proofreading and copyediting the manuscript. We would particularly like to express gratitude to Renee Fall, Elena Manzelli and Kristen McMahon for their unfailing support and research assistance with the day-to-day operations of putting together an edited volume. We are most appreciative of President Linda Wilson of Radcliffe College for her encouragement and support of interdisciplinary scholarship.

CONTRIBUTORS

Susan Bordo is Professor of Philosophy and holds the Singletary Chair in the Humanities at the University of Kentucky. Her publications include *Twilight Zones: The Hidden Life of Cultural Images From Plato to O.J.* (University of California Press, 1997), *Unbearable Weight: Feminism, Western Culture, and the Body* (University of California Press, 1993), which was named one of the New York Times' Notable Books for 1993, and *The Flight to Objectivity: Essays in Cartesianism and Culture* (University of California Press, 1987). She is currently completing a book entitled *Feminist Intepretations of Rene Descartes (Re-reading the Canon)*, due in March 1999 (Penn. State University Press).

Kathleen Canning is Associate Professor of History and Women's Studies at the University of Michigan. She is the author of *Languages of Labor and Gender: Female Factory Work in Germany, 1850–1914* (Cornell University Press, 1996). She is currently working on a new book manuscript entitled *Body, Class and Citizenship: Gender in the Aftermath of War and Revolution in Germany, 1918–1930*.

Patricia Hill Collins is Professor of African-American Studies and Sociology at the University of Cincinnati, and she is a former member of the Council of the American Sociological Association. She has written *Black Feminist Thought: Knowledge, Consciousness, and the Politics of Empowerment* (Unwin Hyman, 1990), which is the winner of the C. Wright Mills Award of the Society for the Study of Social Problems. She has also written *Fighting Words: Black Women and the Search for Justice* (University of Minnesota Press, 1998).

Monique Deveaux is a doctoral student in the Faculty of Social Political Sciences at the University of Cambridge. She is interested in most aspects of moral and political philosophy, and her thesis concerns the relationship between ethical attachments and the construction of political communities. Her article on Foucault, feminism, and empowerment appears in *Feminist Studies* and is reprinted in *Feminist Interpretations of Foucault: Re-reading the Canon* (Penn. State University Press, 1996).

Heidi Hartmann is an economist and director of the Institute for Women's Policy Research (IWPR) and has written extensively on feminist theory and policy issues. Her publications include the National Research Council Report *Women, Work, and Wages: Equal Pay for Jobs of Equal Value,* co-edited with Donald Trieman (National Academy Press, 1981); articles such as "The Unhappy Marriage of Marxism and Feminism" and "Capitalism, Patriarchy, and Job Segregation by Sex"; and numerous essays and reports produced at IWPR with Roberta Spalter-Roth and others. She has recently been awarded a MacArthur Fellowship.

bell hooks is a Distinguished Professor of English at City College in New York. She is a writer and professor who speaks widely on issues of race, class, and gender. Her recent books include *Bone Black: Memories of Girlhood* (Henry Holt, 1997), *Killing Rage: Ending Racism* (Owlet, 1996), *Reel to Real: Race, Sex and Class at the Movies* (Routledge, 1996), *Outlaw Culture: Resisting Representation* (Routledge, 1994), and *Teaching to Transgress: Education as the Practice of Freedom* (Routledge, 1994).

Deniz Kandiyoti is a senior lecturer at the School of Oriental and African Studies at the University of London in London, England. She is the co-author of *Women in Turkish Society (Social, Economic and Political Studies of the Middle East)* (Brill Academic Publishers, 1997), and the editor of volumes titled *Gendering the Middle East: Emerging Perspectives.* (Syracuse University Press, 1996), and *Women, Islamic and The State* (Temple University Press, 1991).

Jayati Lal is currently a Postdoctoral Faculty Fellow in the Program in Women's Studies at New York University, where she teaches courses on feminist theory, gender and the politics of development in the global economy, and globalization. She has also taught women's studies and sociology at Boston College and Cornell University. Her research interests include examining the impacts of liberalization on the feminization and informalization of labor and the gendered transformation of labor processes in India, as well as the impact of neoliberalism on workers and class formation more globally. She is a founding member of the Homeworker's Advocacy Working Group in New York City, and is active in antisweatshop campaigns. She is currently working on a book-length manuscript on the construction of a gendered working class in the television and garment industries in India since the late eighties.

Susan Lanser is Professor of Comparative Literature and English and affiliate Professor of Women's Studies at the University of Maryland. She is the author of *The Narrative Act: Point of View in Prose Fiction* (Princeton University Press, 1981), *Fictions of Authority: Women Writers and Narrative Voice* (Cornell University Press, 1992), and numerous essays on women writers, lesbian and feminist criticism, eighteenth-century cultures, narrative theory, and the professing and teaching of literature. A co-editor of *Women Critics 1660–1820: An Anthology* (Indiana University Press, 1995) and an executive board member of the American Society for Eighteenth-Century Studies. She is interested in discourses of enlightenment and patriarchy in eighteenth-century England, France, and Germany.

Emily Martin is Professor of Anthropology at Princeton University. Her work on ideology and power in Chinese society was published in *The Cult of the Dead in a Chinese Village* (Stanford University Press, 1973) and *Chinese Ritual and Politics* (Cambridge University Press). Beginning with The *Woman In the Body: A Cultural Analysis of Reproduction* (Beacon Press, 1992), she has been working on the anthropology of science and reproduction in the United States. Her latest research is described in *Flexible Bodies: Tracking Immunity in America from the Days of Polio to the Age of AIDS* (Beacon Press, 1995).

Chandra Talpade Mohanty is Associate Professor of Women's Studies at Hamilton College and Core Faculty at the Union Institute Graduate School. Her work focuses on cultural studies and antiracist education. She co-edited *Third World Women and the Politics of Feminism* (Indiana University Press, 1991), and *Feminist Genealogies, Colonial Legacies, Democratic Futures* (Routledge, 1997) and is currently working on a book entitled *Feminisms Without Borders: Multiculturalism, Globalization and the Politics of Solidarity*. She is a member of the editorial collective of *Cultural Critique*, and of the national advisory board of *Signs: A Journal of Women in Culture and Society*, and of the British journal *Gender, Place and Culture: A Journal of Feminist Geography*.

Cindy Patton has been intensively involved in gay and AIDS activism throughout the 1980s. She now teaches lesbian and gay studies in the Graduate Institute for Liberal Arts at Emory University. Some of her works include *Sex and Germs: The Politics of AIDS* (South End Press, 1985), *Inventing AIDS* (Routledge, 1990), *Last Served? Gendering the HIV Pandemic* (Taylor and Francis, 1994), *Fatal Advice* (Duke University Press, 1996), and a forthcoming volume, *Who I Am: Making American Political Identities* (with Harry Denny).

Anne Raine holds a master's degree in Feminism and the Visual Arts from the University of Leeds and is now a doctoral candidate in American Literature at the University of Washington, Seattle. She is interested in the intersections of modernist aesthetics, critical geography, and environmental history and theory. Her dissertation explores how American women modernist writers, like their contemporaries in the conservation and wilderness preservation movements, construct landscape and the artifact as cultural-material spaces where relations and distinctions between subject and object, human and nonhuman, culture and nature, are made and unmade.

Catherine Raissiguier is currently Assistant Professor and Associate Director of the Center for Women's Studies at the University of Cincinnati. She has taught women's studies, sociology, and education courses at other various institutions. Her research and intellectual interests include feminist theory, gender and immigration, international issues in feminism, processes of identity formation, women's education, and sexual politics. She is the author of *Becoming Women/Becoming Workers: Identity Formation in a French High School* (SUNY Press, 1994) and she is currently working on her next book, an in-depth study of gender and immigration in France.

Rayna Rapp teaches in the Department of Anthropology, New School for Social Research, where she chairs the Master's Program in Gender Studies and Feminist Theory. She is editor of *Toward an Anthropology of Women* (Monthly Review Press, 1976), and the co-editor of *Promissory Notes: Women in the Transition to Socialism* (Monthly Review Press, 1989); *Articulating Hidden Histories;* and *Conceiving the New World Order: The Global Politics of Reproduction* (University of Californian Press, 1995). Her book, *Testing Women, Testing the Fetus: The Social Impact of Amniocentesis in America*, forthcoming from Routledge, analyzes the social impact and cultural meaning of prenatal diagnosis in the United States.

Joan Scott is Professor of Social Science at the Institute for Advanced Study in Princeton, New Jersey. She has written extensively on feminist theory and history. Her publications include *Only Paradoxes to Offer: French Feminists and the Rights of Man* (Harvard University Press, 1996), *Gender and the Politics of History* (Columbia University Press, 1988), and an edited volume *Feminism and History* (Oxford University Press, 1996).

Roberta Spalter-Roth obtained her doctorate in Sociology. She is currently Director of Research for the Discipline at the American Sociological Association and is an Adjunct Professor in the Sociology Department at the American University, teaching graduate seminars on social policy research. She was previously Acting Research Director at the Women's Research and Education Institute, consultant to the Women's Bureau, U.S. Department of Labor, and Research Director at the Institute for Women's Policy Research (IWPR). She has researched and published widely on topics including the impact of restructuring gender inequalities in the work force, economic security and the low-wage labor market, welfare to work, family and medical leave, and unemployment insurance.

Valerie Traub is Associate Professor of English at Vanderbilt University. She is the author of *Desire and Anxiety: Circulations of Sexuality in Shakespearean Drama* (Routledge, 1992). Her essay is drawn from a book project on discourses of female erotic pleasure in early modern England, forthcoming from Cambridge University Press.

About the Editors

Sharlene Hesse-Biber is Professor of Sociology at Boston College. She is a co-founder and former director of the college's Women's Studies program, and she also directs the National Association of Women in Catholic Higher Education. Her current focus for research is women and health, especially the effects of race and class on eating disorders. Her most recent publications are *Am I Thin Enough Yet? The Cult of Thinness and the Commercialization of Identity* (Oxford University Press, 1996) and a co-authored book, *Working Women in American Society: Split Dreams* (Oxford University Press, 1999).

Christina Gilmartin is Associate Professor of History and Director of Women's Studies at Northeastern University. She is author of *Engendering the Chinese Revolution: Radical Women, Communist Politics, and Mass Movements in the 1920s* (University of California, 1995) co-editor of *Engendering China: Women, Culture, and the State* (Harvard University Press, 1994), and she has written essays on gender violence, marriage migrations, and marriage reforms in Post-Mao China.

Robin Lydenberg is Professor of English at Boston College where she teaches critical theory, psychoanalysis and literature, and interdisciplinary approaches to the avant-garde. She is the author of *Word Cultures: Radical Theory and Practice in William S. Burroughs' Fiction* (University of Illinois Press, 1987), co-editor of *William S. Burroughs At the Front: Critical Reception, 1959–89* (Southern Illinois University Press, 1990), and she has published essays on nineteenth and twentieth century fiction, collage aesthetics, and Freud.

Introduction

F or three decades, feminist research has been explicitly connected with inter-disciplinarity. This linkage was initially motivated by the recognition of two realities: the fields of knowledge that had sprung up within disciplinary terrains largely reflected male interests, and the artificial barriers dividing these domains obstructed a complete view of women's situations and the social structures that perpetuated gender inequalities. Many years before feminist scholars began to imagine that they might "engender" the disciplines, they set out to make the disciplinary landscapes more hospitable to feminist analysis and interpretation.

The theoretical work for this undertaking has mainly occurred in three localities: at the margins of the disciplines, in interdisciplinary women's studies programs,[1] and in interdisciplinary journals like *Signs: Journal of Women in Culture and Society* and *Feminist Studies*. Over time a rich language has developed to describe the nature of feminist work in these disciplinary and interdisciplinary sites, revealing a variety of views. While some feminists, such as Joan Wallach Scott, focus their efforts on transforming their disciplines (Scott, 1988), others call attention to the difficulties inherent in such undertakings. Deborah Steinberg, for instance, points out the problematic aspects of working within one's "home" discipline:

> Most of us who are feminists forging interdisciplinary scholarship and pedagogy, I imagine, find it more the case that "home" is a place of profound estrangement and considerable danger. . . . Indeed, the metaphor of "home," if we consider the conventional sexual politics of home, is unfortunately appropriate. (Steinberg, 1997:201)

Other scholars are less concerned with the dilemmas related to their disciplinary affiliations than with the viability of the interdisciplinary spaces they have come to inhabit. Both Jane Marcus and Gloria Anzaldúa portray these sites as unsafe, transitory places to which scholars have been exiled. Those who enter these sites, which have been "created by the emotional residue of an unnatural boundary," become "foreigners" and must assume "dangerous identifications" (Marcus, 1989:23; Anzaldúa, 1987:3).

---

[1]In 1960, there were approximately sixteen courses devoted to the topic of women and gender. In 1970, the first women's studies program in the United States was approved at San Diego State University (Stimpson, 1992:257 as cited in Klein, 1996:115). By the mid-1990s, the number of women's studies programs had grown to approximately 620 (Howe, 1997:410). A study conducted by the American Council on Education found that 68 percent of American universities offered courses in women's studies, 48.9 percent of four-year colleges, and 26.5 percent of two-year colleges ("Women's Studies," 1990:214 as cited in Klein, 1996:116)

Despite its risks, interdisciplinarity opens up possibilities for tremendous growth and change; many feminist scholars, therefore, perceive interdisciplinary sites in more neutral or even positive terms. Paula Gunn Allen (1992) uses the term *border* studies to describe the work of scholars whose research crosses multiple disciplines. The anthropological term *contact zone* is used by Margaret Higonnet to characterize the nature of interdisciplinary work in these sites, which she sees as "improvisational and interactive." The value for Higonnet of this formulation is its dynamic nature, for it allows scholars to move beyond "one way questions" (Higonnet, 1994:3). The interdisciplinary bordersite takes on a more explicitly political function in bell hooks's description of a space from which one can "participate in the formation of counter-hegemonic cultural practice" (hooks, 1990:145). Thus, hooks celebrates her position on the border:

> I am located at the margin. I make a definite distinction between that marginality which is imposed by oppressive structures and that marginality one chooses as site for resistance—as location of radical openness and possibility. (hooks, 1990:153)

These sites provide what hooks calls "radical creative space[s]" for the emergence of a body of interdisciplinary work that at first was "sustained by the 'dream of a common language'" (Hirsh and Fox Keller, 1990:379) and presumed to grow out of shared feminist goals. Much attention has been devoted to exposing the underlying male biases in the disciplines, exploring differences between men and women and between sex and gender, and critiquing positivism's knowledge claims. Those working in the social sciences, in particular, interrogated the opposition between researcher/researched, the concepts of "objectivity" and "subjectivity," as well as the role of power and authority in knowledge building. Central to an emerging interdisciplinary feminist methodology are issues such as: Who gets to be a knower? What is knowledge? How are competing knowledge claims resolved? (Harding, 1987:1991). In addition, the encounter of feminist theory with poststructuralism, which occurred in the context of the material and ideological complexities of a global, postcolonial, postindustrial, postmodern culture, at once transformed and intensified feminism's critique of the disciplines and of its own interdisciplinary practice.

The impact of poststructuralism on feminist theory led to a dynamic expansion of interdisciplinary domains and a further fracturing of disciplinary boundaries. The conventional tools, working concepts, and dominant epistemologies of the disciplines were critically re-evaluated. Throughout this process, the question of how knowledge is divided up among and within the disciplines remains central to feminist interdisciplinary scholarship. By asking "who is doing the carving" and "in whose interests," feminists have begun to probe much more deeply into the nature of knowledge production and the operations of power within the academy. In so doing, interdisciplinary feminist practice has developed into what some critics see as a process of "political intervention" (namaste, 1992:58). Indeed, for Konrad Jarusch, the nature of feminist interdisciplinarity has been so transformed under poststructuralist influences that it can legitimately be termed a "new interdisciplinarity," which he sees as being based "on a triple meeting ground: a post-structuralist reading of the text within context, a historical approach to gender issues and an anthropological sensitivity to culture" (Jarusch, 1989:438).

Another significant impact of poststructuralism on feminism is the infusion of serious debate among its practitioners. In the words of Liz Stanley, "it was the emergence of interdisciplinary feminist work that opened up a 'space between' for debate, contention, and disagreement" (Stanley, 1997:1). Assumptions about feminist solidarity were fundamentally challenged as theorists working in a range of different disciplines simultaneously exposed to critical analysis the unexamined universalist and essentialist categories that were so central to the notion of feminism as a political movement. At the same time, they launched assaults against the unquestioned authority of master narratives, totalizing systems of interpretation, and hierarchical and binary structures of categorization. Deconstructing and tracing the genealogy of such fundamental concepts as nature, truth, the unitary subject, and objective knowledge, theorists like Jacques Derrida, Michel Foucault, and Jacques Lacan led many to believe that everything we accept as given—reality, the body, subjecthood—is socially and discursively constructed.

Although the impact of these and other poststructuralist theorists produced different results in individual disciplines, by the 1990s their destabilizing and invigorating effects had been felt more broadly across the disciplines. Many academics resisted this theoretical incursion, and some feminist critics articulated their resistance as politically and even ethically motivated. They were, as Elaine Showalter puts it, protecting the "expressive and dynamic enterprise" of feminist criticism from the "falsely objective . . . pernicious masculine discourse" of the new "masters" who had sprung up in place of the old (1981:181).

The different responses of feminist critics to the "linguistic turn" of poststructuralist theory created a major conflict within the field. For example, while some fought against it, other feminist critics were among the first to bring the work of the new theorists to bear on their own disciplines. They recognized an affinity between their feminist political goals for social change and the new theorists' attacks on the most entrenched and oppressive ideological assumptions of traditional knowledge systems. Rejecting the binary thinking that set male theory in opposition to feminist politics, these poststructuralist feminists not only appropriated the new theoretical modes of inquiry but extended and revised them to address the complexities of gender. The work of feminist scholars like Joan Scott (1988) in history, Gayle Rubin (1975) in anthropology, Judith Butler (1990, 1993) in philosophy, and Sylvia Walby (1992) in sociology influenced feminist scholars across the disciplines, contributing to the emergence of an interdisciplinary feminist theory "whose intention is to destabilize" (Barrett and Phillips 1992:1).

One of the most intense areas of debate in this recent stage of feminist theory and practice crystallized around the tension between essentialist and social constructionist interpretations of the categories of woman, sex, gender, and the body. The development of feminist theoretical discourse of the 1980s and 1990s made possible a powerful rearticulation of the question feminists had been debating at least since the 1920s: Is a woman's destiny, psyche, sexual and social behavior determined by anatomy and nature (and thus universal and unchanging) or constructed by her particular social and cultural environment (and thus historically variable)?

The binary alternative laid out by this formulation of the question polarized feminist theory in the 1980s about conceptions of the body: French feminists like Hélène Cixous (1986), Luce Irigaray (1991), and Julia Kristeva (1986) were accused by social constructionists of biological essentialism, of establishing the female body and maternity as the foundational and symbolic sources of woman's psychic and sexual difference (Faure, 1981). As philosopher Susan Bordo points out, this turn from understanding the body as a "fixed, unitary, primarily physiological reality" to interpreting the body "as a historical, plural, culturally mediated form" can be traced back at least to Mary Wollstonecraft's 1792 analysis of "the social construction of femininity as delicacy and domesticity" (Bordo 1993:288; 17–18). Continuing this constructionist line of reasoning, contemporary feminists influenced by Michel Foucault and Jacques Derrida theorized the body in more complex ways as a site of disciplinary control where discursive and social practices are simultaneously imposed and resisted. Destabilizing the distinction between gender as socially constructed and sex as biologically given, poststructuralist critics like Judith Butler expose even the materiality of the body as "already gendered, already constructed." Extending her argument that gender and sex are the result of the "ritualized repetition" of certain behaviors designed to render the body either "intelligible" (normative, heterosexual) or abject (unthinkable, homosexual), Judith Butler asserts that the body itself is "forcibly produced" by power and discourse (1993:xi).

Feminists are then faced with a political dilemma: if one cannot uncritically assume the commonality of the category *woman* based on the lived experience of the female body, what is the basis, the "essence," of feminist praxis? Some feminists responded to this impasse by arguing that a decentered, fragmented, multiple postmodern subject whose body is socially and discursively constructed could be deployed as a political lever. Critics like Gayatri Chakravorty Spivak (1990), Donna Haraway (1985, 1988), Teresa de Lauretis (1988, 1994), and Chandra Talpade Mohanty (1992, 1995) imagined opportunities for the strategic use of essentialism and a politics of constantly shifting coalitions. One might even argue, as Diana Fuss does, that the "very tension [of the essentialism/constructionism debate] is constitutive of the field of feminist theory" (1989:1). Characterized in this most recent stage of its development by internal debate and rigorous self-criticism, feminist theory opened the field of feminist research to interventions that would transform it dramatically.

In the 1980s feminist scholarship that prioritized sexual differences between men and women began to be criticized explicitly for neglecting differences among women stemming from class, race, ethnicity, or sexual orientation, and for implicitly privileging a norm of womanhood as white, heterosexual, middle class, and Western. New scholarship by black feminists, postcolonial critics, queer theorists, and others exposed this normative ideology as racist, ethnocentric, heterosexist, and elitist. Efforts to represent difference, however, often fell into stereotypes and generalizations that once again obscured the specificity of difference. Mohanty describes, for example, the "discursive colonization" by which "material and historical heterogeneities" of third-world women's experience were lost in Western feminists' construction of a "composite, singular 'Third World Woman'"(1995:260). Furthermore, feminist critics like Patricia Hill Collins (1990), Evelyn Nakano Glenn (1992), Evelyn Brooks Higginbotham (1992), Trinh Minh-ha (1989, 1991) and others demonstrate in their own work the importance of examining the complex and shifting intersections of various categories of difference, and of analyzing those interlocking relations in particular historical contexts. The often painful but increasingly open discussion of the difficulties, risks, and rewards involved in trying to negotiate what Ann duCille calls the "impossible space" of difference has invigorated and transformed the practice of feminist theory and research (1996:56).

While some have found these theoretical and political upheavals threatening, others see them as occasions for the continuing evolution of feminist theory, research, and activism. Teresa de Lauretis celebrates the ongoing self-critique within feminism as "not merely an expansion or reconfiguration of boundaries, but a qualitative shift in political and historical consciousness" (1988:138–39). Practitioners of feminist theory and research struggle to prevent their own foundational categories and modes of representation from obstructing the emergence of subjugated knowledges and identities. The continuing challenge to feminists, as Hirsch and Fox Keller suggest, is to learn to use the conflicts within feminism constructively (1990:379) and perhaps even, as bell hooks hopes, pleasurably (1990:153).

The complex history of the intersection of feminism and interdisciplinarity discussed here provided the background against which a group of academic feminists in the Boston area gathered in 1992 to discuss ways of consolidating and increasing the availability of feminist research and teaching across the disciplines and across institutions. The program that eventually emerged was the Graduate Consortium in Women's Studies at Radcliffe College. The mandate of the program was to bring together faculty from different fields to teach interdisciplinary courses on topics of interest to feminist graduate students from many disciplines. The founders of the consortium (including Joyce Antler, Constance Buchanan, Laura Frader, Carol Hurd Green, Barbara Haber, Alice Jardine, Ruth Perry, and Christiane Zehl Romero) set forth the intellectual criteria for these new team-taught courses to include rigorous attention to the intersection of disciplinary knowledges around a set of wide-ranging and complex questions. The first course addressed interdisciplinary feminist methodologies and epistemologies. Its original developers—Laura Frader, a historian; Mary Loeffelholz, a literary critic; and Shulamit Reinharz, a sociologist—created a coherent yet complex basis for subsequent variations in the syllabus and course design. Over the three years during which the editors of this volume revised and team taught this course, we were surprised to discover that as contested as the terrain of feminism has become, the interdisciplinary aspects of the course proved equally if not more problematic. While we eventually reached some shared understandings about feminism—that although its methodologies were rooted in social activism, it could not be reduced to an easily defined set of propositions, theoretical claims, or research methods—the nature and practice of interdisciplinarity remained more elusive. The decision to publish an anthology of readings based on our collective work in this course, titled "Feminist Perspectives in Research: Interdisciplinary Practice in the Study of Gender," provided an additional opportunity to investigate the question of what constitutes truly interdisciplinary scholarship, and how such work may be uniquely suited to serve the goals of feminist research and activism.

It is not possible in the space of a single volume of this size to include representative examples of interdisciplinary feminist scholarship stretching back twenty to thirty years. It is encouraging for the field, however, that even limiting selections to the best and most representative recent scholarship, we found many more fine essays than we could include. As we experimented with different criteria for the final selections, certain topics emerged as most frequently debated in the literature and as areas in which path-breaking work had been accomplished. The seventeen essays in this anthology are grouped within these six key categories: feminist critiques within the disciplines; the politics of identity and experience; the social construction of difference; power and resistance; representations of the body; social policy and female agency.

The continuing efforts of feminist scholars to expose the male biases embedded in disciplinary paradigms is the focus of our selections for Part I, Feminist Critiques Within the Disciplines. The fact that this endeavor has retained such a central place in feminist scholarship for more than two decades reveals the enormous difficulty of transforming disciplinary practices and paradigms. Emily Martin's article, "The Egg and the Sperm: How Science Has Constructed a Romance Based on Stereotypical Male-Female Roles," is a masterful exposure of the ways in which a presumably neutral medical discourse describes the female body and reproduction in markedly sexist terms. Feminist philosopher Susan Bordo's article "Feminist Skepticism and the 'Maleness' of Philosophy" analyzes a similar pattern of male bias and dominance in the history and structures of philosophical discourse. Kathleen Canning, in her article "Feminist History After the Linguistic Turn: Historicizing Discourse and Experience," brilliantly shows how the poststructuralist encounter with feminism has transformed the practice of historical theory and research.

The essays in Part II, The Politics of Identity and Experience, grapple with dramatic changes in our understanding of two foundational concepts in feminist theory and research. Identity and experience are presented here not as innate and unproblematic, but as constituted by discourse, representation, and the effects of power. As Joan Scott theorizes in "The Evidence of Experience," the goal is not to eliminate identity and experience as categories of analysis but to trace the politics of their construction. In a bold deconstructive problematization of experience as a "linguistic event" shaped by "established meanings," Scott illuminates the historical processes of constructing identity and knowledge. Catherine Raissiguier's "The Construction of Marginal Identities: Working-class Girls of Algerian Descent in a French School" and Jayati Lal's "Situating Locations: The Politics of Self, Identity and 'Other' in Living and Writing the Text" reflect both the impact of poststructuralist challenges to identity and experience and the persistence of these categories in feminist analyses of specific historical contexts. While Raissiguier exposes the often conflicting identities imposed on her research subjects by both religious and secular discursive systems, Lal extends her critique to the constraints imposed by the class differential operating in the research situation itself. Although there are differences in their theoretical assumptions and methods, all three essays in this section stress the ways in which female subjects exercise agency and resistance in spite of the discursive constructions and power relations that shape their daily lives.

Responding to the inability of feminist essentialism to represent the differences within and between women, the essays in Part III, The Social Construction of Difference, focus on the complex terrain in which difference is used as a tool of oppression and of resistance both inside and outside feminist praxis. In "Learning from the Outsider Within: The Sociological Significance of Black Feminist Thought," Patricia Hill Collins cautiously retrieves the categories of identity and experience in order to consolidate a common "black feminist thought." She argues that recognition of this different and more comprehensive standpoint of the "outsider within" is important not only for the self-definition of black women, but also as a source of critical insight for academic and social change. Once difference is represented, however, it can readily be misread and appropriated. In "Eating the Other," bell hooks asserts that when commodified images of "blackness" in the popular media are appropriated by whites and reduced to a depoliticized spectacle by blacks, there is a danger that "difference will be eaten and forgotten." Susan Lanser's "Feminist Criticism, 'The Yellow Wallpaper,' and the Politics of Color in America" uncovers a subtext of racial anxiety "forgotten" by two decades of feminist interpretations that reduce Gilman's story to a parable of sexual difference and oppression. A corrective to such partial readings has been offered by the tenet of black feminist thought, endorsed by critics like Patricia Hill Collins, Evelyn Brooks Higginbotham, and others, that differences must be studied in their interlocking relations.

Part IV of this anthology, Power and Resistance, deals with the importance in feminist scholarship of historicizing systems of domination and of resisting the inclination to view women as passive and powerless victims. Deniz Kandiyoti, in her essay "Islam and Patriarchy: A Comparative Perspective," presents a forceful analysis of the vital workings of patriarchy as a system of gender domination and of young women's abilities to "bargain" with the system. In "Feminism and Empowerment: A Critical Reading of Foucault," Monique Deveaux exposes the weaknesses in Michel Foucault's notions of "biopolitics" and the omnipresence of power in all relationships, and criticizes his neglect of the specificity of women's experience of male domination. Deveaux encourages the development of a feminist scholarly methodology that focuses on women's subjective experiences, the ways in which they mediate relations of power, and their capacity for implementing personal and collective activism.

The power of various knowledge discourses to control female agency and regulate women's bodies is the focus of Part V, Representations of the Body. The familiar trope linking the female body with nature, for example, has been deployed at different historical periods with strikingly different ideological effects. Anne

Raine's "Embodied Geographies: Subjectivity and Materiality in the Work of Ana Mendieta" places the work of this Cuban American artist in the context of a long history of representations of the female body and landscape in Western art. Mendieta's photographs suggest the modern (and particularly diasporan) subject's simultaneous fusion with and alienation from homeland, the maternal, and the materiality of the body. The discourse surrounding the maternal body is explored further by Rayna Rapp in her article "The Power of 'Positive' Diagnosis: Medical and Maternal Discourses on Amniocentesis," in which she exposes how contemporary medical language produces a mythic terror in women who must cope with diagnoses indicating a birth defect. Representations of maternity and reproduction belong to a larger discursive context in which sexuality is regulated and heterosexuality is imposed as the norm. In "The Psychomorphology of the Clitoris," Valerie Traub offers historical and textual interpretations of early discourses in anatomy, travel literature, and psychoanalysis that produced and regulated sexual knowledge by mapping it onto the female body. She proceeds from this historical account to contest contemporary constructions of compulsory heterosexuality and the aberrant lesbian subject.

The essays in Part VI, Social Policy and Female Agency, present the reader with some methodological and political dilemmas feminists encounter as they expose underlying distortions in existing social policy. Roberta Spalter-Roth and Heidi Hartmann's work on social welfare policy, "Small Happinesses: The Feminist Struggle to Integrate Social Research with Social Activism," argues for a "dualistic perspective" on social policy research that combines the range of women's "lived experience" with research that is also grounded in standards of scientific methodology. Cindy Patton's essay "From Nation to Family: Containing African AIDS," demonstrates how social policy is often embedded in dominant discourse and used as a mechanism of social control by the state. She examines how AIDS policy in developing nations of Africa grew out of the legacy of colonial advocacy of the "idealized nuclear family." In a postcolonial non-Western context, global capitalism is served by new ideological constructions. Chandra Talpade Mohanty's article, "Women Workers and Capitalist Scripts: Ideologies of Domination, Common Interests, and the Politics of Solidarity," reveals capitalists' efforts to create a docile and cheap female work force through ideological domination and recolonization of women as "domesticated" workers. While cognizant of the "differences and discontinuities" of third-world women's lived experiences, she argues for the "strategic use" of essentialism whereby women identify the "common interests" and agency they share as workers, across class, race, ethnic, sexual, and national divisions to consolidate collective action against capitalist domination.

The final selection and organization of essays reproduced here is only one variation among many we constructed and others we failed to imagine. The particular configuration of this anthology was guided throughout, however, by our desire to bring the work of leading scholars and emerging new critics into productive dialogue, and to illustrate the crucial contribution of feminist research that is interdisciplinary and global in perspective, combining theoretical debate with empirical application. For the editors, discussing these essays with colleagues and students, compiling the volume, and writing the introduction have been dynamic and challenging ventures in feminist interdisciplinary and collaborative learning.

References

Allen, Paula Gunn (1992). "'Border Studies': The Intersections of Gender and Color." In Joseph Gibaldi, ed., *Introduction to Scholarship in Modern Languages and Literatures*, Second Edition. New York: Modern Language Association of America.

Anzaldúa, Gloria (1987). *Borderlands/La Frontera: The New Mestiza*. San Francisco: Spinsters/Aunt Lute.

Barrett, Michèle and Anne Phillips, eds. (1992). *Destabilizing Theory: Contemporary Feminist Debates*. Stanford, Calif.: Stanford University Press.

Bordo, Susan (1993). *Unbearable Weight: Feminism, Western Culture and the Body*. Berkeley: University of California Press.

Butler, Judith (1990). *Gender Trouble: Feminism and the Subversion of Identity*. New York: Routledge.

Butler, Judith (1993). *Bodies That Matter: On the Discursive Limits of "Sex."* New York: Routledge.

Cixous, Hélène and Catherine Clément (1986). *The Newly Born Woman*. Trans. Betsy Wing. Minneapolis: University of Minnesota Press.

Collins, Patricia Hill (1990). *Black Feminist Thought: Knowledge, Consciousness, and the Politics of Empowerment*. New York: Routledge.

de Lauretis, Teresa (1988). "Displacing Hegemonic Discourses: Reflections on Feminist Theory in the 1980s." *Inscriptions* 3(4):127–45.

de Lauretis, Teresa (1994). "The Essence of the Triangle or, Taking the Risk of Essentialism Seriously: Feminist Theory in Italy, the U.S, and Britain." In Naomi Schor and Elizabeth Weed, eds., *The Essential Difference*. Bloomington: Indiana University Press, pp. 1–39.

duCille, Ann (1996). *Skin Trade*. Cambridge, Mass.: Harvard University Press.

Faure, Christine (1981). "The Twilight of the Goddesses or the Intellectual Crisis of French Feminism." Trans. Lillian S. Robinson. *Signs: Journal of Women in Culture and Society* 7(1):81–86.

Fuss, Diana (1989). *Essentially Speaking: Feminism, Nature and Difference*. New York: Routledge.

Glenn, Evelyn Nakano (1992). "From Servitude to Service Work: Historical Continuities in the Racial Division of Paid Reproductive Labor." *Signs* 18:1:1–43.

Haraway, Donna (1985). "A Manifesto for Cyborgs: Science, Technology and Socialist Feminism in the 1980s." *Socialist Review* 80:65–108.

Haraway, Donna (1988). "Situated Knowledges: The Science Question in Feminism and the Privilege of Partial Perspective." *Feminist Studies* 14 (13):575–99.

Harding, Sandra, ed. (1987). *Feminism and Methodology*. Bloomington: Indiana University Press.

Harding, Sandra (1991). *Whose Science? Whose Knowledge?* Ithaca, N.Y: Cornell University Press.

Higginbotham, Evelyn Brooks (1992). "African-American Women's History and the Metalanguage of Race." *Signs* 17(2):251–274.

Higonnet, Margaret R. (1994). "Introduction." In Margaret R. Higonnet, ed., *Borderwork:*

Feminist Engagements with Comparative Literature. Ithaca, N.Y.: Cornell University Press, pp. 1–16.

Hirsch, Marianne and Evelyn Fox Keller (1990). "Practicing Conflict in Feminist Theory." In Marianne Hirsch and Evelyn Fox Keller, eds., *Conflicts in Feminism.* New York: Routledge, pp. 370–85.

hooks, bell (1990). *Yearning: Race, Gender and Cultural Politics.* Boston, Mass.: South End Press.

Howe, Florence (1997). "Promises to Keep: Trends in Women's Studies Worldwide." *Women's Studies Quarterly* 1 & 2: 404–21.

Irigaray, Luce (1991). In Margaret Whitford, ed., *The Irigaray Reader.* Oxford: Blackwell Publishers.

Jarusch, Konrad H. (1989). "Towards a Social History of Experience: Postmodern Predicaments in Theory and Interdisciplinarity." *Central European History* 22:427–43.

Klein, Julie Thompson (1996). *Crossing Boundaries: Knowledge, Disciplinarities, and Interdisciplinarities.* Charlottsville: University Press of Virginia.

Kristeva, Julia (1986). Toril Moi, ed., In *The Kristeva Reader* New York: Columbia University Press.

Marcus, Jane (1989). "Alibis and Legends: The Ethics of Elsewhereness, Gender and Estrangement." In Mary Lynn Broe and Angela Ingram, eds., *Women's Writing in Exile.* Chapel Hill: University of North Carolina Press.

Mohanty, Chandra Talpade (1992). "Feminist Encounters: Locating the Politics of Experience." In Michele Barrett and Anne Phillips, eds., *Destabilizing Theory: Contemporary Feminist Debates.* Stanford, Calif.: Stanford University Press, pp. 74–92.

Mohanty, Chandra Talpade (1995). "Under Western Eyes: Feminist Scholarship and Colonial Discourses." In B. G. Griffiths and H. Tiffin, eds., *The Post-Colonial Studies Reader.* London: Routledge.

namaste ki (1992). "Deconstruction, Lesbian and Gay Studies and Interdisciplinary Work: Theoretical, Political and Institutional Strategies. In Henry L. Minton, ed., *Gay and Lesbian Studies.* New York: Haworth Press, pp. 49–64.

Rubin, Gayle (1975). "The Traffic in Women: Notes on the 'Political Economy' of Sex," In Rayna R. Reiter, ed., *Toward an Anthropology of Women.* New York: Monthly Review Press, pp. 157–210.

Scott, Joan Wallach (1988). "Gender: A Useful Category of Historical Analysis." In Joan Wallach Scott, ed., *Gender and the Politics of History.* New York: Columbia University Press, pp. 28–50.

Showalter, Elaine (1981). "Feminist Criticism in the Wilderness." *Critical Inquiry* 8(2):179–206.

Spivak, Gayatri Chakravorty (1990). *The Postcolonial Critic: Interviews, Strategies, Dialogue.* New York: Routledge.

Stanley, Liz (1997). "Introduction: On Academic Borders, Territories, Tribes and Knowledges." In *Knowing Feminisms: On Academic Borders, Territories and Tribes.* London: Sage Publications, pp. 1–17.

Steinberg, Deborah Lynn (1997). "All Roads Lead to . . . Problems with Discipline." In Joyce and Debbie Epstein, eds., *A Question of Discipline: Pedagogy, Power, and the Teaching of Cultural Studies,* Boulder, Co.: Westview Press, pp. 192–204.

Stimpson, Catherine R. (1992). "Feminist Criticism." In Stephen Greenblatt and Giles Gunn, eds., *Redrawing the Boundaries: the Transformation of English and American Literary Studies.* New York: Modern Language Association, pp. 251–70.

Trinh, T. Minh-ha (1989). *Woman, Native, Other.* Bloomington: Indiana University Press.

Trinh, T. Minh-ha (1991). *Framer Framed.* New York: Routledge.

Walby, Sylvia (1992). "Post-Post-Modernism? Theorizing Social Complexity." In Michèle Barrett and Anne Phillips, eds., *Destabilizing Theory: Contemporary Feminist Debates.* Stanford, Calif.: Stanford University Press, pp. 74–92

"Women's Studies." (1990). In *Liberal Learning and the Arts and Sciences Major.* V.II. Reports from the Fields, 207–24.

PART 1

Feminists Critiques Within the Disciplines

Feminist scholars have focused much effort during the last few decades on challenging the presumed objectivity and value neutrality of the natural sciences. Drawing upon the insights of interdisciplinary feminist theory, they have revealed much about the connections between the creation of scientific knowledge and culturally embedded gender ideologies. In "The Egg and the Sperm: How Science Has Constructed a Romance Based on Stereotypical Male-Female Roles," anthropologist Emily Martin insightfully reveals how biological explanations of reproduction that are commonly assumed to be based on objective scientific truth are in fact laden with cultural stereotypes about male superiority. Gender biases infuse medical textbook descriptions with the result that male physiological processes such as sperm production are privileged over egg production. Martin warns biologists that by projecting culturally sexist imagery into their work, they not only impair their understanding and future investigations of natural processes, but they also give greater legitimacy to increased technological and political surveillance and manipulation of women's pregnant bodies.

In "Feminist Skepticism and the 'Maleness' of Philosophy," Susan Bordo argues that the discipline of philosophy from its origins until the present can meaningfully be characterized as "male." In so doing she seeks to retain the right to generalize about the existence of "men's perspectives" and "women's perspectives." She supports her bold contention, which challenges prevailing contemporary antiessentialist modes of analysis, by drawing upon a body of interdisciplinary theory, especially the works of Nancy Chodorow, Carol Gilligan and Michel Foucault. Bordo makes this argument in order to caution feminists against the dangers of what she calls a postmodern "theoretics of heterogeneity" that questions the legitimacy of historical and cultural generalizations about the commonalities of women. What is ultimately at stake for Bordo is the survival of gender as a feminist analytical category. In another article on this topic, Bordo has instructively queried: "Why, it must be asked, are we so ready to deconstruct what have historically been the most ubiquitous elements of the gender axis, while so willing to defer to the authority and integrity of race and class axes as fundamentally grounding?" (Bordo, 1990:146) In Bordo's view, it is critical for feminists to acknowledge that no matter how attentive scholars are to the axes that constitute social identity, some of them will be ignored or marginalized and others will be selected.

Kathleen Canning's article, "Feminist History After the Linguistic Turn: Historicizing Discourse and Experience," looks at the destabilizing impact on the discipline of history caused by a shift of emphasis from material "reality" to representation and textuality. No longer is the concept of class understood as a social fact but rather as a postulated social identity. What has become most disturbing to some social historians about this new approach is the contention that language does not simply reflect historical reality but constitutes it. Canning offers a concrete example of how historians can grapple with the poststructuralist challenge "on the terrain of history" through her exploration of the efforts of women workers in post World War I Germany to transform the male-dominant discourse about working conditions and class relations. Female textile workers developed a special vocabulary known as *Eigenart* to articulate the "particularities of female needs, activities and sentiments and consciousness." By deploying *Eigenart* and insisting on the lived bodily experience of working women, they "repudiated the seamless integration of women into male spheres and undermined universalist claims of class struggle." The category of class was thus transformed by sexual difference, evolving gender roles, and the "politics of the body." Canning's work is particularly valuable for showing not only how discourse shapes experience, but how human agency can transform and manipulate discourse in specific historical situations.

Reference
Susan Bordo, "Feminism, Postmodernism, and Gender-Skepticism," in Linda J. Nicholson, ed., *Feminism/Postmodernism*. New York: Routledge, 1990, pp. 133–156.

CHAPTER ONE

The Egg and the Sperm

How Science Has Constructed a Romance Based on Sterotypical Male-Female Roles

EMILY MARTIN

> The theory of the human body is always a part of
> a world picture. . . . The theory of the human
> body is always a part of a *fantasy*.
> *James Hillman*, The Myth of Analysis[1]

As an anthropologist, I am intrigued by the possibility that culture shapes how biological scientists describe what they discover about the natural world. If this were so, we would be learning about more than the natural world in high school biology class; we would be learning about cultural beliefs and practices as if they were part of nature. In the course of my research I realized that the picture of egg and sperm drawn in popular as well as scientific accounts of reproductive biology relies on stereotypes central to our cultural definitions of male and female. The stereotypes imply not only that female biological processes are less worthy than their male counterparts but also that women are less worthy than men. Part of my goal in writing this article is to shine a bright light on the gender stereotypes hidden within the scientific language of biology. Exposed in such a light, I hope they will lose much of their power to harm us.

Egg and Sperm: A Scientific Fairy Tale

At a fundamental level, all major scientific textbooks depict male and female reproductive organs as systems for the production of valuable substances, such as eggs and sperm.[2] In the case of women, the monthly cycle is described as being designed to produce eggs and prepare a suitable place for them to be fertilized and grown—all to the end of making babies. But the enthusiasm ends there. By extolling the female cycle as a productive enterprise, menstruation must necessarily be viewed as a failure. Medical texts describe menstruation as the "debris" of the uterine lining, the result of necrosis, or death, of tissue. The descriptions imply that a system has gone awry, making products of no use, not to specifica-

Emily Martin, "The Egg and the Sperm: How Science Has Constructed a Romance Based on Stereotypical Male-Female Roles," *Signs* 16:3 (1991): 485–501. Reprinted by permission.

tion, unsalable, wasted, scrap. An illustration in a widely used medical text shows menstruation as a chaotic disintegration of form, complementing the many texts that describe it as "ceasing," "dying," "losing," "denuding," "expelling."[3]

Male reproductive physiology is evaluated quite differently. One of the texts that sees menstruation as failed production employs a sort of breathless prose when it describes the maturation of sperm: "The mechanisms which guide the remarkable cellular transformation from spermatid to mature sperm remain uncertain. . . . Perhaps the most amazing characteristic of spermatogenesis is its sheer magnitude: the normal human male may manufacture several hundred million sperm per day."[4] In the classic text *Medical Physiology*, edited by Vernon Mountcastle, the male/female, productive/destructive comparison is more explicit: "Whereas the female *sheds* only a single gamete each month, the seminiferous tubules *produce* hundreds of millions of sperm each day" (emphasis mine).[5] The female author of another text marvels at the length of the microscopic seminiferous tubules, which, if uncoiled and placed end to end, "would span almost one-third of a mile!" She writes, "In an adult male these structures produce millions of sperm cells each day." Later she asks, "How is this feat accomplished?"[6] None of these texts expresses such intense enthusiasm for any female processes. It is surely no accident that the "remarkable" process of making sperm involves precisely what, in the medical view, menstruation does not: production of something deemed valuable.[7]

One could argue that menstruation and spermatogenesis are not analogous processes and, therefore, should not be expected to elicit the same kind of response. The proper female analogy to spermatogenesis, biologically, is ovulation. Yet ovulation does not merit enthusiasm in these texts either. Textbook descriptions stress that all of the ovarian follicles containing ova are already present at birth. Far from being *produced,* as sperm are, they merely sit on the shelf, slowly degenerating and aging like overstocked inventory: "At birth, normal human ovaries contain an estimated one million follicles [each], and no new ones appear after birth. Thus, in marked contrast to the male, the newborn female already has all the germ cells she will ever have. Only a few, perhaps 400, are destined to reach full maturity during her active productive life. All the others degenerate at some point in their development so that few, if any, remain by the time she reaches menopause at approximately 50 years of age."[8] Note the "marked contrast" that this description sets up between male and female: the male, who continuously produces fresh germ cells, and the female, who has stockpiled germ cells by birth and is faced with their degeneration.

Nor are the female organs spared such vivid descriptions. One scientist writes in a newspaper article that a woman's ovaries become old and worn out from ripening eggs every month, even though the woman herself is still relatively young: "When you look through a laparoscope . . . at an ovary that has been through hundreds of cycles, even in a superbly healthy American female you see a scarred, battered organ."[9]

To avoid the negative connotations that some people associate with the female reproductive system, scientists could begin to describe male and female processes as homologous. They might credit females with "producing" mature ova one at a time, as they're needed each month, and describe males as having to face problems of degenerating germ cells. This degeneration would occur throughout life among spermatogonia, the undifferentiated germ cells in the testes that are the long-lived, dormant precursors of sperm.

But the texts have an almost dogged insistence on casting female processes in negative light. The texts celebrate sperm production because it is continuous from puberty to senescence, while they portray egg production as inferior because it is finished at birth. This makes the female seem unproductive, but some texts will also insist that it is she who is wasteful.[10] In a section heading for *Molecular Biology of the Cell,* a best-selling text, we are told that "Oogenesis is wasteful." The text goes on to emphasize that of the seven million oogonia, or egg germ cells, in the female embryo, most degenerate in the ovary. Of those that do go on to become oocytes, or eggs, many also degenerate, so that at birth only two million eggs remain in the ovaries. Degeneration continues throughout a woman's life: by puberty 300,000 eggs remain, and only a few are present by menopause. "During the 40 or so years of a woman's reproductive life, only 400 to 500 eggs will have been released," the authors write. "All the rest will have degenerated. It is still a mystery why so many eggs are formed only to die in the ovaries."[11]

The real mystery is why the male's vast production of sperm is not seen as wasteful.[12] Assuming that a man "produces" 100 million (10^8) sperm per day (a conservative estimate) during an average reproductive life of sixty years, he would produce well over two trillion sperm in his lifetime. Assuming that a woman "ripens" one egg per lunar month, or thirteen per year, over the course of her forty-year reproductive life, she would total five hundred eggs in her lifetime. But the word "waste" implies an excess, too much produced. Assuming two or three offspring, for every baby a woman produces, she wastes only around two hundred eggs. For every baby a man produces, he wastes more than one trillion (10^{12}) sperm.

How is it that positive images are denied to the bodies of women? A look at language—in this case, scientific language—provides the first clue. Take the egg and the sperm.[13] It is remarkable how "femininely" the egg behaves and how "masculinely" the sperm.[14] The egg is seen as large and passive.[15] It does not *move* or *journey,* but passively "is transported," "is swept,"[16] or even "drifts"[17] along the fallopian tube. In utter contrast, sperm are small, "streamlined,"[18] and invariably active. They "deliver" their genes to the egg, "activate the developmental program of the egg,"[19] and have a "velocity" that is often remarked upon.[20] Their tails are "strong" and efficiently powered.[21] Together with the forces of ejaculation, they can "propel the semen into the deepest recesses of the vagina."[22] For this they need "energy," "fuel,"[23] so that with a "whiplashlike motion and strong lurches"[24] they can "burrow through the egg coat"[25] and "penetrate" it.[26]

At its extreme, the age-old relationship of the egg and the sperm takes on a royal or religious patina. The egg coat, its protective barrier, is sometimes called its "vestments," a term usually reserved for sacred, religious dress. The egg is said to have a "corona,"[27] a crown, and to be accompanied by "attendant cells."[28] It is holy, set apart and above, the queen to the sperm's king. The egg is also passive, which means it must depend on sperm for rescue. Gerald Schatten and Helen Schatten liken the egg's role to that of Sleeping Beauty: "a dormant bride awaiting her mate's magic kiss, which instills the spirit that brings her to life."[29] Sperm, by contrast, have a "mission,"[30] which is to "move through the female genital tract in quest of the ovum."[31] One popular account has it that the sperm carry out a "perilous journey" into the "warm darkness," where some fall away "exhausted." "Survivors" "assault" the egg, the successful candidates "surrounding the prize."[32] Part of the urgency of this journey, in more scientific terms, is that "once released from the supportive environment of the ovary, an egg will die within hours unless rescued by a sperm".[33] The wording stresses the fragility and dependency of the egg, even though the same text acknowledges elsewhere that sperm also live for only a few hours.[34] In 1948, in a book remarkable for its early insights into these matters, Ruth Herschberger argued that female reproductive organs are seen as biologically interdependent, while male organs are viewed as autonomous, operating independently and in isolation:

> At present the functional is stressed only in connection with women: it is in them that ovaries, tubes, uterus, and vagina have endless interdependence. In the male, reproduction would seem to involve "organs" only.
> Yet the sperm, just as much as the egg, is dependent on a great many related processes. There are secretions which mitigate the urine in the urethra before ejaculation, to protect the sperm. There is the reflex shutting off of the bladder connection, the provision of prostatic secretions, and various types of muscular propulsion. The sperm is no more independent of its milieu than the egg, and yet from a wish that it were, biologists have lent their support to the notion that the human female, beginning with the egg, is congenitally more dependent than the male.[35]

Bringing out another aspect of the sperm's autonomy, an article in the journal *Cell* has the sperm making an "existential decision" to penetrate the egg: "Sperm are cells with a limited behavioral repertoire, one that is directed toward fertilizing eggs. To execute the decision to abandon the haploid state, sperm swim to an egg and there acquire the ability to effect membrane fusion."[36] Is this a corporate manager's version of the sperm's activities—"executing decisions" while fraught with dismay over difficult options that bring with them very high risk?

There is another way that sperm, despite their small size, can be made to loom in importance over the egg. In a collection of scientific papers, an electron micrograph of an enormous egg and tiny sperm is titled "A Portrait of the Sperm."[37] This is a little like showing a photo of a dog and calling it a picture of the fleas. Granted, microscopic sperm are harder to photograph than eggs, which are just large enough to see with the naked eye. But surely the use of the term "portrait," a word associated with the powerful and wealthy, is significant. Eggs have only micrographs or pictures, not portraits.

One depiction of sperm as weak and timid, instead of strong and powerful— the only such representation in western civilization, so far as I know—occurs in Woody Allen's movie *Everything You Always Wanted to Know About Sex But Were Afraid to Ask.* Allen, playing the part of an apprehensive sperm inside a man's testicles, is scared of the man's approaching orgasm. He is reluctant to launch himself into the darkness, afraid of contraceptive devices, afraid of winding up on the ceiling if the man masturbates.

The more common picture—egg as damsel in distress, shielded only by her sacred garments; sperm as heroic warrior to the rescue—cannot be proved to be dictated by the biology of these events. While the "facts" of biology may not always be constructed in cultural terms, I would argue that in this case they are. The degree of metaphorical content in these descriptions, the extent to which differences between egg and sperm are emphasized, and the parallels between cultural stereotypes of male and female behavior and the character of egg and sperm all point to this conclusion.

New Research, Old Imagery

As new understandings of egg and sperm emerge, textbook gender imagery is being revised. But the new research, far from escaping the stereotypical representations of egg and sperm, simply replicates elements of textbook gender imagery in a different form. The persistence of this imagery calls to mind what Ludwik Fleck termed "the self-contained" nature of scientific thought. As he described it, "the interaction between what is already known, what remains to be learned, and those who are to apprehend it, go to ensure harmony within the system. But at the same time they also preserve the harmony of illusions, which is quite secure within the confines of a given thought style."[38] We need to understand the way in which the cultural content in scientific descriptions changes as biological discoveries unfold, and whether that cultural content is solidly entrenched or easily changed.

In all of the texts quoted above, sperm are described as penetrating the egg, and specific substances on a sperm's head are described as binding to the egg. Recently, this description of events was rewritten in a biophysics lab at Johns Hopkins University—transforming the egg from the passive to the active party.[39]

Prior to this research, it was thought that the zona, the inner vestments of the egg, formed an impenetrable barrier. Sperm overcame the barrier by mechanically burrowing through, thrashing their tails and slowly working their way along. Later research showed that the sperm released digestive enzymes that chemically broke down the zona; thus, scientists presumed that the sperm used mechanical *and* chemical means to get through to the egg.

In this recent investigation, the researchers began to ask questions about the mechanical force of the sperm's tail. (The lab's goal was to develop a contraceptive that worked topically on sperm.) They discovered, to their great surprise, that the forward thrust of sperm is extremely weak, which contradicts the assumption that sperm are forceful penetrators.[40] Rather than thrusting forward, the sperm's head was now seen to move mostly back and forth. The sideways motion of the sperm's tail makes the head move sideways with a force that is ten times stronger than its forward movement. So even if the overall force of the sperm were strong enough to mechanically break the zona, most of its force would be directed sideways rather than forward. In fact, its strongest tendency, by tenfold, is to escape by attempting to pry itself off the egg. Sperm, then, must be exceptionally efficient at *escaping* from any cell surface they contact. And the surface of the egg must be designed to trap the sperm and prevent their escape. Otherwise, few if any sperm would reach the egg.

The researchers at Johns Hopkins concluded that the sperm and egg stick together because of adhesive molecules on the surfaces of each. The egg traps the sperm and adheres to it so tightly that the sperm's head is forced to lie flat against the surface of the zona, a little bit, they told me, "like Br'er Rabbit getting more and more stuck to tar baby the more he wriggles." The trapped sperm continues to wiggle ineffectually side to side. The mechanical force of its tail is so weak that a sperm cannot break even one chemical bond. This is where the digestive enzymes released by the sperm come in. If they start to soften the zona just at the tip of the sperm and the sides remain stuck, then the weak, failing sperm can get oriented in the right direction and make it through the zona provided that its bonds to the zona dissolve as it moves in.

Although this new version of the saga of the egg and the sperm broke through cultural expectations, the researchers who made the discovery continued to write papers and abstracts as if the sperm were the active party who attacks, binds, penetrates, and enters the egg. The only difference was that sperm were now seen as performing these actions weakly.[41] Not until August 1987, more than three years after the findings described above, did these researchers conceptualize the process to give the egg a more active role. They began to describe the zona as an aggressive sperm catcher, covered with adhesive molecules that can capture a sperm with a single bond and clasp it to the zona's surface.[42] In the words of their published account: "The innermost vestment, the *zona pellucida*, is a glycoprotein shell, which captures and tethers the sperm before they penetrate it. . . . The sperm is captured at the initial contact between the sperm tip and the *zona*. . . . Since the thrust [of the sperm] is much smaller than the force needed to break a single affinity bond, the first bond made upon the tip-first meeting of the sperm and zona can result in the capture of the sperm."[43]

Experiments in another lab reveal similar patterns of data interpretation. Gerald Schatten and Helen Schatten set out to show that, contrary to conventional wisdom, the "egg is not merely a large, yolk-filled sphere into which the sperm burrows to endow new life. Rather, recent research suggests the almost heretical view that sperm and egg are mutually active partners."[44] This sounds like a departure from the stereotypical textbook view, but further reading reveals Schatten and Schatten's conformity to the aggressive-sperm metaphor. They describe how "the sperm and egg first touch when, from the tip of the sperm's triangular head, a long, thin filament shoots out and harpoons the egg." Then we learn that "remarkably, the harpoon is not so much fired as assembled at great speed, molecule by molecule, from a pool of protein stored in a specialized region called the acrosome. The filament may grow as much as twenty times longer than the sperm head itself before its tip reaches the egg and sticks."[45] Why not call this "making a bridge" or "throwing out a line" rather than firing a harpoon? Harpoons pierce prey and injure or kill them, while this filament only sticks. And why not focus, as the Hopkins lab did, on the stickiness of the egg, rather than the stickiness of the sperm?[46] Later in the article, the Schattens replicate the common view of the sperm's perilous journey into the warm darkness of the vagina, this time for the purpose of explaining its journey into the egg itself. "[The sperm] still has an arduous journey ahead. It must penetrate farther into the egg's huge sphere of cytoplasm and somehow locate the nucleus, so that the two cells' chromosomes can fuse. The sperm dives down into the cytoplasm, its tail beating. But it is soon interrupted by the sudden and swift migration of the egg nucleus which rushes toward the sperm with a velocity triple that of the movement of chromosomes during cell division, crossing the entire egg in about a minute."[47]

Like Schatten and Schatten and the biophysicists at Johns Hopkins, another researcher has recently made discoveries that seem to point to a more interactive view of the relationship of egg and sperm. This work, which Paul Wassarman conducted on the sperm and eggs of mice, focuses on identifying the specific molecules in the egg coat (the zona pellucida) that are involved in egg-sperm interaction. At first glance, his descriptions seem to be the model of an egalitarian relationship. Male and female gametes "recognize one another," and "interactions . . . take place between sperm and egg."[48] But the article in *Scientific American* in which those descriptions appear begins with a vignette that presages the dominant motif of their presentation: "It has been more than a century since Hermann Fol, a Swiss zoologist, peered into his microscope and became the first person to see a sperm penetrating an egg, fertilize it and form the first cell of a new embryo."[49] This portrayal of the sperm as the active party—the one that *penetrates* and *fertilizes* the egg and *produces* the embryo—is not cited as an example of an earlier, now outmoded view. In fact, the author reiterates the point later in the article: "Many sperm can bind to and penetrate the zona pellucida, or outer coat, of an unfertilized mouse egg, but only one sperm will eventually fuse with the thin plasma membrane surrounding the egg proper *(inner sphere)*, fertilizing the egg and giving rise to a new embryo.[50]

The imagery of sperm as aggressor is particularly startling in this case: the main discovery being reported is isolation of a particular molecule *on the egg coat* that plays an important role in fertilization! Wassarman's choice of language sustains the picture. He calls the molecule that has been isolated, ZP3, a "sperm receptor." By allocating the passive, waiting role to the egg, Wassarman can continue to describe the sperm as the actor, the one that makes it all happen: "The basic process begins when many sperm first attach loosely and then bind tenaciously to receptors on the surface of the egg's thick outer coat, the zona pellucida. Each sperm, which has a large number of egg-binding proteins on its surface, binds to many sperm receptors on the egg. More specifically, a site on each of the egg-binding proteins fits a complementary site on a sperm receptor, much as a key fits a lock."[51] With the sperm designated as the "key" and the egg the "lock," it is obvious which one acts and which one is acted upon. Could this imagery not be reversed, letting the sperm (the lock) wait until the egg produces the key? Or could we speak of two halves of a locket matching, and regard the matching itself as the action that initiates the fertilization?

It is as if Wassarman were determined to make the egg the receiving partner.

Usually in biological research, the *protein* member of the pair of binding molecules is called the receptor, and physically it has a pocket in it rather like a lock. As the diagrams that illustrate Wassarman's article show, the molecules on the sperm are proteins and have "pockets." The small, mobile molecules that fit into these pockets are called ligands. As shown in the diagrams, ZP3 on the egg is a polymer of "keys"; many small knobs stick out. Typically, molecules on the sperm would be called receptors and molecules on the egg would be called ligands. But Wassarman chose to name ZP3 on the egg the receptor and to create a new term, "the egg-binding protein," for the molecule on the sperm that otherwise would have been called the receptor.[52]

Wassarman does credit the egg coat with having more functions than those of a sperm receptor. While he notes that "the zona pellucida has at times been viewed by investigators as a nuisance, a barrier to sperm and hence an impediment to fertilization," his new research reveals that the egg coat "serves as a sophisticated biological security system that screens incoming sperm, selects only those compatible with fertilization and development, prepares sperm for fusion with the egg and later protects the resulting embryo from polyspermy [a lethal condition caused by fusion of more than one sperm with a single egg]."[53] Although this description gives the egg an active role, that role is drawn in stereotypically feminine terms. The egg *selects* an appropriate mate, *prepares him* for fusion, and then *protects* the resulting offspring from harm. This is courtship and mating behavior as seen through the eyes of a sociobiologist: woman as the hard-to-get prize, who, following union with the chosen one, becomes woman as servant and mother.

And Wassarman does not quit there. In a review article for *Science*, he outlines the "chronology of fertilization."[54] Near the end of the article are two subject headings. One is "Sperm Penetration," in which Wassarman describes how the chemical dissolving of the zona pellucida combines with the "substantial propulsive force generated by sperm." The next heading is "Sperm-Egg Fusion." This section details what happens inside the zona after a sperm "penetrates" it. Sperm "can make contact with, adhere to, and fuse, with (that is, fertilize) an egg."[55] Wassarman's word choice, again, is astonishingly skewed in favor of the sperm's activity, for in the next breath he says that sperm *lose* all motility upon fusion with the egg's surface. In mouse and sea urchin eggs, the sperm enters at the *egg's* volition, according to Wassarman's description: "Once fused with egg plasma membrane [the surface of the egg], how does a sperm enter the egg? The surface of both mouse and sea urchin eggs is covered with thousands of plasma membrane-bound projections, called microvilli [tiny "hairs"]. Evidence in sea urchins suggests that, after membrane fusion, a group of elongated microvilli cluster tightly around and interdigitate over the sperm's head. As these microvilli are resorbed, the sperm is drawn into the egg. Therefore, sperm motility, which ceases at the time of fusion in both sea urchins and mice, is not required for sperm entry."[56] The section called "Sperm Penetration" more logically would be followed by a section called "The Egg Envelops," rather than "Sperm-Egg Fusion." This would give a parallel—and more accurate sense that both the egg and the sperm initiate action.

Another way that Wassarman makes less of the egg's activity is by describing components of the egg but referring to the sperm as a whole entity. Deborah Gordon has described such an approach as "atomism" ("the part is independent of and primordial to the whole") and identified it as one of the "tenacious assumptions" of Western science and medicine.[57] Wassarman employs atomism to his advantage. When he refers to processes going on within sperm, he consistently returns to descriptions that remind us from whence these activities came: they are part of sperm that penetrate an egg or generate propulsive force. When he refers to processes going on within eggs, he stops there. As a result, any active role he grants them appears to be assigned to the parts of the egg, and not to the egg itself. In the quote above, it is the microvilli that actively cluster around the sperm. In another example, "the driving force for engulfment of a fused sperm comes from a region of cytoplasm just beneath an egg's plasma membrane."[58]

Social Implications: Thinking Beyond

All three of these revisionist accounts of egg and sperm cannot seem to escape the hierarchical imagery of older accounts. Even though each new account gives the egg a larger and more active role, taken together they bring into play another cultural stereotype: woman as a dangerous and aggressive threat. In the Johns Hopkins lab's revised model, the egg ends up as the female aggressor who "captures and tethers" the sperm with her sticky zona, rather like a spider lying in wait in her web.[59] The Schatten lab has the egg's nucleus "interrupt" the sperm's dive with a "sudden and swift" rush by which she "clasps the sperm and guides its nucleus to the center."[60] Wassarman's description of the surface of the egg "covered with thousands of plasma membrane bound projections, called microvilli" that reach out and clasp the sperm adds to the spider-like imagery.[61]

These images grant the egg an active role but at the cost of appearing disturbingly aggressive. Images of woman as dangerous and aggressive, the femme fatale who victimizes men, are widespread in Western literature and culture.[62] More specific is the connection of spider imagery with the idea of an engulfing, devouring mother.[63] New data did not lead scientists to eliminate gender stereotypes in their descriptions of egg and sperm. Instead, scientists simply began to describe egg and sperm in different, but no less damaging, terms.

Can we envision a less stereotypical view? Biology itself provides another model that could be applied to the egg and the sperm. The cybernetic model—with its feedback loops, flexible adaptation to change, coordination of the parts within a whole, evolution over time, and changing response to the environment—is common in genetics, endocrinology, and ecology and has a growing influence in medicine in general.[64] This model has the potential to shift our imagery from the negative, in which the female reproductive system is castigated both for not producing eggs after birth and for producing (and thus wasting) too many eggs overall, to something more positive. The female reproductive system could be seen as responding to the environment (pregnancy or menopause), adjusting to monthly changes (menstruation), and flexibly changing from reproductivity after puberty to nonreproductivity later in life. The sperm and egg's interaction could also be described in cybernetic terms. J. F. Hartman's research in reproductive biology demonstrated fifteen years ago that if an egg is killed by being pricked with a needle, live sperm cannot get through the zona.[65] Clearly, this evidence shows that the egg and sperm do interact on more mutual terms, making biology's refusal to portray them that way all the more disturbing.

We would do well to be aware, however, that cybernetic imagery is hardly neutral. In the past, cybernetic models have played an important part in the imposition of social control. These models inherently provide a way of thinking about a "field" of interacting components. Once the field can be seen, it can become the object of new forms of knowledge, which in turn can allow new forms of social control to be exerted over the components of the field. During the 1950s, for example, medicine began to recognize the psychosocial *environment* of the patient: the patient's family and its psychodynamics. Professions such as social work began to focus on this new environment, and the resulting knowledge became one way to further control the patient. Patients began to be seen not as isolated, individual bodies, but as psychosocial entities located in an "ecological" system: management of "the patient's psychology was a new entree to patient control."[66]

The models that biologists use to describe their data can have important social effects. During the nineteenth century, the social and natural sciences strongly influenced each other: the social ideas of Malthus about how to avoid the natural increase of the poor inspired Darwin's *Origin of Species*.[67] Once the *Origin* stood as a description of the natural world, complete with competition and market struggles, it could be reimported into social science as social Darwinism, in order to justify the social order of the time. What we are seeing now is similar: the importation of cultural ideas about passive females and heroic males into the "personalities" of gametes. This amounts to the "implanting of social imagery on representations of nature so as to lay a firm basis for reimporting exactly that same imagery as natural explanations of social phenomena."[68]

Further research would show us exactly what social effects are being wrought from the biological imagery of egg and sperm. At the very least, the imagery keeps alive some of the hoariest old stereotypes about weak damsels in distress and their strong male rescuers. That these stereotypes are now being written in at the level of the *cell* constitutes a powerful move to make them seem so natural as to be beyond alteration.

The stereotypical imagery might also encourage people to imagine that what results from the interaction of egg and sperm—a fertilized egg—is the result of deliberate "human" action at the cellular level. Whatever the intentions of the human couple, in this microscopic "culture" a cellular "bride" (or femme fatale) and a cellular "groom" (her victim) make a cellular baby. Rosalind Petchesky points out that through visual representations such as sonograms, we are given "*images of younger and younger, and tinier and tinier, fetuses being 'saved.'*" This leads to "the point of visibility being 'pushed back' indefinitely."[69] Endowing egg and sperm with intentional action, a key aspect of personhood in our culture, lays the foundation for the point of viability being pushed back to the moment of fertilization. This will likely lead to greater acceptance of technological developments and new forms of scrutiny and manipulation, for the benefit of these inner "persons": court-ordered restrictions on a pregnant woman's activities in order to protect her fetus, fetal surgery, amniocentesis, and rescinding of abortion rights, to name but a few examples.[70]

Even if we succeed in substituting more egalitarian, interactive metaphors to describe the activities of egg and sperm, and manage to avoid the pitfalls of cybernetic models, we would still be guilty of endowing cellular entities with personhood. More crucial, then, than what *kinds* of personalities we bestow on cells is the very fact that we are doing it at all. This process could ultimately have the most disturbing social consequences.

One clear feminist challenge is to wake up sleeping metaphors in science, particularly those involved in descriptions of the egg and the sperm. Although the literary convention is to call such metaphors "dead," they are not so much dead as sleeping, hidden within the scientific content of texts—and all the more powerful for it.[71] Waking up such metaphors, by becoming aware of when we are projecting cultural imagery onto what we study, will improve our ability to investigate and understand nature. Waking up such metaphors, by becoming aware of their implications, will rob them of their power to naturalize our social conventions about gender.

Notes

1. James Hillman, *The Myth of Analyses* (Evanston, Ill.: Northwestern University Press, 1972), 220.
2. The textbooks I consulted are the main ones used in classes for undergraduate premedical students or medical students (or those held on reserve in the library for these classes) during the past few years at Johns Hopkins University. These texts are widely used at other universities in the country as well.
3. Arthur C. Guyton, *Physiology of the Human Body*, 6th ed. (Philadelphia: Saunders College Publishing, 1984), 624.
4. Arthur J. Vander, James H. Sherman, and Doroffiy S. Luciano, *Human Physiology: The Mechanisms of Body Function*, 3d ed. (New York: McGraw Hill, 1980), 483–84.
5. Vernon B. Mountcastle, *Medical Physiology*, 14th ed. (London: Mosby, 1980), 2:1624.
6. Eldla Pearl Solomon, *Human Anatomy and Physiology* (New York: CBS College Publishing, 1983), 678.
7. For elaboration, see Emily Martin, *The Woman in the Body: A Cultural Analysis of Reproduction* (Boston: Beacon, 1987), 27–53.
8. Vander, Sherman, and Luciano, 568.
9. Melvin Konner, "Childbearing and Age," *New York Times Magazine* (December 27, 1987), 22–23, esp. 22.
10. I have found but one exception to the opinion that the female is wasteful: "Smallpox being the nasty disease it is, one might expect nature to have designed antibody molecules with combining sites that specifically recognize the epitopes on smallpox virus. Nature differs from technology, however: it thinks nothing of wastefulness. (For example, rather than improving the chance that a spermatozoon will meet an egg cell, nature finds it easier to produce millions of spermatozoa.)" (Niels Kaj Jerne, "The Immune System," *Scientific American* 229, no. 1 [July 1973]: 53). Thanks to a *Signs* reviewer for bringing this reference to my attention.
11. Bruce Alberts et al., *Molecular Biology of the Cell* (New York: Garland, 1983), 795.

12. In her essay "Have Only Men Evolved?" (in *Discovering Reality: Feminist Perspectives on Epistemology, Metaphysics, Methodology, and Philosophy of Science,* eds. Sandra Harding and Merrill B. Hintikka [Dordrecht: Reidel, 1983], 45–69, esp. 60–61), Ruth Hubbard points out that sociobiologists have said the female invests more energy than the male in the production of her large gametes, claiming that this explains why the female provides parental care. Hubbard questions whether it "really takes more 'energy' to generate the one or relatively few eggs than the large excess of sperms required to achieve fertilization." For further critique of how the greater size of eggs is interpreted in sociobiology, see Donna Haraway, "Investment Strategies for the Evolving Portfolio of Primate Females," in *Body/Politics,* eds. Mary Jacobus, Evelyn Fox Keller, and Sally Shuttleworth (New York: Routledge, 1990), 155–56.

13. The sources I used for this article provide compelling information on interactions among sperm. Lack of space prevents me from taking up this theme here, but the elements include competition, hierarchy, and sacrifice. For a newspaper report, see Malcolm W. Browne, "Some Thoughts on Self Sacrifice," *New York Times* (July 5, 1988), C6. For a literary rendition, see John Barth, "Night-Sea Journey" in his *Lost in the Funhouse* (Garden City, N.Y.: Doubleday, 1968), 3–13.

14. See Carol Delaney, "The Meaning of Paternity and the Virgin Birth Debate, *Man 21,* no. 3 (September 1986): 494–513. She discusses the difference between this scientific view that women contribute genetic material to the fetus and the claim of long–standing Western folk theories that the origin and identity of the fetus come from the male, as in the metaphor of planting a seed in soil.

15. For a suggested direct link between human behavior and purported eggs and active sperm, see Erik H. Erikson, "Inner and Outer Space: Reflections on Womanhood," *Daedalus* 93, no. 2 (Spring 1964): 582–606, esp. 591.

16. Guyton (n. 3 above), 619; Mountcastle (n. 5 above), 1609.

17. Jonathan Miller and David Pelham, *The Facts Of Life* (New York: Viking Penguin, 1984), 5.

18. Alberts et al. (n. 11 above), 796.

19. Ibid., 796.

20. See, e.g., William F. Ganong, *Review of Medical Physiology,* 7th ed. (Los Altos, Calif: Lange Medical Publications, 1975), 322.

21. Alberts et al. (n. 11 above), 796.

22. Guyton (n. 3 above), 615.

23. Solomon (n. 6 above), 683.

24. Vander, Sherman, and Luciano (n. 4 above), 4th ed. (1985), 580.

25. Alberts et al. (n. 11 above), 796.

26. All biology texts quoted above use the word "penetrate."

27. Solomon (n. 6 above), 700.

28. A. Beldecos et al., "The Importance of Feminist Critique for Contemporary Cell Biology," *Hypatia 3,* no. 1 (Spring 1988): 61–76.

29. Gerald Schatten and Helen Schatten, "The Energetic Egg," *Medical World News 23* (January 23, 1984): 51–53, esp. 51.

30. Alberts et al. (n. 11 above), 796.

31. Guyton (n. 3 above), 613.

32. Miller and Pelham (n. 17 above), 7.

33. Alberts et al. (n. 11 above), 804.

34. Ibid., 801.

35. Ruth Herschberger, *Adam's Rib* (New York: Pelligrini & Cudaby, 1948), esp. 84. I am indebted to Ruth Hubbard for telling me about Herschberger's works, although at a point when this paper was already in draft form.

36. Bennett M. Shapiro, "The Existential Decision of a Sperm," *Cell 49*, no. 3 (May 1987): 293–94, esp. 293.

37. Lennart Nilsson, "A Portrait of the Sperm," in *The Functional Anatomy of the Spermatozoan*, ed. Bjorn A. Afzelius (New York: Pergamon, 1975), 79–82.

38. Ludwik Fleck, *Genesis and Development of a Scientific Fact*, eds. Thaddeus J.Treun and Robert K. Merton (Chicago: University of Chicago Press, 1979), 38.

39. Jay M. Baltz carried out the research I describe when he was a graduate student in the Thomas C. Jenkins Department of Biophysics at Johns Hopkins University.

40. Far less is known about the physiology of sperm than about comparable female substances, which some feminists claim is no accident. Greater scientific scrutiny of female reproduction has long enabled the burden of birth control to be placed on women. In this case, the researchers' discovery did not depend on development of any new technology. The experiments made use of glass pipettes, a manometer, and a simple microscope, all of which have been available for more than one hundred years.

41. Jay Baltz and Richard A. Cone, "What Force Is Needed to Tether a Sperm" (abstract for Society for the Study of Reproduction, 1985), and "Flagellar Torque on the Head Determines the Force Needed to Tether a Sperm" (abstract for Biophysical Society, 1986).

42. Jay M. Baltz, David F. Katz, and Richard A. Cone, "The Mechanics of the Sperm-Egg Interaction at the Zona Pellucida," *Biophysical Journal 54*, no. 4 (October 1988): 643–54. Lab members were somewhat familiar with work on metaphors in the biology of female reproduction. Richard Cone, who runs the lab, is my husband, and he talked with them about my earlier research on the subject from time to time. Even though my current research focuses on biological imagery and I heard about the lab's work from my husband every day, I myself did not recognize the role of imagery in the sperm research until many weeks after the period of research and writing I describe. Therefore, I assume that any awareness the lab members may have had about how underlying metaphor might be guiding this particular research was fairly inchoate.

43. Ibid., 643, 650.

44. Schatten and Schatten (n. 29 above), 51.

45. Ibid., 52.

46. Surprisingly, in an article intended for a general audience, the authors do not point out that these are sea urchin sperm and note that human sperm do not shoot out filaments at all.

47. Schatten and Schatten (n. 29 above), 53.

48. Paul M. Wassarman, "Fertilization in Mammals," *Scientific American 257* (December 6, 1988): 78–84, esp. 78, 84.

49. Ibid., 78.

50. Ibid., 79.

51. Ibid., 78.

52. Since receptor molecules are relatively *immotile* and the ligands that bind to them relatively *motile*, one might imagine the egg being called the receptor and the sperm the ligand. But the molecules in question on egg and sperm are immotile molecules. It is the sperm as a *cell* that has motility, and the egg as a cell that has relative immotility.

53. Wassarman (n. 48 above), 78–79

54. Paul M. Wassarman, "The Biology and Chemistry of Fertilization," *Science*, no. 4788 (January 30, 1978): 553–60, esp. 554.

55. Ibid., 557

56. Ibid., 557–58. Tbis finding throws into question Schatten and Schatten's description (n. 29 above) of the sperm, its tail beating, diving down into the egg.

57. Deborah R. Gordon, "Tenacious Assumptions in Western Medicine," in *Biomedicine Ex-*

amined, eds. Margaret Lock and Deborah Gordon (Dordrecht: Kluwery, 1988), 19–56, esp. 26.

58. Wassarman (n. 54 above), 558.

59. Baltz, Katz, and Cone (n. 42 above), 643, 650.

60. Schatten and Schatten (n. 29 above), 53.

61. Wassarman (n. 54 above), 557.

62. Mary Ellman, *Thinking About Women* (New York: Harcourt Brace Jovanovich, 1968), 140; Nina Auerbach, *Women and the Demon* (Cambridge, Mass.: Harvard University Press, 1982), esp. 186.

63. Kenneth Alan Adams, "Arachnophobia: Love American Style," *Journal of Psychoanalytic Anthropology 4,* no. 2 (1981): 157–97.

64. William Ray Arney and Bernard Bergen, *Medicine and the Management of Living* (Chicago: University of Chicago Press, 1984).

65. J. F. Hartman, R. B. Gwatkin, and C. F. Hutchison, "Early Contact Interconnections Between Mammalian Gametes *in Vitro,*" *Proceedings of the National Academy of Sciences (U.S.) 69,* no. 10 (1972): 2767–69.

66. Arney and Bergen (n. 64 above), 68.

67. Ruth Hubbard, (n. 12 above), 51–52.

68. David Harvey, personal communication, November 1989.

69. Rosalind Petchesky, "Fetal Images: The Power of Visual Culture in the Politics of Reproduction," *Feminist Studies 13,* no. 2 (Summer 1987): 263–92, esp. 272.

70. Rita Arditti, Renate Klein, and Shelley Minden, *Test-Tube Women* (London: Pandora, 1984); Ellen Goodman, "Whose Right to Life?" *Baltimore Sun* (November 17, 1987); Tamar Lewin, "Courts Acting to Force Care of the Unborn" *New York Times* (November 23, 1987), A1 and B10; Susan Irwin and Brigitte Jordan, "Knowledge, Practice, and Power: Court Ordered Cesarean Sections," *Medical Anthropology Quarterly 1,* no. 3 (September 1987): 319–34.

71. Thanks to Elizabeth Fee and David Spain, who in February 1989 and April 1989, respectively, made points related to this.

CHAPTER TWO

Feminist Skepticism and the "Maleness" of Philosophy

SUSAN BORDO

I n the late 1970s in the United States, contemporary American feminism took an important turn. From an initial emphasis on legal, economic, and social discrimination against women, feminists began to consider the deep effects of the gender organization of human life on Western culture—on the literary, scientific, and philosophical canon that we call "the Western intellectual tradition." Earlier feminist works had criticized that tradition for its explicit gender biases: objectionable images of women, misogynist theory, the lack of representation of women's concerns and voices, and so forth. In the late 1970s, however, a deeper "hermeneutics of suspicion" emerged among feminists. We began to realize that gender bias may be revealed in one's *perspective* on the nature of reality, in one's style of thinking, in one's approach to problems—quite apart from any explicit gender content or attitudes toward the sexes.

Recently, some contemporary feminists have taken yet another critical turn. Criticizing what they see as the historical oversimplifications and unconscious ethnocentrism of earlier feminist readings of culture, more recent perspectives urge a new caution, a new skepticism about the use of gender as an analytical category. These perspectives, like much contemporary thought, are informed by what might be called a "theoretics of heterogeneity"—an attunement to multiple interpretive possibilities, to the plurality of interpenetrating factors that comprise any object of analysis and to the "differences" that fragment all general claims about culture. According to such perspectives, to theorize culture or history along gender lines—to speak of "male" and "female" realities or perspectives—is to homogenize diversity and obscure particularity.

Although most commonly associated with postmodern continental perspectives,[1] such a theoretics of heterogeneity, particularly with respect to its implications for a cultural understanding of philosophy, is strikingly and articulately exemplified by the Anglo-American analyst Jean Grimshaw. In *Philosophy and Feminist Thinking*, emphasizing what she describes as the "extremely variegated na-

Susan Bordo, "Feminist Skepticism and the 'Maleness' of Philosophy," in Elizabeth D. Harvey and Kathleen Okruhlik, eds. *Women and Reason* (Ann Arbor: University of Michigan Press, 1992): 143–62. Reprinted by permission.

ture" of human experience,[2] Grimshaw presents two major skeptical challenges to the notion that the history of philosophy can meaningfully and nonreductively be characterized as "male." One such challenge concerns the assumption that the historical traditions of Western philosophy, culturally heterogeneous as they are, can be said to exhibit characteristic enough features to permit any generalizations about content or style, gender based or otherwise. At stake here is the question of how one "reads" the history of *philosophy*. Her other challenge concerns the legitimacy, however one resolves this first issue, of characterizing philosophical perspectives (or, indeed, *any* perspectives) as "male." At stake here is the question of whether philosophy's historical concerns reflect, in some meaningful way, the historical fact of male dominance within the discipline.

Grimshaw does not deny, it should be emphasized, the explicit misogyny of many philosophers, or the persistent exclusion of women from their conceptions of human nature and human excellence. Indeed, she devotes many pages to examining the *sexism* of philosophy. What she questions, rather, is the notion that there is anything distinctively "male" about the *perspective* (or perspectives) that philosophy brings to problems, quite apart from beliefs and attitudes about women and men. In her book, she presents many interesting substantive criticisms of particular accounts of the "maleness" of philosophy. These will not be dealt with here. Rather, my goal is to describe a context of legitimacy for a certain *kind* of enterprise. There are complexities and cautions that must be taken into account in approaching the question of philosophy's "maleness." But, I argue, the question is neither ill founded nor unanswerable. In defending such a notion, I will also indicate a context in which the insights of Grimshaw's skepticism may be profitably employed. Finally, I briefly discuss some of my own concerns about gender skepticism as a potential theoretical turn within feminism, and advocate a more practical, contextual approach to problems of heterogeneity and generality.

Before I do any of these, however, it is necessary to present some theoretical background to the issue. In the United States, two works—Dorothy Dinnerstein's *Mermaid and the Minotaur*[3] and Nancy Chodorow's *Reproduction of Mothering*[4]—were especially influential in charting two important directions that feminist conceptions of the "maleness" of philosophy were to take.

Dinnerstein's central focus was on destructive cultural attitudes toward nature, the human body, mortality, and sexuality. These attitudes are gender biased, Dinnerstein argued, not in the sense that they are exclusively or even distinctively held by men, but, rather, in the sense that they ultimately derive from a gynophobia to which both men and women are vulnerable, insofar as they have been raised within a system of female-dominated infant care. Within such a system, everything pleasurable *and* everything terrifying about bodily needs, desires, and vulnerabilities are first experienced in the arms of a woman—the mother. As a consequence, the entire arena of spontaneous bodily experience becomes associated with "woman" in general and remains split off from the cultural psyche— now identified with all that is "mind," and coded as male. Split off in this way, our ambivalence toward the body remains culturally unintegrated and destructive, particularly for those on whom it is "projected": woman and nature.

Dinnerstein's cultural emphasis has affinities with developments in French feminism. Inspired by Lacanian psychoanalysis, the key category here is that of phallocentrism, the reign of the phallus operating as a metaphor for the cultural privileging of unity, stability, identity, and self-mastery over the "maternally connoted" values of body, spontaneity, multiplicity, loss of self, and so on.[5] Both men and women, Julia Kristeva argues, find reality constructed for them through the template of this symbolic system; for her (although not for other French feminists), there is no specifically feminine form of discourse. Women, insofar as they participate fully in the dominant symbolic order, are just as "phallic" as men; some men, on the other hand (e.g., iconoclastic artists and philosophers), have often been inspired disrupters of that order.

Nancy Chodorow's emphasis, in contrast, was on *differences* in the psychology and "cognitive style" of men and women, differences stemming from contrasting patterns in the development of male and female infants. Because a more rigorous individuation from the mother is demanded of boys, they grow up, Chodorow argued, insisting on clear and distinct boundaries between self and others, self and world, and defining achievement in terms of emotional detachment and autonomy. Possibilities for the application of Chodorow's ideas to the analysis of our male-dominated intellectual traditions immediately presented themselves to feminists from many disciplines. Adopting her emphasis on gender difference, many U.S. feminists began to see the individual and objectivist biases of dominant traditions in the disciplines and professions as "masculine"— that is, as connected to characteristic features of the construction of male psychology and personality. Carol Gilligan's influential *In a Different Voice* emerged from this stream of feminist thought.[6] In it, she elaborated the consequences of the privileging of detachment and individual autonomy in developmental theory and in our dominant ideals of moral reasoning. Created by men, such theories and ideals establish, as normative, a view of social relations and a hierarchy of ethical values that, Gilligan argued, do not reflect the more relational picture of reality underlying the ethical reasoning of women. (It should be noted, however, that Gilligan does not view the different "voices" she describes as essentially or only related to gender. She discovers them in her clinical work exploring gender difference, but the chief aim of her book, as she describes it, is to "highlight a distinction between two modes of thought and to focus a problem of interpretation rather than to represent a generalization about either sex."[7])

The feminist critique of the Western philosophical tradition has been nourished by insights from what I have here characterized in terms of "Dinnersteinian/Kristevan" (on the one hand) and "Chodorovian" (on the other hand) approaches. Writing from a variety of perspectives, feminist philosophers have by now produced a formidable body of gender analysis directed at the traditions of Western philosophy and specific authors within it.[8] Many argue that philosophy has been "masculine" in a psychological sense; others have focused on the persistence of gynophobic themes and/or phallocentric structurings of reality.

Feminist controversy surrounds the historical generalizations involved in such characterizations of philosophy. What I will call the skeptical position on the history of philosophy has been articulated in a number of different (and sometimes contradictory) ways. Grimshaw, pointing to the many conceptual transformations that have marked the history of Western metaphysics and epistemology, has argued that attempts to specify dominant continuing themes in Western thought necessarily involve a homogenizing and distorting ahistoricism. The so-called mind/body problem, for example, so central to modern epistemology, has no equivalent in classical Greek culture—for the concept of mind in the modern sense of consciousness was philosophically developed only in the modern era. To speak of a "mind/body problem" in Plato or Aristotle, thus, is to ahistorically map the categories of the present onto those of the past.[9] Other feminists, pointing to the contradictions and debates within historical periods, have argued that it is illegitimate to identify distinct historical periods. Rosalind Petchesky, tracing continuing organic images and metaphors into the seventeenth century, has argued that any marking of a "transformation" from an organic to a mechanistic worldview, which some feminists have seen as a decisive historic moment in a modern "masculinization" of thought,[10] is a distorting construction. The existence of multiple and competing voices, discoverable at every historical juncture, renders suspect any reading of history that claims to mark the end of one worldview and the triumph of another.[11]

I share the historicist and pluralist sensibilities of such critics. It should be noted, however, that one cannot hold both Grimshaw's and Petchesky's pluralisms at the same time. If history is read, as Petchesky advocates, as absolute heterogeneity, then the deep conceptual transformations that Grimshaw points to become *her* distortingly univocal rendering of multiple voices of history. A more consistent pluralism would acknowledge that philosophy is marked both by important historical rupture such as the birth of modern science—*and* by constant contestation debate within the philosophical conversation of particular periods. What is difficult to see, however, is how acknowledging such heterogeneity entails denying that there have been continuing dominant perspectives both within historical eras and across them. Grimshaw's and Petchesky's conceptions of history and philosophy appear to assume an unsupportable "either/or" conception of change/continuity and dominance/multiplicity. Let me elaborate this criticism.

First, as Michel Foucault's very different conception of history suggests, in "reading" particular periods, one need not *choose* between reading that reveals heterogeneity and one that acknowledges the hegemony of a particular historical discourse. Within the history of philosophy, resistant and alternative voices frequently have spoken against a dominant discourse; indeed, often within the work of a single thinker it is possible to discern both a dominant and a "recessive" strain, the latter speaking for the excluded and the devalued.[12] Grimshaw and Petchesky both present such examples as counterevidence against various feminist attempts to describe general coherencies in the history of philosophy. In their frameworks, apparently, hegemony must be seamless or it cannot be counted as hegemony. A more Foucauldian approach, on the other hand, emphasizes that cultural dominance is never *total*.

In fact, precisely by virtue of its dominance, a reigning discourse creates its own sites of resistance and contestation. First, in the very process of establishing its norms, it constructs and defines all those who are deviant as resistant, "outside," as the constant shadow (to use Jung's term) of the cultural norm. Moreover, intellectual dominance does not take the form of univocal, magisterial decree, but exercises itself through perpetual local "battles" (Foucault's metaphor) organized around "innumerable points of confrontation (and) focuses of instability."[13] Dominance emerges *through*, not in the absence of, contestation. At certain points dominant categories, precisely because they are so ubiquitously present in culture, may even spawn "reverse discourses that employ those categories on behalf of the marginalized. The movements for women's and homosexual rights, for example, drew their initial rhetoric from the categories of liberal humanism and possessive individualism. Today, we are beginning to recognize the losses as well as the gains from that strategy. But, in fact, in the early stages of these movements, no other political rhetoric was as culturally available to as many people: the language of individual rights seemed as natural as the air we breathed. The appearance of naturalness, of course, is a chief mode through which discourses establish and maintain their dominance.

Second, when reading *across* particular periods, a reading that reveals continuity and one that reveals discontinuity are not, as Grimshaw appears to believe, mutually exclusive interpretive strategies. Examples of conceptual change (e.g., of concepts of Mind, Reason, and so forth) do not constitute evidence that there are no transhistorical elements in Western philosophy. For example, although the "mind/body problem" as such may have been invented in the seventeenth century, there is no denying that the body is constituted as a problem for many philosophers. Certainly, the connotations and images have changed with historical circumstances from era to era. For Plato, for example, living in a culture whose imperialist conquests had opened the doors to an influx of diverse peoples, customs, and morals, raising the spectre of cultural relativism in the face of a once-stable system of values, "the body" is imagined as the site of epistemological and moral confusion, its unreliable senses and volatile passions continually deceiving us into mistaking the transient and illusory for the permanent and the real. For the ruling philosophy of the Middle Ages, on the other hand, "the body" is imagined quite differently. Scientific and moral knowledge is stable and in order, as yet unperturbed by the geographical discoveries, religious upheavals, and technological innovations that were to so upset the prevailing picture of the world in the sixteenth and seventeenth centuries. Within this closed universe, whose contours were shaped by the narratives, images, and values of Christianity, the quest for spiritual purity rather than epistemological certainty was the constant struggle. The body now becomes dominantly imagined as the site of unwanted desire—"the slimy desires of the flesh," as Augustine called sexual passion—threat to spiritual progress and ultimate union with God, and symbolized, for him, in the spontaneously and rebelliously tumescent penis, insisting on its "law of lust" against the attempts of the spiritual will to gain control. We thus see considerable conceptual versatility in the construction of "the body." What remains ubiquitous, however, is the casting of the body as the enemy of purity and control, whether spiritual (as for Augustine) or epistemological (as for Plato and Descartes).

The construction of body-as-enemy is one variant of a more general motif that

French feminism has helped us to discern. Helene Cixous and Luce Irigaray work with categories derived from both de Beauvoir and Derrida and argue that, despite major conceptual shifts, a distinctive *form* and a characteristic *logic* run throughout the history of Western philosophy.[14] The form is that of hierarchical opposition: the bifurcation of reality into mutually opposed elements, one of which is privileged and identified with Self, the other of which is disdained and designated as Other. To Anglo-American philosophers, the term *dualism* may be more familiar. But it must be stressed that the dualism discussed here is not a self-conscious philosophical "position"' to be contrasted to materialism, monism, and so forth. It is, rather, the implicit and sometimes unconscious structuring that underlies virtually all such "positions"—a structuring that Derrida has called "*the* metaphysical exigency."[15] Although the specific content of this structuring is not fixed, indeed it varies culturally, what remains constant is its binary logic, which posits a ground, a center, a positivity—and then, defined against that positivity, that which is inferior, derivative, negative, a "fall" from the higher term. For example, we see a frequent philosophical identification of Self with mind, and body with threatening Other. Western philosophy's historical obsessions with "pure" thought, certainty, clear and distinct perception, its search for ultimate categories with which to order the world—these projects, too, assume a hierarchical, oppositional construction of reality. For the hope that they may succeed depends upon the conceptualization and circumscription of a privileged human faculty—whether "reason" or observation—whose *essential* relation to objects is transparent and pure (Rorty's "mirror of nature" is one historical variant) and that is capable of transcending that which threatens to mire it in obscurity and chaos: emotion, perspective, human interest, and so forth. The agonistic struggle implied in this description derives from the precariousness of the dualist construction itself: on some level, the Other is felt to be the part of the self that it actually is; hence, the necessity for constant vigilance against it.[16]

Even if Grimshaw were to concede that such a reading of the history of philosophy does provide at least some partial illumination of that history, the question would rightfully remain: in what sense, if any, is a binary structuring of reality "male"? Clearly, dualism is not "male" in any innate sense—for many male philosophers have protested strongly against philosophy's implicit dualisms and have eloquently presented perspectives that are critical of the philosopher's quest for purity, ultimacy, grounding, and authority. Nietzsche, Dewey, and Derrida come immediately to mind. Some insight on the "maleness" of binary thinking might seem to be provided by the fact, pointed out by French and American feminists alike, that the hierarchical oppositions of Western thought have consistently been gender coded. Reason, for example (and, after the seventeenth century, science), is frequently conceptualized as a distinctively male capacity. In contrast, those faculties against which reason variously has been defined, and which it must transcend—the instincts, the emotions, sense perception, materiality, the body—typically have been coded as female.[17]

If Dinnerstein and Kristeva are right, however, such coding is a consequence of "maternal connotations" and associations that both men *and* women develop through the infantile experience of body care by a woman. In that case, responsibility for such a symbolic system is appropriately attributed to the patriarchal division of labor, which has designated the woman as chief infant caretaker. This is not the same, however, as connecting hierarchical dualisms to a distinctively "masculine" perspective of reality. To establish that, one needs to show that there are significant differences in the perspectives of men and women, differences that dispose men, at least more so than women, to see the world dualistically.

One way of approaching this, as noted earlier, is through an examination of differences in the psychological development of males and females—for example, the work of Nancy Chodorow. This approach, in its focus on patterns of child rearing specific to the bourgeois, nuclear family, has obvious limitations. The developmental scenarios Chodorow describes—requiring an unprecedented emphasis on infant nurturing and on the socialization of children into "masculine" and "feminine" roles—are clearly historically specific. Arising alongside industrialization and the rigid designation of "public" and "private" spheres, such developmental patterns cannot provide an illumination of the construction of male personality during the classical period of Greek philosophy or in the Middle Ages (when it is not even clear that childhood existed, let alone a gendered childhood). For this reason, analyses such as Chodorow's can have only a limited historical application to the interpretation of philosophical themes and concerns. Thus circumscribed, however, they may be tremendously useful—for example, in exploring the Enlightenment emphasis on objectivity, autonomy, and individual rights. It is striking that such an emphasis emerges historically alongside the development of the modern bourgeois family and its ideologies of autonomous, public "masculinity" and nurturant, other-oriented "femininity."

The fact that one cannot provide an account of philosophy's "maleness" in terms of some transhistorical male personality development does not entail, however, that there are no transhistorical practices that have conditioned Western men's and women's perspectives in significantly different ways. Although the rigidly dualistic sexual division of labor that we inherited (and its highly developed ideologies of "masculinity" and "femininity") is the product of industrial culture, the organization of human labor into male and female spheres goes back as far as the ancient Greeks. If Foucault and Bourdieu are right (as I believe they are) about the primacy of the habits of everyday life, the concrete practices that organize the time, space, and activity of the body, then we would expect such an organization (which exhibits a good deal of historical variation, but presents significant continuities as well) to have some important consequences for the construction of male and female experience.

For Grimshaw, of course, the "lack of consensus" (as she calls it) in the interpretation and conceptualization of such practices precludes the possibility of legitimate generalizations along such lines. Women have perceived childbearing, for example, "as both the source of their greatest joy and as the root of their worst suffering"[18]; thus, she concludes, the practices of reproduction cannot be used as a source of insight into the difference gender makes. I do not dispute the obvious existence of multiple valuations and cultural constructions of events such as giving birth. But one does not require an "essentialist" view of reproduction in order to make the sorts of arguments that Grimshaw dismisses a priori. In Iris Young's essay on "Pregnant Embodiment,"[19] for example, one does not find a statement of one, invariant experience of pregnancy, but an exploration of pregnancy (experienced within certain cultural conditions) as one source of nondualistic perspective on mind and body. Philosophy has historically been deprived of such sources of alternative insight by its lack of inclusion of women's perspectives. Grimshaw, however, appears to take the White Rabbit's more Cartesian view of such matters. "What does it matter," he asks Alice, "where my body happens to be? My mind goes on working all the same!"

The thorny question of whether there exist significant transcultural patterns and coherencies in the gender organization of human life is a major source of feminist debate. But even if Grimshaw were to allow that such elements exist, she would insist that we are methodologically prohibited from isolating and describing them.

> The experience of gender, of being a man or a woman, inflects much if not all of people's lives. . . . But even if one is always a man or a woman, one is never *just* a man or a woman. One is young or old, sick or healthy, married or unmarried, a parent or not a parent, employed or unemployed, middle class or working class, rich or poor, black or white, and so forth. Gender of course inflects one's experience of these things, so the experience of any one of them may well be radically different according to whether one is a man or a woman. But it may also be radically different according to whether one is, say, black or white or working class or middle class. The relationship between male and female experience is a very complex one. Thus there may in some respects be more similarities between the experience of factory labor for example, or of poverty and unemployment—than between a working-class woman and a middle-class woman—experiences of domestic labor and childcare, of the constraints and requirements that one be "attractive" or "feminine," for example.
>
> Experience does not come neatly in segments, such that it is always impossible to abstract what in one's experience is due to "being a woman" from that which is due to "being married," "being middle class," and so forth.[20]

Grimshaw emphasizes, absolutely on target, that gender never exhibits itself in "pure" form, but in the context of lives that are shaped by a multiplicity of influences that cannot be "neatly" sorted out. This does not mean, however (as Grimshaw goes on to suggest), that abstractions about gender are methodologically illicit or perniciously homogenizing of differences among people. Certainly, we shall never find the kind of theoretical "neatness" that Grimshaw, nostalgic for a Cartesian universe of clear and distinct "segments," requires of such abstraction.[21] But as anyone who has taught courses in gender knows, there are many junctures at which, for example, women of color and white women discover profound commonalities in their experience (as well as profound differences). One can, of course, adjust one's methodological tools so that these commonalities become indiscernible under the finely meshed grid of various "inflections" (or the numerous counterexamples that can always be produced). But what then becomes of social criticism? The theoretical criteria such as Grimshaw's, which measure the adequacy of generalizations in terms of their "justice" to the "extremely variegated nature of human life" (102), must find nearly all social criticism guilty of distorting abstraction. Her "inflection" argument, although designed to display the fragmented nature of gender, in fact deconstructs race, class, and historical coherencies as well. For the "inflections" that modify experience are endless, and *some* item of difference can always be produced that will shatter any proposed generalizations. If generalization is only permitted in the absence of multiple inflections or interpretive possibilities, then cultural generalizations of any sort—about race, about class, about historical eras—are ruled out. What remains is a universe composed entirely of counterexamples, in which the way men and women "see" the world is purely as particular individuals, shaped by the unique configurations that form that particularity.[22]

Grimshaw presents her skeptical methodological point as an argument against the legitimacy of specifying "male" and "female" points of view. In the context of the history of philosophy, however, her point may be employed differently—to illuminate rather than dispute the "maleness" of philosophy. For a *particular* intersection of gender, race, and class has been typical of Western philosophy, and only in terms of such an intersection can we get a handle on the particular constructions of masculinity that have informed the history of the discipline.

The authors of our classical philosophical traditions have predominantly been white, economically and socially privileged males. (The "Western intellectual tradition" is thus, as Lucius Outlaw once remarked, properly speaking, a minority tradition.) We have no way of imagining what their work would look like if they had written "'only" as white, or "only" as males. Nor can we isolate the "maleness" of philosophy from the contexts of dominance and subordination that have constructed gender, class, and race in our culture. The fact that philosophy has been dominated by white, privileged men has meant that it has developed from the center of power rather than the margins of culture. This has surely had as significant an effect on its development as the fact that it has been authored by men. But given the particular conjunction of gender and power characteristic of Western history, we have no way of separating these elements. The "phallicness" of Western metaphysics is inseparable from its "centrism" (or its whiteness).[23]

It should be no surprise when we find, then, that dominant historical dualisms are overdetermined with respect to race, gender, and class. So, for example, the hierarchical, oppositional construction of reason/unreason may be coded in a variety of ways, including (but not exclusively) as male/female. We also find unreason coded as African (e.g., in Hegel), and class linked and associated with practical, manual activity (a continual subtheme, as Dewey has pointed out, in Greek philosophy). But despite this flexibility with regard to the content of the duality, its hierarchical form is constant; it posits a revered identity (reason, mind, spirit, the white race, the male sex, and so forth), and then defines what is different, Other, and inferior to it (body, matter, practical activity, woman, African).

This structuring has served a multitude of philosophical and ideological purposes; it is overdetermined, after all, by the intersection of at least three separate axes of privilege and power. As regards gender, it can be seen that, through the consistent philosophical identification of women with the bodily arena of unreason, a powerful ideological support is created for keeping women in their "material" place, excluded from those activities seen as requiring rationality and objectivity. Instead, we are relegated to the corruptible practical realm of which the "man of reason" wishes to have no part: the mundane care of the body, food preparation, the management of everyday dirt and disorder, and so forth.[24] Along the same lines, Lucius Outlaw has described the mind-body distinction as essentially a master-slave distinction, establishing for the "man of reason" that "the other folks have the bodies . . . I am the mind."[25] (Thus, it is justified to treat those other folks the way one would soulless matter: to be owned, sold, traded.)

It is not women alone, then, who have been relegated to the "material" arena. But being overdetermined by gender, race, and class is not equivalent to being undetermined by gender. The hierarchical dualisms of Western culture did not descend from an androgynous heaven; they are the product of a historical conversation that has been almost exclusively male and reflect the material privileges that male dominance has entailed. It is difficult to conceive of any marginalized or subordinated group dreaming up such a metaphysics—although, of course, we often reproduce and perpetuate it, living within a culture that is organized, though not seamlessly, along such lines. Examples of women who "think like men" (especially as we attain position and authority) do not invalidate correlations of gender and perspective; rather, they reveal the sedimented and entrenched power of our male-created institutions and symbolic systems. At the same time, the position of marginality, as Kristeva argues, confers a certain potential for disruption of those systems. It is no accident, surely, that the beginnings of the current philosophical reassessment of objectivism and foundationalism followed close on the heels of the public emergence, in the 1960s and 1970s, of those groups marginalized by the dominant metaphysics.

Feminist skepticism has operated as a necessary corrective to the sometimes unitary and universalizing notions of identity, perspective, and voice that emerged from early gender theory. That theory, usually based on the experiences of white, middle-class men and women, has often been guilty, as Grimshaw and others have rightly pointed out, of perpetuating the exclusion of difference that has been characteristic of "male-normative" theories. From another, equally valid perspective, the universalizations of gender theory—along with the work of those who attempted to speak for "black experience" and "black culture"—performed a crucial cultural work on the shoulders of which we all stand. This work, understood in the context of historical process, played an essential role in demystifying the Enlightenment ideology of abstract, universal "man," the featureless bearer of "human" rights and responsibilities, the disembodied mirrorer of nature. For this conception, the particularities of human locatedness—race, class, gender, religion, geography, ethnicity, historical place, personal autobiography—are so much obscuring (and ultimately irrelevant) detritus that must be shaken loose from the mirror of mind if it is to attain impartial moral judgment or clear and distinct insight into the nature of things. Such unclouded and disinterested insight is possible for all persons (as Descartes most clearly articulated) given the right method—a method that will allow reason (or our powers of observation) to rise above the limitations of located, embodied, partial perspective, to achieve what Thomas Nagel has called "the view from nowhere."[26]

Although Nietzsche was the first to mount a direct assault on the notion of perspectiveless thought, it was Marx who initially discerned the first fault lines in the mythology of Enlightenment humanism and forged the tools of political and social analysis to reveal them: Man, he insisted, is fragmented by history and by class. The liberation movements of the 1960s and 1970s added race and gender to class, completing the powerful modernist triumvirate of demystifying and "locating" categories, shattering the myth of unity assumed by the "universal voice" of the "Western intellectual tradition" and exposing its pretensions to neutral perspective. The official stories of that tradition—of its philosophy, religion, literature, material history—now required radical reconstruction. Not only were vast areas of human experience unrepresented, but what *had* been privileged in the dominant traditions of Western culture now had to be seen as the products of historically situated individuals with very particular class, race, and gender interests. The imperial categories that had provided justification for those stories— Reason, Truth, Human Nature, and Tradition—now were displaced by the (historical, social) questions: *Whose* Truth? *Whose* Nature? *Whose* Tradition?

For many contemporary critics, the difficulty of specifying adequate answers to such questions has become a central theoretical issue. Gender, as Grimshaw and others have emphasized, is only one axis of a complex, heterogeneous construct, constantly interpenetrating, in historically specific ways, with race, class, age, ethnicity, sexual orientation, and so forth. This, I believe, is a crucial and sobering insight that ought to keep us on guard against facile and homogenizing generalizations about gender (or any aspect of social identity). However, the corollary notion that is often covert in these critiques, that it is somehow possible (given the right method or the correct politics) to do "justice" (as Grimshaw puts it) to the heterogeneity of things, is another matter. Here, the modernist epistemological fantasy of adequate representations returns—in the new, postmodern form of what I have elsewhere called a "dream of everywhere,"[27] no longer allied with the quest for unity or fixity, but configured around the adequate representation of "difference."

Such a fantasy is no less grandiose than the Cartesian dream of Archimedean detachment or any other ambition to achieve representational mastery. No matter how attentive the scholar is to the axes that constitute social identity, some of these axes will be ignored or marginalized and others selected. (Attending to the "intersection of race, class, and gender" does not overcome this.) This is an inescapable fact of human embodiment, as Nietzsche was the first to point out: "The eye in which the active and interpreting forces, through which alone seeing becomes seeing *something*, are supposed to be lacking" is "an absurdity and a nonsense."[28] This selectivity, moreover, is never innocent. We always "see" from points of view that are invested with our social, political, and personal interests, inescapably "centric" in one way or another, even in the desire to do justice to heterogeneity.

Nor does attentiveness to difference assure the adequate representation of difference. Certainly, we often err on the side of exclusion and, thus, submerge and ignore large areas of human history and experience. But attending too vigilantly to difference can just as problematically construct an Other who is an exotic alien, a breed apart. As Foucault has reminded us, "everything is dangerous"—and every new context demands that we reassess the "main danger."[29] This requires a hyper- and pessimistic activism, not an alliance with "correct" theory. For no theory—not even one that measures its adequacy in terms of justice to heterogeneity, locality, nuance—can place itself beyond danger.

In practical terms, this means that we can never be reassured that our ideas will be "politically correct"; they will be forever haunted by a voice from the "margins," already speaking (or perhaps presently muted but awaiting the conditions for speech), awakening us to what we have excluded, effaced, damaged. This is how we learn, as Minnie Bruce Pratt recognizes.

> When I am trying to understand myself in relation to folks different from me, when there are discussions, conflicts about antisemitism and racism among women, criticisms, criticisms of me, and I get afraid when, for instance, in a group discussion about race and class, I say I feel we have talked too much about race, not enough about class, and a woman of color asks me in anger and pain if I don't think her skin has something to do with class, and I get afraid; when, for instance, I say carelessly to my Jewish lover that there were no Jews where I grew up, and she begins to ask me: how do I know? do I hear what I'm saying? and I get afraid: when I feel my racing heart, breath, the tightening of my skin around me, literally defenses to protect my narrow circle, I try to say to myself: . . . Yes, that fear is there, but I will try to be at the edge between my fear and outside, on the edge at my skin, listening, asking what new things will I hear, will I see, will I let myself feel, beyond the fear.[30]

Pratt does not imagine that the "correct" methodological approach could ever enable the self to transcend ethnocentrism. Rather, she realizes that confrontation with what she calls the "narrow circle of the self" and what it has excluded is a constant risk/inevitability. She dares to speak anyway, to interact with concrete others and allow their actual differences to put her in *her* place (reveal her locatedness to her) rather than put "difference" in its place, through "theorizing" it "adequately."

The best strategies for "doing justice" to heterogeneity, I believe, are institutional, not epistemological. Here, the requirement is shifted from the methodological dictum that we forswear talk of "male" and "female" realities, to the messier, practical struggle to create institutions, communities, conversations that will not permit *some* groups of people to make determinations about "reality" for *all*. For academics, this means not only struggling against explicit racism and sexism and seeking cultural diversity in the recruitment of faculty and students, but attention to the practical arenas (hiring, tenure, promotion, publication criteria, etc.) that privilege certain styles, language, and orientations over others. It means recognition that sexism, racism, and heterosexism are deep psychocultural currents that cannot be cured merely by better theory. And it requires suspicion of and resistance to the hegemony of intellectual discourses and professional practices whose very language requires "membership" to understand and that remain fundamentally closed to difference (regarding it as "politically incorrect," "theoretically unsophisticated," "unrigorous," and so forth). We deceive ourselves if we believe that theory is attending to the inclusion of "difference" so long as so many actual differences—individual and cultural—are excluded from the conversation.

For the remainder of this essay, I would like to displace the discourse of adequation, acknowledge that generalizations about gender can obscure and exclude as well as reveal and illuminate (determinations, I believe, that must be made from context to context, not by methodological fiat), and raise some concerns about what may be obscured by too relentless an emphasis on heterogeneity. I want to advocate a more practical, contextual approach to problems of heterogeneity and generality. From such a standpoint, general categories of identity—race, class, gender, and so forth—remain vital, in certain contexts, for social criticism. Let me mention just some of those.

Identity politics, for example, require such totalizations (e.g., the "black women" of the Combahee River Collective) at particular moments in their development; they are useful, "life-enhancing fictions" (as Nietzsche might say) that lift veils of personal mystification and enable the recognition of solidarity with others. General categories of social identity continue to be essential, too, to the ongoing exposure and analysis of the biases of Western culture. One of my arguments in this essay has been that too wholesale a commitment to the representation of historical heterogeneity can obscure the transhistorical hierarchical patterns that inform our traditions. The biases of philosophy reflect not only the particular historical situations of various authors but also configurations of race, class, and gender that have been characteristic of the social situations of the authors of our classical canon. What has been called the phallogocentrism of Western metaphysics is the product of the overdetermined privilege—racial, class, and gender privileges—that has allowed imaginations of the pure, the transparent, the one, the true, the clean, the clear, the authoritative, to form such a central motif in the historical conversation of those for whom the messy, the bodily, the "vicissitudes of (everyday, practical) existence" (as Dewey described it) can always be constructed as Other, because they are *taken care of* by others.

More generally, I worry that the intellectual dominance of a "theoretics of heterogeneity" will (once again) obscure the dualistic nature of the actualities of power in Western culture. Contemporary feminism, like many social movements arising in the 1960's, developed out of the recognition that to live in our culture is not (despite powerful social mythology to the contrary) to participate equally in some free play of individual diversity. Rather, one always finds oneself located within structures of dominance and subordination—not least important of which have been those organized around gender. Certainly, the duality of male/female is a "discursive formation," a "social construct." So, too, is the racial duality of black/white. But as such, each of these constructed dualities has had profound consequences for the experiences of those who "live" them.

Feminism, in exposing the *gendered* nature of Western thought, has contributed significantly to intellectually dismantling the Enlightenment mythology of abstract, universal man and its epistemological corollary of an abstract, universal reason. There is no "view from nowhere," feminists have insisted; all thought is socially located. Disquietingly, skeptical feminism may be in the process of installing a *new* version of the "view from nowhere" by deconstructing gender right out of operation as a tool for relocating reason from the Cartesian heavens of disembodied rationality and into the bodies of actual human beings. Without such general categories of identity, the notions of social interest, location, and perspective—notions that give content and force to the critique of abstract humanism and the "view from nowhere"—are no longer usable. They remain theoretically in force, while we are hobbled in making the general claims that drive them home in practice.

This is a practical, not a theoretical, worry. Past feminist efforts have begun to produce visible results in the philosophy curriculum, as more and more philosophers are acknowledging the patterns of exclusion and bias in our discipline and are attempting to reconceive their courses accordingly. But there are others, we should remember, who would reinstate the "great works," undisturbed by gender, race, class, or cultural analysis, to the center of our curriculum, and recrown the future Philosopher-King as the only student worth teaching. Within this institutional struggle, feminists would do well to hold fast to the analytical category of gender and not allow it to become lost in a Sargasso Sea of counterexamples and endlessly multiple meanings. This is not to say that a cultural understanding of philosophy requires univocal, fixed conceptions of social identity and location. Rather, we need to reserve *practical* spaces for both old-fashioned generalist criticism (which still provides, as I have argued, crucial kinds of insights into history and culture) and attention to complexity and nuance as well. At this particular juncture, we may pay a very high institutional and political price for our intellectual deconstructions.

Notes

1. See Susan Bordo, "Feminism, Postmodernism, and Gender Skepticism," in *Feminism/Postmodernism*, ed. Linda Nicholson (New York: Routledge, 1989), for discussion of these perspectives.
2. Jean Grimshaw, *Philosophy and Feminist Thinking* (Minneapolis: University of Minnesota Press, 1986), 102.
3. Dorothy Dinnerstein, *The Mermaid and the Minotaur* (New York: Harper and Row, 1977).
4. Nancy Chodorow, *The Reproduction of Mothering* (Berkeley: University of California Press, 1978).
5. See Julia Kristeva, *About Chinese Women* (New York: Urizen, 1977).
6. Carol Gilligan, *In a Different Voice* (Cambridge, Mass.: Harvard University Press, 1982).
7. Gilligan, *Different Voice*, 2.
8. See the March, 1989, issue of the *Newsletter on Feminism and Philosophy* for a representative bibliography.
9. Grimshaw, *Philosophy*, 66.
10. See Susan Bordo, *The Flight to Objectivity: Essays on Cartesianism and Culture* (Albany, N.Y.: SUNY Press, 1987); Brian Easlea, *Witch Hunting, Magic, and the New Philosophy* (Atlantic Highlands, N.J..: Humanities Press, 1980); Sandra Harding, "Is Gender a Variable in Conceptions of Rationality?", *Dialectica* 36 (1982): 225–42; James Hillman, *The Myth of Analysis* (New York: Harper and Row, 1972).

11. Rosalind Petchesky, "Body Politics in the Seventeenth Century," colloquium on Women, Science, and the Body, Cornell University, May, 1987.
12. Bordo, *Flight to Objectivity*, 114–18.
13. Michel Foucault, *Discipline and Punish* (New York: Vintage, 1979), 27.
14. Helene Cixous, "The Laugh of the Medusa," *Signs 1* (Summer, 1976): 875–93; Helene Cixous with Catherine Clement, *The Newly Born Woman* (Minneapolis: University of Minnesota Press, 1986); Luce Irigaray, *Speculum of the Other Woman* (Ithaca, N.Y: Cornell University Press, 1985).
15. Jacques Derrida, "Limited Inc.," *Glyph 2* (1988): 66.
16. Some specific examples of such hierarchical, binary oppositions are: intelligible/sensible, transcendental/empirical, literal/metaphorical, objective/subjective, reality/appearance, rigorous/soft and (in ethics) duty/compassion.
17. Cixous, "Laugh"; Cixous with Clement, *Newly Born Woman*; Irigaray, *Speculum*; Genevieve Lloyd, *The Man of Reason: "Male" and "Female" in Western Philosophy* (Minneapolis: University of Minnesota Press, 1984).
18. Grimshaw, *Philosophy*, 73.
19. Iris Young, "'Pregnant Embodiment: Subjectivity and Alienation," *Journal of Medicine and Philosophy* 9 (1984): 45-62.
20. Grimshaw, *Philosophy*, 84–85.
21. Grimshaw consistently creates a "straw woman" out of feminist gender theory by suggesting (incorrectly) that it typically argues for "a radical, total disjunction between male and female realities," a "distinctively female point of view that is in all respects inaccessible to men," or "uniquely female" perspectives on reality. This reified, rigidly dichotomous understanding of gender difference is Grimshaw's projection and rarely to be found, in my opinion, in the works she criticizes.
22. Lynne Arnault makes a similar point in "The Uncertain Future of Feminist Standpoint Epistemology" (LeMoyne College, Syracuse, N.Y., typescript).
23. The authors of our classical philosophical canon have also overwhelmingly been Christian. I thank Bat-Ami Bar On for reminding me of this crucial fact, which bears not only on the "structural" motifs discussed in this essay, but on the dominance of particular categories and themes in the nature of philosophy.
24. Here, it is particularly and bitingly ironic when conceptions of philosophy employ images of "cleaning the litter with which the world is filled" (as James called it) in describing the task of the philosopher: Danto's "conceptual housekeeping," Raphael's "mental clearance": Raphael even reminds us, in the style of a *Good Housekeeping* article, that mental clearance, like cleaning the house, "is not a job that can be done once and for all. You have to do it every week. The mere business of living continues to produce more rubbish which has to be cleared regularly." Raphael here picks up on Locke's famous description of the philosopher as an "under-labourer . . . removing some of the rubbish that lies in the way of knowledge." Such metaphors evoke the realm of the material, practical, and everyday precisely to offer a vision of their transcendence. The conceptual "housekeeper" it turns out, "executes" his tasks in a hierarchical, dualistic neighborhood within which it is the Other that makes all the mess. For Danto, this messy side of town is inhabited by the other disciplines, constantly generating conceptual confusion, but too "robustly busy," as he says, to tend to the cleaning of their own houses. Quine's use of the cleaning metaphor is even more suggestive of class associations: he speaks, in *Word and Object*, of the philosopher's task as "clearing the ontological slums." See D. Raphael, *Problems of Political Philosophy* (London: Macmillan, 1976), 16; Arthur Danto, *What Philosophy Is* (New York: Harper and

Row, 1968), 10; W. U. 0. Quine, *Word and Object* (Cambridge: Cambridge University Press, 1960), 275.

25. Workshop on racism and the history of philosophy, Le Moyne College, Syracuse, N.Y., June 1987.
26. Thomas Nagel, *The View from Nowhere* (Oxford University Press, 1986).
27. Susan Bordo, "The View from Nowhere and the Dream of Everywhere: Heterogeneity, Adequation, and Feminist Theory," *Feminism and Philosophy Newsletter* (March 1989): 19–25. See also Bordo, "Feminism, Postmodernism":
28. Friedrich Nietzsche, *On the Genealogy of Morals* New York: Vintage, 1969), 119.
29. Michel Foucault, "On the Genealogy of Ethics," in *Beyond Structuralism and Hermeneutics*, ed. Hubert Dreyfus and Paul Rabinow (Chicago: University of Chicago Press,1983), 232.
30. Minnie Bruce Pratt, "Identity: Skin, Blood, Heart," in *Yours in Struggle*, ed. Elly Balkin, Minnie Bruce Pratt, and Barbara Smith (New York: Long Haul Press, 1984), 18.

CHAPTER THREE

Feminist History After the Linguistic Turn

Historicizing Discourse and Experience

KATHLEEN CANNING

T he starting point of this article is the ongoing and uneasy encounter between feminism and poststructuralist theory across the disciplines. I explore, here, the implications of what has come to be termed the *linguistic turn* for the history of women and gender and analyze the controversies among feminists about its far-ranging consequences for historical research and writing. The very interdisciplinarity implied by the term *linguistic turn* constitutes one of the uneasy moments in this encounter: the boundary crossings between disciplines have challenged the foundations of individual fields while at the same time creating new domains of interdisciplinary inquiry that seem to render obsolete the familiar tools, concepts, and epistemologies of the traditional disciplines. Indeed, because much of the provocative rethinking and recasting of these terms has taken place outside of history, attempts to redefine keywords in the vocabulary of social history and women's history—*experience, agency, discourse,* and *identity*—must be embedded in debates across disciplines.[1]

However fruitful the fracturing of disciplinary boundaries has been, it has also opened up difficult questions regarding the meanings and methods and historical practice in the wake of the linguistic turn. For this reason it is imperative to grapple with the poststructuralist challenge not only across the disciplines but also specifically on the terrain of history by reexamining the historical narratives, concepts, chronologies, and boundaries that have been displaced in the context of our own historical research and writing. In this article, therefore, I rethink the contested terms *discourse, experience,* and *agency* through a study of gender and the politics of work in the German textile industry during late Imperial and Weimar Germany. I focus in particular on two moments of crisis and transformation in German history that intertwine the histories of experiences and discourses: the emergence of female factory labor as a new social question in the

Kathleen Canning, "Feminist History After the Linguistic Turn: Historicizing Discourse and Experience," *Signs* 19:2 (1994): 368–404. Reprinted by permission.

1890s and the feminization of union politics during the 1920s, when a politics of the body transformed the politics of class.

Feminist History and the Linguistic Turn

In the field of history the term *linguistic turn* denotes the historical analysis of representation as opposed to the pursuit of a discernible, retrievable historical "reality." Any attempt to define the linguistic turn should acknowledge that in popular academic usage—in graduate seminars, conference debates, and even in many scholarly papers—"the linguistic turn" (like the term *postmodernism*) has become a catch-all phrase for divergent critiques of established historical paradigms, narratives, and chronologies, encompassing not only poststructuralist literary criticism, linguistic theory, and philosophy but also cultural and symbolic anthropology, new historicism, and gender history.[2] It is difficult to disentangle the complex ways in which each of these strands of inquiry have (depending on one's subject position) challenged, threatened, or revitalized the discipline of history or to discern how these strands (separately or in convergence with one another) have engendered a sense of epistemological crisis, a "crisis of self-confidence" among social historians in particular.[3] What is new and controversial about the linguistic turn for social historians is the pivotal place that language and textuality occupy in poststructuralist historical analysis. Rather than simply reflecting social reality or historical context, language is seen instead as constituting historical events and human consciousness.[4]

While most historians would likely define the linguistic turn in terms of the influence of Foucault, Derrida, and/or Lacan, I view feminist history as occupying a central place in its genealogy. In fact, women's history began to interrogate and subvert the historical canon before Foucault, or certainly Derrida, had found an audience among social historians. The reception of various strains of poststructuralism, including French feminism, took place in the interdisciplinary arenas of university women's studies programs and journals like *Signs* and *Feminist Studies* during the late 1970s and 1980s.[5] Thus, those feminist historians who came to reject biological essentialism as an explanation of the inequalities between the sexes were among the first historians to discover the power of discourses to construct socially sexual difference and to anchor difference in social practices and institutions. In dissolving the myth of "natural" divisions between public and private, between women and men, women's history prepared the way for the shift toward a self-conscious study of gender as a symbolic system or a signifier of relations of power.[6] Together, if not always hand-in-hand, feminist and poststructuralist critiques of historical "master-narratives" interrogated, disassembled, and recast historical paradigms in light of new histories of women and gender and of race, ethnicity, and sexuality.

The decentering of the Western white male subject and the reformulation of subjectivity as a site of disunity and conflict initially appeared to open up an emancipatory space in which feminist historians could constitute female subjects while exposing and rectifying the historical exclusion of women and the identification of human with male. The relentless uncovering of binary oppositions, of their hierarchies and orders of subordination, helped, in the words of Mary Poovey, to "reveal the figurative nature of all ideology" and to expose the artifices and exclusions inherent in the categories of nature, gender, class, and citizen (Poovey 1988a, 58). Yet the process of unmasking and deconstructing categories and boundaries also meant that the once unitary category *woman* began to fracture. As women of color rose to challenge racism within feminist movements and in the academy during the late 1970s and early 1980s, feminist scholars and activists became increasingly, and often painfully, aware of the ways in which the "feminist dream of a common naming of experience" was illusory, totalizing, and racist (Haraway 1991, 173). As feminists of color rewrote histories of slavery, colonialism, and feminism from their oppositional locations, they also contested their own colonization in the discourses of Western feminist humanism (Mohanty 1991, 53.)[7]

In a related but distinct vein of inquiry, Denise Riley's *Am I That Name? Feminism and the Category of "Women" in History* (1988) also interrogated and deconstructed the category *women*. Riley analyzed the inherent instability of the term *women*, emphasizing its embeddedness in other concepts such as "the social" and "the body," through several centuries of European history. Grounded in historical analysis, Riley dismissed notions of tangible unities among women, of fixed notions of identities or counteridentities, and sought to redefine feminism as a contested arena in which the instability of the category women would have to be continually fought out (Riley 1988, 4–7, 99).[8] Historian Joan W. Scott also posed a fundamental challenge to the historical profession with her pathbreaking essay of 1986, "Gender: A Useful Category of Historical Analysis." This article, together with her essay collection *Gender and the Politics of History* (1988), marked and theorized the shift from women's history to gender history that had been underway for some time and summoned so-called mainstream historians to consider gender as an essential category of historical analysis. In introducing poststructuralist theory into women's/gender history, Scott laid the foundation for a critical reinterpretation of concepts such as experience, agency, and identity and placed gender at the heart of nascent historical discussions of poststructuralism. Even though women's history/gender history prepared the ground in many respects for the linguistic turn, the often vitriolic responses to Scott's challenge make clear that it is also a field in which the stakes of the debate are particularly high.[9]

As a historian of women and gender who came of age during this sea change, it is evident to me that feminist historical scholarship is still contending with the destabilizing effects of the linguistic turn. While it is impossible to do justice here to the diverse and imaginative ways in which feminists have sought to contend with this challenge, I will briefly allude to three possible outcomes of the encounter between feminism and poststructuralism. First, and for a wide variety of complex and diverse reasons, many feminists have resisted what they perceive as the fragmenting and paralyzing effects of multiple and indeterminate female identities. Indeed, attempts to decenter a (female, gay, African-American, or Latino) subject whose own subjectivity is still in the process of being historically constituted created profound dilemmas for feminist historians, whose main task until recently was to recover the female subject and render her visible in history. Thus, many have come to see poststructuralism as a particularly disempowering, even dangerous, approach for marginalized groups to adopt, as it undermines their efforts to name themselves, to "act as subjects rather than objects of history" (Hartsock 1990, 163). These feminists have sought to uphold "the visionary and critical energy of feminism as a movement of cultural resistance and transformation," to emphasize their own agency as well as that of their historical subjects against the poststructuralist axiom of the discursive character of all practices (Bordo 1990, 135).

Feminist poststructuralists, by contrast, salute this crisis in feminism as fruitful and invigorating in both the scholarly and political sense. In their recent volume *Feminists Theorize the Political* (1992), editors Judith Butler and Joan W. Scott address some of their critics' objections by explicating a kind of methodology for feminist poststructuralist inquiry. Thus, a feminist deconstruction of the historical subject or agent suggests not the negation, dismissal, or censorship of the concept but rather requires its "critical reinscription and redeployment." Categories can be reinscribed and redeployed once "all commitments to that to which the term . . . refers" are suspended and the ways in which it consolidates and conceals authority are unmasked (Butler 1992, 15; Butler and Scott 1992, xiv). Significantly, Butler and Scott invite feminists to reinscribe concepts like subject or agency but do not suggest a rewriting of deconstruction or poststructuralism itself. The third group of feminists to which I refer here envision an encounter, a strategic engagement between feminism and poststructuralism, that transforms both sides in significant ways. Nancy Fraser and Linda Nicholson, for example, seek to meld the analytical and critical power of both strands, to "combine a postmodern incredulity toward metanarratives with the social-critical power of feminism" (1990, 34–35).[10] Literary scholar Mary Poovey calls upon feminists to first rewrite deconstruction in order to render it useful—to endow it with tools for analyzing specificity, to historicize it, to enrich it with a model of change, and finally to deploy it upon itself. And because deconstruction challenges feminism in fundamental ways, this act of rewriting will transform not only deconstruction but also feminism (Poovey 1988a, 51, 60–63).

Feminist projects of "rewriting," "reinscribing," or "redeploying" key concepts of political and historical vocabulary have emerged as one primary outcome of the encounter between feminism and poststructuralism. In this article I aim to rewrite the terms *experience* and *discourse* and, by implication, the notions of agency, subjectivity, and identity. Specifically, I mean to untangle the relationships between discourses and experiences by exploring the ways in which subjects mediated or transformed discourses in specific historical settings. To do so, I contemplate the sites of subjectivity and agency, in particular, the enigmatic place of the body in the making of subjectivity or identity. My own search for answers takes as its starting point the assertion that there is no turning back to the unreflective use of concepts such as experience or class (although many historians still seem to hope that the power of the poststructuralist challenge will dissipate with time).[11] My inquiry is also grounded in the recognition that the ongoing encounter between poststructuralism and feminism is itself indeterminate and fluid. It is therefore incumbent upon those of us who have found this challenge stimulating to rewrite, reinscribe, and redeploy the concepts we consider crucial in our own work. Because of the importance of Joan W. Scott's work for my own, I seek here to read two of her most compelling essays—one on experience, the other on discourse—against my own analysis of the discourses of social reform in late Imperial Germany and the experiences of female textile workers in Germany after the First World War (Scott 1988, 1991).

Rereading and Rewriting History: Experience and Discourse

Experience

Experience has been a keyword in social history, particularly in histories of subjugated or invisible groups, since the 1960s. In the narratives of labor history, for example, experience denoted the "vast, multiple, contradictory realm" that lay between the relations of production and the awakening of class-consciousness (Sewell 1990, 55–56). One of the most innovative fields of German history, *Alltagsgeschichte* (the history of everyday life), for instance, has focused on everyday life experiences as the site at which "abstract structures of domination and exploitation were directly encountered" (Eley 1989, 324). Women's history and feminist theory have long relied on similar notions of experience as mediating between the experiences of sexual oppression and the development of feminist consciousness and as creating the basis for unity or identity among women (Mohanty 1992, 76). Dorothy Smith's study of *The Everyday World as Problematic* (1987), for example, views experience as the foundation of a feminist sociology, as "the ground of a new knowledge, a new culture" that is located in "one's bodily and material existence." For Smith, experience constitutes an alternative site at which dominant sociological paradigms and theory can be contested, as women's standpoints are usually "situated outside textually mediated discourses in the actualities of our everyday lives" because they are excluded from "the making of cultural and intellectual discourse" (1987, 107).

Joan W. Scott's "The Evidence of Experience" challenges the "authority of experience," that is, "the appeal to experience as uncontestable evidence and as an ordinary point of explanation." She is interested in not only interrogating the experience of the historical subject but also that of "the historian who learns to see and illuminate the lives of those others in his or her texts" (Scott 1991, 777). The starting point of Scott's discussion of experience is Samuel Delany's *The Motion of Light in Water* (1988), which she describes as "a magnificent autobiographical meditation . . . that dramatically raises the problem of writing the history of difference, the history, that is, of the designation of 'other.'" Scott's aim here is to critique Delany's focus on his own experience, his "apprehension of massed bodies," in a gay bathhouse as the basis of knowledge, identity formation, and political power (1991, 775). His mission of documenting the "lives of those omitted or overlooked in accounts of the past"—in this case black, gay men—is one that he shares with many historians (especially women's historians), and his tendency to portray knowledge as "gained through vision" and writing as "reproduction, transmission—the communication of knowledge gained through (visual, visceral) experience"—is indeed emblematic of much historical research and writing (Scott 1991, 775–76). For Scott however, the "project of making experience visible" obscures "the workings of the ideological system itself [and] its categories of representation (homosexual/heterosexual, man/woman, black/white) as fixed immutable identities" and in fact "precludes" the central task of analyzing "how difference is established, how it operates, how and in what way it constitutes subjects who see and act in the world" (1991, 777–78). Here Scott constructs the task of analyzing the experience and/or identity of difference as oppositional rather than complementary to the task of examining how difference was constituted in the first place.

Scott's call to scholars to historicize rather than take as self-evident the identities of those whose experience is being documented is well taken, although much recent work in the history of women and gender already does this, even if it is not always explicitly theorized.[12] Scott's agenda might signal a whole new kind of historical investigation, the history of homosexuality instead of homosexuals; of "blackness" instead of blacks; of the construction of the feminine instead of women. It is the "instead of" that both intrigues and concerns me. Although Scott does not explicitly posit this, it is implicit in the opposition she establishes between the discursive construction of difference and the ways in which people experienced it (and, by extension, how identities were formed based on that experience), and it underlies her claim that the exploration of the latter somehow precludes the former.[13]

Even if Scott rejects the notion that historians can capture experience in the sense of "lived reality" or "raw events," she concedes that "experience is not a word we can do without" (1991, 797). The closest Scott comes to a definition of experience, however, is that it is a "linguistic event" that "doesn't happen outside established meanings": "Experience is a subject's history; language is the site of history's enactment [and] historical explanation cannot, therefore, separate the two" (1991, 792–93). Although many historians would agree that historical analysis should not (or, indeed, cannot) separate language and experience, even sympathetic readers may find problematic the one-dimensional notion that language or discourses "position subjects and *produce* their experiences" (1991, 779). Moreover, Scott's rhetorical strategy allows concepts to flow into one another, making it difficult to disentangle them from one another (language from discourse, for instance). "Experience," for example, "is a subject's history"; "language is the site of history's enactment"; "discourses produce experiences"; subjects are constituted "through experience." Scott's arguments sometimes appear to follow an almost circular path; at other times they seem to establish new oppositions. In either case it is difficult to imagine what these postulates might mean in concrete historical settings. Scott offers a masterful deconstruction of the concept of experience but stops short of actually redefining or rewriting it. So even if we might agree with her about what experience is *not* (transparent, visceral), we are left unsure as to what it might be.

What traces of experience might we be able to discover in various historical sources, then? Labor and feminist historians usually mean by *experience* more than the mere "living through of events"; the term also encompasses the way in which "people construed events as they were living through them" (Sewell 1990, 64). In his dialogue with Scott, for instance, William H. Sewell, Jr., defines experience as "the linguistically shaped process of weighing and assigning meaning to events as they happen," a process that is embedded in the "cultural understandings and linguistic capacities" of historical subjects (Sewell 1989a, 19). Alf Lüdtke's notion of *Eigensinn*, a key concept in German *Alltagsgeschichte*, likewise signifies a particular way of responding to or making meanings of events as they happen, a "striving for time and space of one's own," a sense of self-preservation and self-presentation as well as a "self-willed distancing" that facilitates a "reframing," "reorganizing," or a "creative reappropriation of the conditions of daily life" (Lüdtke 1985, 304–5, 312–15).[14] This emphasis on construing, reframing, and reappropriating implies that subjects do have some kind of agency, even if the meanings they make "depend on the ways of interpreting the world, on the discourses available to [them] at any particular moment" (Weedon 1987, 79). Indeed, experience, as the rendering of meaning, is inextricably entwined with the notion of agency, with a vision of historical subjects as actors who, in Sewell's terms, "put into practice their necessarily structured knowledge" (1989b, 5).

In her discussion of Delany, Scott acknowledges that "subjects do have agency," and she clarifies that "they are not unified, autonomous individuals exercising free will."[15] Scott circumvents the thorny problem of agency in her discussion of Samuel Delany as subject in the making: she emphasizes the ways in which "agency [is] created through situations and statuses conferred on individuals" but leaves open the question of how subjects mediate, challenge, resist, or transform discourses in the process of defining their identities (1991, 792–93). While Scott acknowledges the "conflicts between discursive systems and the contradictions within any one of them," the transformations of individual identities take place within discursive systems that remain seemingly fixed (1991, 793). Her skeptical stance toward stories of emancipation in which "resistance and agency are presented as driven by uncontainable desire" not only obscures the ways in which discourse and experience are entwined but also disregards the fact that desire (a very interesting kind of agency) has figured importantly in many stories of transformation or revolution (778).

Key, however, in analyzing how discourses change, how subjects contest power in its discursive form, and how their desires and discontents transform or explode discursive systems is the concept of agency. How can discourses figure as anything but fixed hegemonic systems without the interventions of agents who render them contingent and permeable? Now that the linguistic turn has stripped agency of the "baggage" of the autonomous enlightened individual, it should undergo the same kind of rethinking and rewriting as the terms *experience, identity,* and *class*.[16] Indeed, we might uncover the ways in which historical subjects mapped, transformed, and "reterritorialized" political location by heeding Sherry Ortner's call to make room for those on the other side of our historical or ethnographic texts, to recognize that as "we attempt to push these people into the molds of our texts, they push back" (1994).[17] A conception of agency as a site of mediation between discourses and experiences serves not only to dislodge the deterministic view in which discourse always seems to construct experience but also to dispel the notion that discourses are, to paraphrase Ortner, shaped by everything but the experiences of "the people the text claims to represent" (1994).

Discourse

Scott's essay "'L'ouvrière! Mot impie, sordide . . .': Women Workers in the Discourse of French Political Economy, 1840–1860" offers a historically specific setting in which to examine the workings of "discursive construction," to consider where discourses begin and end, how they are constituted and transformed, and how they empower and disempower, engender and deflect resistance (in Scott 1988, 139–63). As such, it provides a different kind of forum for debate than her essay on experience. The starting point of the essay is a mid-century discourse of political economy that "define[d] the terms of a new science of economics, . . . codif[ied] its laws and disciplined its practitioners." The political economists who shaped this discourse, she holds, "established the intellectual and institutional power of their science through control of knowledge and access to government [and] were able to provide the conceptual framework within (and against) which those addressing economic questions had to work" (1988, 141). Scott argues convincingly that working women figured in their discourses in a dual way, serving "at once as an object of study and a means of representing ideas about social order and social organization" (1988, 162).

Scott explores the contradictions within this discourse "by attending to the rhetorical as well as the literal functions of these writings, by examining the contrasts used to constitute meaning" (1988, 154). She delivers a fascinating analysis of the ways in which female sexuality was used metaphorically to talk about working-class misery. Women workers came to inhabit a "world of turbulent sexuality, subversive independence and dangerous insubordination" that placed them in close discursive proximity to prostitutes: "The interchangeable uses of *femmes isolées* suggested that all such working women were potential prostitutes, inhabiting a marginal and unregulated world in which good order—social, economic, moral, political—was subverted" (1988, 143). I found this instance of "reading Scott reading" particularly valuable for the insight it offers into the significance of "reading" in historical analysis, which is something that social and labor historians seldom problematize.[18] The ability to attend to the rhetorical aspects of historical texts, to their contrasts, exclusions, and/or binary oppositions, makes it possible to uncover, for example, the metaphors of female sexuality that might otherwise be difficult to see or interpret. In fact, learning how to read in new ways may be a prerequisite for pursuing the history of experience as a process of making, assigning, or contesting meanings.

Yet Scott's arguments foreground the discursive in the construction of women's work while leaving obscure its relationship to the social context in which it emerged. She insists, for example, that "the prominence of the woman worker in the nineteenth century, then, came not so much from an increase in her numbers or a change in the location, quality or quantity of her work, as from contemporaries' preoccupation with gender as a sexual division of labor. This preoccupation was not *caused* by objective conditions of industrial development; rather it *helped shape* those conditions, giving relations of production their gendered form, women workers their secondary status, and home and work, reproduction and production their oppositional meanings" (Scott 1989, 43; emphasis mine). She draws the reader into a compelling analysis of the intertextual process, the meanings internal to this discursive system, but resists the urge to pursue the historical question of what this discourse meant or signified in the broader context of nineteenth-century French history. When and why did political economists begin to "see" women workers? What was the outcome of this discursive explosion during the midcentury, of the attempts of political economists to address public opinion and to translate their views into policy?

To answer these questions I offer a reading of the origins and outcomes of discourses of social reform in Germany during the late nineteenth century. My notion of discourse is a modified Foucauldian one of a convergence of statements, texts, signs, and practices across different, even dispersed, sites (from courtrooms to street corners, e.g.).[19] Implicit in the term *discourse*, as both a textual and a social relation, is a certain expertise, the power and authority to speak, and the existence of a public sphere that transcends local settings.[20] Historical analysis of discourse is complicated by the need to distinguish between singular discourses and the wider discursive systems or domains to which they belong. Chris Weedon explains, for example, that the ideology of "natural" biological difference between the sexes was cast and anchored within a domain of "conflicting discourses, from medicine and sociobiology to radical feminism" during the mid-nineteenth century (Weedon 1987, 127). While the constitutive and subjugative power of discourses is a central focus of my discussion, I take up Sonya Rose's notion of a "double vision of text and context" and consider Judith Walkowitz's suggestion that material reality is a force that pressures and destabilizes the discursive domain, requiring representations "to be reworked, shored up, reconstructed" (Walkowitz, Jehlen, and Chevigny 1989, 31; Rose 1991, 7–8). Finally, like Walkowitz and Mary Poovey, I examine the multiple subject positions within discourses, the discrepancies in access to social space and power, that are essential to an understanding of both the subjugation and the resistance of individual subjects.[21]

Similar to the political economic texts that Scott analyzes, the discourses of social reform in Germany depicted female factory work as constituting a new "social question" during the last two decades of the nineteenth century, as Germany underwent its rapid second wave of industrialization. The 1890s saw a marked shift from a focus on the generalized "worker question" to that of the woman worker and, in particular, the married woman worker, whom many social reformers sought to exclude from factory labor. Along with growing anxieties about social democracy, social unrest, and imperial expansion came fears about the working-class family, rent apart by the expansion of the female factory workforce—children left to fend for themselves, men driven into the pubs by the dirty, inhospitable living quarters in the absence of wives and mothers. Reformers sought to preserve the working-class family as an anchor in a rapidly changing world, a bulwark against social distress and disorder, some by "regulating" and "protecting" women workers, others by banning them altogether from factories.

The narratives of danger about female factory labor ranged from scholarly treatises on *Geschlechtscharakter* (sexual/gender characteristics) to shocking revelations about the effects of women's work—women's bodies ravaged by machines and long hours of labor, infant mortality, filth and squalor in workers' living quarters—that stimulated popular interest in the problem. These narratives evoked dramatic visions of social dissolution that were replete with analogues among the destruction of the social body, the body of the family, and the physical bodies of women workers and the children they bore. As the public sphere expanded and was redefined by mass politics during the 1890s, a wide spectrum of voices shaped this discursive domain: employers, politicians, state bureaucrats, liberals, Catholics, socialists, and feminists, in addition to some of Germany's leading social scientists: Lujo Brentano, Gustav Schmoller, Ferdinand Tönnies, and Max Weber. The voices of the latter, who spoke as "scientific" experts, were juxtaposed with those of the *Betroffene*, those directly affected—male weavers and union leaders who embraced a virulent rhetoric against the feminization (*Verweiblichung*) of factory production and the displacement (*Verdrängung*) of men from their jobs.

The discursive domain of social reform consisted of several overlapping, often competing, discourses: medical-biological-eugenicist; bourgeois feminist; industrialist-capitalist; Social Democratic; social Catholic; liberal social reformist; and the paternalist/interventionist discourses of the welfare state. Although located in discrete social spaces, structured by definite languages, and implementing distinct rhetorical strategies, these discourses were nonetheless ordered by what Denise Riley terms "webs of cross-references."[22] Singular discourses converged to form a discursive domain as each sought to resolve the growing discrepancy between the continued expansion of the female workforce and dominant notions about the character of the sexes. Furthermore, the discourses examined here were constituted across a range of texts, encompassing "scientific" studies of workplace or household budgets; parliamentary debates; factory inspections and state surveys; protective labor legislation; employers' sanctions and union programs; and even calls to strikes against the hiring of women workers. During the 1890s the agitation at these diverse sites (parliaments, pubs, strike lines) formed a groundswell of social pressure that ultimately prompted the state to mediate, intervene, and sanction an official resolution of the new social question through labor legislation.

My reading of the discourses of social reform differs from Scott's in several respects. First, I am interested in how and why discourses emerge, how the historical world was internalized or inscribed in texts (Spiegel 1990, 84). Particularly interesting are, of course, the moments of inscription that lead to discursive shifts or transformations. Inscribed in the discourses of social reform in late Imperial Germany was a transformation of the labor market, namely, the steady and perceptible expansion of the female factory workforce during the last quarter of the century. As the economy boomed at the end of the century, employers faced a continuous labor shortage in nearly all industrial sectors, including the so-called women's industries of textiles, garments, and cigar making. The married female workforce nearly doubled between 1882 and 1907, and the percentage of married women among adult female factory workers increased from 21 to 29 percent in the four-year period between 1895 and 1899.[23] These social and economic changes were inscribed in the discursive domain of social reform, in the vision of men displaced and "transformed into maidens" by mechanization and feminization, in the widespread perception of a sexual and social order gone awry.[24]

Thus, to embed the discourses of social reform in a specific historical context (in this case the rapid expansion of industry and the female labor market in Germany) is not necessarily to postulate that they "reflect a reality." While Scott's analysis suggests an opposition between a discourse's "being caused by industrial conditions" or its "helping to shape them," these are two central and intertwined aspects of the discourse about female factory labor in Germany. I agree that discourses about social reform and female factory labor helped shape the industrial order in Germany, but certainly the increasing numbers of female factory workers and the transformation of the industrial labor market were not imaginary creations of the minds of social reformers. Understanding the reformers' imaginations is crucial, however, in grasping the meanings they ascribed to these social and economic transformations and in mapping out the emergence of female factory labor as a new social question. Contextualizing or historicizing discourse makes it possible to see both of these things at once. In fact, locating the discourses of social reform in the context of the changing industrial landscape renders more visible the power of discourse to shape a new sexual division of labor.

The second way in which my inquiry differs from Scott's is that I am interested in both the material consequences and the ideological effects not only of discourses that become hegemonic but also of those that were contested and transformed. The emergence of female factory labor as a new social question in the late 1880s and 1890s marks a discursive shift away from the prevalent acceptance during the 1870s of "the notion that lower-class women had to work, even if this meant outside the home in factories" (Quataert 1983, 108). The representations of men "transformed into maidens," of women "abducted" from home and family, of a morally degenerate and physically declining workers' estate had complex moralizing as well as regulative outcomes (Martin 1896, 399–400).[25] As they came to realize that married women could not be banned from factories, social reformers sought to import the home into the workplace, to instill female factory workers with domestic skills, and to supplant the imagery of disorder, the specter of feminization and disintegration of gender roles, with a new order founded on the division between the male breadwinner and the female "secondary" earner. Thus, a new ideology of women's work emerged around the turn of the century in the discursive domain of social reform that remade the workplace and demarcated its boundaries and hierarchies of gender. It shaped the structures of production: the sexual division of labor and its hierarchies of wage and skill, the design and implementation of textile technology, and the factory regime of discipline and punishment, as well as employers' moral regime of charity and tutelage. Moreover, this discursive shift and the ideology it engendered had important implications for the world beyond the mill gate. Not only did it define a new industrial order, but it also marked the female body as a new site of intervention for both the moralizing and regulatory regimes of industrial paternalism and social reform. It recast the relationship between family and state, between sexual and social order, and in doing so, it shaped the formation and expansion of the German welfare state.

Third, I am interested in both the subjects and the objects of the discourses of social reform. I aim not only to recover the loud and powerful voices of political economists holding forth on the perils of the industrial world but also to render as subjects those whose labor was inscribed with ideologies of gender. In seeking to break the silence of women workers (however difficult this may be), I resist the tendency of discourse analysis to displace the subject or to reduce her "to a mere bearer of systemic processes" by analyzing the reception, the contestation, the multiple meanings of texts (Smith 1990, 161). In my own work, for example, I attempt to uncover work cultures and work identities, that is, the meanings workers derived from their waged work and the ways this work was embedded in family, neighborhood, and community.[26] Such an examination might uncover the complex ways in which male and female workers interpreted, subverted, or internalized discourses of labor or ideologies of work. Exploration of the expressive cultural practices—the everyday struggles over pride and honor, gossip and respectability, bodies and sexuality, charity and tutelage—through which workers adapted to and subverted ordained locations within the factory regime reveals not only complicity and resistance (including discursive resistance) but also the multiple subject positions that they occupied at any given moment.[27] In the next section of this article I explore one moment of profound disruption in German history, when women workers, armed with the consciousness of their multiple subject positions as workers, wives, and mothers, succeeded in contesting the terms of the discourses that defined them.

Experience, Discourse, and "the Body"
During the Weimar Republic

The First World War, the revolution of 1918, and the subsequent realignment of military and civilian society in Germany brought about a profound transformation of women's experiences of citizenship and class and of family and sexuality, as well as a rapid disordering of the discursive domain of gender. The gender imagery of the early Weimar Republic was replete with contradictions: women's newly acquired right to vote and their prominent place in the strikes and bread riots of 1917–18 and in the revolution of 1918 stood in stark contrast to the mass displacement of women from their jobs during demobilization. Soon after the war the castigation of "double-earners" by state, union, and labor councils nullified their wartime salutations of women's sacrifices for the fatherland. The rhetoric of civic equality for the sexes was supplanted by the rapid erosion of women's rights as the new Social Democratic government struggled to stabilize and regenerate the wounded nation. Central to the tasks of reconstituting the national body politic, of dissolving the boundaries between "male" front and "female" home-front, was a new attention to the political meanings of male and female bodies (Domansky 1994).[28]

Recent feminist scholarship makes clear that the history of the body is essential to understanding the ruptures in discourses and experiences during the war and the Weimar Republic. Weimar society was haunted not only by the visions of male bodies ripped apart or numbed by war but also by the wounds inflicted on women's bodies, as Elisabeth Domansky has argued: "They (women) did not recall a generalized immiseration, but the ceasing of menstruation, their inability to breast-feed their children, and the erosion of their good looks. They interpreted the loss of weight not simply as a loss of strength and health, but as a loss of attractiveness. War defeminized them and turned them into prematurely old women. War wounded them as it wounded the men" (1990). The postwar task of healing the ailing body politic gave the female body a new visibility as a site of discursive intervention. Women's bodies, constructed in the discursive space between medicine and politics, formed a key link in solving physical and social pathologies that were now more acute and widespread than during the 1890s.[29] They figured centrally in both the coercive pronatalism of wartime and in the eugenicist population policies of Weimar. The ideology of motherhood was revitalized across the political spectrum after the war: the Socialist and Communist parties repudiated the punitive population policies advocated by the nationalist Right but pursued their own programs of improving the conditions of maternity for working women (Usborne 1992, 209). The female body was also at the heart of the discourse of the sexually emancipated "new woman," one of the most profound ruptures in postwar culture: she was the woman who could not be sent back into the home, a figure of transgression in the dual sense of economic independence and the pursuit of sexual pleasure.[30]

The female body has also been a key site of contention in the encounter between feminism and poststructuralism.[31] In much feminist theory and historiography the body has figured as a feminist site of lived experience that serves to ground agency and resistance, to give it concrete origins.[32] Feminists and others who disavow the poststructuralist emphasis on discursive construction have mobilized the body as a tangible limit to the power of representation. Susan Bordo points out that poststructuralist feminists have fashioned a "body whose own unity has been shattered by the choreography of multiplicity." Bordo cites the example of Donna Haraway's cyborg as a postmodern body that "invites us to take pleasure in the 'confusion of boundaries,' in the fragmentation and fraying of the edges of the self that have already taken place" (Bordo 1990, 144; Haraway 1991, 151). I seek to transcend these dichotomies through a historical case study of the female body in both its discursive and experiential dimensions. I also explore Regenia Gagnier's suggestions that examination of material culture (as the social space in which discourses are located) necessarily leads one to the body, that the body is located at a crossroads between material culture and subjectivity, and that bodily experiences of desire and deprivation shape subjectivity in important ways (Gagnier 1991, 10–11, 57–58). My focus here is on a new "moment of inscription," when women workers enunciated their own embodied experiences of work, war, and revolution within the segmented realms of formal politics (the fragmented labor movement and the myriad coalition governments that composed "the state") and across the terrain of the diffuse and often contested discourses about the body. It is a moment when women's experiences of wartime and postwar disjunctures were inscribed in the discourse of class, when a politics of the body transformed the politics of class.

The convergence during the early years of Weimar of a crisis of nation with a crisis of class—the fracturing and (re)formation of the working class—also altered the political landscape of the social democratic textile union. The extent to which both were also crises of gender became clear during the sudden and powerful transformation of the social climate surrounding women's work during demobilization. This rupture posed particular dilemmas for the social democratic textile union (DTAV) as female membership in the union increased by over 450 percent between 1918 and 1920 (Deutscher Textilarbeiterverband [DTAV] 1928, 147). It formed the basis for the "feminization" of union politics, for a rewriting of class by gender, as women responded to the rapid discursive shifts about gender and women's waged work after the First World War.

The DTAV, founded in 1891 under the shadow of the protracted transition from home weaving and spinning to mechanized mills, was a site of gender contest from the outset. The profound anxiety of male weavers and spinners about women's waged work in textiles, their perceptions of feminization, dislocation, and displacement, formed an essential subtext of official social democratic theories of women's emancipation. Thus, while the first social democratic weavers' associations granted women the right to vote and to be elected for office, union members frequently raised public demands for legal sanctions against women's work in textile mills.[33] Until 1908, when the revised Prussian Law of Association permitted women to join political associations, the DTAV's policies toward women were unofficial, localized, and lacked an administrative backbone in the union bureaucracy. A marked dissonance prevailed between its endorsement, on the one hand, of "equal pay for equal work" and a shorter working day for women and its evocation, on the other hand, of threatening visions of female competitors (or "wage-cutters") who displaced male breadwinners from their jobs and then acquiesced in their own exploitation. Nonetheless, by 1908 some 48,000 women belonged to the DTAV, constituting over one-third of its membership and the largest female contingent among the industrial unions (Canning 1988, 317–20).

In the political culture and practice of the DTAV between 1908 and 1914, the "woman question" signified contests about men's wages and female competition, about the meanings of female *Eigenart* for union politics. *Eigenart* became a complex political slogan that designated the particularities of female needs, activities, sentiments, and consciousness.[34] Female union activists in the DTAV sought recognition of *Eigenart* in their everyday struggles in the textile mills—for higher wages, a shorter work day, and greater protection of pregnant workers—and through their campaigns to create space within the union for separate women's meetings, a women's column in the union paper, and better training for female union functionaries. The fact that female particularities were embedded in working women's bodies was seldom acknowledged explicitly: at this juncture the politics of *Eigenart* did not represent a new body politics. In emphasizing that female particularities made women different from but not inferior to men, women activists opposed the universalist (male) claims of class and repudiated the possibility of seamless integration of women into male spheres of work or politics (Stoehr 1983, 228–29). They implemented the vocabulary of *Eigenart* to subvert the social identity and the discourse of class by staking political claim to the multiple subject positions women workers inhabited simultaneously, by refusing the assignment of one or the other socially sanctioned subject position ("mother" to the detriment of "worker" or vice versa, depending on the historical circumstances).[35] Male labor leaders, by contrast, utilized their own rhetoric of *Eigenart* to disparage women's needs and experiences and the burdens they might represent for the labor movement. Female *Eigenart* undermined the universalist claims of class and refuted the assertion of DTAV leaders that the union had already achieved equality between the sexes.

The struggle for a social and discursive space for women in the DTAV was suspended by the outbreak of the First World War. The experiences of war, in both their social and discursive dimensions, are crucial to understanding the feminization of union politics that took place during the mid-1920s. First, the fixed boundaries between *Frauen-* and *Männerindustrien* (women's and men's industries) dissolved during the war as women ventured into previously male sectors of production and acquired new skills.[36] The discursive construction of women's work also shifted as employers, factory inspectors, union leaders, and the militarized state acknowledged that the mobilization of female workers was of critical importance to the war effort. Women's paid labor for the fatherland was imbued, if only for a few years, with the honor and esteem that had otherwise been reserved for skilled male breadwinners.

A parallel process took place in the DTAV as thousands of men left for the front and women took their places at local union posts.[37] Within a few years, the DTAV became a predominantly female union: by 1916 women made up some 60 percent of members, increasing to 74 percent by 1918, forcing the DTAV leadership to acknowledge that women had become "the core of the organization" (DTAV 1917b, 127–29). Indeed, the politics of *Eigenart* seem to have flourished in the spaces vacated by the union men during the war.[38] Outside the unions, women workers recast civil society as they negotiated the confusing terrain of consumption restrictions and rations. After the turning point of the "turnip winter" of 1916–17, they played a vital role in fracturing the "civil peace" between unions and state by waging illegal strikes (Domansky 1994; Davis 1994).[39]

Although the DTAV had become a predominantly female union by 1918, female activists faced new challenges when the war came to a close. In 1918 unemployment among textile workers exceeded that of the worst months of the war, as military production ceased and all available raw materials remained under control of the War Ministry (DTAV 1919, 72–73). At the same time, men began returning from the front, hoping to reclaim their former jobs. The demobilization decrees, drafted by the state and supported and enforced by unions and factory labor councils, sought to restore social stability by returning newly discharged veterans to their jobs as quickly as possible. The decrees stigmatized thousands of women as "double-earners" (those whose husbands, fathers, or brothers were employed and could presumably provide for them) and forced them to relinquish their jobs in favor of men.[40] By 1920 the DTAV confirmed that some 8,100 married women had been dismissed from their jobs in the textile industry in order to make room for men (DTAV 1921a, 91–92). Despite the relatively small numbers of demobilized women, the decrees can be viewed as the first step toward a postwar realignment of sexual and social order.

In the meantime, a kind of political demobilization took place within the union as men returned after the war to dominate its bureaucracy and to reclaim their former posts on the local level. Although women joined the union in unprecedented numbers between 1918 and 1921, the dissension within the union among Majority Socialists, Independent Socialists, and Communists—as well as the spread of politically charged labor unrest and general strikes during 1920—meant that union leaders scarcely took note of the new female majority.[41] In 1919 the DTAV executive even voted to dismantle the Women's Bureau when its members concluded "that a special type of training for women was unnecessary" (DTAV 1921b, 146). Male leaders now invoked women's experiences of war, revolution, and democracy as proof of their "equal" abilities and status, as testimony against the politics of *Eigenart*. Female activists, however, quickly renewed their efforts to recast union policies and programs. Drawing on the presence by 1920 of nearly one-half million female members, female activists were now empowered to speak more openly and forcefully in the arena of national union conventions and in the union press. Embracing the new democratic rhetoric of rights, they disrupted the union's congress in 1921 to demand restoration of the Women's Bureau and the appointment of a salaried female member of the executive branch, insisting also that, "in view of the strength of our female membership, we have a right to have a representative here at this congress" (DTAV 1921b, 90–91). The fulfillment of women's postwar demands was delayed by the political upheavals of 1920 and 1921 and then by the crisis of 1923–24, when women's demands were again submerged while the union contended with the effects of economic collapse and drastic unemployment (DTAV 1924, 60). The new crisis, like that of 1918–20, was inscribed by gender conflicts as state and unions alike revived the rhetoric of double-earners and as women were subjected to *Bedürftigkeitsprüfungen* (tests of need) in order to receive unemployment benefits. Indeed, the shift toward a feminization of politics began in the wake of this crisis, during which the DTAV lost nearly 60 percent of its female members.[42]

This crisis served as a turning point in the history of gender politics in the DTAV. As the discursive field of body politics widened during the mid-1920s, female union activists embedded their own bodily experiences of pregnancy, birth control, abortion, and housework in their political demands. The backdrop for the emergence of the female body in the arena of class politics after 1925 was formed by the discourses of national population policy, racist eugenics, and feminist and socialist sexual reform, which sought to discipline sexuality and reproduction, as well as by the revitalized science of work, which sought to rationalize and maximize the body's productivity. This shift is remarkable not only because it represented a fundamental transformation of the discourse of class within the German labor movement but also because it occurred in a predominantly female union that was led until 1927 almost exclusively by men. It attests to the ways in which women workers broke the silence about their bodies in a public arena and in doing so contested the oppositions between production and reproduction, public and private that underlay the politics of class.

The opening act in the DTAV's politics of the body was the battle it initiated with textile mill owners over the protection of pregnant women at work in 1925.[43] The union launched an inquiry into the effects of factory employment on pregnant textile workers: of the 1,110 surveyed, some 70 percent of them (or their babies) had experienced prenatal or postnatal complications (DTAV 1925a; Usborne 1992, 48). Later that year the DTAV presented its shocking findings to the Reichstag in the form of a petition, speaking now not primarily in the name of class but on behalf of its 330,000 female members (40 percent of whom were married) and particularly for the ninety thousand pregnant women who were working full-time in the mills in 1925. Physician Max Hirsch endorsed the DTAV petition and confirmed its claims that some two-thirds of pregnant textile workers experienced complications in childbirth, including very high rates of miscarriage and stillbirth (Hirsch 1925). With this survey, published as a brochure in 1925, the DTAV shifted the terms of the anxiety-ridden discourse about sexual emancipation and the declining birth rate and brought into sharper focus the conditions of birthing and motherhood, transforming what Thomas Laqueur calls "the statistical body" into "the lived (female pregnant) body" that now had a bearing on national politics (1989, 194–95). Hirsch's brochure (appended to the DTAV's petition) visualized these conditions through numerous photographs of pregnant women at work. In each case the task being performed was different—weaving, spinning, winding, finishing—but the shared representation was the woman's swollen belly pressed up against moving machinery. Despite the adamant protests of the employers' association that the DTAV's figures were exaggerated and that many childbirth complications could be attributed to venereal disease, the mill owners conceded that some 25 percent of pregnant textile workers declined the partially paid maternity leave and remained at work until the day of delivery.[44]

The DTAV now sought to create a space within the union for a politics of the body through instituting "women's evenings" and women's conferences. The first was a Conference of Pregnant Workers, held in Crimmitschau in June 1923 in order to organize and outline the planned survey of pregnant women's experiences in the textile mills (DTAV 1925a, 48–50; 1925b, 43). Then, galvanized by its results in 1925, the DTAV convened another women's congress in October 1926. The meeting, held in the textile center of Gera, drew some 280 female and sixty-three male delegates, most of whom were longtime union activists, in addition to factory inspectors, doctors' and midwives' organizations, representatives from the Labor Ministry and the Prussian Ministry of Commerce and Industry, and officials of the Social Democratic and Communist Parties (DTAV 1927a, 4–12). Female *Eigenart*-the special needs of pregnant women, new mothers, unwed mothers, and women in need of birth control or abortion—was the theme and preoccupation of the congress (DTAV 1927a, 3, 15). While the delegates heard testimony from mothers who were forced to stand at their machines until the moment before they gave birth, medical doctors discussed the availability and legality of birth control and presented the grim statistics about the epidemic of illegal and dangerous abortion among working-class women (DTAV 1927a, 74–89, 98; Grossmann 1983).[45] On the last day of the meeting some eight thousand textile workers—mostly women—marched through the streets of Gera, raising banners that linked reproductive issues with the politics of the workplace. They called for a restoration of the eight-hour day; expanded maternity leave; access to birth control; repeal of Paragraph 218, the law that banned abortion; and, finally, the liberation of women from housework (DTAV 1927a, 39–40, 140). In response to the DTAV's two-pronged campaign, the German government voted in 1927 to sign the Washington Agreement that extended mandatory maternity leave from eight to twelve weeks, improved maternity benefits, protected pregnant women or new mothers from being fired, and guaranteed women the right to breaks at work during which they could nurse their infants (DTAV 1927a, 36, 49). While motherhood had figured prominently in the rhetoric of *Eigenart* before the war (one element of which had been to appeal to the woman worker as mother), the feminized politics of the 1920s centered on freedom from the *Gebärzwang* (compulsory childbearing). Underlying the new location of the body in DTAV politics was a renewed commitment to gender equality based on a recognition of female *Eigenart*.

Entwined with the new politics of the body in the DTAV was the emergence of housework, of the sexual division of the labor in the "private" sphere of home and family, as an issue of debate in the union. Female delegates to the Gera congress had raised demands for day care, communal laundries, kitchens, and cafeterias in order to liberate women from housework; at the union's 1927 general congress they called upon DTAV members to recognize the benefits of a socialization of housework for women, men, and the union itself (DTAV 1927a, 51–56; 1927b, 142). The union undertook its own investigation of the double burden soon after, sponsoring an essay contest for female textile workers on the theme *mein Arbeitstag—mein Wochenende* (my working day, my weekend) in 1928. Like its petition to the Reichstag on pregnancy and work, the DTAV's publication of 150 selected essays in a brochure of the same title inserted the everyday lives of working women into its campaign for expanded health and safety protection, shortened work hours, higher wages, and consumer co-ops (DTAV 1930; Lüdtke 1991). Despite the abbreviated and edited form in which they appeared, the published essays point to the fluid boundaries between waged work and housework. The main theme of the essays is time, and many recount in minute detail how much time the author required for preparing meals, cleaning, darning, and walking to and from work and the scarcity of time for children, husband, parents, leisure, self-education, or cultivation of new domestic or political skills.[46] While offering powerful testimony about the ways in which fatigue "defined the limits of the working body," the essays also seem to reflect working women's own internalization of Taylorist norms of efficiency and discipline, of the body as a "human motor" (Rabinbach 1992; Grossman 1986, 70–77; Usborne 1992, 98). The female workers' essays attest to the power of sexual difference as experienced in everyday life in household and neighborhood, even if they efface the sexual or desiring body, the pregnant or nursing body, the body ravaged by frequent abortions. They lack the passion, the urgency of the brochure of 1925 on "Wage Labor, Pregnancy, Women's Suffering." Yet they insert into political debate, in particular the campaign for the eight-hour day, a female body that is hassled, hurried, and depleted by the daily double burden.

Conclusion: Inscription/Reinscription

How does the politicized female body that emerged during the mid-1920s represent the experiences of working women? What is the meaning of the discursively constructed body for women's bodily abjection, not only in extraordinary times of war and revolution, but also in the everyday sufferings of factory work, childbirth, and back-alley abortions? What are the implications of this analysis of the female body and the politics of class for a rewriting of the contested terms *discourse, experience*, and *agency*? First, if the female body appeared at all in union politics prior to the mid-1920s, it was a body that occupied a singular subject position, a body circumscribed by factory work—by its encounters with machines, its submission to production quotas and speed-ups, its vulnerability to accidents and chronic illness. Second, in representing the multiple subject positions working women simultaneously inhabited, the explicitly politicized female body that emerged during the mid-1920s disrupted the singular social identity of motherhood ascribed to working women through dominant discourses. The female body that appears in the DTAV's petitions to the *Reichstag*, in the brochure on women's reproductive "suffering," in the public demonstration for accessible birth control and abortion, and in essays like "The Clock Ticks On" (in *Mein Arbeitstag—mein Wochenende*), marks a discursive shift precisely because it performs different kinds of work all at once: weaving or spinning, birthing and nursing, cooking, cleaning, and caring for children. Furthermore, in joining rather than severing the different spheres of work, the female body of the 1920s was emblematic of the politics of *Eigenart*. Its emergence attests not only to the growing presence of women in the union but also to the ways in which they mobilized their own subjugated and embodied knowledges to contest and recast the dominant meanings of body politics and of class.

My analysis of the feminization of politics suggests that women's embodied experiences of war, revolution, and demobilization—hunger, stealing, striking, demonstrating, and birthing or aborting—opened the way for the transformations of consciousness and subjectivities. The erosion of civil society and the escalated policing by the pronatalist military dictatorship of the spheres of work, consumption, and sexuality meant that women experienced their bodies as sites of intensified intervention and regulation (and perhaps also as political weapons) during war and demobilization. As the female body became an increasingly unpredictable threat to the success of total war and as military and civilian authorities put new systems of codification and supervision in place, women became acutely aware that "the front was everywhere," that the front was inscribed in their bodies (Domansky 1994). While the war represented an indisputable turning point in the body's politicization, what likely propelled women into the streets of Gera in 1926 was the accumulated experiences of the female body in all the realms of "work," its day-to-day wounding—the endless cycle of cooking, washing, cleaning, and mending, work without recognition or pay that decided a family's day-to-day survival; the mechanization and depletion of the body by machines in the mills; the body's vulnerability to illness, injury, or rape; the miscarriages, stillbirths, and pregnancies plagued by pain and complications; the danger and death associated with illegal abortion and the persistently high rates of infant mortality among urban working-class families. Indeed, the insurmountable limits of the body were inscribed in the protests of female textile workers during the 1920s. It was the body stripped of "the natural frontier of the self" that became a site of resistance (Gagnier 1991, 60).

Regenia Gagnier's remarkable examination of subjectivity, the body, and material culture explores how female bodies, permeated by discourses and transfigured by the experiences of work and pain, became sites of resistance at certain historical junctures (1991, 55–98). Her analysis of the ways in which the body figures in the self-representations of working-class women raises important questions about poststructuralist notions of subjectivity. "Reproductive suffering," she argues, "was an essential component of the subjectivity in question: that is what it was like to be a working-class woman" (1991, 60).[47] In Gagnier's view, women's experiences of "extreme physical abjection or loss of boundaries" shaped their resistance, their transformation into subjects. She invokes their own powerful terminology to explain this loss of boundaries: "They suffered continually from misplacements, womb displacement, falling of the womb, gathered breasts, breasts in slings, childbed fever, husbands' abuse of the organs of reproduction, cold in the ovaries, varicose veins, marble leg, . . . untimely flooding, growth of the afterbirth inside the mother, confinement in body-belts and leg-bands, severe hemorrhaging . . . , whiteleg, and the psychologically maddening grinding of machinery in the factory," the sense that their bodies were "going round with the machinery." Finally, there was the despair of the "mother [who] wonders what she has to live for; if there is another baby coming she hopes it will be dead when it is born" (Gagnier 1991, 59–60). Gagnier's reading of these working-class women's letters about maternity offers an interesting parallel to my analysis of the feminization of politics in the DTAV. This story of subjectivity is one of transformation from "subjective isolation within their bodies to subjects with claims upon the State," subjects who resisted alienation from their laboring bodies and who learned how to "use their bodies to change culture," in this instance to obtain insurance coverage for maternity benefits and to establish municipal maternity centers (Gagnier 1991, 63).

The notion of the body as a historically contingent site of subjectivity also offers a more complex understanding of the positions female workers assumed within the discourses of class, nation, citizenship, and/or maternity in Weimar Germany. It is important to note that discourses (both those that empower and those that disempower) constitute not merely the domain in which subjectivities emerge, but they also actually create the conditions for this transformation in quite concrete ways. The discourses of the "new woman," sexual reform, eugenics, and the controversies over birth control and abortion, for example, focused the attention of a wide range of political and social groups on female sexuality. At the same time, however, this saturation of the social field created a social and discursive space in which women were encouraged and empowered to conceptualize their own sexuality.[48] More specifically, the natalist and eugenicist obsessions with population loss and birth rate massed women together as potentially maternal bodies, compelling them to position themselves within this mass. Thus the discursive domain of body politics intruded in women's experiences of their bodies in quite concrete ways during and after the First World War. This intrusion represents one example of how, as Elizabeth Grosz suggests, power in its discursive and material forms "actively marks or brands bodies as social, inscribing them with the attributes of subjectivity" (Grosz 1990, 63). As important as this discursive intervention was in constituting female subjectivities, it makes up only one side of the story.

The emergence of a counterdiscourse about the female body during the 1920s suggests that Weimar body politics was a particularly contested and fractured discursive domain, one that was particularly vulnerable to dispersal, resistance, and transformation (Terdiman 1985, 44–46). Underlying this formulation is a notion of agency as a site of mediation; here agency signifies the way in which female activists mobilized and recast their embodied experiences within the discursive fields of Weimar body politics. Both Gagnier's poignant reading of British working-class women's letters on maternity and my abbreviated discussion of the emergence of female body in the arena of union politics during the 1920s raise particular questions about the realm of experience embedded in the body. The notion that discourses marked, branded, or massed together bodies should make clear that I do not conceive of the body as an unmediated site of experience. Yet I am fascinated by Grosz's notion of the recalcitrant body, which, because it is capable of being self-marked and self-represented, "always entails the possibility of a counterstrategic reinscription" (Grosz 1990, 64). This is one way of understanding Gagnier's letters on maternity or the female textile workers' demonstration in Gera. When female union members marked their bodies, represented themselves through their bodies—the pregnant bodies pushed up against the looms, the bodies maimed or made sterile by illegal abortion, the desiring, sexualized bodies—they sought to reinscribe (as a counterstrategy) both the universalist, seemingly disembodied (male) discourses of class politics and the colonizing claims of natalist reproductive politics on female bodies. In the two cases examined here, women's embodied experiences proved to be the most compelling means of contesting dominant discourses, of appropriating discursive space, and of altering the discourses that excluded or sought to define them. Thus, the body, if understood as a complex site of inscription and of subjectivity/resistance, offers an interesting and intricate way of retheorizing agency. Indeed, the notions of bodily inscription and reinscription seem to defy both the illusion of autonomous agency/subjectivity and the vision of discourse as singularly determinant of subjects and their experiences.

Notes

1. Gabrielle Spiegel 1990, 73, points to the "one-sided nature of the discussion, which has largely been in the hands of literary critics rather than historians"—e.g., Weedon 1987; Poovey 1988a; Nicholson 1990; Rhode 1991; Sawicki 1991, Butler and Scott 1992; and Barrett and Phillips 1992. Joan W. Scott's pathbreaking essay collection, *Gender and the*

Politics of History (1988), and Sonya O. Rose's essay "Text and Context: A 'Double Vision' as Historical Method" (1991) are important exceptions to this rule.

2. See Stone 1991. For an insightful discussion of the terminology of the linguistic turn, see Weedon 1987, esp. her chapter "Principles of Post-structuralism" (12–42); Caplan 1989b; Sewell 1989b; Terdiman 1989; and Butler and Scott 1992, xiii–xvii. Butler and Scott emphasize, correctly in my view, that "'post-structuralism' indicates a field of critical practices that cannot be totalized," that "poststructuralism is not, strictly speaking, a *position*, but rather a critical interrogation of the exclusionary operations by which 'positions' are established" (xiii–xiv).

3. On the crisis of self-confidence among historians, see Stone 1991, 217–18. For discussions of the challenges of postmodernism to German history, see also the special issue of *Central European History, vol. 22*, nos. 3–4, titled "German Histories: Challenges in Theory, Practice, Technique" and edited by Michael Geyer and Konrad Jarausch; and the provocative volume, *Probing the Limits of Representation: Nazism and the Final Solution* (Friedlander 1992).

4. While some view the linguistic turn as representing the "dissolution of history," others embrace the opportunities it has created for rethinking and recasting historical categories and narratives. See especially Spiegel 1990, 60; Joyce and Kelly 1991. Also insightful on the linguistic turn are Scott 1986; Toews 1987; Hull 1989; Schottler 1989; Berlanstein 1991; Mayfield and Thorne 1992; and Eley 1994.

5. Newton 1989 makes a powerful case for the importance of feminism in the reception of poststructuralism (153–55); on this point see also Rabine 1988 and Singer 1992 on the "family resemblance" between feminism and postmodernism. On French feminism, see Marks and de Courtivron 1981 and Fraser and Bartky 1992. I thank Kali Israel for reminding me of the crucial importance of these interdisciplinary arenas in the genealogy of the linguistic turn.

6. A key text in mapping out a self–conscious study of gender was *Sex and Class in Women's History* (Newton, Ryan, and Walkowitz 1983). On the current relationship between women's history and gender history, see Hull 1989 and "Women's History/Gender History: Is Feminist Scholarship Losing Its Critical Edge?" *Journal of Women's History, vol. 5*, no. 1 (Spring 1993): 89–128. Contributors include Sonya O. Rose, Kathleen Canning, Anna Clark, Marcia Sawyer, and Mariana Valverde.

7. Some of the most provocative readings on gender, race, and the category woman include: Anzaldua and Moraga 1981; hooks 1981, 1990; Smith 1983; Spillers 1985; Trinh 1988; Collins 1989, Hurtado 1989, Mohanty, Russo, and Torres 1991, Higginbotham 1992. It is perhaps important to note that many theoretically inclined (including poststructuralist) feminists, as well as many feminist historians of Europe, began to grapple with the challenges of women of color within feminism considerably later than scholars of American or Third World history. See Jane Gallop's remarks on this point (in Gallop, Hirsch, and Miller 1990): "Race only posed itself as an urgent issue to me in the last couple of years. . . . I didn't feel the necessity of discussing race until I had moved myself out of a French post–structural orbit and began talking about American literary criticism" (363–64).

8. On this point, see also Fraser and Nicholson 1990, 34–35, and Auslander 1992, an insightful review of *Am I That Name?*, Butler 1990, and Fraser 1989. Judith Butler 1992 makes a similar point: the term *women*, she argues, "has become "a site of permanent openness and resignifiability." Thus, "the constant rifting" over this term "ought to be safeguarded and prized . . . as the ungrounded ground of feminist theory" (16).

9. See, e.g., Claudia Koonz's energetic critique (1989) of Scott 1988; Jane Caplan's more measured and favorable review (1989b); Catherine Hall's review (1991); the review by

Mariana Valverde (1990); Bryan Palmer's chapter on gender, especially the section, "The Scott Files" (1990, 172–83); Geoff Eley's discussion of the particular reception of poststructuralism in feminist studies (1994, 3); and finally, the somewhat acrimonious debate between Scott and Linda Gordon in *Signs* (Gordon 1990a; Scott 1990b).

10. See also Weedon 1987; Poovey 1988a; Sawicki 1991; Singer 1992, 469–71.

11. I argue this point regarding the concept of class in Canning 1992.

12. I found some interesting parallels between Scott's argumentation in "The Evidence of Experience" and Donna Haraway's views of experience as discussed in her essay,"Reading Buchi Emecheta" (in Haraway 1991, 109–13). Examples of recent feminist historiography that also historicize identities include Walkowitz 1980, Davidoff 1983; and Davidoff and Hall's pathbreaking *Family Fortunes* (1987).

13. I cannot do justice to the complex issue of identity formation within the scope of this article. For a recent discussion of this issue that also engages with poststructuralism, see Laura Downs's discussion of the work of Scott, Carolyn Steedman, and Jessica Benjamin (1993). Somers and Gibson 1994 offer an excellent theoretical reading of narrative and the social constitution of identity. Caulfield's 1993 study of "dishonest women, modern girls and women-men" in Rio de Janeiro during the 1920s offers an interesting comparison of Scott and Butler on the issue of gender identity.

14. For more extensive discussions of *Alltagsgeschichte,* see also Crew 1989, Lüdtke 1989; and the important three-volume work of the LUSIR project, *Lebensgeschichte und Sozialkultur im Ruhrgebiet zwischen 1930 und 1960* (Niethammer 1983; and Niethammer and von Plato 1985).

15. Scott refers here to Adams and Minson (1978) 1990, who qualify *agency* as "subject to definite conditions of existence, conditions of endowment of agents and conditions of exercise" (91).

16. Ortner 1994, 3–4, examines the "baggage surrounding the term *agency.*" The following texts helped me think through the problem of agency: Poovey 1988a, 1988b, 1991; Walkowitz, Jehlen, and Chevigny 1989; Spiegel 1990; Gagnier 1991; Rose 1991, and Mohanty 1992. Particularly helpful were Donna Haraway's notion of "situated knowledges" (Haraway 1991, 2–3, 110–11, 188–89); Somers and Gibson's discussion of narrative identity (1994, 30–34); and Caulfield's 1993 comparative reading of Butler and Scott.

17. Haraway also suggests that our quest to disentangle discursive construction from experience and agency might best be served by a view of history, ethnography, or even social theory as a "conversation" in which "the agency of people studied itself transforms the entire project" (1991, 98).

18. Laura Downs offers a somewhat different reading of Scott's "L'ouvrière" (1993, 422 –24)

19. My own working definition of discourse and discursive domains has been shaped by readings of Foucault 1980; Terdiman 1985; Stallybrass and White 1986; Weedon 1987; Poovey 1988b, 1991; Walkowitz, Jehlen, and Chevigny 1989, 1992; Smith 1990; and Rose 1991. Terdiman 1985 defines discourse as "a complex of signs and practices which organize social existence and social reproduction" (54) and that comprise "a culture's determined and determining structures of representation and practice" (12). My analysis of the discursive construction of male and female labor forms only one part of my larger investigation, *Languages of Labor and Gender: Female Factory Work in Germany, 1850–1914,* although, of course, it shapes the whole story.

20. On the dispersed sites of discourse, see Walkowitz 1992, 6, and Stallybrass and White 1986, 194. Terdiman 1985 analyzes the relationships between dominant discourses and counterdiscourses in the specific historical context of nineteenth-century France when

the emergence of a literate middle-class public, newspapers, and new disciplines and bodies of knowledge such as statistics transformed both the "techniques for assuring discursive control" and those of "symbolic subversion" (44–46). On discourse as a social relation in a new kind of public arena, see Smith 1990, 161–67.

21. On the reciprocal relationship between the discursive and material domains, see especially Walkowitz, Jehlen, and Chevigny 1989, 30, 31, 43; Poovey 1990, 29, 43; and Spiegel 1990, 71; Walkowitz 1992, 9–11, 233–41.

22. As cited by Scott 1988, 141. In practice this occurred when a union leader cited a middle-class social reformer's study in a speech to a union assembly or when parliamentary representatives drew on local stories to enhance their campaigns for restrictions on women's work. The term *webs of cross-references* also applies to counterdiscourses (such as feminist critiques of social reformers' punitive solutions to the social problem of female factory labor).

23. "Married women" here denotes married and formerly married women (widows and women who were divorced or separated from husbands). The married female workforce grew by 90 percent and the single female workforce by 78 percent between 1882 and 1907. Figures here based on Pohle 1901, 158–61; Otto 1910, 10; Simon 1910, 7; Dorn 1911/12, 8687; Bajohr 1979, 25.

24. This term is from Wilbrandt 1906, 31. The implication of the word "maiden" here is also that of "hand-maiden" of a machine.

25. On moralizing and regulative outcomes of discourses of social reform, see Poovey 1991, 65, and introduction to Jacobus, Keller, and Shuttleworth 1990, 1–10.

26. I do not claim to "reconstruct" identities as they somehow might have "really" existed; rather I attempt to "read" them using a variety of sources that can be compared and contrasted with one another.

27. Kali Israel's work (1990, 1991) has influenced my thinking about multiple subject positions.

28. On the political meanings of the body during the Weimar Republic, see Grossmann 1983, 1984, 1986, 1994; Hagemann 1990, 196–305; and Usborne 1992.

29. On the social pathologies of body politics during the last quarter of the nineteenth century, see Rabinbach 1992, 21–22.

30. On the "new woman" in Germany, see Grossman 1983, 1986, and Usborne 1992, 69–101. For a fascinating French comparison, see Roberts 1992, 1994.

31. Jacobus, Keller, and Shuttleworth 1990, 3–4, contend that there has been "no issue more vexed" in contemporary feminist theory than that of the female body. See also Sawicki 1991, 13–14, 70–83, 107; Butler 1992, 17; Turner 1992, 48.

32. Haraway 1991, 134, and Riley 1988, 104, make this point. On the 'lived experiences" of the body in history, see Outram 1989 and Duden 1991.

33. See Hauff 1912, 11–13. The Internationale Gewerksgenossenschaft der Manufaktur-, Fabrik- und Handarbeiter, founded in Saxony in 1869, had one thousand female members in 1870, who constituted 15 percent of its membership.

34. I define *Eigenart* more extensively in Canning 1992, 761–63.

35. DTAV 1908, 214; 1910b, 227. See also DTAV 1910a.

36. Hauptstaatsarchiv Dusseldorf (HStAD), Regierung Dusseldorf 335–81, "Bericht der Gewerbeinspektor für Crefeld Stadt und Land und Kreis Kempen von 30.3.1917." According to this report, many women received specialized job training, including some who learned to repair machines. Ute Daniel 1989 dispenses with the myth that the majority of women who went to work in factories during the war were housewives, employed for the first time. Her work demonstrates that most of the women employed in armaments production during the war had worked before the war in other industrial sectors, above all textiles.

37. The number of women who held union posts grew from some 1,800 in 1913 to 3,000 in 1917 (DTAV 1916, 282, 307; 1918, 72–74). By 1915, 25 percent of 316 locals were headed by women.
38. DTAV 1915a, 19; 1915b, 152; 1916, 283.
39. DTAV 1917a, 95–97; 1918, 63–71. In 1916 women made up 62 percent of striking textile workers and in 1917 they represented 75 percent. Only 26 percent of those involved (male and female) in 1916 and only 36 percent in 1917 were unionized.
40. We still know too little about demobilization, particularly about its effect on women workers. See Bessel 1983 and Rouette 1991.
41. Female membership in the DTAV increased by over 450 percent, as some 260,000 women joined the union between December 1918 and the end of 1920. Male membership increased by an even faster rate of 740 percent between 1918 and 1920 as men returned to their jobs and to the union after the war (DTAV 1917b, 53, 77; 1920, 3; 1921b, 100–101, 108, 130).
42. According to my calculation the male membership declined by 46 percent between 1923 and 1925, while female membership declined by 57 percent during the same period. Although the percentage of women declined steadily after 1923, women continued to constitute the majority of DTAV members.
43. Hauptstaatsarchiv Detmold (HStADet), Regierung Minden MIG 172, 256–57: "Offener Brief des Hauptvorstandes des DTV an den Arbeitgeberverhand der Deutschen Textilindustrie" (no date) 260–68: "Schreiben des Arbeitgeberverbandes der Deutschen Textilindustrie betr. Antrag des DTAV vom 1. April 1925 auf Erweiterung der gesetzlichen Bestimmungen zum Schutze schwangerer Arbeiterinnen"; 273–300: "Eingabe des Arbeitgeberverbandes der Deutschen Textilindustrie vom 28.10.1926 an die Reichsregierung mit zwei ärztlichen Gutachten beigefugt." See also Hirsch 1925 and DTAV 1925b, 43.
44. HStDet, Regierung Minden 172, 256–57: "Offener Brief," 260–68 273–300. See also Usborne 1992, 48).
45. DTAV 1927a, 74, 89, 98. See Grossmann 1983; and Wolf 1930.
46. See Atina Grossman's excellent discussion of *Mein Arbeitstag, mein Wochenende* (Grossman 1986, 70–75) as well as Lüdtke's introduction to the new edition of *Mein Arbeitstag* (Lüdtke 1991, 11–12). The titles of the first two essays are "Die Uhr ruckt vor" (The clock ticks on) and "Zicke-zacke die Maschine . . ." (The tick-tock of the machine). On rationalized housework in the Weimar Republic, also see Hagemann 1990, 99–132, and Nolan 1990.
47. Gagnier's main source here is a collection of 160 letters written by members of the British Women's Cooperative Guild and published in 1915, entitled *Maternity: Letters from Working-Women* ([1915] 1980).
48. On the saturation of the social field by the discursive, see Terdiman 1985, 42–46. I found Terdiman and Poovey 1990, 29–30, 43, particularly useful in understanding the specific ways in which the discourses of body politics positioned subjects.

References

Adams, Parveen, and Jeff Minson. (1978) 1990. "The 'Subject' of Feminism." *mlf*, vol. 2, reprinted in *The Woman in Question*, ed. Parveen Adams and Elizabeth Cowie, 81–101. Boston: MIT Press.

Anzaldua, Gloria, and Cherrie Moraga, eds. 1981. *This Bridge Called My Back: Writings of Radical Women of Color*. Watertown, Mass.: Persephore.

Auslander, Leora. 1992. "Feminist Theory and Social History: Explorations in the Politics of Identity." *Radical History Review* 54:158–76.

Bajohr, Stefan. 1979. *Die Hälfte der Fabrik, Geschichte der Frauenarbeit in Deutschland.* Marburg: Verlag Arbeiterbewegung und Gesellschaftswissenschaften.

Barrett, Michele, and Anne Phillips. 1992. *Destabilizing Theory: Contemporary Feminist Debates.* Stanford, Calif.: Stanford University Press.

Berlanstein, Lenard. 1991. "Working with Language: The Linguistic Turn in French Labor History: A Review Article." *Comparative Studies of Society and History* 33(2):426–40.

Bessel, Richard. 1983. "'Eine nicht allzu große Beunruhigung des Arbeitsmarktes,' Frauenarbeit und Demobilmachung in Deutschland nach dem Ersten Weltkrieg." *Geschichte und Gesellschaft* 9:211–29.

Bordo, Susan. 1990. "Feminism, Postmodernism, and Gender-Scepticism." In *Feminism/Postmodernism,* ed. Linda J. Nicholson, 133–56. New York: Routledge.

Butler, Judith. 1990. *Gender Trouble: Feminism and the Subversion of Identity.* New York: Routledge.

———. 1992. "Contingent Foundations: Feminism and the Question of 'Postmodernism.'" In Butler and Scott 1992, 3–21.

Butler, Judith, and Joan W. Scott, eds. 1992. *Feminists Theorize the Political.* New York and London: Routledge.

Canning, Kathleen. 1988. "Class, Gender and Working-Class Politics: The Case of the German Textile Industry, 1890–1933." Ph.D. dissertation, Johns Hopkins University.

———. 1992. "Gender and the Politics of Class Formation: Rethinking German Labor History." *American Historical Review* 97 (3):736–68.

Caplan, Jane. 1989a. "Gender Is Everywhere." *Nation* (January 9 and 16), 62–65.

———. 1996. *Languages of Labor and Gender: Female Factory Work in Germany, 1850–1914.* Ithaca, NY: Cornell University Press.

———. 1989b. "Postmodernism, Post-Structuralism, Deconstruction." *Central European History* 22:260–78.

Caulfield, Sueann. 1993. "Getting into Trouble: Dishonest Women, Modern Girls, and Women-Men in the Conceptual Language of *Vida Policial,* 1925–1927." *Signs: Journal of Women in Culture and Society* 19(1):146–76.

Collins, Patricia Hill. 1989. "The Social Construction of Black Feminist Thought." *Signs* 14(4):745–73.

Crew, David F. 1989. "*Alltagsgeschichte:* A New Social History 'From Below'?" *Central European History* 22(3–4):394–407.

Daniel, Ute. 1989. *Arbeiterfrauen in der Kriegsgesellschaft: Beruf, Familie und Politik im Ersten Weltrieg.* Göttingen: Vandenhoeck & Ruprecht.

Davidoff, Leonore. 1983. "Class and Gender in Victorian England." In Newton, Ryan, and Walkowitz 1983, 17–71.

Davidoff, Leonore, and Catherine Hall. 1987. *Family Fortunes: Men and Women of the English Middle Class, 1780–1850.* Chicago: University of Chicago Press.

Davis, Belinda. 1994. "Gender, Women and the 'Public Sphere' in World War I Berlin." In *Society, Culture and State in Germany, 1870–1930,* ed. Geoff Eley. Ann Arbor: University of Michigan Press.

Delany, Samuel R. 1988. *The Motion of Light in Water: Sex and Science Fiction Writing in the East Village, 1957–1965.* New York: W. Morrow/Arbor House.

Deutscher Textilarbeiterverband (DTAV). 1908. *Protokoll der 9. ordentlichen Generalversammlung, abgehalten 1908 in Leipzig.* Berlin: DTAV.

———. 1910a. "An unsere Kolleginnen." *Der Textilarbeiter* 22/30 (July 29, 1910).

———. 1910b. *Protokoll der 10. Generalversammlung, abgehalten 1910 in Berlin.* Berlin: DTAV.

———. 1915a. "Frauenversammlungen Während des Krieges." *Der Textilarbeiter* 27/5 (January 29, 1915).

———. 1915b. "Kriegszusammenkunfte der Arbeiterinnen." *Der Textilarbeiter* 27/38 (September 17, 1915).

———. 1916. *Jahrbuch, 1914–1915.* Berlin: DTAV.

———. 1917a. *Jahrbuch, 1916.* Berlin: DTAV.

———. 1917b. *Protokoll der 13. Generalversammlung, abgehalten 1917 in Augsburg.* Berlin: DTAV.

———. 1918. *Jahrbuch, 1917.* Berlin: DTAV.

———. 1919. *Jahrbuch, 1918.* Berlin: DTAV.

———. 1920. *Jahrbuch, 1919.* Berlim DTAV.

———. 1921 a. *Jahrbuch, 1920.* Berlin: DTAV.

———. 1921b. *Protokoll des 14. Verbandstages des Deutschen Textilarbeiterverbandes, abgehalten in Breslau.* Berlin: DTAV.

———. 1924. *Protokoll des 15. Verbandstags des Deutschen Textilarbeiterverband abgehalten 1924 in Cassel.* Berlin: DTAV.

———. 1925a. *Jahrbuch, 1923–1924.* Berlin: DTAV.

———. 1925b. *Umbang der Frauenarbeit in der deutschen Textilindustrie: (Erwerb) Schuangerschaft, Frauenleid.* Berlin: Verlag DTAV.

———. 1927a. *Protokoll vom 1. Kongress der Textilarbeiterinnen Deutschlands abgehalten 1926 in Gera.* Berlin: Verlag Textilpraxis.

———. 1927b. *Protokoll des 16. Verbandstages abgehalten 1927 in Hamburg.* Berlin: DTAV.

———. 1928. *Jahrbuch 1927.* Berlin: DTAV.

———. 1930. *Mein Arbeitstag—mein Wochenende: 150 Textilarbeiterinnen berichten!* Berlin: Verlag Textilpraxis.

Domansky, Elisabeth. 1990. "World War I as Gender Conflict in Germany." Paper presented at the Kaiserreich conference, University of Pennsylvania, February.

———. 1994. "Militarization and Reproduction in World War I Germany." In *Society, Culture and State in Germany. 1870–1930,* ed. Geoff Eley. Ann Arbor: University of Michigan Press.

Dorn, Hanns. 1911/12. "Die Frauenerwerbsarbeit und ihre Aufgaben für die Gesetzgebung." *Archiv für Rechts- und Wirtschaftsphilosophie* 5(1911–12): 86–87.

Downs, Laura Lee. 1993. "If 'Woman' Is Just an Empty Category, Then Why Am I Afraid to Walk Alone at Night? Identity Politics Meets the Postmodern Subject." *Comparative Studies in Society and History* 35(2):414–37.

Duden, Barbara. 1991. *The Woman Beneath the Skin: A Doctor's Patients in Eighteenth-Century Germany.* Cambridge, Mass.: Harvard University Press.

Eley, Geoff. 1989. "Labor History, Social History, *Alltagsgeschichte:* Experience, Culture, and the Politics of the Everyday—a New Direction for German Social History?" *Journal of Modern History* 61 (2):297–343.

———. 1994. "Is All the World a Text? From Social History to the History of Society Two Decades Later." In McDonald 1994.

Foucault, Michel. 1980. *History of Sexuality. Vol. 1: An Introduction.* New York: Vintage.

Fraser, Nancy. 1989. *Unruly Practices: Power, Discourse and Gender in Contemporary Social Theory.* Minneapolis: University of Minnesota Press.

Fraser, Nancy, and Sandra Bartky. 1992. *Revaluing French Feminisms: Critical Essays on Difference, Agency and Culture.* Bloomington: Indiana University Press.

Fraser, Nancy, and Linda J. Nicholson. 1990. "Social Criticism without Philosophy: An Encounter between Feminism and Postmodernism." In Nicholson 1990, 19–38.

Friedlander, Saul, ed. 1992. *Probing the Limits of Representation: Nazism and the Final Solution.* London and Cambridge, Mass.: Harvard University Press.

Gagnier, Regenia. 1991. *Subjectivities: A History of Self-Representation in Britain 1832–1920.* New York: Oxford University Press.

Gallop, Jane, Marianne Hirsch, and Nancy K. Miller. 1990. "Criticizing Feminist Criticism." In Hirsch 1990, 349–69.

Gordon, Linda. 1990a. "Response to Scott." *Signs* 15(4):852–53.

———. 1990b. Review of *Gender and the Politics of History* by Joan Wallach Scott. *Signs* 15(4): 853–58.

Grossmann, Atina. 1983. "The New Woman and the Rationalization of Sexuality, in Weimar Germany." In *Powers of Desire: The Politics of Sexuality* ed. Ann Snitow, Christine Stansell, and Sharon Thompson, 153–76. New York: Monthly Review.

———. 1984. "Abortion and Economic Crisis: The Campaign against Paragraph 218 in Germany." In *When Biology Became Destiny: Women in Weimar and Nazi Germany,* ed. Renate Bridenthal, Atina Grossmann, and Marion Kaplan, 66–86. New York: Monthly Review.

———. 1986. "*Girikultur* or Thoroughly Rationalized Female: A New Woman in Weimaer Germany?" In *Women in Culture and Politics: A Century of Change,* ed. Judith Friedlander, Blanche W. Cook, Alice Kessler-Harris, and Carroll Smith-Rosenberg, 62–80. Bloomington: Indiana University Press.

———. 1994. *Reforming Sex: German Sex Reform* 1920 *to* 1950. New York: Oxford University Press.

Grosz, Elizabeth. 1990. "Inscriptions and Body-Maps: Representations and the Corporeal." In *Feminine, Masculine and Representation,* ed. Terry Threadgold and Anne Cranny-Francis, 62–75. Sydney and London: Allen & Unwin.

Hagemann, Karen. 1990. *Frauenalltag und Männerpolitik: Alltagsleben und gesellschaftliches Handeln von Arbeiterfrauen in der Weimarer Republik.* Bonn: Dietz.

Hall, Catherine. 1991. "Politics, Post-structuralism and Feminist History." *Gender and History* 3(2):204–10.

Haraway, Donna J. 1991. *Simians, Cyborgs and Women: The Reinvention of Nature.* New York and London: Routledge.

Hartsock, Nancy. 1990. "Foucault on Power: A Theory for Women?" In Nicholson 1990, 157–75.

Hauff, Lilly. 1912. *Die Arbeiterinnen-Organisationen.* Halle, a.S.: E. Karras.

Higginbotham, Evelyn Brooks. 1992. "African-American Women's History and the Metalanguage of Race." *Signs* 17(2):251–74.

Hirsch, Marilyn, and Evelyn Fox Keller, eds. 1990. *Conflicts in Feminism.* New York and London: Routledge.

Hirsch, Max. 1925. *Die Gefahren der Frauenerwerbsarbeit für Schwangerschaft, Geburt, Wochenbett und Kindesaufzucht mit besonderer Berücksichtigung der Textilindustrie.* Special Issue *Archiv für Frauenkunde und Konstitutionsforschung vol.* 11, no. 4. Leipzig: Curt Kabitzsch.

hooks, bell. 1981. *Ain't I a Woman? Black Women and Feminism.* Boston: South End.

———. 1990. *Yearning: Race, Gender and Cultural Politics.* Boston: South End.

Hull, Isabel. 1989. "Feminist and Gender History through the Literary Looking Glass: German Historiography in Postmodern Times." *Central European History* 22(3–4):279–300.

Hurtado, Aida. 1989. "Relating to Privilege: Seduction and Rejection in the Subordination of White Women and Women of Color." *Signs* 14(4):833–55.

Israel, Kali. 1990. "Writing inside the Kaleidoscope: (Re)Representing Victorian Women Public Figures." *Gender and History* 2(1):40–48.

———. 1991. "Working-Class Women as Selves and Others: The Feminist Trades Unionism of Emilia Dilke." Paper presented at the annual meeting of the American Historical Association, Chicago, December 27–30.

Jacobus, Mary, Evelyn Fox Keller, and Sally Shuttleworth, eds. 1990. *Body Politics: Women and the Discourses of Science.* New York and London: Routledge.

Journal of Women's History. 1993. "Women's History/Gender History: Is Feminist Scholarship Losing Its Critical Edge?" *Journal of Women's History* 5 (Spring): 89–128.

Joyce, Patrick, and Catriona Kelly. 1991. "History and Post-Modernism 11." *Past and Present* no. 133, 204–13.

Koonz, Claudia. 1989. Review of *Gender and the Politics of History* by Joan W. Scott. *Women's Review of Books* 6(4):19–20.

Laqueur, Thomas W. 1989. "Bodies, Details, and the Humanitarian Narrative." In *The New Cultural History,* ed. Lynn Hunt, 176–204. Berkeley: University of California Press.

Lüdtke, Alf. 1985. "Organizational Order or *Eigensinn?* Workers' Privacy and Workers' Politics in Imperial Germany." In *Rites of Power: Symbolism, Ritual and Politics Since the Middle Ages,* ed. Sean Wilentz, 303–33. Philadelphia: Temple University Press.

———. ed. 1989. *Alltagsgeschichte: Zur Rekonstruktion historischer Erfahrungen und Lebensweisen.* Frankfurt and New York: Campus Verlag.

———. ed. 1991. *Mein Arbeitstag—mein Wochende: 150 Arbeiterinnen berichten,* new ed. with introduction by Alf Lüdtke. Hamburg: Ergebnisse Verlag.

McDonald, Terence J., ed. 1994. *The Historic Turn in the Human Sciences.* Ann Arbor: University of Michigan Press.

Marks, Elaine, and Isabelle de Courtivron. 1981. *New French Feminisms.* New York: Schocken.

Martin, Rudolf. 1896. "Die Ausschliessung der verheirateten Frauen aus der Fabrik: Eine Studie an der Textilindustrie." *Zeitschrift für die gesamte Staatswissenschaft* 52:104–46, 383–418.

Mayfield, David, and Susan Thorne. 1992. "Social History and Its Discontents: Gareth Stedman Jones and the Politics of Language." *Social History* 17(2): 166–88.

Mohanty, Chandra Talpade. 1991. "Under Western Eyes: Feminist Scholarship and Colonial Discourses." In *Third World Women and the Politics of Feminism,* ed. Chandra Talpade Mohanty, Ann Russo, and Lourdes Torres, 51–80. Bloomington: Indiana University Press.

———. 1992. "Feminist Encounters: Locating the Politics of Experience." In *Destabilizing Theory: Contemporary Feminist Debates,* ed. Michele Barret and Anne Phillips, 74–92. Stanford, Calif.: Stanford University Press.

Newton, Judith L. 1989. "History as Usual? Feminism and the 'New Historicism.'" In *The New Historicism,* ed. H. Aram Veeser, 152–67. New York and London: Routledge.

Newton, Judith L., Mary P. Ryan, and Judith R. Walkowitz, eds. 1983. *Sex and Class in Women's History.* London and Boston: Routledge, Kegan, Paul.

Nicholson, Linda J., ed. 1990. *Feminism/Postmodernism.* New York and London: Routledge.

Niethammer, Lutz, ed. 1983. *Lebensgeschichte und Sozialkultur im Ruhrgebiet zwischen 1930 und 1960,* 2 vols. Berlin and Bonn: Dietz.

Niethammer, Lutz, and Alexander von Plato, eds. 1985. *"Wir kriegen jetzt andere Zeiten."* Berlin and Bonn: Dietz.

Nolan, Mary. 1990. "'Housework Made Easy': The Taylorized Housewife in Weimar Germany's Rationalized Economy." *Feminist Studies* 16:549–77.

Ortner, Sherry. 1994. "Some Theoretical Problems in Anthropological History and Historical Anthropology." In McDonald 1994.

Otto, Rose. 1910. *Über die Fabrikarbeit verheirateter Frauen. Münchener Volkswirtschaftliche Studien 4.* Stuttgart and Berlin: J. G. Cotta.

Outram, Dorinda. 1989. *The Body and the French Revolution: Sex, Class and Political Culture.* New Haven, Conn.: Yale University Press.

Palmer, Bryan. 1990. *Descent into Discourse: The Reification of Language and the Writing of Social History.* Philadelphia: Temple University Press.

Pohle, Ludwig. 1901. "Die Erhebungen der Gewerbeaufsichtsbeamten über die Fabrikarbeit verheirateter Frauen." *Jahrbuch für Gesetzgebung Verwaltung and Volkswirtschaft* 25:158–61.

Poovey, Mary. 1988a. "Feminism and Deconstruction." *Feminist Studies* 14(1):51–65.

———. 1988b. *Uneven Developments: The Ideological Work of Gender in Mid-Victorian England.* Chicago: University of Chicago Press.

———. 1990. "Speaking of the Body: Mid-Victorian Constructions of Female Desire." In Jacobus, Keller, and Shuttleworth 1990, 29–46.

———. 1991. "Domesticity and Class Formation: Chadwick's *Sanitary Report.*" In *Subject to History,* ed. David Simpson, 65–81. Ithaca, N.Y.: Cornell University Press.

Quataert, Jean H. 1983. "A Source Analysis in German Women's History: Factory Inspectors' Reports and the Shaping of Working-Class Lives, 1878–1914." *Central European History* 16(2):99–121.

Rabinbach, Anson. 1992. *The Human Motor: Energy Fatigue and the Origins of Modernity.* Berkeley: University of California Press.

Rabine, Leslie Wahl. 1988. "A Feminist Politics of Non-Identity." *Feminist Studies* 14:11–31.

Rhode, Deborah L., ed. 1991. *Theoretical Perspectives on Sexual Difference.* New Haven, Conn.: Yale University Press.

Riley, Denise. 1988. *Am I That Name? Feminism and the Category of "Women" in History.* Minneapolis: University of Minnesota Press.

Roberts, Mary Louise. 1992. "'This Civilization No Longer Has Sexes': *La Garconne* and Cultural Crisis in France after World War I." *Gender and History* 4(1) :49–69.

———. 1994. *Civilization Without Sexes: Reconstructing Gender in Post-War France 1917–1927.* Chicago: University of Chicago Press.

Rose, Sonya O. 1991. "Text and Context: A 'Double Vision' as Historical Method." Paper presented at the annual meeting of the Social Science History Association, New Orleans, November 1–3.

Rouette, Susanne. 1991. "Die sozialpolitische Regulierung der Frauenarbeit: Arbeitsmarkt- und Fürsorgepolitik in den Anfangsjahren der Weimarer Republik: Das Beispiel Berlin." Ph.D. dissertation, Technische Universitat Berlin.

Rubin, Gayle. 1975. "The Traffic in Women: Notes on the 'Political Economy' of Sex." In *Toward an Anthropology of Women,* ed. Rayna R. Reiter, 157–210. New York: Monthly Review.

Sawicki, Jana. 1991. *Disciplining Foucault: Feminism, Power and the Body.* London and New York: Routledge.

Schottler, Peter. 1989. "Historians and Discourse Analysis." *History Workshop* 27:37–65.

Scott, Joan W. 1986."Gender: A Useful Category of Historical Analysis," *American Historical Review* 91(5):1053–75.

———. 1988. *Gender and the Politics of History.* New York: Columbia University Press.

———. 1990a. Review of *Heroes of Their Own Lives: The Politics and History of Family Violence* by Linda Gordon. *Signs* 15(4):848–52.

———. 1990b. "Response to Gordon." *Signs* 15(4):859–60.

———. 1991. "The Evidence of Experience." *Critical Inquiry* 17(3):773–97.

———. 1993. "The Woman Worker in the Nineteenth Century." In *History of Women in The West,* ed. Georges Duby and Michelle Perrot. Cambridge, Ma: BelKnap of Harvard University Press. vol. 4.

Sewell, William H., Jr. 1989a. "Gender, History and Deconstruction: Joan Wallach Scott's *Gender and the Politics of History.*" CSST Working Paper, no. 34. Program in the Comparative Study of Social Transformation, Ann Arbor, Mich.

———. 1989b. "Toward a Theory of Structure: Duality, Agency, and Transformation." CSST Working Paper, no. 29. Program in the Comparative Study of Social Transformation, Ann Arbor, Mich.

———. 1990. "How Classes Are Made: Critical Reflections on E. P. Thompson's Theory of

Working-Class Formation." In *E. P. Thompson: Critical Perspectives,* ed. Harvey J. Kaye and Keith McClelland, 50–77. Philadelphia: Temple University Press.

Simon, Helene. 1910. *Der Anteil der Frau an der deutschen Industrie.* Jena: G. Fischer.

Singer, Linda. 1992. "Feminism and Postmodernism." In Butler and Scott 1992, 464–75.

Smith, Barbara. 1983. *Home Girls: A Black Feminist Anthology.* New York: Kitchen Table, Women of Color Press.

Smith, Dorothy. 1987. *The Everyday World as Problematic: A Feminist Sociology.* Boston: Northeastern University Press.

———. 1990. *Texts, Facts and Femininity: Exploring the Relations of Ruling.* New York and London: Routledge.

Somers, Margaret R., and Gloria D. Gibson. 1994. "Reclaiming the Epistemological 'Other': Narrative and the Social Constitution of Identity." In *Social Theory and the Politics of Identity,* ed. Craig Calhoun. London: Basil Blackwell.

Spiegel, Gabrielle M. 1990. "History, Historicism, and the Social Logic of the Text in the Middle Ages." *Speculum* 65:59–86.

Spillers, Hortense. 1985. *Conjuring: Black Women Fiction and Literary Tradition.* Bloomington: Indiana University Press.

Stallybrass, Peter, and Allon White. 1986. *The Politics and Poetics of Transgression.* Ithaca, N.Y.: Cornell University Press.

Stoehr, Irene. 1983. "'Organisierte Mütterlichkeit': Zur Politik der deutschen Frauenbewegung um 1900." In *Frauen suchen ihre Geschichte,* ed. Karin Hausen, 221–49. Munich: Beck.

Stone, Lawrence. 1991. "History and Post-Modernism." *Past and Present* no. 131, 217–18.

Terdiman, Richard. 1985. *Discourse/Counter-Discourse: The Theory and Practice of Symbolic Resistance in Nineteenth-Century France.* Ithaca, N.Y., and London: Cornell University Press.

———. 1989. "Is There Class in This Class?" In *The New Historicism,* ed. H. Aram Veeser, 225–30. New York and London: Routledge.

Toews, John. 1987. "Intellectual History after the Linguistic Turn: The Autonomy of Meaning and the Irreducibility of Experience." *American Historical Review* 92(4):879–907.

Trinh, Minh-ha. 1988. "Not You/Like You: Post-Colonial Women and the Interlocking Questions of Identity and Difference." *Inscriptions* 3(4):71–76.

Turner, Bryan S. 1992. *Regulating Bodies: Essays in Medical Sociology.* London and New York: Routledge.

Usborne, Cornelie. 1992. *The Politics of the Body in Weimar Germany: Women's Reproductive Rights and Duties.* Ann Arbor: University of Michigan Press.

Valverde, Mariana. 1990. "Poststructuralist Gender Historians: Are We Those Names?" *Labour/Le Travail* 25:227–36.

Walkowitz, Judith R. 1980. *Prostitution and Victorian Society: Women, Class and the State.* Cambridge and New York: Cambridge University Press.

———. 1992. *City of Dreadful Delight: Narratives of Sexual Danger in Late-Victorian London.* Chicago: University of Chicago Press.

Walkowitz, Judith R., Myra Jehlen, and Bell Chevigny. 1989. "Patrolling the Borders: Feminist Historiography and the New Historicism." *Radical History Review* no. 43, 23–43.

Weedon, Chris. 1987. *Feminist Practice and Poststructuralist Theory.* Oxford and New York: Basil Blackwell.

Wilbrandt, Robert. 1906. *Die Weber in der Gegenwart: Sozialpolitische Wanderungen durch die Hausweberei und die Webfabrik.* Jena: G. Fischer.

Wolf, Julius. 1930. *Mutter oder Embryo: Zum Kampf gegen die Abtreibungsparagraphen.* Berlin: Carl Heymanns Verlag.

Women's Cooperative Guild. (1915) 1980. *Maternity: Letters from Working Women.* New York: Garland.

PART 2

The Politics of Identity and Experience

Joan Scott's "The Evidence of Experience" explores the effect produced when the notion of "experience" appears to take on a foundational authority. A very disparate group of scholars—including those seeking to restore the occluded narratives of race, gender, and sexual practices; those challenging the false objectivity of empiricism or the limits of Marxism; and those resisting the "linguistic turn"—all look to experience as an authentic, accessible, and communicable source of knowledge. This recourse to experience is perceived by those practicing it as oppositional and progressive, but as Scott points out, it leaves the dominant ideological system intact: it shores up the belief in a prediscursive reality, a unitary subject preceding experience, and the objective authority of the historian. In response to this reaffirmation of the dominant paradigms of the discipline, Scott calls for a critical genealogy of the most basic premises of historical research. Recognizing that such a fundamental challenge cannot be launched from within a discipline, Scott calls for an interdisciplinary encounter in which literary and historical ways of reading might, in Gayatri Spivak's words, "'interrupt' each other, bring each other to crisis." The crisis provoked in historians by more literary ways of reading involves a destabilizing of the correspondence between words and things, of the singularity of meaning, of the possibility of resolving contradictions in a linear narrative of progress and unification. Anticipating objections to this literary turn in the practice of history, Scott insists she is not promoting linguistic determinism and the obliteration of human agency. Her goal, instead, is to expose the historical context in which identity, experience and agency are constituted and constrained. From her own encounter with "reading for the literary," Scott emerges with the conviction that an historical understanding of the ways in which identity and experience are discursively constituted will not preclude agency but rather open up the possibility of more dramatic individual and collective transformations.

In "Situating Locations: The Politics of Self, Identity, and 'Other' in Living and Writing the Text," Jayati Lal points out that studies focusing on gender and development often inadvertently produce a power structure in which the "Third World [is] a resource for Western theory." The oppositional logic of self versus other, white versus black, is problematized by Lal's demonstration that the designation of who is Other or outsider shifts with each new situation. She finds on returning home to India from her advanced training in the West that her research status as an "authentic insider" is undermined by power differentials tied to class and Westernization. She cannot assume an affinity or shared standpoint with the New Delhi female factory workers who are the subjects of her fieldwork. Influenced by theories of Insider/Outsider positionality in the work of black feminist scholars like Patricia Hill Collins, and by theories of multiple subjectivity articulated by postmodern feminist theorists like Trinh Minh-ha and Donna Haraway, Lal challenges the reductive binary oppositions of knower/known, home/work, personal/professional, private/public which provide the foundation for much social science research. Even as she follows the imperative of feminist standpoint methodology to examine self-reflexively her own position as a researcher, Lal is aware of the danger that such scrutiny may become an end in itself, further silencing her research subjects. To counteract this methodological danger, Lal focuses on her subjects' agency and resistance, not just in relation to patriarchal dominance in the family and workplace, but also in relation to the research situation. Lal acknowledges that hierarchies of gender and class are too thoroughly embedded in everyday life to be eliminated from the fieldwork process, but she also demonstrates how one might begin, as she puts it, to "'work the hyphens' between Self and Other . . . rather than reproduce the tensions between Us and Them.'"

In "The Construction of Marginal Identities: Working-class Girls of Algerian Descent in a French School," Catherine Raissiguier offers a "nonessentialist" empirical analysis that stresses the impact of ethnicity and class, of group allegiances as well as individual identity in the process of self-definition. Acknowledging the influence of feminist theorists from across the disciplines (including Audre Lorde, bell hooks, and Trinh Minh-ha), she emphasizes the complex and shifting identities of her research subjects as they are shaped by discourse. While family and community discourses position these girls as upholders and symbols of Islamic tradition, they are also encouraged to achieve financial stability through advanced education and assimilation. In the popular media in France Algerian girls are represented as a mythic Other set in opposition to normative "modern" French girls, but they are held up in the media as more malleable and acceptable young female foreigners in contrast to the specter of a fanatically violent and unassimilable *male* Other. Raissiguier's research reveals her subjects' alternating accommodation and resistance to these multiple discourses, their often acute analysis of their own culture, and their insights into the dominant culture that surrounds them. As these Algerian girls exercise agency in reformulating their sense of self in the different contexts of family, school, and the media, identity is shown to be multiple and relational rather than essential.

The Evidence of Experience

JOAN W. SCOTT

Becoming Visible

There is a section in Samuel Delany's magnificent autobiographical meditation, *The Motion of Light in Water*, that dramatically raises the problem of writing the history of difference, the history, that is, of the designation of "other," of the attribution of characteristics that distinguish categories of people from some presumed (and usually unstated) norm.[1]

Delany (a gay man, a black man, a writer of science fiction) recounts his reaction to his first visit to the St. Marks bathhouse in 1963. He remembers standing on the threshold of a "gym-sized room" dimly lit by blue bulbs. The room was full of people, some standing, the rest

> an undulating mass of naked, male bodies, spread wall to wall.
> My first response was a kind of heart-thudding astonishment, very close to fear.
> I have written of a space at certain libidinal saturation before. That was not what frightened me. It was rather that the saturation was not only kinesthetic but visible.[2]

Watching the scene establishes for Delany a "fact that flew in the face" of the prevailing representation of homosexuals in the 1950s as "isolated perverts," as subjects "gone awry." The "apprehension of massed bodies gave him (as it does, he argues, anyone, "male, female, working or middle class") a "sense of political power":

> what *this* experience said was that there was a population—not of individual homosexuals . . . not of hundreds, not of thousands, but rather of millions of gay men, and that history had, actively and already, created for us whole galleries of institutions, good and bad, to accommodate our sex. [*M*, p. 174]

The sense of political possibility is frightening and exhilarating for Delany. He emphasizes not the discovery of an identity, but a sense of participation in a movement; indeed, it is the extent (as well as the existence) of these sexual practices that matters most in his account. Numbers—massed bodies—constitute a movement and this, even if subterranean, belies enforced silences about the range

Joan Scott, "The Evidence of Experience," in *Critical Inquiry* 178:3 (1991):773–97. Reprinted by permission.

and diversity of human sexual practices. Making the movement visible breaks the silence about it, challenges prevailing notions, and opens new possibilities for everyone. Delany imagines, even from the vantage of 1988, a future utopian moment of genuine sexual revolution, "once the AIDS crisis is brought under control":

> That revolution will come precisely because of the infiltration of clear and articulate language into the marginal areas of human sexual exploration, such as this book from time to time describes, and of which it is only the most modest example. Now that a significant range of people have begun to get a clearer idea of what has been possible among the varieties of human pleasure in the recent past, heterosexuals and homosexuals, females and males will insist on exploring them even further. [*M,* p. 175]

By writing about the bathhouse Delany seeks not, he says, "to romanticize that time into some cornucopia of sexual plenty," but rather to break an "absolutely sanctioned public silence" on questions of sexual practice, to reveal something that existed but that had been suppressed.

> Only the coyest and the most indirect articulations could occasionally indicate the boundaries of a phenomenon whose centers could not be spoken or written of, even figuratively: and that coyness was medical and legal as well as literary; and, as Foucault has told us, it was, in its coyness, a huge and pervasive discourse. But what that coyness means is that there is no way to gain from it a clear, accurate, and extensive picture of extant public sexual institutions. That discourse only touched on highly select margins when they transgressed the legal and/or medical standards of a populace that firmly wished to maintain that no such institutions existed. [*M,* pp. 175–76]

The point of Delany's description, indeed of his entire book, is to document the existence of those institutions in all their variety and multiplicity, to write about and thus to render historical what has hitherto been hidden from history.

As I read it, a metaphor of visibility as literal transparency is crucial to his project. The blue lights illuminate a scene he has participated in before (in darkened trucks parked along the docks under the West Side Highway, in men's rooms in subway stations), but understood only in a fragmented way. "No one ever got *to see* its whole" (*M,* p. 174; emphasis added). He attributes the impact of the bathhouse scene to its visibility: "You could *see* what was going on throughout the dorm" (*M,* p. 173; emphasis added). Seeing enables him to comprehend the relationship between his personal activities and politics: "the first direct sense of political power comes from the apprehension of massed bodies." Recounting that moment also allows him to explain the aim of his book: to provide a "clear, accurate, and extensive *picture* of extant public sexual institutions" so that others may learn about and explore them (*M,* pp. 174,176; emphasis added). Knowledge is gained through vision; vision is a direct apprehension of a world of transparent objects. In this conceptualization, the visible is privileged; writing is then put at its service.[3] Seeing is the origin of knowing. Writing is reproduction, transmission—the communication of knowledge gained through (visual, visceral) experience.

This kind of communication has long been the mission of historians documenting the lives of those omitted or overlooked in accounts of the past. It has produced a wealth of new evidence previously ignored about these others and has drawn attention to dimensions of human life and activity usually deemed unworthy of mention in conventional histories. It has also occasioned a crisis for orthodox history by multiplying not only stories but subjects, and by insisting that histories are written from fundamentally different—indeed irreconcilable—perspectives or standpoints, none of which is complete or completely "true." Like Delany's memoir, these histories have provided evidence for a world of alternative values and practices whose existence gives the lie to hegemonic constructions of social worlds, whether these constructions vaunt the political superiority of white men, the coherence and unity of selves, the naturalness of heterosexual monogamy, or the inevitability of scientific progress and economic development. The challenge to normative history has been described, in terms of conventional historical understandings of evidence, as an enlargement of the picture, a correction to oversights resulting from inaccurate or incomplete vision, and it has rested its claim to legitimacy on the authority of experience, the direct experience of others, as well as of the historian who learns to see and illuminate the lives of those others in his or her texts.

Documenting the experience of others in this way has been at once a highly successful and limiting strategy for historians of difference. It has been successful because it remains so comfortably within the disciplinary framework of history, working according to rules that permit calling old narratives into question when new evidence is discovered. The status of evidence is, of course, ambiguous for historians. On the one hand, they acknowledge that "evidence only counts as evidence and is only recognized as such in relation to a potential narrative, so that the narrative can be said to determine the evidence as much as the evidence determines the narrative."[4] On the other hand, historians' rhetorical treatment of evidence and their use of it to falsify prevailing interpretations, depends on a referential notion of evidence which denies that it is anything but a reflection of the real.[5] Michel de Certeau's description is apt. Historical discourse, he writes,

> gives itself credibility in the name of the reality which it is supposed to represent, but this authorized appearance of the "real" serves precisely to camouflage the practice which in fact determines it. Representation thus disguises the praxis that organizes it.[6]

When the evidence offered is the evidence of "experience," the claim for referentiality is further buttressed—what could be truer, after all, than a subject's own account of what he or she has lived through? It is precisely this kind of appeal to experience as uncontestable evidence and as an originary point of explanation—as a foundation on which analysis is based—that weakens the critical thrust of histories of difference. By remaining within the epistemological frame of orthodox history, these studies lose the possibility of examining those assumptions and practices that excluded considerations of difference in the first place. They take as self-evident the identities of those whose experience is being documented and thus naturalize their difference. They locate resistance outside its discursive construction and reify agency as an inherent attribute of individuals, thus decontextualizing it. When experience is taken as the origin of knowledge, the vision of the individual subject (the person who had the experience or

the historian who recounts it) becomes the bedrock of evidence on which explanation is built. Questions about the constructed nature of experience, about how
subjects are constituted as different in the first place, about how one's vision is
structured—about language (or discourse) and history—are left aside. The evidence of experience then becomes evidence for the fact of difference, rather than
a way of exploring how difference is established, how it operates, how and in
what ways it constitutes subjects who see and act in the world.[7]

To put it another way, the evidence of experience, whether conceived through
a metaphor of visibility or in any other way that takes meaning as transparent,
reproduces rather than contests given ideological systems—those that assume that
the facts of history speak for themselves and those that rest on notions of a natural or established opposition between, say, sexual practices and social conventions, or between homosexuality and heterosexuality. Histories that document the
"hidden" world of homosexuality, for example, show the impact of silence and
repression on the lives of those affected by it and bring to light the history of their
suppression and exploitation. But the project of making experience visible precludes critical examination of the workings of the ideological system itself, its categories of representation (homosexual/heterosexual, man/woman, black/white
as fixed immutable identities), its premises about what these categories mean and
how they operate, and of its notions of subjects, origin, and cause. Homosexual
practices are seen as the result of desire, conceived as a natural force operating
outside or in opposition to social regulation. In these stories homosexuality is presented as a repressed desire (experience denied), made to seem invisible, abnor-
mal, and silenced by a "society" that legislates heterosexuality as the only normal practice.[8] Because this kind of (homosexual) desire cannot ultimately be
repressed—because experience is there—it invents institutions to accommodate
itself. These institutions are unacknowledged but not invisible; indeed, it is the
possibility that they can be seen that threatens order and ultimately overcomes
repression. Resistance and agency are presented as driven by uncontainable desire; emancipation is a teleological story in which desire ultimately overcomes social control and becomes visible. History is a chronology that makes experience
visible, but in which categories appear as nonetheless ahistorical: desire, homosexuality, heterosexuality, femininity, masculinity, sex, and even sexual practices
become so many fixed entities being played out over time, but not themselves
historicized. Presenting the story in this way excludes, or at least understates, the
historically variable interrelationship between the meanings "homosexual" and
"heterosexual," the constitutive force each has for the other, and the contested
and changing nature of the terrain that they simultaneously occupy. "The
importance—an importance—of the category 'homosexual,'" writes Eve Kosofsky Sedgwick,

> comes not necessarily from its regulatory relation to a nascent or already-constituted
> minority of homosexual people or desires, but from its potential for giving whoever
> wields it a structuring definitional leverage over the whole range of male bonds that
> shape the social constitution.[9]

Not only does homosexuality define heterosexuality by specifying its negative limits, and not only is the boundary between the two a shifting one, but both

operate within the structures of the same "phallic economy"—an economy whose workings are not taken into account by studies that seek simply to make homosexual experience visible. One way to describe this economy is to say that desire is defined through the pursuit of the phallus—that veiled and evasive signifier which is at once fully present but unattainable, and which gains its power through the promise it holds out but never entirely fulfills.[10] Theorized this way, homosexuality and heterosexuality work according to the same economy, their social institutions mirroring one another. The social institutions through which gay sex is practiced may invert those associated with dominant heterosexual behavior (promiscuous versus restrained, public versus private, anonymous versus known, and so on), but they both operate within a system structured according to presence and lack.[11] To the extent that this system constructs desiring subjects (those who are legitimate as well as those who are not), it simultaneously establishes them and itself as given and outside of time, as the way things work, the way they inevitably are.

The project of making experience visible precludes analysis of the workings of this system and of its historicity; instead, it reproduces its terms. We come to appreciate the consequences of the closeting of homosexuals and we understand repression as an interested act of power or domination; alternative behaviors and institutions also become available to us. What we don't have is a way of placing those alternatives within the framework of (historically contingent) dominant patterns of sexuality and the ideology that supports them. We know they exist, but not how they have been constructed; we know their existence offers a critique of normative practices, but not the extent of the critique. Making visible the experience of a different group exposes the existence of repressive mechanisms, but not their inner workings or logics; we know that difference exists, but we don't understand it as relationally constituted. For that we need to attend to the historical processes that, through discourse, position subjects and produce their experiences. It is not individuals who have experience, but subjects who are constituted through experience. Experience in this definition then becomes not the origin of our explanation, not the authoritative (because seen or felt) evidence that grounds what is known, but rather that which we seek to explain, that about which knowledge is produced. To think about experience in this way is to historicize it as well as to historicize the identities it produces. This kind of historicizing represents a reply to the many contemporary historians who have argued that an unproblematized "experience" is the foundation of their practice; it is a historicizing that implies critical scrutiny of all explanatory categories usually taken for granted, including the category of "experience."

The Authority of Experience

History has been largely a foundationalist discourse. By this I mean that its explanations seem to be unthinkable if they do not take for granted some primary premises, categories, or presumptions. These foundations (however varied, whatever they are at a particular moment) are unquestioned and unquestionable; they are considered permanent and transcendent. As such they create a common ground for historians and their objects of study in the past and so authorize and legitimize analysis; indeed, analysis seems not to be able to proceed without them.[12] In the minds of some foundationalists, in fact, nihilism, anarchy, and moral confusion are the sure alternatives to these givens, which have the status (if not the philosophical definition) of eternal truths.

Historians have had recourse to many kinds of foundations, some more obviously empiricist than others. What is most striking these days is the determined embrace, the strident defense, of some reified, transcendent category of explanation by historians who have used insights drawn from the sociology of knowledge, structural linguistics, feminist theory, or cultural anthropology to develop sharp critiques of empiricism. This turn to foundations even by anti-foundationalists appears, in Fredric Jameson's characterization, as "some extreme form of the return of the repressed."[13]

"Experience" is one of the foundations that has been reintroduced into historical writing in the wake of the critique of empiricism; unlike "brute fact" or "simple reality," its connotations are more varied and elusive. It has recently emerged as a critical term in debates among historians about the limits of interpretation and especially about the uses and limits of post-structuralist theory for history. In these debates those most open to interpretive innovation—those who have insisted on the study of collective mentalities, of economic, social, or cultural determinations of individual behavior, and even of the influences of unconscious motives on thought and action—are among the most ardent defenders of the need to attend to "experience." Feminist historians critical of biases in "malestream" histories and seeking to install women as viable subjects, social historians insisting on the materialist basis of the discipline on the one hand and on the "agency" of individuals or groups on the other, and cultural historians who have brought symbolic analysis to the study of behavior, have joined political historians whose stories privilege the purposive actions of rational actors and intellectual historians who maintain that thought originates in the minds of individuals. All seem to have converged on the argument that experience is an "irreducible" ground for history.

The evolution of "experience" appears to solve a problem of explanation for professed anti-empiricists even as it reinstates a foundational ground. For this reason it is interesting to examine the uses of "experience" by historians. Such an examination allows us to ask whether history can exist without foundations and what it might look like if it did.

In *Keywords* Raymond Williams sketches the alternative senses in which the term *experience* has been employed in the AngloAmerican tradition. These he summarizes as "(i) knowledge gathered from past events, whether by conscious observation or by consideration and reflection; and (ii) a particular kind of consciousness, which can in some contexts be distinguished from 'reason' or 'knowledge.'"[14] Until the early eighteenth century, he says, experience and experiment were closely connected terms, designating how knowledge was arrived at through testing and observation (here the visual metaphor is important). In the eighteenth century, experience still contained this notion of consideration or reflection on observed events, of lessons gained from the past, but it also referred to a particular kind of consciousness. This consciousness, in the twentieth century, has come to mean a "full and active 'awareness,'" including feeling as well as thought (*K*, p. 127). The notion of experience as subjective witness, writes Williams, is "offered not only as truth, but as the most authentic kind of truth," as "the ground for all (subsequent) reasoning and analysis" (*K*, p. 128). According to Williams, experience has acquired another connotation in the twentieth century different from these notions of subjective testimony as immediate, true, and authentic. In this usage it refers to influences external to individuals—social conditions, institutions, forms of belief or perception—"real" things outside them that they react to, and does not include their thought or consideration.[15]

In the various usages described by Williams, "experience," whether conceived as internal or external, subjective or objective, establishes the prior existence of individuals. When it is defined as internal, it is an expression of an individual's being or consciousness; when external, it is the material on which consciousness then acts. Balking about experience in these ways leads us to take the existence of individuals for granted (experience is something people have) rather than to ask how conceptions of selves (of subjects and their identities) are produced.[16] It operates within an ideological construction that not only makes individuals the starting point of knowledge, but that also naturalizes categories such as man, woman, black, white, heterosexual, and homosexual by treating them as given characteristics of individuals.

Teresa de Lauretis's redefinition of experience exposes the workings of this ideology. "Experience," she writes, is the

> process by which, for all social beings, subjectivity is constructed. Through that process one places oneself or is placed in social reality, and so perceives and comprehends as subjective (referring to, originating in, oneself) those relations—material, economic, and interpersonal—which are in fact social and, in a larger perspective, historical.[17]

The process that de Lauretis describes operates crucially through differentiation; its effect is to constitute subjects as fixed and autonomous, and who are considered reliable sources of a knowledge that comes from access to the real by means of their experience.[18] When talking about historians and other students of the human sciences it is important to note that this subject is both the object of inquiry—the person one studies in the present or the past—and the investigator him- or herself—the historian who produces knowledge of the past based on "experience" in the archives or the anthropologist who produces knowledge of other cultures based on "experience" as a participant observer.

The concepts of experience described by Williams preclude inquiry into processes of subject-construction; and they avoid examining the relationships between discourse, cognition, and reality, the relevance of the position or situatedness of subjects to the knowledge they produce, and the effects of difference on knowledge. Questions are not raised about, for example, whether it matters for the history they write that historians are men, women, white, black, straight, or gay; instead, as de Certeau writes, "the authority of the 'subject of knowledge' [is measured] by the elimination of everything concerning the speaker" ("H," p. 218).

His knowledge, reflecting as it does something apart from him, is legitimated and presented as universal, accessible to all. There is no power or politics in these notions of knowledge and experience.

An example of the way "experience" establishes the authority of an historian can be found in R. G. Collingwood's *Idea of History*, the 1946 classic that has been required reading in historiography courses for several generations. For Collingwood, the ability of the historian to re-enact past experience is tied to his autonomy, "where by autonomy I mean the condition of being one's own authority, making statements or taking action on one's own initiative and not because those statements or actions are authorized or prescribed by anyone else."[19] The question of where the historian is situated—who he is, how he is defined in relation to others, what the political effects of his history may be—never enters the discussion. Indeed, being free of these matters seems to be tied to Collingwood's definition of autonomy, an issue so critical for him that he launches into an uncharacteristic tirade about it. In his quest for certainty, the historian must not let others make up his mind for him, Collingwood insists, because to do that means

> giving up his autonomy as an historian and allowing someone else to do for him what, if he is a scientific thinker, he can only do for himself. There is no need for me to offer the reader any proof of this statement. If he knows anything of historical work, he already knows of his own experience that it is true. If he does not already know that it is true, he does not know enough about history to read this essay with any profit, and the best thing he can do is to stop here and now.[20]

For Collingwood it is axiomatic that experience is a reliable source of knowledge because it rests on direct contact between the historian's perception and reality (even if the passage of time makes it necessary for the historian to imaginatively reenact events of the past). Thinking on his own means owning his own thoughts, and this proprietary relationship guarantees an individual's independence, his ability to read the past correctly, and the authority of the knowledge he produces. The claim is not only for the historian's autonomy, but also for his originality. Here "experience" grounds the identity of the researcher as an historian.

Another, very different use of "experience" can be found in E. P. Thompson's *Making of the English Working Class*, the book that revolutionized social and labor history. Thompson specifically set out to free the concept of "class" from the ossified categories of Marxist structuralism. For this project "experience" was a key concept. "We explored," Thompson writes of himself and his fellow New Left historians, "both in theory and in practice, those junction-concepts (such as 'need,' 'class,' and 'determine') by which, through the missing term, 'experience,' structure is transmuted into process, and the subject re-enters into history."[21]

Thompson's notion of experience joined ideas of external influence and subjective feeling, the structural and the psychological. This gave him a mediating influence between social structure and social consciousness. For him experience meant "social being"—the lived realities of social life, especially the affective domains of family and religion and the symbolic dimensions of expression. This definition separated the affective and the symbolic from the economic and the rational. "People do not only experience their own experience as ideas, within thought and its procedures," he maintained, "they also experience their own experience as *feeling*" ("PT," p. 171). This statement grants importance to the psychological dimension of experience, and it allows Thompson to account for agency. Feeling, Thompson insists, is "handled" culturally as "norms, familial and kinship obligations and reciprocities, as values or (through more elaborated forms) within art and religious beliefs" ("PT," p. 171). At the same time it somehow precedes these forms of expression and so provides an escape from a strong structural determination: "For any living generation, in any 'now,'" Thompson asserts, "the ways in which they 'handle' experience defies prediction and escapes from any narrow definition of determination" ("PT," p. 171).[22]

And yet in his use of it, experience, because it is ultimately shaped by relations of production, is a unifying phenomenon, overriding other kinds of diversity. Since these relations of production are common to workers of different ethnicities, religions, regions, and trades they necessarily provide a common denominator and emerge as a more salient determinant of "experience" than anything else. In Thompson's use of the term, experience is the start of a process that culminates in the realization and articulation of social consciousness, in this case a common identity of class. It serves an integrating function, joining the individual and the structural, and bringing together diverse people into that coherent (totalizing) whole which is a distinctive sense of class.[23] "'Experience' (we have found) has, in the last instance, been generated in 'material life', has been structured in class ways, and hence 'social being' has determined 'social consciousness'" ("PT," p. 171). In this way unequivocal and uniform identity is produced through objective circumstances and there is no reason to ask how this identity achieved predominance—it had to.

The unifying aspect of experience excludes whole realms of human activity by simply not counting them as experience, at least not with any consequences for social organization or politics. When class becomes an overriding identity, other subject-positions are subsumed by it, those of gender, for example (or, in other instances of this kind, of history, race, ethnicity, and sexuality). The positions of men and women and their different relationships to politics are taken as reflections of material and social arrangements rather than as products of class politics itself; they are part of the "experience" of capitalism. Instead of asking how some experiences become more salient than others, how what matters to Thompson is defined as experience, and how differences are dissolved, experience becomes itself cumulative and homogenizing, providing the common denominator on which class consciousness is built.

Thompson's own role in determining the salience of certain things and not others is never addressed. Although his author's voice intervenes powerfully with moral and ethical judgments about the situations he is recounting, the presentation of the experiences themselves is meant to secure their objective status. We forget that Thompson's history, like the accounts offered by political organizers in the nineteenth century of what mattered in workers' lives, is an interpretation, a selective ordering of information that through its use of originary categories and teleological accounts legitimizes a particular kind of politics (it becomes the only possible politics) and a particular way of doing history (as a reflection of what happened, the description of which is little influenced by the historian if, in this case, he only has the requisite moral vision that permits identification with the experiences of workers in the past).

In Thompson's account class is finally an identity rooted in structural relations that preexist politics. What this obscures is the contradictory and contested process by which class itself was conceptualized and by which diverse kinds of subject-positions were assigned, felt, contested, or embraced. As a result, Thompson's brilliant history of the English working-class, which set out to historicize the category of class, ends up essentializing it. The ground may seem to be displaced from structure to agency by insisting on the subjectively felt nature of experience, but the problem Thompson sought to address isn't really solved. Working-class "experience" is now the ontological foundation of working-class identity, politics, and history.[24]

This kind of use of experience has the same foundational status if we substitute "women's" or "black" or "lesbian" or "homosexual" for "working-class" in the previous sentence. Among feminist historians, for example, "experience" has helped to legitimize a critique of the false claims to objectivity of traditional historical accounts. Part of the project of some feminist history has been to unmask all claims to objectivity as an ideological cover for masculine bias by pointing out the shortcomings, incompleteness, and exclusiveness of mainstream history. This has been achieved by providing documentation about women in the past that calls into question existing interpretations made without consideration of gender. But how do we authorize the new knowledge if the possibility of all historical objectivity has been questioned? By appealing to experience, which in this usage connotes both reality and its subjective apprehension—the experience of women in the past and of women historians who can recognize something of themselves in their foremothers.

Judith Newton, a literary historian writing about the neglect of feminism by contemporary critical theorists, argues that women, too, arrived at the critique of objectivity usually associated with deconstruction or the new historicism. This feminist critique came "straight out of reflection on our own, that is, women's experience, out of the contradictions we felt between the different ways we were represented even to ourselves, out of the inequities we had long experienced in our situations."[25] Newton's appeal to experience seems to bypass the issue of objectivity (by not raising the question of whether feminist work can be objective) but it rests firmly on a foundational ground (experience). In her work the relationship between thought and experience is represented as transparent (the visual metaphor combines with the visceral) and so is directly accessible, as it is in historian Christine Stansell's insistence that "social practices," in all their "immediacy and entirety," constitute a domain of "sensuous experience" (a prediscursive reality directly felt, seen, and known) that cannot be subsumed by "language."[26] The effect of these kinds of statements, which attribute an indisputable authenticity to women's experience, is to establish incontrovertibly women's identity as people with agency. It is also to universalize the identity of women and thus to ground claims for the legitimacy of women's history in the shared experience of historians of women and those women whose stories they tell. In addition, it literally equates the personal with the political, for the lived experience of women is seen as leading directly to resistance to oppression, that is, to feminism.[27] Indeed, the possibility of politics is said to rest on, to follow from, a preexisting women's experience.

"Because of its drive towards a political massing together of women," writes Denise Riley, "feminism can never wholeheartedly dismantle 'women's experience,' however much this category conflates the attributed, the imposed, and the lived, and then sanctifies the resulting melange." The kind of argument for a women's history (and for a feminist politics) that Riley criticizes closes down inquiry into the ways in which female subjectivity is produced, the ways in which agency is made possible, the ways in which race and sexuality intersect with gender, the ways in which politics organize and interpret experience—in sum, the ways in which identity is a contested terrain, the site of multiple and conflicting claims. In Riley's words, "it masks the likelihood that . . . [experiences] have accrued to women not by virtue of their womanhood alone, but as traces of domination, whether natural or political."[28] I would add that it masks the necessarily discursive character of these experiences as well.

But it is precisely the discursive character of experience that is at issue for some historians because attributing experience to discourse seems somehow to deny its status as an unquestionable ground of explanation. This seems to be the case for John Toews, who wrote a long article in the *American Historical Review* in 1987 called "Intellectual History after the Linguistic Turn: The Autonomy of Meaning and the Irreducibility of Experience." The term *linguistic turn is* a comprehensive one used by Toews to refer to approaches to the study of meaning that draw on a number of disciplines, but especially on theories of language "since the primary medium of meaning was obviously language."[29] The question for Toews is how far linguistic analysis has gone and should go, especially in view of the post-structuralist challenge to foundationalism. Reviewing a number of books that take on questions of meaning and its analysis, Toews concludes that

> the predominant tendency [among intellectual historians] is to adapt traditional historical concerns for extralinguistic origins and reference to the semiological challenge, to reaffirm in new ways that, in spite of the relative autonomy of cultural meanings, human subjects still make and remake the worlds of meaning in which they are suspended, and to insist that these worlds are not creations *ex nihilo* but responses to, and shapings of, changing worlds of experience ultimately irreducible to the linguistic forms in which they appear. ["IH," p. 882]

By definition, he argues, history is concerned with explanation; it is not a radical hermeneutics, but an attempt to account for the origin, persistence, and disappearance of certain meanings "at particular times and in specific sociocultural situations" ("IH," p. 882). For him explanation requires a separation of experience and meaning: experience is that reality which demands meaningful response. "Experience," in Toews's usage, is taken to be so self-evident that he never defines the term. This is telling in an article that insists on establishing the importance and independence, the irreducibility of "experience." The absence of definition allows experience to resonate in many ways, but it also allows it to function as a universally understood category—the undefined word creates a sense of consensus by attributing to it an assumed, stable, and shared meaning.

Experience, for Toews, is a foundational concept. While recognizing that meanings differ and that the historian's task is to analyze the different meanings produced in societies and over time, Toews protects "experience" from this kind of relativism. In doing so he establishes the possibility for objective knowledge and for communication among historians, however diverse their positions and views. This has the effect (among others) of removing historians from critical scrutiny as active producers of knowledge. The insistence on the separation of meaning and experience is crucial for Toews, not only because it seems the only way to account for change, but also because it protects the world from "the hubris of wordmakers who claim to be makers of reality" ("IH," p. 906). Even if Toews here uses "wordmakers" metaphorically to refer to those who produce texts, those who engage in signification, his opposition between "words" and "reality" echoes the distinction he makes earlier in the article between language (or meaning) and experience. This opposition guarantees both an independent status for human agents and the common ground on which they can communicate and act. It produces a possibility for "inter-subjective communication" among individuals despite differences between them, and also reaffirms their existence as thinking beings outside the discursive practices they devise and employ.

Toews is critical of J. G. A. Pocock's vision of "inter-subjective communication" based on rational consensus in a community of free individuals, all of whom are equally masters of their own wills. "Pocock's theories," he writes, "often seem like theoretical reflections of familiar practices because the world they assume is also the world in which many contemporary Anglo-American historians live or think they live" ("IH," p. 893). Yet the separation of meaning and experience that Toews offers does not really provide an alternative. A more diverse community can be posited, of course, with different meanings given to experience. Since the phenomenon of experience itself can be analyzed outside the meanings given to it, the subjective position of historians then can seem to have nothing to do with the knowledge they produce.[30] In this way experience authorizes historians and it enables them to counter the radical historicist stance that, Toews says, "undermines the traditional historians' quest for unity, continuity, and purpose by robbing them of any standpoint from which a relationship between past, present, and future could be objectively reconstructed" ("IH," p. 902). Here he establishes as self-evident (and unproblematic) the reflective nature of historical representation, and he assumes that it will override whatever diversity there is in the background, culture, and outlook of historians. Attention to experience, he concludes, "is essential for our self-understanding, and thus also for fulfilling the historian's task of connecting memory with hope" ("IH," p. 907).[31]

Toews's "experience" thus provides an object for historians that can be known apart from their own role as meaning makers and it then guarantees not only the objectivity of their knowledge, but their ability to persuade others of its importance. Whatever diversity and conflict may exist among them, Toews's community of historians is rendered homogeneous by its shared object (experience). But as Ellen Rooney has so effectively pointed out, using the field of literary theory as her example, this kind of homogeneity can exist only because of the exclusion of the possibility that "historically irreducible interests divide and define reading communities."[32] Inclusiveness is achieved by denying that exclusion is inevitable, that difference is established through exclusion, and that the fundamental differences that accompany inequalities of power and position cannot be overcome by persuasion. In Toews's article no disagreement about the meaning of the term *experience* can be entertained, since experience itself lies somehow outside its signification. For that reason, perhaps, Toews never defines it.

Even among those historians who do not share all of Toews's ideas about the objectivity or continuous quality of history writing, the defense of "experience" works in much the same way: it establishes a realm of reality outside of discourse and it authorizes the historian who has access to it. The evidence of experience works as a foundation providing both a starting point and a conclusive kind of explanation, beyond which few questions can or need to be asked. And yet it is precisely the questions precluded—questions about discourse, difference, and subjectivity, as well as about what counts as experience and who gets to make that determination—that would enable us to historicize experience, and to reflect critically on the history we write about it, rather than to premise our history on it.

Historicizing "Experience"

Gayatri Chakravorty Spivak begins an essay addressed to the Subaltern Studies collective with a contrast between the work of historians and literary scholars:

> A historian confronts a text of counterinsurgency or gendering where the subaltern has been represented. He unravels the text to assign a new subject-position to the subaltern, gendered or otherwise.
>
> A teacher of literature confronts a sympathetic text where the gendered subaltern has been represented. She unravels the text to make visible the assignment of subject-positions. . . .
>
> The performance of these tasks, of the historian and the teacher of literature, must critically "interrupt" each other, bring each other to crisis, in order to serve their constituencies; especially when each seems to claim all for its own.[33]

Spivak's argument here seems to be that there is a difference between history and literature that is both methodological and political. History provides categories that enable us to understand the social and structural positions of people (as workers, subalterns, and so on) in new terms, and these terms define a collective identity with potential political (maybe even revolutionary, but certainly subversive) effects. Literature relativizes the categories history assigns, and exposes the processes that construct and position subjects. In Spivak's discussion, both are critical operations, although she clearly favors the deconstructive task of literature.[34] Although her essay has to be read in the context of a specific debate within Indian historiography, its general points must also be considered. In effect, her statements raise the question of whether historians can do other than construct subjects by describing their experience in terms of an essentialized identity.

Spivak's characterization of the Subaltern Studies historians' reliance on a notion of consciousness as a *"strategic* use of positivist essentialism" doesn't really solve the problem of writing history either, since whether it's strategic or not, essentialism appeals to the idea that there are fixed identities, visible to us as social or natural facts.[35] A refusal of essentialism seems particularly important once again these days within the field of history, as disciplinary pressure builds to defend the unitary subject in the name of his or her "experience." Neither does Spivak's invocation of the special political status of the subaltern justify a history aimed at producing subjects without interrogating and relativizing the means of their production. In the case of colonial and postcolonial peoples, but also of various others in the West, it has been precisely the imposition of a categorical (and universal) subject-status (*the* worker, *the* peasant, *the* woman, *the* black) that has masked the operations of difference in the organization of social life. Each category taken as fixed works to solidify the ideological process of subject-construction, making the process less rather than more apparent, naturalizing rather than analyzing it.

It ought to be possible for historians (as for the teachers of literature Spivak so dazzlingly exemplifies) to "make visible the assignment of subject-positions," not in the sense of capturing the reality of the objects seen, but of trying to understand the operations of the complex and changing discursive processes by which identities are ascribed, resisted, or embraced, and which processes themselves are unremarked and indeed achieve their effect because they are not noticed. To do this a change of object seems to be required, one that takes the emergence of concepts and identities as historical events in need of explanation. This does not mean that one dismisses the *effects* of such concepts and identities, nor that one does not explain behavior in terms of their operations. It does mean assuming that the appearance of a new identity is not inevitable or determined, not something that was always there simply waiting to be expressed, not something that will always exist in the form it was given in a particular political movement or at a particular historical moment. Stuart Hall writes:

> The fact is "black" has never been just there either. It has always been an unstable identity, psychically, culturally and politically. It, too, is a narrative, a story, a history. Something constructed, told, spoken, not simply found. People now speak of the society I come from in totally unrecognizable ways. Of course Jamaica is a black society, they say. In reality it is a society of black and brown people who lived for three or four hundred years without ever being able to speak of themselves as "black." Black is an identity which had to be learned and could only be learned in a certain moment. In Jamaica that moment is the 1970s.[36]

To take the history of Jamaican black identity as an object of inquiry in these terms is necessarily to analyze subject-positioning, at least in part, as the effect of discourses that placed Jamaica in a late twentieth-century international racist political economy; it is to historicize the "experience" of blackness.[37]

Treating the emergence of a new identity as a discursive event is not to introduce a new form of linguistic determinism, nor to deprive subjects of agency. It is to refuse a separation between "experience" and language and to insist instead on the productive quality of discourse. Subjects are constituted discursively, but there are conflicts among discursive systems, contradictions within any one of them, multiple meanings possible for the concepts they deploy.[38] And subjects do have agency. They are not unified, autonomous individuals exercising free will, but rather subjects whose agency is created through situations and statuses conferred on them. Being a subject means being "subject to definite conditions of existence, conditions of endowment of agents and conditions of exercise."[39] These conditions enable choices, although they are not unlimited. Subjects are constituted discursively and experience is a linguistic event (it doesn't happen outside established meanings), but neither is it confined to a fixed order of meaning. Since discourse is by definition shared, experience is collective as well as individual. Experience can both confirm what is already known (we see what we have learned to see) and upset what has been taken for granted (when different meanings are in conflict we re-adjust our vision to take account of the conflict or to resolve it— that is what is meant by "learning from experience," though not everyone learns the same lesson or learns it at the same time or in the same way). Experience is a subject's history. Language is the site of history's enactment. Historical explanation cannot, therefore, separate the two. The question then becomes how to analyze language, and here historians often (though not always and not necessarily) confront the limits of a discipline that has typically constructed itself in opposition to literature. (These are not the same limits Spivak points to; her contrast is about the different kinds of knowledge produced by history and literature, mine is about different ways of reading and the different understandings of the relationship between words and things implicit in those readings. In neither case are the limits obligatory for historians; indeed, recognition of them makes it possible for us to get beyond them.) The kind of reading I have in mind would not assume a direct correspondence between words and things, nor confine itself to single meanings, nor aim for the resolution of contradiction. It would not render process as linear, nor rest explanation on simple correlations or single variables. Rather it would grant to "the literary" an integral, even irreducible, status of its own. To grant such status is not to make "the literary" foundational, but to open new possibilities for analyzing discursive productions of social and political reality as complex, contradictory processes.

The reading I offered of Delany at the beginning of this essay is an example of the kind of reading I want to avoid. I would like now to present another reading—one suggested to me by literary critic Karen Swann—as a way of indicating what might be involved in historicizing the notion of experience. It is also a way of agreeing with and appreciating Swann's argument about "the importance of 'the literary' to the historical project."[40]

For Delany, witnessing the scene at the bathhouse (an "undulating mass of naked male bodies" seen under a dim blue light) was an event. It marked what in one kind of reading we would call a coming to consciousness of himself, a recognition of his authentic identity, one he had always shared, would always share with others like himself. Another kind of reading, closer to Delany's preoccupation with memory and the self in this autobiography, sees this event not as the discovery of truth (conceived as the reflection of a prediscursive reality), but as the substitution of one interpretation for another. Delany presents this substitution as a conversion experience, a clarifying moment, after which he sees (that is, understands) differently. But there is all the difference between subjective perceptual clarity and transparent vision; one does not necessarily follow from the other even if the subjective state is metaphorically presented as a visual experience. Moreover, as Swann has pointed out, "the properties of the medium through which the visible appears—here, the dim blue light, whose distorting, refracting qualities produce a wavering of the visible"—make any claim to unmediated transparency impossible. Instead, the wavering light permits a vision beyond the visible, a vision that contains the fantastic projections ("millions of gay men" for whom "history had, actively and already, created . . . whole galleries of institutions") that are the basis for political identification. "In this version of the story," Swann notes, "political consciousness and power originate, not in a presumedly unmediated experience of presumedly real gay identities, but out of an apprehension of the moving, differencing properties of the representational medium— the motion of light in water."

The question of representation is central to Delany's memoir. It is a question of social categories, personal understanding, and language, all of which are connected, none of which are or can be a direct reflection of the others. What does it mean to be black, gay, a writer, he asks, and is there a realm of personal identity possible apart from social constraint? The answer is that the social and the personal are imbricated in one another and that both are historically variable. The meanings of the categories of identity change and with them the possibilities for thinking the self:

> At that time, the words "black" and "gay"—for openers—didn't exist with their current meanings, usage, history. 1961 had still been, really, part of the fifties. The political consciousness that was to form by the end of the sixties had not been part of my world. There were only Negroes and homosexuals, both of whom—along with artists—were hugely devalued in the social hierarchy. It's even hard to speak of that world. [M, p. 242]

But the available social categories aren't sufficient for Delany's story. It is difficult, if not impossible, to use a single narrative to account for his experience. Instead he makes entries in a notebook, at the front about material things, at the back about sexual desire. These are "parallel narratives, in parallel columns" (M, p. 29). Although one seems to be about society, the public, and the political, and the other about the individual, the private, and the psychological, in fact both narratives are inescapably historical; they are discursive productions of knowledge of the self, not reflections either of external or internal truth. "That the two columns must be the Marxist and the Freudian—the material column and the column of desire—is only a modernist prejudice. The autonomy of each is subverted by the same excesses, just as severely" (M, p. 212). The two columns are constitutive of one another, yet the relationship between them is difficult to specify. Does the social and economic determine the subjective? Is the private entirely separate from or completely integral to the public? Delany voices the desire to resolve the problem: "Certainly one must be the lie that is illuminated by the other's truth" (M,

p. 212). And then he denies that resolution is possible since answers to these questions do not exist apart from the discourses that produce them:

> If it is the split—the space between the two columns (one resplendent and lucid with the writings of legitimacy, the other dark and hollow with the voices of the illegitimate)—that constitutes the subject, it is only after the Romantic inflation of the private into the subjective that such a split can even be located. That locus, that margin, that split itself first allows, then demands the appropriation of language—now spoken, now written—in both directions, over the gap. [*M*, pp. 29–30]

It is finally by tracking "the appropriation of language . . . in both directions, over the gap," and by situating and contextualizing that language that one historicizes the terms by which experience is represented, and so historicizes "experience" itself.

Conclusion

Reading for "the literary" does not seem at all inappropriate for those whose discipline is devoted to the study of change. It is not the only kind of reading I am advocating, although more documents than those written by literary figures are susceptible to such readings. Rather it is a way of changing the focus and the philosophy of our history, from one bent on naturalizing "experience" through a belief in the unmediated relationship between words and things, to one that takes all categories of analysis as contextual, contested, and contingent. How have categories of representation and analysis—such as class, race, gender, relations of production, biology, identity, subjectivity, agency, experience, even culture—achieved their foundational status? What have been the effects of their articulations? What does it mean for historians to study the past in terms of these categories and for individuals to think of themselves in these terms? What is the relationship between the salience of such categories in our own time and their existence in the past? Questions such as these open consideration of what Dominick LaCapra has referred to as the "transferential" relationship between the historian and the past, that is, of the relationship between the power of the historian's analytic frame and the events that are the object of his or her study.[41] And they historicize both sides of that relationship by denying the fixity and transcendence of anything that appears to operate as a foundation, turning attention instead to the history of foundationalist concepts themselves. The history of these concepts (understood to be contested and contradictory) then becomes the evidence by which "experience" can be grasped and by which the historian's relationship to the past he or she writes about can be articulated. This is what Foucault meant by genealogy:

> If interpretation were the slow exposure of the meaning hidden in an origin, then only metaphysics could interpret the development of humanity. But if interpretation is the violent or surreptitious appropriation of a system of rules, which in itself has no essential meaning, in order to impose a direction, to bend it to a new will, to force

its participation in a different game, and to subject it to secondary rules, then the development of humanity is a series of interpretations. The role of genealogy is to record its history: the history of morals, ideals, and metaphysical concepts, the history of the concept of liberty or of the ascetic life; as they stand for the emergence of different interpretations, they must be made to appear as events on the stage of historical process.[42]

Experience is not a word we can do without, although given its usage to essentialize identity and reify the subject, it is tempting to abandon it altogether. But *experience* is so much a part of everyday language, so imbricated in our narratives that it seems futile to argue for its expulsion. It serves as a way of talking about what happened, of establishing difference and similarity, of claiming knowledge that is "unassailable."[43] Given the ubiquity of the term, it seems to me more useful to work with it, to analyze its operations and to redefine its meaning. This entails focussing on processes of identity production, insisting on the discursive nature of experience and on the politics of its construction. Experience is at once always already an interpretation *and* something that needs to be interpreted. What counts as experience is neither self-evident nor straightforward; it is always contested, and always therefore political. The study of experience, therefore, must call into question its originary status in historical explanation. This will happen when historians take as their project *not* the reproduction and transmission of knowledge said to be arrived at through experience, but the analysis of the production of that knowledge itself. Such an analysis would constitute a genuinely nonfoundational history, one which retains its explanatory power and its interest in change but does not stand on or reproduce naturalized categories.[44] It also cannot guarantee the historian's neutrality, for deciding which categories to historicize is inevitably political, necessarily tied to the historian's recognition of his or her stake in the production of knowledge. Experience is, in this approach, not the origin of our explanation, but that which we want to explain. This kind of approach does not undercut politics by denying the existence of subjects; it instead interrogates the processes of their creation and, in so doing, refigures history and the role of the historian and opens new ways for thinking about change.[45]

Notes

1. For an important discussion of the "dilemma of difference," see Martha Minow, "Justice Engendered," foreword to "The Supreme Court, 1986 Term," *Harvard Law Review* 101 (Nov. 1987): 10–95.
2. Samuel R. Delany, *The Motion of Light in Water: Sex and Science Fiction Writing in the East Village, 1957–1965* (New York, 1988), p. 173; hereafter abbreviated *M*.
3. On the distinction between seeing and writing in formulations of identity, see Homi K. Bhabha, "Interrogating Identity," in *Identity The Real Me*, ed. Lisa Appignanesi (London, 1987), pp. 5–11.
4. Lionel Gossman, *Towards a Rational Historiography*, Transactions of the American Philosophical Society, n.s. 79, pt. 3 (Philadelphia, 1989), p. 26.
5. On the "documentary" or "objectivist" model used by historians, see Dominick LaCapra, "Rhetoric and History," *History and Criticism* (Ithaca, N.Y., 1985), pp. 15–44.

6. Michel de Certeau, "History: Science and Fiction," in *Heterologies: Discourse on the Other,* trans. Brian Massumi (Minneapolis, 1986), p. 203; hereafter abbreviated "H."

7. Vision, as Donna Haraway points out, is not passive reflection. "All eyes, including our own organic ones, are active perceptual systems, building in translations and specific ways of seeing—that is, ways of life" (Donna Haraway, "Situated Knowledges: The Science Question in Feminism and the Privilege of Partial Perspective," *Feminist Studies* 14 [Fall 1988]: 583). In another essay she pushes the optical metaphor further: "The rays from my optical device diffract rather than reflect. These diffracting rays compose *interference* patterns, not reflecting images. . . . A diffraction pattern does not map where differences appear, but rather where the *effects* of differences appear" (Haraway, "The Promises of Monsters: Reproductive Politics for Inappropriate/d Others," typescript). In this connection, see also Minnie Bruce Pratt's discussion of her eye that "has only let in what I have been taught to see," in her "Identity: Skin Blood Heart," in Elly Bulkin, Pratt, and Barbara Smith, *Yours in Struggle: Three Feminist Perspectives on Anti-Semitism and Racism* (Brooklyn, N.Y., 1984), and the analysis of Pratt's autobiographical essay by Biddy Martin and Chandra Talpade Mohanty, "Feminist Politics: What's Home Got to Do with It?," in *Feminist Studies/Critical Studies,* ed. Teresa de Lauretis (Bloomington, Ind., 1986), pp. 191–212.

8. On the disruptive, antisocial nature of desire, see Leo Bersani, *A Future for Astyanax: Character and Desire in Literature* (Boston, 1976).

9. Eve Kosofsky Sedgwick, *Between Men: English Literature and Male Homosocial Desire* (New York, 1985), p. 86.

10. See Jane Gallop, *The Daughter's Seduction: Feminism and Psychoanalysis* (Ithaca, N.Y., 1982); de Lauretis, *Alice Doesn't: Feminism, Semiotics, Cinema* (Bloomington, Ind., 1984), esp. chap. 5, "Desire in Narrative," pp. 103–57; Sedgwick, *Between Men;* and Jacques Lacan, "The Signification of the Phallus," *Ecrits: A Selection,* trans. Alan Sheridan (New York, 1977), pp. 281–91.

11. Discussions with Elizabeth Weed on this point were helpful.

12. I am grateful to Judith Butler for discussions on this point.

13. Fredric Jameson, "Immanence and Nominalism in Postmodern Theory," *Postmodernism, or, the Cultural Logic of Late Capitalism* (Durham, N.C., 1991), p. 199.

14. Raymond Williams, *Keywords: A Vocabulary of Culture and Society,* rev. ed. (New York, 1985), p. 126; hereafter abbreviated *K.*

15. On the ways knowledge is conceived "as an assemblage of accurate representations," see Richard Rorty, *Philosophy and the Mirror of Nature* (Princeton, N.J., 1979), esp. p. 163.

16. Bhabha puts it this way: *"To see* a missing person, or to *look* at Invisibleness, is to emphasize the subject's *transitive* demand for a *direct* object of self-reflection; a point of presence which would maintain its privileged enunciatory position *qua subject"* (Bhabha, "Interrogating Identity," p. 5).

17. De Lauretis, *Alice Doesn't,* p. 159.

18. Gayatri Chakravorty Spivak describes this as "positing a metalepsis":

> A subject-effect can be briefly plotted as follows: that which seems to operate as a subject may be part of an immense discontinuous network . . . of strands that may be termed politics, ideology, economics, history, sexuality, language, and so on. . . . Different knottings and configurations of these strands, determined by heterogeneous determinations which are themselves dependent upon myriad circumstances, produce the effect of an operating subject. Yet the continuist and homogenist deliberative consciousness symptomatically requires a continuous and homogeneous cause for this effect and thus posits a sovereign and determining subject. This latter is, then, the effect of an effect, and its positing a metalepsis, or the substitution of an effect for a cause. [Gayatri Chakravorty Spivak, *In Other Worlds: Essay in Cultural Politics* (New York, 1987), p. 204].

19. R. C. Collingwood, *The Idea of History* (Oxford, 1946), pp. 274–75.

20. Ibid., p. 256.

21. E. P. Thompson, "The Poverty of Theory or an Orrery of Errors," *The Poverty of Theory and Other Essays* (New York, 1978), p. 170; hereafter abbreviated "PT."

22. Williams's discussion of "structures of feeling" takes on some of these same issues in a more extended way. See Williams, *The Long Revolution* (New York, 1961), and the interview about it in his *Politics and Letters: Interviews with New Left Review* (1979; London, 1981), pp. 133–74. I am grateful to Chun Lin for directing me to these texts.

23. On the integrative functions of "experience," see Judith Butler, *Gender Trouble: Feminism and the Subversion of Identity* (New York, 1990), pp. 22–25.

24. For a different reading of Thompson on experience, see William H. Sewell, Jr., "How Classes Are Made: Critical Reflections on E. P. Thompson's Theory of Working-class Formation," in *E. P. Thompson: Critical Debates,* ed. Harvey J. Kay and Keith McClelland (Philadelphia, 1990), pp. 50–77. I also have benefitted from Sylvia Schafer's "Writing about 'Experience': Workers and Historians Tormented by Industrialization," typescript.

25. Judith Newton, "History as Usual? Feminism and the 'New Historicism,'" *Cultural Critique* 9 (Spring 1988): 93.

26. Christine Stansell, "A Response to Joan Scott," *International Labor and Working Class History,* no. 31 (Spring 1987): 28. Often this kind of invocation of experience leads back to the biological or physical "experience" of the body. See, for example, the arguments about rape and violence offered by Mary E. Hawkesworth, "Knowers, Knowing, Known: Feminist Theory and Claims of Truth," *Signs* 14 (Spring 1989): 533–57.

27. This is one of the meanings of the slogan "the personal is the political." Personal knowledge, that is, the experience of oppression is the source of resistance to it. This is what Mohanty calls "the feminist osmosis thesis: females are feminists by association and identification with the experiences which constitute us as female" (Mohanty, "Feminist Encounters: Locating the Politics of Experience," *Copyright* 1 [Fall 1987]: 32). See also an important article by Katie King, "The Situation of Lesbianism as Feminism's Magical Sign: Contests for Meaning and the U.S. Women's Movement, 1968–1972," *Communication* 9 (1986): 65–91.

28. Denise Riley, *"Am I That Name?" Feminism and the Category of Women in History* (Minneapolis, 1988), pp. 100, 99.

29. John E. Toews, "Intellectual History after the Linguistic Turn: The Autonomy of Meaning and the Irreducibility of Experience," *American Historical Review* 92 (Oct. 1987): 881; hereafter abbreviated "IH."

30. De Certeau puts it this way:
    > That the particularity of the place where discourse is produced is relevant will be naturally more apparent where historiographical discourse treats matters that put the subject-producer of knowledge into question: the history of women, of blacks, of Jews, of cultural minorities, etc. In these fields one can, of course, either maintain that the personal status of the author is a matter of indifference (in relation to the objectivity of his or her work) or that he or she alone authorizes or invalidates the discourse (according to whether he or she is "of it" or not). But this debate requires what has been concealed by an epistemology, namely, the impact of subject-to-subject relationships (men and women, blacks and whites, etc.) on the use of apparently "neutral" techniques and in the organization of discourses that are, perhaps, equally scientific. For example, from the fact of the differentiation of the sexes, must one conclude that a woman produces a different historiography from that of a man? Of course, I do not answer this question, but I do assert that this interrogation puts the place of the subject in question and requires a treatment of it unlike the epistemology that constructed the "truth" of the work on the foundation of the speaker's irrelevance. ["H," pp. 217–18]

31. Here we have an example of what Foucault characterized as "continuous history":"the indispensable correlative of the founding function of the subject: the guarantee that everything that has eluded him may be restored to him; the certainty that time will disperse nothing without restoring it in reconstituted unity" (Michel Foucault, *The Archaeology of Knowledge*, trans. A. M. Sheridan Smith [New York, 1972], p. 12).

32. Ellen Rooney, *Seductive Reasoning: Pluralism as the Problematic of Contemporary Theory* (Ithaca, N.Y., 1989), p. 6.

33. Spivak, "A Literary Representation of the Subaltern: A Woman's Text from the Third World," in *In Other Worlds*, p. 241.

34. Her argument is based on a set of oppositions between history and literature, male and female, identity and difference, practical politics and theory, and she repeatedly privileges the second set of terms. These polarities speak to the specifics of the debate she is engaged in with the (largely male) Subaltern Studies collective, historians working within a Marxist, especially Cramscian, frame.

35. Spivak, "Subaltern Studies: Deconstructing Historiography," in *In Other Worlds*, p. 205. See also Spivak (with Rooney), "In a Word. *Interview*," *differences* I (Summer 1989): 124–54, esp. p. 128. On essentialism, see Diana Fuss, *Essentially Speaking: Feminism, Nature, and Difference* (New York, 1989).

36. Stuart Hall, "Minimal Selves," in *Identity The Real Me*, p. 45. See also Barbara J. Fields, "Ideology and Race in American History," in *Region, Race and Reconstruction: Essays in Honor of C. Vann Woodward*, ed. J . Morgan Kousser and James M. McPherson (New York, 1982), pp. 143–77. Fields's article is notable for its contradictions: the way, for example, that it historicizes race, naturalizes class, and refuses to talk at all about gender.

37. An excellent example of the historicizing of black women's "experience" is Hazel Carby's *Reconstructing Womanhood: The Emergence of the Afro-American Woman Novelist* (New York, 1987).

38. For discussions of how change operates within and across discourses, see James J. Bono, "Science, Discourse, and Literature: The Role/Rule of Metaphor in Science," in *Literature and Science: Theory and Practice*, ed. Stuart Peterfreund (Boston, 1990), pp. 59–89. See also, Mary Poovey, *Uneven Developments: The Ideological Work of Gender in Mid-Victorian England* (Chicago, 1988), pp. 123.

39. Parveen Adams and Jeff Minson, "'The 'Subject' of Feminism," *m/f* no. 2 (1978), p. 52. On the constitution of the subject, see Foucault, *The Archaeology of Knowledge*, pp. 95–96; Felicity A. Nussbaum, *The Autobiographical Subject: Gender and Ideology in Eighteenth Century England* (Baltimore, 1989); and Peter de Bolla, *The Discourse of the Sublime: Readings in History, Aesthetics, and the Subject* (New York, 1989).

40. Karen Swann's comments on this paper were presented at the Little Three Faculty Colloquium on "The Social and Political Construction of Reality" at Wesleyan University in January 1991. The comments exist only in typescript.

41. See LaCapra, "Is Everyone a *Mentalité* Case? Transference and the 'Culture' Concept," in *History and Criticism*, pp. 71–94.

42. Foucault, "Nietzsche, Genealogy, History," in *Language, Counter-Memory, Practice: Selected Essays and Interviews*, trans. Donald F. Bouchard and Sherry Simon, ed. Bouchard (Ithaca, N.Y., 1977), pp. 151–52.

43. Ruth Roach Pierson, "Experience, Difference, and Dominance in the Writings of Women's History," typescript.

44. Conversations with Christopher Fynsk helped clarify these points for me.

45. For an important attempt to describe a post-structuralist history, see de Bolla, "Disfiguring History," *Diacritics* 16 (Winter 1986): 49–58.

CHAPTER FIVE

Situating Locations: The Politics of Self, Identity and "Other" in Living and Writing the Text[1]

JAYATI LAL

> [As] ethnography is moving into areas long occupied by sociology, . . . it has become clear that every version of an "other," wherever found, is also the construction of a self," and the making of ethnographic texts . . . has always involved a process of "self-fashioning". . . . Cultural *poesis*—and politics—is the constant reconstitution of selves and others through specific exclusions, conventions, and discursive practices.
>
> —*James Clifford, "Partial Truths"*

> . . . we need to observe the life we participate in when we are "back from the field" critically, and question the roles we play with respect to those from all over the world who are affected by our actions . . . There is no corner of life so private and personal that issues of race, class, color and culture do not permeate it; if anthropologists have connected the kitchens and bedrooms of other societies to their theories they have no excuse for closing the doors on their own.
>
> —*Deborah D'Amico-Samuels, "Undoing Fieldwork"*

Deconstructing "Fieldwork"

The very notion of what it means to do research on gender and development in the contemporary historical arena has been urgently called into question by recent critical discourses on anticolonialism. For instance, debates on postcoloniality have interrogated the excavation of the Third World as a resource for Western theory. Additionally, feminist discourses on difference and antiuniversalism have challenged the construction of the "Third World woman" as an essentialized Other. And finally, methodological writings in sociology and anthropology have also articulated a deep skepticism about methodological vantage points that colonize, or objectify, the subjects of one's research. The common theme that underlies these strands of questioning is their collective interrogation of the foun-

Jayati Lal, "Situating Locations: The Politics of Self, Identity, and 'Other' in Living and Writing the Text," in Diane L. Wolf, ed. *Feminist Dilemmas in Fieldwork* (Boulder, Colo.: Westview Press, 1996): 185–214. Reprinted by permission.

dationalism that is embedded in much extant social science research, which rests on an essential division between "Self" and "Other," or between the knowing subject (the researcher) and the known, or soon-to-be-known, object (the researched).

In this chapter, I examine the politics of representation and the epistemologies of locations in attempting to articulate a non-universalizing feminist methodology that goes beyond colonialist representations of "Third World women." In so doing, I bring together anthropological discourses on rethinking the project of ethnographic fieldwork and the politics of ethnographic writing, feminist discourses on and critiques of canonical ways of knowing and dominant epistemologies, and sociological discourses on feminist methodologies and critiques of malestream social science research. Despite the overlapping areas of concern in these disciplinary discourses, they have by and large not been engaged in an interdisciplinary dialogue which could be very productive.[2] In developing my arguments in this chapter, I draw on my experiences of "fieldwork"—a term that I will attempt to deconstruct as I proceed—in a mix of writing genres. Utilizing narrative, interpretive, and reflexive modes I examine fieldwork encounters and my own background for their theoretical and epistemic implications.

Postmodern Disjunctures

In the postmodern era of intensified globalization, the international movements of capital, labor, and commodities shape not just the objects of our academic inquiry—factories and finance capital, workers, and products—but critically determine the forms that such inquiry and the discourse surrounding it takes. In the first instance, these international circuits mark us as individual scholars and locate us in a complex web of lived material realities that shape our notions of ourselves, our identities, our politics, and our writing. Furthermore, in this "global, ethnoscape" (Appadurai, 1991), the subjects of our research on the globalization of the economy increasingly inhabit locations that do not "fit" our historically derived theoretical expectations of where they might be, giving rise to "new genre of neuroses" for researchers in the field (Fox, 1991a:4). Although the "native" subject might be increasingly likely to inhabit the privileged world of the first world anthropologist, many Third World scholars who immigrated to the United States for higher studies are also increasingly (dis)located when they return "home."[3]

There is a growing body of literature which acknowledges this historical moment in the disciplinary fields of anthropology and, to a lesser extent, in other social science disciplines. A generation of Third World scholars returning home have foregrounded epistemological concerns raised by scholars studying their own cultures within the West, particularly those studying "Third World" cultures and communities within the United States.[4] These concerns have coalesced with those stemming from a paradigmatic movement that is informed by poststructuralist concerns regarding representations of the Other and the author/ity of researcher-ethnographer and ethnographic texts.[5] Issues of nativity have once again come to the fore in analyses of "non-western" and "third-world" societies, but it is now the nativity of the *researcher* rather than the research subject that is problematized.[6] This 'return of the native' in recent anthropological debates specifically problematizes the assumption of an "authentic insider" (Narayan, 1993), arguing instead for the recognition that we all occupy multiple and fluid locations—a theme that I will pursue in more detail later.

This chapter thus situates the researcher-in-practice by addressing the multiple location(s) in the production of my identity as a Third World woman and United States based graduate student returning "home" from the academy to conduct research on women. Exploring my construction as a researcher around the multiple locations and positionalities that constitute the politics of self and identity—Third World woman in United States, scholar and graduate student in the academy, feminist, middle class researcher in India—I examine the epistemological implications of such multiple locations and positionalities in the political practice of "fieldwork."

There are three interlinked issues that I address in this context: First, I analyze the *politics of locations* in living the text in the field. In particular, I discuss the implications of these locations for the author/ity of the text in light of academic discourses on epistemic privilege and the presumed authenticity of native accounts. Second, I explore the *politics of representation* in writing the text by examining how engaging with research subjects' agency and resistances to ethnographic authority provide their own (less partial) account through self-presentations. In conclusion, I suggest that our texts have potential for *pedagogical empowerment*, which is an important avenue for political activism within the locational setting that assumes particular salience in contextualizing my identity at this juncture: the academy. In developing this analysis, I draw on my own locations both within and outside of the academy to ground my arguments. In so doing, I seek to explicate the manner in which my positionalities within those locations is implicated in the account that I provide or, in other words, that "the problem of *voice* ('speaking for' and 'speaking to') intersects with the problem of *place* (speaking 'from' and speaking 'of')" (Appadurai, 1988:17, emphasis mine).

The feminist dilemmas in and of "fieldwork" that I examine are thus broadly conceived in this discussion. My focus is on identity and (inter)subjectivity as they crosscut the boundaries of the dualisms of home:work, field:academy, and personal:professional. I thus attempt to erase the boundaries that mark the domains of private:public in my life while simultaneously writing within them as they have been constituted, demarcated, and redrawn in the process of the encounters and intersections of my history with the history of various disciplinary developments and the history of Others. More specifically, my focus in this discussion is on the research, reading, and writing that extends beyond that narrowly demarcated period of being in the "field."[7] This reconceptualization of what constitutes the field has been a powerful contribution of a poststructuralist informed ethnography, because it foregrounds the authorial role in constructions and representations of the subject (i.e., the author as subject), thereby rendering positivist depictions of social scientists in the "researcher-as-detached-observer" mode obsolete.[8]

Questions That Ensue from the "Fieldwork"

My discussion draws on the experiences of eighteen months of research in Delhi, with women workers and their employers and managers in fourteen garment and seven television firms. In the course of this fieldwork, I visited the factories, workshops, sweatshops, and homes where the production related work of these firms was conducted. With the help of two research assistants, I conducted interviews with 196 workers (90 percent of whom were women), and 57 managers and owners. I conducted all the interviews with the managers, owners, and contractors, and sixty of the worker interviews. The episodes that I relate in this paper are drawn from the interviews conducted by me and the quoted statements that I reproduce here are from transcripts of these interviews. Additionally, I relied on non-participatory ethnographic methods of observation, the analysis of firm records, and archival research. The goals of research were to examine processes of gendered class formation and factory level gender politics that undergird the widely noted feminization of the workforce in these industries under new conditions of globalization.

My primary sources of information were structured and semi-structured interviews which lasted from one and a half hours to three hours, depending on the respondent and the location of the interview. Although the bulk of interviews were conducted on the firms' premises, interviews of domestic workers and of workers in one firm where on-site factory access to workers was denied were conducted in the homes of workers or co-workers. There were additional opportunities for meeting with workers outside of the formal interview situation, especially during tea and lunch breaks, which I spent with workers, and the brief mingling that would occur after work hours and while commuting.

In the process of doing this research, I encountered several dilemmas that have made me deeply skeptical of our ability to realize feminist methodologies in practice—especially in light of the prescriptive methodological guidelines, canonical texts, and authorizing forms of discourse that have been put forth in this literature. In this chapter, I focus on the implications of feminist research practice for the (re)consideration of epistemological and political projects. I thus address three closely related sets of questions that were suggested by my research experiences and which bear on current debates on representation and reflexive methodologies that are in evidence across the social sciences.

The first question, broadly conceived, involves the issue of the authority of my voice. I am concerned with the epistemological question, "How do I know?," specifically as it is premised on my particular history and identities. In examining this issue, I attempt to initiate a move away from an identity-based epistemology that rests on a self conceived identity as a Native or Indian Woman to an epistemology that is based on an engagement with one's *politics of location* in articulating partial perspectives based on "situated knowledges" (Haraway, 1988a). The second question is, What do research subjects' actions and responses tell me about the construction of ethnographic authority? How do subjects assert their agency and shape their own representations? How does this inform endeavors towards postcolonial ethnographic representations? The third question is, How and where can I effect change? That is to say, from which site—among the multiplicity of sites that I currently inhabit—can I practice my feminist politics: in the field, in the academy, or both? In this context I examine the limits on praxis in Third World industrial settings and the limits of a postmodern ethnography in which the possibilities for politics are often limited to *textual* practices. In what follows, I do not aim to provide answers to these questions, so much as I seek to reintroduce and re-frame these issues into ongoing and well-established debates.

Situating Identities/Locating Self and Other

Disciplinary Conjunctures

The issue of disciplinarity is one of the first "locations" that needs to be addressed, for it is perhaps the most important determiner of how one defines a research area and what methods one chooses to study it. Even among closely allied disciplines in the social sciences, responses to the current crisis in representation have been quite disparate. For example, although feminist anthropologists have attempted to address the challenges posed by postmodernism to ethnographic writing and responsibility quite seriously,[9] debate about these issues seems curiously lacking in methodological writings on qualitative fieldwork in sociology, although there are some recent important exceptions to this.[10] My training as a sociologist left me unprepared for the complex concerns that surfaced during my fieldwork around issues of representation and identity.

Reflecting on the historical moment of my graduate training, I realize that I am in-between a new generation of scholars who have had exposure to a variety of methodologies within the social sciences and courses that are explicitly labeled as "feminist methodologies," and an older generation of scholars who are now turning their experiences of trial-and-error in the field into inter-disciplinary feminist course offerings (see, for example, Reinharz, 1992; DeVault, 1996; Wolf, 1996). Clearly, these generational differences reflect the paradigmatic developments and disjunctures experienced within various disciplines.[11] Yet epistemic shifts are never uncontroversial: Kuhn (1970) and Foucault (1984) both recognized the power of defining/defending the paradigm/canon. In the social sciences, this canonical construction of appropriate research and adequate proof has often meant the outright rejection of ethnographic approaches, based on the concern for a "statistically significant sample size." My point here is that those who are relatively powerless in the academy—students—rarely have the ability to choose approaches that do not fit the desired model for appropriate research designs.[12]

Issues of disciplinarity are further complicated in the interdisciplinary field of women's studies. Not only is doing fieldwork looked upon skeptically within dominant constructions of appropriate sociological research, often hegemonically constructed through the availability of computerized survey data files as hypothesis-driven number crunching but, in addition, feminist work is still likely to be viewed with suspicion even within more openly constituted sociology departments.[13] Despite the "knowledge explosion" (Kramarae and Spender, 1992) of feminist scholarship in the academy, it has not translated into its uniform distribution among (and in) disciplines and across university campuses.[14] Although women's studies is best conceived as an interdisciplinary, or even a postdisciplinary field of inquiry, the fact remains that The Academy is still structured around disciplines seeking to retain the boundaries around their special turfs of academic inquiry, especially in the age of privatization and budget cutbacks that we currently bear witness to. These politics, once again, translate into special difficulties for those who are relatively powerless within the academy: students and untenured junior faculty, particularly in the arena of defining and defending intellectually "appropriate" research projects which go against the grain of disciplinarity and hegemonic neopositivism. In articulating my research design, I felt these tensions and pressures quite strongly. As I worked through these issues and progressed into the research, I moved further and further away from my initial design of interview-based surveys and relied increasingly on ethnographic observations and open-ended interviews.

In/Essential Identities (Native, Indian, Woman)

> If anthropology [and ethnography] is to be decolonized, it must start by situating itself, its practitioners, and the objects of its research within the same plenary space and time and with reference to the same world political, economic and cultural hierarchy. (D'Amico-Samuels, 1991: 68–69)

What is the nature of reality that is presumed in constructions of a researcher's identity that has stable boundaries? Who is the assumed historical subject in such a construction? How have such constructions undergirded critical political practices of representation of Third World subjects? In other words, what happens when the traditional boundaries between the Knower and the Known begin to break down, are reversed, or crosscut with mixed and hybrid identities? What are the implications of this for the politics of field based research? Unavoidably, the many locations that shape my identity and notions of self influenced my choices, access, and procedures in/of research and also permeate the representation of research subjects in my writing. Among these, is the subjective construction of my identity as an "Indian woman."

Living and growing up in a very sheltered non-urban university town setting in India for most of my childhood, I had and have a very definite sense of myself as "Indian," even though my Yugoslavia-born, naturalized American immigrant-citizen, relocated-to-India-by-marriage mother stood out in this small and cloistered community. In such a construction of my mother as Other, I do not mean to naturalize my father's "Indianess": Like most Indians of his generation, his travels to the West (for graduate education in both the United Kingdom and America) were deeply implicated in the larger post-independence, postcolonial relations of exchange, immigration, and return.

My speaking English at home and attending an English-medium convent school made Hindi a language I was never completely comfortable in, and I struggled with Hindi throughout high school with the help of a home-tutor. Although my poor Hindi subjected me to humiliating taunts in high school, in college, since Hindi as a "Modern Indian Language" was something that I just had to pass, I was less likely to be marked as "different." These postcolonial institutional structures (i.e., English-medium schools) have shaped generations of students into varying degrees of trained incapacity, or "sanctioned ignorance" (John, 1991:72) in their mother tongue and have also assisted in shaping the devaluation of our own culture's heritage that many of us display/ed in a variety of forms of internalized racism. In college, my incapacity in Hindi did not define me as inferior but as Westernized, and hence, in the neocolonial mentality of "postcolonials," as exotically different.[15] Upper middle class Indian culture, floating as it does above the Indian reality of the masses, is constituted as a complex hybrid mix of East and West—the latter embodying both British and American cultures. Within such a scenario, being marked as different because of a white mother did not construct me as Other. In many ways I was as "Indian" as all my urban college classmates who were just as out of touch with Indian reality.[16]

Perhaps equally unremarkable for my generation of Delhi University students, was my lack of sustained political investments in ongoing events and a relatively underdeveloped sense of myself as a feminist. In India, my relatively cloistered middle-class existence (both at home and away from home) had not really allowed for the development of a feminist consciousness. Like many upper middle class women, I took for granted class privileges—such as a good college education—that crosscut gender boundaries. Feminism was an encounter that unfortunately was, and sadly unfortunately continues to be, primarily defined through academic debates and theories. Mary John, in examining her transformations toward becoming a postcolonial feminist in the United States, makes a similar observation: "Discrepant locations do . . . produce unintended effects: For some of us, the dislocation from a sheltered Indian middle class environment, where a consciousness of privilege dominates, to a milieu as highly sexualized, and with such intensified and refined technologies of gender, as this one, does lead to the espousal of a more explicitly feminist politics" (John, 1991:17).

Furthermore, it was only after relocating to the United States for graduate studies that I began to develop a political sensibility and a sense of myself as "Other"—both in the immediate sense of everyday interactions which situated me as such and in my growing awareness of myself as a member of a minority—as a South Asian/Third World woman of color in the United States. As Lata Mani (Frankenberg and Mani, 1993:297) has noted, this process of "Othering," of defining oneself as "Third World," often begins within the racialized context of contemporary American immigrant relations and begs differentiation from the situation of those Others who are "native" to and have come of age in the United States.

By historically locating myself within the specific geopolitical context in which I did my fieldwork research, I have tried to disrupt the notions of power that are often assumed in discussions of nativity. Prevailing relations of power define what constitutes Other as unacceptably different and what remains within the boundaries of acceptably different. "Inauthentic natives" can circumvent the status of Other through the privilege of class and its attendant forms of cultural capital which, while being culturally and historically specific, are often manifested within postcolonial contexts though idealized/idolized "Western" trappings. My privileged and secular upper middle class Indian background situates me *within* this class less as Other than as Self/same, while simultaneously demarcating Us from the "real" Others outside our class. Furthermore, I have sought to bring out the ways in which I am constituted as a historical subject, deeply imbricated in the larger postcolonial relations of exchange of commodities, labor, and capital between East and West. That my labor power is realized in the West is, of course, the thorniest issue of all. For it is the fact that our sites of enunciation center in and on The West that is the most problematic, and potentially most compromising, aspect of a postcolonial feminist critique (John, 1991).[17]

On Fieldwork (or, "Going Home?")

After a six-year stay in the United States pursuing graduate work, I returned to Delhi for my dissertation research, to a familiar city where I had spent critical years of my life as a college student. Yet in many ways, I entered a world that was completely foreign to me. I was traveling to factories in the industrial districts and zones in and around the city that were surrounded by working class neighborhoods and squatter slums; I was searching for addresses of fly-by-night operations in the narrow *galis* (lanes) of neighborhoods that few (middle class) people knew existed—areas that can best be characterized as villages within the city. These communities were often nestled cheek by jowl alongside the more affluent communities that were on the map of my familiar. I was a "native" returning to a foreign country. Shapur Jat, Laddo Sarai, Amrit Nagar—these neighborhoods were behind, beside, and between the more familiar locations of South Extension, East of Kailash, and Siri Fort, not to mention other areas widely recognized as being on the map to which I had also never been before, such as the industrial zones of Naraina, Shahibabad, Okhla, Mayapuri, and Noida.

I will never forget the sense of excitement that I experienced when I walked into my first "real" factory, a large garment manufacturing unit. Until then, I had only been to smaller firms which didn't fit my notions of what a factory should look like. This sense of discovery was repeated when I visited the fabrication units to which work was sent out. "These are *sweatshops,*" I thought to myself, appalled at the filth, dingy lighting, and cramped quarters of the fabrication units. These workshops are often one-room quarters that house both *karigars* (tailors) and the sewing-machines that they work on. As rural migrants, the predominantly male craft piece-workers in these workshops eat, sleep, and work in the fabrication units while they live in Delhi. "Just like the old putting-out system!" I thought excitedly of all the great theoretical, historical, and comparative possibilities that this would generate. After these initial moments of recognition and several hours spent talking to workers and contractors, observing their work and relationships to firms, I moved quite naturally to seeing the fabrication units as more complex lived realities and not as mere manifestations of theoretical constructs. Immersion in the field provides its own corrective. As we begin to develop "nativised selves" (Karim, 1993:248), we see phenomenon that we explore more from the perspectives of those who *live* the realities rather than from our imperialist academic vantage points, ever ready to appropriate the experience of others into our preordained theoretical categories (Smith, 1987:116–17; Hale, 1988). Furthermore, when writing the text, exploring the interpellation of the local social phenomenon that we investigate into larger global histories also serves to denaturalize and de-exotify their existence, to work against a romanticization of Third World phenomenon as somehow existing outside of history (Jordan, 1991).

Just how invested are we in locating exploitation? In doing and writing our research, we must vigilantly question our own investments in looking for the exotic—that truly paradigmatic theoretical subject of our disciplines. In crossing the class barriers of my upbringing and moving into the arena of industrial man-ufacturing in Delhi, I was confronting that Other for the first time. For a first-time fieldworker, self-consciousness about our (trained) tendencies to re-present the Other comes quickly, and it is a self-consciousness we must strive hard *not* to let subside once we return from the "field" into that other field of re-presentation—the academy—because it is in the academy that we feel the pressure to reproduce colonizing discourses on the Other most strenuously. As Ganguly (1990:76) notes, ". . . the best way to make a "splash" in ethnographic circles is still to write about something exotic." In moving from "living" to "writing" the text, then, we can work against reproducing colonizing discourses if we assiduously maintain the perception of the academy as just another "field" location and of writing as a con-tinuation of "fieldwork."

Non-participant Urban Industrial Fieldwork:
The Researcher as Outsider

In many ways my own marginality in Indian society fueled a preoccupation with my identity before and during the actual research. As an Indian returning home, I had assumed that I would not face many of the difficulties that an outsider might, because of our partially shared histories as Indian women. Yet because of my privileged class background, I also realized that our differences were much more significant than our similarities. I was very aware that this would limit the shared cultural expectations that we might have and associate with the socially constructed identity "Indian woman." Coming to grips with these differences made me realize my dislocation even within that space that I had thought of as "home" (see Martin and Mohanty, 1986). In the actual practice of research, of course, one is faced with the need to constantly negotiate between the positions of insider and outsider, rather than being fixedly assigned one or the other sub-ject position. More important than a sameness that might be assumed in my pos-sible identity as an insider are the power differentials and class inequities that di-vide those insiders and the divisions between researched and researcher that are created by the very act of observation.

While initiating contact with firms, I was never sure of what conditions would be provided for the worker interviews. Although these varied greatly from firm to firm, all television manufacturers were much more reluctant to let me on to the shop floor. Most garment worker interviews were conducted on the shop floor, with us sitting on the floor in quiet corners of particular production departments. In these cases, I often interviewed women as they were doing their work—checking garments, thread cutting, or embroidering. In the television factories, I was typically assigned a private space to conduct the interviews—a manager's office, an office worker's desk, or a guest room. These differences in the provi-sions for my setup speak directly to differing forms, and intensities, of labor con-trol within firms. In smaller garment manufacturing firms, there are fewer divi-sions amongst workers and there is a close and personal supervision of work and hence contact between workers, managers, and owners. In these paternalistically run firms, my close contact with workers during interviews was therefore not seen as disruptive of larger factory-based class configurations, since managers and owners themselves rely heavily on informal, personal, and direct forms of labor control.

Larger firms, which included most television firms and one garment firm, rely on more formal systems of control and regulation. For example, they hire managers for different functions (e.g., personnel, production), who are absent in smaller firms where control is directly managed by the owner, or a single manager. In these firms, the more formal setup of a clean and private space (such as an office) that was provided for my interviews clearly served to protect my class privileges. But in protecting my class privileges, firms also acted to maintain the class boundaries and hierarchies within the firm, and to reinforce the hierarchical factory regime upon which production itself was predicated. The spatial locations in which the interviews were conducted thus provide a vivid mapping of class and gender hierarchies within the factory and set the boundaries within which my desired subject location (as researcher) could be positioned.

The research situation routinely places the researcher in an overtly powerful position vis-à-vis research subjects, and this inequality is exacerbated by the researcher's often necessary relationships with access providers who may have control over other research subjects. This is an especially likely outcome of non-participatory industrial ethnographic research, where the researcher does not have unmediated or immediate access to the research subjects. In my research, managers and owners of firms were simultaneously both research subjects and access providers, making for a contradictory power imbalance in my relationships with them. Thus, while they were clearly flattered at being interviewed, managers were often quick to (re)establish their authority over me and also took every opportunity to demonstrate their authority over the workers. Most often this would be done while I was attempting to schedule interviews with workers, such that "this department is too busy today" or "you will have to come back tomorrow" were lines I came to read not just as simple statements of fact.

Gaining access to firms with the consent of managers and owners often meant that women were called to a room that was assigned to me for interviewing, without knowing why they had been called upon. This situation was understandably seen as extremely threatening by some of the women, who sometimes assumed that I was a *sarkari* (government) employee and hence someone to be wary of. This was especially true for those women who were not in stable jobs. After I explained the research project and the nature of the interview to each prospective interviewee, with one exception, not a single woman who was approached refused participation in the study.

This does not suggest that participation in the project was voluntary, since women who were summoned to the room allocated for the interviews most likely perceived this as an order from management and hence did not see themselves as having a choice about whether they would be interviewed. Because they also saw that I toured production facilities accompanied by the owner, manager, or the supervisor, this tended to place me in a powerful and potentially authoritative position merely by association. Often this was evidenced in the questions that they posed once *outside* the factory premises, while we walked to a common bus stop or while we commuted in a company bus at the end of the workday. Word about the study would spread after the first interview on the first day, and subsequent interviewees were clearly more comfortable as women came to them in the context of information provided by previous interviewees.

The following encounter highlights—through the curious juxtaposition of researcher, interviewee, and potential inter viewee that ensued—the incredibly paradoxical position that one might be forced to adopt as a researcher seeking to minimize her power and distance from her research subjects. This conversation was extracted from an interview with the production manager of a large garment manufacturing firm, who was responsible for hiring all production workers in the factory. The manager's objectification of women workers, although not directly caused by me, was indirectly the result of my interviewing him: I asked him how he recruited new workers. He responded,

> For production jobs we never advertise. That's only for clerical or typists jobs, for office jobs. We just tell the girls. If someone comes to the gates looking for a job . . . if she's a good *phurti* [smart, agile, prompt] girl, we'll take her. We don't advertise on a board outside the factory gates either. No, it is not hard finding people for production jobs in this industry. For one vacancy I sometimes get up to 20 applicants. So then we see which ones are educated, agile . . . like 8th [grade] or 10th pass, we'll take them. So I'll take those who look like they are quick. I look for *phurtipan* (*Mein phurtipan dekhta hu*), that's what I look for . . . that they are quick and agile in their work. I can tell that by just looking at them. Someone who can work fast, that's more important than an education.

I have trouble understanding his use of the word and want him to be explicit about what he means, so I ask him, "What exactly do you mean by *phurtipan*?" He turns to the contractor for "pressmen" (men who iron the garments prior to packing), who had been sitting in the room during our interview, and tells him to bring a particular person into the room. I am puzzled, because I'm not sure what this is leading up to. He says, "I'll show you what I mean. I'm calling this girl, and you will see for yourself truly what I mean, you will understand immediately upon looking at her."

At this point the woman who was summoned enters the room. She is young, around 20 years old, neatly dressed and does not appear to be intimidated as she comes into the room. "You called for me, Sir?" she asks him. "Like her, she looks active, doesn't she?" He directs this question to me, pointing to her as he does so. Then he dismisses her and asks her to send another person to his office, whom he refers to by name. He turns to me and says, "Now I'll show you what I mean by a *dhila* [loose, lethargic] person."

I am very embarrassed by this and now that I know what he is about to do, try to dissuade him from calling on anybody else. I tell him that I have understood what he means by *phurtipan*, but he insists on calling the second woman in, arguing that the workers won't object to it as they are not very busy. He wants to prove to me that *phurtipan*, his sole criterion for hiring women, or at least for their placement in the band, is a tangible, embodied quality that can be seized upon and discerned in the few seconds that the women he had called were in his office. In response to his second summons, an older Nepalese woman who looks quite tired and is easily forty years old comes into the room a little diffidently and looks at him questioningly, not saying anything. "You see?" he says to me, "Now this is what I mean by 'dead weight,' just look at her, you see what I mean?"[18]

He dismisses the woman after saying this to me while she is in the room. Despite my attempts to dissuade him from calling upon "examples" of alert and lethargic women, the manager was proud to display what he felt was a clever and keen ability on his part to visibly distinguish between the two on the basis of this very important characteristic and predictor of future productivity—*phurtipan*. This episode clearly located me (along with the manager) in a position of power over the two women who were called upon to exhibit the meaning of *phurtipan* through their physical appearance. Demonstrating his power over the women who worked under him in this fashion could be seen as a deliberate attempt on his part to minimize the incongruity of the class and gender based power relations between us as middle class female researcher and working class male production manager. Although it may have closed the distance between us in his eyes, it had the reverse effect on me. Moreover, this episode only served to distance me even further from these two women and possibly from all the workers on the shop floor at that time who witnessed the women being called into the production manager's office.

These contradictions constitute an essential component of the process of doing social science research in the "real" world. Because social science research is always "a social interaction in its own right" (Stanley, 1990:8), it unavoidably reflects the social world into which it and we are situated. And where the social world that is being investigated is a sexist and hierarchical one, the process of research is sure to become a *sexist* and *hierarchical* social interaction. For the feminist researcher, being situated into this sexist and hierarchical interaction which reflects the nature of the reality that she is attempting to understand, critique, and change generates insurmountable contradictions. Moreover, if the men one is researching have power over other female subjects and they assert that power in the context of the research situation—either as a means to impress the foreign-returned female scholar and hence reclaim an inverted gender hierarchy created by the research diad, or as a means to innocently illustrate responses to queries— then they act to undermine and subvert a researcher's goal for non-hierarchical and non-objectifying relationships.

Despite my intention to minimize the distance between me and the women I interviewed, I was not able to avert episodes such as the one that I have just described. Furthermore, my research choices and entré into factories inevitably located me well before I was able to proceed to the stage of interviewing workers. This is because within the factories, I would first conduct the interviews with managers, owners, and contractors. This served the purpose of providing background information on the firms, such as on the distribution of workers by departments, work that was subcontracted out, and so forth. Clearly, the methods of non-participatory industrial ethnography and interviewing worked to shape my position as an outsider within the factories. Yet, given the overdetermined configurations of class within a factory setting, and within the larger societal configurations in contemporary postcolonial India, I am not convinced that other methods would enable a researcher to transcend the boundaries of "outsider."

In examining the range of assigned subject positions available to me as a researcher within different factory settings, it would seem that I was constituted as a powerful outsider. Yet I have also been simultaneously working *against* this construction of the "researcher as outsider." This is because I found myself deeply imbricated in the very class hierarchy that I was investigating through my construction as Other *within* local factory class configurations. This clearly reduces the utility of an insider-outsider distinction, because with each threshold of an insider boundary that one crosses, there would seem to be another border zone available for one's definition as outsider. What is it, then, that one is then ultimately "inside" of (Aguilar, 1981:25)? I have been constantly shifting the connotation of insider in my discussions thus far—as insider to India, to women, to factory, to workers—to highlight the problematical nature of such a distinction. Within such a configuration of locations, it is only someone who is not Indian, not a woman, and not fieldworker who can mark me as an insider.

One's identity within the research context is thus neither fixed nor predetermined.[19] The degree to which others and the research situation itself manipulate one's identity (Narayan, 1993:674) would seem to suggest that identity is not a useful site for the exploration of one's positioning into the research situation, because one is constantly being situated into it by the micropolitics of the research interactions and the macropolitics of societal inequality. To expect a researcher to become an insider is to demand that she transcend these politics, that she escape the differences that are embedded in the everyday life that she inhabits and is examining. The feminist injunction for non-hierarchical research relations can thus only be met by an *escape* from reality—it is a search for a location "outside the text"—a position which is politically irresponsible, empirically impossible, and epistemologically indefensible.

Toward a Postcolonial Methodology

I'd like to briefly explore the epistemological implications of my multiple locations in terms of debates on feminist methodologies and epistemic privilege—a notion that is fraught with difficulties for feminists. In the context of feminist methodological and epistemological debates, the issue of representations has been largely contained within a discussion on the notion of a *feminist standpoint*, which privileges the experiences of women as a vantage point for developing knowledge (e.g., Hartsock, 1987; Smith, 1987). Much like Hegel's slave who, from her subjugated standpoint, has a less partial view than the master (Hegel, 1967: 228–240), oppressed women's vision in patriarchal settings is argued to have greater power and objectivity because of its subjugated status (see Harding, 1986:26, 158). However, notions of epistemic privilege that derive from a feminist standpoint were argued to essentialize women (see, for e.g., Stanley and Wise, 1990; Harding, 1991), and later reworking of the idea of women's standpoints have attempted to account for differences among women, while still privileging particular perspectives. An example of this is Patricia Hill Collins' formulation that Black women's locations as "outsiders within" society are a critical site of marginality from which knowledge of the sex-race-class system may be gleaned (Collins, 1991).

Ironically, acknowledgment of the critique of universalism leveled against feminist theory by women of color on the grounds of the exclusion of their perspectives has led to two divergent outcomes. On the one hand, this has led to the widely noted trend by women's studies scholars of making the obligatory pronouncements of one's positioning into the analysis without ever actually contending with these differences *in* the analysis (John, 1991:2–3; Rao, 1992:41); toward a mere invoking of what has been called the "mantra" of self positioning vis-à-vis the axes of race-sex-class-sexuality (Patai and Koertge, 1994:68). However, this lip service to difference does not inform an assessment of how these positionings are implicated in one's analysis and, as such, it is therefore a politically *disengaged* response (Strickland, 1994; Robinson, 1994:249). As John (1991) notes, this practice has become prevalent partly because dislocation has become a privileged trope in feminist and postcolonial theorizing. But the mere recitation of locations is dissatisfying if it remains at this level and does not go on to examine how they might impact our analysis. "Static connotations of 'positions,' however multiple and contradictory they may be, can sometimes elide the need to confront 'what one is' through a more extensive questioning of the imbrications of one's history within History" (John, 1991:3).

On the other hand, in the corrective epistemological project of working against hegemonically universalist subject positions available in dominant modes of theorizing, subjugated epistemological standpoints have had a special appeal. Notwithstanding Hartsock's (1987:159) careful enunciation of a feminist standpoint as something that is *achieved* through political struggle rather than by merely claiming it, this epistemological privileging of marginality has resulted in special claims to knowledge by Third World women, based on the "authenticity of their personal experience of oppression" (Martin and Mohanty, 1986:199).[20] It has also resulted in widespread expectations of, and demands for, third world women to speak *from* the location of their authentic otherness (Minh-ha, 1988 and 1989).

I do not contest the fact that notions of epistemic privilege play an important political function to account for the implications of categorical aspects of identities (such as race, gender, nativity or ethnicity) in the production of knowledge. But if the representations are assumed to be innocent, authentic, and natural outcomes of this identity, then it leads to the epistemological equivalent of identity politics, or "identity epistemology" (Patai and Koertge, 1994:60).[21] Positing privileged epistemic standpoints from the specific ontological location of the oppressed thus downplays the very real possibility that such representations can be colonialist, while simultaneously obscuring the possibility of non-colonizing representations emerging from non-subjugated standpoints.[22] Clearly, both responses (i.e., mere mantra-like evocation of identities *and* standpoint epistemologies) err in being excessive: one is irresponsibly disengaged and the other is so deeply engaged that it questions our ability to see from non-subjugated standpoints.

The problems associated with standpoint epistemologies are paralleled in the presumed epistemology of the native insider. Both constructions are essentialist, and reduce either the native or Third World woman to an assumed homogeneous entity. Both suggest subjectivist, ideographic methodologies in the assumption that experience is the basis for knowledge. Both reduce the politics of location to the experience of (a presumed homogeneous) identity. Furthermore, such constructions have the unintended effect of reinforcing the very distinctions that they are supposed to erase. This is because the construction of subjugation, nativity, and insiderness, as privileged epistemic standpoints from which to counter the universalism of Western theory, are all premised on maintaining the same borderlines between Us and Them, Self and Other, and Subject and Object they purport to question in the first place. In other words, reversing the binaries does not go far enough in questioning the grounds for *either* epistemology—subjectivist-insiderism nor objectivist-outsiderism; both rely on a "naïve empiricism" (Aguilar, 1981:23). As Lennon and Whitford (1994:14) note, "we must be wary of making a fetish of 'otherness,' simply reversing the hierarchy of the original categories. The danger here is that the binary structure remains intact, dividing the world along pre-determined faultlines, attributing a spurious homogeneity to the categories."

These binaries are deeply embedded in conventional research practices that rely on realist epistemologies, such as traditional survey techniques and ethnographic fieldwork methods (e.g., participant observation). They are founded on the assumed division between the researcher as observer and researched as observed, between a knowing subject and a research object, and between research in the field and writing it up in the academy.[23] Since these dualisms have provided the grounding assumptions for foundationalist epistemologies, most conventional social science methodologies rest on these assumptions.

Initial questioning of where the "field" lies were raised by anthropologists in the context of studying their "own" societies. Yet in phrasing this issue in terms of the methods appropriate to the study of one's own society, at "home" in North America (cf. Messerschmidt, 1981a), these authors did not question the very self-other distinction which gives rise to the here:there, home:abroad distinctions that they initially set out to question. For example, although the definition of anthropology was sought to be broadened to include the study of one's own society, it was assumed that because home was the here-modern society of the West it required a new set of methods for its analysis. The paramount question was thus perceived to be:

> ... whether ... [methods] developed in the study of *less complex tribal and peasant societies*, have utility and relevance in studying *today's complex and highly industrialized society*. This question has been the focus for debate as long as anthropologists have been returning from, or turning away from, doing research in traditional, exotic, "primitive" or "other" cultures elsewhere; that is for as long as we have been doing research among our own kind. (Messerschmidt, 1981b:6, emphasis added)

Despite these limitations, contributors to this anthology did question dogmatic constructions of the "field" and of "natives" as being synonymous with the "third world." For example, Aguliar (1981:25) explicitly critiques the notion of an "insider" on the grounds that it renders invisible internal differences within that which one is conceived to be inside of. The critique of dualisms has been furthered more recently by the endeavor to decolonize anthropology (see Harrison, 1991a), by postmodern ethnographers (e.g., Clifford and Marcus, 1986), and by feminist questioning of the role of the native female researcher (e.g., Abu-Lughod, 1991; Narayan, 1993; Visweswaran, 1994).

There have been several recent attempts to theorize from the locations of multiple and hybrid identities.[24] Because these identities are not easily transcribed into either separate halves or synthetic composites that fit into one or the other end of the locational poles provided by realist epistemologies, they have worked against the reductionism and essentialism of the nativist epistemologies depicted in the positions of Native and Insider. The dis/locations of these mixed (or multiple) identities serve to highlight the point that there is no easy or comfortable in-between location that "transcends" these dualisms.

In the foregoing examination of my histories, I have indicated how the identity "Indian woman" is deeply divided by class privileges, among other differences, thereby disrupting the essentialism of an assumed universalist vantage point of the Third World woman. Furthermore, my own inhabitations of, and positionings within, the class specific location of upper-middle- class Indian woman were sharply demarcated by my divergent political and epistemic projects before and after I had lived in the United States as an adult. As a middle-class Indian, and Western-educated feminist researcher, I was clearly only able to partially access the lives and worlds of working class women in Delhi.[25] I have examined the constitution of my subject position(s) in order to argue that an epistemology of locations cannot spring out of an a priori ontological location. As Donna Haraway (1988a:586) notes

> There is no way to "be" simultaneously in all, or wholly in any of the privileged (i.e. subjugated) positions structured by gender, race, nation and class. And that is a short list of critical positions. The search for a "full" and total position is the search for the fetishized perfect subject of oppositional history, sometimes appearing as the essentialized third world woman. *Subjugation is not grounds for an ontology, [though] it might be a visual clue.* (emphasis mine)

In this discussion, I have been working to denaturalize the stability in the boundaries that are assumed in the binary pairs of oppositions and dualisms that are immanent in realist conventions of ethnographic and sociological research which rest on foundational epistemologies. But in displacing this boundary, I do not mean to suggest that the postcolonial intellectual has the ability to surpass these dualisms.[26] In other words, I am arguing against the possibilities of a unique synthetic position, which surmounts the dialectic embedded in these terms. Rather, I would suggest that *all* of us live in contradictory locations, and not just those of us who are involuntarily placed into those contradictions. There can be no blood count that determines postcoloniality. As a politics it is a feminist and anticolonial intellectual location that we choose to position ourselves into, rather than being assigned into it on the basis of our gender, class, race, ethnicity, sexuality, nationality, or other identity-based ontological categories.

There is, however, the very real danger of fetishizing hybridity as a new site of epistemic privilege. The postcolonial intellectuals' dislocation as a historical site is merely a useful starting point from which we can begin to enunciate and theorize a "postcolonial methodology." But this identification is not an essentialist move; indeed, I have borrowed this phrase from Jennifer Robinson who, as a white South African attempting to study the Indian community in South Africa, refuses to be constrained by an epistemology of identity: "It is within the postcolonial idiom that I find some of the most useful pathways through—though not solutions to—this relationship [between researcher and researched]" (Robinson, 1994:218–19). It is this sense of an "imagined community" (Anderson, 1991) of postcolonial intellectuals that rise above national, racial, and gendered boundaries in the articulation of politically responsible representations that I have been working to explicate in this chapter.

Articulating this as a methodology has the advantage of shifting our gaze from questions of identity and experience to those of "positioning," which Donna Haraway posits as the "politics and epistemologies of location" (1988a:589). It is only through an examination of one's politics and accountability, in questioning where and how we are located, that will get us out of mere reversals of dualisms of native:non-native and insider:outsider positionings and on to a more productive engagement with nature of our relationships with those whom we study and represent, and to questioning the nature of one's insertion into the research process and its resultant representations, in ensuring that the "object of knowledge be pictured as an actor and agent, not as a screen or a ground or a resource" (Haraway, 1988a:592).[27] A postcolonial methodology, then, enjoins us to focus our attention to "examine the hyphen at which Self-Other join in the politics of everyday life" (Fine, 1994:70), and to work against inscribing the Other.

The Politics of Representations

Let us be clear of the silences that are initiated by the focus on a reflexive mode, clearly evidenced thus far in this discussion: the "voices" of the subjects of my research (with the exception of a manager) are conspicuously absent. Although my focus has been on reflections prior and subsequent to the actual "fieldwork," this marginalization of the subjects of my research, whose voices were *not* heard here, is a problematic result of reflexive accounts. As even a cursory reading of the literature on experimental ethnography indicates, although the discussion regarding the *representation* of the anthropological subject that is so central to this movement is sensitive to textual practices that serve to undermine and distance the "subject," the undeniable effect of the discourse is to displace her (Balsamo, 1990). As a textual strategy, reflexivity gives voice to the already speaking author. As a rhetorical device to foreground this silencing, in the previous section I sought to concentrate primarily on my own experiences and subjectivity, rather than deploying the strategy of both narrative and reflexivity.

In this section, I recount examples of conversations and dialogues that arose during the interviews in a consciously reflexive mode. Such "ethnographic encounters" (most often narrated through a conversation between researcher and researched) serve to illustrate some of the difficulties one faces in doing industrial ethnography: for example, in negotiating the stereotypical representations of Indian women workers voiced in numerous managers' interviews, or even those that come from workers' own interviews. These encounters also serve to bring alive the processes of confrontation and acceptance that occurred between me and the women I interviewed—as researcher and researched, as women, as Indians, as Self and Other—and the ways in which we "worked the hyphens" (Fine, 1994) at these borders. Yet one must also wonder to what extent such a narrative serves to whet the readers' or audiences' desire to know, and the narrator's need to prove, that one was really "There," or, in other words, to what extent they merely serve as an authorizing gesture for the ethnographic text. In a reflexive mode, there is thus always a danger that ". . . the people studied are treated as garnishes and condiments, tasty only in relationship to the main course, the sociologist," (Richardson, 1988:205).

I am therefore uneasy about the strategy of calling on my research subjects' voices selectively to buttress my arguments, ever aware that feminist and anticolonial discourses "are engaged in this very subtle and delicate effort to build affinities, and not to produce one's own and another's experience as a resource for another closed narrative" (Haraway, 1988b:111). The issue of how one works against the tendency to appropriate another's experience while making the connections remains a productive source of tension that is perhaps never resolved.[28] Writing the text thus becomes a key arena in which the authorial Self confronts and inscribes the Other as a "captive" object: an object that we capture via new technologies of inscription—such as tapes, surveys, interviews, word processing, videos, and so forth. Conceiving of writing as an extension of fieldwork foregrounds this process of inscription, a process which deserves much closer scrutiny than it typically receives.

In the foregoing analysis, I have examined how the configuration of factory level class politics overdetermined my position within the factory. Yet, I would also like to suggest that, in the microdynamics of the interview, these hierarchies are easily displaced although we may often fail to see that this has occurred. How one reads into the conversation can just as easily replace the research Subject *back* into her location as Object, even though she actively claims the space of Subject. As Kaplan suggests, ". . . scrupulous attention to the micropolitics of the 'elicited situation,' the context of interviewer and interviewee, raises critical questions about how women's subjectivity is formed, reported, and interpreted" (1992:125). Let us examine two brief examples of my interactions with women workers which suggest that subject-object relations within the interview context are easily displaced.

Representing Sunita's Self-Presentations

Sunita is a married garment worker between the age of thirty-six and thirty-eight, who works in a small garment factory that is located behind South Extension Market and has been working there for approximately three years. She travels for about an hour and takes two buses to get to this factory from her home in

Meherauli. She has been working off and on for the last ten years, and has lived in Delhi most of her life. All but one of these jobs (her first) have been in the garment industry. Her first job was with an informal *Masala* (spice) packing company. Sunita first started to work after she was married, when her three children were between the ages of two and six. Before she started this job she quit work for about two years because her children had started fighting a lot amongst each other, so much so that they were getting complaints from their neighbors that her children were spoiled and troublesome (*"Bacche bigarh gaye hain"*).

She left one of her previous jobs, also at a garment factory, because of the oppressive conditions of work and often involuntary overtime that workers were subjected to, including enforced overnight stays. Her husband would not allow her to stay overnight at the factory after the first time that this happened (when they were unable to make special arrangements for her to be picked up from work). After this episode, she left that job as soon as she could find another one. The next job was as a temporary worker without benefits or minimum wages. She worked at that job until she found her current one, which is permanent and pays minimum unskilled wages although, as a garment checker, she is performing semi-skilled work.

The factory where she works is owned and operated by a woman. It is a small business, a family-run affair which is actually run by her alone, with only about 20 workers on the premises, excluding contract workers. The atmosphere is cozy, friendly, and all the women know and talk to one another. The owner does require overtime, but makes arrangements to drop off the workers to their homes in a van when she needs them to stay late at night. Both of the contractors to whom work is sent out (and who bring contract workers into the factory) are women. Sunita says that her husband has met "Madam" (the owner) and is very happy that she is working here. The owner tells me that she makes a point of meeting the families of workers—the familial and m/paternalistic disciplining of workers is thus readily evidenced in this firm. The workers tell me they feel like "daughters."

Sunita came across as a very strong and confident woman. She has managed to get her younger sister a job in the same factory, and tells me that she first began working partly because they needed the money and partly because, as she put it, "If everybody else is going out to work, then why not me?" She also enjoys the opportunities for friendships that work gives her outside her family, and for the very extra-familial experience that work provides. "Its good to get out, by coming out one has one's friends . . . [and] one learns to do various things." There is a mixture of shyness and eager curiosity in her manner with me that characterized her interview. I have this written down in the notes that I wrote after the interview. Several times during the interview she asked me, "Is it over yet?" But this wasn't out of impatience or boredom, because when I was interviewing someone else after her interview, she came repeatedly to where we were sitting to see how we were doing and what we were talking about. After my second day there and intensive interviews with several of the workers, several of us were talking about the perceptions among workers, their families, and the wider community regarding garment export work.

My interest in generating such conversations was in contrasting the conditions, definitions, and discourses of and on work in the television and garment industries. These discussions revealed that definitions of garment export work as "cheap" rest primarily on the looser regulation of work conditions and sexuality in dispersed, informal, and fragmented garment production. The workers told me about the bad working conditions, the late nights, about how it is looked upon as unseemly and questionable work. And this is what Sunita says,

> Yes, many people think this (and some husbands don't like it either)—that these girls are characterless, they work in factories and so on. But not in our house, because they know that we go to work, and work in a nice place. They have even come here and seen the place. Among our neighbors, not everyone knows that we work in factories, and we don't tell everybody that we are working in exports; they just know that we are working. So if other people get to know, it won't be very nice. So our names should not appear anywhere and our photographs should not come out anywhere, O.K.? If my family saw it, *Meri bejti ho jati* (I would be shamed) . . . because we have never done anything like this before: had our picture taken or our interview; this is the first time that someone has taken my interview. So if my husband hears that my photo has been printed in a newspaper or in a book, then he'll be upset and wouldn't like it.

At this point another woman who was listening to Sunita adds: *"Aap ko malum hain, 'medium-type' ke log ko ye pasand nahin hain, hena?* (You know 'medium-type' of people don't like these things, isn't that so?)"

Although a complex discussion of the range of intersecting discourses that situate the comments made by Sunita and her co-worker, and of the interesting theoretical issues that this raises on the interrelationships between gender and class, is outside the scope of the present discussion, let us examine the available referents that we have from the limited information that I have provided here to see how they might impact a possible interpretation and representation of Sunita. The ambivalence and contradictions regarding her "work" identity are indicative, I think, of the way in which work within this particular factory has been contained within, and (re)defined through, "home." This is expressed, for example, in statements such as, "She [the owner] is like a mother to us"; "we are like daughters to her." That is, expressed through readily available gendered identities constituted through the idiom of family. The class anxieties expressed in these statements are thus primarily articulated through gendered idioms.

Rather than constructing this as an instance of a "nonfeminist, non-western other," as a "failure to achieve modernity" (Ong, 1988:80), it helps to look at the play, the active juggling, between the idioms of worker and wife that are expressed in Sunita's voiced sentiments "not to get found out" by "society." As Sunita *tells me* how to represent her, I see Sunita's ambivalence regarding her gendered status as a "worker," as an attempt to actively work through the contradictions of "modernity" and "tradition." Although it would be easy to try to impose our own narrative of liberation onto her experience of work (an approach which would inevitably see this as a "lack" of a modern, public work identity), this would erase completely her own creative use of the work opportunities provided by this "modern" factory (relative to her previous work experiences) to suit her construction of her gender identities. This firm provides women workers access to "good femininity" through a regime of labor discipline that is at best paternalistic (or more appropriately maternalistic). This allows her to continue to work, which she needs to do for the sake of her family and which she *enjoys* doing. In fact, as she tells me, it is work that allows her to "get out" from her household.

To represent her concerns with her public work identity as a co-optation of the "liberating aspects of work" would be to buy into the narrative of modernization where capitalism is seen to improve women's status vis-à-vis traditional patriarchy, and would completely obscure the active renegotiation with and transformation of patriarchy that is occurring (cf. Elson and Pearson, 1981; Kandiyoti, 1988). Yet this is certainly the dominant representation of Third World women in the literature on gender and development. As Aihwa Ong (1988:86) notes, "The 'non- western woman' as a trope of feminist discourse is either nonmodern or modern, she is seldom perceived as living in a situation where there is a deeply felt tension between tradition and modernity."

If we are to be truly open to what our research subjects tell us, we must be willing to read against the grain and yet within the larger contexts that situate their responses. Although partial truths are an inevitable outcome of research that is situated and constructed around specific locations, this should not necessarily lead to, or be an excuse for, distorted representations (Birth, 1990). There is always a need to situate responses into larger historical and societal contexts that can frame a meaning, in order to avoid the risk of either giving voice *to* stereotypes (cf. Bhavnani, 1993) or perpetuating stereotypes *about* one's research subjects.

Listening to Prema and Amit's Silences and Resistance

Other respondents' silences during and resistance to interviews is also suggestive of the degree to which research subjects shape their own self-presentations. The second example I'd like to draw on is from an interview with another garment worker, who is employed in a factory located in the industrial zone of Mayapuri. Prema is 20 years old and has worked in this factory as an unskilled thread cutter for about one and a half years. Her natal home is in the rural village of *Bhori Pur* in the *Farukabad* District of *Uttar Pradesh*. Her husband, Amit, is from *Eta* (also in *Uttar Pradesh*) and has been working in the same firm that she is employed in for about 4–5 years. She tells me that they have been married for less than two years.

Prema has been in Delhi only a short while longer than she has been working; when I met her she was shy and clearly still not at home in Delhi. After she had been working for about 4 months, she went home to her village for a few months. Although she works now, she is unsure that she will continue to work after she starts a family. Her home (in Delhi) is only a ten minute bike ride away from the factory, and so she comes to work riding on the back of her husband's bicycle. Her husband works in the factory as a "packing in-charge" for which he is paid unskilled helper wages, even though this is a semi-skilled occupational designation.

The firm that Prema is working in is a mid-sized firm, with about 40 workers on the books, though there are several departments (such as finishing and packing) which are filled with contract workers, bringing the number of workers on the premises closer to about 65–80. In this firm there are two separate rooms for thread-cutters, and I have noticed right away that there are differences amongst the two groups of women working in them. The first room, which is on the mid-level of the factory off a courtyard, is a small room set off to itself and has women that clearly look more "rural." The other, one level down, is larger, and has a more mixed crowd of women who seem more like "Delhites." To get to this second thread-cutting room, one has to walk through a room that runs the length of the building. This is where the predominantly male finishing contract workers' work on spotting, washing, ironing, and packing the finished garments.

Prema was working in the upstairs room, which is where we met for her interview. She was shy and often silent, unlike many other workers who kept up a steady stream of conversation during their interviews. The interview was made more difficult by the fact that her husband, Amit, was nervous about the interview and came into the room where we are talking several times, although his visits were ostensibly to check on some ongoing work. At one point he asks her: "What are you doing sitting around here doing nothing, don't you have any other work?" And he explicitly tells me, "Ask her only *matlab ka savaal* (relevant questions), not anything else—ask her about her job, not other things."

I was not too happy about this scenario but continued with the interview, since there was not much that I could do about Amit's interruptions. Prema does not want to talk about several issues. Her initial response to some questions is, "I don't want to talk about it," after which she would respond anyway. But when it came to questions about possible work interruptions due to childbirth and about the couple's desired family size and reproductive decisions, she just responded, "Don't ask this," and so we moved on to other questions.

After the interview is over, I chat with some other workers over lunch in the downstairs room. In the course of a casual conversation, I discover that Prema and Amit have been married for about six years. This unsolicited information is provided by Sheela, who has worked in the factory for several years, and who was an employee in the firm when Amit was initially employed there. From her I learn that Prema was in the village for several years after they were married and that they "still" do not have any children. Furthermore, Sheela tells me, they have been to many places to get "treatment," but they don't want others to know about it. All this in a conspiratorial tone of someone trying to "help" me get the facts straight. I am mortified for Prema and Amit because this lunchtime conversation is not a very private one.

Later, I talk casually to Prema and her husband Amit together as they leave work. On another day, I meet Amit and talk to him again. Without trying to pry, I tell him I'm confused about how long they've been married. Amit responds, "What did she tell you? That we've been married one year? Then that's how long we've been married."

Prema and Amit's attempts to hide their infertility from me was one of those moments when I hated asking all the questions that I did, I hated my impulses to probe further, to "get to the bottom" of the story. Both actively resist responding to questions that they deemed too probing, and misrepresent when they got married and the length of time that Prema has lived in Delhi. I initially accepted their responses and would not have deemed them suspect had it not been for the "helpful" interventions of Sheela. Obviously, what became more important than the "fact" of their infertility and the "facts" of their work histories was the extent to which Amit and Prema were intensely engaged in this attempt to create an image of fertility or rather to deflect an image of infertility. In order not to be perceived as a childless couple, both Amit and Prema misrepresent how long they've been married.

This brief example highlights an element that often gets underplayed in discussions on ethnographic responsibility and angst over authority in feminist and anthropological discussions on the politics of representation. The fact is that our research subjects are often not just "responding" to our agendas and to our questions, but they are also engaged in actively shaping their presentations to suit their own agendas of how they wish to be represented.

Moving away from the subjective and reflexive mode of analysis deployed earlier in this chapter, in this discussion I have drawn on interactions with workers during the more formal interview process as well as on casual conversations that were less structured. These encounters illustrate the ways in which workers actively responded to as well as resisted the interview process and particular inquiries that I directed at them during the course of my research. Sunita told me how I could and could not represent her, which *must* be read against the grain if we are to avoid stereotyping her as an "unliberated" Third World woman. Prema's silence in response to specific questions and her conscious misrepresentation of herself in other responses also signal an active process of resistance to my attempts to represent her and are also to be read as an act of self-presentation and empowerment (Bhavnani, 1988).

Researchers contributing to debates on feminist methodology and experimental ethnography recommend creating a polyvocal text that incorporates research subjects' voices as one strategy to decolonize the subject. Yet we often fail to take account of research subjects' self-presentations, the resultant contests for meaning, and the challenges that they provide to extant modes of representation. We need to acknowledge this agency, to treat the researched as subjects with whom we are engaged in a *mutual*, though unequal, "power-charged social relation of 'conversation'" (Haraway, 1988a: 593). In other words, we must develop the art of "listening to" and (not just) "talking with" if we are to avoid the "rape of the scientists' 'looking at'" (Tyler, 1986:139–40). Otherwise, we risk getting into the trap of just giving voice to subjugated positions, which, as we well know, are never innocent. As Sherry Gorelick (1991) has persuasively argued, just "giving voice" is not enough. Unreflexive attempts to get beyond the binarisms of Self and Other, through textually experimental tactics deployed by poststructuralist ethnographers, can thus end up *reconstituting* them (Ganguly, 1990:74) unless they are deployed critically.

Academic Politics and the Pedagogy of Empowerment

Whereas the reflexive methodology employed in this chapter clearly derives from postmodernism's focus on the multiple and fragmented self, a focus on identity often elides politics, thereby circumventing the intent of such analyses (Hutcheon, 1989). Furthermore, a focus on textuality has also displaced politics to matters of stylistic conventions, away from real world interventions (Rosenau, 1992). Although postmodern ethnographies, as the "discourse of the postmodern world," avowedly seek "evocation" rather than "presentation" or "representation" (Tyler, 1986:123), the point, as Birth (1990) has pointed out, is not just to evoke understanding, but also to "provoke action." This "retreat into the politics of textuality" (Said, 1989:209), although an interesting and necessary intervention, cannot adequately support the feminist project of revisioning and reshaping The Canon.[29] As feminists demand new subject positions within the academy (Heald, 1992:139–140), we need to think through the ways in which we can "organize collectively for "doing academia" differently," (McKenna, 1992:127). We cannot allow the text to serve as a *pretext* for not seeking a political moment of engagement with either one's research subjects or readers.

I am keenly aware that a focus on reflexivity and on the politics of representation that are in currency in overlapping debates on feminist and anticolonialist research have tended to displace and obscure the research subject and instead place the *researcher* at the center. Yet I am unhappy with attempts to bring in research subjects into the analysis in what I perceive to be a necessarily incomplete and exploitative fashion in an attempt to redress this power imbalance. My response to a critique of self-absorption, then, has been to argue for the use of reflexive analyses of Self and Other, and Self-Other dynamics in the ethnographic encounter, as part of my rationale for making the point that these academic discourses *must* be put to political use through their pedagogical value to other scholars and to new entrants into critical and feminist ethnography and fieldwork.[30]

This tendency of silencing the subjects of our research is made even more disturbing in light of the fact that the conditions under which we produce and labor as intellectuals tend to push us to being more accountable to The Academy than to the communities we study. That the relations of production within the academy are more constraining for younger and untenured academics than for established scholars is perhaps the reason for the widely noted fact that "reflexive pieces" often follow the substantive work rather than preceding it (Visweswaran, 1994:11). However, if academic politics make students and junior scholars *more* accountable in the legitimate appropriation of new writing genres than established scholars with more power (Marcus, 1994), then these politics also effectively serve to silence potential critiques of and counter-hegemonic discourses in The Canon.

As *pedagogical praxis*, reflexive methodological practices can thus serve an extra-textual political end through their intervention in and disruption of routinized and hierarchical academic practices. Erasing the boundaries between theory, methodology, and political practice, and between the field and home, this reflexive genre can work to empower feminist researchers seeking to write without the erasure of their own subjectivity.[31] What I have in mind is an approach in which we explicitly employ the practice of deconstructing our fieldwork experiences, thereby rendering them non-transparent. Given the commonplace dislocation(s) of feminist researchers within the field and in the academy, this practice has tremendous value in its potential for the pedagogical empowerment of a new generation of feminist scholars within social science disciplines. It also introduces a new dimension of power into feminist discussions of power relations in research, for it posits the empowerment of fellow and future social researchers, and not just that of research subjects. This is an especially meaningful avenue for critical interventions for me, given my relative powerlessness in the industrial and factory setting in which I did my research.[32]

I have been arguing for the acceptance of an epistemology based on situated knowledges that results, at best, in partial truths. However, despite the powerful critique against foundationalist discourses and positivist epistemologies that I have endorsed in this chapter, I am reluctant to forgo completely the all important political work that remains to be done in the arena of empiricist reconstructions. The *feminist empiricist* project thus continues to be an important political arena for academics and public intellectuals.[33] To take an example of census definitions: feminist economists have often pointed to distortions in available census data because of gender biases that are built into the measurement of such basic social science categories as "work" (see for e.g. Waring, 1988; Benería, 1992). This project is located squarely within the empiricist effort to have more accurate data on the nature and extent of work done by women and, relatedly, by a nation, as counted by national accounts statistics. Similarly, in India, in a joint project with UNIFEM academic feminist economists have contributed to the 1991 Indian census redefinition of what constitutes "work" (see Krishnaraj, 1990). Such empiricist reformulations have an impact not just on social policy, but also on our discursive constructions and representations of Indian women workers.[34]

Conclusions: Into the Future[35]

Amidst the current theoretical movement towards deconstruction and prevailing critiques of representations, when we've thrown out our "technoscience booster literature" (Haraway, 1988a:576), what do we have left in the way of new technologies for writing the subject? In this chapter, drawing on narrative, interpretive, and reflexive modes of analysis, I have been engaged with articulating new modes for writing The Text. I have attempted to do this by disrupting the boundaries between Self and Other in three primary ways.

First, I have attempted to destabilize the notion of the field, as well as several other dualisms (such as insider- outsider) which accompany the construction of the field as the Third World. In articulating the academy as a site for feminist politics in the conduct of research, I have also acted to expand our vision of where the field lies and where one practices empowering methodologies. Second, in locating myself as a political and historical subject, and as part of the same forces that shape my research subjects, I have attempted to break down the divisions between subject and object. For example, I argued that our labor power in the academic mode of production can be fetishized as a product of difference— epistemic privilege—a division of labor that should be resisted on political and epistemic grounds. It is rather the conditions under which our labor is realized that constitute the more important divisions in the production of knowledge. In both these respects then, I have been viewing the researcher as Object, or the Self as Other. Third, I have argued that examining the self-presentations, silences, and resistances of research subjects in the ethnographic encounter also works to disrupt this binary. Here the researched Other acts as Subject, transforming the Other into the knowing, acting, Self.

We must, however, be wary of the potential paralysis of analysis that ensues from the reflexive mode of analysis and concentrated attentiveness to the authorial strategies and powers of representations, especially when situated within the context of the current postmodernist theoretical moment, characterized by ". . . the contemporary crisis of representation, the profound uncertainty about what constitutes an adequate depiction of social 'reality'" (Lather, 1991:21). As Lather notes, "In an era of rampant reflexivity, *just getting on with it* may be the most radical action one can make" (p. 20, emphasis mine). We cannot allow reflexivity to become an end in itself—another academic fad that is pursued for its own sake. A reflexive and self-critical methodological stance can become meaningful only when it engages in the politics of "reality" and intervenes in it in some significant way. Otherwise, we risk the charge of self-absorbed navel gazing or "soul searching" (Harding, 1987:9). Within the current moment, then, and especially in the context of the relativist politics that can ensue from some versions of postmodernism, the task before us is to critically engage in "passionate scholarship" (DuBois, 1983) where we "work the hyphens" between Self and Other (Fine, 1994) rather than reproduce the tensions between Us and Them.

Notes

1. I have found Steven Epstein's distinction between the terms "self" and "identity" a useful one in thinking through many of the issues that I raise in this chapter. "*Self* refers to the person's conscious and unconscious striving for continuity and individuality over time; *identity* refers to the placement of self in relation to social categories. . . . While both self and identity are social constructs, identity refers more specifically to one's location in the social world," (Epstein, 1991: 864). I also draw on poststructuralist critiques of the unitary subject in humanist discourse (cf. Weedon, 1987) in my analysis of factory women's subjectivities—self and identities—and their representations. This chapter teases out the epistemological and methodological implications of such critiques.

2. For example, "giving voice" is an issue that comes up in each of them in varying ways: in the literature on feminist methodology, giving voice to research subjects is one way of breaking down power relations between the researcher and researched. Similarly, in anthropology there is an attempt to create "polyvocal texts" to disrupt the authority of the ethnographer. Feminist epistemological articulations of a subjugated "standpoint epistemology" and recent attention in Indian historiography to subaltern perspectives also indicate parallel moves to attend to marginalized perspectives.

3. Appadurai uses the example of the (dis)location of his wife's informant, a priest from the Meenakshi temple in the town of Madurai, South India, to Texas, USA, to describe this "deterritorialization" that characterizes contemporary ethnography in the global terrain (1991:194).

4. See for example the collected essays in Messerschmidt (1981a), Fahim (1982), Harrison (1991b), and Panini (1991), which provide some examples of anthropological work being done in one's "own" society. This focus is relatively recent, given Anthropology's historical project of studying "Other," which necessitates a focus on authenticity and subjectivity and hence too on "getting close to the natives" and relying on native informants. The discipline of sociology, on the other hand, has historically been premised on studying "self" and hence obsessively concerned with creating and maintaining distance rather than on undermining it. In the context of India, Kirin Narayan describes this as the, ". . . division of labor between anthropologists who focus on the Other (tribal groups) and sociologists who research the Self (village and urban dwellers)," (Narayan, 1993:675). From the vantage point of the historical construction and sociology of knowledge, then, it should come as no surprise that the ex-colony is the terrain upon which the anthropology of the other devolves into the sociology of the self. My own training in India, in a department of sociology, staffed primarily by British trained anthropologists, reflects the undisciplined and intertwined history of these fields in the "postcolonial." As will be clear from my discussion in this chapter, along with a rich body of recent interdisciplinary feminist research, I locate my work at the intersections of these disciplines.

5. In anthropology, this discourse is variously labeled as either experimental or reflexive (see for example Marcus and Cushman, 1982; Clifford and Marcus, 1986; and Fox, 1991b). However, these concerns cross disciplinary lines and form part of a more over-arching questioning of positivist assumptions of the possibilities of Truth and Knowledge (see for example: Clough, 1992; Rosenau, 1992; Denzin and Lincon, 1994; and Hollinger, 1994).

6. I use the terms "native," "home," "third world," and "non-western" advisedly and work to deconstruct these terms in my analysis. Critical students of development as well as scholars influenced by postmodernism clearly suggest the problematical constructions of specific countries as "third" world (often used synonymously with "underdeveloped") in the unstated assumptions of a master narrative of development that might indeed be replicated outside of the historical experience of the Western, first world. Although later references to these terms will be without quotes, the reader should always read them critically.

7. Other researchers have also argued for a reconceptualization of what we conceive of as the field (e.g. Visweswaran and Tsing in Scott and Shah, 1993). D'Amico-Samuels (1991:69) uses the term "research experience" to cover the three geographical locations in which she did her work (data collection, write-up etc.) thereby expanding the notion of what constitutes the field. Similarly Kamala Ganesh (1993) identifies her fields as the research site, herself, *and* academia. See also articles in Messerschmidt (1981) and Harrison (1991b) for others who question this separation between the "field" and the "academy," or home.

8. As Patricia Clough (1992:136) notes, "The problems of writing are still viewed as different from the problems of method or fieldwork itself. Thus the solution offered is experiments in writing, that is, a self-consciousness about writing. It is only when writing is seen to provide the mechanisms of scientific conceptions itself . . . that it becomes clearer that it is this insistence on the difference of writing and field methods that must be deconstructed if the general function of ethnography is to be analyzed."

9. For examples of this anthropological work, see the collected essays in a special issue of *Inscriptions* on "Feminism and the Critique of Colonial Discourse" (Nos. 3/4, 1988), diLeonardo (1991) and M. Wolf (1992). The challenge of postmodernism, in its broadest sense, refers to the deep skepticism posed to "epistemological foundationalism." It is outside the scope of this chapter to discuss in detail the grounds for epistemologi-

cal foundationalism, or the challenges to it that are posed by a postmodern epistemology. Anna Yeatman (1994) would provide a useful starting point for such a review.
At its most basic, "The authority of a foundationalist science constitutes the scientist
as Subject to all those who, brought under the regime of the scientist's observation, are
constituted as Object" (ibid:189). Within this realist epistemology, the assumption is
that if the knower is properly trained, s/he can access reality objectively. Knowledge
thus derives from the knowing Subject's (scientist's) detached observation of the research Object and the correct application of research techniques. The ensuing knowledge and representation are believed to mirror Reality and approximate Truth. On the
other hand, post-foundationalist epistemologies foreground the politics of representational authority, thereby undermining claims to Truth and the possibility of a non-
partial or unbiased representations. Post-foundationalist (postmodern) epistemologies
focus rather on the necessarily incomplete and distorted representations of reality that
circulate in knowledge, by asking the questions: Whose representations prevail? Who
is silenced? (see also Clough, 1992; Fine, 1994; and Morrow, 1994a and 1994b).

10. The essays in Denzin and Lincon (1994) are an example of such recent work. Further
examples are Richardson (1988), Rosenau (1994), and articles in recent special issues
of two journals, *Current Perspectives in Social Theory* and *Current Issues in Symbolic Interaction*. While the literature on feminist methodologies is large and diverse, it has
only recently begun to engage with the postmodern critique (Fine, 1994; Olesen, 1994).

11. For a wonderful account of the generational shifts among feminist sociologists, see the
collected essays in Laslett and Thorne (1997).

12. I recall having gone into the field with the words of one of my advisors ringing in my
ears, that I had better come back with some "real data." This powerlessness is also
manifest in the writing of ethnographic research. For example, the editor of a recent
anthology (Clifford, 1986:21) has argued that most of the contributors to the collection
were established scholars in the field, because junior and marginal scholars could not
afford the luxury of reflexivity currently in fashion in anthropology (see also Marcus,
1994). It is interesting that an alternative reading of this statement could well define
this as a form of gatekeeping in the process of defining a new canon within the discipline (see Gordon, 1988).

13. Clearly not *all* Sociology departments are hegemonically positivist. One public example is provided by a co-authored book that was the result of Berkeley Sociology professor Micheal Buroway's course on participant observation field methods (see
Buroway et al., 1991).

14. A recent example of the trials of doing feminist scholarship in the field of South Asian
studies is provided by Trivedi's (1994) account of her travails at the University of
Chicago. When it was made clear to her that her advisor (and the department) "did
not feel that gender was a useful form of analysis for South Asia" (ibid:14), she decided to pursue her Ph.D. elsewhere. Examples of sociology's resistance to feminist
scholarship—as examined by Stacey and Thorne (1985) a decade ago—still abound (see
for e.g. Itzin, 1984 and Bannerji et al., 1992). For a recent comment on the perception
of feminists and women sociologists as "narrow" scholars, despite the obvious ad-
vances and visibility of feminist scholarship within the discipline, see the statement by
the Chair of the Sex and Gender Section of the American Sociological Association to
this effect (cf. Risman, 1994).

15. For an interesting and complex discussion of the critique of "Westernization" leveled
against third world feminists, see Narayan (1997). It should be clear from this discussion that I am critical of the term "postcolonial" in as much as it signifies the closure
of a historical period of dependence and the consequent erasure of neo-colonial power
relations. Many of the ideological mechanisms that supported colonialism—such as in-

ternalized beliefs in the superiority of the West and Western products—are manifested in ongoing discourses over Westernization that continue to permeate Indian society. Equally significant are the continuing economic dependencies of many third world nations on Western economies (and on the multilateral institutions of global governance that are controlled by them) as manifested in their debt, reliance on foreign capital investments and export markets. While neo-colonial might thus be a more accurate term, I retain the use of "post"colonial, because it helps to foreground the methodological arguments that I make later in this chapter for a *politics* of postcoloniality. For further discussions on the problematic connotations of "post" in the term postcolonial, see Dirlik (1994), McClintock (1992) and Shohat (1992).

16. I do not mean to suggest that the reality of the "masses" is either homogeneous or untouched by Western influence. I am grateful to Suzanne Rudolph (personal communication) for taking issue with this implication of my comments and hence making me aware of the need for this clarification. Clearly, working-class, rural, and tribal peoples' lifestyles differ from one another just as they differ from "middle-class" lifestyles and lived experiences. My point here is merely to indicate the extent to which "Western" is valorized and emulated among the middle class. Unlike the upper classes for whom such lifestyles are a realizable goal, the middle class feels the tensions of a desired, but less easily acquired, lifestyle. As a consequence, the pressures to adapt are perhaps felt more strongly here than among other classes. It is also important to note the historical context of the late seventies and early eighties that serve as a background for this discussion.

17. For John (1991), naming the "sites of enunciation" of theory (and theorists) foregrounds this rupture between the locations of the theoretical objects and subjects of postcolonial theory, i.e. that the audience for and locations of many postcolonial feminists are in the first world: "What might it mean for me—a third world feminist whose current institutional home is in the first," John asks (ibid:2), to examine this? For an insightful reading of Gayatri Spivak's (1990) site of enunciation as perhaps an unresolved issue in this critical postcolonial feminists work, see Ray (1992).

18. The reference to "dead weight" is to a phrase that he coined earlier on in this interview. He refers to the majority of women in the production department who are working in low-skilled jobs as "dead" labor, to which he assigns mostly married and older women, ". . . this is dead labor . . . [I am] giving them a salary for free. . . . I call them dead because even if they don't work, things still go on." This is just one instance of the ways in which women are discursively constructed as cheap labor on the shop floor and in the labor process.

19. Even outside the specific research situation, one's identity needs to be de-naturalized. Sociologists working on issues of identity have made this point about the social construction (and contestation) of identity quite emphatically: "identity is not simply imposed. It is also chosen, and actively used. . . ." (Pettman, 1991:191).

20. Collins herself is quite clear that it is not just Black women who can gain from this subjugated standpoint: "A variety of individuals can learn from Black women's experience as outsiders within. . . . all individuals who, while benefitting from the same social strata that provided them with the benefits of white male insiderism, have never felt comfortable with its taken-for-granted assumptions." (Collins, 1991:53).

21. The problematic nature of this assumption can be illustrated quite simply by examining the potential political differences that one may hold while inhabiting same-space locations within categorical axes of identity: Black women may be for or against the Nation of Islam, while Jewish women might be either for or against Palestinian nationhood. For a nuanced discussion of the range of political options open to those who occupy positions of potential epistemic privilege, see Uma Narayan (1989).

22. I do not intend to imply that standpoint epistemologies completely close out these possibilities. For example, Uma Narayan (1988) argues that the concept of epistemic privilege does not preclude the possibilities that oppressed groups can have distorted perceptions, and that nonmembers can gain knowledge on/of the oppressed. For an insightful discussion of colonialist representations by insiders of their own communities, see Jennifer Robinson's discussion of Fatihma Meer's construction of Indians in South Africa. Robinson argues that Meer ". . . is clearly presenting a picture of Indian people for outside consumption . . . the 'outsider within' sociology, [who] constructs Indian people through a lens of exotica and 'sameness'" (Robinson, 1994:215–6). My point here is simply that we should not be closed to these possibilities purely on ontological grounds.

23. Further examples of such dualisms might include: global/local, macro/micro, modern/primitive, heterogeneous/homogeneous, First World/Third World, theory/case study, author/object, citizen/native, thought/experience, now-here/then-there, representer/represented, self/other, outsider/insider and so on. Although not all these oppositions may be assumed in the actual practices of research, listing them together in this fashion serves the function of making us more self-conscious about the assumptions that guide our research, especially in the field of gender and development.

24. Various identity descriptors have been used by different scholars to describe their (dis)locations within the boundaries that are produced in foundationalist discourses. Some of these are: "outsider within" (Collins, 1991), "native informant" (John, 1988 and 1991), "postcolonial intellectual" (Robinson, 1994), "multiplex identity" (Narayan, 1993), "inappropriate other" (Minh-ha, 1988 and 1989), "postfoundationalist intellectual" (Yeatman, 1994), and "nativised self" (Karim, 1993). In my discussion, I have used the term "inauthentic native" to disrupt the boundaries between inside-outside, native-other, and self-other.

25. I do not wish to normalize the subject location of upper-middle-class, western-educated, Third World researcher. There are certainly other subject positions that are obtained among "native" postcolonial feminists: immigrant academics like myself from working class backgrounds who have returned "home" for research. Even within such a trajectory, discrepant locations in the politics of fieldwork are likely.

26. There is some slippage in my usage of the term "postcolonial" that the reader should be alert to—between referring to an historical subject such as myself whose personal history is shaped by and in a geographic region with a colonial history on the one hand and a political subject who is committed to the politics of anti-colonialism regardless of their personal histories on the other. This slippage may result in some confusion, but the context should help the reader locate the meaning in which it is used. Furthermore, this conflation reinforces the point that I am making here: that "postcoloniality" is a politically engaged location that we may all choose to position ourselves into, regardless of our individual histories and particular identity configurations. This argument extends the coalitional (as opposed to identity) politics of second wave feminism (cf. Combahee River Collective, 1983; Reagon, 1983,) onto the transnational, global arena (see also, for example, Brah, 1991; Sandoval, 1991; Grewal and Kaplan, 1994; and Kaplan, 1994).

27. Following Haraway, Kirin Narayan (1993) also proposed that instead of the insider-outsider dualism, the more fruitful focus is on the nature of our relationships with our research subjects: do we treat them as exemplars of a "generalized Other," or do we see them as subjects?

28. Although the strategy of selective presentation of my subjects could serve to *exacerbate* the unequal power that I hold vis-a-vis my research subjects, it is also clearly the case that the encounters which I recount here illustrate worker's resistances to my au-

thor(ity)/ial power. I would note that just as it is possible to select examples which reflect rather than challenge dominant discursive constructions of Third World women as "victim" and "oppressed" (cf. Mohanty, 1984), it is equally possible to err in the constructions of overly agentic representations. This intellectual romance with resistance (Handler, 1993; Abu-Lughod, 1990) has equally damaging results in that it can lead to a form of blaming the victim, when, for example, subaltern agency cannot inadequately "resist" the structures of colonialism.

29. For example, it is disturbing to me that for Visweswaran (1994) important issues of ethnographic betrayal and resistance get displaced by the textual style that she deploys in reading this as a play in three acts (see her chapter 3). The textuality of the text does serve to direct attention to the politics of representation, but one must wonder, along with Birth (1990:555), whether such textual experimentation serves its purpose, for "When highly trained, intelligent people—that is, informed readers—have trouble reading an article, . . . [this] writing subverts its own primary purpose—changing the reader." This issue becomes especially problematic in a pedagogic context.

30. It must be noted that this approach is already being self-consciously adopted in narrative ethnographies and consciously reflexive texts (e.g. Kondo, 1990; Abu Lughod, 1993). Whether it is reading Diane Wolf's honest account which depicts the "intellectual and methodological shifts" in her approach and personalized reactions to the field (Wolf, 1992:6), or Kamala Visweswaran's engaging account of her recovery/discovery of self and identity in the realist fiction, *Sari Stories* (Visweswaran, 1994)—I find them empowering, in no small part because they are fragments of *my* history in text. Losing the transparency of the mechanics of doing research also contributes to what Harding (1992) refers to as "strong objectivity" within a postpositivist, feminist framework.

31. U.S. feminists of color have also chosen to theorize through modes of writing that challenge those of "high" theory (Anzaldúa, 1987; 1990a) . Choosing a language and speaking in a voice that draws on the experiences of marginality, and which have been typically excluded from the dominant modes of theorizing, this work has been articulated in a hybrid voice of the borderlands that insistently locates the subjectivity of the author as a historically constituted, embodied, and gendered being. "When we, the objects, become the subjects, and look at and analyze our own experiences, the danger arises that we may look through the master's gaze, speak through his tongue . . .—in Audre Lorde's words, use the "master's tools," notes Gloria Anzaldúa (1990b:xxiii). She continues, "it is *vital* that we occupy theorizing space . . . by bringing our own approaches and methodologies, we transform that theorizing space. . . . We need theories that will point out ways to maneuver between our particular experiences. . . . In our mestizaje theories we create new categories for those of us left out or pushed out of existing ones" (ibid: xxv).

32. One's relative powerlessness as a researcher in a field setting where access to research subjects is controlled and may be withdrawn at any time is a feature that tends to get downplayed in feminist injunctions for non-hierarchical relations in research, but it is a defining feature of non-participatory industrial fieldwork. The limits of acting within industrial factory settings in which the research is conducted, especially when the research design does not rely on participant observation that allows for close and sustained interactions with ones research subjects, are readily apparent. These limits to feminist praxis in field settings notwithstanding, the expectation that feminist research include a transformative political moment of concientization for research subjects was routinely invoked as a principle of feminist research in earlier writing on feminist methodologies (see, for example, Nebraska Feminist Collective, 1983; Cook and Fonow, 1986; Bristow and Esper, 1988; Fonow and Cook, 1991).

33. It is the feminist empiricist project which often provides an important first step away from the "add-women-and- stir-approach" that merely adds women to existing curriculum without challenging extant male biased constructs and theories (Anderson, 1993:10; Minnich, 1990:27). Perhaps this accounts for the tendency to devalue the feminist empiricism as an early phase in the development of feminist knowledge. For example, it is argued that empiricist epistemologies have been superseded by standpoint and postmodern epistemologies, which challenge gender-blind knowledge and constructs more thoroughly (cf. Harding, 1991). I am suggesting that rather than constructing a (positivist) historical narrative of the progression of feminist epistemologies, the political project of feminist empiricism must be retained alongside postpositivist feminist epistemologies. This argument is analogous to Sandoval's (1991) re/conceptualization of the different strands of hegemonic US feminism—that of Liberals, Radicals, Marxists, and Socialists feminists—as a topography of modes of feminist oppositional consciousness or feminist political tactics in a postmodern world, rather than as a typology of second wave feminism. Sandoval suggests that we conceive of these forms of feminist consciousness as the gears of a car, as differential modes which enable different political objectives, that work through the clutch of a differential consciousness enabled by U.S. third world feminisms (ibid:14).

34. While a truly transformative project cannot end there (i.e. with a new accounting system), it is a *critical* first step in the reformulation of knowledge that must *continually* engage feminists. This is also a form of feminist realpolitik: as long as censuses continue to be important means of defining and identifying segments of populations, for providing state social services and forms of protection, this project must remain an ongoing part of a larger feminist project of revisioning the grounds and challenging the assumptions of malestream science and knowledge. In my research, this translates into a carefully detailed empirical analysis of women's work-histories, which provide a useful window into the inadequacies of census data on "women's work" and the basis of a feminist critique of "class."

35. The reference here is to Fonow and Cook's (1991) article on feminist methodologies, entitled "Back to the Future: A Look at the Second Wave of Feminist Epistemology and Methodology." Although I echo their desire to move this debate forward, as the title of their anthology *"Beyond Methodology"* suggests, I believe we must question the very epistemological grounds upon which feminist methodologies have been heretofore articulated.

References

Abu-Lughod, Lila. 1990. "The Romance of Resistance: Tracing Transformations of Power Through Bedouin Women." *American Ethnologist* 17(1): 41–55.

———. 1991. "Writing Against Culture." In *Recapturing Anthropology: Working in the Present*, edited by Richard G. Fox, 137–62. Santa Fe, New Mexico: School of American Research Press.

———. 1993. *Writing Women's Worlds: Bedouin Stories.* Berkeley: University of California Press.

Anzaldúa, Gloria. 1987. *Borderlands: La Frontera, The New Mestiza.* San Francisco: Spinisters Aunt Lute books.

———. 1990a. ed. *Making Face, Making Soul, Haciendo Caras: Creative and Critical Perspectives by Feminists of Color.* San Francisco: aunt lute books.

————. 1990b. "Haciendo Caras, una entrada." Pp. xv–xxviii in *Making Face, Making Soul, Haciendo Caras: Creative and Critical Perspectives by Feminists of Color*, edited by Gloria Anzaldua. San Francisco: aunt lute books.

Aguilar, John. 1981. "Insider Research: An Ethnography of a Debate." In *Anthropologists at Home in North America: Methods and Issues in the Study of One's Own Society*, edited by Donald Messerschmidt, 15–28. Cambridge: Cambridge University Press.

Anderson, Benedict. 1991. *Imagined Communities: Reflections on the Origins and the Spread of Nationalism*. London: Verso.

Anderson, Margaret L. 1993. *Thinking About Women: Sociological Perspectives on Sex and Gender*. New York: Macmillan Publishing Company. Third Edition.

Appadurai, Arjun. 1988. "Introduction: Place and Voice in Anthropological Theory." *Cultural Anthropology* 3(1)(February): 16–20.

————. 1991. "Global Ethnoscapes: Notes and Queries for a Transnational Anthropology." In *Recapturing Anthropology: Working in the Present*, edited by Richard G. Fox, 191–210. Santa Fe, New Mexico: School of American Research Press.

Balsamo, Anne. 1990. "Rethinking Ethnography: A Work for the Feminist Imagination." *Studies in Symbolic Interaction* 11: 45–57.

Bannerji, Himani, Linda Carty, Kari Delhi, Susan Heald, and Kate McKenna. 1992. *Unsettling Relations: The University as a Site of Feminist Struggle*. Boston: South End Press.

Benería, Lourdes. 1992. Accounting for Women's Work: The Progress of Two Decades." *World Development* 20 (11): 1547–1560.

Bhavnani, Kum-Kum. 1988. "Empowerment and Social Research: Some Comments." *Text* 8(1–2): 41–50.

————. 1993. "Tracing the Contours: Feminist Research and Feminist Objectivity." *Women's Studies International Forum* 16(2): 95–104.

Birth, Kevin. 1990. "Reading and the Righting of Writing Ethnographies." Review Article. *American Ethnologist* 17: 549–57.

Brah, Avtar. 1991. "Questions of Difference and International Feminism." Pp. 168–176 in *Out of The Margins: Women's Studies in the Nineties*, edited by Jane Aaron and Sylvia Walby. London, New York, and Philadelphia: The Falmer Press.

Bristow, Ann R., and Jody A. Esper. 1988. "A Feminist Research Ethos." Pp. 68–81 in *A Feminist Ethic for Social Science Research*, edited by Nebraska Sociological Women's Collective. Ontario: The Edwin Mellen Press.

Buroway, Micheal et al. 1991. *Ethnography Unbound: Power and Resistance in the Modern Metropolis*. Berkeley: University of California Press.

Clifford, James. 1986. "Introduction: Partial Truths." In *Writing Culture: The Poetics and Politics of Ethnography*, edited by James Clifford and George Marcus, 1–26. Berkeley: University of California Press.

Clifford, James, and George Marcus. 1986. eds. *Writing Culture: The Poetics and Politics of Ethnography*. Berkeley: University of California Press.

Clough, Patricia T. 1992. *The End(s) of Ethnography: From Social Realism to Social Criticism*. Newbury Park, CA: Sage Publications.

Collins, Patricia. 1991. "Learning From the Outsider Within: The Sociological Significance of Black Feminist Thought." In *Beyond Methodology: Feminist Scholarship as Lived Research*, edited by Mary M. Fonow and Judith A. Cook, 35–59. Bloomington: Indiana University Press.

Combahee River Collective. 1983. "The Combahee River Collective Statement." Pp. 272–282 in *Home Girls: A Black Feminist Anthology*, edited by Barbara Smith. New York: Kitchen Table/Women of Color Press.

Cook, Judith A., and Mary M. Fonow. 1986. "Knowledge and Women's Interests: Issues of Epistemology and Methodology in Feminist Sociological Research." *Sociological Inquiry* 56:2–29.

D'Amico-Samuels, Deborah. 1991. "Undoing Fieldwork: Personal, Political, Theoretical and Methodological Implications." In *Decolonizing Anthropology: Moving Further Toward an Anthropology for Liberation,* edited by Faye V. Harrison, 68–87. Washington, D.C.: American Anthropological Association.

Denzin, Norman K., and Yvonna S. Lincon. 1994. eds. *Handbook of Qualitative Research.* Thousand Oaks, CA: Sage Publications.

DeVault, Marjorie. 1996. "Talking Back to Sociology: Distinctive Contributions of Feminist Methodology." *Annual Review of Sociology* 22:29–50.

di Leonardo, Micaela. 1991. ed. *Gender at the Crossroads of Knowledge: Feminist Anthropology in the Postmodern Era.* Berkeley: University of California Press.

Dirlik, Arif. 1994. "The Postcolonial Aura: Third World Criticism in the Age of Global Capitalism." *Critical Inquiry* 20:328–356.

DuBois, Barbara. 1983. "Passionate Scholarship: Notes on Values, Knowing and Method in Feminist Social Science." In *Theories of Women's Studies,* edited by Gloria Bowles and Renate D. Klien, 2–29. London: Routledge and Kegan Paul.

Elson, Diane, and Ruth Pearson. 1981. "The Subordination of Women and the Internationalisation Process." Pp. 18–40 in *Of Marriage and the Market: Women's Subordination Internationally and Its Lessons,* edited by Kate Young, Carol Wolkowitz and Roslyn Mc-Cullagh. London: Routledge & Kegan Paul.

Epstein, Steven. 1991. "Sexuality and Identity: The Contribution of Object Relations Theory to a Constructionist Theory." *Theory and Society* 20:825–874.

Fahim, Hussein. 1982. ed. *Indigenous Anthropology in Non-western Societies: Proceedings of a Burg Wartenstein Symposium.* Durham, North Carolina: Carolina Academic Press.

Fine, Michele. 1994. "Working the Hyphens: Reinventing Self and Other in Qualitative Research." In *Handbook of Qualitative Research,* edited by Norman K Denzin and Yvonna S. Lincon, 70–82. Thousand Oaks, CA: Sage Publications.

Fonow, Mary M., and Judith A. Cook. 1991. "Back to the Future: A Look at the Second Wave of Feminist Epistemology and Methodology." Pp. 1–15 in *Beyond Methodology: Feminist Scholarship as Lived Research,* edited by Mary M. Fonow and Judith A. Cook. Bloomington: Indiana University Press.

Foucault, Michel. 1984. *The Foucault Reader.* Edited with an introduction by Paul Rabinow. New York: Pantheon Books.

Fox, Richard. 1991a. "Introduction: Working in the Present." In *Recapturing Anthropology: Working in the Present,* edited by Richard G. Fox, 1–16. Santa Fe, New Mexico: School of American Research Press.

―――. 1991b. ed. *Recapturing Anthropology: Working in the Present.* Santa Fe, New Mexico: School of American Research Press.

Frankenberg, Ruth, and Lata Mani. 1993. "Crosscurrents, Crosstalk: Race, 'Postcoloniality' and the Politics of Location." *Cultural Studies* 7 (2): 292–310.

Ganesh, Kamala. 1993. "Breaching the Wall of Difference: Fieldwork and a Personal Journey to Srivaikuntam, Tamilnadu." In *Gendered Fields: Women, Men and Ethnography,* edited by Diane Bell, Pat Caplan, and Karim Wazir, 128–42. London and New York: Routledge.

Ganguly, Keya. 1990. "Ethnography, Representation, and the Reproduction of Colonialist Discourse." *Studies in Symbolic Interaction* 11: 69–79.

Gordon, Deborah. 1988. "Writing Culture, Writing Feminism: The Poetics and Politics of Experimental Ethnography." *Inscriptions,* no. 3/4: 1–7.

Gorelick, Sherry. 1991. "Contradictions of Feminist Methodology." *Gender and Society* 5, no. 4(Dec.): 459–77.

Grewal, Inderpal, and Caren Kaplan. 1994. "Introduction: Transnational Feminist Practices and Questions of Postmodernity." Pp. 1–36 in *Scattered Hegemonies: Postmodernity and Transnational Feminist Practices*, edited by Inderpal Grewal and Caren Kaplan. Minneapolis and London: University of Minnesota Press.

Hale, Sylvia M. 1988. "Using the Oppressor's Language in the Study of Women and Development." *Women and Language* XI (2): 38–43.

Handler, Richard. 1993. "Anthropology Is Dead! Long Live Anthropology!" Review Article. *American Anthropologist* 95 (4):991–999.

Haraway, Donna. 1988a. "Situated Knowledges: The Science Question in Feminism and the Privilege of Partial Perspective." *Feminist Studies* 14 (3): 575–599.

———. 1988b. "Reading Buchi Emecheta: Contests for Women's Experience in Women's Studies." *Inscriptions*, no. 3/4: 107–124.

Harding, Sandra. 1986. *The Science Question in Feminism*. Ithaca: Cornell University Press.

———. 1987. ed. *Feminism and Methodology: Social Science Issues*. Bloomington: Indiana University Press.

———. 1991. *Whose Science? Whose Knowledge? Thinking from Women's Lives*. Ithaca: Cornell University Press.

———. 1992. "After the Neutrality Ideal: Science, Politics, and 'Strong Objectivity.'" *Social Research* 59, no.3: 567–587.

Harrison, Faye. 1991a. "Anthropology as an Agent of Transformation: Introductory Comments and Queries." Pp. 1–14 in *Decolonizing Anthropology: Moving Further Toward an Anthropology of Liberation*, edited by Faye Harrison. Washington, D.C.: American Anthropological Association/Association of Black Anthropologists.

———. 1991b. ed. *Decolonizing Anthropology: Moving Further Toward an Anthropology for Liberation*. Washington, D.C.: Association of Black Anthropologists, American Anthropological Association.

Hartsock, Nancy C.M. 1987. "The Feminist Standpoint:Developing the Ground for a Specifically Feminist Historical Materialism." In *Feminism and Methodology: Social Science Issues*, edited by S. Harding, 157–80. Bloomington: University of Indiana Press.

Heald, Susan. 1992. "Pianos to Pedagogy: Pursuing the Educational Subject." In *Unsettling Relations: The University as a Site of Feminist Struggle*, edited by H. Bannerji et al., 129–150. Boston: South End Press.

Hegel, Fredrich, G.W. 1967. *The Phenomenology of Mind*. Translated with an introduction and notes by J. B. Baille. Introduction to Torchbook edition by George Lichtheim. New York: Harper Torchbooks.

Hollinger, Robert. 1994. *Postmodernism and the Social Sciences: A Thematic Approach*. Thousand Oaks, CA: Sage Publications.

Hutcheon, Linda. 1989. *The Politics of Postmodernism*. London and New York: Routledge.

Itzin, Catherine. 1984. "'You Can't Do It Like That': The Conflict Between Feminist Methodology and Academic Critieria in Research on Women in Aging." *Studies in Sexual Politics* 2:33–60.

John, Mary. 1988. "Postcolonial Feminists in the Western Intellectual Field: Anthropologists *and* Native Informants?" *Inscriptions* 5: 49–73.

———. 1991. *Discrepant Locations: Feminism, Theory and the Post-Colonial Condition*. Ph.D Diss., University of California, Santa Cruz.

Jordan, Glenn H. 1991. "On Ethnography in an Intertextual Situation: Reading Narratives or Deconstructing Discourse?" In *Decolonizing Anthropology: Moving Further Toward an*

Anthropology for Liberation, edited by Faye Harrison, 42–67. Washington, D.C.: Association of Black Anthropologists, American Anthropological Association.

Kandiyoti, Deniz. 1988. "Bargaining with Patriarchy." *Gender and Society* 2(3)(Sept.): 274–90.

Kaplan, Caren. 1992. "Resisting Autobiography: Outlaw Genres and Transnational Feminist Subjects." In *De/Colonizing the Subject: The Politics of Gender in Women's Autobiography*, edited by Sidone Smith and Julia Watson, 115–138. Minneapolis: University of Minnesota Press.

———. 1994. "The Politics of Location as Transnational Feminist Practice." Pp. 137–152 in *Scattered Hegemonies: Postmodernity and Transnational Feminist Practices*, edited by Inderpal Grewal and Caren Kaplan. Minneapolis and London: University of Minnesota Press.

Karim, Wazir J. 1993. "Epilogue: The 'Nativised' Self and the 'Native.'" In *Gendered Fields: Women, Men and Ethnography*, edited by Diane Bell, Pat Caplan, and Karim Wazir, 248–51. London and New York: Routledge.

Kondo, Dorinne. 1990. *Crafting Selves: Power, Gender and Discourses of Identity in a Japanese Workplace*. Chicago: University of Chicago Press.

Kramarae, Cheris, and Dale Spender. eds. *The Knowledge Explosion, Generations of Feminist Scholarship*. New York: Teachers College Press, Columbia University.

Krishnaraj, Maithreyi. 1990. "Women's Work in Indian Census: Beginnings of Change." *Economic and Political Weekly* 25(48–49) (Dec.1–8): 2663–2672.

Kuhn, Thomas. S. 1970. *The Structure of Scientific Revolutions*. Chicago: University of Chicago Press. Second Edition, enlarged.

Laslett, Barbara, and Barrie Thorne. 1997. eds. *Feminist Sociology: Life Histories of a Movement*. New Brunswick: Rutgers University Press.

———. 1991. *Getting Smart: Feminist Research and Pedagogy with/in the Postmodern*. New York: Routledge, Chapman and Hall, Inc.

Lennon, Kathleen, and Margaret Whitford. 1994. "Introduction." In *Knowing the Difference: Feminist Perspectives in Epistemology*, edited by Kathleen Lennon and Margaret Whitford, 1–16. New York and London: Routledge.

Marcus, George E. 1994. "What Comes (Just) After "Post"? The Case of Ethnography." In *Handbook of Qualitative Research*, edited by Norman K. Denzin, and Yvonna S. Lincon, 563–574. Thousand Oaks, CA: Sage Publications.

Marcus, George, and Dick Cushman. 1982. "Ethnographies as Texts." *Annual Review of Anthropology* 11: 25–69.

Martin, Biddy, and Chandra Mohanty. 1986."Feminist Politics: What's Home Got to Do with It?" In *Feminist Studies, Critical Studies,* edited by Teresa de Lauretis, 191–212. Bloomington: Indiana University Press.

McClintock, Anne. 1992. "The Angel of Progress: Pitfalls of the Term 'Post-Colonialism.'" *Social Text* 31/32:84–98.

McKenna, Kate. 1992. "Subjects of Discourse: Learning the Language That Counts." In *Unsettling Relations: The University as a Site of Feminist Struggle*, edited by H. Bannerji et al., 109–128. Boston: South End Press.

Messerschmidt, Donald. 1981a. ed. *Anthropologists at Home in North America: Methods and Issues in the Study of One's Own Society*. Cambridge: Cambridge University Press.

———. 1981b. "On Anthropology 'at Home.'" In *Anthropologists at Home in North America: Methods and Issues in the Study of One's Own Society*, edited by Donald Messerschmidt, 3–14. Cambridge: Cambridge University Press.

Minnich, Elizabeth Kamarck. 1990. *Transforming Knowledge*. Philadelphia: Temple University Press.

Mohanty, Chandra Talpade. 1984. "Under Western Eyes: Feminist Scholarship and Colonial Discourses." *Boundary 2* (XII):333–358.

Morrow, Raymond. 1994a. *Critical Theory and Methodology.* Thousand Oaks, California: Sage Publications.

———. 1994b. "Critical Theory, Poststructuralism, and Critical Realism: Reassessing the Critique(s) of Positivism." *Current Perspectives in Social Theory* 14: 27–51.

Narayan, Kirin. 1993. "How Native Is a "Native" Anthropologist?" *American Anthropologist* 95: 671–686.

Narayan, Uma. 1988. "Working Together Across Differences." *Hypatia* (Summer).

———. 1989. "The Project of Feminist Epistemology: Perspectives from a Non-Western Feminist." In *Gender/Body/Knowledge: Feminist Reconstruction of Being and Knowing*, edited by Alison Jaggar and Susan Bordo, 256–272. New Brunswick: Rutgers University Press.

———. 1997. "Contesting Cultures: "Westernization," Respect for Cultures, and Third-World Feminisms." Pp. 396–414 in *The Second Wave: A Reader in Feminist Theory*, edited by Linda Nicholson. London and New York: Routledge.

The Nebraska Feminist Collective. 1983. "A Feminist Ethic for Social Science Research." *Women's Studies International Forum* 6:535–543.

Olesen, Virginia. 1994. "Feminisms and Models of Qualitative Research." In *Handbook of Qualitative Research*, edited by Norman K. Denzin, and Yvonna S. Lincon, 158–74 . Thousand Oaks, CA: Sage Publications.

Ong, Aihwa. 1988. "Colonialism and Modernity: Feminist Re-presentations of Women in Non-western Societies." *Inscriptions*, no. 3/4: 79–93.

Panini, M.N. 1991. ed. *From the Female Eye: Accounts of Women Fieldworkers Studying Their Own Communities.* New Delhi: Hindustan Publishing Corporation.

Patai, Daphne Noretta Koertge. 1994. *Professing Feminism: Cautionary Tales from the Strange World of Women's Studies.* New York: Basic Books.

Pettman, Jan. 1991. "Racism, Sexism and Sociology." In *Intersexions: Gender/Class/Culture/Ethnicity*, edited by G Bottomley, de Lepervanche, and J. Martin, 187–202. Sydney: Allen and Unwin.

Rao, Brinda. 1992. "Dry Wells and 'Deserted' Women: Gender, Ecology, and Agency in Rural India." Ph.D. Diss. University of California, Santa Cruz.

Ray, Sangeeta. 1992. "Shifting Subjects Shifting Ground: The Names and Spaces of the Post-Colonial." *Hypatia* 7, no. 2:188–201.

Reagon, Bernice Johnson. 1983. "Coalition Politics: Turning the Century." Pp. 356–369 in *Home Girls: A Black Feminist Anthology*, edited by Barbara Smith. New York: Kitchen Table/Women of Color Press.

Reinharz, Shulamit. 1992. *Feminist Methods in Social Research.* New York: Oxford University Press.

Richardson, Laurel. 1988. "The Collective Story: Postmodernism and the Writing of Sociology." *Sociological Focus* 21(3)(August): 199–208.

Risman, Barbara. 1994. "From the Chair: Feminist Scholarship: Just Another Area or Transformational?" In *Section Sex and Gender Newsletter*, American Sociological Association, (Fall):2–3.

Robinson, Jennifer. 1994. "White Women Researching/Representing 'Others': From Anti-apartheid to Postcolonialism?" Pp. 197–229 in *Writing, Women, and Space*, edited by Alison Blunt and Gillian Rose. New York and London: The Guilford Press.

Rosenau, Pauline M. 1992. *Post-Modernism and the Social Sciences: Insights, Inroads, and Intrusions.* Princeton, N.J.: Princeton University Press.

———. 1994. "Revitalizing Sociology: Post-modern Perspectives on Methododology." *Current Perspectives in Social Theory* 14: 89–99.

Trihn, Minh-ha. 1988. "Not You/Like You: Post-Colonial Women and the Interlocking Questions of Identity and Difference." *Inscriptions* 3, no.4: 71–77.

———. 1989. *Woman, Native, Other: Writing Postcoloniality and Feminism.* Bloomington: Indiana University Press.

Said, Edward W. 1989. "Representing the Colonized: Anthropology's Interlocutors." *Critical Inquiry* 15 (Winter): 205–25.

Sandoval, Chela. 1991. "U.S. Third World Feminism: The Theory and Method of Oppositional Consciousness in the Postmodern World." *Genders* 10:1–24.

Scott, Ellen, and Bindi Shah. 1993. "Future Projects/Future Theorizing in Feminist Field Research Methods: Commentary on Panel Discussion." *Frontiers* XIII (3): 90–101.

Shohat, Ella. 1992. "Notes on the 'Post-Colonial.'" *Social Text* 31/32:99–113.

Smith, Dorothy E. 1987. "Women's Perspective as a Radical Critique of Sociology." In *Feminism and Methodology: Social Science Issues,* edited by S. Harding, 84–96. Bloomington: Indiana University Press.

Spivak, Gayatri Chakravorty. 1990. *The Post-Colonial Critic: Interviews, Strategies, Dialogues,* edited by Sarah Harasym. London and New York:Routledge.

Stacey, Judith, and Barry Thorne. 1985. "The Missing Revolution in Sociology." *Social Problems* 23 (4): 301–316.

Stanley, Liz, and Sue Wise. 1990. "Method, Methodology and Epistemology in Feminist Research Process." In, *Feminist Praxis: Research, Theory and Epistemology in Feminist Sociology,* edited by L. Stanley, 20–60. London: Routledge.

Stanley, Sue. 1990. "Feminist Praxis and the Academic Mode of Production: An Editorial Introduction." In *Feminist Praxis: Research, Theory and Epistemology in Feminist Sociology,* edited by L. Stanley, 3–19. London: Routledge.

Strickland, Susan. 1994. "Feminism, Postmodernism and Difference." In *Knowing the Difference: Feminist Perspectives in Epistemology,* edited by Kathleen Lennon and Margaret Whitford, 265–74. New York: Routledge.

Trivedi, Lisa N. 1994. "' Can't Take a Joke . . . Graduate School in the Men's Room." *Women's Review of Books,* XI (5) (February):14.

Tyler, Stephen A. 1986. "Post-Modern Ethnography: From Document of the Occult to Occult Document." In *Writing Culture: The Poetics and Politics of Ethnography,* edited by James Clifford and George Marcus, 122–40. Berkeley: University of California Press.

Visweswaran, Kamala. 1988. "Defining Feminist Ethnography." *Incriptions,* no. 3/4: 27–46.

———. 1994. *Fictions of Feminist Ethnography.* Minneapolis and London: University of Minnesota Press.

Yeatman, Anna. 1994. "Postmodern Epistemological Politics and Social Science." In *Knowing the Difference: Feminist Perspectives in Epistemology,* edited by Kathleen Lennon and Margaret Whitford, 187–202. New York: Routledge.

Waring, Marilyn. 1988. *If Women Counted: A New Feminist Economics.* New York: HarperCollins Publishers.

Weedon, Chris. 1987. *Feminist Practice and Poststructuralist Theory.* Oxford and New York: Basil Blackwell.

Wolf, Diane. 1992. *Factory Daughters: Gender, Household Dynamics, and Rural Industrialization in Java.* Berkeley and Los Angeles: University of California Press.

Wolf, Diane. 1996. ed. *Feminist Dilemmas in Fieldwork.* Boulder, Colorado: Westview Press.

Wolf, Marjorie. 1992. *A Thrice-Told Tale: Feminism, Postmodernism, and Ethnographic Responsibility.* Stanford: Stanford University Press.

CHAPTER SIX

The Construction of Marginal Identities

Working-class Girls of Algerian Descent in a French School

CATHERINE RAISSIGUIER

Introduction and Theoretical Debates

This chapter analyzes the processes of identity formation among working-class female students of Algerian descent in a French school. It argues that the school—as a social space—is at once a contested terrain within which these young women's identities are being constructed and a powerful tool for their own identity formation.

Indeed, the public (state) school, because it is a secular space, brings different groups into contact with one another materially and symbolically and pulls competing and conflicting discourses onto a shared terrain. This chapter explores how a particular group of young women actively engage in a work of self-definition within and against these competing discourses.

The first half analyzes how the Algerian community and French mass media create a potent discursive link between the young women and school. The second part explores the ways in which the young women construct themselves within the school in relation to others—in particular to French women in their age-group and similar class background and men within their own community.

As I pose the seemingly simple research question "How do young women construct themselves in relation to others in a given context?," the raucous, explosive, troubled debates that have emerged at the margins of feminist and postmodern scholarship come to mind. How does one frame a non-essentialist analysis of the construction of subjectivity that allows for agency while still recognizing

Catherine Raissiguier, "The Construction of Marginal Identities: Working-class girls of Algerian descent in a French school," in Marianne H. Marchand, ed. *Feminism, Postmodernism, Development* (New York: Routledge, 1994): 79–93. Reprinted by permission. *Editors' note:* The reference list for this chapter was culled from the bibliography for *Feminism, Postmodernism, Development.*

the existence of material and discursive boundaries within which the agent is constituted?

Foucault's work on discourse, power, and knowledge informs my own attention to language in the process of identity formation. However, it is also in the spirit of Audre Lorde, Trinh Minh-ha, bell hooks and Patribha Parmar—to name just a few—that I have included in my analysis a discursive layer. Indeed, one of the greatest Master's tools is language and its ability to represent the other(s). While it is crucial to recognize that discourses always shape the ways in which we can apprehend reality, it is as important to locate these discourses in the lived, historical and material situations in which they circulate. Dorothy Smith calls for a similar grounding of our discursive analyses when she writes that "textually-mediated discourse is a distinctive feature of contemporary society" which "must not be isolated from the practices in which they are embedded and which they organize" (1988: 38–9).

Because discourse and knowledge are constitutive of Man/Woman as subject, "identity" and "subjectivity" become dubious concepts under a Foucauldian gaze (Foucault 1972; 1979; 1980). Linda Alcoff speaks to this tension when she writes, "In attempting to speak for women, feminism often seems to presuppose that it knows what women truly are, but such an assumption is foolhardy given that every source of knowledge about women has been contaminated with misogyny and sexism" (1988: 406). Similarly, and in earlier formulations, feminists of color have pointed out the danger of a feminism which ignores its own racial location (hooks 1984; Hull, Scott, and Smith 1982; Moraga and Anzaldúa 1981; Smith 1983).

In return, this postmodern suspicion of subjectivity is problematic for feminist, anti-racist, and post-colonial thinkers especially when they are beginning "to remember their selves and to claim an agentic subjectivity available before only to a few privileged white men" (Flax 1990: 220). In a context where politics finds more and more its point of departure in subordinated people's claim for their marginal identities (Melucci 1980; Wexler 1987), and their disidentification with hegemonic representation of them as others (Roman, Smith and Ellsworth 1988), it is important to find ways to conceptualize women, blacks, Arabs, gays and other Others as subjects in their own right. Speaking more specifically about black experiences and subjectivities, bell hooks suggests, however, that a critique of essentialism—when it is not solely the province of white intellectuals and when it critically engages with its exclusionary practices—can generate a liberatory and oppositional affirmation of "multiple black identities, varied black experience. It also challenges colonial imperialist paradigms of black identity which represent blackness one-dimensionally in ways that reinforce and sustain white supremacy" (1990: 28).

In interesting efforts to come to terms with this set of contradictions, de Lauretis and Alcoff argue that "identity"—a necessary component of the subject's agency—is attained through an ongoing process of people's self-analysis, interpretation and "reworking" of their actual social positions and meanings given to these positions through discourse (Alcoff 1988; de Lauretis 1984). In light of this brief theoretical discussion, and paraphrasing Linda Alcoff, I would define identity as the product of an individual or a group of individuals' interpretation and reconstruction of their personal history and particular social location, as mediated through the cultural and discursive context to which they have access. Similarly, I would define the process of identity formation as the set of self-definitions and practices through which people constantly modify this construction.

Methods and Sources of Data

This study is based on data collected during 1989–90, when I spent several days a week in the vocational Lycée Lurçat.[1] The school, located in a working-class suburb of Paris, offers primarily short clerical training programs to its students, most of whom are female. At the time of the study, approximately 70 percent of the students were female, half were of migrant descent or were migrants themselves, and over 25 percent were of North African parentage.

I "followed" two classes of girls in a short secretarial track, who were studying for a *Brevet d'Etudes Professionnelles* (BEP = Vocational Studies Certificate). Among the two classes (48 students), 20 students were French, 11 were of Algerian descent, and the rest were of other migrant parentage. Only one student was male. I spent the first trimester observing classroom processes and the last two trimesters doing semi-directive interviews (individual and collective) of students as well as intermittent classroom observations. I also interviewed school officials and informally talked to teachers.

Algerian Migrants and the French School

What I want to explore first is the specific positioning of the Algerian community in France *vis-à-vis* schooling and education and its particular manifestations where young women are concerned. It has been argued that schooling and education are of prime importance for a community whose collective trajectory is that of rupture and displacement. Migration itself marks the beginning of that trajectory and school education for one's children represents one of the powerful means to further this process. Dispossessed of their land, Algerian men were theoretically "free" to leave their country and try their luck in France. In that limited space of choice, some decided to migrate, to change, "to give a different meaning to their lives." At first, the idea of leaving was closely connected to the idea of *going back* "richer, freer" (Begag and Chaouite 1990: 37). However, most stayed and settled with their families.[2] Again, in that very thin slice of choice—staying rather than returning to a post-colonial shattered economy and tormented civil society—the education of the children in French schools would perhaps fulfill the initial dream of being "richer, freer," but in France rather than Algeria this time.[3]

Where girls are concerned, this collective positioning in favor of school and education furthers the dynamic of rupture and displacement because it necessitates the breaking of certain "traditional" rules and the taking of certain risks. For instance, girls must be allowed to venture into public space. This breach in the "law" of the Father by fathers and brothers themselves is portentous of future trouble and has been beautifully captured (in the Algerian setting) by the Algerian writer Assia Djebar. Interestingly, Djebar draws links between knowledge, sexuality and self-realization for young Algerian women.

> As soon as the young girl goes out to learn the alphabet, neighbours cast the sly look of those who are sorry 10 or 15 years in advance, for the audacious father, the irresponsible brother. Doom is bound to fall on them. Each knowledgeable virgin will know how to write, will surely write "the" letter. The time will come for her when love that can be written is more dangerous than love that can be sequestered. (Djebar 1985: 11, translation mine)

Young women in the changing context of the Algerian community in France seem to be called to play contradictory roles: on the one hand they are still considered the bearers and keepers of "tradition" and culture, and on the other hand they are expected to engage with a new culture and new traditions.

In the interviews I conducted, mothers stand out as an important force around this issue. Even when not directly telling their daughters to stay in school, their experiences and stories strongly suggest the importance of school for their children, and for girls in particular.

> Aïcha: My mom never went to school. I get the feeling that she's telling us that we [the girls] should keep on studying. Since we have the opportunity, she wants us to stay in school; it's fundamental for me too. . . . Yes school is useful, it can help me enjoy all the things that my mother has missed; youth, work, *real life.* (emphasis added)

It's not only mothers who—through their very lived experiences—suggest the importance of school. Parents in general play a similar role and sometimes even a father will push for his daughter's education.

> Soraya: My parents want me to stay in school, they don't want me to get a bad job. . . . The job my father had at the plant was hard. He's still working very hard; he doesn't want me to get this kind of job. He wants me to get a good job, a good salary, and most of all a good education, because he never got the opportunity to study.

What I find interesting here is the fact that "real" material conditions—postcolonial economic relations between France and Algeria, the world economic crisis, French deindustrialization, and migratory flows—as well as the discursive insistence of the idea of school as opportunity, create specific boundaries within which young women of Algerian descent in France come to construct themselves within and in relation to school. The positioning in favor of school and education within the Algerian community in France, and its resonance among young women within that community must also be looked at in light of mass discourse in the dominant culture.

The French Media, Girls of Algerian
Descent and the School

In France, in the recent past and within the larger context of the rise of all religious fundamentalisms, the media has fueled racism and xenophobia by constructing the "Arab" (in France read: the migrant) as a potential threat to national unity. According to these constructions, men are caught in "tradition" and "religious fundamentalism" and women silenced and oppressed by Islam.[4] Second-generation immigrants, as they are often labeled (the term itself locks youth of migrant parentage in a fictive temporary state in the host country), are often presented as a "social time bomb."[5]

Young males, in particular, are often depicted as potential or actual delinquents. Girls of North African descent however—in part because of their supposedly better results in school—are increasingly represented as a potential integrating/assimilating force for the North African communities in France (Andre 1991). While doing my research at Lurçat, Paris billboards and press stands regularly presented headlines and images constructing this powerful scenario[6]:

> Le Point, 6 March 1989: "France: the Islamic shock" The picture shows Moslem men praying in the street during a post-Rushdie demonstration in Paris. The caption reads "France counts more Moslems than all the Arab Emirates."
>
> L'Evènement du Jeudi, 6–12 July 1989: "The courage of the beurettes[7]: they are doing better [in school] than their brothers and they might be the bridge between two worlds."
>
> Le Point, 7–13 August 1989: "Immigration: a bet and its risks" The picture shows two North African men getting into a police car. One of them—young—is handcuffed, the second is gathering suitcases closely watched by a French policeman.
>
> L'US (Teachers' union magazine), 8 December 1989: "Islam, an obstacle [to integration/assimilation]?"
>
> Le Point, 5 February 1990: "Beurettes: Integration in the feminine form"

As these captions and images suggest, while men are represented as criminals/religious fanatics—potential outcasts in any case, young women emerge as the "bridge between two worlds." The best example of this mediatic construction which developed in the fall of 1989 and lasted for most of the academic year 1989–90 is what has been called in France the "Veil Case." On 18 September 1989 a junior high school principal suspended three North African girls from a school in a Paris suburb because they refused to remove their hijeb (koranic scarf) in school. In a few weeks "the veil case" became a national debate dramatically splitting France into two opposing camps. One side favored the exclusion of religious signs in public schools and saw "the veil" as a symbol both of militant fundamentalism and of the oppression of women. The other side condemned the exclusion of the three girls on anti-racist and multi-cultural grounds and often argued that being in school would be the best way to "save" young women from Islamic fanaticism and gender oppression. Indeed, in the press, "the veil" (note the linguistic slippage from hijeb to "veil") often conflated in a single symbol Arab, Woman, Islam and Tradition.

Conflicting discourses depicted the French school—and its secular tradition—as the target of Islamic militants in their holy war against the French nation (Le Pen's[8] scenario) or as the powerful tool for the assimilation of North African migrants' children (the liberal scenario). School in either case is central and female students of North African descent are center stage but are represented without a voice of their own; even when shown with a clenched fist it is assumed and/or suggested that they must be manipulated by their fathers and their brothers (*Le Nouvel Observateur*, 26 October–l November 1989).

Work of Identity Formation in the School

When mass culture is constructing such powerful representations of a certain group of people, when so much has already been said and written about "them," the work of self-formation—the construction of a "we"—becomes very tricky and difficult. It is to this process of self-definition that I will now turn by analyzing the ways in which several girls at Lurçat understand and interpret their position as young women of Algerian parentage in French society. This work of self-definition necessitates a careful negotiation and recoding of the symbols and common sense ideas widely spread in mass culture. It also necessitates exchange and communication. School, as Djamila, one of the students, aptly points out, offers a space where this kind of exchange can happen for girls of Algerian descent.

> DJAMILA   You can criticize school all you want, but at the end of the day that's where you learn a lot. Okay, there's also TV, but with your parents . . . even among the French they don't talk about certain things like menstruation, drugs etc. Okay, I'm not saying that teachers talk easily about all this but at school you can know more and the contact with your schoolmates teaches you a lot.

The learning and knowing to which Djamila seems to be referring also happens in collective subjective positioning, in the difficult game of defining "us" *vis-à-vis* "them." In the two classes I observed, ethnicity plays a central role in the ways in which individuals and groups position themselves. In both classes, young women formed friendship networks primarily within their own ethnic circle; girls of French descent sat with and hung out with other French girls. Similar patterns were found among girls of Portuguese descent and girls of Algerian descent.

For girls of Algerian descent, the locus of difference between themselves and their schoolmates of French descent lies in their respective relation to sexuality. In an informal interview for instance, Soraya, Acia and Farida brought to the fore the issue of sexuality which they perceived as the main difference between them and the French students and which made it very diffficult for them to feel comfortable among French girls.

> SORAYA   All they talk about is sex, sex, sex! After a while we get fed up, it's too much in the end.
> ACIA   That's right, that's all they have on their mind: sex!

FATIDA   It's true, we're more comfortable among ourselves.
ACIA   Yeah! See, we've been in the same class for almost two years but the other day I got here late and there were only French girls and I felt uneasy.

In an individual interview another student added:

LAÏLA   They are freer. Their parents give them more freedom. They can do what they want. . . . Some of them take advantage of this freedom in ways that I really dislike. They dress crazy, they sleep with several guys, I think it's . . . stupid. Anyway I'm of Algerian descent, I don't envy them too much. I feel that because of all this freedom they have they go overboard, it's getting ridiculous.

When asked why she thought the two groups of young women had such a different attitude toward sexuality one student answered:

SORAYA   It's French society, because now French society does not keep its customs, see. For us our culture [is important] . . . but for the French, no, they don't keep their culture. . . . When they are told you should not do this, the Bible says this or that, they don't care, it surprises us.

It is interesting to note that Soraya conflates customs, culture and religion. We get the feeling that girls of Algerian descent know that French girls have a greater latitude in general and particularly in relation to sexuality. However, none of them expressed the desire to enjoy similar freedom. This might be simply a realistic appraisal of what is possible in their families and their communities, or a refusal to totally disidentify with Algerian customs, culture and religion. But it might also reflect a subtle understanding of the pernicious side effects of pseudo sexual freedom for women in a society shaped by otherwise deeply entrenched gender inequalities.

The particular ways in which girls of Algerian descent understand the issue of sexuality, and how they position themselves in relation to it, needs to be explored from various angles. While they seem to take on a rather "conformist" stance when comparing themselves to girls of French descent, they nevertheless take on a critical point of view *vis-à-vis* their own community and its particular gendered boundaries.

Indeed, the interviews suggest a great awareness of gender asymmetry within the family among girls of Algerian parentage. This awareness seems to be linked not only to actual differential treatments of male children within Algerian households,[9] but also to the fact that the issue of gender oppression in Islamic communities is part and parcel of French mass discourse on immigration.

The following excerpts discuss whether my informants felt their parents treated them differently from their brothers.

FELLA   For us, the girls, my parents like to know who we go out with. It's true, they kind of like to know . . . if I tell them at what time I'll be back they will always worry more than for my brothers, see . . . Okay, it's not like I am locked up or anything but with my parents it's always "who's that boy? bla bla bla" see what I mean? Things like that. But, it's alright, I'm not locked up—it's okay because sometimes I can go out with my brothers.
AÏCHA   My parents want the same thing for their sons and daughters as far as school

is concerned, but in the family it's a different story. Boys have more freedom. They can go out at night. . . . My parents don't trust us (the girls). If we go out with male friends; we must be doing . . . dishonest things (she laughs). They think we are wild.

These responses clearly underscore that girls of Algerian descent feel much more controlled in their movements than their brothers. On the one hand they resent the existence of such control. Aïcha, for instance, using moderate language, laments that "Boys have more freedom," "My parents don't trust us." She also hints at the driving force behind such control: "When we go out with boys we must be doing dishonest things." As I will show later, those young women are quite aware that their use of space is tightly controlled because their parents, and their fathers in particular, want to keep a check on their sexuality.

On the other hand, they seem to accept, at a certain level, the legitimacy of such constraints. Fella's insistence on the fact that she's not "locked up" can be interpreted here as an effort to dispel the idea that Algerian girls are ultimately without freedom and agency—an idea widely spread within the dominant French discourse.

These responses begin to illustrate the complex process of identity formation in which girls of Algerian descent work/play to self-(de)construct themselves (de Lauretis 1990: 136). What we have here is neither pure resistance nor pure accommodation to already available scripts (i.e. the liberated French girl/the traditional Algerian girl). What seems to emerge echoes Martin and Mohanty's reading of Minnie Bruce Pratt's attempts at self-definition as involving "a series of successive displacements from which each configuration of identity is examined in its contradiction and deconstructed but not simply discarded" (de Lauretis 1990: 136).

One of these configurations lies in the critical gaze of these young women on the gendered organization of their families. Indeed, in the interviews, girls of Algerian descent point out that boys get more attention and greater care from Algerian parents. Nasma's comments are quite telling and stress her own discontent at such blatant preferential treatment.

NASMA My mom, she adores my brothers! She's always after them. She talks to them like they are babies. "Have you eaten? You haven't eaten, have you? Should I give you something to eat?" But, us [the girls], we could be dying right there, she wouldn't lift a finger!

Boys have certain advantages, certain privileges because they are thought of by Algerian parents as the ones who will be in charge of the family. Acia told me that her parents would prefer it if she quit school after this cycle of study, but when asked if they would react the same way if she were a boy, she answered:

ACIA No, if I was a boy they would prefer me to stay in school. Because when a boy gets married he must be in charge; he's the head of the family, he must . . . I don't know. But for a woman it's different—if she doesn't find a job, she can always stay at home.

Anifa elaborated further what was expected of boys in the Algerian family and how that affected the ways women were treated and thought of by their parents.

ANIFA   If there is a woman in the family they are more careful with her. They go "he's a boy, he's *the man.*" And he can go out too, he doesn't even have to make his bed! . . .

C.R.   The man?

ANIFA   Yeah, a man, he's the man in the family. He's the one in charge . . . I can't stand it! They [Algerian men] are very proud, I mean. A Man . . . my father tells me, he makes me feel it . . . a woman is nothing . . . he really makes me feel it and that's why I want to show him the opposite. See, in fact I'm struggling for that too, to make him understand that perhaps I can *make something of myself,* I hope so. (emphasis added)

Anifa, who openly resents this unequal treatment, sees in her education (and in staying in school) the possibility of challenging what her father and the men in her community think of women and of transcending the future they have in mind for her. The unequal treatment sensed by girls of Algerian descent also gets translated in the ways they describe their brothers taking on the role of male controllers in the family and the community. Soraya broaches this issue when talking about her rapport with her male siblings:

SORAYA   I personally get along with all my brothers. But my brother always tells my sister what to do, "You go out too much! You're wearing too much make up! You think you live in a hotel, or what?" And yet she is the oldest!

Soraya, who has chosen not to go out and to concentrate on her education, does not encounter the rebuke of her brothers. Her sister, on the contrary, "goes out a lot, is always on the phone, complains all the time and fights against [their] parents." Such assertive behavior, however, is met by her younger brother's disapproval. Soraya's sister is seeking self-determination outside acceptable boundaries and that gets her into trouble with the male members of her family. Soraya, however, never clearly expressed her resentment at this situation even when I asked her directly.

SORAYA   With the Moslems it's like that, you know. If we want to go out, if we want to do what we haven't been able to do when we were younger, we must get married. If your husband does not let you go out, then it's too bad . . .

C.R.   Does it bother you?

SORAYA   Frankly no! It's never bothered me. It doesn't bother me at all.

The potential contradictions in Soraya's interviews are also a sign of the lack of "purity" within these emerging identities. This lack of purity reminds us that identity "is a locus of multiple and variable positions" which at times may be "ideologically with the 'oppressor' whose position it may occupy in certain socio-sexual relations [if not in others]" (de Lauretis 1990: 137).

In another set of interviews, these young women, individually and collectively, critically analyze how particular social constraints work to define the boundaries of acceptable female behaviors particularly in relation to sexuality.

ACIA   I can receive as many phone calls as I want to, as long as they are not from men! (They all start laughing)

FARIDA AND SORAYA   Same here!

C.R.   Really?

SORAYA   Of course, no phone calls from boys! My mother never stops telling me: "Beware of boys!"

ACIA   Sure! My mom, ever since I turned eight, she's been telling me "Watch out for the boys!"

C.R.   What about you Farida?

FARIDA   They don't say it, but I can guess it. They make me understand. They don't gossip or anything, but I can hear when they talk about certain girls. So I figure that they'd feel the same way about their daughter!

These comments reveal a strict check on female sexuality in their respective families. While none of them is willing to criticize this control in front of an outsider (a potential arrogant eye), their comments and their insiders' laughter might suggest it is something they talk and perhaps complain about among themselves.

In the same vein, Anifa, one of the most rebellious of the North African girls, explicitly points out that it is indeed her sexuality that men, and her father, in particular, are trying to control:

ANIFA   Sometimes my father sees me and I'm talking with a guy and I don't know but deep inside it must break his heart to see me. For him it's like, I don't know, to see his daughter talk with a boy. I try to tell him "It's nothing; he was just asking for directions" or something, "that's all." But he cannot accept it, I don't know, and it also has to do with being a virgin and the whole deal, see. They smother me—"don't do this, don't do that"—because I am a girl.

Abla, who is less openly rebellious than Anifa, also clearly underlines the link between young women's inability to move around freely and male control over their sexuality.

ABLA   Being a virgin is really important for us. For our parents it's like a matter of honor. That's why we cannot go places. But for a boy it doesn't matter; it bothers me that they make a difference between boys and girls. My mother does not make a difference but my father does; he's old-fashioned, backward.

Of all these students Djamila is the most articulate about and the most angry at such inequalities.

DJAMILA   It's because at home he's [the Moslem man] got all the power. He can do anything! He can shut you up! He can tell you "do this, do that," we can't say a thing! Even with my brothers! Yeah, my brothers, for instance, with housework. These are little things but they kill you, they kill the life of a person. They don't do a thing. . . . Even when they are born in France, you get the impression that they think like men who are born over there [in Algeria] . . . Because we are girls we cannot do anything! As women. Because we've got a different sex than they have, that's it. I can't stand this way of thinking! . . . Men have got everything; when they come home, perhaps a couple of them clean up. But men are waited on, whereas the woman does her schoolwork and after that she's got to prepare dinner, she's got to do house chores. She tries to do it all because she tells herself if I don't do it, if I don't go to school I know I'll get married at fifteen, at eighteen.

Djamila, like Anifa, stresses the importance of school for North African girls. At home, some of them "can't say a thing" and school in this context represents a space where women can escape to a certain degree the male gaze of family members:

> ANIFA   I told my father that he is not always behind my back, I tell him that at school I do talk with boys and that it doesn't mean that I'm getting into trouble, and all that. When I talk like this he gets really quiet but it breaks his heart because I'm telling him the truth, see.

Concluding Remarks

School, then, emerges as a space where young North African women can bide time, where perhaps they can "make something of themselves," where, in spite of the double burden described by Djamila, they gain some control over their lives. While school is often presented in liberal discourses on immigration as a great "assimilating" tool, it is clear that it does not necessarily "erase" differences and turn children of migrants into bona fide—even if second rate—French products. In fact, as we have seen, female students of Algerian descent are actively engaged in the work of positioning themselves between, within and against different discourses, and school, in this respect, offers them a space to conduct this work.

The particular positioning of working-class female students of Algerian descent in a French vocational school in the late 1980s puts them at the crossroad of several contradictory discourses. Strong media projections of them as at once oppressed within their own communities and as the potential integrating agents of that community into larger French society; mounting xenophobia and racism; and conflicting messages they receive from their own families and communities regarding school as an appropriate space for them and as a step toward advancement with accompanying clear and restricting delineations of their roles within the community and society at large.

This specific location—which starts, as discussed at the beginning of the paper, with immigration as a trajectory of displacement—seems to create for them the possibility, in certain circumstances, of critical insights (of multiple displacements, dislocations) and the potential for a rebellious consciousness. At the same time it can also anchor them in some of the more "traditional" values of their communities. To resolve and envision the potential outcomes of these contradictions is definitely beyond the scope of this paper. However, this close "micro" analysis of identity formation might enable us—in our empirical works—to explore beyond the limiting dualities of resistance/accommodation, freedom/determination, and to conceptualize identities as multiple, varied and constituted through an ongoing struggle to re-invent selves within specific material and discursive boundaries.[10] Furthermore, it suggests the importance of moving beyond representations of a homogeneous, Euro-American notion of Northern womanhood, to an acknowledgment that the North as well as the South is a site of difference and diversity among women.

Notes

1. For a full discussion of the study see Catherine Raissiguier (1994), *Becoming Women/Becoming Workers: Identity Formation in a French Vocational School,* Albany: State University of New York Press.
2. Recent French immigration policies have favored immigration on a permanent basis for migrants of European origin but encouraged returning home for African and North African workers (Abadan-Unat 1984). In 1974 the French government halted all work migration and allowed migrants to enter and remain in the country for family reunification purposes only. Ironically, the policy changed what had started as a transient male worker immigration into an immigration of settlement.
3. This relation of trust and hope *vis-à-vis* the French educational system is far from monolithic. Some Algerian families perceive and resent the French school as one of the many barriers which prevent them from achieving social mobility (Zeroulou 1987; 1988). In spite of a remarkable broadening of the social base of the French educational system since World War II, educational outcomes are still widely unequal (Baudelot and Establet 1971; Bourdieu and Passeron 1964). Working-class youth and students of migrant parentage are systematically overrepresented in non-prestigious short vocational tracks (Boulot and Boyzon-Fradet 1988).
4. This is also happening in "high" academic discourse. For a critique of Eurocentric analyses of Islam and of women in Islamic societies see Mernissi 1975; Ahmed 1982; and particularly Lazreg 1988.
5. For a discussion of the phrase and its implications in the former West Germany in particular, see Castles 1980 and Castles and Kosack 1985.
6. The papers and magazines selected here cover a wide spectrum of political agendas and all belong, except for the US, to the non-specialized media.
7. *Beurette* is the feminine form of *beur* which is a slang word used to describe youth of North African parentage in France. While initially the term was coined and used by the youth themselves, it has now been recuperated by the dominant culture. It is interesting to note that *beur* is a double reversal of the original term *Arabe*. French working-class youth talk *verlan* (reversed talk); in this game of language *Arabe* became *re-beu,* and then again *beur* (Aissou 1987).
8. Jean-Marie Le Pen is the leader of the National Front (FN) in France which has been at the forefront of all racist, anti-immigrant campaigns of the past ten years. This political party, which was a marginal force in the 1970s, now carries more weight than the Communist Party (traditionally the fourth force in the French political scene).
9. Of course asymmetric treatments of boys and girls exist within French families also, but the locus of the difference is less visible perhaps because it complies more with wider social gender practices.
10. For recent discussions and explorations of these possibilities see Kondo 1990; Kruks 1992; Mahoney and Yngvesson 1992.

References

Abadan-Unat, N. (1984). "International Labour Migration and Its Effects upon Women's Occupation and Family Rules: A Turkish View." In UNESCO, *Women on the Move.* Paris: UNESCO.

Ahmed, L. (1982). "Western Ethnocentrism and Perceptions of the Harem." *Feminist Studies* 8:521–34.

Aissou, A. (1987). *Les Beurs, l'école et la France*. Paris: Centre d'Information et d'Etudes sur les Migrations Internationales.

Alcoff, L. (1988). "Cultural Feminism versus Poststructrualism: The Identity Crisis in Feminist Theory." *Signs* 13(3):405–36.

Andre, M. (1991). "L'Intégration au Féminin." *Hommes et Migrations* 1141:3.

Baudelot, C. and R. Establet (1971). *L'Ecole capitaliste*. Paris: Maspéro.

Begag, A. and A. Chaouite (1990). *Ecarts d'Identité*. Paris: Editions du Seuil.

Boulot, S. and D. Boyzon-Fradet (1988). *Les Immigrés et l'école: Une course d'obstacles*. Paris: L'Harmattan et Centre d'Information et d'Etudes sur les Migrations Internationales.

Castles, S. (1980). "The Social Time-bomb: Education of an Underclass in West Germany." *Race and Class* 21 (4): 369–87.

Castles, S. and G. Kosack (1985; first published 1973). *Immigrant Workers and Class Structure in Western Europe*. New York: Oxford University Press.

de Lauretis, T. (1984). *Alice Doesn't*. Bloomington, IN: Indiana University Press.

de Lauretis, T. (1990). "Eccentric Subjects: Feminist Theory and Historical Consciousness." *Feminist Studies* 16 (1): 115–50.

Djebar, A. (1985). *L'Amour, la fantasia*. Paris: Editions J.C. Lattes.

Flax, J. (1990). *Thinking Fragments: Psychoanalysis, Feminism, and Postmodernism in the Contemporary West*. Berkeley: University of California Press.

Foucault, M. (1972). *The Archaeology of Knowledge and the Discourse on Language*. New York: Tavistock Publications & Harper Colophon.

hooks, b. (1984). *Feminist Theory: From Margin to Center*. Boston: South End Press.

hooks, b. (1990). *Yearning: Race, Gender and Cultural Politics*. Boston: South End Press.

Hull, G.T., P. Scott and B. Smith, eds. (1982). *All the Women are White, All the Blacks are Men, but Some of Us Are Brave: Black Women's Studies*. New York: Feminist Press.

Kondo, D. (1990). *Crafting Selves*. Chicago: University of Chicago Press.

Kruks, S. (1992). "Gender and Subjectivity: Simone de Beauvoir and Contemporary Feminism." *Signs* 18 (1): 89–110.

Lazreg, M. (1988). "Feminism and Difference: The Perils of Writing as a Woman on Women in Algeria." *Feminist Studies* 14 (1): 81–107.

Mahoney, M.A. and B. Yngvesson (1992). "The Construction of Subjectivity and the Paradox of Resistance: Reintegrating Feminist Anthropology and Psychology." *Signs* 18 (1): 44–73.

Melucci, A. (1980). "The New Social Movements: A Theoretical Approach." *Social Science Information* 19 (2): 199–226.

Mernissi, F. (1975). *Beyond the Veil: Male and Female Dynamics in Modern Muslim Society*. Cambridge, MA: Schenkman.

Moraga, C. and G. Anzaldúa, eds. (1981). *This Bridge Called My Back: Writings of Radical Women of Color*. Watertown, MA: Persephone Press.

Roman, L., L. Christian Smith and E. Ellsworth, eds. (1988). *Becoming Feminine: The Politics of Popular Culture*. London, New York: Falmer Press.

Smith, B., ed. (1983). *Home Girls: A Black Feminist Anthology*. New York: Kitchen Table, Women of Color Press.

Smith, D.E. (1988). "Femininity as Discourse." In L. Roman, L. Christian Smith, and E. Ellsworth, eds. (1988) *Becoming Feminine: The Politics of Popular Culture*. London, New York: Falmer Press.

Wexler, P. (1987). *Social Analysis of Education: After the New Sociology*. London, New York: Routledge & Kegan Paul.

Zeroulou, Z. (1987). "A L'Ile et dans la Région du Nord: la Seconde génération entre en faculté." *Hommes et Migrations* 1108.

Zeroulou, Z. (1988). "Famille Immigrées et 'Ecole Française': Quels types de rapports." *Migrants-Formation* (December): 21–6.

3

Social Construction
of Difference

Over the past twenty years, the work of black feminist scholars has had a major impact on the understanding of the category of difference in feminist scholarship. The imperative to strive for a nonracist, nonoppressive feminist theory, research, and activism has been heard both within and beyond the disciplines. Patricia Hill Collins' article "Learning from the Outsider Within: The Sociological Significance of Black Feminist Thought" describes a black woman's standpoint as the "outsider within" a dominant white culture, a positionality shared with other nondominant groups and allowing for the recovery of subjugated knowledges. Collins isolates three key themes, however, that characterize the uniqueness of a black feminist epistemology: an emphasis on "self-definition and self-evaluation"; a recognition of "the interlocking nature of oppression"; and the importance of "Afro-American women's culture." In addition to new and powerful analyses of self, family, and society, the standpoint of black feminist or "womanist" thought provides insights and models that challenge the hegemony of traditional disciplines and the tendency of white middle-class feminists to overgeneralize in their knowledge building without reference to the diversity of women's experience. Although contextualized here within the specific field of sociological research, Collins' theorizing of the "outsider within" standpoint has been widely used by feminist critics challenging the biases operating in other academic disciplines, and has provided a bridge between disciplines for those working in an interdisciplinary context.

In the work of feminist scholars focusing on issues of race, class, and ethnicity, gender difference has been shown to be inseparable from other categories of difference. These complex intersections of differences have been obscured by the promotion of a white, Eurocentric, middle-class, heterosexual identity as normative, and by the dependence of that norm on the construction of a simplified Other as their excluded opposite. In "Eating the Other," bell hooks examines the commodification of the Other in "white supremacist capitalist patriarchy," particularly as seen in representations of "blackness" in advertising, film, and popular music. An early version of the erotic nature of this commodification is found in the imperialist desire to "possess" the Other, and in early modernism's preoccupation with "primitivism" as a creative force to be assimilated. Hooks sees the reduction of the potentially revolutionary consciousness of the Other to mere stereotype and spectacle for the white gaze as an effect of what she calls " imperial nostalgia." Following the narratives of several popular films, hooks uncovers the fantasies behind stories of aging white males incorporating the vitality of the black man, and of white women living on the margins of society appropriating the black woman as a "personal metaphor." The danger, as she puts it, is that "difference will be eaten and forgotten." Although she is skeptical about popular culture narratives in which racial conflict is ultimately "resolved," she does hold out hope that a nonappropriative encounter between blacks and whites could emerge from a "mutual recognition of racism." It might then be possible, she argues, to move toward an acknowledgment (by blacks and whites) of the complexity of "blackness" as not only an imaginary fantasy of power and pleasure but a lived experience of pain. Drawing on her own insight into such disparate disciplines as history, cultural criticism, film theory, and psychoanalysis, hooks provides an important theoretical base for explorations of the objectification and appropriation of difference in other fields of research.

In "Feminist Criticism, 'The Yellow Wallpaper,' and the Politics of Color in America," Susan Lanser interrogates the blind spots within white feminist academic literary criticism, taking as her focus one of its canonical texts. In the 1970s and 1980s, most feminist readings of this Charlotte Perkins Gilman story made sexual difference and sexual oppression its central and illuminating theme. Lanser points out that in producing such readings, feminist critics mirrored the story's protagonist: by repressing many of the contradictions and ambiguities of both the wallpaper and the story, they generated coherent interpretations reflecting what they wanted or needed to see. Lanser shows how the literary text always exceeds such ideological reduction, and her own reading restores at least one of the story's repressed meanings—its undercurrent of deep racial anxiety. Taking the acknowledged risk of overreading "The Yellow Wallpaper," Lanser places it within a "psychic geography" of racial obsession at a particular moment in American history. She demonstrates how white American anxiety about increased immigration produced a racial discourse in which "yellow" designated not only all Asians, but also some African Americans, Eastern Europeans, Jews, and the Irish—striking evidence of the discursive construction of racial difference. Lanser finds echoes in Gilman's fiction and nonfiction of the racist language of legislators, journalists, and intellectuals, and she holds Gilman accountable for her engagement with the racist discourse and ideology of her time. Lanser's alternative reading of "The Yellow Wallpaper" also holds feminist literary analysis accountable for an essentialist reading strategy that is "built on the repression of difference," that allows gender to obscure differences of race, class, and ethnicity. By extending her analysis beyond disciplinary boundaries to include nonliterary texts, and by focusing not only on gender but on racial difference as well, Lanser is able to deconstruct some of the ideological blindspots of what might be termed white feminist literary criticism.

CHAPTER SEVEN

Learning from the Outsider Within

The Sociological Significance of Black Feminist Thought

PATRICIA HILL COLLINS

A fro-American women have long been privy to some of the most intimate secrets of white society. Countless numbers of Black women have ridden buses to their white "families," where they not only cooked, cleaned, and executed other domestic duties, but where they also nurtured their "other" children, shrewdly offered guidance to their employers, and frequently became honorary members of their white "families." These women have seen white elites, both actual and aspiring, from perspectives largely obscured from their Black spouses and from these groups themselves. [1]

On one level, this "insider" relationship has been satisfying to all involved. The memoirs of affluent whites often mention their love for their Black "mothers," while accounts of Black domestic workers stress the sense of self-affirmation they experienced at seeing white power demystified—of knowing that it was not the intellect, talent, or humanity of their employers that supported their superior status, but largely just the advantages of racism.[2] But on another level, these same Black women knew they could never belong to their white "families." In spite of their involvement, they remained "outsiders."[3]

This "outsider within" status has provided a special standpoint on self, family, and society for Afro-American women.[4] A careful review of the emerging Black feminist literature reveals that many Black intellectuals, especially those in touch with their marginality in academic settings, tap this standpoint in producing distinctive analyses of race, class, and gender. For example, Zora Neal Hurston's 1937 novel, *Their Eyes Were Watching God*, most certainly reflects her skill at using the strengths and transcending the limitations both of her academic training and of her background in traditional Afro American community life.[5] Black feminist historian E. Frances White (1984) suggests that Black women's ideas

Patricia Hill Collins, "Learning from the Outsider Within: The Social Significance of Black Feminist Thought," in M. Fonow and J. Cook, eds. *Beyond Methodology*. (Bloomington: Indiana University Press, 1991): 35–59. Reprinted by permission.

have been honed at the juncture between movements for racial and sexual equality and contends that Afro-American women have been pushed by "their marginalization in both arenas" to create Black feminism. Finally, Black feminist critic bell hooks captures the unique standpoint that the outsider within status can generate. In describing her small-town Kentucky childhood, she notes, "living as we did—on the edge—we developed a particular way of seeing reality. We looked both from the outside in and from the inside out . . . we understood both" (1984:vii).

In spite of the obstacles that can confront outsiders within, such individuals can benefit from this status. Simmel's (1921) essay on the sociological significance of what he called the "stranger" offers a helpful starting point for understanding the largely unexplored area of Black female outsider within status and the usefulness of the standpoint it might produce. Some of the potential benefits of outsider within status include (1) Simmel's definition of "objectivity" as "a peculiar composition of nearness and remoteness, concern and indifference"; (2) the tendency for people to confide in a "stranger" in ways they never would with each other; and (3) the ability of the "stranger" to see patterns that may be more difficult for those immersed in the situation to see. Mannheim (1936) labels the "strangers" in academia "marginal intellectuals" and argues that the critical posture such individuals bring to academic endeavors may be essential to the creative development of academic disciplines themselves. Finally, in assessing the potentially positive qualities of social difference, specifically marginality, Lee notes, "for a time this marginality can be a most stimulating, albeit often a painful, experience. For some, it is debilitating . . . for others, it is an excitement to creativity" (1973:64).[6]

Sociologists might benefit greatly from serious consideration of the emerging cross-disciplinary literature that I label Black feminist thought, precisely because, for many Afro-American female intellectuals, "marginality" has been an excitement to creativity. As outsiders within, Black feminist scholars may be one of many distinct groups of marginal intellectuals whose standpoints promise to enrich contemporary sociological discourse. Bringing this group—as well as others who share an outsider within status vis-à-vis sociology—into the center of analysis may reveal aspects of reality obscured by more orthodox approaches.

In the remainder of this essay, I examine the sociological significance of the Black feminist thought stimulated by Black women's outsider within status. First, I outline three key themes that characterize the emerging cross-disciplinary literature that I label Black feminist thought.[7] For each theme, I summarize its content, supply examples from Black feminist and other works that illustrate its nature, and discuss its importance. Second, I explain the significance these key themes in Black feminist thought may have for sociologists by describing why Black women's outsider within status might generate a distinctive standpoint vis-à-vis existing sociological paradigms. Finally, I discuss one general implication of this essay for social scientists: namely, the potential usefulness of identifying and using one's own standpoint in conducting research.

Three Key Themes in Black Feminist Thought

Black feminist thought consists of ideas produced by Black women that clarify a standpoint of and for Black women. Several assumptions underlie this working definition. First, the definition suggests that it is impossible to separate the structure and thematic content of thought from the historical and material conditions shaping the lives of its producers (Berger and Luckmann, 1966; Mannheim, 1936). Therefore, while Black feminist thought may be recorded by others, it is produced by Black women. Second, the definition assumes that Black women possess a unique standpoint on, or perspective of, their experiences and that there will be certain commonalities of perception shared by Black women as a group. Third, while living life as Black women may produce certain commonalities of outlook, the diversity of class, region, age, and sexual orientation shaping individual Black women's lives has resulted in different expressions of these common themes. Thus, universal themes included in the Black women's standpoint may be experienced and expressed differently by distinct groups of Afro-American women. Finally, the definition assumes that, while a Black woman's standpoint exists, its contours may not be clear to Black women themselves. Therefore, one role for Black female intellectuals is to produce facts and theories about the Black female experience that will clarify a Black woman's standpoint for Black women. In other words, Black feminist thought contains observations and interpretations about Afro-American womanhood that describe and explain different expressions of common themes.

No one Black feminist platform exists from which one can measure the "correctness" of a particular thinker; nor should there be one. Rather, as I defined it above, there is a long and rich tradition of Black feminist thought. Much of it has been oral and has been produced by ordinary Black women in their roles as mothers, teachers, musicians, and preachers.[8] Since the civil rights and women's movements, Black women's ideas have been increasingly documented and are reaching wider audiences. The following discussion of three key themes in Black feminist thought is itself part of this emerging process of documentation and interpretation. The three themes I have chosen are not exhaustive but, in my assessment, they do represent the thrust of much of the existing dialogue.

The Meaning of Self-Definition and Self-Valuation

An affirmation of the importance of Black women's self-definition and self-valuation is the first key theme that pervades historical and contemporary statements of Black feminist thought. Self-definition involves challenging the political knowledge-validation process that has resulted in externally defined, stereotypical images of Afro-American womanhood. In contrast, self-valuation stresses the content of Black women's self-definitions—namely, replacing externally derived images with authentic Black females images.

Both Mae King's (1973) and Cheryl Gilkes's (1981) analyses of the importance of stereotypes offer useful insights for grasping the importance of Black women's self-definition. King suggests that stereotypes represent externally-defined, controlling images of Afro-American womanhood that have been central to the dehumanization of Black women and the exploitation of Black women's labor. Gilkes points out that Black women's assertiveness in resisting the multifaceted oppression they experience has been a consistent threat to the status quo. As punishment, Black women have been assaulted with a variety of externally-defined negative images designed to control assertive Black female behavior.

The value of King's and Gilkes's analyses lies in their emphasis on the function of stereotypes in controlling dominated groups. Both point out that replacing negative stereotypes with ostensibly positive ones can be equally problematic if the function of stereotypes as controlling images remains unrecognized. John Gwaltney's (1980) interview with Nancy White, a 73-year-old Black woman, suggests that ordinary Black women may also be aware of the power of these controlling images in their everyday experiences. In the following passage, Ms. White assesses the difference between the controlling images applied to Afro-American and white women as being those of degree, and not of kind:

> My mother used to say that the black woman is the white man's mule and the white woman is his dog. Now, she said that to say this: we do the heavy work and get beat whether we do it well or not. But the white woman is closer to the master and he pats them on the head and lets them sleep in the house, but he ain't goin' treat neither one like he was dealing with a person. (1980:148)

This passage suggests that while both groups are stereotyped, albeit in different ways, the function of the images is to dehumanize and control both groups. Seen in this light, it makes little sense, in the long run, for Black women to exchange one set of controlling images for another even if, in the short run, positive stereotypes bring better treatment.

The insistence on Black female self-definition reframes the entire dialogue from one of determining the technical accuracy of an image to one stressing the power dynamics underlying the very process of definition itself. Black feminists have questioned not only what has been said about Black women, but the credibility and the intentions of those possessing the power to define. When Black women define themselves, they clearly reject the taken-for-granted assumption that those in positions granting them the authority to describe and analyze reality are entitled to do so. Regardless of the actual content of Black women's self-definitions, the act of insisting on Black female self-definition validates Black women's power as human subjects.

The related theme of Black female self-valuation pushes this entire process one step further. While Black female self-definition speaks to the power dynamics involved in the act of defining images of self and community, the theme of Black female self-valuation addresses the actual content of these self-definitions. Many of the attributes extant in Black female stereotypes are actually distorted renderings of those aspects of Black female behavior seen as most threatening to white patriarchy (Gilkes, 1981; White, 1985). For example, aggressive Afro-American women are threatening because they challenge white patriarchal definitions of femininity. To ridicule assertive women by labeling them Sapphires reflects an effort to put all women in their place. In their roles as central figures in socializing the next generation of Black adults, strong mothers are similarly threatening, because they contradict patriarchal views of family power relations. To ridicule strong Black mothers by labeling them matriarchs (Higginbotham, 1982) reflects a similar effort to control another aspect of Black female behavior that is especially threatening to the status quo.

When Black females choose to value those aspects of Afro-American womanhood that are stereotyped, ridiculed, and maligned in academic scholarship and the popular media, they are actually questioning some of the basic ideas used to control dominated groups in general. It is one thing to counsel Afro-American women to resist the Sapphire stereotype by altering their behavior to become meek, docile, and stereotypically "feminine." It is quite another to advise Black women to embrace their assertiveness, to value their sassiness, and to continue to use these qualities to survive in and transcend the harsh environments that circumscribe so many Black women's lives. By defining and valuing assertiveness and other "unfeminine" qualities as necessary and functional attributes for Afro-American womanhood, Black women's self-valuation challenges the content of externally-defined controlling images.

This Black feminist concern—that Black women create their own standards for evaluating Afro-American womanhood and value their creations—pervades a wide range of literary and social science works. For example, Alice Walker's 1982 novel, *The Color Purple*, and Ntozake Shange's 1978 choreopoem, *For Colored Girls Who Have Considered Suicide*, are both bold statements of the necessity for Black female self-definition and self-valuation. Lena Wright Myers' (1980) work shows that Black women judge their behavior by comparing themselves to Black women facing similar situations and thus demonstrates the presence of Black female definitions of Afro-American womanhood. The recent spate of Black female historiography suggests that self-defined, self-valuating Black women have long populated the ranks of Afro-American female leaders (Giddings, 1984; Loewenberg and Bogin, 1976).

Black women's insistence on self-definition, self-valuation, and the necessity for a Black female-centered analysis is significant for two reasons. First, defining and valuing one's consciousness of one's own self-defined standpoint in the face of images that foster a self-definition as the objectified "other" is an important way of resisting the dehumanization essential to systems of domination. The status of being the "other" implies being "other than" or different from the assumed norm of white male behavior. In this model, powerful white males define themselves as subjects, the true actors, and classify people of color and women in terms of their position vis-à-vis this white male hub. Since Black women have been denied the authority to challenge these definitions, this model consists of images that define Black women as a negative other, the virtual antithesis of positive white male images. Moreover, as Brittan and Maynard (1984.199) point out, "domination always involves the objectification of the dominated; all forms of oppression imply the devaluation of the subjectivity of the oppressed."

One of the best examples of this process is described by Judith Rollins (1985). As part of her fieldwork on Black domestics, Rollins worked as a domestic for six months. She describes several incidents where her employers treated her as if she were not really present. On one occasion while she sat in the kitchen having lunch, her employers had a conversation as if she were not there. Her sense of invisibility became so great that she took out a pad of paper and began writing field notes. Even though Rollins wrote for 10 minutes, finished lunch and returned to work, her employers showed no evidence of having seen her at all. Rollins notes,

> It was this aspect of servitude I found to be one of the strongest affronts to my dignity as a human being. . . . These gestures of ignoring my presence were not, I think, intended as insults; they were expressions of the employers' ability to annihilate the humanness and even, at times, the very existence of me, a servant and a black woman. (1985:209)

Racist and sexist ideologies both share the common feature of treating dominated groups—the "others"—as objects lacking full human subjectivity. For example, seeing Black women as obstinate mules and viewing white women as obedient dogs objectifies both groups, but in different ways. Neither is seen as fully human, and therefore both become eligible for race/gender specific modes of domination. But if Black women refuse to accept their assigned status as the quintessential "other," then the entire rationale for such domination is challenged. In brief, abusing a mule or a dog may be easier than abusing a person who is a reflection of one's own humanness.

A second reason that Black female self-definition and self-valuation are significant, concerns their value in allowing Afro-American women to reject internalized, psychological oppression (Baldwin, 1980). The potential damage of internalized control to Afro-American women's self-esteem can be great even to the prepared. Enduring the frequent assaults of controlling images requires considerable inner strength. Nancy White, cited earlier, also points out how debilitating being treated as less than human can be if Black women are not self-defined. She notes, "Now, you know that no woman is a dog or a mule, but if folks keep making you feel that way, if you don't have a mind of your own, you can start letting them tell you what you are" (Gwaltney 1980:152). Seen in this light, self-definition and self-valuation are not luxuries—they are necessary for Black female survival.

The Interlocking Nature of Oppression

Attention to the interlocking nature of race, gender, and class oppression is a second recurring theme in the works of Black feminists (Beale, 1970; Davis, 1981; Dill, 1983; hooks, 1981; Lewis, 1977; Murray, 1970; Steady, 1981).[9] While different socio-historical periods may have increased the saliency of one or another type of oppression, the thesis of the linked nature of oppression has long pervaded Black feminist thought. For example, Ida Wells Barnett and Frances Ellen Watkins Harper, two prominent Black feminists of the late 1800s, both spoke out against the growing violence directed against Black men. They realized that civil rights held little meaning for Black men and women if the right to life itself went unprotected (Loewenberg and Bogin, 1976:26). Black women's absence from organized feminist movements has mistakenly been attributed to a lack of feminist consciousness. In actuality, Black feminists have possessed an ideological commitment to addressing interlocking oppression yet have been excluded from arenas that would have allowed them to do so (Davis, 1981).

As Barbara Smith points out, "the concept of the simultaneity of oppression is still the crux of a Black feminist understanding of political reality and . . . is one of the most significant ideological contributions of Black feminist thought" (1983:xxxii). This should come as no surprise since Black women should be among the first to realize that minimizing one form of oppression, while essential, may still leave them oppressed in other equally dehumanizing ways. Sojourner Truth knew this when she stated, "there is a great stir about colored men getting their rights, and not colored women theirs, you see the colored men will be masters over the women, and it will be just as bad as before" (Loewenberg and Bogin, 1976:238). To use Nancy White's metaphors, the Black woman as "mule" knows that she is perceived to be an animal. In contrast, the white woman as "dog" may be similarly dehumanized, and may think that she is an equal part of the family when, in actuality, she is a well-cared-for pet. The significant factor shaping Truth's and White's clearer view of their own subordination than that of Black men or white women is their experience at the intersection of multiple structures of domination.[10] Both Truth and White are Black, female, and poor. They therefore have a clearer view of oppression than other groups who occupy more contradictory positions vis-à-vis white male power—unlike white women, they have no illusions that their whiteness will negate female subordination, and unlike Black men, they cannot use a questionable appeal to manhood to neutralize the stigma of being Black.

The Black feminist attention to the interlocking nature of oppression is significant for two reasons. First, this viewpoint shifts the entire focus of investigation from one aimed at explicating elements of race or gender or class oppression to one whose goal is to determine what the links are among these systems. The first approach typically prioritizes one form of oppression as being primary, then handles remaining types of oppression as variables within what is seen as the most important system. For example, the efforts to insert race and gender into Marxist theory exemplify this effort. In contrast, the more holistic approach implied in Black feminist thought treats the interaction among multiple systems as the object of study. Rather than adding to existing theories by inserting previously excluded variables, Black feminists aim to develop new theoretical interpretations of the interaction itself.

Black male scholars, white female scholars, and more recently Black feminists like bell hooks, may have identified one critical link among interlocking systems of oppression. These groups have pointed out that certain basic ideas crosscut multiple systems of domination. One such idea is either/or dualistic thinking, claimed by hooks to be "the central ideological component of all systems of domination in Western society" (1984:29).

While hooks's claim may be somewhat premature, there is growing scholarly support for her viewpoint.[11] Either/or dualistic thinking, or what I will refer to as the construct of dichotomous oppositional difference, may be a philosophical lynchpin in systems of race, class, and gender opposition. One fundamental characteristic of this construct is the categorization of people, things, and ideas in terms of their difference from one another. For example, the terms in dichotomies such as black/white, male/female, reason/emotion, fact/opinion, and subject/object gain their meaning only in *relation* to their difference from their oppositional counterparts. Another fundamental characteristic of this construct is that difference is not complementary in that the halves of the dichotomy do not enhance each other. Rather, the dichotomous halves are different and inherently opposed to one another. A third and more important characteristic is that these oppositional relationships are intrinsically unstable. Since such dualities rarely represent different but equal relationships, the inherently unstable relationship is resolved by subordinating one half of each pair to the other. Thus, whites rule Blacks, males dominate females, reason is touted as superior to emotion in ascertaining truth, facts supercede opinion in evaluating knowledge, and subjects rule objects. Dichotomous oppositional differences invariably imply relationships of superiority and inferiority, hierarchical relationships that mesh with political economies of domination and subordination.

The oppression experienced by most Black women is shaped by their subordinate status in an array of either/or dualities. Afro-American women have been assigned the inferior half of several dualities, and this placement has been central to their continued domination. For example, the allegedly emotional, passionate nature of Afro-American women has long been used as a rationale for their sexual exploitation. Similarly, denying Black women literacy—then claiming that they lack the facts for sound judgment—illustrates another case of assigning a group inferior status, then using that inferior status as proof of the group's inferiority. Finally, denying Black women agency as subjects and treating them as objectified "others" represents yet another dimension of the power that dichotomous oppositional constructs have in maintaining systems of domination.

While Afro-American women may have a vested interest in recognizing the connections among these dualities that together comprise the construct of dichotomous oppositional difference, that more women have not done so is not surprising. Either/or dualistic thinking is so pervasive that it suppresses other alternatives. As Dill points out, "the choice between identifying as black or female is a product of the patriarchal strategy of divide-and-conquer and the continued importance of class, patriarchal, and racial divisions, perpetuates such choices both within our consciousness and within the concrete realities of our daily lives" (1983:136). In spite of this difficulty, Black women experience oppression in a personal, holistic fashion and emerging Black feminist perspectives appear to be embracing an equally holistic analysis of oppression.

Second, Black feminist attention to the interlocking nature of oppression is significant in that this view implicitly involves an alternative humanist vision of societal organization. This alternative world view is cogently expressed in the following passage from an 1893 speech delivered by the Black feminist educator, Anna Julia Cooper:

> We take our stand on the solidarity of humanity, the oneness of life, and the unnaturalness and injustice of all special favoritisms, whether of sex, race, country, or

condition. . . . The colored woman feels that woman's cause is one and universal; and that . . . not till race, color, sex, and condition are seen as accidents, and not the substance of life; not till the universal title of humanity to life, liberty, and the pursuit of happiness is conceded to be inalienable to all; not till then is woman's lesson taught and woman's cause won—not the white woman's nor the black woman's, nor the red woman's, but the cause of every man and of every woman who has writhed silently under a mighty wrong. (Loewenberg and Bogin, 1976:330–31)

I cite the above passage at length because it represents one of the clearest statements of the humanist vision extant in Black feminist thought.[12] Black feminists who see the simultaneity of oppression affecting Black women appear to be more sensitive to how these same oppressive systems affect Afro-American men, people of color, women, and the dominant group itself. Thus, while Black feminist activists may work on behalf of Black women, they rarely project separatist solutions to Black female oppression. Rather, the vision is one that like Cooper's, takes its "stand on the solidarity of humanity."

The Importance of Afro-American Women's Culture

A third key theme characterizing Black feminist thought involves efforts to redefine and explain the importance of Black women's culture. In doing so, Black feminists have not only uncovered previously unexplored areas of the Black female experience, but they have also identified concrete areas of social relations where Afro-American women create and pass on self-definitions and self-valuations essential to coping with the simultaneity of oppression they experience.

In contrast to views of culture stressing the unique, ahistorical values of a particular group, Black feminist approaches have placed greater emphasis on the role of historically specific political economies in explaining the endurance of certain cultural themes. The following definition of culture typifies the approach taken by many Black feminists. According to Mullings, culture is composed of

> the symbols and values that create the ideological frame of reference through which people attempt to deal with the circumstances in which they find themselves. Culture . . . is not composed of static, discrete traits moved from one locale to another. It is constantly changing and transformed, as new forms are created out of old ones. Thus culture . . . does not arise out of nothing: it is created and modified by material conditions. (1986a :13)

Seen in this light, Black women's culture may help provide the ideological frame of reference—namely, the symbols and values of self-definition and self-valuation—that assist Black women in seeing the circumstances shaping race, class, and gender oppression. Moreover, Mullings' definition of culture suggests that the values which accompany self-definition and self-valuation will have concrete, material expression: they will be present in social institutions like church and family, in creative expression of art, music, and dance, and, if unsuppressed, in patterns of economic and political activity. Finally, this approach to culture stresses its historically concrete nature. While common themes may link Black women's lives, these themes will be experienced differently by Black women of different classes, ages, regions, and sexual preferences as well as by Black women in different historical settings. Thus there is no monolithic Black women's culture—rather, there are socially-constructed Black women's cultures that collectively form Black women's culture.

The interest in redefining Black women's culture has directed attention to several unexplored areas of the Black female experience. One such area concerns the interpersonal relationships that Black women share with each other. It appears that the notion of sisterhood—generally understood to mean a supportive feeling of loyalty and attachment to other women stemming from a shared feeling of oppression—has been an important part of Black women's culture (Dill, 1983:132). Two representative works in the emerging tradition of Black feminist research illustrate how this concept of sisterhood, while expressed differently in response to different material conditions, has been a significant feature of Black women's culture. For example, Debra Gray White (1985) documents the ways Black slave women assisted each other in childbirth, cared for each other's children, worked together in sex-segregated work units when pregnant or nursing children, and depended on one another when married to males living on distant farms. White paints a convincing portrait of Black female slave communities where sisterhood was necessary and assumed. Similarly, Gilkes's (1985) work on Black women's traditions in the Sanctified Church suggests that the sisterhood Black women found had tangible psychological and political benefits.[13]

The attention to Black women's culture has stimulated interest in a second type of interpersonal relationship: that shared by Black women with their biological children, the children in their extended families, and with the Black community's children. In reassessing Afro-American motherhood, black feminist researchers have emphasized the connections between (1) choices available to Black mothers resulting from their placement in historically specific political economies, (2) Black mothers' perceptions of their children's choices as compared to what mothers thought those choices should be, and (3) actual strategies employed by Black mothers both in raising their children and in dealing with institutions that affected their children's lives. For example, Janice Hale (1980) suggests that effective Black mothers are sophisticated mediators between the competing offerings of an oppressive dominant culture and a nurturing Black value-structure. Dill's (1980) study of the childrearing goals of Black domestics stresses the goals the women in her sample had for their children and the strategies these women pursued to help their children go further than they themselves had gone. Gilkes (1980) offers yet another perspective on the power of Black motherhood by observing that many of the Black female political activists in her study became involved in community work through their role as mothers. What typically began as work on behalf of their own children evolved into work on behalf of the community's children.

Another dimension of Black women's culture that has generated considerable interest among Black feminists is the role of creative expression in shaping and sustaining Black women's self-definitions and self-valuations. In addition to documenting Black women's achievements as writers, dancers, musicians, artists, and actresses, the emerging literature also investigates why creative expression has been such an important element of Black women's culture.[14] Alice Walker's (1974) classic essay, "In Search of Our Mothers' Gardens," explains the necessity of Black women's creativity, even if in very limited spheres, in resisting objectification and asserting Black women's subjectivity as fully human beings. Illustrating Walker's thesis, Willie Mae Ford Smith, a prominent gospel singer featured in the 1984 documentary, "Say Amen Somebody," describes what singing means to her. She notes, "it's just a feeling within. You can't help yourself . . . I feel like I can fly away. I forget I'm in the world sometimes. I just want to take off." For Mother Smith, her creativity is a sphere of freedom, one that helps her cope with and transcend daily life.

This third key theme in Black feminist thought—the focus on Black women's culture—is significant for three reasons. First, the data from Black women's culture suggest that the relationship between oppressed people's consciousness of oppression and the actions they take in dealing with oppressive structures may be far more complex than that suggested by existing social theory. Conventional social science continues to assume a fit between consciousness and activity; hence, accurate measures of human behavior are thought to produce accurate portraits of human consciousness of self and social structure (Westkott, 1979). In contrast, Black women's experiences suggest that Black women may overtly conform to the societal roles laid out for them, yet covertly oppose these roles in numerous spheres, an opposition shaped by the consciousness of being on the bottom. Black women's activities in families, churches, community institutions, and creative expression may represent more than an effort to mitigate pressures stemming from oppression. Rather, the Black female ideological frame of reference that Black women acquire through sisterhood, motherhood, and creative expression may serve the added purpose of shaping a Black female consciousness about the workings of oppression. Moreover, this consciousness is not only shaped through abstract, rational reflection, but also is developed through concrete rational action. For example, while Black mothers may develop consciousness through talking with and listening to their children, they may also shape consciousness by how they live their lives, the actions they take on behalf of their children. That these activities have been obscured from traditional social scientists should come as no surprise. Oppressed peoples may maintain hidden consciousness and may not reveal their true selves for reasons of self-protection.[15]

A second reason that the focus on Black women's culture is significant is that it points to the problematic nature of existing conceptualizations of the term "activism." While Black women's reality cannot be understood without attention to the interlocking structures of oppression that limit Black women's lives, Afro-American women's experiences suggest that possibilities for activism exist even within such multiple structures of domination. Such activism can take several forms. For Black women under extremely harsh conditions, the private decision to reject external definitions of Afro-American womanhood may itself be a form of activism. If Black women find themselves in settings where total conformity is expected, and where traditional forms of activism such as voting, participating in collective movements, and officeholding are impossible, then the individual women who in their consciousness choose to be self-defined and self-evaluating are, in fact, activists. They are retaining a grip over their definition as subjects, as full humans, and rejecting definitions of themselves as the objectified "other." For example, while Black slave women were forced to conform to the specific oppression facing them, they may have had very different assessments of themselves and slavery than did the slaveowners. In this sense, consciousness can be viewed as one potential sphere of freedom, one that may exist simultaneously with unfree, allegedly conforming behavior (Westkott, 1979). Moreover, if Black women simultaneously use all resources available to them—their roles as mothers, their participation in churches, their support of one another in Black female networks, their creative expression—to be self-defined and self-valuating and to encourage others to reject objectification, then Black women's everyday behavior itself is a form of activism. People who view themselves as fully human, as subjects, become activists, no matter how limited the sphere of their activism may be. By returning subjectivity to Black women, Black feminists return activism as well.

A third reason that the focus on Black women's culture is significant is that an analytical model exploring the relationship between oppression, consciousness and activism is implicit in the way Black feminists have studied Black women's culture. With the exception of Dill (1983), few scholars have deliberately set out to develop such a model. However, the type of work done suggests that an implicit model paralleling that proposed by Mullings (1986a) has influenced Black feminist research.

Several features pervade emerging Black feminist approaches. First, researchers stress the interdependent relationship between the interlocking oppression that has shaped Black women's choices and Black women's actions in the context of those choices. Black feminist researchers rarely describe Black women's behavior without attention to the opportunity structures shaping their subjects' lives (Higginbotham, 1985; Ladner, 1971; Myers, 1980). Second, the question of whether oppressive structures and limited choices stimulate Black women's behavior characterized by apathy and alienation, or behavior demonstrating subjectivity and activism, is seen as ultimately dependent on Black women's perceptions of their choices. In other words, Black women's consciousness—their analytical, emotional, and ethical perspective of themselves and their place in society—becomes a critical part of the relationship between the working of oppression and Black women's actions. Finally, this relationship between oppression, consciousness, and action can be seen as a dialectical one. In this model, oppressive structures create patterns of choices which are perceived in varying ways by Black women. Depending on their consciousness of themselves and their relationships to these choices, Black women may or may not develop Black-female spheres of influence where they develop and validate what will be appropriate Black-female sanctioned responses to oppression. Black women's activism in constructing Black-female spheres of influence may, in turn, affect their perceptions of the political and economic choices offered to them by oppressive structures, influence actions actually taken, and ultimately alter the nature of oppression they experience.

The Sociological Significance of Black Feminist Thought

Taken together, the three key themes in Black feminist thought—the meaning of self-definition and self-valuation, the interlocking nature of oppression, and the importance of redefining culture—have made significant contributions to the task of clarifying a Black women's standpoint of and for Black women. While this accomplishment is important in and of itself, Black feminist thought has potential contributions to make to the diverse disciplines housing its practitioners.

The sociological significance of Black feminist thought lies in two areas. First, the content of Black women's ideas has been influenced by and contributes to ongoing dialogues in a variety of sociological specialties. While this area merits attention, it is not my primary concern in this section. Instead, I investigate a second area of sociological significance: the process by which these specific ideas were produced by this specific group of individuals. In other words, I examine the influence of Black women's outsider within status in academia on the actual thought produced. Thus far, I have proceeded on the assumption that it is impossible to separate the structure and thematic content of thought. In this section, I spell out exactly what form the relationship between the three key themes in Black feminist thought and Black women's outsider within status might take for women scholars generally, with special attention to Black female sociologists.

First, I briefly summarize the role sociological paradigms play in shaping the facts and theories used by sociologists. Second, I explain how Black women's outsider within status might encourage Black women to have a distinctive standpoint vis-à-vis sociology's paradigmatic facts and theories. I argue that the thematic content of Black feminist thought described above represents elements of just such a standpoint and give examples of how the combination of sociology's paradigms and Black women's outsider within status as sociologists directed their attention to specific areas of sociological inquiry.

Two Elements of Sociological Paradigms

Kuhn defines a paradigm as the "entire constellation of beliefs, values, techniques, and so on shared by the members of a given community" (1962:175). As such, a paradigm consists of two fundamental elements: the thought itself and its producers and practitioners.[16] In this sense, the discipline of sociology is itself a paradigm—it consists of a system of knowledge shared by sociologists—and simultaneously consists of a plurality of paradigms (e.g., functionalism, Marxist sociology, feminist sociology, existential sociology), each produced by its own practitioners.

Two dimensions of thought itself are of special interest to this discussion. First, systems of knowledge are never complete. Rather, they represent guidelines for "thinking as usual." Kuhn (1962) refers to these guidelines as "maps," while Schutz (1944) describes them as "recipes." As Schutz points out, while "thinking as usual" is actually only partially organized and partially clear, and may contain contradictions, to its practitioners it provides sufficient coherence, clarity, and consistency. Second, while thought itself contains diverse elements, I will focus mainly on the important fact/theory relationship. As Kuhn (1962) suggests, facts or observations become meaningful in the context of theories or interpretations of those observations. Conversely, theories "fit the facts" by transforming previously accessible observations into facts. According to Mulkay, "observation is not separate from interpretation, rather these are two facets of a single process" (1979:49).

Several dimensions of the second element of sociological paradigms—the community formed by a paradigm's practitioners—are of special interest to this discussion. First, group insiders have similar worldviews, acquired through similar educational and professional training, that separate them from everyone else. Insider worldviews may be especially alike if group members have similar social class, gender, and racial backgrounds. Schutz describes the insider worldview as the "cultural pattern of group life"—namely, all the values and behaviors which characterize the social group at a given moment in its history. In brief, insiders have undergone similar experiences, possess a common history, and share taken-for-granted knowledge that characterizes thinking as usual."

A second dimension of the community of practitioners involves the process of becoming an insider. How does one know when an individual is really an insider and not an outsider in disguise? Merton suggests that socialization into the life of a group is a lengthy process of being immersed in group life, because only then can "one understand the fine-grained meanings of behavior, feeling, and values . . . and decipher the unwritten grammar of conduct and nuances of cultural idiom" (1972:15). The process is analogous to immersion in a foreign culture in order to learn its ways and its language (Merton, 1972; Schutz, 1944). One becomes an insider by translating a theory or worldview into one's own language until, one day, the individual converts to thinking and acting according to that worldview.

A final dimension of the community of practitioners concerns the process of remaining an insider. A sociologist typically does this by furthering the discipline in ways described as appropriate by sociology generally, and by areas of specialization particularly. Normal foci for scientific sociological investigation include: (1) determining significant facts; (2) matching facts with existing theoretical interpretations to "test" the paradigm's ability to predict facts; and (3) resolving ambiguities in the paradigm itself by articulating and clarifying theory (Kuhn, 1962).

Black Women and the Outsider Within Status

Black women may encounter much less of a fit between their personal and cultural experiences and both elements of sociological paradigms than that facing other sociologists. On the one hand, Black women who undergo sociology's lengthy socialization process, who immerse themselves in the cultural pattern of sociology's group life, certainly wish to acquire the insider skills of thinking in and acting according to a sociological worldview. But on the other hand, Black women's experienced realities, both prior to contact and after initiation, may provide them with "special perspectives and insights available to that category of outsiders who have been systematically frustrated by the social system" (Merton, 1972:29). In brief, their outsider allegiances may militate against their choosing full insider status, and they may be more apt to remain outsiders within.[17]

In essence, to become sociological insiders, Black women must assimilate a standpoint that is a quite different from their own. White males have long been the dominant group in sociology, and the sociological worldview understandably reflects the concerns of this group of practitioners. As Merton observes, "white male insiderism in American sociology during the past generations has largely been of the tacit or de facto . . . variety. It has simply taken the form of patterned expectations about the appropriate . . . problems for investigation" (1972:12). In contrast, a good deal of the Black female experience has been spent coping with, avoiding, subverting, and challenging the workings of this same white male insiderism. It should come as no surprise that Black women's efforts in dealing with the effects of interlocking systems of oppression might produce a standpoint quite distinct from, and in many ways opposed to, that of white male insiders.

Seen from this perspective, Black women's socialization into sociology represents a more intense case of the normal challenges facing sociology graduate students and junior professionals in the discipline. Black women become, to use Simmel's (1921) and Schutz's terminology, penultimate "strangers."

> The stranger . . . does not share the basic assumptions of the group. He becomes essentially the man who has to place in question nearly everything that seems to be unquestionable to the members of the approached group. . . . To him the cultural patterns of the approached group do not have the authority of a tested system of recipes . . . because he does not partake in the vivid historical tradition by which it has been formed. (Schutz, 1944:502)

Like everyone else, Black women may see sociological "thinking as usual" as partially organized, partially clear, and contradictory, and may question these existing recipes. However, for them, this questioning process may be more acute, for the material that they encounter—white male insider-influenced observations and interpretations about human society—places white male subjectivity at the center of analysis and assigns Afro-American womanhood a position on the margins.

In spite of a lengthy socialization process, it may also be more difficult for Afro-American women to experience conversion and begin totally to think in and act according to a sociological worldview. Indeed, since past generations of white male insiderism have shaped a sociological worldview reflecting this group's concerns, it may be self-destructive for Black women to embrace that worldview. For example, Black women would have to accept certain fundamental and self-devaluing assumptions: (1) white males are more worthy of study because they are more fully human than everyone else; and (2) dichotomous oppositional thinking is natural and normal. More importantly, Black women would have to act in accordance with their place in a white male worldview. This involves accepting one's own subordination or regretting the accident of not being born white and male. In short, it may be extremely difficult for Black women to accept a worldview predicated upon Black female inferiority.

Remaining in sociology by doing normal scientific investigation may also be less complicated for traditional sociologists than for Afro-American women. Unlike Black women, learners from backgrounds where the insider information and experiences of sociology are more familiar may be less likely to see the taken-for-granted assumptions of sociology and may be more prone to apply their creativity to "normal science." In other words, the transition from student status to that of a practitioner engaged in finding significant facts that sociological paradigms deem important, matching facts with existing theories, and furthering paradigmatic development itself may proceed more smoothly for white middle-class males than for working-class Black females. The latter group is much more inclined to be struck by the mismatch of its own experiences and the paradigms of sociology itself. Moreover, those Black women with a strong foundation in Black women's culture (e.g., those that recognize the value of self-definition and self-valuation, and that have a concrete understanding of sisterhood and motherhood) may be more apt to take a critical posture toward the entire sociological enterprise. In brief, where traditional sociologists may see sociology as "normal" and define their role as furthering knowledge about a normal world with taken-for-granted assumptions, outsiders within are likely to see anomalies.

The types of anomalies typically seen by Black female academicians grow directly from Black women's outsider within status and appear central in shaping the direction Black feminist thought has taken thus far. Two types of anomalies are characteristically noted by Black female scholars. First, Black female sociologists typically report the omission of facts or observations about Afro-American women in the sociological paradigms they encounter. As Scott points out, "from reading the literature, one might easily develop the impression that Black women have never played any role in this society" (1982:85). Where white males may take it as perfectly normal to generalize findings from studies of white males to other groups, black women are more likely to see such a practice as problematic, as an anomaly. Similarly, when white feminists produce generalizations about "women," Black feminists routinely ask "which women do you mean?" In the same way that Rollins (1985) felt invisible in her employer's kitchen, Afro-American female scholars are repeatedly struck by their own invisibility, both as full human subjects included in sociological facts and observations, and as practitioners in the discipline itself. It should come as no surprise that much of Black feminist thought aims to counter this invisibility by presenting sociological analyses of Black women as fully human subjects. For example, the growing research describing Black women's historical and contemporary behavior as mothers, community workers, church leaders, teachers, and employed workers, and Black women's ideas about themselves and their opportunities reflects an effort to respond to the omission of facts about Afro-American women.

A second type of anomaly typically noted by Black female scholars concerns distortions of facts and observations about Black women. Afro-American women in academia are frequently struck by the difference between their own experiences and sociological descriptions of the same phenomena. For example, while Black women have and are themselves mothers, they encounter distorted versions of themselves and their mothers under the mantle of the Black matriarchy thesis. Similarly, for those Black women who confront racial and sexual discrimination.

and know that their mothers and grandmothers certainly did, explanations of Black women's poverty that stress low achievement motivation and the lack of Black female "human capital" are less likely to ring true. The responses to these perceived distortions has been one of redefining distorted images—for example, debunking the Sapphire and Mammy myths.

Since facts or observations become meaningful in the context of a theory, this emphasis on producing accurate descriptions of Black women's lives has also re-focused attention on major omissions and distortions in sociological theories them-selves. By drawing on the strengths of sociology's plurality of sub-disciplines, yet taking a critical posture toward them, the work of Black feminist scholars taps some fundamental questions facing all sociologists. One such question concerns the fundamental elements of society that should be studied. Black feminist re-searchers' response has been to move Black women's voices to the center of the analysis, to study people, and by doing so to reaffirm human subjectivity and in-tentionality. They point to the dangers of omission and distortion that can occur if sociological concepts are studied at the expense of human subjectivity. For ex-ample, there is a distinct difference between conducting a statistical analysis of Black women's work, where Afro-American women are studied as a reconstituted amalgam of researcher-defined variables (e.g., race, sex, years of education, and father's occupation), and examining Black women's self-definitions and self-valuations of themselves as workers in oppressive jobs. While both approaches can further sociological knowledge about the concept of work, the former runs the risk of objectifying Black women, of reproducing constructs of dichotomous oppositional difference, and of producing distorted findings about the nature of work itself.

A second question facing sociologists concerns the adequacy of current in-terpretations of key sociological concepts. For example, few sociologists would question that work and family are two fundamental concepts for sociology. How-ever, bringing Black feminist thought into the center of conceptual analysis raises issues of how comprehensive current sociological interpretations of these two con-cepts really are. For example, labor theories that relegate Afro-American women's work experiences to the fringe of analysis miss the critical theme of the inter-locking nature of Black women as female workers (e.g., Black women's unpaid domestic labor) and Black women as racially oppressed workers (e.g., Black women's unpaid slave labor and exploited wage labor). Examining the extreme case offered by Afro-American women's unpaid and paid work experiences raises questions about the adequacy of generalizations about work itself. For example, Black feminists' emphasis on the simultaneity of oppression redefines the eco-nomic system itself as problematic. From this perspective, all generalizations about the normal workings of labor markets, organizational structure, occupa-tional mobility, and income differences that do not explicitly see oppression as problematic become suspect. In short, Black feminists suggest that all generaliza-tions about groups of employed and unemployed workers (e. g., managers, wel-fare mothers, union members, secretaries, Black teenagers) that do not account for interlocking structures of group placement and oppression in an economy are simply less complete than those that do.

Similarly, sociological generalizations about families that do not account for Black women's experience will fail to show how the public/private split shaping household composition varies across social and class groupings, how racial/ethnic family members are differentially integrated into wage labor, and how families alter their household structure in response to changing political economies (e.g., adding more people and becoming extended, fragmenting and becoming femaleheaded, and migrating to locate better opportunities). Black women's family experiences represent a clear case of the workings of race, gender, and class oppression in shaping family life. Bringing undistorted observations of Afro-American women's family experiences into the center of analysis again raises the question of how other families are affected by these same forces.

While Black women who stand outside academia may be familiar with omissions and distortions of the Black female experience, as outsiders to sociology, they lack legitimated professional authority to challenge the sociological anomalies. Similarly, traditional sociological insiders, whether white males or their nonwhite and/or female disciples, are certainly in no position to notice the specific anomalies apparent to Afro-American women, because these same sociological insiders produced them. In contrast, those Black women who remain rooted in their own experiences as Black women—and who master sociological paradigms yet retain a critical posture toward them—are in a better position to bring a special perspective not only to the study of Black women, but to some of the fundamental issues facing sociology itself.

Toward Synthesis: Outsiders Within Sociology

Black women are not the only outsiders within sociology. As an extreme case of outsiders moving into a community that historically excluded them, Black women's experiences highlight the tension experienced by any group of less powerful outsiders encountering the paradigmatic thought of a more powerful insider community. In this sense, a variety of individuals can learn from Black women's experiences as outsiders within: Black men, working-class individuals, white women, other people of color, religious and sexual minorities, and all individuals who, while from social strata that provided them with the benefits of white male insiderism, have never felt comfortable with its taken-for-granted assumptions.

Outsider within status is bound to generate tension, for people who become outsiders within are forever changed by their new status. Learning the subject matter of sociology stimulates a reexamination of one's own personal and cultural experiences; and, yet, these same experiences paradoxically help to illuminate sociology's anomalies. Outsiders within occupy a special place—they become different people, and their difference sensitizes them to patterns that may be more difficult for established sociological insiders to see. Some outsiders within try to resolve the tension generated by their new status by leaving sociology and remaining sociological outsiders. Others choose to suppress their difference by striving to become bonafide, "thinking as usual" sociological insiders. Both choices rob sociology of diversity and ultimately weaken the discipline.

A third alternative is to conserve the creative tension of outsider within status by encouraging and institutionalizing outsider within ways of seeing. This alternative has merit not only for actual outsiders within, but also for other sociologists as well. The approach suggested by the experiences of outsiders within is one where intellectuals learn to trust their own personal and cultural biographies as significant sources of knowledge. In contrast to approaches that require submerging these dimensions of self in the process of becoming an allegedly unbiased, objective social scientist, outsiders within bring these ways of knowing back into the research process. At its best, outsider within status seems to offer its occupants a powerful balance between the strengths of their sociological training and the offerings of their personal and cultural experiences. Neither is subordinated to the other. Rather, experienced reality is used as a valid source of knowledge for critiquing sociological facts and theories while sociological thought offers new ways of seeing that experienced reality.

What many black feminists appear to be doing is embracing the creative potential of their outsider within status and using it wisely. In doing so, they move themselves and their disciplines closer to the humanist vision implicit in their work—namely, the freedom both to be different and to be part of the solidarity of humanity.

Notes

1. In 1940, almost 60 percent of employed Afro-American women were domestics. The 1970 census was the first time this category of work did not contain the largest segment of the Black female labor force. See Rollins (1985) for a discussion of Black domestic work.

2. For example, in *Of Women Born: Motherhood as Experience and Institution*, Adrienne Rich has fond memories of her Black "mother," a young, unstereotypically slim Black woman she loved. Similarly, Dill's (1980) study of black domestic workers reveals Black women's sense of affirmation at knowing that they were better mothers than their employers, and that they frequently had to teach their employers the basics about children and interaction in general. Even though the Black domestic workers were officially subordinates, they gained a sense of self-worth at knowing they were good at things that they felt mattered.

3. For example, in spite of Rich's warm memories of her Black "mother," she had all but forgotten her until beginning research for her book. Similarly, the Black domestic workers in both Dill's (1980) and Rollins' (1985) studies discussed the limitations that their subordinate roles placed on them.

4. For a discussion of the notion of a special standpoint or point of view of oppressed groups, see Hartsock (1983). See Merton's (1972) analysis of the potential contributions of insider and outsider perspectives to sociology. For a related discussion of outsider within status, see his section "Insiders as 'Outsiders'" (1972:29-30).

5. Hurston has been widely discussed in Black feminist literary criticism. For example, see selected essays in Walker's (1979) edited volume on Hurston.

6. By stressing the potentially positive features of outsider within status, I in no way want to deny the very real problem this social status has for large numbers of Black women. American sociology has long identified marginal status as problematic. However, my sense of the "problems" diverge from those espoused by traditional sociologists. For example, Robert Park states, "the marginal man . . . is one whom fate has condemned to live in two societies and in two not merely different but antagonistic cultures" (1950:373). From Park's perspective, marginality and difference themselves were problems. This perspective quite rationally led to the social policy solution of assimilation, one aimed at eliminating difference, or if that didn't work, pretending it was not important. In contrast, I argue that it is the meaning attached to difference that is the problem. See Lorde (1984:114–23 and passim) for a Black feminist perspective on difference.

7. In addition to familiarizing readers with the contours of Black feminist thought, I place Black women's ideas in the center of my analysis for another reason. Black women's ideas have long been viewed as peripheral to serious intellectual endeavors. By treating Black feminist thought as central, I hope to avoid the tendency of starting with the body of thought needing the critique—in this case sociology—fitting in the dissenting ideas, and thus, in the process, reifying the very systems of thought one hopes to transform.

8. On this point, I diverge somewhat from Berger and Luckmann's (1966) definition of specialized thought. They suggest that only a limited group of individuals engages in theorizing and that "pure theory" emerges with the development of specialized legitimating theories and their administration by fulltime legitimators. Using this approach, groups denied the material resources to support pure theorists cannot be capable of developing specialized theoretical knowledge. In contrast, I argue that "traditional wisdom" is a system of thought and that it reflects the material positions of its practitioners.

9. Emerging Black feminist research is demonstrating a growing awareness of the importance of including the simultaneity of oppression in studies of Black women. For example, Paula Giddings' (1984) history of Afro-American women emphasizes the role of class in shaping relations between Afro-American and white women, and among Black women themselves. Elizabeth Higginbotham's (1985) study of Black college women examines race and class barriers to Black women's college attendance. Especially noteworthy is the growing attention to Black women's labor market experiences. Studies such as those by Dill (1980), Rollins (1985), Higginbotham (1983), and Mullings (1986b) indicate a new sensitivity to the interactive nature of race, gender, and class. By studying Black women, such studies capture the interaction of race and gender. Moreover, by examining Black women's roles in capitalist development, such work taps the key variable of class.

10. The thesis that those affected by multiple systems of domination will develop a sharper view of the interlocking nature of oppression is illustrated by the prominence of Black lesbian feminists among Black feminist thinkers. For more on this, see Smith (1983), Lorde (1984), and White (1984:22–24).

11. For example, African and Afro-American scholars point to the role dualistic thinking has played in domestic racism (Asante, 1980; Baldwin, 1980; Richards, 1980). Feminist scholars note the linkage of duality with conceptualizations of gender in Western cultures (Chodorow, 1978; Keller, 1983; Rosaldo, 1983). Recently, Brittan and Maynard, two British scholars, have suggested that dualistic thinking plays a major role in linking systems of racial oppression with those of sexual oppression. They note that "there is an implicit belief in the duality of culture and nature. Men are the creators and me-

diators of culture—women are the manifestations of nature. The implication is that men develop culture in order to understand and control the natural world, while women, being the embodiment of forces of nature, must be brought under the civilizing control of men. . . . This duality of culture and nature . . . is also used to distinguish between so-called higher nations or civilizations and those deemed culturally backward. . . . Non-European peoples are conceived of as being nearer to nature than Europeans. Hence, the justification . . . for slavery and colonialism." (1984:193–94).

12. This humanist vision takes both religious and secular forms. For religious statements, see Andrews' (1986) collection of the autobiographies of three nineteenth century Black female evangelical preachers. For a discussion of the humanist tradition in Afro-American religion that has contributed to this dimension of Black feminist thought, see Paris (1985). Much of contemporary Black feminist writing draws on this religious tradition but reframes the basic vision in secular terms.

13. During a period when Black women were widely devalued by the dominant culture, Sanctified Church members addressed each other as "Saints." During the early 1900s, when basic literacy was an illusive goal for many Blacks, Black women in the Church not only stressed education as a key component of a sanctified life, but supported each other's efforts at educational excellence. In addition to these psychological supports, the Church provided Afro-American women with genuine opportunities for influence, leadership, and political clout. The important thing to remember here is that the Church was not an abstract, bureaucratic structure that ministered to Black women. Rather, the Church was a predominantly female community of individuals in which women had prominent spheres of influence.

14. Since much Black feminist thought is contained in the works of Black women writers, literary criticism by Black feminist critics provides an especially fertile source of Black women's ideas. See Tate (1983) and Christian (1985).

15. Audre Lorde (1984:114) describes this conscious hiding of one's self as follows: "in order to survive, those of us for whom oppression is as American as apple pie have always had to be watchers, to become familiar with the language and manners of the oppressor, even sometimes adopting them for some illusion of protection."

16. In this sense, sociology is a special case of the more generalized process discussed by Mannheim (1936). Also, see Berman (1981) for a discussion of Western thought as a paradigm, Mulkay (1979) for a sociology of knowledge analysis of the natural sciences, and Berger and Luckmann (1966) for a generalized discussion of how everyday knowledge is socially constructed.

17. Jackson (1974) reports that 21 of the 145 Black sociologists receiving doctoral degrees between 1945 and 1972 were women. Kulis et al. (1986) report that Blacks comprised 5.7 percent of all sociology faculties in 1984. These data suggest that historically, Black females have not been sociological insiders, and currently, Black women as a group comprise a small portion of sociologists in the United States.

References

Andrews, William L. (ed.) 1986. *Sisters of the Spirit*. Bloomington: Indiana University Press.

Asante, Molefi Kete. 1980. "International/intercultural relations." Pp. 43–58 in Molefi Kete Asante and Abdulai S. Vandi (eds.), *Contemporary Black Thought*. Beverly Hills, CA: Sage.

Baldwin, Joseph A. 1980. "The psychology of oppression." Pp. 95–110 in Molefi Kete Asante and Abdulai S. Vandi (eds.), *Contemporary Black Thought*. Beverly Hills, CA: Sage.

Beale, Frances. 1970. "Double jeopardy: To be Black and female." Pp. 90–110 in Toni Cade (ed.), *The Black Woman*. New York: Signet.

Berger, Peter L., and Thomas Luckmann. 1966. *The Social Construction of Reality*. New York: Doubleday.

Berman, Morris. 1981. *The Reenchantment of the World*. New York: Bantam.

Brittan, Arthur, and Mary Maynard. 1984. *Sexism, Racism and Oppression*. New York: Basil Blackwell.

Chodorow, Nancy. 1978. *The Reproduction of Mothering*. Berkeley, CA: University of California Press.

Christian, Barbara. 1985. *Black Feminist Criticism: Perspectives on Black Women Writers*. New York: Pergamon.

Davis, Angela. 1981. *Women, Race and Class*. New York: Random House.

Dill, Bonnie Thornton. 1980. "'The means to put my children through': child-rearing goals and strategies among Black female domestic servants." Pp. 107–23 in LaFrances Rodgers-Rose (ed.), *The Black Woman*. Beverly Hills, CA.: Sage.

———. 1983. "Race, class, and gender: prospects for an all-inclusive sisterhood." *Feminist Studies* 9:131–50.

Giddings, Paula. 1984. *When and Where I Enter . . . the Impact of Black Women on Race and Sex in America*. New York: William Morrow.

Gilkes, Cheryl Townsend. 1980. "'Holding back the ocean with a broom': Black women and community work." Pp. 217–31 in LaFrances Rodgers-Rose (ed.), *The Black Woman*. Beverly Hills, CA: Sage.

———. 1981. "From slavery to social welfare: racism and the control of Black women." Pp. 288–300 in Amy Smerdlow and Helen Lessinger (eds.), *Class, Race, and Sex: The Dynamics of Control*. Boston: G. K. Hall.

———. 1985. "'Together and in harness': women's traditions in the sanctified church." *Signs* 10:678–99.

Gwaltney, John Langston. 1980. *Drylongso, a Self-portrait of Black America*. New York: Vintage.

Hale, Janice. 1980. "The Black woman and child rearing." Pp. 79–88 in LaFrances Rodgers-Rose (ed.), *The Black Woman*. Beverly Hills, CA: Sage.

Hartsock, Nancy M. 1983. "The feminist standpoint: developing the ground for a specifically feminist historical materialism." Pp. 283–310 in Sandra Harding and Merrill Hintikka (eds.), *Discovering Reality*. Boston: D. Reidel.

Higginbotham, Elizabeth. 1982. "Two representative issues in contemporary sociological work on Black women." Pp. 93–98 in Gloria T. Hull, Patricia Bell Scott, and Barbara Smith (eds.), *But Some of Us Are Brave*. Old Westbury, NY: Feminist Press.

———. 1983 "Laid bare by the system: work and survival for Black and Hispanic women." Pp. 200–15 in Amy Smerdlow and Helen Lessinger (eds.), *Class, Race, and Sex: The Dynamics of Control*. Boston: G. K. Hall.

———. 1985 "Race and class barriers to Black women's college attendance." *Journal of Ethnic Studies* 13:89–107.

hooks, bell. 1981. *Ain't I a Woman: Black Women and Feminism*. Boston: South End Press.

———. 1984. *From Margin to Center*. Boston: South End Press.

Jackson, Jacquelyn. 1974. "Black female sociologists." Pp. 267–98 in James E. Blackwell and Morris Janowitz (eds.), *Black Sociologists*. Chicago: University of Chicago Press.

Keller. Evelyn Fox. 1983. "Gender and science." Pp. 187–206 in Sandra Harding and Merrill Hintikka (eds.), *Discovering Reality*. Boston: D. Reidel.

King, Mae. 1973. "The politics of sexual stereotypes." *Black Scholar* 4:12–23.

Kuhn, Thomas S. 1970. *The Structure of Scientific Revolutions.* 2d Edition. [1962] Chicago: University of Chicago Press.

Kulis, Stephen, Karen A. Miller, Morris Axelrod, and Leonard Gordon. 1986. "Minority representation of U.S. departments." *ASA Footnotes* 14:3.

Ladner, Joyce. 1971. *Tomorrow's Tomorrow: The Black Woman.* Garden City, NY: Anchor.

Lee, Alfred McClung. 1973. *Toward Humanist Sociology.* Englewood Cliffs, NJ: Prentice-Hall.

Lewis, Diane. 1977. "A response to inequality: Black women, racism and sexism. *Signs* 3:339–61.

Loewenberg, Bert James, and Ruth Bogin (eds.). 1976. *Black Women in Nineteenth-Century Life.* University Park, PA: Pennsylvania State University.

Lorde, Audre. 1984. *Sister Outsider.* Trumansburg, NY: The Crossing Press.

Mannheim, Karl. 1954. *Ideology and Utopia: An Introduction to the Sociology of Knowledge.* [1936] New York: Harcourt, Brace & Co.

Merton, Robert K. 1972. "Insiders and outsiders: a chapter in the sociology of knowledge." *American Journal of Sociology* 78:9–47.

Mulkay, Michael. 1979. *Science and the Sociology of Knowledge.* Boston: George Allen & Unwin.

Mullings, Leith. 1986a. "Anthropological perspectives on the Afro-American family." *American Journal of Social Psychiatry* 6:11–16.

———. 1986b. "Uneven development: class, race and gender in the United States before 1900." Pp. 41–57 in Eleanor Leacock and Helen Safa (eds.), *Women's Work, Development and the Division of Labor by Gender.* South Hadley, MA: Bergin & Garvey.

Murray, Pauli. 1970. "The liberation of Black women." Pp. 87–102 in Mary Lou Thompson (ed.), *Voices of the New Feminism.* Boston: Beacon Press.

Myers, Lena Wright. 1980. *Black Women: Do They Cope Better?* Englewood Cliffs, NJ: Prentice-Hall.

Paris, Peter J. 1985. *The Social Teaching of the Black Churches.* Philadelphia: Fortress Press.

Park, Robert E. 1950. *Race and Culture.* Glencoe, IL: Free Press.

Rich, Adrienne. 1976. *Of Woman Born: Motherhood as Experience and Institution.* New York: Norton.

Richards, Dona. 1980. "European mythology: The ideology of 'progress.'" Pp. 59–79 in Molefi Kete Asante and Abdulai S. Vandi (eds.), *Contemporary Black Thought.* Beverly Hills, CA: Sage.

Rollins, Judith. 1985. *Between Women: Domestics and Their Employers.* Philadelphia: Temple University Press.

Rosaldo, Michelle Z. 1983. "Moral/analytic dilemmas posed by the intersection of feminism and social science." Pp. 76–96 in Norma Hann, Robert N. Bellah, Paul Rabinow, and William Sullivan (eds.). *Social Science as Moral Inquiry.* New York: Columbia University Press.

Schutz, Alfred. 1944. "The stranger: an essay in social psychology." *American Journal of Sociology* 49:499–507.

Scott, Patricia Bell. 1982. "Debunking sapphire: toward a non-racist and non-sexist social science." Pp. 85–92 in Gloria T. Hull, Patricia Bell Scott, and Barbara Smith (eds.), *But Some of Us Are Brave.* Old Westbury, NY: Feminist Press.

Simmel, Georg. 1921. "The sociological significance of the 'stranger.'" Pp. 322–27 in Robert E. Park and Ernest W. Burgess (eds.), *Introduction to the Science of Sociology.* Chicago: University of Chicago Press.

Smith, Barbara (ed.). 1983. *Home Girls: A Black Feminist Anthology.* New York: Kitchen Table, Women of Color Press.

Steady, Filomina Chioma. 1981. "The Black woman cross-culturally: an overview." Pp. 7–42 in Filomina Chioma Steady (ed.), *The Black Woman Cross-culturally.* Cambridge, MA: Schenkman.

Tate, Claudia. 1983. *Black Women Writers at Work.* New York: Continuum.

Walker, Alice (ed.). 1974. "In search of our mothers' gardens." Pp. 231–43 in *In Search of Our Mothers' Gardens.* New York: Harcourt Brace Jovanovich.

Walker, Alice. 1979. *I Love Myself When I Am Laughing . . . A Zora Neal Hurston Reader.* Westbury, NY: Feminist Press.

Westkott, Marcia. 1979. "Feminist criticism of the social sciences." *Harvard Educational Review* 49:422–30.

White, Deborah Gray. 1985. *Art'n't I a Woman? Female Slaves in the Plantation South.* New York: W.W. Norton.

White, E. Frances. 1984. "Listening to the voices of Black feminism." *Radical America* 18:7–25.

CHAPTER EIGHT

Eating the Other

Desire and Resistance

BELL HOOKS

> This is theory's acute dilemma: that desire expresses itself most
> fully where only those absorbed in its delights and torments are
> present, that it triumphs most completely over other human pre-
> occupations in places sheltered from view. Thus it is paradoxi-
> cally in hiding that the secrets of desire come to light, that
> hegemonic impositions and their reversals, evasions, and sub-
> versions are at their most honest and active and that the identi-
> ties and disjunctures between felt passion and established cul-
> ture place themselves on most vivid display.
>
> — *Joan Cocks*
> The Oppositional Imagination

Within current debates about race and difference, mass culture is the contemporary location that both publicly declares and perpetuates the idea
that there is pleasure to be found in the acknowledgment and enjoyment of racial
difference. The commodification of Otherness has been so successful because it is
offered as a new delight, more intense, more satisfying than normal ways of doing and feeling. Within commodity culture, ethnicity becomes spice, seasoning
that can liven up the dull dish that is mainstream white culture. Cultural taboos
around sexuality and desire are transgressed and made explicit as the media bom-
bards folks with a message of difference no longer based on the white supremacist assumption that "blondes have more fun." The "real fun" is to be had by
bringing to the surface all those "nasty" unconscious fantasies and longings about
contact with the Other embedded in the secret (not so secret) deep structure of
white supremacy. In many ways it is a contemporary revival of interest in the
"primitive," with a distinctly postmodern slant. As Marianna Torgovnick argues
in *Gone Primitive: Savage Intellects, Modern Lives:*

> What is clear now is that the West's fascination with the primitive has to do with
> its own crises in identity, with its own need to clearly demarcate subject and object
> even while flirting with other ways of experiencing the universe.

bell hooks, "Eating the Other," *Black Looks: Race and Representation* (Boston: South End
Press, 1992): 21–39. Reprinted by permission. *Editors' note:* The reference list for this
chapter was compiled by the editors and does not appear in the original.

Certainly from the standpoint of white supremacist capitalist patriarchy, the hope is that desires for the "primitive" or fantasies about the Other can be continually exploited, and that such exploitation will occur in a manner that reinscribes and maintains the *status quo*. Whether or not desire for contact with the Other, for connection rooted in the longing for pleasure, can act as a critical intervention challenging and subverting racist domination, inviting and enabling critical resistance, is an unrealized political possibility. Exploring how desire for the Other is expressed, manipulated, and transformed by encounters with difference and the different is a critical terrain that can indicate whether these potentially revolutionary longings are ever fulfilled.

Contemporary working-class British slang playfully converges the discourse of desire, sexuality, and the Other, evoking the phrase getting "a bit of the Other" as a way to speak about sexual encounter. Fucking is the Other. Displacing the notion of Otherness from race, ethnicity, skin-color, the body emerges as a site of contestation where sexuality is the metaphoric Other that threatens to take over, consume, transform via the experience of pleasure. Desired and sought after, sexual pleasure alters the consenting subject, deconstructing notions of will, control, coercive domination. Commodity culture in the United States exploits conventional thinking about race, gender, and sexual desire by "working" both the idea that racial difference marks one as Other and the assumption that sexual agency expressed within the context of racialized sexual encounter is a conversion experience that alters one's place and participation in contemporary cultural politics. The seductive promise of this encounter is that it will counter the terrorizing force of the status quo that makes identity fixed, static, a condition of containment and death. And that it is this willingness to transgress racial boundaries within the realm of the sexual that eradicates the fear that one must always conform to the norm to remain "safe." Difference can seduce precisely because the mainstream imposition of sameness is a provocation that terrorizes. And as Jean Baudrillard suggests in *Fatal Strategies*:

> Provocation—unlike seduction, which allows things to come into play and appear in secret, dual and ambiguous—does not leave you free to be; it calls on you to reveal yourself as you are. It is always blackmail by identity (and thus a symbolic murder, since you are never that, except precisely by being condemned to it).

To make one's self vulnerable to the seduction of difference, to seek an encounter with the Other, does not require that one relinquish forever one's mainstream positionality. When race and ethnicity become commodified as resources for pleasure, the culture of specific groups, as well as the bodies of individuals, can be seen as constituting an alternative playground where members of dominating races, genders, sexual practices affirm their power-over in intimate relations with the Other. While teaching at Yale, I walked one bright spring day in the downtown area of New Haven, which is close to campus and invariably brings one into contact with many of the poor black people who live nearby, and found myself walking behind a group of very blond, very white, jock type boys. (The downtown area was often talked about as an arena where racist domination of blacks by whites was contested on the sidewalks, as white people, usually male, often jocks, used their bodies to force black people off the sidewalk, to push our bodies aside, without ever looking at us or acknowledging our presence.) Seemingly unaware of my presence, these young men talked about their plans to fuck as many girls from other racial/ethnic groups as they could "catch" before graduation. They "ran" it down. Black girls were high on the list, Native American girls hard to find, Asian girls (all lumped into the same category), deemed easier to entice, were considered "prime targets." Talking about this overheard conversation with my students, I found that it was commonly accepted that one "shopped" for sexual partners in the same way one "shopped" for courses at Yale, and that race and ethnicity was a serious category on which selections were based.

To these young males and their buddies, fucking was a way to confront the Other, as well as a way to make themselves over, to leave behind white "innocence" and enter the world of "experience." As is often the case in this society, they were confident that non-white people had more life experience, were more worldly, sensual, and sexual because they were different. Getting a bit of the Other, in this case engaging in sexual encounters with non-white females, was considered a ritual of transcendence, a movement out into a world of difference that would transform, an acceptable rite of passage. The direct objective was not simply to sexually possess the Other; it was to be changed in some way by the encounter. "Naturally," the presence of the Other, the body of the Other, was seen as existing to serve the ends of white male desires. Writing about the way difference is recouped in the West in "The 'Primitive' Unconscious of Modern Art, or White Skin, Black Masks," Hal Foster (1985) reminds readers that Picasso regarded the tribal objects he had acquired as "witnesses" rather than as "models." Foster critiques this positioning of the Other, emphasizing that this recognition was "contingent upon instrumentality": "In this way, through affinity and use, the primitive is sent up into the service of the Western tradition (which is then seen to have partly produced it)." A similar critique can be made of contemporary trends in inter-racial sexual desire and contact initiated by white males. They claim the body of the colored Other instrumentally, as unexplored terrain, a symbolic frontier that will be fertile ground for their reconstruction of the masculine norm, for asserting themselves as transgressive desiring subjects. They call upon the Other to be both witness and participant in this transformation.

For white boys to openly discuss their desire for colored girls (or boys) publicly announces their break with a white supremacist past that would have such desire articulated only as taboo, as secret, as shame. They see their willingness to openly name their desire for the Other as affirmation of cultural plurality (its impact on sexual preference and choice). Unlike racist white men who historically violated the bodies of black women/women of color to assert their position as colonizer/conqueror, these young men see themselves as non-racists, who choose to transgress racial boundaries within the sexual realm not to dominate the Other, but rather so that they can be acted upon, so that they can be changed utterly. Not at all attuned to those aspects of their sexual fantasies that irrevocably link them to collective white racist domination, they believe their desire for contact represents a progressive change in white attitudes towards non-whites. They do not see themselves as perpetuating racism. To them the most potent indication of that change is the frank expression of longing, the open declaration of desire, the need to be intimate with dark Others. The point is to be changed by this convergence of pleasure and Otherness. One dares—acts—on the assumption that the exploration into the world of difference, into the body of the Other, will provide a greater, more intense pleasure than any that exists in the ordinary world of one's familiar racial group. And even though the conviction is that the familiar world will remain intact even as one ventures outside it, the hope is that they will reenter that world no longer the same.

The current wave of "imperialist nostalgia"(defined by Renato Rosaldo in *Culture and Truth* as "nostalgia, often found under imperialism, where people mourn the passing of what they themselves have transformed" or as "a process of yearning for what one has destroyed that is a form of mystification") often obscures contemporary cultural strategies deployed not to mourn but to celebrate the sense of a continuum of "primitivism." In mass culture, imperialist nostalgia takes the form of reenacting and reritualizing in different ways the imperialist, colonizing journey as narrative fantasy of power and desire, of seduction by the Other. This longing is rooted in the atavistic belief that the spirit of the "primitive" resides in the bodies of dark Others whose cultures, traditions, and lifestyles may indeed be irrevocably changed by imperialism, colonization, and racist domination. The desire to make contact with those bodies deemed Other, with no apparent will to dominate, assuages the guilt of the past, even takes the form of a defiant gesture where one denies accountability and historical connection. Most importantly, it establishes a contemporary narrative where the suffering imposed by structures of domination on those designated Other is deflected by an emphasis on seduction and longing where the desire is not to make the Other over in one's image but to become the Other.

Whereas mournful imperialist nostalgia constitutes the betrayed and abandoned world of the Other as an accumulation of lack and loss, contemporary longing for the "primitive" is expressed by the projection onto the Other of a sense of plenty, bounty, a field of dreams. Commenting on this strategy in "Readings in Cultural Resistance," Hal Foster (1985) contends, "Difference is thus used productively; indeed, in a social order which seems to know no outside (and which must contrive its own transgressions to redefine its limits), difference is often fabricated in the interests of social control as well as of commodity innovation." Masses of young people dissatisfied by U.S. imperialism, unemployment, lack of economic opportunities, afflicted by the postmodern malaise of alienation, no sense of grounding, no redemptive identity, can be manipulated by cultural strategies that offer Otherness as appeasement, particularly through commodification. The contemporary crises of identity in the west, especially as experienced by white youth, are eased when the "primitive" is recouped *via* a focus on diversity and pluralism which suggests the Other can provide life-sustaining alternatives. Concurrently, diverse ethnic/racial groups can also embrace this sense of specialness, that histories and experience once seen as worthy only of disdain can be looked upon with awe.

Cultural appropriation of the Other assuages feelings of deprivation and lack that assault the psyches of radical white youth who choose to be disloyal to western civilization. Concurrently, marginalized groups, deemed Other, who have been ignored, rendered invisible, can be seduced by the emphasis on Otherness, by its commodification, because it offers the promise of recognition and reconciliation. When the dominant culture demands that the Other be offered as sign that progressive political change is taking place, that the American Dream can indeed be inclusive of difference, it invites a resurgence of essentialist cultural nationalism. The acknowledged Other must assume recognizable forms. Hence, it is not African American culture formed in resistance to contemporary situations that surfaces, but nostalgic evocation of a "glorious" past. And even though the focus is often on the ways that this past was "superior" to the present, this cultural narrative relies on stereotypes of the "primitive," even as it eschews the term, to evoke a world where black people were in harmony with nature and with one another. This narrative is linked to white western conceptions of the dark Other, not to a radical questioning of those representations.

Should youth of any other color not know how to move closer to the Other, or how to get in touch with the "primitive," consumer culture promises to show the way. It is within the commercial realm of advertising that the drama of Otherness finds expression. Encounters with Otherness are clearly marked as more exciting, more intense, and more threatening. The lure is the combination of pleasure and danger. In the cultural marketplace the Other is coded as having the capacity to be more alive, as holding the secret that will allow those who venture and dare to break with the cultural anhedonia (defined in Sam Keen's *The Passionate Life* as the " insensitivity to pleasure, the incapacity for experiencing happiness") and experience sensual and spiritual renewal. Before his untimely death, Michel Foucault, the quintessential transgressive thinker in the west, confessed that he had real difficulties experiencing pleasure:

> I think that pleasure is a very difficult behavior. It's not as simple as that to enjoy one's self. And I must say that's my dream. I would like and I hope I die of an overdose of pleasure of any kind. Because I think it's really difficult and I always have the feeling that I do not feel *the* pleasure, the complete total pleasure and, for me, it's related to death. Because I think that the kind of pleasure I would consider as *the* real pleasure, would be so deep, so intense, so overwhelming that I couldn't survive it. I would die.

Though speaking from the standpoint of his individual experience, Foucault voices a dilemma felt by many in the west. It is precisely that longing for *the* pleasure that has led the white west to sustain a romantic fantasy of the "primitive" and the concrete search for a real primitive paradise, whether that location be a country or a body, a dark continent or dark flesh, perceived as the perfect embodiment of that possibility.

Within this fantasy of Otherness, the longing for pleasure is projected as a force that can disrupt and subvert the will to dominate. It acts to both mediate and challenge. In Lorraine Hansberry's play *Les Blancs*, it is the desire to experience closeness and community that leads the white American journalist Charles to make contact and attempt to establish a friendship with Tshembe, the black revolutionary. Charles struggles to divest himself of white supremacist privilege, eschews the role of colonizer, and refuses racist exoticization of blacks. Yet he continues to assume that he alone can decide the nature of his relationship to a black person. Evoking the idea of a universal transcendent subject, he appeals to Tshembe by repudiating the role of oppressor, declaring, "I am a man who feels like talking." When Tshembe refuses to accept the familiar relationship offered him, refuses to satisfy Charles's longing for camaraderie and contact, he is accused of hating white men. Calling attention to situations where white people have oppressed other white people, Tshembe challenges Charles, declaring that "race is a device—no more, no less," that "it explains nothing at all." Pleased with this disavowal of the importance of race, Charles agrees, stating "race hasn't a thing to do with it." Tshembe then deconstructs the category "race" without minimizing or ignoring the impact of racism, telling him:

> I believe in the recognition of devices as *devices*—but I also believe in the reality of those devices. In one century men choose to hide their conquests under religion, in another under race. So you and I may recognize the fraudulence of the device in both cases, but the fact remains that a man who has a sword run through him because he will not become a Moslem or a Christian—or who is lynched in Mississippi or Zatembe because he is black—is suffering the utter reality of that device of conquest. And it is pointless to pretend that it doesn't *exist*—merely because it is a lie. . . .

Again and again Tshembe must make it clear to Charles that subject to subject contact between white and black which signals the absence of domination, of an oppressor/oppressed relationship, must emerge through mutual choice and negotiation. That simply by expressing their desire for "intimate" contact with black people, white people do not eradicate the politics of racial domination as they are made manifest in personal interaction.

Mutual recognition of racism, its impact both on those who are dominated and those who dominate, is the only standpoint that makes possible an encounter between races that is not based on denial and fantasy. For it is the ever present reality of racist domination, of white supremacy, that renders problematic the desire of white people to have contact with the Other. Often it is this reality that is most masked when representations of contact between white and non-white, white and black, appear in mass culture. One area where the politics of diversity and its concomitant insistence on inclusive representation have had serious impact is advertising. Now that sophisticated market surveys reveal the extent to which poor and materially underprivileged people of all races/ethnicities consume products, sometimes in a quantity disproportionate to income, it has become more evident that these markets can be appealed to with advertising. Market surveys revealed that black people buy more Pepsi than other soft drinks and suddenly we see more Pepsi commercials with black people in them.

The world of fashion has also come to understand that selling products is heightened by the exploitation of Otherness. The success of Benneton ads, which with their racially diverse images have become a model for various advertising strategies, epitomize this trend. Many ads that focus on Otherness make no explicit comments, or rely solely on visual messages, but the recent fall *Tweeds* catalogue provides an excellent example of the way contemporary culture exploits notions of Otherness with both visual images and text. The catalogue cover shows a map of Egypt. Inserted into the heart of the country, so to speak, is a photo of a white male (an *Out of Africa* type) holding an Egyptian child in his arms. Behind them is not the scenery of Egypt as modern city, but rather shadowy silhouettes resembling huts and palm trees. Inside, the copy quotes Gustave Flaubert's comments from *Flaubert in Egypt*. For seventy-five pages Egypt becomes a landscape of dreams, and its darker-skinned people background, scenery to highlight whiteness, and the longing of whites to inhabit if only for a time, the world of the Other. The front page copy declares:

> We did not want our journey to be filled with snapshots of an antique land. Instead, we wanted to rediscover our clothing in the context of a different culture. Was it possible, we wondered, to express our style in an unaccustomed way, surrounded by Egyptian colors, Egyptian textures, even bathed in an ancient Egyptian light?

Is this not imperialist nostalgia at its best—potent expression of longing for the "primitive"? One desires "a bit of the Other" to enhance the blank landscape of whiteness. Nothing is said in the text about Egyptian people, yet their images are spread throughout its pages. Often their faces are blurred by the camera, a strategy which ensures that readers will not become more enthralled by the images of Otherness than those of whiteness. The point of this photographic attempt at defamiliarization is to distance us from whiteness, so that we will return to it more intently.

In most of the "snapshots," all carefully selected and posed, there is no mutual looking. One desires contact with the Other even as one wishes boundaries to remain intact. When bodies contact one another, touch, it is almost always a white hand doing the touching, white hands that rest on the bodies of colored people, unless the Other is a child. One snapshot of "intimate" contact shows two women with their arms linked, the way close friends might link arms. One is an Egyptian woman identified by a caption that reads "with her husband and baby, Ahmedio A'bass, 22, leads a gypsy's life"; the second woman is a white-skinned model. The linked hands suggest that these two women share something, have a basis of contact and indeed they do, they resemble one another, look more alike than different. The message again is that "primitivism," though more apparent in the Other, also resides in the white self. It is not the world of Egypt, of "gypsy" life, that is affirmed by this snapshot, but the ability of white people to roam the world, making contact. Wearing pants while standing next to her dark "sister" who wears a traditional skirt, the white woman appears to be cross-dressing (an ongoing theme in *Tweeds*). Visually the image suggests that she and first world white women like her are liberated, have greater freedom to roam than darker women who live peripatetic lifestyles.

Significantly, the catalogue that followed this one focused on Norway. There the people of Norway are not represented, only the scenery. Are we to assume that white folks from this country are as at "home" in Norway as they are here so there is no need for captions and explanations? In this visual text, whiteness is the unifying feature—not culture. Of course, for *Tweeds* to exploit Otherness to dramatize "whiteness" while in Egypt, it cannot include darker-skinned models since the play on contrasts that is meant to highlight "whiteness" could not happen nor could the exploitation that urges consumption of the Other whet the appetite in quite the same way; just as inclusion of darker-skinned models in the Norway issue might suggest that the west is not as unified by whiteness as this visual text suggests. Essentially speaking, both catalogues evoke a sense that white people are homogeneous and share "white bread culture."

Those progressive white intellectuals who are particularly critical of "essentialist" notions of identity when writing about mass culture, race, and gender have not focused their critiques on white identity and the way essentialism informs representations of whiteness. It is always the non-white, or in some cases the non-heterosexual Other, who is guilty of essentialism. Few white intellectuals call attention to the way in which the contemporary obsession with white consumption of the dark Other has served as a catalyst for the resurgence of essentialist based racial and ethnic nationalism. Black nationalism, with its emphasis on black separatism, is resurging as a response to the assumption that white cultural imperialism and white yearning to possess the Other are invading black life, appropriating and violating black culture. As a survival strategy, black nationalism surfaces most strongly when white cultural appropriation of black culture threatens to decontextualize and thereby erase knowledge of the specific historical and social context of black experience from which cultural productions and distinct black styles emerge. Yet most white intellectuals writing critically about black culture do not see these constructive dimensions of black nationalism and tend to see it instead as naive essentialism, rooted in notions of ethnic purity that resemble white racist assumptions.

In the essay "Hip, and the Long Front of Color," white critic Andrew Ross interprets Langston Hughes's declaration ("You've taken my blues and gone—You sing 'em on Broadway—And you sing 'em in Hollywood Bowl—And you mixed 'em up with symphonies—And you fixed 'em—So they don't sound like me. Yep, you done taken my blues and gone.") as a "complaint" that "celebrates folk purism." Yet Hughes's declaration can be heard as a critical comment on appropriation (not a complaint). A distinction must be made between the longing for ongoing cultural recognition of the creative source of particular African American cultural productions that emerge from distinct black experience, and essentialist investments in notions of ethnic purity that undergird crude versions of black nationalism.

Currently, the commodification of difference promotes paradigms of consumption wherein whatever difference the Other inhabits is eradicated, via exchange, by a consumer cannibalism that not only displaces the Other but denies the significance of that Other's history through a process of decontextualization. Like the "primitivism" Hal Foster maintains "absorbs the primitive, in part via the concept of affinity," contemporary notions of "crossover" expand the parameters of cultural production to enable the voice of the non-white Other to be heard by a larger audience even as it denies the specificity of that voice, or as it recoups it for its own use.

This scenario is played out in the film *Heart Condition* when Mooney, a white racist cop, has a heart transplant and receives a heart from Stone, a black man he has been trying to destroy because Stone has seduced Chris, the white call girl that Mooney loves. Transformed by his new "black heart," Mooney learns how to be more seductive, changes his attitudes towards race, and, in perfect Hollywood style, wins the girl in the end. Unabashedly dramatizing a process of "eating the Other" (in ancient religious practices among so called "primitive" people, the heart of a person may be ripped out and eaten so that one can embody that person's spirit or special characteristics), a film like *Heart Condition* addresses the fantasies of a white audience. At the end of the film, Mooney, reunited with Chris through marriage and surrounded by Stone's caring black kin, has become the "father" of Chris and Stone's bi-racial baby who is dark-skinned, the color of his father. Stone, whose ghost has haunted Mooney, is suddenly "history"—gone. Interestingly, this mainstream film suggests that patriarchal struggle over "ownership" (i.e., sexual possession of white women's bodies) is the linchpin of racism. Once Mooney can accept and bond with Stone on the phallocentric basis of their mutual possession and "desire" for Chris, their homosocial bonding makes brotherhood possible and eradicates the racism that has kept them apart. Significantly, patriarchal bonding mediates and becomes the basis for the eradication of racism.

In part, this film offers a version of racial pluralism that challenges racism by suggesting that the white male's life will be richer, more pleasurable, if he accepts diversity. Yet it also offers a model of change that still leaves a white supremacist capitalist patriarchy intact, though no longer based on coercive domination of black people. It insists that white male desire must be sustained by the "labor" (in this case the heart) of a dark Other. The fantasy, of course, is that this labor will no longer be exacted *via* domination, but will be given willingly. Not surprisingly, most black folks talked about this film as "racist." The young desirable handsome intelligent black male (who we are told *via* his own self-portrait is "hung like a shetland pony") must die so that the aging white male can both restore his potency (he awakens from the transplant to find a replica of a huge black penis standing between his legs) and be more sensitive and loving. Torgovnick reminds readers in *Gone Primitive* that a central element in the western fascination with primitivism is its focus on "overcoming alienation from the body, restoring the body, and hence the self, to a relation of full and easy harmony with nature or the cosmos." It is this conceptualization of the "primitive" and the black male as quintessential representative that is dramatized in *Heart Condition*. One weakness in Torgovnick's work is her refusal to recognize how deeply the idea of the "primitive" is entrenched in the psyches of everyday people, shaping contemporary racist stereotypes, perpetuating racism. When she suggests, "our own culture by and large rejects the association of blackness with rampant sensuality and irrationality, with decadence and corruption, with disease and death," one can only wonder what culture she is claiming as her own.

Films like *Heart Condition* make black culture and black life backdrop, scenery for narratives that essentially focus on white people. Nationalist black voices critique this cultural crossover, its decentering of black experience as it relates to black people, and its insistence that it is acceptable for whites to explore blackness as long as their ultimate agenda is appropriation. Politically "on the case" when they critique white cultural appropriation of black experience that reinscribes it within a "cool" narrative of white supremacy, these voices cannot be dismissed as naive. They are misguided when they suggest that white cultural imperialism is best critiqued and resisted by black separatism, or when they evoke outmoded notions of ethnic purity that deny the way in which black people exist in the west, are western, and are at times positively influenced by aspects of white culture.

Steve Perry's essay "The Politics of Crossover" deconstructs notions of racial purity by outlining the diverse inter-cultural exchanges between black and white musicians, yet he seems unable to acknowledge that this reality does not alter the fact that white cultural imperialist appropriation of black culture maintains white supremacy, and is a constant threat to black liberation. Even though Perry can admit that successful black crossover artists, such as Prince, carry the "cross over impulse" to the point where it "begins to be a denial of blackness," he is unable to see this as threatening to black people who are daily resisting racism, advocating ongoing decolonization, and in need of an effective black liberation struggle.

Underlying Perry's condescension, and at times contemptuous attitude towards all expressions of black nationalism, is a traditional leftist insistence on the primacy of class over race. This standpoint inhibits his capacity to understand the specific political needs of black people that are addressed, however inadequately, by essentialist-based black separatism. As Howard Winant clarifies in "Postmodern Racial Politics in the United States: Difference and Inequality," one must understand race to understand class because "in the postmodern political framework of the contemporary United States, hegemony is determined by the articulation of race and class." And most importantly it is the "ability of the right to represent class issues in racial terms" that is "central to the current pattern of conservative hegemony." Certainly an essentialist-based black nationalism imbued with and perpetuating many racial stereotypes is an inadequate and ineffective response to the urgent demand that there be a renewed and viable revolutionary black liberation struggle that would take radical politicization of black people, strategies of decolonization, critiques of capitalism, and ongoing resistance to racist domination as its central goals.

Resurgence of black nationalism as an expression of black people's desire to guard against white cultural appropriation indicates the extent to which the commodification of blackness (including the nationalist agenda) has been reinscribed and marketed with an atavistic narrative, a fantasy of Otherness that reduces protest to spectacle and stimulates even greater longing for the "primitive." Given this cultural context, black nationalism is more a gesture of powerlessness than a sign of critical resistance. Who can take seriously Public Enemy's insistence that the dominated and their allies "fight the power" when that declaration is in no way linked to a collective organized struggle. When young black people mouth 1960s' black nationalist rhetoric, don Kente cloth, gold medallions, dread their hair, and diss the white folks they hang out with, they expose the way meaningless commodification strips these signs of political integrity and meaning, denying the possibility that they can serve as a catalyst for concrete political action. As signs, their power to ignite critical consciousness is diffused when they are commodified. Communities of resistance are replaced by communities of consumption. As Stuart and Elizabeth Ewen emphasize in *Channels of Desire*:

> The politics of consumption must be understood as something more than what to buy, or even what to boycott. Consumption is a social relationship, the dominant relationship in our society—one that makes it harder and harder for people to hold together, to create community. At a time when for many of us the possibility of meaningful change seems to elude our grasp, it is a question of immense social and political proportions. To establish popular initiative, consumerism must be transcended—a difficult but central task facing all people who still seek a better way of life.

Work by black artists that is overly political and radical is rarely linked to an oppositional political culture. When commodified, it is easy for consumers to ignore political messages. And even though a product like rap articulates narratives of coming to critical political consciousness, it also exploits stereotypes and essentialist notions of blackness (like black people have natural rhythm and are more sexual). The television show *In Living Color* is introduced by lyrics that tell listeners "do what you wanna do." Positively, this show advocates transgression, yet it negatively promotes racist stereotypes, sexisms and homophobia. Black youth culture comes to stand for the outer limits of "outness." The commercial nexus exploits the culture's desire (expressed by whites and blacks) to inscribe blackness as "primitive" sign, as wildness, and with it the suggestion that black people have secret access to intense pleasure, particularly pleasures of the body. It is the young black male body that is seen as epitomizing this promise of wildness, of unlimited physical prowess and unbridled eroticism. It was this black body that was most "desired" for its labor in slavery, and it is this body that is most represented in contemporary popular culture as the body to be watched, imitated, desired, possessed. Rather than a sign of pleasure in daily life outside the realm of consumption, the young black male body is represented most graphically as the body in pain.

Regarded fetishistically in the psycho-sexual racial imagination of youth culture, the real bodies of young black men are daily viciously assaulted by white racist violence, black on black violence, the violence of overwork, and the violence of addiction and disease. In her introduction to *The Body in Pain*, Elaine Scarry states that "there is ordinarily no language for pain," that "physical pain is difficult to express; and that this inexpressibility has political consequences." This is certainly true of black male pain. Black males are unable to fully articulate and acknowledge the pain in their lives. They do not have a public discourse or audience within racist society that enables them to give their pain a hearing. Sadly, black men often evoke racist rhetoric that identifies the black male as animal, speaking of themselves as "endangered species," as "primitive," in their bid to gain recognition of their suffering.

When young black men acquire a powerful public voice and presence *via* cultural production, as has happened with the explosion of rap music, it does not mean that they have a vehicle that will enable them to articulate that pain. Providing narratives that are mainly about power and pleasure, that advocate resistance to racism yet support phallocentrism, rap denies this pain. True, it was conditions of suffering and survival, of poverty, deprivation, and lack that characterized the marginal locations from which breakdancing and rap emerged. Described as "rituals" by participants in the poor urban non-white communities where they first took place, these practices offered individuals a means to gain public recognition and voice. Much of the psychic pain that black people experience daily in a white supremacist context is caused by dehumanizing oppressive forces, forces that render us invisible and deny us recognition. Michael H. (commenting on style in Stuart Ewen's book *All Consuming Images*) also talks about this desire for attention, stating that breakdancing and rap are a way to say "listen to my story, about myself, life, and romance." Rap music provides a public voice for young black men who are usually silenced and overlooked. It emerged in the street outside the confines of a domesticity shaped and informed by poverty, outside enclosed spaces where a young male's body had to be contained and controlled.

In its earliest stages, rap was "a male thing." Young black and brown males could not breakdance and rap in cramped living spaces. Male creativity, expressed in rap and dancing, required wide-open spaces, symbolic frontiers where the body could do its thing, expand, grow, and move, surrounded by a watching crowd. Domestic space, equated with repression and containment, as well as with the "feminine," was resisted and rejected so that an assertive patriarchal paradigm of competitive masculinity and its concomitant emphasis on physical prowess could emerge. As a result, much rap music is riddled with sexism and misogyny. The public story of black male lives narrated by rap music speaks directly to and against white racist domination, but only indirectly hints at the enormity of black male pain. Constructing the black male body as site of pleasure and power, rap and the dances associated with it suggest vibrancy, intensity, and an unsurpassed joy in living. It may very well be that living on the edge, so close to the possibility of being "exterminated" (which is how many young black males feel) heightens one's ability to risk and make one's pleasure more intense. It is this charge, generated by the tension between pleasure and danger, death and desire, that Foucault evokes when he speaks of that *complete total pleasure* that is related to death. Though Foucault is speaking as an individual, his words resonate in a culture affected by anhedonia—the inability to feel pleasure. In the United States, where our senses are daily assaulted and bombarded to such an extent that an emotional numbness sets in, it may take being "on the edge" for individuals to feel intensely. Hence the overall tendency in the culture is to see young black men as both dangerous and desirable.

Certainly the relationship between the experience of Otherness, of pleasure and death, is explored in the film *The Cook, the Thief, His Wife and Her Lover*, which critiques white male imperialist domination even though this dimension of the movie was rarely mentioned when it was discussed in this country. Reviewers of the film did not talk about the representation of black characters; one would have assumed from such writing that the cast was all white and British. Yet black males are a part of the community of subordinates who are dominated by one controlling white man. After he has killed her lover, his blonde white wife speaks to the dark-skinned cook, who clearly represents non–white immigrants, about the links between death and pleasure. It is he who explains to her the way blackness is viewed in the white imagination. The cook tells her that black foods are desired because they remind those who eat them of death, and that this is why they cost so much. When they are eaten (in the film, always and only by white people), the cook as native informant tells us it is a way to flirt with death, to flaunt one's power. He says that to eat black food is a way to say "death, I am eating you" and thereby conquering fear and acknowledging power. White racism, imperialism, and sexist domination prevail by courageous consumption. It is by eating the Other (in this case, death) that one asserts power and privilege.

A similar confrontation may be taking place within popular culture in this society as young white people seek contact with dark Others. They may long to conquer their fear of darkness and death. On the reactionary right, white youth may be simply seeking to affirm "white power" when they flirt with having contact with the Other. Yet there are many white youths who desire to move beyond whiteness. Critical of white imperialism and "into" difference, they desire cultural spaces where boundaries can be transgressed, where new and alternative relations can be formed. These desires are dramatized by two contemporary films, John Waters' *Hairspray* and the more recent film by Jim Jarmusch, *Mystery Train*. In *Hairspray*, the "cool" white people, working-class Traci and her middle class boyfriend, transgress class and race boundaries to dance with black folks. She says to him as they stand in a rat-infested alley with winos walking about, "I wish I was dark-skinned." And he replies, "Traci, our souls are black even though our skin is white." Blackness—the culture, the music, the people—is once again associated with pleasure as well as death and decay. Yet their recognition of the particular pleasures and sorrows black folks experience does not lead to cultural appropriation but to an appreciation that extends into the realm of the political— Traci dares to support racial integration. In this film, the longing and desire whites express for contact with black culture is coupled with the recognition of the culture's value. One does not transgress boundaries to stay the same, to reassert white domination. *Hairspray* is nearly unique in its attempt to construct a fictive universe where white working class "undesirables" are in solidarity with black people. When Traci says she wants to be black, blackness becomes a metaphor for freedom, an end to boundaries. Blackness is vital not because it represents the "primitive" but because it invites engagement in a revolutionary ethos that dares to challenge and disrupt the *status quo*. Like white rappers MC Search and Prime Minister Pete Nice who state that they "want to bring forth some sort of positive message to black people, that there are white people out there who understand what this is all about, who understand we have to get past all the hatred," Traci shifts her positionality to stand in solidarity with black people. She is concerned about her freedom and sees her liberation linked to black liberation and an effort to end racist domination.

Expressing a similar solidarity with the agenda of "liberation," which includes freedom to transgress, Sandra Bernhard, in her new film *Without You I'm Nothing*, also associates blackness with this struggle. In the March issue of *Interview* she says that the movie has "this whole black theme, which is like a personal metaphor for being on the outside." This statement shows that Bernhard's sense of blackness is both problematic and complex. The film opens with her pretending she is black. Dressed in African clothing, she renders problematic the question of race and identity, for this representation suggests that racial identity can be socially constructed even as it implies that cultural appropriation falls short because it is always imitation, fake. Conversely, she contrasts her attempt to be a black woman in drag with the black female's attempt to imitate a white female look. Bernhard's film suggests that alternative white culture derives its standpoint, its impetus from black culture. Identifying herself with marginalized Others, Bernhard's Jewish heritage as well as her sexually ambiguous erotic practices are experiences that already place her outside the mainstream. Yet the film does not clarify the nature of her identification with black culture. Throughout the film, she places herself in a relationship of comparison and competition with black women, seemingly exposing white female envy of black women and their desire to "be" imitation black women; yet she also pokes fun at black females. The unidentified black woman who appears in the film, like a phantom, looking at herself in the mirror has no name and no voice. Yet her image is always contrasted with that of Bernhard. Is she the fantasy Other Bernhard desires to become? Is she the fantasy Other Bernhard desires? The last scene of the film seems to confirm that black womanhood is the yardstick Bernhard uses to measure herself. Though she playfully suggests in the film that the work of black women singers like Nina Simone and Diana Ross is derivative, "stolen" from her work, this inversion of reality ironically calls attention to the way white women have "borrowed" from black women without acknowledging the debt they owe. In many ways, the film critiques white cultural appropriation of "blackness" that leaves no trace. Indeed, Bernhard identifies that she had her artistic beginnings working in black clubs, among black people. Though acknowledging where she is coming from, the film shows Bernhard clearly defining an artistic performance space that only she as a white woman can inhabit. Black women have no public, paying audience for our funny imitations of white girls. Indeed, it is difficult to imagine any setting other than an all black space where black women could use comedy to critique and ridicule white womanhood in the way Bernhard mocks black womanhood.

Closing the scene shrouded in a cloak that resembles an American flag, Bernhard unveils her nearly nude body. The film ends with the figure of the black woman, who has heretofore only been in the background, foregrounded as the only remaining audience watching this seductive performance. As though she is seeking acknowledgment of her identity, her power, Bernhard stares at the black woman, who returns her look with a contemptuous gaze. As if this look of disinterest and dismissal is not enough to convey her indifference she removes a tube of red lipstick from her purse and writes on the table "fuck Sandra Bernhard." Her message seems to be: "you may need black culture since without us you are nothing, but black women have no need of you." In the film, all the white women strip, flaunt their sexuality, and appear to be directing their attention to a black male gaze. It is this standpoint that the film suggests may lead them to ignore black women and only notice what black women think of them when we are "right up in their face."

Bernhard's film walks a critical tightrope. On one hand it mocks white appropriation of black culture, white desire for black (as in the scene where Bernhard with a blonde white girl persona is seen being "boned" by a black man whom we later find is mainly concerned about his hair—i.e., his own image) even as the film works as spectacle largely because of the clever ways Bernhard "uses" black culture and standard racial stereotypes. Since so many of the representations of blackness in the film are stereotypes it does not really go against the Hollywood cinematic grain. And like the *Tweeds* catalogue on Egypt, ultimately black people are reduced, as Bernhard declares in *Interview*, to a "personal metaphor." Blackness is the backdrop of Otherness she uses to insist on and clarify her status as Other, as cool, hip, and transgressive. Even though she lets audiences know that as an entertainment "rookie" she had her start working in close association with black people, the point is to name where she begins to highlight how far she has come. When Bernhard "arrives," able to exploit Otherness in a big time way, she arrives alone, not in the company of black associates. They are scenery, backdrop, background. Yet the end of the film problematizes this leave-taking. Is Bernhard leaving blackfolks or has she been rejected and dismissed? Maybe it's mutual. Like her entertainment cohort Madonna, Bernhard leaves her encounters with the Other richer than she was at the onset. We have no idea how the Other leaves her.

When I began thinking and doing research for this piece, I talked to folks from various locations about whether they thought the focus on race, Otherness, and difference in mass culture was challenging racism. There was overall agreement that the message that acknowledgment and exploration of racial difference can be pleasurable represents a breakthrough, a challenge to white supremacy, to various systems of domination. The over-riding fear is that cultural, ethnic, and racial differences will be continually commodified and offered up as new dishes to enhance the white palate—that the Other will be eaten, consumed, and forgotten. After weeks of debating with one another about the distinction between cultural appropriation and cultural appreciation, students in my introductory course on black literature were convinced that something radical was happening, that these issues were "coming out in the open." Within a context where desire for contact with those who are different or deemed Other is not considered bad, politically incorrect, or wrong-minded, we can begin to conceptualize and identify ways that desire informs our political choices and affiliations. Acknowledging ways the desire for pleasure, and that includes erotic longings, informs our politics, our understanding of difference, we may know better how desire disrupts, subverts, and makes resistance possible. We cannot, however, accept these new images uncritically.

References

Baudrillard, Jean. (1990). *Fatal Strategies.* New York: Autonomedia.
Ewen, Stuart. (1990). *All Consuming Images: The Politics of Style in Contemporary Culture.* New York: Basic.

Ewen, Stuart and Elizabeth Ewen. (1982). *Channels of Desire: Mass Images and the Shaping of American Consciousness.* New York: McGraw Hill.

Foster, Hal. (1985). *Recoding: Art, Spectacle, Cultural Politics.* Seattle: Bay Press.

Hansberry, Lorraine. (1972). *Les Blancs: The Collected Last Plays of Lorraine Hansberry.* Ed. Robert Nemiroff. New York: Random House.

Keen, Sam. (1983). *The Passionate Life.* San Francisco: Harper.

Perry, Steve. "The Politics of Crossover." [*Editors' note:* Source not available.]

Rosaldo, Renato. (1989). *Culture & Truth: The Remaking of Social Analysis.* Boston: Beacon.

Ross, Andrew. (1989). "Hip, and the Long Front of Color." In *No Respect: Intellectuals and Popular Culture.* New York: Routledge.

Scarry, Elaine. (1985). *The Body in Pain: The Making and Unmaking of the World.* New York: Oxford University Press.

Torgovnick, Marianna. (1990). *Gone Primitive: Savage Intellects, Moderns Lives.* Chicago: University of Chicago Press.

Winant, Howard. (1990). "Postmodern Racial Politics in the United States." *Socialist Review* 20. 1: 121–47.

CHAPTER NINE

Feminist Criticism, "The Yellow Wallpaper," and the Politics of Color in America

Susan S. Lanser

> "The difference between mad people and sane people," Brave Orchid explained to the children, "is that sane people have variety when they talk-story. Mad people have only one story that they talk over and over."
>
> — *Maxine Hong Kingston,* The Woman Warrior: Memoirs of a Girlhood among Ghosts, p. 184

I n 1973, a new publishing house with the brave name of The Feminist Press reprinted in a slim volume Charlotte Perkins Gilman's "The Yellow Wallpaper," first published in 1892 and out of print for half a century. It is the story of an unnamed woman confined by her doctor-husband to an attic nursery with barred windows and a bolted-down bed. Forbidden to write, the narrator-protagonist becomes obsessed with the room's wallpaper, which she finds first repellent and then riveting; on its chaotic surface she eventually deciphers an imprisoned woman whom she attempts to liberate by peeling the paper off the wall. This brilliant tale of a white, middle-class wife driven mad by a patriarchy controlling her "for her own good" has become an American feminist classic; in 1987, the Feminist Press edition numbered among the ten best-selling works of fiction published by a university press.[1]

The canonization of "The Yellow Wallpaper" is an obvious sign of the degree to which contemporary feminism has transformed the study of literature. But Gilman's story is not simply one to which feminists have "applied" ourselves; it is one of the texts through which white, American academic feminist criticism has constituted its terms.[2] My purpose here is to take stock of this criticism through the legacy of "The Yellow Wallpaper" in order to honor the work each has fostered and to call into question the status of Gilman's story—and the story of academic feminist criticism—as sacred texts.[3] In this process I am working from the inside, challenging my own reading of "The Yellow Wallpaper," which had deepened but not changed direction since 1973.

Susan Lanser, "Feminist Criticism: 'The Yellow Wallpaper,' and the Politics of Color in America," *Feminist Studies* 15:3(1989):414–41. Reprinted by permission.

My inquiry will make explicit use of six well-known studies of "The Yellow Wallpaper," but I consider these six to articulate an interpretation shared by a much larger feminist community. The pieces I have in mind are written by Elaine Hedges, Sandra Gilbert and Susan Gubar, Annette Kolodny, Jean Kennard, Paula Treichler, and Judith Fetterley, respectively, and their publication dates span from 1973 to 1986.[4] Reading these essays as a body, I am struck by a coherence that testifies to a profound unity in white, American feminist criticism across apparent diversity.[5] That is, although Hedges is concerned primarily with biography, Gilbert and Gubar with female authorship, Treichler with textual form, and Fetterley, Kolodny, and Kennard with interpretation, and although each discussion illuminates the text in certain unique ways, the six readings are almost wholly compatible, with one point of difference which is never identified as such and to which I will return. I will also return later to the significance of this redundancy and to the curiously unchallenged, routine elision from nearly all the discussion of one of the story's key tropes.

The theoretical positions that "The Yellow Wallpaper" helped to shape and perhaps reify may be clearer if we recall some of the critical claims with which U.S. academic feminist criticism began. In the late sixties and early seventies, some academic women, most of them trained in Anglo-American methods and texts, began to take a new look at those works by men and a few white women that comprised the standard curriculum. The earliest scholarship—Kathryn Rogers' *The Troublesome Helpmate* (1966), Mary Ellmann's *Thinking About Women* (1968), Kate Millett's *Sexual Politics* (1970), Elaine Showalter's "Women Writers and the Double Standard" (in *Women in Sexist Society*, 1971)—was asserting against prevailing New Critical neutralities that literature is deeply political, indeed steeped in (patriarchal) ideology. Ideology, feminists argued, makes what is cultural seem natural and inevitable, and what had come to seem natural and inevitable to literary studies was that its own methods and great books transcended ideology.[6]

This conception of literature as a privileged medium for universal truths was defended by the counterclaim that those who found a work's content disturbing or offensive were letting their "biases" distract them from the aesthetic of literature.[7] Feminist criticism was bound to challenge this marginalization of social content and to argue that literary works both reflect and constitute structures of gender and power. In making this challenge, feminist criticism was implying that canonical literature was not simply *mimesis*, a mirror of the way things are or the way men and women are, but *semiosis*—a complex system of conventional (androcentric) tropes. And by questioning the premises of the discipline, feminists were of course arguing that criticism, too, is political, that no methodology is neutral, and that literary practice is shaped by cultural imperatives to serve particular ends.[8] Although the word "deconstruction" was not yet in currency, these feminist premises inaugurated the first major opposition to both (old) scholarly and (New) critical practices, generating what has become the most widespread deconstructive imperative in the American academy.

Yet the feminist project involved, as Gayle Greene and Coppélia Kahn have put it, not only "deconstructing dominant male patterns of thought and social practice" but also "reconstructing female experience previously hidden or overlooked."[9] In the early 1970s, the rediscovery of "lost" works like "The Yellow Wallpaper," Kate Chopin's *The Awakening,* and Susan Glaspell's "A Jury of Her Peers" offered not only welcome respite from unladylike assaults on patriarchal practices and from discouraging expositions of androcentric "images of women in literature" but also an exhilarating basis for reconstructing literary theory and literary history. The fact that these works which feminists now found so exciting and powerful had been denounced, ignored, or suppressed seemed virtual proof of the claim that literature, criticism, and history were political. The editor of the *Atlantic Monthly* had rejected "The Yellow Wallpaper" because "I could not forgive myself if I made others as miserable as I have made myself!"[10] Even when William Dean Howells reprinted Gilman's story in 1920 he wrote that it was "terrible and too wholly dire," "too terribly good to be printed."[11] Feminists could argue convincingly that Gilman's contemporaries, schooled on the "terrible" and "wholly dire" tales of Poe, were surely balking at something more particular: the "graphic" representation of "'raving lunacy'" in a middle-class mother and wife that revealed the rage of the woman on a pedestal.[12]

As a tale openly preoccupied with questions of authorship, interpretation, and textuality, "The Yellow Wallpaper" quickly assumed a place of privilege among rediscovered feminist works, raising basic questions about writing and reading as gendered practices. The narrator's double-voiced discourse—the ironic understatements, asides, hedges, and negations through which she asserts herself against the power of John's voice—came for some critics to represent "women's language" or the "language of the powerless."[13] With its discontinuities and staccato paragraphs, Gilman's narrative raised the controversial question of a female aesthetic; and the "lame uncertain curves," "outrageous angles," and "unheard of contradictions" of the wallpaper came for many critics to symbolize both Gilman's text and, by extension, the particularity of female form.[14] The story also challenged theories of genius that denied the material conditions—social, economic, psychological and literary—that make writing (im)possible, helping feminists to turn questions like "Where is your Shakespeare?" back upon the questioners. Gilbert and Gubar, for example, saw in the narrator's struggles against censorship *"the* story that all literary women would tell if they could speak their 'speechless woe.'"[15]

"The Yellow Wallpaper" has been evoked most frequently, however, to theorize about reading through the lens of a "female" consciousness. Gilman's story has been a particularly congenial medium for such a revision not only because the narrator herself engages in a form of feminist interpretation when she tries to read the paper on her wall but also because turn-of-the-century readers seem to have ignored or avoided the connection between the narrator's condition and patriarchal politics, instead praising the story for its keenly accurate "case study" of a presumably inherited insanity. In the contemporary feminist reading, on the other hand, sexual oppression is evident from the start: the phrase "John says" heads a litany of "benevolent" prescriptions that keep the narrator infantilized, immobilized, and bored literally out of her mind. Reading or writing her self upon the wallpaper allows the narrator, as Paula Treichler puts it, to "escape" her husband's "sentence" and to achieve the limited freedom of madness which, virtually all these critics have agreed, constitutes a kind of sanity in the face of the insanity of male dominance.

This reading not only recuperated "The Yellow Wallpaper" as a feminist text but also reconstituted the terms of interpretation itself. Annette Kolodny theorized that emerging feminist consciousness made possible a new, female-centered interpretive paradigm that did not exist for male critics at the turn of the century. Defining that paradigm more specifically, Jean Kennard maintained that the circulation of feminist conventions associated with four particular concepts—"patriarchy, madness, space, quest"—virtually ensured the reading that took place in the 1970s. Furthermore, the premise that "we engage not texts but paradigms,"[16] as Kolodny puts it in another essay, explodes the belief that we are reading what is "there." Reading becomes the product of those conventions or strategies we have learned through an "interpretive community"—Stanley Fish's term to which Kolodny and Kennard give political force; to read is to reproduce a text according to this learned system or code.

These gender-based and openly ideological theories presented a radical challenge to an academic community in which "close reading" has remained the predominant critical act. A theory of meaning grounded in the politics of reading destabilizes assumptions of interpretive validity and shifts the emphasis to the contexts in which meanings are produced. A text like "The Yellow Wallpaper" showed that to the extent that we remain unaware of our interpretive conventions, it is difficult to distinguish "*what* we read" from "how we have learned to read it."[17] We experience meaning as given in "the text itself." When alternative paradigms inform our reading, we are able to read texts differently or, to put it more strongly, to read different texts. This means that traditional works may be transformed through different interpretive strategies into new literature just as patriarchy's "terrible" and repellent "Yellow Wallpaper" was dramatically transformed into feminism's endlessly fascinating tale.

It is, I believe, this powerful theoretical achievement occasioned by "The Yellow Wallpaper" that has led so much critical writing on the story to a triumphant conclusion despite the narrator's own unhappy fate. I have found it striking that discussions of the text so frequently end by distinguishing the doomed and "mad" narrator, who could not write her way out of the patriarchal prison-house, from the sane survivor Charlotte Perkins Gilman, who could.[18] The crucial shift from narrator to author, from story to text, may also serve to wrest readers from an unacknowledged over-identification with the narrator-protagonist. For just as the narrator's initial horror at the wallpaper is mirrored in the earlier critics' horror at Gilman's text, so now-traditional feminist re-readings may be reproducing the narrator's next move: her relentless pursuit of a single meaning on the wall. I want to go further still and suggest that feminist criticism's own persistent return to the "Wallpaper"—indeed, to specific aspects of the "Wallpaper"—signifies a somewhat uncomfortable need to isolate and validate a particular female experience, a particular relationship between reader and writer, and a particular notion of subjectivity as bases for the writing and reading of (women's) texts. Fully acknowledging the necessity of the feminist reading of "The Yellow Wallpaper" which I too have produced and perpetuated for many years, I now wonder whether many of us have repeated the gesture of the narrator who *"will* follow that pointless pattern to some sort of conclusion" (p. 19)—who will read until she finds what she is looking for—no less and no more. Although—or because—we have read "The Yellow Wallpaper" over and over, we may have stopped short, and our readings, like the narrator's, may have reduced the text's complexity to what we need most: our own image reflected back to us.

Let me return to the narrator's reading of the paper in order to clarify this claim. The narrator is faced with an unreadable text, a text for which none of her interpretive strategies is adequate. At first she is confounded by its contradictory style: it is "flamboyant" and "pronounced," yet also "lame," "uncertain," and "dull" (p. 13). Then she notices different constructions in different places. In one "recurrent spot" the pattern "lolls," in another place "two breadths didn't match," and elsewhere the pattern is torn off (p. 16). She tries to organize the paper geo-metrically but cannot grasp its laws: it is marked vertically by "bloated curves and flourishes," diagonally by "slanting waves of optic horror like a lot of wal-lowing seaweeds in full chase," and horizontally by an order she cannot even fig-ure out. There is even a centrifugal pattern in which "the interminable grotesques seem to form around a common centre and rush off in headlong plunges of equal distraction" (p. 20). Still later, she notices that the paper changes and moves ac-cording to different kinds of light (p. 25). And it has a color and smell that she is never able to account for. But from all this indecipherability, from this immensely complicated text, the narrator—by night, no less—finally discerns a single image, a woman behind bars, which she then expands to represent the whole. This is hardly a matter of "correct" reading, then, but of fixing and reducing possibili-ties, finding a space of text on which she can locate whatever self-projection will enable her to move from "John says" to "I want." The very excess of description of the wallpaper, and the fact that it continues after the narrator has first identi-fied the woman behind the bars, actually foregrounds the seductiveness of her interpretive act. And if the narrator, having liberated the paper woman, can only imagine tying her up again, is it possible that our reading too has freed us mo-mentarily only to bind us once more?

Most feminist analyses of "The Yellow Wallpaper" have in fact recognized this bind without pursuing it. Gilbert and Gubar see the paper as "otherwise in-comprehensible hieroglyphics" onto which the narrator projects "her own pas-sion for escape."[19] Treichler notes that the wallpaper "remains indeterminate, complex, unresolved, disturbing."[20] Even Fetterley, who seems least to question the narrator's enterprise, speaks of the narrator's "need to impose order on the 'impertinence' of row after row of unmatched breadths."[21] Kolodny implicates all critical practice when she says that the narrator obsessively and jealously "em-phasiz[es] one section of the pattern while repressing others, reorganiz[es] and regroup[s] past impressions into newer, more fully realized configurations—*as one might with any complex formal text.*"[22] And Kennard states openly that much more goes on in both the wallpaper and the story than is present in the standard account and that the feminist reading of "The Yellow Wallpaper" is far from the final and "correct" one that replaces the patriarchal "misreading" once and for all. Still, Kennard's position in 1981 was that "despite all these objections . . . it is the feminist reading I teach my students and which I believe is the most fruitful"; although suggesting that a new interpretive community might read this and other stories differently, she declined to pursue the possibility on grounds of insufficient "space"—a term that evokes the narrator's own confinement.[23] In light of these more-or-less conscious recognitions that the wallpaper remains incompletely read, the redundancy of feminist readings of Gilman's story might well constitute the return of the repressed.

I want to suggest that this repressed possibility of another reading reveals larger contradictions in white, academic feminist theories and practices. Earlier I named as the two basic gestures of U.S. feminist criticism "deconstructing dominant male patterns of thought and social practice" and "reconstructing female experience previously hidden or overlooked." This formulation posits as oppositional an essentially false and problematic "male" system beneath which essentially true and unproblematic "female" essences can be recovered—just as the figure of the woman can presumably be recovered from beneath the patriarchal pattern on Gilman's narrator's wall (a presumption to which I will return). In designating gender as the foundation for two very different critical activities, feminist criticism has embraced contradictory theories of literature, proceeding as if men's writings were ideological sign systems and women's writings were representations of truth, reading men's or masculinist texts with resistance and women's or feminist texts with empathy. If, however, we acknowledge the participation of women writers and readers in "dominant . . . patterns of thought and social practice," then perhaps our own patterns must also be deconstructed if we are to recover meanings still "hidden or overlooked." We would then have to apply even to feminist texts and theories the premises I described earlier: that literature and criticism are collusive with ideology, that texts are sign systems rather than simple mirrors, that authors cannot guarantee their meanings, that interpretation is dependent on a critical community, and that our own literary histories are also fictional. The consequent rereading of texts like "The Yellow Wallpaper" might, in turn, alter our critical premises.

It is understandably difficult to imagine deconstructing something one has experienced as a radically reconstructive enterprise. This may be one reason—though other reasons suggest more disturbing complicities—why many of us have often accepted in principle but ignored in practice the deconstructive challenges that have emerged from within feminism itself. Some of the most radical of these challenges have come from women of color, poor women, and lesbians, frequently with primary allegiances outside the university, who have exposed in what has passed for feminist criticism blindnesses as serious as those to which feminism was objecting. In 1977, for example, Barbara Smith identified racism in some of the writings on which feminist criticism had been founded; in 1980, Alice Walker told the National Women's Studies Association of her inability to convince the author of *The Female Imagination* to consider the imaginations of women who are Black; in 1978, Judy Grahn noted the "scathing letters" the Women's Press Collective received when it published Sharon Isabell's *Yesterday's Lessons* without standardizing the English for a middle-class readership; at the 1976 Modern Language Association meetings and later in *Signs*, Adrienne Rich pointed to the erasure of lesbian identity from feminist classrooms even when the writers being taught were in fact lesbians; in the early 1980s, collections like *This Bridge Called My Back: Writings by Radical Women of Color* and *Nice Jewish Girls: A Lesbian Anthology* insisted that not all American writers are Black or white; they are also Latina, Asian, Arab, Jewish, Indian.[24]

The suppression of difference has affected the critical canon as well. In 1980, for example, *Feminist Studies* published Annette Kolodny's groundbreaking "Dancing Through the Minefield: Some Observations on the Theory, Practice, and Politics of a Feminist Literary Criticism" to which my own elucidation of feminist premises owes a considerable and respectful debt. In Fall 1982, *Feminist Studies* published three responses to Kolodny, criticizing the essay not only for classism, racism, and homophobia in the selection and use of women's texts but also for perpetuating patriarchal academic values and methodologies. One respondent, Elly Bulkin, identified as a crucial problem "the very social and ethical issue of *which* women get published by whom and why—of what even gets *recognized* as 'feminist literary criticism.'"[25] Bulkin might have been speaking prophetically, because none of the three responses was included when "Dancing Through the Minefield" was anthologized.[26]

All these challenges occurred during the same years in which the standard feminist reading of "The Yellow Wallpaper" was produced and reproduced. Yet none of us seems to have noticed that virtually all feminist discourse on "The Yellow Wallpaper" has come from white academics and that it has failed to question the story's status as a universal woman's text. A feminist criticism willing to deconstruct its own practices would re-examine our exclusive reading of "The Yellow Wallpaper," rethink the implications of its canonization, and acknowledge both the text's position in ideology and our own. That a hard look at feminism's "Yellow Wallpaper" is now possible is already evident by the publication in 1986 of separate essays by Janice Haney-Peritz and Mary Jacobus which use psychoanalytic theory to expose the limits of both the narrator's and feminist criticism's interpretive acts.[27] I believe we have also entered a moment not only of historical possibility but of historical urgency to stop reading a privileged, white, New England woman's text as simply—a woman's text. If our traditional gesture has been to repeat the narrator's own act of underreading, of seeing too little, I want now to risk overreading, seeing perhaps too much. My reading will make use of textual details that traditional feminist interpretations have tended to ignore, but I do not propose it as a coherent or final reading; I believe no such reading is either possible or desirable and that one important message of "The Yellow Wallpaper" is precisely that. At the same time, I concur with Chris Weedon when she insists that meanings, however provisional, "have real effects."[28]

One way back to "The Yellow Wallpaper" is through the yellow wallpaper itself: through what I mentioned earlier as the point of difference and the point of silence in the feminist interpretations I have been discussing here. I begin with the difference that occurs within and among otherwise consistent readings when critics try to identify just whose text or what kind of text the wallpaper represents. For Hedges and for Gilbert and Gubar, the wallpaper signifies the oppressive situation in which the woman finds herself; for Kolodny the paper is the narrator's "own psyche writ large"; for Treichler it is a paradigm of women's writing; and for Fetterley it is the husband's patriarchal text which, however, becomes increasingly feminine in form. Haney-Peritz alone confronts the contradiction, seeing the wallpaper as both John's and his wife's discourse, because the narrator "relies on the very binary oppositions" that structure John's text.[29]

It seems, then, that just as it is impossible for the narrator to get "that top pattern . . . off from the under one" (p. 31), so it is impossible to separate the text of a culture from the text of an individual, to free female subjectivity from the patriarchal text. Far from being antitheses, the patriarchal text and the woman's text are in some sense one. And if the narrator's text is also the text of her culture, then it is no wonder that the wallpaper exceeds her ability to decipher it. If, instead of grasping as she does for the single familiar and self-confirming figure in the text, we understand the wallpaper as a pastiche of disturbed and conflicting discourses, then perhaps the wallpaper's chaos represents what the narrator (and we ourselves) must refuse in order to construct the singular figure of the woman behind bars: the foreign and alien images that threaten to "knock [her] down, and trample upon [her]" (p. 25), images that as a white, middle-class woman of limited consciousness she may neither want nor know how to read. In avoiding certain meanings while "liberating" others from the text, in struggling for the illusion of a fully "conscious knowing, unified, rational subject,"[30] is the narrator going "mad" not only from confinement, or from the effort to interpret, but also from the effort to repress? In this case, are those of us who reproduce the narrator's reading also attempting to constitute an essential female subject by shunting aside textual meanings that expose feminism's own precarious and conflicted identity? If the narrator is reading in the paper the text of her own unconscious, an unconscious chaotic with unspeakable fears and desires, is not the unconscious, by the very nature of ideology, political?

If we accept the culturally contingent and incomplete nature of readings guaranteed only by the narrator's consciousness, then perhaps we can find in the yellow wallpaper, to literalize a metaphor of Adrienne Rich, "a whole new psychic geography to be explored."[31] For in privileging the questions of reading and writing as essential "woman questions," feminist criticism has been led to the paper while suppressing the politically charged adjective that colors it.[32] If we locate Gilman's story within the "psychic geography" of Anglo-America at the turn of the century, we locate it in a culture obsessively preoccupied with race as the foundation of character, a culture desperate to maintain Aryan superiority in the face of massive immigrations from Southern and Eastern Europe, a culture openly anti-Semitic, anti-Asian, anti-Catholic, and Jim Crow. In New England, where Gilman was born and raised, agricultural decline, native emigration, and soaring immigrant birth rates had generated "a distrust of the immigrant [that] reached the proportions of a movement in the 1880's and 1890's."[33] In California, where Gilman lived while writing "The Yellow Wallpaper," mass anxiety about the "Yellow Peril" had already yielded such legislation as the Chinese Exclusion Act of 1882. Across the United States, newly formed groups were calling for selective breeding, restricted entry, and "American Protection" of various kinds. White, Christian, American-born intellectuals—novelists, political scientists, economists, sociologists, crusaders for social reform—not only shared this racial anxiety but, as John Higham puts it, "blazed the way for ordinary nativists" by giving popular racism an "intellectual respectability."[34]

These "intellectual" writings often justified the rejection and exclusion of immigrants in terms graphically physical. The immigrants were "human garbage": "'hirsute, low-browed, big-faced persons of obviously low mentality,'" "oxlike men" who "belong in skins, in wattled huts at the close of the Great Ice age," ready to "pollute" America with "non-Aryan elements." Owen Wister's popular Westerns were built on the premise that the eastern United States was being ruined by the "debased and mongrel" immigrants, "encroaching alien vermin, that turn our cities to Babels and our citizenship to a hybrid farce, who degrade our commonwealth from a nation into something half pawn-shop, half broker's office." In the "clean cattle country," on the other hand, one did not find "many Poles or Huns or Russian Jews," because pioneering required particular Anglo-Saxon abilities. Jack London describes a Jewish character as "yellow as a sick persimmon" and laments America's invasion by "the dark-pigmented things, the half-castes, the mongrel-bloods." Frank Norris ridicules the "halfbreed" as an "amorphous, formless mist" and contrasts the kindness and delicacy of Anglo-Saxons with "the hot, degenerated blood" of the Spanish, Mexican, and Portuguese.[35]

Implicit or explicit in these descriptions is a new racial ideology through which "newcomers from Europe could seem a fundamentally different order" from what were then called "native Americans." The common nineteenth-century belief in three races—black, white, yellow—each linked to a specific continent, was reconstituted so that "white" came to mean only "Nordic" or Northern European, while "yellow" applied not only to the Chinese, Japanese, and light-skinned African-Americans but also to Jews, Poles, Hungarians, Italians, and even the Irish. Crusaders warned of "yellow inundation." The California chapter of the Protestant white supremacist Junior Order of United American Mechanics teamed up with the Asiatic Exclusion League to proclaim that Southern Europeans were "semi-Mongolian" and should be excluded from immigration and citizenship on the same basis as the Chinese; Madison Grant declared Jews to be "a Mongrel admixture . . . of Slavs and of Asiatic invaders of Russia"; and a member of Congress announced that "the color of thousands" of the new immigrants "differs materially from that of the AngloSaxon." The greatest dangers were almost always traced back to Asia; in a dazzling conflation of enemies, for example, Grant warned that "in the guise of Bolshevism with Semitic leadership and Chinese executioners, [Asia] is organizing an assault upon Western Europe." Lothrop Stoddard predicted that "colored migration" was yielding the "very immediate danger that the white stocks may be swamped by Asiatic blood." Again and again, nativists announced that democracy "simply will not work among Asiatics," that "non-Aryans," especially Slavs, Italians, and Jews, were "impossible to Americanize." The threat of "Yellow Peril" thus had "racial implications" much broader than anxiety about a takeover of Chinese or Japanese: "in every section, the Negro, the Oriental, and the Southern European appeared more and more in a common light."[36] In such a cultural moment, "yellow" readily connoted inferiority, strangeness, cowardice, ugliness, and backwardness. "Yellow-belly" and "yellow dog" were common slurs, the former applied to groups as diverse as the Irish and the Mexicans. Associations of "yellow" with disease, cowardice, worthlessness, uncleanliness, and decay may also have become implicit associations of race and class.[37]

If "The Yellow Wallpaper" is read within this discourse of racial anxiety, certain of its tropes take on an obvious political charge. The very first sentence constructs the narrator in class terms, imagining an America in which, through democratic self-advancement, common (British) Americans can enjoy upper-class (British) privileges. Although the narrator and John are "mere ordinary people" and not the rightful "heirs and coheirs," they have secured "a colonial mansion, a hereditary estate," in whose queerness she takes pride (p. 9); this house with its "private wharf" (p. 15) stands "quite alone . . . well back from the road, quite three miles from the village" like "English places that you read about, for there are hedges and walls and gates that lock, and lots of separate little houses for the gardeners and people" (p. 11). I am reminded by this description of another neglected "gentleman's manor house" that people "read about"—Thornfield—in which another merely ordinary woman "little accustomed to grandeur" comes to make her home. Charlotte Brontë's Jane Eyre is given a room with "gay blue chintz window curtains" that resemble the "pretty old-fashioned chintz hangings" (p. 12) in the room Gilman's narrator wanted for herself; Jane is not banished to Thornfield's third floor, where "wide and heavy beds" are surrounded by outlandish wall-hangings that portray "effigies of strange flowers, and stranger birds, and strangest human beings,—all of which would have looked strange, indeed, by the pallid gleam of moonlight"—and where, if Thornfield had ghosts, Jane tells us, these ghosts would haunt. Like Gilman's narrator, Jane longs for both the freedom to roam and the pleasures of human society, and her "sole relief" in those moments is to walk around the attic and look out at the vista of road and trees and rolling hills so much like the view the narrator describes from her nursery in the writing that is her own sole "relief" (pp. 10, 21). It is from her attic perch that Jane feels so keenly that women, like men, need "exercise for their faculties" and "suffer from too rigid a restraint,"[38] as in her attic Gilman's narrator lies on the "great immovable bed" (p. 19) and longs for company and exercise.

But the permanent, imprisoned inhabitant of Thornfield's attic is not Jane; she is a dark Creole woman who might well have been called "yellow" in Gilman's America. Is Gilman's narrator, who "thought seriously of burning the house" (p. 29) imagining Bertha Mason's fiery revenge? Does the figure in the paper with its "foul, bad yellow" color (p. 28), its "strange, provoking, formless sort of figure" (p. 18), its "broken neck" and "bulbous eyes" (p. 16), resemble Bertha with her "bloated features" and her "discoloured face"? Surely the narrator's crawling about her room may recall Bertha's running "backwards and forwards . . . on all fours." And like Brontë's "mad lady," who would "let herself out of her chamber" at night "and go roaming about the house" to ambush Jane,[39] the "smouldering" yellow menace in Gilman's story gets out at night and "skulk[s] in the parlor, [hides] in the hall," and "[lies] in wait for me" (pp. 13, 28–29). When the narrator tells John that the key to her room is beneath a plantain leaf, is she evoking not only the North American species of that name but also the tropical plant of Bertha's West Indies? When she imagines tying up the freed woman, is she repeating the fate of Bertha, brought in chains to foreign shores? Finally, does the circulation of Brontë's novel in Gilman's text explain the cryptic sentence at the end of the story—possibly a slip of Gilman's pen—in which the narrator cries to her husband that "I've got out at last . . . in spite of you and Jane" (p. 36)?

Is the wallpaper, then, the political unconscious of a culture in which an Aryan woman's madness, desire, and anger, repressed by the imperatives of "reason," "duty" (p. 14), and "proper self-control" (p. 11), are projected onto the "yellow" woman who is, however, also the feared alien? When the narrator tries to liberate the woman from the wall, is she trying to purge her of her color, to peel her from the yellow paper, so that she can accept this woman as herself? If, as I suggested earlier, the wallpaper is at once the text of patriarchy and the woman's text, then perhaps the narrator is both resisting and embracing the woman of color who is self and not-self, a woman who might need to be rescued from the text of patriarchy but cannot yet be allowed to go free. Might we explain the narrator's pervasive horror of a yellow color and smell that threaten to take over the "ancestral halls," "stain[ing] everything it touched," as the British-American fear of a takeover by "aliens"? In a cultural moment when immigrant peoples and African Americans were being widely caricatured in the popular press through distorted facial and bodily images, might the "interminable grotesques" (p. 20) of "The Yellow Wallpaper"—with their lolling necks and "bulbous eyes" "staring everywhere," with their "peculiar odor" and "yellow smell" (p. 29), their colors "repellent, almost revolting," "smouldering" and "unclean" (p. 13), "sickly" and "particularly irritating' (p. 18), their "new shades of yellow" (p. 28) erupting constantly—figure the Asians and Jews, the Italians and Poles, the long list of "aliens" whom the narrator (and perhaps Gilman herself) might want at once to rescue and to flee?

For if anxieties about race, class, and ethnicity have inscribed themselves as a political unconscious upon the yellow wallpaper, they were conscious and indeed obsessive problems for Gilman herself, as I discovered when, disturbed by my own reading of "The Yellow Wallpaper," I turned to Gilman's later work.[40] Despite her socialist values, her active participation in movements for reform, her strong theoretical commitment to racial harmony, her unconventional support of interracial marriages, and her frequent condemnation of America's racist history,[41] Gilman upheld white Protestant supremacy; belonged for a time to eugenics and nationalist organizations; opposed open immigration; and inscribed racism, nationalism, and classism into her proposals for social change. In *Concerning Children* (1900), she maintains that "a sturdy English baby would be worth more than an equally vigorous young Fuegian. With the same training and care, you could develop higher faculties in the English specimen than in the Fuegian specimen, because it was better bred."[42] In the same book, she argues that American children made "better citizens" than "the more submissive races" and in particular that "the Chinese and the Hindu, where parents are fairly worshipped and blindly obeyed," were "not races of free and progressive thought and healthy activity." Gilman advocated virtually compulsory enlistment of Blacks in a militaristic industrial corps, even as she opposed such regimentation for whites. In *The Fore-runner,* the journal she produced single-handedly for seven years, "yellow" groups are singled out frequently and gratuitously: Gilman chides the "lazy old orientals" who consider work a curse, singles out Chinatown for "criminal conditions," and uses China as an example of various unhealthy social practices. And she all but justifies anti-Semitism by arguing, both in her "own" voice and more boldly through her Herlandian mouthpiece Ellador, that Jews have not yet "'passed the tribal stage'" of human development, that they practice an "'unethical'" and "'morally degrading'" religion of "'race egotism'" and "'concentrated pride,'" which has unfortunately found its way through the Bible into Western literature, and that in refusing to intermarry they "'artifically maintain characteristics which the whole world dislikes, and then complain of race prejudice.'"[43]

Like many other "nativist" intellectuals, Gilman was especially disturbed by the influx of poor immigrants to American cities and argued on both race and class grounds that these "undesirables" would destroy America. Although she once theorized that immigrants could be "healthier grafts upon our body politic," she wrote later that whatever "'special gifts" each race had, when that race was transplanted, "their 'gift' is lost."[44] While proclaiming support for the admission of certain peoples of "assimilable stock," she declared that even the best of "Hindus . . . would make another problem" like the existing "problem" of African Americans, and that an "inflow" of China's "'oppressed'" would make it impossible to preserve the American "national character." This "character," it is clear, requires that "Americans" be primarily people "of native born parentage," who "should have a majority vote *in their own country.*"[45] Surprisingly perhaps for a socialist, but less surprisingly for a woman whose autobiography opens with a claim of kinship with Queen Victoria,[46] Gilman seems to equate class status with readiness for democracy. Repeatedly she claims to favor immigration so long as the immigrants are of "better" stock. In her futurist utopia, *Moving the Mountain,* for instance, a character remembers the "'old'" days when "'we got all the worst and lowest people'"; in the imaginary new America, immigrants may not enter the country until they "'come up to a certain standard'" by passing a "'microscopic'" physical exam and completing an education in American ways. It is surely no accident that the list of receiving gates Gilman imagines for her immigrant groups stops with Western Europe: "'There's the German Gate, and the Spanish Gate, the English Gate, and the Italian Gate—and so on.'"[47]

Classism, racism, and nationalism converge with particular virulence when Ellador, having established her antiracist credentials by championing the rights of Black Americans, observes that "'the poor and oppressed were not necessarily good stuff for a democracy'" and declares, in an extraordinary reversal of victim and victimizer to which even her American partner Van protests, that "'it is the poor and oppressed who make monarchy and despotism.'"[48] Ellador's triumph is sealed with the graphic insistence that you cannot "'put a little of everything into a meltingpot and produce a good metal,'" not if you are mixing "'gold, silver, copper and iron, lead, radium, pipe, clay, coal dust, and plain dirt.'" Making clear the racial boundaries of the melting pot, Ellador challenges Van, "'And how about the yellow? Do they 'melt'? Do you want them to melt? Isn't your exclusion of them an admission that you think some kinds of people unassimilable? That democracy must pick and choose a little?'" Ellador's rationale—and Gilman's—is that "'the human race is in different stages of development, and only some of the races—or some individuals in a given race—have reached the democratic stage.'" Yet she begs the question and changes the subject when Van asks, "'But how could we discriminate?'"[49]

The aesthetic and sensory quality of this horror at a polluted America creates a compelling resemblance between the narrator's graphic descriptions of the yellow wallpaper and Gilman's graphic descriptions of the cities and their "swarms of jostling aliens."[50] She fears that America has become "bloated" and "verminous," a "dump" for Europe's "social refuse," "a ceaseless offense to eye and ear and nose,"[51] creating "multiforeign" cities that are "abnormally enlarged" and "swollen," "foul, ugly and dangerous," their conditions "offensive to every sense: assailing the eye with ugliness, the ear with noise, the nose with foul smells."[52] And when she complains that America has "stuffed" itself with "uncongenial material," with an "overwhelming flood of unassimilable characteristics," with "such a stream of non-assimilable stuff as shall dilute and drown out the current of our life," indeed with "'the most illassorted and unassimilable mass of human material that was ever held together by artificial means,'" Gilman might be describing the patterns and pieces of the wallpaper as well.[53] Her poem "The City of Death" (1913) depicts a diseased prison "piped with poison, room by room,"

> Whose weltering rush of swarming human forms,
> Forced hurtling through foul subterranean tubes
> Kills more than bodies, coarsens mind and soul.
> . . .
> And steadily degrades our humanness . . .[54]

Such a city is not so different from the claustrophobic nursery which finally "degrades" the "humanness" of "The Yellow Wallpaper's" protagonist.

The text of Gilman's imagining, then, is the text of an America made as uninhabitable as the narrator's chamber, and her declaration that "children ought to grow up in the country, all of them,"[55] recalls the narrator's relief that her baby does not have to live in the unhappy prison at the top of the house. Clearly Gilman was recognizing serious social problems in her concern over the ghettos and tenements of New York and Chicago—she herself worked for a time at Hull House, although she detested Chicago's "noisome" neighborhoods. But her conflation of the city with its immigrant peoples repeats her own racism even as her nostalgia about the country harks back to a New England in the hands of the New English themselves.[56] These "'little old New England towns'" and their new counterparts, the "'fresh young western ones,'" says Ellador, "'have more of America in them than is possible—could ever be possible—in such a political menagerie as New York,'" whose people really "'belong in Berlin, in Dublin, in Jerusalem.'"[57]

It is no accident that some of the most extreme of Gilman's anti-immigrant statements come from the radical feminist Ellador, for race and gender are not separate issues in Gilman's cosmology, and it is in their intersection that a fuller reading of "The Yellow Wallpaper" becomes possible. For Gilman, patriarchy is a racial phenomenon: it is primarily non-Aryan "yellow" peoples whom Gilman holds responsible for originating and perpetuating patriarchal practices, and it is primarily Nordic Protestants whom she considers capable of change. In *The Man-Made World: or, Our Androcentric Culture*, Gilman associates the oppression of women with "the heavy millions of the unstirred East," and the "ancestorworship[ping]" cultures of the "old patriarchal races" who "linger on in feudal Europe." The text singles out the behaviors of "savage African tribes," laments the customs of India, names the "Moslem" religion as "rigidly bigoted and unchanging," and dismisses "to the limbo of all outworn superstition that false Hebraic and grossly androcentric doctrine that the woman is to be subject to the man."[58] Elsewhere, Gilman declares that except for "our Pueblos," where "the women are comparatively independent and honored," nearly all "savages" are "decadent, and grossly androcentric."[59] In one of two essays in *The Forerunner* attacking Ida Tarbell, Gilman identifies Tarbell's "androcentrism" as "neither more nor less than the same old doctrine held by India, China, Turkey, and all the ancient races, held by all ignorant peasants the world over; held by the vast mass of ordinary, unthinking people, and by some quite intelligent enough to know better: that the business of being a woman is to bear and rear children, to 'keep house,' and nothing else."[60] "The most progressive and dominant races" of the present day, she claims, are also "those whose women have most power and liberty; and in the feeblest and most backward races we find women most ill-treated and enslaved." Gilman goes on to make clear that this is an explicitly Aryan accomplishment: "The Teutons and Scandinavian stocks seem never to have had that period of enslaved womanhood, that polygamous harem culture; their women never went through that debasement; and their men have succeeded in preserving the spirit of freedom which is inevitably lost by a race which has servile women."[61] That the "progressive and dominant races" Gilman lauds for not "enslaving" women were at that very moment invading and oppressing countries around the globe seems to present Gilman with no contradiction at all; indeed, imperialism might provide the opportunity, to paraphrase Gayatri Spivak, to save yellow women from yellow men.[62]

In this light, Gilman's wallpaper becomes not only a representation of patriarchy but also the projection of patriarchal practices onto non-Aryan societies. Such a projection stands, of course, in implicit tension with the narrative, because it is the modern-minded, presumably Aryan husband and doctor who constitutes the oppressive force. But for Gilman, an educated, Protestant, social-democratic Aryan, America explicitly represented the major hope for feminist possibility. The superiority of this "wider and deeper" and "more human" of religions is directly associated with the fact that "in America the status of women is higher," for example, than in "Romanist" Spain.[63] Not all people are equally educable, after all, particularly if they belong to one of those "tribal" cultures of the East: "you could develop higher faculties in the English specimen than in the Fuegian." And Gilman's boast that "The Yellow Wallpaper" convinced S. Weir Mitchell to alter his practices suggests that like Van, the sociologist-narrator of two of Gilman's feminist utopias, educated, white Protestant men could be taught to change. The immigrant "invasion" thus becomes a direct threat to Gilman's program for feminist reform.

As a particular historical product, then, "The Yellow Wallpaper" is no more *"the* story that all literary women would tell" than the entirely white canon of *The Madwoman in the Attic* is *the* story of all women's writing or the only story those (white) texts can tell. "The Yellow Wallpaper" has been able to pass for a universal text only insofar as white, Western literatures and perspectives continue to dominate academic American feminist practices even when the most urgent literary and political events are happening in Africa, Asia, and Latin America, and among the new and old cultures of Color in the United States. We might expand our theories of censorship, for example, if we read "The Yellow Wallpaper" in the context of women's prison writings from around the world—writings like Ding Links memoirs and Alicia Partnoy's *The Little School: Tales of Disappearance and Survival in Argentina* and some of the stories of Bessie Head. We might have something to learn about interpretation if we examined the moment in Partnoy's narrative when her husband is tortured because he gives the "wrong" reading of his wife's poems.[64] We might better understand contemporary feminist racial politics if we studied the complex but historically distanced discourses of feminists a century ago.[65] Perhaps, like the narrator of Gilman's story, white, American academic feminist criticism has sought in literature the mirror of its own identity, erasing the literary equivalent of strange sights and smells and colors so that we can have the comfort of reproducing, on a bare stage, that triumphant moment when a woman recognizes her self. Perhaps white, American feminist practice too readily resembles that of Gilman, who deplores that historically "we have cheated the Indian, oppressed the African, robbed the Mexican,"[66] and whose utopian impulses continue to insist that there is only "one race, the human race,"[67] but for whom particular, present conditions of race and class continue to be blindnesses justified on "other"—aesthetic, political, pragmatic—grounds.

"The Yellow Wallpaper" also calls upon us to recognize that the white, female, intellectual-class subjectivity which Gilman's narrator attempts to construct, and to which many feminists have also been committed perhaps unwittingly, is a subjectivity whose illusory unity, like the unity imposed on the paper, is built on the repression of difference. This also means that the conscious biographical experience which Gilman claims as the authenticating source of the story is but one contributing element.[68] And if we are going to read this text in relation to its author, we may have to realize that there are dangers as well as pleasures in a feminist reading based on a merging of consciousnesses.[69] Once we recognize Gilman as a subject constituted in and by the contradictions of ideology, we might also remember that she acknowledges having been subjected to the narrator's circumstances but denies any relationship to the wallpaper itself—that is, to what I am reading as the site of a political unconscious in which questions of race permeate questions of sex. A recent essay by Ellen Messer-Davidow in *New Literary History* argues that literary criticism and feminist criticism should be recognized as fundamentally different activities, that feminist criticism is part of a larger interdisciplinary project whose main focus is the exploration of "ideas about sex and gender," that disciplinary variations are fairly insignificant differences of "medium," and therefore that feminist literary critics need to change their subject from "literature" to "ideas about sex and gender" as these happen to be expressed in literature.[70] I suggest that one of the messages of "The Yellow Wallpaper" is that textuality, like culture, is more complex, shifting, and polyvalent than any of the ideas we can abstract from it, that the narrator's reductive gesture is precisely to isolate and essentialize one "idea about sex and gender" from a more complex textual field.

Deconstructing our own reading of the wallpaper, then, means acknowledging that Adrienne Rich still speaks to feminist critics when she calls on us to "[enter] an old text from a new critical direction," to "take the work first of all as a clue to how we live . . . how we have been led to imagine ourselves, how our language has trapped as well as liberated us . . . and how we can begin to see and name—and therefore live—afresh," so that we do not simply "pass on a tradition but . . . break its hold over us."[71] Feminist critical theory offers the Reconstructive principles for this continuing revision, so long as we require ourselves, as we have required our non-feminist colleagues, to look anew at what have become old texts and old critical premises. Still, the revision I am proposing here would have been impossible without the first revision of "The Yellow Wallpaper" that liberated the imprisoned woman from the text. Adrienne Rich has addressed the poem "Heroines" to nineteenth-century white feminists who reflected racism and class privilege in their crusades for change. It is both to Gilman herself and to all of us whose readings of "The Yellow Wallpaper" have been both transformative and limiting, that, in closing, I address the final lines of Rich's poem:

> How can I fail to love
>   your clarity and fury
> how can I give you
>   all your due
>   take courage from your courage
> honor your exact
>   legacy as it is
> recognizing
>   as well
>   that it is not enough?[72]

Notes

1. In an 11 Oct. 1987 *New York Times Book Review* listing of the best-selling works of university-press fiction for the past twenty-five years, "The Yellow Wallpaper" ranked seventh (145,000 copies) and Zora Neale Hurston's *Their Eyes Were Watching God* ranked fourth (240,000 copies). These figures are all the more astonishing, because these two books have been in print for considerably less than twenty-five years and "The Yellow Wallpaper" is also reprinted in several anthologies. The top entries are Eugene O'Neill's *Long Day's Journey into Night* (900,500 copies), Tom Clancy's *The Hunt for Red October* (358,000 copies), and Ovid's *Metamorphoses* (304,278 copies).
2. I use the term "American" here to refer not to the nationality of practitioners but to a

set of practices that has dominated the discourse of feminist criticism in U.S. universities during the 1970s and into the 1980s. Elaine Showalter's *New Feminist Criticism* (New York: Pantheon, 1985) offers a representative collection of this work. When I say "academic," I mean a criticism aligned predominantly with professional-class interests and produced primarily for academic settings: "scholarly" journals, university presses, classrooms, conferences, colloquia.

3. Janice Haney-Peritz and Mary Jacobus have also written critiques of feminism's "Yellow Wallpaper." I thank the anonymous reviewer of my essay for *Feminist Studies* for introducing me to Jacobus' essay, which I had not seen before submitting this paper. I will discuss the two essays more specifically below.

4. The six critical studies, in chronological order, are Elaine Hedges, "Afterword" to The Feminist Press edition of "The Yellow Wallpaper" (Old Westbury, N.Y.: The Feminist Press, 1973), 37–63; Sandra Gilbert and Susan Gubar, *The Madwoman in the Attic: The Woman Writer and the Nineteenth-Century Literary Imagination* (New Haven: Yale University Press, 1979, 89–92; Annette Kolodny, "A Map for Re-Reading: Or, Gender and the Interpretation of Literary Texts," *New Literary History* 11 (Spring 1980): 451–67; Jean Kennard, "Convention Coverage or How to Read Your Own Life," *New Literary History* 13 (Autumn 1981): 69–88; Paula Treichler, "Escaping the Sentence," *Tulsa Studies in Women's Literature* 3 (Spring/Fall 1984): 61–77; Judith Fetterley, "Reading about Reading: 'A Jury of Her Peers,' 'The Murderers in the Rue Morgue,' and 'The Yellow Wallpaper,'" in *Gender and Reading: Essays on Readers, Texts, and Contexts,* ed. Elizabeth Flynn and Patrocinio Schweikart (Baltimore: Johns Hopkins, 1986), 147–64. Similar, often briefer readings abound.

5. Kennard's essay is based precisely on this recognition of unity: she writes in 1981 that although her interpretation, Gilbert and Gubar's, Hedges', and Kolodny's all "emphasize different aspects of the text, they do not conflict with each other" (p. 74).

6. Although "ideology" is now in currency through European theory, American feminism also used the term to designate what Catherine Belsey describes as the unacknowledged underpinnings of our social, political, intellectual, sexual, and emotional lives, our "imaginary relation" to real conditions, which presents "partial truths," smooths contradictions, and "appears to provide answers to questions which in reality it evades" (see her *Critical Practice* [London: Methuen, 1980], 57–58). For an early use of "ideology" as a feminist concept, see Sandra Bem and Daryl Bem, "Case Study of a Nonconscious Ideology: Training a Woman to Know her Place," in *Beliefs, Attitudes, and Human Affairs,* ed. Daryl Bem (Brooks/Cole Publishing Company, 1970) 89–99.

7. Certainly these values linger. One of the most revealing defenses of the now-old New Criticism appeared in a 10 July 1988 letter by John W. Aldridge responding to *The New York Times Magazine's* essay of 5 June 1988, "The Battle of the Books":

> Our mission—if it had ever been defined—was to identify and promote the most artistically successful and esthetically satisfying works produced in that culture. It was also part of our mission to work as critics to try to educate public taste so as to be better able to make esthetic discriminations among contemporary works—in particular, to develop appreciation for neglected writers and to reexamine the work of those whose reputations had become overinflated. In the service of the first, we had Malcolm Cowley on Faulkner, Edmund Wilson on the early Hemingway, Cleanth Brooks on T S Eliot, and Eliot on the metaphysical poets. In the service of the second, we had Wilson on Kafka and murder mysteries, Dwight Macdonald on James Gould Cozzens, Norman Podhoretz on the Beats, and, in more recent years, if I may say so, myself writing negatively on John Updike, Mary McCarthy, William Styron, James Baldwin, and some others. . . .
>
> I do not believe that once in this long course of reassessment were considerations of an

author's race, sex, politics, religion or ethnic origin allowed to intrude upon the process of critical judgment. All this is to say that criticism must, to deserve the name, be impartial and politically disinterested. When it ceases to be by yielding to external pressures, it abdicates its primary reponsibility as a monitor and conservator of taste. (P. 6)

8. In an essay that precedes Terry Eagleton's *Literary Theory* by a decade, for example,
   Fraya Katz-Stoker read in the agenda of New Criticism not only the attempt to hold
   poetry to a coherence absent in an era of fascism, McCarthyism, and world war but
   also an imposition on literature of the same political stance it sought to ignore. See
   "The Other Criticism: Feminism vs. Formalism," in *Images of Women in Fiction*, ed. Susan Koppelman Cornillon (Bowling Green, Ohio: Popular Press, 1972), 315–27.

9. Gayle Greene and Coppélia Kahn, "Feminist Scholarship and the Social Construction
   of Woman," in *Making a Difference: Feminist Literary Criticism*, ed. Gayle Greene and
   Coppélia Kahn (London: Methuen, 1985), 6.

10. Cited in Charlotte Perkins Gilman, *The Living of Charlotte Perkins Gilman* (New York:
    D. Appleton, 1935), 119.

11. The story was reprinted in *The Great Modern American Stories: An Anthology* (New York:
    Boni & Liveright, 1920), vii; William Dean Howells, cited in Conrad Shumaker, "'Too
    Terribly Good to be Printed': Charlotte Gilman's 'The Yellow Wallpaper,'" *American
    Literature* 57 (December 1985): 588.

12. Anonymous letter to the Boston *Transcript*, cited in Gilman, *The Living of Charlotte
    Perkins Gilman*, 120.

13. On the difference between these terms, see William M. O'Barr and Bowman K. Atkins,
    "'Women's Language' or 'Powerless Language'?" in *Women and Language in Literature
    and Society*, ed. Sally McConnell-Ginet, Ruth Borker, and Nelly Furman (New York:
    Praeger, 1980), 93–110. On double-voiced "coding"strategies, see Joan Radner and Su-
    san Lanser, "The Feminist Voice: Coding in Women's Folklore and Literature," *Jour-
    nal of American Folklore* 100 (October 1987): 412–25.

14. Charlotte Perkins Gilman, *The Yellow Wallpaper* (Old Westbury, N.Y.: The Feminist
    Press, 1973), 13. All references are to this edition; further citations appear in paren-
    thesis in the text.

15. Gilbert and Gubar, 89.

16. Kennard, 74; Annette Kolodny, "Dancing through the Minefield: Some Observations
    on the Theory, Practice, and Politics of a Feminist Literary Criticism," *Feminist Studies*
    6 (Spring 1980): 10.

17. Ibid., 12.

18. See, for example, Fetterley, 164; Gilbert and Gubar, 91–92; Hedges, 55; Treichler, 68–69.

19. Gilbert and Gubar, 90.

20. Treichler, 73.

21. Fetterley, 162.

22. Kolodny, "Map for Re-Reading," 458 (emphasis mine).

23. Kennard, 78, 84.

24. Barbara Smith, "Toward a Black Feminist Criticism," *Conditions Two* (October 1977):
    29–30; rpt. in *The New Feminist Criticism*, 168–85; Alice Walker, "*One* Child of One's
    Own: A Meaningful Digression within the Work(s)," in *In Search of Our Mothers' Gar-
    dens: Womanist Prose* (New York: Harcourt Brace Jovanovich, 1983), 361–83; Judy Grahn,
    "Murdering the King's English," in *True to Life Adventure Stories*, 2 vols. (Oakland: Di-
    ana Press, 1978), 1: 6–14; Adrienne Rich, "It Is the Lesbian in Us . . . " in *On Lies, Se-
    crets, and Silence: Selected Prose, 1966–78* (New York: Norton, 1979), 199–202, and "Com-
    pulsory Heterosexuality and Lesbian Existence," *Signs* 5 (Summer 1980): 631–60;
    Cherrie Moraga and Gloria Anzaldúa, *This Bridge Called My Back: Writings by Radical
    Women of Color* (Watertown, Mass.: Persephone Press, 1981); and Evelyn Torton Beck,

Nice Jewish Girls:A Lesbian Anthology (Watertown, Mass.: Persephone Press, 1982). *This Bridge Called My Back* has been reprinted by Kitchen Table Press; *Nice Jewish Girls* is due out in fall 1989 in a revised third edition from Beacon Press.

25. Elly Bulkin, in Judith Kegan Gardiner, Elly Bulkin, Rena Grasso Patterson, and Annette Kolodny, "An Interchange on Feminist Criticism: On 'Dancing Through the Minefield,'" *Feminist Studies* 8 (Fall 1982): 636.

26. I am thinking in particular of Showalter's *New Feminist Criticism* (1985), which mentions the responses briefly in its introduction but does not discuss or excerpt them. Dale Spender's *Men's Studies Modified* (Oxford, England: Pergamon, 1981), which also reprints "Dancing Through the Minefield," was published before the responses to Kolodny appeared.

27. In "Monumental Feminism and Literature's Ancestral House: Another Look at 'The Yellow Wallpaper'" *(Women's Studies* 12 [December 1986]: 113–28), Janice Haney-Peritz argues from a Lacanian perspective that like the narrator, American feminist critics "see in literature a really distinctive body which they seek to liberate through identification" and which is "usually presented as essential to a viable feminist literary criticism and celebrated as something so distinctive that it shakes, if it does not destroy, the very foundations of patriarchal literature's ancestral house" (p. 123). In this process, says Haney-Peritz, gender hierarchies are not dismantled but merely reversed, and the material nature of feminist struggle is erased. Mary Jacobus' "An Unnecessary Maze of Sign-Reading" (in *Reading Woman: Essays in Feminist Criticism* [New York: Columbia University Press, 1986], 229–48), was, as I said earlier, introduced to me by an anonymous reader for *Feminist Studies.* Although my interpretation of Gilman's story is very different from Jacobus', our analyses of earlier feminist readings are strikingly similar, and we focus on some of the same key elements of the tale. Because all three readings seem to have been undertaken independently of one another, they clearly signify a new interpretive moment in both feminist criticism generally and criticism of "The Yellow Wallpaper" in particular.

28. Chris Weedon, *Feminist Practice and Poststructuralist Theory* (Oxford: Basil Blackwell, 1987), 86.

29. See Hedges, 51; Gilbert and Gubar, 90; Kolodny, "Map for Re-Reading," 458; Treichler, 62ff; Fetterley, 162; Haney–Peritz, 116.

30. Weedon, 21.

31. Adrienne Rich, "When We Dead Awaken: Writing As Re-Vision" (1971) in *On Lies, Secrets, and Silence,* 35.

32. Before 1986, only Jean Kennard had noted the degree to which "yellow" failed to figure in the standard feminist analysis (pp. 78–79). For other new readings of the long unread trope of color, see Jacobus, 234ff, and William Veeder, "Who Is Jane? The Intricate Feminism of Charlotte Perkins Gilman," *Arizona Quarterly* 44 (Autumn 1988): 40–79. Sometimes readers associate Gilman's paper with "yellow journalism," but that phrase was not coined until 1895.

33. Thomas F. Gossett, *Race: The History of an Idea in America* (Dallas: Southern Methodist University Press, 1975), 299.

34. John Higham, *Strangers in the Land: Patterns of American Nativism, 1860–1925,* 2d ed. (New York: Atheneum, 1975), 133, 39.

35. Ibid., 42; E.A. Ross, *The Old World and the New;* John W. Burgess, "The Ideal of the American Commonwealth"; Owen Wister, "The Evolution of the Cow Puncher"; and Jack London, *Burning Daylight,* all quoted in Gossett, 293, 307, and 219. See also Jack London's *Valley of the Moon,* quoted in Higham, 172; Frank Norris' *Collected Writings* and *The Octopus,* both quoted in Gossett, 219, 221–22.

36. Higham, 133. Roger Daniels and Harry Kitano, *American Racism: Exploration of the Na-*

ture of Prejudice (Englewood Cliffs, (N.J.: Prentice-Hall, 1970), 44; Higham, 174; Madison Grant, *The Conquest of a Continent* (New York: Scribners, 1933), 255; Higham, 168; Madison Grant, *The Passing of the Great Race* (1916), cited in Daniels and Kitano, 55; Lothrop Stoddard, cited in Daniels and Kitano, 55; Grant, *The Conquest of a Continent*, 356; and Higham, 166, 173

37. See, for example, *Dictionary of American Slang,* ed. Harold Wentworth and Stuart Berg Flexner (New York: Thomas Y. Crowell, 1960). The association of the color yellow with artistic decadence, which Mary Jacobus also suggests (p. 234), may not be irrelevant to these other cultural practices.

38. Charlotte Brontë, *Jane Eyre*, Norton Critical Edition (New York: Norton, 1971), 86, 85, 92, 93, 96. Mary Jacobus also discusses briefly resonances between "The Yellow Wallpaper" and *Jane Eyre.*

39. Brontë, 258, 249, 257–58.

40. I want to stress that my reading of "The Yellow Wallpaper" emerged from my experience of and discomfort with the text and not from prior knowledge of Gilman's radical ideology. When I began to imagine political implications for the color "yellow" in the story, I thought the text might be reflecting unconscious anxieties, but I did not expect to find overt evidence of racism in Gilman's writings.

41. See, for example, Gilman's "My Ancestors," *Forerunner* 4 (March 1913): 73–75, in which the narrator represents all humans as one family; "Race Pride," *Forerunner* 4 (April 1913): 88–89, in which she explicitly criticizes Owen Wister's *The Virginian* for white supremacy; and *With Her in Ourland, Forerunner* 7 (1916): passim, in which America is chastised for its abuse of Negroes, Mexicans, and Indians.

42. *Concerning Children,* 4, cited in Gary Scharnhorst, *Charlotte Perkins Gilman* (Boston: Twayne, 1985), 66. Scharnhorst gives much more attention to Gilman's racism than does Mary Hill in *Charlotte Perkins Gilman: The Making of a Radical Feminist, 1860–1896* (Philadelphia: Temple University Press, 1980). This may be because Scharnhorst is dealing with the whole of Gilman's life and work, Hill with only the first half. But I do not want to rule out the possibility that Scharnhorst's gender and/or ethnic identity, or the five years' difference between his book and Hill's, made it easier for him to confront Gilman's racism.

43. Gilman, *Concerning Children,* 89 and 55; Gilman, in the *American Journal of Sociology,* (July 1908), 78–85, both cited in Scharnhorst, 66, 127. See Gilman, "Why We Honestly Fear Socialism," *The Forerunner* 1 (December 1909): 9. This charge is also made of the Jews in Gilman's *The Man-Made World: or, Our Androcentric Culture* (New York: Charlton, 1911), 231. See Gilman, review of "The Woman Voter," *Forerunner* 3 (August 1912): 224; and see, for example, *Forerunner* 4 (February 1913): 47, and 3 (March 1912): 66. Gilman, *With Her in Ourland, Forerunner* 7 (October 1916): 266–67. See similar statements in "Growth and Combat," *Forerunner* 7 (April 1916): 108; and the following example from "Race Pride," *Forerunner* 4 (April 1913): 89: "Perhaps the most pronounced instance of this absurdity [of race superiority] is in the historic pride of the Hebrews, firmly believing themselves to be the only people God cared about, and despising all the other races of the earth for thousands upon thousands of years, while all those other races unanimously return the compliment." In at least one earlier text, however, Gilman does note without blaming the victim that "the hideous injustice of Christianity to the Jew attracted no attention through many centuries." See *Women and Economics* (1898; rpt. New York: Harper & Row, 1966), 78.

44. Gilman, personal correspondence, cited in Scharnhorst, 127.

45. Gilman, "Immigration, Importation, and Our Fathers," *Forerunner* 5 (May 1914): 1–18; "Let Sleeping Forefathers Lie," *Forerunner* 6 (October 1915): 263 (emphasis mine)

46. Gilman, *Living of Charlotte Perkins Gilman,* 1.

47. Gilman, "Moving the Mountain," in *Forerunner* 2 (March 1911): 80.

48. *Forerunner* 7 (June 1916): 154.

49. *With Her in Ourland,* in *Forerunner* 7 (June 1916): 155. It may not be accidental that Ellador changes the subject from race to sex.

50. Gilman, cited in Scharnhorst.

51. Gilman, "Let Sleeping Forefathers Lie," 261; Gilman, "Growth and Combat," *Forerunner* 7 (December 1916): 332.

52. Gilman, *Living of Charlotte Perkins Gilman,* 317; Gilman, *The Forum* 70 (October 1923): 1983–89; *Forerunner* 7 (October 1916): 277.

53. Gilman, "Immigration, Importation, and Our Fathers," 118; "Let Sleeping Forefathers Lie," 262; *With Her in Ourland,* in *Forerunner* 7 (June 1916): 153.

54. Gilman, "The City of Death," *Forerunner* 4 (April 1913): 104.

55. Gilman, "The Power of the Farm Wife," *Forerunner* 6 (December 1915): 316. See also "Growth and Combat," 332.

56. Gilman's autobiography echoes these sentiments when she names New York "that unnatural city where everyone is an exile, none more so than the American," and laments that New York has "but 7 per cent native-born" and that one-third of New Yorkers are Jews. When she travels one summer to coastal Maine, she "could have hugged the gaunt New England farmers and fishermen—I had forgotten what my people looked like!" (*Living of Charlotte Perkins Gilman,* 316).

57. Gilman, *With Her in Ourland,* 151,155. Ellador's racism (and Gilman's) is often tempered with "fairness." Here, for example, Ellador insists that "'I do not mean the immigrants solely. There are Bostonians of Beacon Hill who belong in London; there are New Yorkers of five generations who belong in Paris.'" But these seem to be exceptions, because only the immigrants belong elsewhere in "'vast multitudes.'"

58. Gilman, *The Man-Made World,* 27–28, 136, 249.

59. Gilman, "Personal Problems," *Forerunner* 1 (July 1910): 23–24.

60. Gilman, "Miss Tarbell's Third Paper," *Forerunner* 3 (April 1912): 95.

61. Gilman, "Personal Problems," 23–24.

62. See Gayatri Spivak, "Can the Subaltern Speak? Speculations on Widow-Sacrifice," *Wedge,* nos. 7/8 (1985).

63. Gilman, *The Man-Made World,* 136.

64. Alicia Partnoy, *The Little School: Tales of Disappearance and Survival in Argentina* (San Francisco: Cleis Press, 1986), 104.

65. Reading Gilman's remarks about polluting the melting pot, for example, helped me to see similarities between anxieties about immigration policy and anxieties about "letting too many groups into" the literary canon.

66. Gilman, "Race Pride," *Forerunner* 4 (April 1913): 90.

67. See, for example, Gilman, "My Ancestors," 74.

68. See Gilman, "Why I Wrote 'The Yellow Wallpaper,'" *Forerunner* 4 (1913).

69. The strongest articulation of the pleasures of such reading is Sydney Janet Kaplan's "Varieties of Feminist Criticism," in *Making a Difference,* 37–58.

70. Ellen Messer-Davidow, "The Philosophical Bases of Feminist Literary Criticisms," *New Literary History* 19 (Autumn 1987): 79, 96.

71. Rich, "When We Dead Awaken," 35.

72. Adrienne Rich, "Heroines," in *A Wild Patience Has Taken Me This Far* (New York: Norton, 1981), 35–36.

PART 4

Power and Resistance

The two articles in this section cover very different terrains, but are linked by a common concern about the ways in which feminist scholarship analyzes systems of domination and their gendered impact. Deniz Kandiyoti, in her essay "Islam and Patriarchy: A Comparative Perspective," presents a brilliant analysis of the powerful workings of patriarchy as a system of gender domination. Patriarchy is not a new category for feminist scholars, but rather has deep roots in the practice of feminist theory and research. Gerda Lerner is perhaps the most well-known historian to examine its operations. Her writings have traced the development of patriarchy from the second millennium BCE until the present, arguing that patriarchy is the most ancient and entrenched form of social difference, predating the establishment of other discriminatory power hierarchies based on class, race, ethnicity, and sexual orientation. However, after the linguistic turn patriarchy has become a problematic term for many feminist scholars because of the rather immutable, timeless, and universalist fashions in which it has often been deployed. Judith Butler for instance, has addressed some of its conceptual inadequacies in her prominent work *Gender Trouble* where she contends: "The very notion of 'patriarchy' has threatened to become a universalizing concept that overrides or reduces distinct articulations of gender asymmetry in different cultural contexts" (1990:35). In the wake of the poststructuralist challenge that has threatened to obliterate patriarchy as a viable feminist concept, Kandiyoti argues persuasively for its retention by defining, contextualizing, and historicizing the term. She contends that patriarchy is essentially a precapitalist social formation based on kinship systems in agrarian contexts. Key to its operations, in her view, is the patrilocally extended household, into which very young women are brought through marriage. Kandiyoti is clearly cognizant of the gender subordination that occurs under such patriarchal systems, but she takes great pains to show that these young women are not victims, but rather are able to bargain with and manipulate the system.

In "Feminism and Empowerment: A Critical Reading of Foucault," Monique Deveaux provides a compelling analysis of three waves of feminist application and revision of Foucault's theories of power. Feminist work comprising the first wave has concerned itself with the impact of power on the body, applying Foucault's "docile bodies" theory of the body as a site of social control to analyses of "contemporary practices of femininity" in which women are actually complicitous in disciplining their own bodies. In addition, the "biopower" concept of state control aimed at the manipulation of entire populations of bodies has proven useful in feminist scholars' research on the state's disciplining of women's sexuality and reproductive capacities. Deveaux argues that some feminist work based on these early Foucauldian models of disciplining the body obscures the possibility of individual and collective resistance to state control and cultural norms. Foucault's later development of an agonistic model of power provides a more complex model of shifting and localized power relations that enables feminists to move beyond totalizing "dualistic accounts of power." However, Deveaux and others still resist Foucault's notion of the omnipresence of power in all relationships and his neglect of the specificity of women's experience of male domination. Responding to the need for a fuller understanding of the role of sexual difference in power relations, a third group of postmodern feminist scholars draws on Foucault's theory of the discursive construction and normalization of sexuality. Theorists like Judith Butler, for example, argue that gender and sexual orientation are not fixed categories of identity or analysis, but are discursively constructed through "performance." While Butler and others see the destabilization of gender, sexuality, and subjectivity as opening up new avenues for agency and resistance, Deveaux argues that such a perspective leaves women with little sense of how feminist politics can be carried out. Deveaux urges feminists to move toward a focus on how women subjectively experience and mediate relations of power, and to take seriously women's capacity for implementing personal and collective activism. She notes that while Foucault's theories of power and resistance have "heuristic usefulness," feminist critics deploying these concepts need to historicize them, grounding them in the variety of women's material as well as internal experiences of power and violence in their daily lives.

Reference
Judith Butler, *Gender Trouble: Feminism and the Subversion of Identity.* New York: Routledge, 1990.

Islam and Patriarchy:
A Comparative Perspective

Deniz Kandiyoti

I n contrast to the growing body of historical scholarship on gender relations in
the West, the question of women in Muslim societies has remained closely tied
to a predominantly ahistorical consideration of the main tenets of Islamic religion
and their implications for women. This has been attributed by some to the more
general shortcomings of Middle Eastern historiography, namely the lingering influence of orientalism and an idealist bias that presents historical facts as flowing
directly from ideology.[1] In the case of scholarship on women, these tendencies
have been compounded by a high degree of confusion between polemical and analytical goals. There is a continuing output of exegetical writing by Muslim scholars, many of whom identify themselves as feminists.[2] This writing typically tries
to establish Islam's compatibility with the emancipation of women. The favored
sources of such works continue to be the Quran, the hadith, and the lives of prominent women in early Islam. There is a clear attempt to resuscitate early Islamic
history and the holy text in order to formulate an indigenous feminist project, or
at the very least to encourage more progressive reading of the texts that are regularly invoked by traditionalists to justify the status quo. That feminists and traditionalists are equally concerned with appropriating the "true" message of Islam indicates that all parties believe it to be the only legitimate ideological terrain
on which issues pertaining to women can be debated. I will not discuss the adequacy or merits of this position, but merely point out that it has been one of the
tendencies giving a longer lease of life to ahistorical approaches to the question
of women in Muslim societies.[3]

There is, on the other hand, a vigorous body of scholarship that locates women
as historical and political actors firmly in the context of temporal processes of so-
cioeconomic transformation.[4] Most work in this genre does not necessarily privilege Islam as an analytic category, but inserts gender into broader discourses
about social transformation or the various theoretical paradigms of different social science disciplines. At one extreme of this spectrum, one finds studies that

Deniz Kandiyoti, "Islam and Patriarchy: A Comparative Perspective," in Nikki R. Kiddie
and Beth Baron, eds. *Women in Middle Eastern History: Shifting Boundaries in Sex and Gender* (New Haven, Conn.: Yale University Press, 1991): 23–42. Reprinted by permission.

are barely distinguishable from work on women and development in any other part of the Third World. The specificity of Muslim women's subordination, if any, and the possible role of Islamic ideology and practice in reproducing it are thus lost from view. This leads to a paradoxical situation whereby Islam sometimes appears to be all there is to know, and at other times to be of little consequence in understanding the condition of women, or more broadly, gender relations in Muslim societies.

I argue in this chapter that this is in part because we have not found adequate ways of talking about the articulation between Islam and different systems of male dominance,[5] which are grounded in distinct material arrangements between the genders but are rather imprecisely labeled with the blanket term *patriarchy*. Indeed, the literature confirms that different systems of male dominance, and their internal variations according to class and ethnicity, exercise an influence that inflects and modifies the actual practice of Islam as well as the ideological constructions of what may be regarded as properly Islamic. Religious practice is necessarily influenced by the history of productive and reproductive relations between the genders, as reflected in the workings of different indigenous kinship systems. It may be, and has been argued, that the spread of Islam has expedited the demise of varied local systems in favor of a more uniformly patriarchal mode, with an emphasis on patrilineality and patrilocality, and with characteristic modes of control of female sexuality and spatial mobility.[6] This does not, however, justify the use of imprecise expressions such as "Muslim patriarchy"[7] to denote the sexual asymmetries encountered in contexts as varied as those of a Bedouin tribe, a Hausa village or an upper-class harem in Cairo or Istanbul. We therefore need to examine critically the concept of patriarchy itself, before moving on to a more detailed consideration of its usefulness for an understanding of gender relations in Muslim societies.

Patriarchy: A Problematic Concept

Although a brief incursion into feminist theory cannot do justice to the complex debates generated around the term *patriarchy*,[8] I will attempt a sketchy outline of some contemporary developments in its usage.

Radical feminists were the first to initiate a fairly liberal usage of the term to apply to almost any form or instance of male dominance. Since patriarchy defined in those terms was an all-pervasive, virtually timeless phenomenon, its manifestations could be sought anywhere, although the symbolic and psychic spheres were singled out as privileged areas of investigation. In spite of numerous modifications and reworkings within radical feminism, patriarchy was by and large allocated to the ideological sphere, with a material basis in the division of labor between the sexes (and in particular the facts of reproductive biology).[9]

In the case of Marxist or socialist feminism, the concept has a somewhat different history. It emerged as a residual category, because forms of exploitation and oppression based on gender proved singularly recalcitrant to reduction to other forms (such as those based on race and class). In those terms, what could not be explained through the workings of capital could be put down to the logic of a related but distinct system with its own laws of motion, namely that of patriarchy. However, the degree of analytic independence assigned to the category of patriarchy, as distinct from capitalism or the class system, could be quite variable, as indeed was the degree of commitment to a systematic consideration of the relations between the two.[10] Nonetheless, this position had advantages in that patriarchy was acknowledged to have a material basis in the social relations between the sexes, which are in turn subject to historical transformations. The emphasis on the reciprocal relations between types and systems of production, the sexual division of labor, and age and gender hierarchies meant that the psychodynamics and cultural constructions of gender could be historicized, and at least in principle, more adequately theorized. In practice, however, most of the debate remained centered on the effects of industrial and postindustrial capitalism on gender relations, with relatively fewer attempts to establish linkages within a broader comparative perspective.

The ways in which such linkages were theorized have in addition been quite diverse. Some concentrated on establishing empirical associations between types of production, kinship systems, and indicators of women's status. Ester Boserup, for instance, made a distinction between male and female farming systems, relating them to population density, technology, and type of cultivation.[11] Female farming systems, most prevalent in sub-Saharan Africa, are characterized by abundant land, low population density, shifting cultivation, and the use of the hoe as a farming implement. Apart from tasks like clearing the land for cultivation, food production is primarily the responsibility of women, who, according to Boserup, have a high degree of mobility and the ability to market their surplus to support themselves and their children. Male farming systems, more characteristic of Asia, are prevalent under conditions of higher population density, the necessity to increase productivity, and the use by men of draught animals and the plow. Plow agriculture is prevalent in areas of private ownership where a landless class whose labor may be hired exists. Ideally, the women of landed households are released from agricultural work in the fields and confined to domesticity, often actually secluded as a symbol of prestige and family honor (as in Muslim veiling or the purdah system). They increasingly come to depend on men for both economic support and symbolic shelter.

Germaine Tillion, in her analysis of codes of honor and female modesty in the Mediterranean, argues that these phenomena may in fact be of more recent origin than suspected and may have evolved as a reaction to the threat posed to endogamous tribal societies, which form the backbone of the postneolithic ancient world, by outside forces, particularly by an expanding urban civilization.[12] She sees the customs and practices related to the seclusion of women as results of the incomplete evolution and degeneration of tribal society and of the structures of defense it erected to maintain its integrity. Islamic rules are incidental to this process, as evidenced by the very selectivity with which they are applied, ignored, or circumvented. For instance, women are either altogether deprived of their inheritance rights when these threaten tribal property and solidarity, or when they are accorded such rights, they are tightly monitored through strict controls over marriage alliances and their spatial mobility. Thus the apparent irony behind the fact that veiled urban women have property rights whereas their unveiled rural sisters, whose contribution to subsistence is typically higher, are deprived of them, disappears. Although Tillion is quite clear about the material forces underpinning tribal endogamy, the process of erosion of such structures through contact with city values and exposure to other civilizational influences (operating through changes in mentality and outlook) remains more nebulous.

Jack Goody followed up Boserup's typology by relating women's contribution to production with kinship systems and modes of inheritance.[13] He notes the empirical association between plow agriculture, male farming, diverging devolution (that is, bilateral inheritance), and monogamy, all characteristic of Eurasia, which stand in contrast to Africa, where female predominance in hoe cultivation is accompanied by homogenous inheritance (matrilineal or patrilineal), polygyny, and bridewealth. This approach has been criticized for trying to explain differences in kinship patterns between very broadly defined regions through ahistorical reference to technological and ecological variations and for trying to understand kinship and systems of production solely in terms of property relations.[14]

At a more general level, approaches to women's subordination stressing their modes of contribution to subsistence were criticized for their "productivist" bias. It was argued that ultimately the position of women could not be explained in terms of participation in production, which could be extremely variable, but could be better understood with reference to their roles in reproduction.[15] Some even turned the productivist argument on its head by suggesting not only that women's status was not predicated on their roles in production but also that productive roles may in fact themselves be defined and limited by the kinds of reproductive tasks assigned to women at different junctures of capital accumulation.[16] Thus Lourdes Beneria and Gita Sen argued in their critique of Boserup that the crucial distinguishing features of African and Asian farming do not reside in the tools used—the hoe or the plow—but in the forms of appropriation of land, surplus, and women's reproductive capacities.[17] They proposed an analysis based on the dual concepts of accumulation and reproduction, it being understood that there are systematic connections between different phases of accumulation, class formation, and gender relations.[18]

Where did these developments leave the concept of patriarchy? To the extent that efforts were made to relate it to processes of accumulation, it became increasingly insubstantial and was often reduced to an epiphenomenon of the workings of capital. The allocation of productive and reproductive tasks between the sexes is frequently presented as functional to the maintenance of a cheap labor force, with gender ideologies merely acting to justify the existing division of labor. In spite of strenuous attempts at disentangling the workings of patriarchy from those of capitalism and the wish to grant the former some analytic autonomy,[19] a great deal was said about the laws of motion of capitalism whereas those of patriarchy have at best remained nebulous and vague. This is partly due to the often implicit assumption that there is such a thing as a unitary and universal system that we may call patriarchy, and that the differences in the character of women's subordination concretely encountered are merely the outcome of different expressions or stages of the same system.[20] This has resulted in an overly abstract and monolithic conception of male dominance, which obfuscates rather than reveals the intimate inner workings of different gender arrangements.

I have proposed elsewhere that a useful point of entry for the identification of different systems of male dominance may be found through analyses of women's strategies in dealing with them.[21] I have argued that women strategize within a set of concrete constraints that reveal and define the blueprint of what I term the *patriarchal bargain*[22] of any given society, which may exhibit variations according to class, caste, and ethnicity. These patriarchal bargains exert a powerful influence on the shaping of women's gendered subjectivity and determine the nature of gender ideology in different contexts. They also influence both the potential for and the actual forms of women's active or passive resistance. Most important, patriarchal bargains are not timeless or immutable entities, but are susceptible to historical transformations that open up new areas of struggle or renegotiation of the relations between genders.

By way of illustration, I will contrast two systems of male dominance, rendered ideal-typical for the purposes of discussing their implications for women. I use these ideal types as heuristic devices that necessarily simplify more complex reality, but can be fleshed out and expanded with comparative, empirical content. These two types are based on examples from sub-Saharan Africa and from the Middle East and southern and eastern Asia. My aim is to highlight a continuum ranging from less corporate forms of householding, involving the relative autonomy of mother-child units evidenced in sub-Saharan polygyny, to the more corporate male-headed entities prevalent in the regions identified by James Caldwell as the "patriarchal belt."[23] Against this background, I will explore the extent to which Islam cut across different systems of male dominance and the possibility that gender relations in the Middle East are influenced by a particular conjunction between Islam and the system I identify as "classic patriarchy." Finally, I will speculate on the impact of contemporary social transformations on patriarchal bargains and gender ideologies.

Autonomy and Protest: Some Examples from Sub-Saharan Africa

As I reviewed the literature on women in agricultural development projects in sub-Saharan Africa, my own background, as a woman born and raised in Turkey, left me totally unprepared for what I found.[24] This literature was rife with instances of women's resistance to attempts to lower the value of their labor, and more significant, women's refusal to allow the total appropriation of their production by their husbands.

Whenever new agricultural schemes provided men with inputs and credit, and the assumption was made that as heads of household they would have access to their wives' unremunerated labor, problems seemed to develop. In the Mwea irrigated rice settlement in Kenya, where women were deprived of access to their own plots, their lack of alternatives and their total lack of control over men's earnings made life so intolerable to them that wives commonly deserted their husbands.[25] In Gambia, in yet another rice-growing scheme, the irrigated land and the credit were made available to men, even though it was the women who traditionally grew rice in tidal swamps and there was a long-standing practice of men and women cultivating their own crops and controlling the produce. Women's customary duties with respect to labor allocation to common and individual plots protected them from demands by their husbands that they provide free labor on men's irrigated rice fields. Men had to pay their wives wages or lend them an irrigated plot to have access to their labor. In the rainy season, when women had the alternative of growing their own swamp rice, they created a labor bottleneck for men, who simply had to wait for the days on which women did not go to their own fields.[26] Pepe Roberts also illustrates the strategies used by women to maximize their autonomy in the African context.[27] Yoruba women in Nigeria negotiate the terms of their farm-labor services to their husbands while they aim to devote more time and energy to the trading activities that will enable them to support themselves. Hausa women in Nigeria,whose observance of Islamic seclusion reduces the demands husbands can make on their services (an important point to which we shall return), allocate their labor to trade, mainly the sale of ready-cooked foodstuffs.

In short, the insecurities of African polygyny for women are matched by areas of relative autonomy that they clearly strive to maximize. Men's responsibility for their wives' support, although normative in some instances, is in actual fact relatively low. Typically, it is the woman who is primarily responsible for her own and her children's upkeep, including meeting the costs of their education, with varying degrees of assistance from her husband. Women have little to gain and a lot to lose by becoming totally dependent on husbands, and quite rightly resist projects that tilt the delicate balance they strive to maintain.

Documentation of a genuine trade-off between women's autonomy and men's responsibility for their wives can be found in some historical examples. Kristin Mann suggests that despite the wifely dependence entailed by Christian marriage, Yoruba women in Lagos accepted it with enthusiasm because of the greater protection they thought they would receive.[28] Conversely, men in contemporary Zambia resist the more modern ordinance marriage, as opposed to customary marriage, because it burdens them with greater obligations for their wives and children.[29] A form of conjugal union in which the partners may openly negotiate the exchange of sexual and labor services seems to lay the groundwork for more explicit forms of bargaining. Commenting on Ashanti marriage, Katherine Abu singles out as its most striking feature "the separateness of spouses' resources and activities and the overtness of the bargaining element in the relationship."[30] Polygyny, and in this case, the continuing obligations of both men and women to their own kin, does not foster a notion of the family or household as a corporate entity.

Clearly, there are important variations in African kinship systems with respect to forms of marriage, residence, descent, and inheritance rules, which are grounded in complex historical processes, including different modes of incorporation of African societies into the world economy.[31] Nonetheless, it is within a broadly defined Afro-Caribbean pattern that we find some of the clearest instances of noncorporateness of the conjugal family both in ideology and in practice, which informs marital and marketplace strategies for women.

It is therefore particularly interesting to see how Islam, which privileges patrilineal bonds and clearly enjoins men to take full responsibility for the support of their wives, acts on gender relations in different African contexts. Enid Schildkrout's study of secluded Hausa women in Kano, Nigeria, suggests that a typically West African pattern of high economic activity and relative autonomy of women persists within a family structure defined by Islamic values concerning the sexual division of labor.[32] She relates how women are able to subvert the idealized structure of the domestic economy through the control they exercise over the labor of their children, which makes it possible for them to trade in cooked foods without having direct contact with the marketplace. Their seclusion obviously restricts their mobility so that they are dependent on manipulating the limited resources their husbands provide for consumption and diverting them to their own productive ends. However, this also puts limits on the services husbands may expect from their wives, as they cannot rely on them as a source of support and are thus at least in theory expected to be the providers. Schildkrout suggests that the widespread adoption of purdah in Kano is possible precisely because women have the ability to play active economic roles while participating in the myth of their total dependence on men. To the extent that this ability is predicated on their control over children's labor, however, it will be increasingly jeopardized as the latter are absorbed by the modern educational system and become unavailable as domestic labor. Ultimately, the structure of all but the wealthiest families in Islamic West Africa may be challenged by such contemporary changes.

In Mette Bovin's work on the Manga women in Bornu, Niger, she detects signs of actual female resistance to Muslim institutions in spite of nine hundred years of "Islamization."[33] Islam in Bornu grafted itself on an older matrilineal system with different pre-Islamic marriage rules, which were superseded but not totally eradicated by a Muslim patrilineal system. Bovin suggests that it is women who maintain and transmit this pre-Islamic cultural heritage, through their struggle to enforce the matrilineal principle, the actual result being a kind of bilateral system. Pre-Islamic influences are also apparent in traces of totemism in women's rituals, the existence of independent statuses for women, and women's vocabulary, which unlike men's does not include Arabic words. It is as though Islamic rules were being negotiated by participants with diverging gender interests, the women stubbornly clinging to aspects of the pre-Islamic system that may have been more empowering.

One does not have to accept this particular interpretation of pre-Islamic survivals to concede a more general and rather obvious point. There may or may not be a good fit between Islamic injunctions concerning kinship and marriage and local pre-Islamic customs and practices. In the latter case, not only local kinship patterns and ideologies are modified but often the practice and interpretation of Islam itself. Presenting women as active participants in this process of reinterpretation and cultural negotiation exercises a corrective influence on depictions of Muslim women as passive victims of patriarchal domination. It is no accident, moreover, that it is in sub-Saharan Africa that we encounter the clearest instances of women's resistance, since they frequently involve the safe-guarding of existing spheres of autonomy.

Subservience and Manipulation: Women Under Classic Patriarchy

The foregoing examples of women's resistance stand in stark contrast to women's accommodations to the system I call classic patriarchy. The clearest instances of classic patriarchy are found in the geographical area that includes North Africa, the Muslim Middle East (including Turkey, Pakistan, and Iran), and southern and eastern Asia (specifically India and China).[34]

The key to the reproduction of classic patriarchy lies in the operations of the patrilocally extended household, which is also commonly associated with the reproduction of the peasantry in agrarian societies.[35] Even though demographic and other constraints may have curtailed the actual predominance of three-generational patrilocal households, there is little doubt that they represented a powerful cultural ideal. It is plausible that the emergence of the patriarchal extended family, which gives the senior man authority over everyone else, including younger men, is bound up in the incorporation and control of the family by the state,[36] and in the transition from kin-based to tributary modes of surplus control.[37] The implications of the patrilineal-patrilocal complex for women are not only remarkably uniform but also entail forms of control and subordination that cut across cultural and religious boundaries, such as those of Hinduism, Confucianism, and Islam.

Under classic patriarchy, girls are given away in marriage at a very young age into households headed by their husband's father. There they are subordinate not only to all the men but also to the more senior women, especially their mothers-in-law. The extent to which this represents a total break with their own kin group, and consequent isolation and hardship, varies in relation to the degree of endogamy in marriage practices. Michael Meeker in his comparison between the rural Arabs of the Levant and the Black Sea Turks draws our attention to the different structuring of conceptions of honor among them and its possible relation to the degree of endogamy they favor in marriage.[38] Among the Turks, he finds much lower rates of endogamy, and that the husband is directly and principally responsible for a woman's honor. Among the rural Arabs of the Levant, there is much greater mutuality among affines, and a woman's natal family retains both an interest and an active involvement in protecting a married daughter's honor. As a result, a Turkish woman's traditional position may more closely resemble the status of the "stranger-bride" of pre-revolutionary China than that of an Arab woman, whose position in the patriarchal household may be somewhat attenuated by endogamy and recourse to her natal kin.

Lila Abu-Lughod, in her study of the Awlad 'Ali, Bedouins of the Western

Desert in Egypt, draws attention to the tension that marriage creates in an ideological system in which agnation is given clear priority as a basis for affiliation, and suggests that one resolution of this tension may be sought in a preference for patrilateral parallel-cousin marriages.[39] She comments on the preferential treatment that wives from the same patrikin as their husbands receive and on their greater sense of security. Unni Wikan in her study of Oman indicates quite perceptively that although in principle men subscribe to the ideal of cousin marriage and agnatic loyalties, in practice they strive to stay clear of such unions.[40] Marrying a stranger enhances the control of the husband by reducing accountability to related in-laws and ensures the wife's exclusive dependence on him.

Under classic patriarchy women frequently have no claim on their father's patrimony, whether the prevalent marriage payment is bride-price or dowry. Their dowries do not qualify as a form of premortem inheritance since they are transferred directly to the bridegroom's kin and do not take the form of productive property, such as land.[41] In the case of the *mahr* (brideprice), the proportion retained by the bride's father and that returned to her in the form of valuables can be extremely variable, despite explicit provision that part of the *mahr* belongs to her. Likewise, women's access to and control over property can vary a great deal. There is substantial historical evidence that women in the Middle East did own and control property, especially if they were urban and middle or upper class.[42] There is equally widespread evidence that the patrilineage expropriates them if productive property takes the form of land or flocks and if their inheritance rights threaten the economic integrity of the family or tribal unit. Thus whether they are members of Muslim, Hindu, or Confucian communities, young brides often enter their husband's household as effectively dispossessed individuals, who can establish their place in the patriliny only by producing male offspring.

A woman's life cycle in the patrilocally extended family is such that the deprivation and hardship she may experience as a young bride are eventually superseded by the control and authority she will have over her own daughters-in-law. The powerful postmenopausal matriarch thus is the other side of the coin of this form of patriarchy. The cyclical nature of women's power and their anticipation of inheriting the authority of senior women encourages a thorough internalization of this form of patriarchy by the women themselves. Subordination to men is offset by the control older women have over younger women. Women have access to the only type of labor power they can control, and to old-age security, however, through their married sons. Since sons are a woman's most critical resource, ensuring their lifelong loyalty is an enduring preoccupation. Older women have a vested interest in the suppression of romantic love between youngsters to keep the conjugal bond secondary and to claim their sons' primary allegiance. Young women have an interest in circumventing and possibly evading their mother-in-law's control. There are culturally specific examples of how this struggle works to the detriment of the heterosexual bond,[43] but there are striking similarities in the overall pattern. In the case of Muslim societies, Fatima Mernissi emphasizes the role of Islamic ideology, which posits the primacy of the male believer's relationship with God, treating all other involvements, especially passionate and exclusive relationships with women, as diversionary if not positively subversive.[44] Although this ideology may indeed constitute a local contributory factor, there is little doubt that what is being played out in the mother-son-bride triangle forms a central structural component of a much broader patriarchal scenario.

The class or caste impact on classic patriarchy produces additional complexities. Among the wealthier strata, the withdrawal of women from nondomestic work is frequently a mark of status institutionalized in such seclusion and exclusion practices as the purdah system and veiling. The women who are thus restricted nonetheless share in the privileges of their class through greater access to and control over property, more leisure, and eventuallly better access to education. For the women of poorer strata, who can ill afford to observe this cultural ideal, the ideology of seclusion and dependence on men still exercises a powerful influence that severely restricts the range of options available to them. Judith Tucker's data on nineteenth-century Egypt suggest that the strongly interventionist state policies of the Muhammad 'Ali period resulted in women's recruitment into public works, state-run industries, and expanding sectors of health and education.[45] Yet at the same time she draws our attention to how women's independent access to income could result in losses on the family front, as when women in certain kinds of employment were legally deprived of the right of guardianship of their children. Ultimately, women's access to resources is mediated through the family. In situations where the observance of restrictive practices is a crucial element in the reproduction of family status, women will resist breaking the rules, even if observing them produces economic hardship. I would therefore agree with Maria Mies's analysis of the lacemakers of Narsapur, India, about whom she observes that the ideology of their domesticity keeps them working at home, for extremely low wages, even though they are producing for the world market.[46] In this instance, ideology acts as a material force that results in a lucrative export commodity produced by conveniently cheap labor.

Women in areas of classic patriarchy thus are often unable to resist unfavorable labor relations in both the household and the market, and frequently adhere as far and as long as they possibly can to rules that result in the devaluation of their labor. The cyclical fluctuations of their power position, combined with status considerations, result in their active collusion in the reproduction of their own subordination. They frequently adopt interpersonal strategies that maximize their security through manipulation of the affections of their sons and husband. As Margery Wolf's insightful discussion of the Chinese uterine family suggests, this strategy can even result in the aging male patriarch losing power to his wife.[47] Even though these individual power tactics do little to alter the structurally unfavorable terms of the overall patriarchal script, women become experts at maximizing their own life chances.

This creates the paradoxical situation noted by Kay Anne Johnson, who comments on female conservatism in China: "Ironically, women through their actions to resist passivity and total male control, became participants with vested interests in the system that oppressed them."[48] One also gains important insights into women's investment in existing gender arrangements through ethnographic studies of the Middle East. Some suggest that far from producing subjective feelings of oppression, this willing participation enhances women's sense of control and self-worth. Wikan, for instance, depicts Omani women in the following terms: "Indeed many of the constraints and limitations imposed on women, such as the *burqa* [veil], restrictions of movement and sexual segregation, are seen by women as aspects of that very concern and respect on the part of the men which provide the basis for their own feeling of assurance and value. Rather than reflecting subjugation, these constraints and limitations are perceived by women as a source of pride and a confirmation of esteem."[49]

The survival of the moral order of classic patriarchy, as well as the positioning of male versus female and young versus old, however, is grounded in specific material conditions. Changes in these conditions can seriously undermine the normative order. As expressed succinctly by Mead Cain, S. R. Khanan, and S. Nahar, it is both the key and the irony of this system that "male authority has a material base, while male responsibility is normatively controlled."[50] Their study of a village in Bangladesh offers a striking example of the strains placed by poverty on bonds of obligation between kin and, more specifically, on men's fulfillment of their normative obligations toward women. Martin Greeley also documents the growing dependence of landless households in Bangladesh on women's wage labor, including that of married women, and discusses the ways in which the stability of the patriarchal family is thereby undermined.[51]

In a purely analogical sense, patriarchal bargains, like scientific paradigms,[52] can be shown to have a normal and a crisis phase, which challenges our very interpretation of what is going on in the world. Thus during what we might call the normal phase of classic patriarchy, there were always large numbers of women who were in fact exposed to economic hardship and insecurity. They were infertile and had to be divorced, or orphaned and without recourse to their natal family, or unprotected because they had no surviving sons or, even worse, had ungrateful sons. They were merely considered "unlucky," however, anomalies and accidental casualties of a system that otherwise made sense. It is at the point of breakdown that every system reveals its internal contradictions and often forces participants in the system to take up new and seemingly contradictory ideological positions.

The Demise of Patriarchal Bargains: Retreat into Conservatism or Radical Protest?

The material bases of classic patriarchy crumble under the impact of new market forces, capital penetration in rural areas,[53] and processes of economic marginalization and immiseration. Although there is no single path leading to the breakdown of this system, its consequences are fairly uniform. The domination of younger men by older men and the shelter of women in the domestic sphere were the hallmarks of a system in which men controlled some form of viable joint patrimony in land, animals, or commercial capital. Among the propertyless and the dispossessed, the necessity of every household member's contribution to survival turns men's economic protection of women—which is central to Muslim men's claims to primacy in the conjugal union—into a myth.

The breakdown of classic patriarchy results in the earlier emancipation from their fathers of younger men and their earlier separation from the paternal household. Whereas this process implies that women escape the control of mothers-in-law and head their own households at a much younger age, it also means that they themselves can no longer look forward to a future surrounded by subservient daughters-in-law. For the generation of women caught in between, this transformation may represent genuine personal tragedy, since they have paid the heavy price of an earlier patriarchal bargain, but are not able to cash in on its promised benefits. Wolf's statistics on suicide among women in China suggest a clear change in the trend since the 1930s, with a sharp increase in the suicide rates of women over forty-five, whereas previously the rates were highest among young women, especially new brides.[54] She relates this change explicitly to the emancipation of sons and their new chance to escape familial control in their choice of spouse, which robs the older woman of her power and respectability as mother-in-law.

In the case of Muslim societies, Mernissi comments on the psychologically distortive effects of the discordance between deeply ingrained images and expectations of male-female roles and the changing realities of everyday life. "The wider the gap between reality and fantasy (or aspiration), the greater the suffering and the more serious the conflict and tension within us. The psychological cost is just barely tolerable. The fact that we cling to images of virility (economic power) and femininity (consumption of the husband's fortune) that have nothing whatever to do with real life contributes to making male-female dynamics one of the most painful sources of tension and conflict."[55] This tension is documented through an analysis of "sexual anomie" in contemporary Morocco, in which she stresses primarily men's frustration and humiliation at being unable to fulfill their traditional role and the threat posed by women's greater spatial mobility and access to paid employment.

The breakdown of classic patriarchy may be equally threatening to women, however, who often resist the process of change because they see the old normative order slipping away from them without any empowering alternatives. In a broader discussion of women's interests, Maxine Molyneux suggests that this may not be put down merely to "false consciousness" but to the possibility that changes realized in a piecemeal fashion "could threaten the short-term practical interests of some women, or entail a cost in the loss of forms of protection that are not then compensated for in some way."[56]

Thus when classic patriarchy enters a crisis, many women may continue to pressure men to live up to their obligations and will not, except under the most extreme circumstances, compromise the basis for their claims by stepping out of line and losing their respectability. Their passive resistance takes the form of claiming their half of this particular patriarchal bargain—protection in exchange for submissiveness and propriety, and a confirmation that male honor is indeed dependent on their responsible conduct.

The response of some women who have to work for wages in this context may be an intensification of traditional modesty markers, such as veiling. Often, through no choice of their own, they are working outside the home and are thus "exposed"; they must now use every symbolic means at their disposal to signify that they continue to be worthy of protection. It is significant that Khomeini's exhortations to keep women at home found enthusiastic support among many Iranian women, despite the obvious elements of repression. The implicit promise of increased male responsibility restores the integrity of their original patriarchal bargain in an environment where the range of options available to women is extremely restricted. Younger women adopt the veil, Farah Azari suggests, because "the restriction imposed on them by an Islamic order was therefore a small price that had to be paid in exchange for the security, stability and presumed respect this order promised them."[57] That this promise has proven to be illusory is strongly suggested by Haleh Afshar's review of social policies under the Islamic Republic.[58] She nonetheless acknowledges a large support base among the poor and working classes. Fadwa El Guindi's analysis of young women taking up the veil in Egypt also speaks of women's concern with retaining respectability and a measure of "untouchability" now that they are present in public spaces in growing numbers.[59]

It would be simpleminded to single out Islam as unique in fulfilling this soothing and restorative function. There is evidence from non-Muslim societies that retreat into social and religious conservatism is one of the possible responses to changes that seem to threaten the moral order, especially when they present challenges to existing gender arrangements. At the ideological level, broken bargains seem to instigate a search for culprits, a hankering for the certainties of a more traditional order, or a more diffuse feeling that change might have gone either too far or badly wrong. The familism of the New Right and the anti-feminist movement in the West thus have been interpreted by some as an attempt to reinstate an older patriarchal bargain, with feminists providing a convenient scapegoat on whom to blame the loss of family values, intimacy, and community.[60] What makes conservative Islamic discourse even more compelling is that it often associates moral decay with contamination by foreign, generally Western values, and assigns women a privileged role in restoring the lost authenticity of the community of believers. This anti-imperialist, populist discourse constructs women upholding Muslim values as radical militants rather than mere traditionalists, adding a significant new dimension to female reaction in the Muslim world. What unites female conservatism in the West with Muslim women's militancy in the Middle East, however, is the common perception that the furtherance of women's gender interests lies in the restoration of an original patriarchal bargain that afforded them protection and dignity.

I have argued here that one of the major weaknesses in our theorizing about women in the Middle East stems from a conflation of Islam, as ideology and practice, with patriarchy. This conflation is encouraged by monolithic and essentialist conceptions of both Islam and patriarchy. In search of an alternative, I presented case materials illustrating women's strategies and coping mechanisms as a means of capturing the nature of patriarchal systems in their cultural, class specific, and temporal concreteness. I have tried to show how two ideal-typical systems of male dominance could provide different base lines from which women negotiate and strategize, and how each affects the potentialities of their resistance and struggles.

Islam cuts across these ideal types and extends well beyond them (as in the case of Southeast Asian societies). Even though Islam brings its own prescriptions to bear on gender relations in each context, it nonetheless achieves different ac-commodations with the diverse cultural complexes it encounters. That the core areas of Islamic civilization have historically coincided with areas of classic pa-triarchy has tended to obscure these variations, and encouraged a confusion be-tween the assumed workings of Islam and those of a specific type of patriarchy.

The different political projects of modern nation-states, the specificities of their nationalist histories, and the positioning of Islam vis-à-vis diverse nationalisms also account for deep and significant variations in policies and legislation affect-ing women.[61] These variations find concrete expression in the degree of access that women have to education, paid employment, social benefits, and political participation.

There is, nonetheless, a sense in which Islam in the contemporary world may be promoting a homogenization of ideology and practice concerning women, the family, and gender relations. This political Islam speaks to the gap created by the breakdown of patriarchal bargains and to the turmoil and confusion created by rapid and often corrosive processes of social transformation. The extensive "ide-ologization" of the sphere of family and gender relations is itself, however, a his-torical phenomenon of fairly recent origin that cannot be imputed to Islam itself.

It should be clear that these different levels at which I have invoked Islam—kinship systems, the state, and political ideologies—cannot be conflated and must be kept analytically distinct. We should now be moving toward finely grained historical analyses of how they intersect, interact, and change.

Notes

1. Nikki R. Keddie, "Problems in the Study of Middle Eastern Women," *International Jour-nal of Middle East Studies* 10 (1979): 225–40; Judith E. Tucker, "Problems in the Histori-ography of Women in the Middle East: The Case of Nineteenth-Century Egypt," *In-ternational Journal of Middle East Studies* 15 (1983): 321–36.

2. Nawal al-Saadawi, "Women and Islam," in *Women and Islam,* ed. Azizah al-Hibri (Ox-ford: Pergamon, 1982), 193–206; Azizah al-Hibri, "A Study of Islamic Herstory," in *Women and Islam,* 207–20; Fatima Mernissi, *Le harem politique* (Paris: Albin Michel, 1987).

3. For critical views on this question, see Azar Tabari, "The Women's Movement in Iran: A Hopeful Prognosis," *Feminist Studies* 12 (1986): 343–60; Mai Ghoussoub, "Feminism—or the Eternal Masculine—in the Arab World," *New Left Review* 161 (1987): 3–18.

4. Lois Beck and Nikki Keddie, eds. *Women in the Muslim World* (Cambridge: Harvard University Press, 1978); Judith E. Tucker, *Women in Nineteenth-Century Egypt* (Cam-bridge: Cambridge University Press, 1985); Elizabeth W. Fernia, ed. *Women and the Fam-ily in the Middle East* (Austin: University of Texas Press, 1985); UNESCO, *Social Science Research and Women in the Arab World* (London: Frances Pinter, 1984).

5. We have likewise not paid enough systematic attention to the articulation between Is-lam, nationalism, and different state-building projects in the Middle East. On this ques-tion, see Deniz Kandiyoti, ed., *Women, Islam and the State* (London: Macmillan, 1991).

6. Leila Ahmed, "Women and the Advent of Islam," *Signs* 11 (1986): 665–91.

7. Mervat Hatem, "Class and Patriarchy as Competing Paradigms for the Study of Mid-dle Eastern Women," *Comparative Studies in Society and History* 29, no. 4 (1987): 811–18.

8. This discussion will not be representative of the broader debate on the question of the origins and causes of women's subordination. On the question of origins, see Gerda Lerner, *The Creation of Patriarchy* (New York: Oxford University Press, 1986). A useful collection of essays may be found in Michelle Zimbalist Rosaldo and Louise Lamphere, eds., *Women, Culture, and Society* (Stanford: Stanford University Press, 1974). This work introduces the public-private dichotomy, which has been particularly influential, as well as contested, in analyses of women in the Middle East.

9. For two very different materialist accounts, see Shulamith Firestone, *The Dialectic of Sex* (London: Women's Press, 1979) and Christine Delphy, *The Main Enemy* (London: Women's Research and Resource Centre, 1977).

10. As in Zillah Eisenstein, "Developing a Theory of Capitalist Patriarchy" in *Capitalist Patriarchy and the Case for Socialist Feminism,* ed. Zillah Eisenstein (New York: Monthly Review Press, 1979), 940; Roisin McDonough and Rachel Harrison, "Patriarchy and Relations of Production" in *Feminism and Materialism,* ed. Annette Kuhn and Ann Marie Wolpe (London: Routledge and Kegan Paul, 1978), 11–41; Heidi Hartmann, "The Unhappy Marriage of Marxism and Feminism: Towards a More Progressive Union," in *Women and Revolution,* ed. Lydia Sargent (London: Pluto, 1981), 1–41; Michele Barrett, *Women's Oppression Today* (London: Verso, 1980).

11. Ester Boserup, *Women's Role in Economic Development* (London: George Allen and Unwin, 1970).

12. Germaine Tillion, *The Republic of Cousins* (London: Al Saqi, 1983).

13. Jack Goody, *Production and Reproduction* (Cambridge: Cambridge University Press, 1976).

14. Ann Whitehead, "Review of Jack Goody's *Production and Reproduction," Critique of Anthropology* 3, nos. 9–10 (1977): 151–59; Karen Sacks, *Sisters and Wives: The Past and Future of Sexual Equality* (Westport, Conn.: Greenwood, 1979).

15. Felicity Edholm, Olivia Harris, and Kate Young, "Conceptualizing Women," *Critique of Anthropology* 3, nos. 9–10 (1977): 101–30.

16. Lourdes Beneria, "Reproduction, Production and the Sexual Division of Labour," *Cambridge Journal of Economics* 3, no. 3 (1979): 203–25.

17. Lourdes Beneria and Gita Sen, "Accumulation, Reproduction and Women's Role in Economic Development: Boserup Revisited," *Signs* 7 (1981): 279–98.

18. There have been many variations on this theme. See, for instance, Maria Mies, *Patriarchy and Accumulation on a World Scale* (London: Zed, 1986).

19. As in Sargent, ed., *Women and Revolution,* and Barrett, *Women's Oppression Today.*

20. Hence the host of such imprecise formulations as "state" patriarchy versus "private" patriarchy, Muslim patriarchy, and so on.

21. Deniz Kandiyoti, "Bargaining with Patriarchy," *Gender and Society* 2, no. 3 (1984): 274–90.

22. This term is intended to indicate the existence of set rules and scripts regulating gender relations, to which both genders accommodate and acquiesce, yet which may nevertheless be contested, redefined, and renegotiated.

23. James C. Caldwell, "A Theory of Fertility: From High Plateau to Destabilization," *Population and Development Review* 4 (1978): 553–77.

24. Deniz Kandiyoti, *Women in Rural Production Systems: Problems and Policies* (Paris: UNESCO, 1985).

25. John Hanger and Jon Moris, "Women and the Household Economy," in *Mwea: An Irrigated Rice Settlement in Kenya,* ed. Robert Chambers and Jon Moris (Munich: Weltforum, 1973), 209–44.

26. Janet Dey, "Gambian Women: Unequal Partners in Rice Development Projects," in

African Women in the Development Process, ed. Nici Nelson (London: Frank Cass, 1981), 109–22.

27. Pepe Roberts, "The Sexual Politics of Labour in Western Nigeria and Hausa Niger," in *Serving Two Masters,* ed. Kate Young (New Delhi: Allied Publishers, 1989), 27–47.

28. Kristin Mann, *Marrying Well: Marriage, Status and Social Change among the Educated Elite in Colonial Lagos* (Cambridge: Cambridge University Press, 1985).

29. Monica Munachonga, "Income Allocation and Marriage Options in Urban Zambia," in *A Home Divided: Women and Income in the Third World,* ed. Daisy Dwyer and Judith Bruce (Stanford: Stanford University Press, 1988), 173–94.

30. Katherine Abu, "The Separateness of Spouses: Conjugal Resources in an Ashanti Town," in *Male and Female in West Africa,* ed. Christine Oppong (London: George Allen and Unwin, 1983), 156–68.

31. Jane I. Guyer and Pauline E. Peters, eds., *Conceptualizing the Household: Issues of Theory and Policy in Africa,* special issue of *Development and Change* 18 (1987).

32. Enid Schildkrout, "Dependence and Autonomy: The Economic Activities of Secluded Hausa Women in Kano, Nigeria," in *Women and Work in Africa,* ed. Edna G. Bay (Boulder Colo.: Westview, 1982), 55–81.

33. Mette Bovin, "Muslim Women in the Periphery: The West African Sahel,"in *Women in Islamic Societies,* ed. Bo Utas (London: Curzon, 1983), 66–103.

34. I am excluding not only Southeast Asia but also the northern Mediterranean, despite important similarities in the latter concerning codes of honor and the overall importance attached to the sexual purity of women, because I want to restrict myself to areas where the patrilocal-patrilineal complex is dominant. Thus societies with bilateral kinship systems such as Greece, in which women do inherit and control property and whose dowries constitute productive property, do not qualify in spite of important similarities in other ideological respects. This is not to suggest, however, that an unqualified homogeneity of ideology and practice exists within the geographical boundaries indicated. There are critical variations within the Indian subcontinent, for example, that have dramatically different implications for women. For these, see Tim Dyson and Mick Moore, "On Kinship Structures, Female Autonomy and Demographic Behavior," *Population and Development Review* 9 (1983): 35–60. Conversely, even in areas of bilateral kinship, there may be instances in which all the facets of classic patriarchy, namely property, residence, and descent through the male line, may coalesce under specified circumstances. See Bette Denich, "Sex and Power in the Balkans," in *Women, Culture, and Society,* ed. Rosaldo and Lamphere, 243–62. What I am suggesting is that the most clear cut and easily identifiable examples of classic patriarchy are found within the boundaries indicated in the text.

35. Eric Wolf, *Peasants* (Englewood Cliffs, N.J.: Prentice-Hall, 1966).

36. Sherry Ortner, "The Virgin and the State," *Feminist Studies* 4 (1978): 19–36.

37. Eric Wolf, *Europe and the People without History* (Berkeley: University of California Press, 1982).

38. Michael Meeker, "Meaning and Society in the Near East: Examples from the Black Sea Turks and Levantine Arabs," *International Journal of Middle East Studies* 7 (1976): 383–422.

39. Lila Abu-Lughod, *Veiled Sentiments* (Berkeley: University of California Press, 1986).

40. Unni Wikan, *Behind the Veil in Arabia* (Baltimore: Johns Hopkins University Press, 1982).

41. Ursula Sharma, *Women, Work and Property in North West India* (London: Tavistock, 1980).

42. Ronald C. Jennings, "Women in Early Seventeenth Century Ottoman Judicial Records: The Sharia Court of Anatolian Kayseri," *Journal of the Economic and Social History of the Orient* 28 (1975): 53–114; Haim Gerber, "Social and Economic Position of Women in an

Ottoman City, Bursa, 1600–1700," *International Journal of Middle East Studies* 12 (1980): 231–44; Tucker, *Women in Nineteenth-Century Egypt.*

43. Abdelwahab Boudhiba, *Sexuality in Islam* (London: Routledge and Kegan Paul, 1985); Kay Anne Johnson, *Women, the Family and Peasant Revolution in China* (Chicago: University of Chicago Press, 1983); Margery Wolf, *Women and the Family in Rural Taiwan* (Stanford: Stanford University Press, 1972).

44. Fatima Mernissi, *Beyond the Veil* (London: Al Saqi, 1985).

45. Tucker, *Women in Nineteenth-Century Egypt.*

46. Maria Mies, "The Dynamics of the Sexual Division of Labour and Integration of Women into the World Market," in *Women and Development: The Sexual Division of Labour in Rural Socities,* ed. Lourdes Beneria (New York: Praeger, 1982), 1–28.

47. Wolf, *Women and the Family in Rural Taiwan.*

48. Johnson, *Women, the Family and Peasant Revolution in China,* 21.

49. Wikan, *Behind the Veil in Arabia,* 184.

50. Mead Cain, S. R. Khanan, and S. Nahar, "Class, Patriarchy and Women's Work in Bangladesh," *Population and Development Review* 5 (1979): 408–16.

51. Martin Greeley, "Patriarchy and Poverty: A Bangladesh Case Study," *South Asia Research* 3 (1983): 35–55.

52. Thomas S. Kuhn, *The Structure of Scientific Revolutions* (Chicago: University of Chicago Press, 1970).

53. Deniz Kandiyoti, "Rural Transformation in Turkey and Its Implications for Women's Status," in *Women on the Move: Contemporary Changes in Family and Society* (Paris: UNESCO, l984), 17–30.

54. Margery Wolf, "Women and Suicide in China," in *Women in Chinese Society,* ed. Margery Wolf and Roxane Witke (Stanford: Stanford University Press, 1975), 111–41.

55. Memissi, *Beyond the Veil,* 149.

56. Maxine Molyneux, "Mobilization without Emancipation? Women's Interests, the State and Revolution in Nicaragua," *Feminist Studies* 11 (1985): 227–54.

57. Farah Azari, "Islam's Appeal to Women in Iran: Illusion and Reality," in *Women of Iran: The Conflict with Fundamentalist Islam,* ed. Farah Azari (London: Ithaca Press, 1983), 1–71.

58. Haleh Afshar, "Behind the Veil: The Public and Private Faces of Khomeini's Policies on Iranian Women," in *Structures of Patriarchy,* ed. Bina Agarwal (London: Zed, 1988), 228–47.

59. Fadwa El Guindi, "Veiling *Infitah* with Muslim Ethic: Egypt's Contemporary Islamic Movement," *Social Problems* 8 (1981): 465–85.

60. Janet S. Chafetz and Anthony G. Dworkin, "In the Face of Threat: Organized Antifeminism in Comparative Perspective," *Gender and Society* 1 (1987): 33–60; Deborah Rosenfelt and Judith Stacey, "Second Thoughts on the Second Wave," *Feminist Studies* 13 (1987): 341–61; Judith Stacey, "Sexism by a Subtler Name? Postindustrial Conditions and Postfeminist Consciousness in the Silicon Valley," *Socialist Review* (November 1987): 7–28.

61. Kandiyoti, ed., *Women, Islam and the State;* see also Deniz Kandiyoti, "Emancipated but Unliberated? Reflections on the Turkish Case," *Feminist Studies* 13 (1987): 317–38.

CHAPTER ELEVEN

Feminism and Empowerment

A Critical Reading of Foucault

MONIQUE DEVEAUX

F ew thinkers have influenced contemporary feminist scholarship on the themes of power, sexuality, and the subject to the extent that Michel Foucault has. Indeed, even scholars who dispute this thinker's claims are compelled to acknowledge the contribution represented by his work in these areas. The years since Foucault's death have been marked by intense interest in his writings, feminist and otherwise. Today, a decade after his death, it seems appropriate to reflect critically upon the central exchanges between feminist thought and Foucauldian theory.

This article looks at three "waves" of Foucauldian literature by feminist political theorists and philosophers. Although neither chronologically separate nor thematically discrete, these waves refer to bodies of work by feminist scholars in which different aspects of Foucault's work—all related primarily to the problematic of *power*—are used for distinctly feminist ends. These waves are first, literature that appropriates Foucault's analysis of the effects of power on bodies, or what is known as the "docile-bodies" thesis, as well as a related aspect of this, the notion of "biopower," which refers to state regulation of the population; second, analyses that take their cue from Foucault's later development of an agonistic model of power,[1] in which multiple, interweaving power relations are viewed as inherently contested, as best expressed by his adage, "where there is power, there is resistance"; and third, postmodern feminist writings on sexual and gender identity informed by Foucault's assertion that prevailing categories of sex identity are the result of the transition to a modern regime of power and a proliferation of subjectifying discourses on sexuality. These three waves are taken up in turn in the first three sections of this article.

In reviewing the three waves of Foucauldian feminist literature, I argue that both the paradigms of power and the treatment of the subject[2] which emerge from Foucault's work are inadequate for feminist projects that take the delineation of women's oppression and the concrete transformation of society as central aims.

Monique Deveaux, "Feminism and Empowerment: A Critical Reading of Foucault," *Feminist Studies* 20:2 (Summer 1994):223–45. Reprinted by permission.

As such, my position stands in contrast to recent, influential feminist Foucauldian arguments, such as those of Susan Hekman and Judith Butler.[3] Although Foucault's writings on power have a certain heuristic value for feminists, I suggest that two major pitfalls recommend against uncritical appropriations of his thought: the tendency of a Foucauldian conceptualization of the subject to erase women's specific experiences with power; and the inability of the agonistic model of power to account for, much less articulate, processes of empowerment. Finally, as an antidote to these problems, section four of the article points to an emerging body of literature by feminist writers on the issue of empowerment which, I argue, serves as a more viable basis for feminist work on the themes of freedom, power, and empowerment.

The First Wave: Surveillance and Biopower

Just So Many Docile Bodies? Feminism and Panopticonism

The transition from sovereign, or monarchical, power to modern regulatory power comprised of disciplinary regimes, systems of surveillance, and normalizing tactics provides the backdrop to Foucault's early "docile bodies" thesis. Modern power requires "minimum expenditure for the maximum return," and its central organizing principle is that of discipline.[4] Aspects of sovereign power are carried over into the modern period but function as ruses, disguising and legitimating the emerging discourse of disciplinary power. This new regime of control is minimalist in its approach (in the sense of lesser expenditures of force and finance) but more far reaching and localized in its effect on bodies.

For Foucault, sex is the pivotal factor in the proliferation of mechanisms of discipline and normalization; it is also at the center of a system of "dividing practices" that separate off the insane, the delinquent, the hysteric, and the homosexual. As the sovereign's rights over the life and death of subjects began to shift in the seventeenth century, two axes or poles emblematic of the modern power paradigm evolved. They were the "anatomo-politics of the human body," which emphasizes a disciplined, useful body (hence, "docile bodies"), and the model Foucault calls the "biopolitics of the population," in which the state's attention turns to the reproductive capacities of bodies, and to health, birth, and mortality.[5] The prime focus of the first axis of power is thus "the body and its forces, their utility and their docility, their distribution and their submission."[6] The body becomes a "political field," inscribed and constituted by power relations.

Although the docile bodies thesis is later amended by Foucault in favor of a less reductionist, agonistic conception of the subject and power—and later still, by an emphasis on the "technologies of the self"[7]—his earlier paradigm has been used by feminists of this first wave of Foucauldian feminist literature to describe contemporary practices of femininity. Two specific areas of Foucault's work are drawn on in this project: the discussion of disciplinary measures in *Discipline and Punish,* encompassing the subthemes of docile bodies, surveillance, and the normalizing gaze; and, in the same text, the thesis on Panopticonism—referring to

Bentham's design for a prison that would leave prisoners perpetually exposed to view and therefore likely to police themselves.[8]

In feminist literature that appropriates the docile bodies paradigm, the transition from sovereign authority to modern, disciplinary forms of power is seen to parallel the shift from more overt manifestations of the oppression of women to more insidious forms of control. This new method is disciplinary in nature and more subtle in its exercise; it involves women in the enterprise of surveillance. The following description of modern power by Foucault provides the basis for an analysis, by scholars of this first wave, of what they call the "techniques of femininity":

> There is no need for arms, physical violence, material constraints. Just a gaze. An inspecting gaze, a gaze which each individual under its weight will end by interiorising to the point that he is his own overseer, each individual thus exercising this surveillance over, and against, himself. A superb formula: power exercised continuously and for what turns out to be at minimal cost.[9]

Feminist scholars who take up this conceptualization of power treat the account of self-surveillance offered by the model of the Panopticon as a compelling explanatory paradigm for women's acquiescence to, and collusion with, patriarchal standards of femininity. However, it is an explanation which must be modified to fit feminist purposes. Sandra Bartky applauds Foucault's work on disciplinary practices in modernity and on the construction of docile bodies, but she cautions that his analysis "treats the body . . . as if bodily experiences of men and women did not differ and as if men and women bore the same relationship to the characteristic institutions of modern life." Thus, Bartky asks: "Where is the account of the disciplinary practices that engender the 'docile bodies' of women, bodies more docile than the bodies of men? . . . [Foucault] is blind to those disciplines that produce a modality of embodiment that is peculiarly feminine."[10]

Bartky's two theses are, first, that femininity (unlike femaleness) is socially constructed, with this feminine mold taking hold most powerfully through the female body; and, second, that the disciplinary practices which produce the feminine subject must be viewed as peculiarly modern in character, symptoms of the "modernization of patriarchal domination." Bartky describes three kinds of practices that contribute to the construction of femininity: exercise and diet regimes aimed at attaining an "ideal" body size and configuration; an attention to comportment and a range of "gestures, postures and movements"; and techniques that display the feminine body as an "ornamental surface," such as the use of cosmetics. These three areas combine to "produce a body which in gesture and appearance is recognizably feminine" and reinforce a "disciplinary project of bodily perfection."[11]

But just *who*, Bartky asks, is the disciplinarian in all this? Her response is that we need to look at the dual nature of feminine bodily discipline, encompassing its socially "imposed" and "voluntary" (or self-disciplining) characteristics. The imposed aspects of feminine bodily discipline are not restricted to messages from the beauty industry and society that women should look a certain way but also include negative repercussions in terms of personal relationships and job opportunities. Bartky accounts for the voluntary, self- disciplining dimension of these techniques of femininity in two ways. Women internalize the feminine ideal so profoundly that they lack the critical distance necessary to contest it and are even fearful of the consequences of "noncompliance," and ideals of femininity are so powerful that to reject their supporting practices is to reject one's own identity.[12]

Bartky's use of the docile bodies and Panopticon theses is problematic for at least two reasons. First, it is not clear why Bartky argues that more subtle and insidious forms of domination characterize the modern era or what she calls the "modernization of patriarchal power." In fact, current examples abound of overt control of women's choices and bodies, like lack of accessible abortions and frighteningly high rates of rape and assault. This is not to suggest that glaring barriers to women's freedom should preclude reflection on less tangible obstacles but, rather, to point out the danger of taking up the latter in isolation from a broader discussion of women's social, economic, and political subordination.

Furthermore, the way Bartky conceives of women's interaction with their bodies seems needlessly reductionist. Women's choices and differences are lost altogether in Bartky's description of the feminine body and its attendant practices:

> To subject oneself to the new disciplinary power is to be up-to-date . . . it represents a saving in the economy of enforcement: since it is women themselves who practice this discipline on and against their own bodies, men get off scot-free. . . . The woman who checks her makeup half a dozen times a day to see if her foundation has caked or her mascara has run, who worries that the wind or the rain may spoil her hairdo, who looks frequently to see if her stockings have bagged at the ankle or who, feeling fat, monitors everything she eats, has become, just as surely as the inmate of the Panopticon, a self-policing subject, a self committed to a relentless self-surveillance.[13]

This description may draw attention to the pernicious effects of cultural standards of attractiveness, but it blocks meaningful discussion of how women feel about their bodies, their appearance, and social norms. It obscures the complex ways in which gender is constructed, and the fact that differences among women—age, race, culture, sexual orientation, and class—translate into myriad variations in responses to ideals of femininity and their attendant practices. Bartky's use of the docile bodies thesis has the effect of diminishing and delimiting women's subjectivity, at times treating women as robotic receptacles of culture rather than as active agents who are both constituted by, and reflective of, their social and cultural contexts.

Susan Bordo, in "The Body and the Reproduction of Femininity," also takes up Foucault's docile bodies thesis to show the ways in which women's bodies serve as a locus for the social construction of femininity. Bordo argues that anorexia nervosa and bulimia are located on a continuum with feminine normalizing phenomena such as the use of makeup, fashion, and dieting, all of which contribute to the construction of docile, feminine bodies. Thus, "anorexia begins, emerges out of . . . conventional feminine practice,"[14] the docile feminine body becomes, in the case of the anorectic, the ultimate expression of the self-disciplining female caught up in an insane culture.

There are similarities between Bordo's and Bartky's appropriation of Foucault's model of disciplining power, but the two treatments are disanalogous in significant ways. Bordo's thesis that cultural practices are inscribed onto bodies is not so extreme as Bartky's "woman-as-Panopticon" picture. In contrast to the thesis that women's bodies and psyches are molded by a patriarchal culture, Bordo focuses on anorectics' and bulimics' relationships to social practices and the ways in which they mediate the demands of a contradictory culture. For instance, she describes a teenage girl's growing awareness of social expectations and values and her impulse to both suppress feminine bodily development and resist the influence of her family by restricting her eating.[15] This does not indicate that it is appropriate to borrow the docile bodies thesis from Foucault unamended; instead, it seems that Bordo is able to steer clear of the totalizing picture of the self-disciplining Panopticon by modifying the paradigm to include accounts of women's understandings of their experiences. The modification is insufficient, however, for Bordo, like Bartky, loosely employs such concepts as "disciplinary techniques" and "normalization" to explain the forms and effects of feminine cultural practices.

This unhelpful account of subjectivity derives from problems inherent in the docile bodies paradigm. Foucault's extreme reluctance to attribute explicit agency to subjects in this early account of power results in a portrayal of individuals as passive bodies, constituted by power and immobilized in a society of discipline. Significantly, this analysis gives way, in Foucault's later works, to a more complex understanding of power as a field of relationships between free subjects. Yet feminists have clearly found this first power paradigm's emphasis on the body a useful analytic tool with which to examine women's subjectification. However, the limitations of Foucault's account of the modernization of power give us reason to take a critical distance from this aspect of his work. The appropriations discussed above indicate that there is a danger in employing the notion of self-policing, disciplined subjects in an ahistorical, metaphorical sense. Bartky—and to a lesser extent, Bordo—uses the docile body and the Panopticon as if these describe a wide range of subjectivities and practices, and this leads her to conflate women's myriad experiences of femininity. Lost are the historical context of Foucault's account of the modernization of power and the subtleties of his usage of "normalization" and bodily discipline by institutions and discourses.[16] Moreover, by treating the metaphor of docile bodies as a paradigm for women's experiences of femininity, Bartky and Bordo foreclose the integration of Foucault's later work, including his admission that resistance is inherent to the strategic model of disciplined bodies. Indeed, given Foucault's subsequent revisions and his preference for a more constitutive understanding of power in his later writings, we should ask whether any version of the "docile bodies" paradigm is useful for feminists.

Feminism and the Rise of Biopower

The second axis of modern power is what Foucault calls the "biopolitics of the population," or simply "biopower." The account of the rise of biopower in the West in the modern period, signaling a whole new politics of population control and management, is used by some Foucauldian feminists of this first wave to cast light on those "discourses"—such as fetal protection laws and new reproductive and genetic technologies (NRGT's)—that directly affect women's control of their bodies and reproductive choices.[17]

Foucault uses the term "biopower" to denote a transformation in the nature of the sovereign's power over its subjects, in which the state's focus on prohibition and juridical authority is replaced by new interests in the birth rate, education, discipline, health, and longevity of its population. Thus, what Foucault calls a "normalizing society" replaces the juridical authority of the sovereign. There is a concurrent shift from struggles for political rights to "life rights"—that is, a right to one's body, health, and the fulfillment of basic needs. As with the "docile bodies" aspect of modern power, sexuality is key to the exercise of biopower: both axes of power—the body and biopower—revolve around sexuality, which in turn becomes "a crucial target of a power organized around the management of life rather than the menace of death." This focus is manifested in the sciences of the "new technology of sex" starting from the end of the eighteenth century—namely, pedagogy, medicine, and demography.[18] Of particular interest to feminists who employ the biopower analysts are the accounts of discourses and innovations which facilitate increased state control of reproduction or what Foucault calls the "socialization of procreation." These developments are used by feminists to theorize about current reproductive practices, ranging from birth control and abortion to new reproductive and genetic technologies.

Jennifer Terry uses Foucault's account of modern power to examine such issues as "prenatal surveillance," fetal rights discourse, and surrogacy. These practices stem from increased state concern for issues of population—birth, longevity, eugenics, health—and the focus for intervention is, not surprisingly, the domain of reproduction and prenatal care. Terry situates fetal rights discourses and "natal Panopticonism" against the backdrop of regulatory prenatal technologies, including "amniocentesis, sonograms, electronic fetal monitoring . . . sonar-produced video images," and "life-style monitoring" of pregnant women, which can include regular Breathalyzer tests for women suspected of alcohol abuse.[19] She also points to legislative proposals in the United States that advocate mandatory HIV antibody testing for any woman who becomes pregnant and wishes to have a child, and notes that there are several states that require HIV testing to obtain a marriage license. This ominous form of medical interference holds particularly serious implications for childbearing women, because it implies that the state should be permitted to override their choices on the grounds that they are potential transmitters of disease.

Similarly, Terry views fetal rights discourse as a new, legitimating ideology whose deeper aspiration is the control of reproduction and the lives of pregnant women. The new prenatal screening technologies are instrumental in allowing both state and medical authorities to view the fetus as separate from the mother, who is then subject to a range of suspicions concerning her behavior during pregnancy. Furthermore, the articulation of distinct fetal rights has been the outcome of a series of civil court cases throughout the 1980s in which mothers were sued for allegedly damaging their fetuses through irresponsible behavior.[20] Terry relates these developments to Foucault's biopower paradigm so as to situate them within the overall context of increased state interest in population regulation.

Although part of Terry's argument falls back on the docile bodies thesis, the biopower paradigm nevertheless seems appropriate to describe the dramatic character of medical and state intervention. Yet like the docile bodies thesis, Foucault's biopower model de-emphasizes agents' capacities to resist regulatory and disciplinary technologies. Terry is able to avoid the worst excesses of the paradigm by inserting descriptions of various resistances, both individual and collective, into her account. She points, for instance, to the Women's AIDS Network, an international group of women in law, health, and education who are concerned with HIV and AIDS and advocate women's rights to freedom from medical surveillance. Without such correctives, readers would be left with a profound sense of disempowerment in the face of ubiquitous state and medical surveillance of our reproductive lives. More importantly, failing to point out women's responses to this intervention would give a false picture of feminist politics: women's health issues have been a constant focus for feminist activism—more so today than ever, as evidenced by the renewed prochoice movement, groups demanding increased funding for breast cancer research and treatment, grassroots initiatives to establish women's community health clinics, and so forth.

Foucault's biopower analysis helps to reveal the implications of the mechanisms for the control and regulation of our bodies discussed by Terry. However, taken unamended, the paradigm obscures both individual women's and collective struggles against coercive medical and social practices. As Terry's work shows, feminist appropriation of Foucault's biopower framework must include discussions of strategies employed by women to mediate and resist encroachments on their bodies and lives.

The Second Wave: "Where There Is Power, There Is Resistance"

A second wave of feminist literature has taken up Foucault's work on power in a different way, stressing the possibilities of resistance over the fact of domination. Here the focus is on Foucault's later development of an agonistic model of power—the notion that "where there is power, there is resistance"—as well as on the assertion that individuals contest fixed identities and relations in ongoing and sometimes subtle ways. This power paradigm has proven particularly helpful for feminists who want to show the diverse sources of women's subordination as well as to demonstrate that we engage in resistance in our everyday lives. Drawing upon Foucault's treatment of power and resistance in his *Power/Knowledge*, *History of Sexuality* (vol. 1), and "The Subject and Power," this literature illustrates how he challenges the assumption that power is located exclusively or even primarily in state apparatuses or in prohibition. By demanding that we look to the productive character of power and to the existence of multiple power relations— rather than to dualistic, top-down force—Foucault helps us move from a "state of subordination" explanation of gender relations, which emphasizes domination and victimization, to a more textured understanding of the role of power in women's lives. Viewing power as *constitutive* has helped many of us to grasp the interweaving nature of our social, political, and personal relationships.

Jana Sawicki points out that Foucault both reminds us of the importance of looking to subjugated knowledges and makes us circumspect about theories or movements that claim to offer a transcendence of power, or a power-free context. Sawicki argues that Foucault's account of power complements feminist concerns in that he "proposes that we think of power outside the confines of State, law or class. . . . Thus, Foucault frees power from the political domain in much the same way as radical feminists did."[21] Similarly, Susan Hekman argues that feminists have much to learn from Foucault's antitotalizing conception of power, because it cautions us against invoking universalisms and quick-fix solutions for complex social and political relations. Moreover, she asserts that a Foucauldian view of power necessarily reveals resistance to discourses and practices that subordinate women, a conclusion she reaches by highlighting—and I would argue, embellishing—accounts of resistance and political action in Foucault's work.[22]

A more critical body of work by feminist scholars takes issue with precisely those aspects of the agonistic model of power that this second wave finds so useful—the notion that power circulates and is *exercised* rather than possessed. However, this criticism stems in part from wrongly reading Foucault as a certain kind of postmodernist thinker, reflected in the allegation that he is a relativist (because antihumanist) and consequently guilty of overlooking the political aspects of power and resistance. Foucault's antimodernist rejection of truth is invoked to corroborate this analysis, as is his reluctance in his middle and later works to speak of social systems of domination. This position is best represented by Nancy Fraser, who contends that Foucault's agonistic notion of power posits that "power is productive, ineliminable, and therefore normatively neutral." By contrast, Fraser asserts that feminism needs to be able to distinguish between social practices which are "good" (less coercive) and "bad" (very coercive) and expresses nostalgia for Weberian distinctions between violence, domination, and authority.[23] Integral to this charge is Fraser's reading of Foucault as an antihumanist thinker who refuses to engage in normative discussions. Nancy Hartsock concurs with the conclusion that feminists cannot find adequate normative grounding in Foucault's work and goes so far as to state that his theory undermines attempts at social change, because his conception of power obscures the systematic nature of gender oppression. Echoing Fraser's criticism, she states that for Foucault, "power is everywhere and ultimately nowhere" and that "domination, viewed from above, is more likely to appear as equality." As an antidote to this distortion, she suggests that feminists need to "develop an account of the world which treats our perspectives not as subjugated or disruptive knowledges, but as primary and constitutive of the real world."[24]

Hartsock's claim that Foucault's model of power does not allow for an understanding of systematic injustice seems, at first glance, credible. Indeed, his account of power renders murky and less tangible numerous social relations, relations which feminists have argued constitute concrete oppression. Yet it is misleading to suggest that for Foucault such a condition does not exist; to the contrary, domination is by his account a frequent and at times inescapable reality.[25] Nor does it seem fair to impute to Foucault, as both Fraser and Hartsock do, a normatively neutral world view, because his work consistently reflects what are manifestly—if not always polemically—political concerns.

Staking out a middle ground between the criticisms of Fraser and Hartsock and the generosity of Sawicki and Hekman, I would like to argue that Foucault's agonistic model of power is double-edged. It is useful for feminists to the extent that it disengages us from simplistic, dualistic accounts of power; at the same time, however, it obscures many important experiences of power specific to women and fails to provide a sustainable notion of agency. This is not an easily negotiated tension for feminists; as one critic comments, Foucault's "lack of a rounded theory of subjectivity or agency conflicts with a fundamental aim of the feminist project to rediscover and reevaluate the experiences of women."[26] Moreover, feminists in particular should be wary of Foucault's assertion that *all* social interactions are defined and thoroughly permeated by the exercise of power, as expressed in his view that "in human relations, whatever they are—whether it be a question of communicating verbally . . . or a question of a love relationship, an institutional or economic relationship—power is always present: I mean the relationship in which one wishes to direct the behavior of another."[27] If we agree with Hartsock's suggestion that feminists need to envisage a nondominated world, we should not slip into fatalistic views about the omnipresence of power. This means rejecting Foucault's assertion that absolutely *no* social or personal relations escape permeation by power.[28]

To illustrate the ramifications of Foucault's approach, it is useful to consider some specific ways in which this model tends to obscure women's experiences of power. This entails a discussion of Foucault's treatment of the subject, first with respect to freedom, then as concerns the issue of violence. In his later work, Foucault emphasizes that in order for a power relationship to exist, the subject on whom that "conduct" or governance is exercised must be a *free* subject. This appears at times as an essentialist freedom and at others as a qualified liberty where "individual or collective subjects . . . are faced with a field of possibilities in which several ways of behaving, several reactions and diverse comportments may be realized." Thus, power is separated off from force, violence, and domination, which do not involve any freedom on the part of the subject.

> A relationship of violence acts upon a body or upon things; it forces, it bends, it breaks on the wheel, it destroys, or it closes the door on all possibilities. Its opposite pole can only be passivity, and if it comes up against any resistance it has no other option but to try to minimize it.

In order for a relationship of power to exist, a subject must be capable of action or resistance and be recognized as a person on whom force or "conduct" is exercised: thus, agonistic power is "a set of actions upon other actions."[29] This does not mean that domination is altogether antithetical to power. Rather, domination is the result of trajectories of force and power relations, culminating in a greater or lesser state of subordination, and correspondingly, with fewer or greater possibilities for resistance by subjects. [30] Yet power and domination remain different phenomena for Foucault.

It is important to ask whether this treatment of the subject enables us to recognize women's experiences of freedom and unfreedom. It would be difficult to argue that Foucault's account of the subject's capacity to resist power is simply untrue. Indeed, much feminist literature now stresses the importance of seeing women not as passive victims uniformly dominated but as active agents mediating their experiences. Nor does it seem accurate to claim that Foucault's reworking of the subject somehow compromises the political claim that women are indeed subordinated—for domination is a state that Foucault is quick to acknowledge. [31] Yet what feminist theory does, and what Foucault does *not* do, is look closely and critically at the issue of freedom where it concerns women's responses to structural inequality and male violence.

To understand the workings of power and the responses that power elicits, it is necessary to ask how women experience freedom and barriers to freedom. This might involve, for instance, looking at what Virginia Held has referred to as internal impediments to women's freedom or empowerment. [32] Held points to Sandra Bartky's work on shame: "The heightened self-consciousness that comes with emotions of self-assessment may become, in the shame of the oppressed, a stagnant self-obsession. Or shame may generate a rage whose expression is unconstructive, even self-destructive. In all these ways, shame is profoundly disempowering." [33] Unlike her earlier "woman-as-Panopticon" analysis, Bartky's theorizing on shame posits women as active subjects capable of a range of responses to social power. Bartky also discusses sources of disempowerment for women often omitted from accounts of power and powerlessness: unreciprocated emotional labor, nurturing, and caregiving. This kind of disempowerment, because it "is more subtle and oblique, one that is rooted in the subjective and deeply interiorized effects upon women ourselves both of the emotional care we give and of the care we fail to get in return," [34] is, I think, easily obscured by Foucault's agonistic model of power, because it reflects neither outright domination nor the intersubjective play of power between two free agents.

Feminists need to look at the *inner* processes that condition women's sense of freedom or choice in addition to external manifestations of power and dominance—and Foucault's understanding of power is decidedly inadequate to this task. Women's "freedom" does not simply refer to objective possibilities for maneuvering or resisting within a power dynamic but concerns whether a woman *feels* empowered in her specific context. Because Foucault's account of the freedom of the subject determines the presence of power or "conduct"—as well as its opposite pole, violence or domination—based on the existence of objective points of resistance, it obscures the subjective aspects of power. As Lois McNay points out, in Foucault's theory, "power relations are only examined from the perspective of how they are installed in institutions and not from the point of view of those subject to power." [35] A feminist response to this failing might borrow from Held's objection to classical liberals and contemporary libertarians' views of freedom as largely determined by the absence of "external impediments": feminists must emphasize, against this account, that "the self-development of women involves changing the affective tastes, the emotional coloration, with which we experience the world, not only the outer obstacles in that experience." Addressing women's freedom requires that we reflect upon internal impediments to exercising choice as well as the tangible obstacles to its realization—and this means considering practices and conventions that may have disempowering effects not easily discernible to theorists who focus exclusively on political power. Finally, it involves recognizing certain experiences as ongoing expressions of resistance to power—"the power to give voice to one's aspiration to be heard is not so much the removal of an external impediment as the beginning of an internal empowerment."[36]

Foucault's agonistic model of power, skewed as it is towards a dynamic of *acting upon,* cannot provide feminists with the conceptual tools needed to understand empowerment and disempowerment, freedom and non-freedom, To illustrate the inability of this framework to consider women's experiences of power, let us next consider the issue of male violence. First, recall Foucault's claim that violence and power are inherently different or separable, the former presupposing a situation of physical determination and the latter connoting a relation of "conduct," a dichotomy expressed by his claim that "where the determining factors saturate the whole there is no relationship of power; slavery is not a power relationship when a man is in chains."[37] Foucault's metaphoric slave in chains has no possibility of movement or resistance and is, in his view, situated in a context of violence and domination, not power. What does this mean for feminists grappling with the question of women's experiences of rape, battery, and psychological abuse? To define male power as an inherently separable phenomenon from male force and domination, as Foucault would have us do, is to disregard the ways in which this power is frequently transformed into violence. A woman living in an abusive relationship feels the continuum of her partner's anger and force, sees that the day-to-day exercise of power is the stuff out of which explosions of abuse and violence are made. Foucault's distinction between power and violence, freedom and domination, do not allow us to ask whether this woman feels complicit or victimized, powerless or empowered to leave the situation of abuse.

The issues of women's relation to violence and power are raised in a response by Monique Plaza to Foucault's position on rape. Foucault's view, expressed during a roundtable discussion, is that "when rape is punished, it is exclusively the physical violence that should be punished," and that one should consider rape "nothing but an assault." Foucault concludes that to treat rape as a sexual offense is to shore up the apparatus of repression, infusing sex with repressive power; thus, he comments that sexuality should not "under any circumstances be the object of punishment."[38]

Plaza's response to Foucault is that he is setting up a false dichotomy between violence and sex. Rape, which is violent, forced sex, thus represents an imbroglio for Foucault, leading him to assert that the sexual part of rape should be exempted from punishment, leaving only force as deserving of sanction—a preposterous distinction. Women's unfreedom (as victims of rape) is thus superseded by the need to maintain men's freedom, that is, their freedom not to be punished for sex or to have their sex repressed. As Plaza writes, "what do they say except that *they want to defend the freedom that men have at the present time to repress us by rape?* What do they say except that *what they call (their) freedom is the repression of our bodies?*"[39]

I have brought up the issues of male violence and rape not to show that Foucault is a bad person or a bad philosopher but rather to illustrate that feminist theorists should approach his notions of the free subject and agonistic power with great caution. To summarize, this caveat is necessary for three reasons: first, because his analysis does not consider women's internal barriers to agency and choice, as with the example of shame; second, because it sets up a false dichotomy between power and violence, as illustrated by the continuum of anger and physical abuse experienced by a battered woman; and third, because it does not question the fact that in many societies, men's freedom (privilege, etc.) is contingent upon women's unfreedom, as in the case of rape, rather than on the presence of a freely maneuvering subject. This does not mean feminists must jettison Foucault's framework of power relations altogether but suggests that if we *do* wish to employ this part of the tool kit,[40] we must amend the thesis drastically to include inquiry into subjective aspects of power and, in particular, to reconceptualize the relationship between social and personal power and privilege, on one hand, and violence, on the other. This requires that we recognize that there are significant connections between the two, connections that are not always immediately obvious to us. However, certain distinctions between power and force are warranted and are crucial for feminists—there are real differences, for instance, between not being considered for a promotion on sexually discriminatory grounds, and being raped. It does not help feminists to insist on the existence of one single, global form of oppression that admits only of degree.[41]

Finally, as the discussion of lesbian and gay identity politics in the next section will show, the omission of an account of empowerment from Foucault's analysis of power should alert us to the limitations of his theory for feminist theory and praxis.

The Third Wave: Sexual Identity and Regimes of Truth/Power

Following the intense interest in recent years in the themes of identity and difference, numerous scholars have used Foucault's work to suggest new ways of thinking about gender and sexual orientation. I will use the example of lesbian and gay politics to show that, despite their initial appeal, Foucault's accounts of the subject and power may contradict the aspirations of those who would mobilize around common, if contingent, identities.

Judith Butler is at the center of the third wave of Foucauldian feminist theory. In *Gender Trouble: Feminism and the Subversion of Identity*, Butler builds on Foucault's account of the proliferation of discourses on sex in the modern era. What we see today, she argues, is the constant reproduction of sexual identities via "an exclusionary apparatus of production" in which meanings of these practices are curtailed, restricted, and reinforced. Whereas Foucault is most interested in the way regimes of power produce discourses on sexual perversion, pathology, delinquency and criminality, and new subjects emerging from these categories, Butler is equally interested in the construction of gender and sexual minority identities. For feminists, her most controversial move is to use Foucault's thesis on modern power to deconstruct the very notion of woman. Butler proposes that we view gender as discursively and materially constructed through repetitive "performances" of "words, acts, gestures and desire." Foucault's influence on Butler's formulation is clear in her claim: "If the inner truth of gender is a fabrication and if a true gender is a fantasy instituted and inscribed on the surface of bodies then it seems that genders can be neither true nor false, but are only produced as the truth effects of a discourse of primary and stable identity." Rather than clinging to fixed notions of femaleness as necessary for feminist praxis, Butler suggests that we reconceptualize identity as "an effect" in order to destabilize gender and open up new, unforeseen possibilities for agency.[42]

A full discussion of Butler's work is not possible here, but I would like to address those aspects of Foucault's analysis of modern power that Butler invokes in her call for a notion of sexuality as a site of contestation and subversion and to consider such a strategy's implications for lesbian and gay politics. Like Foucault, Butler suggests that sexual identities are constituted by regulatory practices and draws our attention to the instability of sexual categories. The backdrop to this thesis is found in Foucault's discussion of the rise of pastoral power in the West in the modern period; this power is salvation-oriented, individualizing (and at the same time totalizing), and "linked with the production of truth—the truth of the individual himself."[43] This combination of tactics culminates in dividing practices and "true discourses" that tie the individual back onto her or his own identity, producing the modern category of the "homosexual" as well as other subject categories.

It is because minority sexual identities are so deeply couched in the dividing practices which first gave them meaning—established "through the isolation, intensification, and consolidation of peripheral sexualities"[44]—that Foucault discourages us from embracing these self-understandings in an uncritical way or as part of a political strategy. Not surprisingly, Foucault is dismissive of struggles that make sex the "rallying point" for resistance to the deployment of sexuality[45]; he contrasts "the homosexual liberation movements" with "the creative and interesting elements in the women's movements" and praises the latter for attempting to overcome their particular form of individualization, promoting "a displacement effected in relation to the sexual centering of the problem, formulating the demand for new forms of culture, discourse, language . . . which are no longer part of that rigid assignation and pinning down to their sex which they had initially . . . been politically obliged to accept in order to make themselves heard." Gay men have not yet tried to desexualize their political platform as much as the feminist movement and instead have unwittingly overemphasized their sexual orientation.[46] Foucault believes there is a need to "desex" struggles, by which he means that the focus of a project of "liberation"—a concept he views with much suspicion—must change in order to prompt a more radical questioning of discourses that have made the categorization and persecution of individuals possible.

> It is the *agency* of sex that we must break away from, if we aim—through a tactical reversal of the various mechanisms of sexuality—to counter the grips of power with the claims of bodies, pleasures, and knowledge in their multiplicity and their possibility of resistance. The rallying point for the counterattack against the deployment of sexuality ought not to be sex-desire, but bodies and pleasures.[47]

Butler concurs with Foucault's view that a politics placed squarely on fixed categories of gender and sexual orientation has the effect of reifying those identities. As an antidote to the production and reinforcement of prevailing notions of sexual identity, Butler argues that homosexuality and heterosexuality—like gender—exist as enactments of culture and aesthetic performances; even as these identities are performed and repeated, they are (in true Foucauldian form) being contested and unraveled. In an analysis that also borrows from Jacques Derrida, Butler claims that emancipatory discourses on sexuality ironically set up heterosexuality as origin, in the sense that homosexuality is viewed as a "copy" of the "original," or authentic, sexual identity.[48] To counteract this reification, Butler proposes to disrupt the logic that makes this dualistic formulation possible by underlining the contingency of the "sign" of sexual identity.

It is considerably less clear how a strategy of displacement translates into effective political action. Butler endorses Foucault's strategy and argues for a concept of politics as the constant undoing of the categories and gender norms that derive from, and are perpetuated by, sexual "performances." Crucially, however, she avoids the topic of how we go about employing for political purposes those same provisional identities. Indeed, it is not at all clear that Butler thinks this can be done successfully—that is, without reifying those subjectivities. Butler's ambivalence points to the sheer difficulty of such a project, as evidenced by her comment: "There is a political necessity to use some sign now, and we do, but how to use it in such a way that its futural significations are not foreclosed? How to use the sign and avow its temporal contingency at once?"[49] Similarly, Jana Sawicki incorporates Foucauldian premises in her assertions that we need to discover new ways of understanding ourselves and new ways of resisting how we have been socially defined and constructed. Unfortunately, as with Butler, Sawicki leaves us with little sense of how feminist politics can proceed if gender is to be displaced.[50]

The political ambivalence of a position stressing the contingency of common self-understandings—or for Butler, the illusory nature of gender and sexual identities—is echoed in Foucault's own work. Foucault's view that subjects must resist the particular forms of subjectification that have oppressed them is linked to his claim that these struggles must expand and critically reflect upon both their definitions of shared identity and their domain of activism. This is as close as Foucault comes to suggesting what political resistance to oppression might look like, and the vagueness of his vision is reproduced by third-wave Foucauldian feminists. If, by the suggestion: "Maybe the target nowadays is not to discover what we are, but to refuse what we are," Foucault is advising that one take up a critical stance toward identities that have been constructed and reinforced by coercive discourses, the point is well taken.[51] This circumspection is also helpful as a caution against the sometimes homogenizing effect of identity politics—the tendency for a particular self-understanding to supersede others by setting up norms for what it means to be, and to live as, a lesbian or gay man. Yet several troubling questions remain. For example, are sexual identities strictly "constructed" via dividing practices that set homosexual off from heterosexual? Aren't a range of issues regarding sexual choice and the conscious appropriation of an identity simply being overlooked? Isn't it necessary, both for reasons of personal affirmation and political efficacy—in order to make rights-based claims, for instance—to assert the existence of the "categories" of women, lesbians, and gay men? And how does a group or an individual simultaneously resist an identity and mobilize around it for the purposes of empowerment and political action? These are questions which the arguments of third-wave Foucauldian feminists, like those of Foucault himself, necessarily raise. The fact that the questions go unaddressed speaks to the difficulties inherent in Foucauldian conceptions of identity and power.

Despite the initial usefulness of a deconstruction of sexual identity, then, Foucault's position leaves feminist theorists in something of a quandary. In particular, there are three concrete political problems raised by this approach that require attention. The first, perhaps most obvious, problem is that Foucault's treatment of sexual identities gives insufficient attention to struggles by particular social movements and to the ways in which their participants perceive and creatively inhabit their own identities. Most lesbian and gay activists today place sexual orientation at the center of their struggles, which range from retrieving accounts of their historical communities to resisting homophobic violence and discrimination as concerns employment, health and pension benefits, and so forth. For Foucault, such activity constitutes a dubious if not illogical strategy, because it casts these sexual identities as essential or biological rather than socially constructed. The end result is, as one critic notes of unmitigated social constructionist theories in general, a tendency to treat lesbians and gay men who understand themselves in identity-bound terms as "victims of 'false consciousness,' unaware of the constructedness of their identities."[52]

Foucault's analysis also negates the importance of personal and group definition and affirmation, resources not easily replaced by the vague notion of identity contestation. Shane Phelan, for instance, has looked at the ways in which the construction of a positive lesbian identity and a community to support it, while rife with difficulties, has provided a base of emotional and political support for many lesbians. She cautions against the pitfalls of fixing a static description of lesbianism—since "every new definition . . . shades another, and this is a choice with political consequences"—agreeing with Foucault insofar as she argues that lesbian feminists fall into "the trap of counterreification" in taking back the task of defining themselves. Yet in the final instance, Phelan shows it is possible and desirable to forge a critical, strategic politics that keeps identity at the center of its project.

Identity politics does mean building our public action on who we are and how that identity fits into and does not fit into our society. This is and must be the basis for political action that addresses nonjuridical, nonstate-centered power. . . . Identity politics must be based, not only on identity, but on an appreciation for politics as the art of living together. Politics that ignores our identities, that makes them "private," is useless; but nonnegotiable identities will enslave us whether they are imposed from within or without.[53]

A second, related problem with a Foucauldian analysis of identity is that it needlessly dichotomizes the debate on strategies for sexual minority politics, offering two disparate alternatives: on the one hand, the decision to keep sexuality and sexual choice at the center of a movement, to reappropriate these experiences as a departure point for political activism; and, on the other, Foucault's preferred option, that of "desexualizing" struggles and exploring new forms of pleasure and discourse that do not feed back into the "pinning down" to one's sex. This ignores the possibility, illustrated by lesbian and gay communities over the past several decades, that these two political methods may be complementary tools of empowerment and political activism, pursued simultaneously. In particular, the idea of strategic essentialism—reappropriating and subverting an identity while maintaining an understanding of its historical contingency—is overlooked by Foucault and is treated rather suspiciously by this third-wave feminist literature.[54]

A final criticism both of Foucault's position on sexual identity and of third-wave feminist appropriations of his thesis is that they leave untouched the subject's understanding of her condition of oppression, and by implication, tend to foreclose discussions of agency and empowerment. This omission is crucially related to the criticisms of Foucault's agonistic model of power and his position on sexual identities. Many forms of resistance may go unnoticed if we begin from Foucault's call to desexualize struggles and so shun the minority identities which have been constructed by discourses on sex. For instance, it is unlikely that this approach to sexual identities can comprehend lesbian feminist politics of the past two decades, Stonewall, ACT UP, or even the institution of Gay Pride Day. Moreover, Foucault's treatment of power obscures the personal experiences behind such activism: these may contain elements of power relations in which the "acting upon" dynamic is appropriate, as, for example, in the case of specific demands directed at decision makers. Yet struggles such as these are also about personal empowerment and acting collectively to set an agenda for change. In effect, Foucault's power analysis prevents us from seeing or conceptualizing relationships in which the object is neither to act upon another in a power relation nor to resist the attempts of governing conduct or a local manifestation of power; it is a framework that seems inappropriate for describing cooperative efforts aimed both at political transformation and personal empowerment or consciousness raising.[55]

Foucault's theory allows little room for an account of the processes involved in developing personal and collective capacities for political activism; empowerment is not simply about actions upon agents in a relationship of power and so cannot be understood within the confines of this analysis. A richer resource of alternative approaches to theorizing agency is to be found in works by such writers as Audre Lorde, Patricia Hill Collins, and bell hooks.

Dualism of power construction — Acting / being Acted
resisting / upon

Conclusion: Feminism, Power, and Empowerment

> Feminist ideology should not encourage (as sexism has done) women to believe they are powerless. It should clarify for women the powers they exercise daily and show them ways these powers can be used to resist sexist domination and exploitation.
>
> — bell hooks, "Changing Perspectives on Power", in
> *Feminist Theory: From Margin to Center*, 1984

If empowerment is much more than a relationship of power, or an attempt to direct the behavior of others, what is the most useful conceptualization of this phenomenon for feminists? Rather than offering a single definition, I would like to hint at an array of useful accounts in feminist literature.

Audre Lorde writes of the importance of erotic power in our lives and the connections between agency and self-understanding: "Our acts against oppression become integral with self, motivated and empowered from within."[56] The relationship between personal experiences of disempowerment and oppression, on the one hand, and broader political action, on the other, has numerous illustrations in contemporary North American feminist politics. For instance, the advent of the direct-action Women's Action Coalition (WAC) in the United States in early 1992 (and soon after, in Canada) was motivated by a surge of frustration and anger in the wake of such events as the Kennedy rape trial and the Supreme Court's disbelief in the testimony of Anita Hill, both of which resonated with the experiences of untold numbers of women.[57] WAC has been successful precisely because it galvanizes this discontent and recognizes the importance of empowerment: the women involved do not expect immediate political changes but know that their dramatic, vocal protests register their anger and convey the message that specific injustices will not be tolerated.

On a similar note, Patricia Hill Collins writes about the empowerment of Black American women as an outcome of changed consciousness, resulting from both internal transformation and the effects of these transformations on the broader community.

> [C]hange can also occur in the private, personal space of an individual woman's consciousness. Equally fundamental, this type of change is also empowering. If a Black woman is forced to remain "motionless on the outside," she can always develop the "inside" of a changed consciousness as a sphere of freedom. Becoming empowered through self-knowledge, even within conditions that severely limit one's ability to act, is essential.

Collins writes of the importance of an alternative vision of power. In her view, "Black women have not conceptualized our quest for empowerment as one of replacing elite white male authorities with ourselves as benevolent Black female ones. Instead, African-American women have overtly rejected theories of power based on domination in order to embrace an alternative vision of power based on a humanist vision of self-actualization, self-definition, and self-determination."[58] bell hooks also believes it is important to consider the possibilities for political transformation which arise from our daily lives. Her notion of a "politics of location" as a revisioning exercise to counter the effects of hege-monic practices, as well as her concept of the dual nature of marginality—as a "site of deprivation" and a "space of resistance"—are useful analytic tools with which to examine Black American struggles as well as women's specific empow-erment.[59]

These feminist writings on empowerment suggest the need to place the sub-ject's interpretation and mediation of her experiences at the center of our inquiries into the how and why of power. Such an analysis might ask: what do relation-ships of power feel like from the inside, where are the possibilities for resistance, and what personal and collective processes will take us there? A feminist analy-sis of power would avoid the omissions and problems of Foucault's understand-ing of power in four key ways. First, by conceptualizing women's relationships to their bodies as both a reflection of social construction *and* of their own responses to (and mediation of) the cultural ideals of femininity, it would avoid the pitfalls of a static, "docile bodies" paradigm of subjectivity. Second, it would reject as-pects of Foucault's agonistic model of power—including his assertion that all relations are permeated by power, and the simplistic, false dichotomy of power versus violence or domination—and instead attend to the myriad sources of disempowerment and oppression experienced by women. Third, it would take seriously the issue of women's empowerment, their capacities for self-determination and freedom, and the conditions in which these flourish. And fourth, a feminist analysis of power would dispute both Foucault's view that sex-ual identities should not form the basis for lesbian and gay struggles and third-wave Foucauldian feminists' assertion that the category of "women" should be displaced from the center of feminist politics. This last point need not prevent those engaged in feminist theory and queer theory—nor, indeed, social move-ments themselves—from appreciating the significance of Foucault's discussion of the historical construction of marginalized identities.

Although the overall tone of this article conveys more criticisms of Foucault than suggestions for feminist uses of his thought, this is not necessarily bad news. I think that feminist theorists have learned, and can learn still more, from Fou-cault. Although it is disappointing that his work does not engage directly with feminism, this does not diminish the heuristic usefulness of certain of Foucault's insights on power, resistance, and sexuality. It is vital, however, to keep a criti-cal edge when attempting to appropriate Foucauldian concepts for feminist ends. In the process, we may discover that there are resources within feminist theory better suited to the task of developing an alternative vision of power and em-powerment than are attempts to make Foucault fit feminist purposes.

Notes

1. Foucault's reference to power as agonic, or agonistic, denotes his assertion that power circulates, is never fixed, and is really a network of relationships of power among sub-jects who are at least in some minimal sense free to act and to resist. This is the con-cept of power developed in his *Power/Knowledge: Selected Interviews and Other Writings:*

1972–1977, ed. Colin Gordon, trans. Colin Gordon et al. (New York: Pantheon Books, 1980), and in "The Subject and Power," afterword to *Michel Foucault: Beyond Structuralism and Hermeneutics,* ed. Paul Rabinow and Hubert Dreyfus (Chicago: University of Chicago Press, 1983). Agonistic comes from the Greek, *agon,* or combat, and connotes both the exercise of power and struggle (see Foucault's account of the agonistic metaphor in "The Subject and Power," 222).

2. I refer to the subject in the singular throughout the essay for simplicity's sake, but do not mean to imply that Foucault asserts the existence of a homogeneous kind of subject or subjectivity. Indeed, in response to this suggestion, Foucault comments:

> (The subject) is not a substance; it is a form and this form is not above all or always identical to itself. You do not have towards yourself the same kind of relationship when you constitute yourself as a political subject who goes and votes or speaks up in a meeting, and when you try to fulfill your desires in a sexual relationship. . . . In each case, we play, we establish with one's self some different form of relationship. And it is precisely the historical constitution of these different forms of subject relating to games of truth that interest me.

See "The Ethic of Care for the Self as a Practice of Freedom: An Interview with Michel Foucault," interview by Raul Fornet-Betancourt et al., trans. Joseph D. Gauthier, in *The Final Foucault,* ed. James Bernauer and David Rasmussen (Boston, MIT Press, 1988), 10.

3. See Susan Hekman, *Gender and Knowledge: Elements of a Postmodern Feminism* (Boston: Northeastern University Press, 1990); and Judith Butler, *Gender Trouble: Feminism and the Subversion of Identity* (New York and London: Routledge, 1990).

4. Michel Foucault, "Two Lectures," in *Power/Knowledge,* 105.

5. Michel Foucault, *History of Sexuality,* vol. 1, *Introduction,* trans. Robert Hurley (New York: Vintage Books, 1980), 139.

6. Michel Foucault, *Discipline and Punish,* trans. Alan Sheridan (New York: Vintage Books, 1979), 25.

7. For example, Foucault, in his 1982 lecture on "Technologies of the Self," stated: "Perhaps I've insisted too much on the technology of domination and power. I am more and more interested in the interaction between oneself and others and in the technologies of individual domination, the history of how an individual acts upon himself, in the technology of the self." Also important here is his emphasis on "governmentality," which is the "contact between the technologies of domination of others and those of the self." See Luther H. Martin et al., *Technologies of the Self: A Seminar with Michel Foucault* (Amherst: University of Massachusetts Press, 1988), 19.

8. See also Foucault, "The Eye of Power," in *Power/Knowledge.*

9. Ibid., 155.

10. Sandra Bartky, "Foucault, Femininity, and the Modernization of Patriarchal Power," in *Feminism and Foucault: Reflections on Resistance,* ed. Irene Diamond and Lee Quimby (Boston: Northeastern University Press, 1988), 63, 63–64.

11. Ibid., 64 and 66. Unfortunately, "femininity" as a construct is at no point historicized or contextualized in Bartky's analysis.

12. Ibid., 77–78.

13. Ibid., 81.

14. Susan Bordo, "The Body and the Reproduction of Femininity," in *Gender, Body, Knowledge,* ed. Alison Jaggar and Susan Bordo (London and New Brunswick, NJ: Rutgers University Press, 1989), 23.

15. Ibid. See also Bordo's "Anorexia Nervosa: Psychopathology as Crystallization of Culture," in *Feminism and Foucault.*

16. Foucault—in *Discipline and Punish* and "Two Lectures"—traces the emergence of specific disciplinary mechanisms such as prisons, hospitals, and schools to account for the formation of a "disciplinary society" beginning in the late seventeenth century and em-

phasizes that the transition from sovereign to disciplinary power is a historically specific phenomenon.

17. Although I have chosen to distinguish between Foucault's "docile bodies" and "biopower" theses, they are frequently run together in the literature. I treat them separately in order to show that the "biopower" analysis, if amended, is much more useful for feminists than is the docile bodies thesis.

18. *History of Sexuality,* 1: 142–43, 145, 147, 116.

19. Jennifer Terry, "The Body Invaded: Medical Surveillance of Women as Reproducers," *Socialist Review* 19 (July-September 1989): 13–43, 20.

20. Terry points out (p. 23) that, since 1984, it has become possible in the United States to charge a vehicle driver, including a pregnant woman, with manslaughter causing the death of a fetus. Additionally, legal theorist Patricia Williams cites one case among many in which a pregnant woman who was a known drug user was ordered put in jail by a judge in order to protect the fetus (Women and the Law lecture series, Law Faculty, McGill University, Montreal, 4 Apr. 1990).

21. Jana Sawicki, "Identity Politics and Sexual Freedom," in *Feminism and Foucault,* 185 and 189 and her "Foucault and Feminism: Toward a Politics of Difference," *Hypatia* 1 (Fall 1986): 32, 26.

22. Hekman, 182–86.

23. Nancy Fraser, "Foucault on Modern Power: Empirical Insights and Normative Confusions," in *Unruly Practices: Power, Discourse, and Gender in Contemporary Social Theory* (Minneapolis: University of Minnesota Press, 1989), 31, 32.

24. Nancy Hartsock, "Foucault on Power: A Theory for Women?," in *Feminism/Postmodernism,* ed. Linda Nicholson (New York and London: Routledge, 1990), 170, 168, 171.

25. Foucault, "The Ethic of Care for the Self as a Practice of Freedom," 12.

26. Lois McNay, "The Foucauldian Body and the Exclusion of Experience," *Hypatia* 6 (Fall 1991): 125.

27. Foucault, "The Ethic of Care for the Self as a Practice of Freedom, " 11.

28. Peta Bowden suggests that Foucault's conception of power precludes a range of emotions and interpersonal experiences, because it insists that all relations are characterized by adversarial agonistic power (seminar presentation, Department of Political Science, McGill University, Montreal, April 1990).

29. To "conduct" in this Foucauldian sense can mean to direct others or even to coerce. Foucault also uses conduct as a noun to denote a way of behaving in an "open field of possibilities." See Foucault, "The Subject and Power," 220–21.

30. Foucault, "Power and Strategies," in *Power/Knowledge,* 42.

31. Ibid. Despite Foucault's references to domination, he is often taken to purport the absence of domination per se. For instance, Biddy Martin argues that "there is the danger that Foucault's challenges to traditional categories, if taken to a 'logical' conclusion . . . could make the question of women's oppression obsolete." See her "Feminism, Criticism, and Foucault," in *Feminism and Foucault,* 17.

32. Virginia Held, "Freedom and Feminism" (paper presented to the conference on "The Intellectual Legacy of C.B. Macpherson," University of Toronto, 4–6 Oct. 1989). For a revised version, see her *Feminist Morality: Transforming Culture, Society, and Politics* (Chicago: University of Chicago Press, 1993), chap. 9.

33. Sandra Bartky, "Shame and Gender," in *Feminism and Domination: Studies in the Phenomenology of Oppression* (New York and London: Routledge, 1991), 97. Held quotes an earlier version of this work on p. 8 of her essay.

34. Sandra Bartky, "Feeding Egos and Tending Wounds: Deference and Disaffection in Women's Emotional Labor," ibid., 111.

35. McNay, 134.

36. Held, 8, 12.

37. Foucault, "The Subject and Power," 221.

38. Monique Plaza, "Our Damages and Their Compensation—Rape: The 'Will Not to Know' of Michel Foucault," *Feminist Issues* 1 (Summer 1981): 25–35. Plaza quotes Foucault from a round-table discussion published in *La Folie Encerclée* (Paris: Seghers/Lafont, 1977), 99. See Plaza, 27, 26.

39. Plaza, 31.

40. Foucault suggests using theory as a "tool kit" in the sense of "instrument"—rather than as a total "system," in "Power and Strategies," *Power/Knowledge*, 145.

41. I am indebted to Virginia Held for pointing out how important distinctions between power and violence are for feminists. Held draws a number of useful distinctions between power, force, coercion, and violence. (Personal communication, 5 June 1993).

42. Butler, *Gender Trouble*, 31–32, 136, 147. Butler's clearest definition of gender is found early (p. 33) on in her text: "Gender is the repeated stylization of the body, a set of repeated acts within a highly regulatory frame that congeal over time to produce the appearance of substance, of a natural sort of being."

43. Foucault, "The Subject and Power," 214.

44. Foucault, *History of Sexuality,* 1: 48.

45. Foucault, "Confessions of the Flesh," *Power/Knowledge*, 219–20; see also interview entitled "The End of the Monarchy of Sex," trans. John Johnson, in *Foucault Live: Interviews, 1966–1984,* ed. Sylvère Lotringer (New York: Semiotext(e), 1989).

46. Foucault, "Confessions of the Flesh," 220. Foucault appears to be referring to gay men, and not to lesbians, when he speaks of "homosexual movements"; moreover, he contrasts this movement with "women," a distinction which is both misleading and ill-informed.

47. Foucault, *History of Sexuality*, 1:157.

48. Judith Butler, "Imitation and Gender Insubordination," in *Inside/Out: Lesbian Theories, Gay Theories,* ed. Diana Fuss (New York and London: Routledge, 1992), 18, 19, 20.

49. Ibid., 19.

50. Sawicki, "Identity Politics and Sexual Freedom," 189.

51. Foucault: "The Subject and Power," 216.

52. Stephen Epstein, "Gay Politics, Ethnic Identity: The Limits of Social Constructionism," *Socialist Review* 7 (May/August 1987): 22.

53. Shane Phelan, *Identity Politics: Lesbianism, Feminism and the Limits of Community* (Philadelphia: Temple University Press, 1989), 79, 156, 170 (emphasis added).

54. See, for instance, Butler, "Imitation and Gender Insubordination," 19, 20.

55. Of the three types of relationships identified by Foucault those of "objective capacities," relationships of communication, and power relations—none come close to describing what we understand as empowerment. The first refers to the *effects* of power, and the others identify the ways in which individuals or groups are brought together in a play of power, acting upon one another. See Foucault's "The Subject and Power," 217–18. Foucault considers even personal communication and love to be constituted by a dynamic of "acting upon." See his "Ethic of Care for the Self as a Practice of Freedom,"11.

56. Audre Lorde, "Uses of the Erotic: The Erotic as Power," in Audre Lorde's *Sister Outsider: Essays and Speeches* (Trumansburg, N.Y.: Crossing Press, 1984), 58.

57. See Karen Houppert, "WAC," *Village Voice* 37 (9 June 1992): 33–38.

58. Patricia Hill Collins, *Black Feminist Thought: Knowledge, Consciousness, and the Politics of Empowerment* (New York and London: Routledge, 1991) 111, 224.

59. bell hooks, "Choosing the Margin as a Space of Radical Openness, " in bell hooks, *Yearning: Race, Gender, and Cultural Politics* (Boston: South End Press, 1990), 145, 149.

PART 5

Representations of the Body

The three articles in this section reveal the capacity of interdisciplinary analysis to expose the ways in which both contemporary and historical visual and discursive constructions of the female body have produced and regulated sexual and reproductive knowledge with detrimental consequences for women. Anne Raine's "Embodied Geographies: Subjectivity and Materiality in the Work of Ana Mendieta" exemplifies the complex and nuanced analysis made possible by the collapsing of disciplinary boundaries; art history here is transformed by its intersection with feminist work in psychoanalysis, cultural studies, ecology, and theology. Examining two major aesthetic conventions in Western art—the female body and landscape—Raine shows how at the intersection of these tropes the female body functions as "the site of negotiation between materiality, psychic drives, and social and cultural inscriptions." In tracing the ideological history of the female body used as metaphor for nature, Raine shows how the body is deployed both to "support and to resist discourses of patriarchal, imperialist and ecological domination." She reads in the hybrid land art/self-portraits of Cuban American artist Ana Mendieta not only the personal narrative of the artist's exile from Cuba, but also the collective narrative of imperialist domination of the New World and more recent struggles for personal and collective identity in the diaspora. Mendieta's identification with nature, Raine argues, is not an essentialist gesture but a political identification with "modern industrial America's excluded others." To understand the ways the body and subjectivity are experienced in this modern political landscape, Raine turns to psychoanalytic theory. The uncanny effect evoked by Mendieta's photographs of the body represented in and by natural matter points to an anxiety about separation and death, to a confrontation with the subject's alienation from the maternal body and from the security of an autonomous self. Raine expands the terrain of the maternal as represented in Freud and Lacan to include feminist theories of subjectivity based on the concept of the "matrix," the maternal body as an ambiguous and uncanny site of both a founding separation and a connection that survives through contiguity and touch. Mendieta's art demonstrates how theory, representation, and politics are all problematized by the subject's entanglement with the incomprehensible otherness of her own body in its strange and irreducible materiality.

In "The Power of the 'Positive' Diagnosis," anthropologist Rayna Rapp examines the capacity of patriarchal medical discourse to control critical reproductive decisions of couples undergoing amniocentesis. Combining a social science investigative approach—based on a sample of forty women and their families, sixteen of whom she interviewed and twenty-four with whom she corresponded—with a discursive analysis of medical diagnostic language, she reveals the largely hidden experiences of would-be parents confronted with the difficult choice of whether to continue with an imperfect pregnancy. The fact that Rapp's sample is self-selected reflects its invisibility as a distinct group in American society and the extreme privatization of its decision-making experience. It is the "deafening" silence coming from women and their families on the emotional tribulations of being enmeshed in a sanitized medical discourse that aims to suppress subjectivity and increasingly defines pregnancy as "pathological" that particularly concerns Rapp, for it leaves women trapped in roles shaped by images of the mother as selfless "madonna" or as the agent of quality control. To remedy this predicament, she urges the creation of social knowledge about the lived realities of disabilities in order to empower women to cope with a "positive" prenatal diagnosis unencumbered by the mythic terror produced by contemporary medical language.

The discipline of psychoanalysis has dominated the theoretical study of female sexuality in the twentieth century, and feminist scholars have been challenging various models of psychosexual development at least since the 1920s. Valerie Traub's "The Psychomorphology of the Clitoris" focuses in particular on Freud's normative mapping of developmental stages onto the female body, tracing a progression from clitoral pleasure and attachment to the mother, to vaginal pleasure, attachment to the father, and a desire for heterosexual reproduction. Rather than contest Freud's developmental theories on the psychoanalytic front alone, Traub launches an interdisciplinary attack, marshaling historical and textual interpretations of earlier discourses that reduced and regulated sexual knowledge. In the emerging science of anatomy and the rising popularity of travel narratives in the sixteenth and seventeenth centuries, Traub finds the simultaneous construction of the heterosexual subject and of the lesbian. She shows how anatomical knowledge produces a normative (white, heterosexual) body, and how travel narratives reinforce that norm by setting it in opposition to an exoticized, eroticized, and racialized "foreigner." Traub's recovery of the particular political, economic, and social determinants that contributed to sexual knowledge before 1900 is a helpful corrective to the essentializing logic of classical psychoanalysis. Her interpretation also challenges some recent studies of homosexuality that seem to accept the reductive concept of a stable and knowable lesbian subject. In order to expose and discredit the constraining stereotypes produced by these conventional ways of thinking about sexuality, Traub traces them back to their roots in early homophobic and racist ideologies.

CHAPTER TWELVE

Embodied Geographies

Subjectivity and Materiality in the Work of Ana Mendieta

ANNE RAINE

Introduction

In her work of the 1970's, the Cuban-American artist Ana Mendieta enacted a series of private rituals which she called "a dialogue between the landscape and the female body."[1] Working at outdoor sites in Mexico and Iowa City, she used materials such as earth, sand, stones, water, gunpowder, fire, plants, flowers, trees, blood, human hair, and her own body, tracing and re-tracing her silhouette on the landscape, mapping its outlines onto and into the earth: attending, discerning, digging, moulding, carving, burning, exploding, plucking, scattering, arranging, and occupying space along the visible and tactile boundaries between the body and the land. Mendieta wrote of this work:

> Through my earth/body sculptures I become one with the earth. . . . I become an extension of nature and nature becomes an extension of my body. This obsessive act of reasserting my ties with the earth is really the reactivation of primeval beliefs . . . [in] an omnipresent female force, the after-image of being encompassed within the womb.[2]

What remains of this intimate practice is a series of photographs and films, optical indexes of concrete meditations; their power draws on other registers of sensory and psychic experience than those organized around vision. Viewed as a series of memory-traces, the inscriptions of the female body through which Mendieta traced her urgent and tentative itinerary are both repetitively familiar and strangely disquieting.

Lucy Lippard has written that visiting ancient stone circles and other prehistoric aesthetic-symbolic sites prompted her "to perceive places as spatial metaphors for temporal distance," and to consider how this dialectic between space and time might relate to "the crucial connections between individual de-

Anne Raine, "Embodied Geographies: Subjectivity and Materiality in the work of Ana Mendieta," in Griselda Pollack, ed. *Generations and Geographies in the Visual Arts: Feminist Readings* (New York: Routledge, 1996): 228–49. Reprinted by permission.

sires (to make something, to hold something) and the social values that determine what we make and why."[3] Lippard's question draws together landscape and history, the psychic and the social into two axes across which I want to read Ana Mendieta's *Silueta* series (Silhouette series) and *Serie árbol de la vida* (Tree of Life series).[4] Using Freud's notion of the uncanny and Bracha Lichtenberg Ettinger's theory of matrixial subjectivity, I want to attend to Mendieta's images and their "dark, incantatory power,"[5] and to read her negotiation of the traditional association between woman and nature for the insights it might provide into something like a politics of space for the 1990's.

In the late twentieth century, we are dealing on a global scale with the personal, social, political and environmental aftermath of colonial imperialism and the industrial revolution. The feminist Christian theologian Sallie McFague argues that these crises demand an ethical and conceptual paradigm that takes seriously the concepts of embodiment, space and place; in her view, "Geography, often considered a trivial subject compared to the more splendid history (the feats of the forefathers) may well be *the* subject of the twenty-first century."[6] I am not arguing against the strategic possibilities of what Donna Haraway calls cyborg politics,[7] and I agree with Haraway that we technological skeptics may need to rethink our notions of the body and space in order to deal effectively with the postmodern world of new biotechnologies, microelectronics, telecommunications and cyberspace, and transnational capital. I am arguing, though, that in such times and spaces it seems all the more urgent, personally and politically, to find ways of being, literally, grounded. Ana Mendieta's work speaks to this desire and this political imperative.

Early in the twentieth century, D. H. Lawrence wrote a fascinating essay[8] in which he argues that the English tradition of landscape painting is rooted in anxiety about the body, and represents an escape from physicality into "optical systems" and "mental concepts." Dismissing painted landscapes as "background with the real subject left out" (139), he champions Cézanne's still life paintings as "the first real sign that man has made for several thousands of years that he is willing to admit that matter *actually* exists" (145–146). In Lawrence's view, Cézanne wanted not to question the possibility of representation in art, but rather to make art *more* "true to life" than what Lawrence calls "the optical vision, a sort of flashy coloured photography of the eye" (138). Lawrence defines Cézanne's project as an attempt "to touch the world of substance once more with the intuitive touch . . . to displace our present mode of mental-visual consciousness . . . and substitute a mode of consciousness that was predominantly intuitive, the awareness of touch" (156). In Cézanne, he writes,

> . . . modern French art made its first tiny step back to real substance, to objective substance, if we may call it so. Van Gogh's earth was still subjective earth, himself projected into the earth, but Cézanne's apples are a real attempt to let the apple exist in its own separate entity, without transfusing it with personal emotion. Cézanne's great effort was, as it were, to shove the apple away from him, and let it live of itself. (145)

Truth, for Lawrence, lies in the "appleyness" of bodies and things, in materiality as irreducible otherness to the meanings imposed by eye and mind. "The only bit of a woman which nowadays escapes being ready-made and ready-known cliché is the appley part of her," and the artist's model should strive to "be primarily an apple," to "sit still and just be physically there, and be truly non-moral," to "leave out all your thoughts, all your feelings, all your mind and all your personality, which we know all about and find boring beyond endurance" (156–157). Lawrence continues, "The eye sees only fronts, and the mind, on the whole, is satisfied with fronts. But intuition needs all-aroundness, and instinct needs insideness" (157). These passages raise intriguing questions, both about how a painting practice could be considered "non-optical" and so *more* true to life," and also about precisely how the desire for "appleyness," or "intuitive reality," is related to the gendering of embodied artists, models, and viewers.

Lawrence says of Cézanne: "It was part of his desire: to make the human form, the *life* form, come to rest. Not static—on the contrary. Mobile but come to rest. And at the same time he set the unmoving material world into motion. Walls twitch and slide, chairs bend or rear up a little, cloths curl like burning paper" (158). I am wondering what desire exactly Lawrence is talking about; and I want to read this passage as being *about landscape*—landscape understood as a way of imagining the relationship between human subjects and the physical environment. In his reading of Cézanne, Lawrence invokes a conception of landscape which gestures toward the strange combination of stillness and unsettledness in Ana Mendieta's earth/body sculptures half a century later, and in which the non-human material world is neither mere "background" nor a "subjective earth" infused with the artist's personal emotions. This is not only a question of painting or other avant garde practices, but also a psychic as well as a social, political and ecological question. It can be separated neither from issues of gender and the formation of subjectivity, nor from concrete political struggles: as Oriana Baddeley and Valerie Fraser argue in their study of contemporary Latin American art, "Landscapes, whether or not they are populated, are about land and land use, space, frontiers, boundaries, territories."[9]

Lucy Lippard and others have located Mendieta's practice in relation to other feminist artists of the 1970's who reclaimed goddess imagery and a celebratory identification with nature. The Cuban art historian Gerardo Mosquera, focusing on Mendieta's Cuban roots, has read in her work both "a harmonious coexistence of Man and his landscape" and "a return to one's origins."[10] More recently, Mendieta's work has been discussed within debates about diasporan identity and cultural politics. In a 1989 article, Luis Camnitzer attributes her success in the 1970's to a misreading of her work as "a programmatic expression of feminism enhanced by a U. S. perception of mysterious exoticism," rather than as "much more simply and modestly, a self-portrait."[11] It seems to me that all of these readings turn on the crucial question of the relationship between human subjects, individually and collectively, and something I have been calling *whatever else there is*: the maternal body, the imaginary self, social and cultural Others, landscape and "nature," the Real. Ana Mendieta distilled into deceptively simple images a number of complex and urgent questions of aesthetic-symbolic production,[12] subjectivity, gender, the body, cultural identity, and what we now call "the environment." I want to think of her work as inscribing not female or "natural" essences, but a gendered physicality, memory, desire, and representation, across a concrete material terrain always already marked by politics and history. In my view, Mendieta's work does represent an engagement with self-portraiture, but one that is not at all simple, and is crucially involved in what I am thinking of as a diffuse and multi-leveled problematic of figure and ground.

Landscape

In *The Culture of Nature*, Alexander Wilson defines landscape as not only an art genre, but a complex discourse socially produced through multiple practices and productions, from abstract attitudes and values to concrete buildings and spaces.

> The way we produce our material culture—our parks and roads and movies—is derived from and in turn shapes our relationships with the physical environment. I call all of this activity *landscape*. . . . In the broadest sense of the term, landscape is a way of seeing the world and imagining our relationship to nature. It is something we think, do, and make as a social collective.[13]

The dominant discourses of landscape in late twentieth century North America have a history which can be traced as far back as the shift from ancient earth-centred goddess cults to patriarchal religions, but is also closely related to the development of "natural science" in sixteenth- and seventeenth-century Europe. As Carolyn Merchant argues in *The Death of Nature*,[14] the revolution in European science coincided with a paradigm shift in which "nature" ceased to be regarded as a nurturing mother and living organism, and became instead an orderly system of inert particles moved by external rather than internal forces. This change from "organismic" to mechanistic constructions of nature both enabled and was demanded by changing agricultural, industrial and commercial practices, which required a different conception of the relationship between human goals and values and the material world. Unlike the personification of the earth as mother, which provided some moral restraint against wholesale plundering of nature's resources,[15] the mechanistic model constructs nature as an object of knowledge, mastery and improvement by human reason and technology, and so facilitates resource extraction, industrial development, and social and ecological disruption on an unprecedented scale. "Landscape" as a fine art genre increased in importance and popularity during the increasing hegemony of scientific discourses and industrial capital; within the dominant paradigm, physics and ethics were worlds apart, and by the late nineteenth century, the concerns of "landscape" could be theorized as neither moral nor political, but optical effects of light, shade and colour—or in D. H. Lawrence's polemical phrase, "delicious nowhereness."[16]

Mechanistic discourses of landscape produced not only landscape painting as art-for-art's sake, but also the bleak topographies of the twentieth century: drained wetlands and deforested hillsides; fertile farmlands made arid by industrial agriculture; sterile suburbs and squalid ghettoes and shanty towns; poisoned air, lakes and rivers; and their damaging and often lethal effects on the bodies of plants, animals and people, especially working class people and those in the Third World. At the same time, modernist landscape discourses have produced other topographies: national park systems, scenic highways and signposted roadside "viewpoints"; summer cottages, outdoor recreation organizations and facilities for picnicking, hiking and camping; anti-modernist communities from the Hutterites and Amish to the "back to the land" counter-culture; and conservationist projects from bird sanctuaries to blockaded logging roads. These alternative approaches to landscape often draw on what Merchant calls the organismic model, the view of nature as living body, which remains an underlying tension in the dominant mechanistic paradigm and has resurfaced at such historical moments as the Romantic reaction to the Enlightenment, American transcendentalism, Marx's early writings, and twentieth-century theories of holism and process philosophy. However, the notion of "unspoiled" nature as living, life-giving and intrinsically worthy of preservation emerged from a society whose self-construction depends on excluding "nature" from its frontiers. The resurgence of the organismic view of nature in the late nineteenth and early twentieth century is closely connected with accelerated resource exploitation and industrial development, an increasingly urban population and a tourist industry based on the automobile; as Wilson notes, the management of Canadian and American national park systems has always been inextricable from that of logging, mining and commercial development. While providing an oppositional alternative to the mechanistic world view, the organismic "nature" of nature tourism and conservationist politics has also been complementary to the dominant culture founded on technological mastery of the material world.

In this critical yet complementary relationship with urban industrial society, the conservationist view of nature that dominates contemporary environmental movements is rooted in the Western pastoral tradition, which Merchant describes as "an escape backward into the motherly benevolence of the past."[17] Originating in the writings of Virgil and other classical authors, pastoralism is based on nostalgia for bucolic landscapes uncorrupted by urbanization, and re-emerged in the Renaissance personification of Nature as a benevolent mother or virginal bride. In pastoral imagery, nature is constructed as a living female body rather than an inert system of particles; however, both nature and woman are essentially passive and subordinate, their primary function to provide material and spiritual nourishment for men weary of urban life. Because of this slippage from nature as "active teacher and parent" to nature as "mindless, submissive body,"[18] the pastoral mode is compatible with human domination over nature (and male domination over women) at the same time as it constructs nature, like women, as a pristine sanctuary that compensates men for the alienation of modern industrial society.

With the discovery of the Americas, distant lands replaced distant times as the idealized space of pastoral imagination. Explorers and colonizers described the "new world" in pastoral terms, indicating that the pastoral mode is complicit not only with technological domination of nature, but also with imperialist domination of newly discovered lands and peoples. For the male, white, urban subject, the Americas and their native inhabitants represent an Edenic state of simplicity, purity and harmony with nature, and are consigned to an idealized past in the narrative of human progress, a nostalgic mirror in which European culture can gaze at its own imagined infancy; or they are removed from history altogether to become part of the landscape, the scenic backdrop across which "history" (the acts of white European men) is staged. Like "nature," indigenous peoples represent a timeless space where, as Wilson writes of Disney nature films, "the cycle of the seasons—'always enthralling, never changing'—sits in for real historical change."[19] Within this discourse of landscape, wildlife and native cultures are consigned to reserve lands, oases of "nature" in a desert of modern culture. History is banished from the pastoral scene; yet underlying and pressing on the borders of that dehistoricized territory are other, non-pastoral landscapes—the city, "progress," imperial civilization. As Sidonie Smith observes, "If the surface of pastoral promotes timeless spatiality, the subtext introduces historical specificity, the very history that undermines the pastoral vision, the very history from which the subject of pastoral would escape."[20]

❦

It is within these complex histories and geographies that I want to locate Ana Mendieta's work, along with that of other American artists who abandoned the art gallery for outdoor sites during the late 1960's and 1970's. John Beardsley has described the land art movement as a return to landscape, which after its apotheosis in Impressionism had been a neglected genre for much of the twentieth century.[21] Landscape, however, was now site rather than subject, for works conceived not as discrete objects but as fully engaged elements of their environments. Like the "dematerialization of the object" in conceptual and performance art, earthworks were a way of resisting the gallery system and the commodification of the art object; they also asserted a specifically American avant garde sculptural practice in resistance to Minimalism's European roots in Rodin and Brancusi. In 1969, Michael Heizer stated that "Art had to be radical. It had to become American." If traditional and Minimal sculpture were both based on the "intrusive, opaque object" which "has little exterior reference" and "is rigid and blocks space," the goal of this new American practice would be "an incorporative work" which is "aerated, part of the material of its place, and refers beyond itself."[22]

Lucy Lippard has argued that forms resembling prehistoric architecture, barrows and standing stones re-emerged in the land art of the late 1960's "in part as a reaction against the cool technology of most Minimal sculpture," but also partly "as a *response* to Minimalism's formal affinities with the simplicity and clarity of ancient monuments."[23] Similarly, the literal return to landscape in art was both a critique of the Minimalist object and an extension of Minimalism's attempt "to exclude all symbolic, metaphorical or referential aspects" to create "a concrete actuality, perceived within the 'real time' of the immediate present."[24] Ana Mendieta was not alone in feeling that "my paintings were not real enough for what I wanted the images to convey"[25]; the trend away from painting and sculpture toward outdoor sites and natural materials reflected a desire not only to "dematerialize" the rigid, commodified art object, but also to "re-materialize" landscape, somehow to escape the mediations of modern culture and make art which, rather than mimicking the "concrete actuality" of nature, *encountered* it in ways that were more direct, palpable, "real." However, Heizer's insistence that "It's about art, not about landscape"[26] indicates that although the earthwork might refer beyond itself to the materials and forms of its surroundings, it often remained embedded in the formalist discourse of high modernism, in which art as such, "incorporative" or not, remains as self-referential as ever.

What is repressed in Heizer's construction of the earthworks movement is that its critique of the sterile isolation of the art object in the gallery space coincided historically with other movements away from the alienated, commodified spaces of modernity. Widespread disillusionment with consumerism, industrial capitalism, technological optimism, and ethnocentric notions of "civilization" and "progress" resulted in such events as the 1960's boom in nature tourism, the increase in environmental activism, the "back to the land" movement, the popular romance with Native American culture, and feminism's reclamation of formerly devalued "feminine" activities and attributes, including goddess spirituality and women's traditional identification with the cycles of nature. Heizer and some of his contemporaries may have resisted the connections between earthworks and these other interventions into social discourses of landscape, but others welcomed such connections as an opportunity for critical engagement with broader issues than those of avant garde aesthetics.

Such artists made earthworks which incorporated not only site-specific materials and forms, but also social, symbolic, or ritual content; the encounter with the "concrete actuality" of the outdoor site could then enact a reintegration, not only of art and nature, but also of nature and the social. In different ways, this desire underlies the synthesis of land art and body art in the work of Charles Simonds and Ana Mendieta, as well as the projects of Robert Smithson, Robert Morris and others who reworked abandoned industrial sites into aesthetically satisfying public environments. This impulse also informs the practices of feminist artists such as Margaret Hicks and Mary Beth Edelson who strove to make earthworks more intimate, less abstract and monumental, through rituals that reaffirmed the work and its site as a locus of social and spiritual values.[27] For many, the "return to landscape" was linked with a revaluation of traditionally feminine values and practices, and also with a growing interest in anthropology, ancient goddess religions, and the aesthetic-symbolic production of Native American and prehistoric societies: both the "feminine" and the "primitive" seemed to offer alternative, more fulfilling ways of constructing "nature" and "culture" than those offered by mainstream American society. Many shared Ana Mendieta's view that animistic and/or matriarchal cultures possessed "an inner knowledge, a closeness to natural resources . . . which gives a reality to the images they have created"[28] and which could provide both formal and philosophical inspiration for modern attempts to reformulate "landscape," to imagine and give concrete form to different kinds of relationships between the human and the physical world.

Figures

The various alternative approaches to landscape in the 1960's and 1970's, including many land art practices, can be seen as attempts to "humanize" the landscape, to affirm its living presence and intrinsic value rather than regarding it as a distant, neutral, passive object of observation and use. As I have argued, the organismic view of nature was compelling in the 1970's: radical feminist texts such as Susan Griffin's *Woman and Nature* (1978) and Mary Daly's *Gyn/Ecology* (1979), as well as J. E. Lovelock's *Gaia: A New Look at Life on Earth* (1979), which popularized the controversial "Gaia hypothesis" of the earth as a living organism,[29] were among many texts and practices which, like Ana Mendieta's *Silueta* and *Árbol de la vida* series, invoked the body as a mediating metaphor between human subjects and societies and the material environment. As Donna Haraway has observed,

> . . . most American socialists and feminists see deepened dualisms of mind and body, animal and machine, idealism and materialism in the social practices, symbolic formulations, and physical artifacts associated with "high technology" and scientific culture. From *One-Dimensional Man* (Marcuse, 1964) to *The Death of Nature* (Merchant, 1980), the analytic resources developed by progressives have insisted on the necessary domination of technics and recalled us to an imagined organic body to integrate our resistance.[30]

Yet as Haraway argues, the organismic model has its limitations as a strategy for intervention into dominant discourses of landscape. The oppositional view of society and the earth as organic body has been an affectively powerful and enabling resource for both feminist and environmental movements, but has also "perhaps restricted too much what we allow as a friendly body and political language"[31] and tended to discourage the adoption of other strategies which might more effectively resist the global spread of economic and ecological domination. For example, anthropomorphic language has sometimes undermined the scientific and political credibility of the environmental movement: as science historian Joel Hagen observes, Lovelock's "Gaia hypothesis" was not taken seriously in the scientific community partly because, despite its appeal to the popular imagination, "naming his hypothesis after a Greek goddess was perhaps a poor strategy for catching the attention of professional biologists."[32]

Scientific debates have identified other problems with organismic conceptual frameworks beyond their tendency to be marginalized and disempowered within the dominant mechanistic paradigm. Some ecologists argue that describing populations and ecosystems in terms of living bodies, anthropomorphic or not, tends to impose arbitrary boundaries and notions of harmonious balance and teleological function onto material phenomena which might be structured by radically different mechanisms, such as indeterminism, instability, and constant change.[33] Discourses of landscape that use the metaphor of the body to establish harmony between nature and the social also tend to assume that the body in question is a human one, and to project human characteristics, values, narratives and desires onto the non-human world. As Sallie McFague argues, the humanist vision embodied in Leonardo da Vinci's drawing of a male figure whose limbs map the four corners of the cosmos can be deeply troubling as a model for the body politic and the cosmic order:

> [T]he body forming the basis for the model was *one* body and it was the *ideal* human body . . . a perfectly proportioned young, physically fit, white, human male body.

... [T]he organic model is a unitary notion that subordinates the members of the body as parts to the whole; it is concerned principally with human and especially male forms of community and organization; and ... if there is only one body with one head, there can be only one point of view.[34]

In contrast to the view of nature as a landscape made friendly through identification with a nurturing female body, this particular organismic model constructs the cosmic order as an ideal male body identified not so much with landscape or the material world as with history: that is, with the universalized subject of Western history and its discourses of anthropocentric, patriarchal, imperialist domination. Despite the emphasis on embodiment and interdependence of parts, rational human (Western, male) consciousness is privileged as the literal and figurative head, paradoxically both part of and sovereign over the body of the material world. Like nature constructed as female body, this model offers a sense of harmony and intimacy with the non-human which is lacking in the view of the physical world as inert object of observation and use. However, imaging the cosmos as an ideal mechanistic human body also renders invisible the multiplicity and diversity of life on earth, and supports the privileging of human bodies, conceptual structures, ambitions and desires over the needs of other life forms. In its complacent self-centredness, this model represents what Lawrence calls "the tyranny of mind, the white, worn-out arrogance of the spirit, the mental consciousness, the enclosed ego in its sky-blue heaven self-painted." Within this claustrophobic world, the non-human can be experienced only as "self projected into the earth"; there is no "outside" to human consciousness, and it is impossible to "get out of the sky-blue prison into real air."[35]

Like Lawrence's reading of Cézanne, the social and aesthetic "return to landscape" in the 1960's and 1970's can be read as both a critique of mechanistic landscape discourses, and an attempt to reach beyond the apparently omnipresent subject of Western history. One strategy toward these dual goals was to embrace that which is marginalized within the classic organic model's "self-painted" universe: the "feminine," ancient and non- Western cultures, materiality, the non-human world. The construction of nature as female body, drawing more on prehistoric cultures than on the Western pastoral tradition, was one such oppositional strategy, offering radically different ways of organizing the body politic and its relations with the non-human environment. However, the desire to "get in touch" with a lost unity between humanity and nature through the metaphor of the earth as female body bears a suspicious resemblance to the pastoral journey, in its fantasy of escaping the mediation of culture to return to an original unalienated state, and its complicity with a set of aligned binaries (male/female, modern/primitive, mechanistic/organic, culture/nature) whose terms are fixed by the dominant spaces of the metropolis. The construction of nature as female body also remains a projection of human forms and desires onto the non-human world; landscape is still "self projected into the earth," although the "self" in question has changed. It remains possible to read a project like Ana Mendieta's "dialogue between the earth and the female body" as John Perreault does, in terms that echo the anthropocentric humanist vision of man as the measure of all things: "Her version of body art aspired to the universal: she used the measurements of her five-foot form to measure the world."[36]

The impulse to give human form to the landscape derives, paradoxically, from the desire in Lawrence's reading of Cézanne: the desire for an "outside" to human subjectivity as defined in dominant Western discourses of selfhood—but crucially, an "outside" which is more than a system of inert particles. This might also be described, in Wilson's words, as a desire to encounter the non-human environment as "an agent of historical processes as well as the field of human action," not merely as object or empty background but, in a sense, as subject.[37] But what kind of subject? The anthropomorphizing of the earth as mother is entangled in what Robert Smithson has called "the ecological oedipal complex,"[38] in which a female "nature" becomes both the pastoral landscape of desire and the repudiated object of domination for the universalized male subject of history, while the female subject can articulate her difference only through identification with that ambivalent figure/landscape, "nature." However, the earthworks movement offered a possible alternative to this impasse in practices like that of Carl Andre,[39] which attempted an explicitly non-anthropocentric perspective from which the material world might be apprehended as a kind of "subject," but one autonomous of and *other than* the human.

Like Michael Heizer's more monumental projects, Andre's influential strategy of "tak[ing] his sculpture back to 'ground level'—to the floor, or the earth—rejecting the pedestal and felling the traditionally anthropomorphic stance of heroic vertical sculpture"[40] critiqued the isolated, fetishized Minimalist object. At the same time, Andre's practice continued Minimalism's critique of the fetishization of individual (human, and usually masculine) subjectivity in the Abstract Expressionist painterly gesture. In lieu of both the subjective gesture and the self-contained object with its anthropomorphic residues, Andre proposed "sculpture as place," which he defined as "an area within an environment altered in such a way as to make the rest of the environment more conspicuous."[41] This attempt to evacuate the human as an organizing principle for art production recalls Lawrence's argument that materiality as vital otherness to human subjectivity—what Minimalism calls "concrete actuality" and Lawrence calls "appleyness," the "real air" beyond the "sky-blue prison" of the ego—can be apprehended only by "deliberately painting *out* the so-called humanness, the personality, the 'likeness,' the physical cliché."[42] What is central in "sculpture as place" is no human or anthropomorphic form, but precisely that non-human otherness which the work's intervention invites viewers to apprehend.

❦

Ana Mendieta's practice of the 1970's appears far removed from Andre's solution to the problem of anthropocentrism in discourses of art and landscape. Although based on encounter with a chosen site or "place," Mendieta's *Silueta* and *Árbol de la vida* works are insistently anthropomorphic; they have been called "overly narcissistic and reductive"[43] for their repeated tracing of the artist's own form onto the land, a literal enactment of the anthropocentric "self projected into the earth" that Lawrence critiques in Van Gogh. Underlying Mendieta's self-inscriptions are both a desire to "become one" with a maternal earth, and "a personal will to continue being 'other'" to dominant white society (including American feminism, which she denounced as "basically a white middle class movement").[44] That is, she used the meeting of female body and land as a deliberately oppositional position of identification with modern industrial America's excluded Others, invoking an animistic view of nature as "omnipresent female force" and drawing on concepts and motifs from ancient and non-Western cultural traditions, particularly Santería, a Cuban syncretic religion based on African Yoruba and popular Catholic beliefs and practices.[45]

As I have argued, such strategies of resistance are implicated in complex ways with pastoralism and anthropocentrism as well as restrictive gender binaries. They are also open to a particular claustrophobic reading in which Mendieta is identified with her own images as a romanticized figure of exotic otherness: defined by her personal trauma of exile and by some "innate" affinity with the "natural" and "primitive" due to her female gender and Cuban origins, she and her work are relegated to a timeless realm removed from contemporary aesthetic, social and political debates. Yet Mendieta was also an artist trained in the United States in the 1960's, whose deployment of landscape, Santería and goddess imagery participated in the social and cultural discourses I have discussed, and was linked not only to a personal longing for the culture of her childhood[46] and a desire to "re-materialize" the landscape through "the reactivation of primeval beliefs," but also to her support for the Non-Aligned Nations in resistance to First World political and economic domination.[47]

The view of Mendieta as an apolitical, ahistorical "primitive" is supported by the fact that in contrast to Andre's ideal of art that points to the specificity of its surroundings, Mendieta's works often appear oddly unlocatable in space or time. Unlike Andre's outdoor installations, the encounters Mendieta staged between work and site are now accessible only as photographic images; their sites, although carefully chosen and identified in the titles, are not encountered directly by viewers, and the images themselves focus on the boundaries of the human form and contain few distinguishing marks of place. This apparent "placelessness" also contrasts with strategies in contemporary Latin American painting, where the land is so infused with bitter tensions—from European conquest to the clearing of rainforest for cash crops—that artists cannot approach landscapes in terms of timeless aesthetic values, but rather insistently identify them as both particular places and sites of particular historical and political struggles.[48] Contemporary Latin American landscape painters resist the dominant narrative of Western history, and its dehistoricizing of landscape as its pastoral Other, by insisting on the specificity of place while refusing to let the continuing realities of political, economic and cultural colonization be consigned to the past. Yet as Irit Rogoff has argued, Mendieta's work too can be read as resisting hegemonic history through a strategic deployment of the geographic: a spatial rather than temporal itinerary which "def[ies] cultural time as a progressive sequence" but does not thereby "impose some other non-specific notion of timelessness."[49]

Such a reading must attend to the particular conception of geography underlying the *Silueta* and *Árbol de la vida* series, a conception quite other than ei-

Figure 12.1. Mendieta, Ana; Untitled (from Tree of Life series); 1977; courtesy of the Estate of Ana Mendieta and Galerie Lelong, New York.

Figure 12.2. Mendieta, Ana; Untitled (from the Silueta series); 1976; courtesy of the Estate of Ana Mendieta and Galerie Lelong, New York.

ther the dehistoricized landscape of pastoral, the "re-historicized" landscapes of contemporary Latin American painting, or any landscape surveyed through Lawrence's "optical vision." Mendieta's intervention into dominant discourses of landscape posits a relationship to the non-human based on the indexical rather than the symbolic; it attempts, as Lawrence writes of Cézanne, "to displace our present mode of mental-visual consciousness . . . and substitute a mode of consciousness that [is] predominantly intuitive, the awareness of touch." As Rogoff argues, Mendieta employs "matter versus contour as the essence of a personalized geography"[50]; her works do not depict landscapes recognizable to the eye, but invoke a landscape encountered as "appleyness," that material otherness beyond the "self-painted" human world, that non-humanness to which Andre's "sculpture as place" attempts to gesture. At the same time, however, her practice resists the notion that a non-anthropocentric approach to landscape requires an evacuation of the human from notions of site or place. In the *Silueta* and *Árbol de la vida* series she attempts, like Cézanne, "to set the unmoving material world into motion" not by banishing the human form, but by making it "come to rest." Within this tactile geography, her insistence on the anthropomorphic represents not so much an imposition of the human on the landscape, as a refusal to evacuate questions of cultural identity and gender—questions both of individual subjectivity and of social and political relations—from her reconfiguration of the relationship between the human and the material world.

Figure 12.3. Mendieta, Ana; Untitled (from the Tree of Life series); 1976; courtesy of the Estate of Ana Mendieta and Galerie Lelong, New York.

Body and Representation

Ana Mendieta's practice posits a relationship to landscape which is insistently an embodied one. The body is the site of negotiation between materiality, psychic drives, and social and cultural inscriptions, and is therefore central to a practice in which the encounter with the non-human and the exploration of human psychic and social existence can occupy the same space, and indeed are posited as inseparable. As Elisabeth Bronfen has written,

> The real body is positioned before or beyond semiosis. As that which is replaced by signs and images, it can serve as the medium through which language hooks back into the world, through which it returns to the referential. But because the body marks a site of real insertion into the world, it also serves to establish social laws and allows culture to materialize ideas. The word turning flesh can serve to establish and authenticate a political, theoretical or aesthetic discourse.[51]

The body functions for human subjects as the boundary between the symbolic order and the real, and at the same time, in Sidonie Smith's words, "the margin joining/separating one subject from the other, one sex from the other, one race from another, the sane from the mad, the whole from the unhealthy . . . whereby the culturally dominant and the culturally marginalized are assigned their 'proper' places in the body politic."[52] It is Mendieta's attention to both of these aspects of embodiment which underlies her insistence on the anthropomorphic; her invocation of the body alludes both to the relationship between subjectivity and materiality, and to the ways in which, as I have argued, the trope of the human body is used to support and to resist discourses of patriarchal, imperialist and ecological domination. In Mendieta's practice, all of these issues come together in the encounter between landscape and self-portraiture, an encounter in which gender is acknowledged as a crucial category. The question is how to read this "dialogue between the landscape and the female body" in terms which are both psychic and political, and which do not reinscribe either pastoral binaries or anthropocentric configurations in their attention to the gendering of both domination and desire.

Many of Mendieta's images appear to document ordinary sights that anyone might pass by during an afternoon walk, an impression reinforced by the apparent transparency and literalness of the photographic medium. Yet this unthinking familiarity is continually disrupted by the sometimes obvious, sometimes barely perceptible presence of a human-like form, which becomes increasingly insistent when the works are viewed as a series. The *Silueta* and *Árbol de la vida* images provoke a double *déjà vu*: because of the ordinariness of the scenes, and because of the continual recurrence of the silhouette, whose roughly anthropomorphic shape evokes a sense of something utterly familiar yet made strange by its repetition across a variety of materials and sites. If these are landscapes, the eye does not traverse their expanses, but rather is drawn to rest on the outlined human form with a satisfying sense of self-recognition, as though on the viewer's own image in a mirror. However, the stillness thus produced seems in its very intensity to be always on the verge of tipping over into restlessness. The images do not provide a safe resting place for narcissistic self-contemplation, since despite its stubborn recurrence, the anthropomorphic form is also utterly tentative, its boundaries vague and subject to immanent dissolution: at any moment, the flowers will scatter or decompose, the mud or sand will wash away, the flames will burn out, the figure will come to life and spirit itself out of the frame—or a second glance will reveal what appeared to be a human form as a momentary trick of light and shadow, a self-projection onto a chance formation of earth or wood. Narcissistic identification is also unsettled by the fact that although the silhouettes are linked to the feminine through references to goddess iconography and through Mendieta's bodily presence in the ritual of making, they often do not bear the visible signs of anatomical sex that uphold stable categories of sexual difference within the symbolic order. Both sensuous and schematic, the anthropomorphic outlines simultaneously insist on the presence of the body and mark its almost palpable absence, like the chalk drawings used by police to mark the position of an absent corpse.[53]

In their ambivalent interplay between establishment/unsettling of boundaries and presence/absence of the body, Mendieta's images can be read as self-portraits which function as uncanny doubles, as theorized by Freud and elaborated by Elisabeth Bronfen in her book *Over Her Dead Body: Death, Femininity and the Aesthetic.* Freud defines the uncanny as a particular category of aesthetic or life experience which produces anxiety by "lead[ing] back to what is known of old and long familiar"[54]; summarizing Freud's discussion, Bronfen writes that the sources of uncanny experiences lie "in the compulsion to repeat, to re-present, double, supplement; in the establishment or re-establishment of similarity; and in a return to the familiar that has been repressed." Bronfen describes instances of the uncanny as "situation[s] of undecidability, where fixed frames or margins are set in motion," where "the question whether something is animate (alive) or inanimate (dead), whether something is real or imagined, unique, original or a repetition, a copy, cannot be decided" (113). The "double," a figure somehow identical to or interchangeable with the self, is one of the most unsettling instances of the uncanny, since it implies a doubling, dividing or exchanging that results in undecidability or blurred boundaries between self and other. Bronfen extends Freud's definition of the double to include the ambivalent distinction between a material, animate body and its inanimate representation: portraits, "similar to but also different from the body they resemble," can function as uncanny doubles, "hover[ing] between an absence/presence of their object of reference" (111).

Freud argues that the double produces uncanny anxiety because it "harks back" to "a time when the ego had not yet marked itself off sharply from the external world and from other people," to ideas and psychic states which were once familiar but have become alien through processes of repression during the formation of the adult self:

> [T]he "double" was originally an insurance against the destruction of the ego . . . and probably the "immortal" soul was the first "double" of the body. . . . Such ideas, however, have sprung from the soil of unbounded self-love, from the primary narcissism which dominates the mind of the child and of primitive man. But when this

stage has been surmounted, the "double" reverses its aspect. From having been an assurance of immortality, it becomes the uncanny harbinger of death.[55]

The urge to "double" the self—through the notion of an immortal soul or the production of self-representations—represents an attempt to protect the self against
the material decomposition of the real body by ensuring its survival within the
imaginary and symbolic registers. Yet the double also memorializes the mortality and lack in the self which produces the drive to supplement the self through
doubling; and by definition, the double involves a split or gap between double
and self which undermines any attempt to construct the self as whole and intact
by means of a reassuring mirror image. Such attempts to ensure self-stability are
also ambivalent in that the more perfectly the double resembles the self, the more
difficult it is to decide which is which: the self's apparent wholeness and fullness
are both reinforced by the mirroring double and at the same time undermined by
the difficulty of distinguishing self from image.

The perfectly "lifelike" portrait thus produces uncanny anxiety through the
confusion it provokes between the symbolic and the real. As Bronfen writes,

> Even though the creation of the portrait can be seen as an effort to privilege a sym-
> bolic form of semiosis that clearly distinguishes signifier from signified (because it al-
> ways contains the artist's signature and a self-referential moment), its perfect execu-
> tion denies the self-referential dimension and evokes a scandalous return to the literal;
> reintroduces an uncertainty about the distinction between a body and its image. (115)

This uncertainty leads to a desire to restore stability of meaning by deciding the
disturbing question posed by the uncanniness of the image, re-establishing safe
boundaries between body and image, self and other. This is often done through
what Bronfen calls "a move to the figural, a posture of scrutiny and judgement
of the portrait, which binds the mobility of meaning to a fixed signified": that is,
the portrait's disturbing undecidability is enclosed within a narrative about the
artistic skill that produced such a lifelike representation, thus re-establishing the
portrait as a symbolic production ontologically distinct from the intact fullness of
the material body to which it refers (115–116).

In contrast to the uncanny likeness of the portraits Bronfen discusses, the uncanny anxiety provoked by Ana Mendieta's *Silueta* and *Árbol de la vida* images
does not derive from a perfect resemblance between portrait and model, since except where Mendieta's body is literally present in the photograph, the silhouettes
are neither marked with individual identity nor visually similar to their model
except in scale (and even this is not clear from the photographs alone, which are
much smaller than life size). The threatening semantic instability in Mendieta's
self-portraits derives from a "scandalous return to the literal" of another sort: the
insistently literal presence of the stones, flowers, mud, water, sticks, and other
materials that constitute the silhouette. The photographic images of these objects
and substances refer indexically and iconically to their material referents in the
physical landscape, even as they are used to construct a symbolic image signifying a human presence. This persistent reference to the elements of the landscape
as "themselves" prevents the perfect resemblance that would create an undecidability between signified (material human body) and signifier (portrait). Instead,

uncanny anxiety is produced through the undecidability between two possible objects of reference: the signified of the anthropomorphic form might be either the human body for which it acts as a double, or the landscape out of which—*in* which—it is made. The threat to the self remains one of substitution or undecidability, but what is potentially substituted for/indistinguishable from the self is precisely *not* a mirroring double, but rather the implacable material presence of the non-human.

Mendieta's uncanny silhouettes, like Bronfen's uncanny portraits, provoke a desire for a recuperating narrative that can restore stability of meaning. In this case, however, the narrative usually invoked draws on Mendieta's description of her work as "a direct result of my having been torn from my homeland (Cuba) during my adolescence,"[56] and constructs her self-portraits as products not of artistic skill but of inner compulsion. In a much-quoted statement, Mendieta universalizes the personal loss produced by her family's response to particular historical events, identifying her own specific exile with alienation from both "nature" and the maternal body: "I am overwhelmed by the feeling of having been cast from the womb (nature). My art is the way I re-establish the bonds that unite me to the universe. It is a return to the maternal source. Through my earth/body sculptures I become one with the earth."[57] This account binds the uncanny mobility of meaning in the silhouette images to a fixed signified, the ritual of healing through restorative union with a female nature; it allows the spatial or geographical sequence of the *Silueta* and *Árbol de la vida* series to be read also as a temporal one, a progressive history leading to spiritual fulfillment. This optimistic narrative offers a reassuring position of identification for viewers, thereby deciding the disturbing question of reference in favour of a human rather than a non-human signified for the silhouette. At the same time, the narrative attempts to hold *both* possible signifieds, human body and landscape, through asserting a utopian unity between them.

I want to compare this ambivalent gesture with Bronfen's reading of another narrative of survival, the Swiss painter Ferdinand Hodler's portraits of his dying mistress Valentine Godé-Darel. This series of portraits documents the visual effects of Godé-Darel's slow, painful death by cancer, followed by images of her corpse and then by a landscape supposedly drawn on the day of her death. Read as a temporal sequence, the images point to a moment of uncanny undecidability between human and non-human in the space between the last portrait of the corpse and the landscape image that follows it; yet as Bronfen argues, this construction also supports the self-stability of the male viewer by "reassuringly suggest[ing] that there is ultimately no distinction to be drawn between death, the corpse, woman, landscapes" (49). Godé-Darel's individual, embodied and violent experience of death is repressed and replaced as signified of the series by a double narrative in which a universalized human body (though not coincidentally female) dissolves peacefully into landscape, while a universalized human (male) subject heroically transforms into art his own disruptive and threatening experience of her death. As in Mendieta's account of her silhouettes as encounters with the earth as "omnipresent female force," the uncanny anxiety provoked by the visual slippage between animate and inanimate is both articulated and repressed through a merging of landscape and the female body into a figure/scene of pleasure and desire, which signifies the survival of the artist (and by extension the viewer) in the face of traumatic loss.

There is, however, a crucial difference between the two narratives. In the narrative surrounding Hodler's images, self-stability is asserted through a gender binary that codes survival as masculine and invites viewers to identify with the artist as a removed, though intimate and privileged, observer of the feminine spectacle of dissolution into landscape. In Mendieta's account of her *Silueta* series, survival and psychic healing occur precisely *through* active participation in a pleasurable union with a female earth; and since few of the silhouettes are unambiguously gendered, the position of survivor is not determined by rigid categories of sexual difference. Female subjects are a privileged audience for this work, but viewers of either sex are invited to identify with, rather than to survey, the figure/scene with which the artist herself identifies during the process of making. The uncanny effects of both Hodler's and Mendieta's series can be read as traces of earlier, now repressed psychic states in which the boundaries of the self were still being formed; however, the slippage from body to landscape in the two series does not refer to the same moment in the development of subjectivity. In the Hodler images and their surrounding narrative, the displacement of the threat of dissolution onto the female body is structured in part by the traumatic recognition of sexual difference during the Oedipal phase.[58] In contrast, Mendieta's uncanny self-portraits invoke a state in which the infant proto-subject has not yet assumed a gender identification, and the threatening apprehension of difference takes the more general, non-gendered form of the recognition of absence as different from presence: specifically, absence and presence as figured by the maternal body from which the infant begins to recognize itself as a distinct subject.

❦

Freud's interpretation of the "fort–da game" in *Beyond the Pleasure Principle* provides a model for understanding representation and self-representation as related to the threatening absence of the maternal body. In the repetitive game Freud describes, an eighteen-month-old child makes a toy reel on a string disappear by throwing it over the edge of his cot, while saying "o-o-o-o," which Freud interprets as the German word *fort* ("gone"). Sometimes the child then draws the reel back on its string until it becomes visible, accompanied by a joyful *"da"* ("there"). Freud argues that through this game, the child copes with the mother's periodic absence by replacing the absent maternal body with a symbolic object whose disappearance and return it can control. Through this symbolic repetition the child assumes the position of active master of the situation rather than passive victim of loss, and compensates itself for the trauma of the mother's real or potential absence by staging in representation her reassuring return. However, the game must perpetually be repeated, since the pleasure of the return to presence is never complete: what returns in representation is always a substitute, and the very act of representation, while speaking desire for the absent maternal body, also negates that body by replacing it with a symbol or mental image. This ambivalent doubling/negation of the maternal body culminates in another version of the fort–da game, where the child watches its own image in a mirror and says "Baby o-o-o-o!" as it crouches down to make the image disappear. As Bronfen argues, in this game "the child doubles the disappearance of the mother, gliding from her to his own effacement. Where the 'complete' game initially included the return ('da') which always confirmed the absent body, this shift from reel (internal image of the mother) to self-image transfers the moment of reassuring return from the mother to the self" (27).

In this substitution between maternal image and self-image in ambivalent play between image/body and absence/presence, the maternal body is a prototype for all uncanny doubles: it both affirms self-stability by "doubling" the self, and at the same time disrupts any sense of stability and points to the possibility of the absence of the self. During primary narcissism, or what Lacan calls the mirror stage, the infant proto-subject begins to structure its chaos of sensations and drives through the satisfying recognition of its own image, both in literal mirrors and in the mirroring figure of the maternal body. This pleasurable self-image provides boundaries between self and other within which the subject can experience itself as stable and whole; but this security is undermined by the troubling awareness that the image is always other than the self and potentially indistinguishable from or substitutable for the self. In response to this threat of absence and lack, the maternal body becomes a figure for an imagined pre-subjective state of presence without possibility of absence, in which no boundaries separated self from mother/other.[59] In its role as imaginary mirror, however, the maternal body, like any image, must already be other than the self, signifying the fragmentation of that imagined earlier unity. Paradoxically, therefore, the maternal body also signifies the trauma of loss, the severing of unity which continually disrupts any sense of wholeness or self-sufficiency. The shift from "o-o-o-o" to "Baby o-o-o-o" involves a relationship between the maternal body, representation and self-representation which is much more complex than the absence/presence dialectic of the first fort–da game: an object of anxiety as well as pleasure and desire, the maternal body represents not only a mirror image or uncanny double of the self, but also the ground out of which the subject differentiates itself as a coherent self-image, and from which the subject is thereby irrevocably severed.

In Ana Mendieta's *Silueta* and *Árbol de la vida* series, union with the earth is equated with a "return to the maternal source": landscape, in the form of various chosen sites, serves as a trope or substitute not only for the homeland of Mendieta's particular exile, but also for the maternal body in its dual role as both "figure" and "ground" for the process of imaginary self-formation. Through an intimate working process of lying on the ground and literally tracing the boundaries of her own body onto the earth, Mendieta re-stages the establishment of a reassuring narcissistic self-image in the imaginary mirror of the maternal body; at the same time, the satisfying fullness of tactile encounter with the earth invokes the fantasy of absolute plenitude in unity with the maternal body. The invitation to viewers to identify with the resulting figure/scene turns not only on the delight of self-recognition in the anthropomorphic figure, but also on the sensory pleasures to which the images of sand, wood, and water indexically refer: the imagined experience of nestling in the curve of the silhouette, feeling the textures of the landscape along the surface of the skin. This combination of narcissistic and tactile pleasures is what made Mendieta's work so compelling to many feminists in the 1970's, offering powerful affective resources for an oppositional politics rooted in celebration of earth-centred female spirituality. However, what is repressed in this reassuring formulation and "returned" by the uncanniness of the images is not only the impossibility of absolute union with the earth/mother, but also the threatening aspect of that union, which signifies both plenitude and the subject's dissolution into undifferentiation. Despite the utopian claims of the surrounding narratives, the relationship between Mendieta's self-inscriptions and the landscape as maternal body is contradictory and ambivalent. In their tactile references and the uncanny undecidability they stage between human and non-human, the silhouettes point to another crucial aspect of imaginary self-formation: they suggest that subjectivity is constituted not only through images of the self and the maternal body, but also in relation to what Bronfen calls "the unencompassable body of 'matter-materiality-maternity,' which indexically figures death" (111).

Like any fort–da game, the obsessive repetition of Mendieta's silhouettes both resists and points to absence and death, because the material/maternal presence they invoke is always a substitute for the imagined state of originary plenitude, and is always already lost before it can be repeated in representation. Encountered in the gallery, the photographic images further repeat the separation from the maternal body, since they refer to the fullness of a tactile encounter which remains always absent from its visual representation. Yet as Bronfen argues, notions of loss and mortality are invoked not only by the mother's absence, but also by her *presence*, because the maternal body indexically figures the position previous to life and so prefigures the absence of the self in death. As I suggested, the tentative boundaries of Mendieta's silhouettes unsettle narcissistic identification by implying a temporal sequence in which the anthropomorphic form, like the feminine corpse in Hodler's series, will eventually dissolve into its material surroundings. In Mendieta's work, this dissolution can be read as utopian fusion of self and landscape/maternal body, but it also points to the maternal body's repressed signified, the terrifyingly unimaginable dissolution of the self in death. At stake in representation as fort–da game is both the ambivalent substitution of images and signifiers for the absent mother and the potentially absent self, and also the impossible signified of the self's inevitable disappearance in the real, material dissolution of the body.

The uncanny effect of the *Silueta* and *Árbol de la vida* images is, however, only partly due to the implied temporal sequence of self-dissolution/mortality; the slippage between animate and inanimate in these images is constructed not only temporally, but spatially. As I have argued, the insistently literal reference to the materials that constitute the silhouettes creates an uncanny undecidability between two possible signifieds, human and non-human, for the anthropomorphic form. This undecidability is experienced not only as a semantic problem, but also as a conflict between the invitation to identify with the pleasurable merging of self and earth and the physical impossibility of such a union. Although viewers can imagine occupying the space of the silhouettes hollowed from sand or mud, the images built of flowers or stones frustrate such a fantasy, filling the space of the human form with insistently non-human materiality, which can be experienced as surface but not as interiority. Mendieta's inscription of the anthropomorphic form literally *in* the landscape produces anxiety as well as pleasure, since it both suggests a palpable intimacy between body and earth, and insists on the unimaginable situation of human body and non-human landscape literally occupying the same space.

This paradox points to the impossible and necessary relationship between subjectivity and soma. It suggests that the threat to the self represented by the maternal body (and its substitute, landscape) is not only mortality and the material dissolution of the body, but also the very constitution of the real body *in* materiality. For the subject constituted in the imaginary and the symbolic, the real body grounds all psychic drives and representations, yet remains inaccessible, since the real is precisely that which image and language are not, the unknowable material referent to which signifiers are arbitrarily linked. Impossible to picture or articulate, materiality, like death, threatens all stability by pointing to the collapse of representation in the unrepresentable, the inadequacy of language and images as means of apprehension, mastery and self-construction. In its complex configuration of representation, self-representation, the maternal body, landscape, mortality and materiality, Ana Mendieta's practice stages what Bronfen describes as "the ambivalent and indeterminant shift between real body and image/symbol, as well as between real body of the mother and maternal body as figure for one's own soma" (34–35). The ambivalent object of both negation and desire is not only the maternal body, but the limit and ground of representation and selfhood: that more global, implacable yet unencompassable otherness of materiality/mortality which cannot be known except through representations, yet which always exceeds and resists representation.

Embodied Geographies

Elisabeth Bronfen argues that repressed anxiety about this "unencompassable body of matter-materiality-maternity" underlies the displacement of loss and lack onto the feminine body, and therefore supports gendered structures of domination:

> What is put under erasure by the gendered concept of castration is the other, so often non-read theme of death, forbidden maybe because far less conducive to efforts of stable self-fashioning than notions of sexual difference. To see the phallus as secondary to the scar of the navel means acknowledging that notions of domination and inferiority based on gender difference are also secondary to a more global and non-individuated disempowerment before death. (35)

The navel is the index of death in that it points both to the subject's irrevocable separation from the maternal body of plenitude, and to the maternal body as figure for the subject's inevitable dissolution in material death. However, through its connection to the maternal body as both imaginary figure and concrete presence, the navel also points to the inseparability of subject and soma, to the implacable yet unknowable presence of materiality which both grounds and disrupts all imaginary and symbolic stability. Rather than claiming utopian identification between woman and landscape in opposition to phallic technocratic civilization, Ana Mendieta's *Silueta* and *Árbol de la vida* series can be read as an aesthetic-symbolic practice organized under the sign of the navel: both non-gendered and related to feminine bodily specificity through its link with the maternal body, this practice displaces the binary structures of the phallic symbolic order and patriarchal social relations by attending to the ambivalent relationship of separation and inseparability, negation and desire between human subjects and materiality/mortality.

To read Mendieta's work as uncanny is to argue that it both inscribes and unsettles the binary opposition between fusion and separation by figuring a state of undecidability between the two. In my view, however, the relationship traced in Mendieta's practice is suggested not so much in her claim that "through my earth/body sculptures I become one with the earth" as in the slightly amended "I become an extension of nature and nature becomes an extension of my body." The second statement suggests a relationship based less on fusion, or even identification, than on proximity: the image of a human body is inscribed in a maternal landscape conceived not as undifferentiated unity with or mirroring double of the self, but as unknownness encountered through touch along the boundaries of the body. This invocation of tactile encounter with the unencompassable unknown suggests a model of subjectivity that is irreducible to the primary narcissism theorized by Freud: it suggests a relationship with landscape, and its analogue the maternal body, that recalls the revisionary psychoanalytic model proposed by Bracha Lichtenberg Ettinger, in which subjectivization is organized not only around the phallus as the sign for "*oneness*, totality, and sameness, and oedipal, symbolic castration," but also around what Lichtenberg Ettinger calls the matrix, a sign for aspects of subjectivity "involving multiplicity, plurality, partiality, difference, strangeness, relations to the unknown other, *prenatal* passages to the symbolic, with processes of change of *I* and *not-I* emerging in co-existence, and of change in their borderlines, limits, and thresholds within and around them."[60]

Within Lacan's exclusively phallic paradigm, the prenatal state represents total fusion with the maternal body and therefore "both a paradise and a state of annihilation."[61] Alongside this, Lichtenberg Ettinger proposes an alternative model in which maternal body represents neither fusion nor dissolution, but an originary *differentiation* figured by the organization of experience in the infant-mother unit "in terms of sensory surfaces, movement, time-intervals, rhythm and tangibility."[62] The matrixial paradigm posits subjectivity not as carved out only through violent differentiation, but also as co-emerging through shared encounter along intimate, shifting boundaries between the known *I* and unknown *not-I(s)*. There is differentiation, but that which is differentiated is neither mere background nor a mirror for the developing subject, but an unknownness whose presence is registered at the level of unconscious desire as non-visual, non-symbolic traces of tactile experience.

This way of figuring the maternal body allows Lichtenberg Ettinger to privilege aspects of unconscious experience that are not reducible to the imaginary and symbolic strata, and which seem crucial to the workings of desire between self and other, body and landscape, human and non-human in Ana Mendieta's self-portraits. As well as an oscillation between presence/absence and pleasure/anxiety, the *Silueta* and *Árbol de la Vita* images invoke a hauntingly undefinable response that might be described as "matrixial": neither pleasure nor displeasure, nor an oscillation between the two, but a distinct pleasure/displeasure affective response shared through "evocations of silent alertness, amazement and wonder, curiosity, empathy, compassion, awe, and uncanniness."[63] In so far as subjectivity has "matrixial" aspects, Lichtenberg Ettinger argues, that which is other than the self is not necessarily perceived as threatening, and can be encountered and acknowledged without either assimilation or rejection:

> The Matrix deals with the possibility of recognizing the other in his/her otherness, difference, and unknownness. . . . The Matrix is a composition of *I* and *not-I(s)*, of self and not-selves while they are unknown or anonymous. Some selves identify one another as *not-I* without aspiring to assimilate in order to become one, without abolishing differences and making the other a *same* in order to accept him/her, and without creating a phallic rejection so that only one of them can occupy the physical/mental space.[64]

This alternative model of subjectivity allows us to read Mendieta's images as staging an intimate, anonymous coexistence in the same space of the known *I* (apprehended through recognition of or identification with the human form) and *not-I(s)* which might become known in part as soma, m/other, landscape, but which also remain unrecognized, unidentified, their unfathomable presence gestured toward by the invocation of boundaries continually re-negotiated through non-verbal, non-visual, tactile encounter. The human body in this configuration is both an imaginary construct through which the self is reinvented in the act of inscription,[65] and a mediating surface through which the self encounters that which is other than the self—including the otherness of its own soma.

In its acknowledgment of "the other in its otherness, difference, and unknownness" and its emphasis on the tactile, Ana Mendieta's practice privileges matrixial aspects of subjectivity and posits the embodied subject as a site of simultaneous inscriptions of the unviewable, out-of-the-signified real as well as of history and acculturation. However, these matrixial traces cannot be separated from the imaginary and symbolic registers through which they must be conveyed in order to participate in cultural production. As Charles Merewether writes in an article on Latin American artists in diaspora, "The issue is how to understand the social formation of the body—the realm of the senses, of memory and the unconscious, as well as vision and visuality—as social facts."[66] Mendieta's oppositional practice is not only the private ritual of the artist's encounter with the earth, but also its documentation and exhibition in photographic form; and within the private encounter, the real body and landscape are always already inscribed with personal, social and historical meanings, and experienced through imaginary and conceptual bodies and landscapes produced by various psychic events and social discourses. Mendieta's self-inscriptions enact an encounter between the human subject and its limit and ground in mortality and materiality, experienced simultaneously as the physical landscape, the imaginary maternal body and unknown *not-I(s)*; yet this encounter is always also an intervention into the interrelated social discourses of patriarchal, imperialist and ecological domination, a resistance to the dominant narrative of Western history and its universalized subject whose relation to its Others (woman, non-Western cultures, landscape) is structured by the phallic either/or of assimilation or rejection. In their undecidability, whether experienced as uncanny anxiety or as matrixial affect, Mendieta's *Silueta* and *Árbol de la vida* series insist on the necessity of acknowledging the limits of selfhood (individual and universalized) in the unrepresentable unknownness of materiality/mortality: both individual death, and the implacable resistance of the biosphere to human attempts to reconstruct it according to our own designs and in our own inflated self-image. The relationship between human and non-human in these images is infused simultaneously with pleasure, anxiety, desire, and an intimate anonymity; it points both to the utter impossibility of knowing the non-human except through representations, and to the utter necessity of adapting our discourses and practices to attend to that other, unencompassable territory.

Notes

1. Ana Mendieta, unpublished statement, 1981; quoted in Petra Barreras del Rio and John Perreault, *Ana Mendieta: A Retrospective* [exh. cat.] (New York: The New Museum of Contemporary Art, 1987), p. 10.
2. Ibid.
3. Lucy R. Lippard, *Overlay: Contemporary Art and the Art of Prehistory* (New York: Pantheon Books, 1983), p. 4.
4. The two series, produced concurrently, have different formal and conceptual emphases, but are similar enough in form and strategy to be treated as one body of work for the purposes of this paper.
5. The phrase is from a review by Ellen Lubell in *Art in America*, vol. 71 no. 6 (Summer 1983), p. 161.
6. Sallie McFague, *The Body of God: An Ecological Theology* (London: SCM Press Ltd., 1993), p. 101.
7. See Donna Haraway, *Simians, Cyborgs and Women: The Reinvention of Nature* (London: Free Association Books, 1991).
8. D. H. Lawrence, "Introduction to These Paintings (Puritanism and the Arts)," *Lawrence on Hardy and Painting* (London: Heinemann Educational Books Ltd., 1973; first published in *The Paintings of D. H. Lawrence*, London, 1929). To avoid an excessive number of footnotes, page references to this text will appear in the body of the essay.
9. Oriana Baddeley and Valerie Fraser, *Drawing the Line: Art and Cultural Identity in Contemporary Latin America* (London and New York: Verso, 1989), p. 11.
10. Gerardo Mosquera, catalogue essay in Ana Mendieta, *Rupestrian Sculptures/Esculturas Rupestres* [exh. cat.] (New York: A.I.R. Gallery, 1981).
11. Luis Camnitzer, "Ana Mendieta," *Third Text*, no. 7 (Summer 1989), p. 48.
12. Gerardo Mosquera suggests "aesthetic-symbolic production" as an alternative to the

term "Art," which is historically and culturally specific to post-Enlightenment Western culture and fails to acknowledge the culturally specific social meanings and functions of past and non-Western cultural practices. See Mosquera, "The History of Art and Cultures" (seminar paper presented at the Centre for Curatorial Studies, Bard College, New York, 15 April 1994).

13. Alexander Wilson, *The Culture of Nature: North American Landscape from Disney to the Exxon Valdez* (Cambridge, Massachusetts and Oxford, UK: Blackwell Publishers, 1992), p. 14.

14. Carolyn Merchant, *The Death of Nature: Women, Ecology, and the Scientific Revolution* (New York: Harper & Row, Publishers, Inc., 1980). This is a detailed analysis of various competing models of nature in relation to gender and to social and environmental history; for reasons of space I have had to oversimplify this complex and contradictory field.

15. See Merchant, pp. 29–41.

16. Lawrence, p. 142.

17. Merchant, p. 6.

18. Ibid., p. 190.

19. Wilson, p. 154.

20. Sidonie Smith, *Subjectivity, Identity and the Body: Women's Autobiographical Practices in the Twentieth Century* (Bloomington and Indianapolis: Indiana University Press, 1993), p. 171.

21. John Beardsley, *Earthworks and Beyond: Contemporary Art in the Landscape* (New York: Abbeville Press, Inc., 1984), p. 7. It should be noted that the notion of a more or less universal twentieth-century devaluation of landscape art comes from a particular perspective based in New York high modernism; in Canada, for instance, landscape was the dominant vocabulary of modernist painting in the first half of the twentieth century.

22. Michael Heizer, quoted in Beardsley, *Earthworks and Beyond*, p. 13.

23. Lucy R. Lippard, "Quite Contrary: Body, Nature, Ritual in Women's Art," *Chrysalis*, vol. 2 (1977), pp. 39–40.

24. Lippard, *Overlay*, p. 78.

25. Mendieta, bilingual wall text for exhibition circa 1981, quoted in Barreras del Rio and Perreault, p. 28.

26. Heizer, quoted in Beardsley, *Earthworks and Beyond*, p. 19.

27. Lippard, "Quite Contrary: Body, Nature, Ritual in Women's Art," p. 40.

28. Ana Mendieta, gallery sheet for *Silueta Series 1977*, an exhibition at Corroboree, Gallery of New Concepts, Iowa City; quoted in Mary Jane Jacob, *Ana Mendieta: The "Silueta" Series, 1973–1980* [exh. cat.] (New York: Galerie Lelong, 1991), p. 8.

29. See Joel B. Hagen, *An Entangled Bank: The Origins of Ecosystem Ecology* (New Brunswick, New Jersey: Rutgers University Press, 1992), pp. 191–192 for a summary of the scientific status of the "Gaia hypothesis," understood more rigorously as proposing not that the earth is literally an organism, but that the biosphere is controlled by living organisms which regulate the conditions essential for life through the complex feedback mechanisms of earth's ecosystems.

30. Haraway, p. 154.

31. Ibid., p. 174.

32. Hagen, p. 191.

33. See Hagen for a history of late nineteenth and twentieth century ecology and its debates over the use of organismic and technological language in scientific discourses.

34. McFague, p. 36.

35. Lawrence, p. 146.

36. John Perreault, "Earth and Fire: Mendieta's Body of Work," in Barreras del Rio and Perreault, p. 13.

37. Wilson, p. 14.

38. Robert Smithson, quoted in Lippard, *Overlay*, p. 57.

39. It would be irresponsible not to note that Carl Andre and Ana Mendieta married in January 1985, and that Mendieta died tragically later that year by falling out of the window of their 34th-storey apartment in circumstances that are still unclear. Luis Camnitzer notes in his article on Mendieta that Andre was acquitted of murder in 1988 because his guilt had not been proven "beyond a reasonable doubt."

40. Lippard, *Overlay*, p. 30.

41. Carl Andre, quoted in Lippard, *Overlay*, p. 141.

42. Lawrence, 'Introduction to These Paintings', p. 157.

43. Donald Kuspit, "Ana Mendieta" [review], *Artforum*, vol. 26, no. 6, p. 144.

44. Ana Mendieta, "Introduction," *Dialectics of Isolation: An Exhibition of Third World Women Artists of the United States* [exh. cat.] (New York: A.I.R. Gallery, 1980).

45. See Mary Jane Jacob, *Ana Mendieta: The "Silueta" Series, 1973–1980* [exh. cat.] (New York: Galerie Lelong, 1991) for the most detailed discussion to date of Mendieta's use of Santería.

46. It should be noted that Mendieta did not grow up practicing Santería, but encountered it through the stories of African-Cuban servants in her parents' household, and later through the writings of Lydia Cabrera and the Santería practices of Cuban communities in New York and Miami. Her deployment of it is thus more a deliberate, strategic identification than an expression of pre-existing identity. See Jacob, p. 4.

47. In the exhibition catalogue *Ana Mendieta: A Retrospective*, Marcia Tucker notes that Mendieta "was outspoken and aggressive about her political views, but at the same time she felt that art's importance lay in the spiritual sphere." She quotes Mendieta as stating that "Art is a material part of culture but its greatest value is its spiritual role, and that influences society, because it's the greatest contribution to the intellectual and moral development of humanity that can be made." See Barreras del Rio and Perreault, p. 6. See also Mendieta's introduction to the exhibition catalogue *Dialectics of Isolation*.

48. See Baddeley and Fraser, Chapter 1, "Mapping Landscapes."

49. See Irit Rogoff, "The Discourse of Exile: Geographies and Representations of Identity," *Journal of Philosophy and the Visual Arts* (July 1989), pp. 72–73.

50. Ibid., p. 72.

51. Elisabeth Bronfen, *Over Her Dead Body: Death, Femininity and the Aesthetic* (Manchester: Manchester University Press, 1992), p. 52. To avoid an excessive number of footnotes, further references to this text will appear in the body of the essay.

52. Smith, p. 10.

53. This point is made by Camnitzer (p. 50).

54. Sigmund Freud, "The 'Uncanny'" (Standard Edition, vol. XVII), p. 220.

55. Ibid., pp. 235–236.

56. Mendieta, unpublished statement, 1981; quoted in Barreras del Rio and Perreault, p. 10. The thirteen-year-old Ana Mendieta and her sister were among a number of children sent in the early 1960's from newly communist Cuba to Catholic orphanages in the United States; their mother joined them three years later. Mendieta revisited Cuba in 1980, and in 1981 she "took the *Silueta* series back to its source" by making her "Rupestrian Sculptures" at Jaruco, Cuba.

57. Ibid.

58. Space does not permit me to support this argument fully, but see Bronfen, pp. 121–124,

for a summary of the workings of sexual difference and fetishism in images of women/Woman.

59. See Kaja Silverman, *The Acoustic Mirror: The Female Voice in Psychoanalysis and Cinema* (Bloomington and Indianapolis: Indiana University Press, 1988) for a useful discussion of the maternal body as imaginary mirror and object of retrospective fantasy.

60. Bracha Lichtenberg Ettinger, "Matrix and Metramorphosis," *Differences*, vol. 4, no. 3 (Fall 1992), pp. 178–179.

61. Lichtenberg Ettinger, "Metramorphic Borderlinks and Matrixial Borderspace" (seminar paper presented at the University of Leeds, 15 March 1994), p. 13.

62. Ibid., p. 14.

63. Lichtenberg Ettinger, "Metramorphic Borderlinks and Matrixial Borderspace," p. 11.

64. Lichtenberg Ettinger, "Matrix and Metramorphosis," p. 200.

65. I am indebted here to Charles Merewether's reading of Mendieta's project: he argues that "Mendieta shifted the location of meaning and identity from the fixity of an image or place (the body represented, or the land) to the actual processes of inscription." See Merewether, "Displacement and the Reinvention of Identity" in Waldo Rasmussen (ed.), *Latin American Artists of the Twentieth Century* [exh. cat.] (New York: The Museum of Modern Art, 1993), p. 146.

66. Merewether, p. 155.

CHAPTER THIRTEEN

The Power of "Positive" Diagnosis

Medical and Maternal Discourses on Amniocentesis

> When we walked into the doctor's office, both my husband and
> I were crying. He looked up and said, "What's wrong? Why are
> you both in tears?" "It's our baby, our baby is going to die," I
> said. "That isn't a baby," he said firmly. "It's a collection of
> cells that made a mistake."
>
> *Leah Rubinstein, age thirty-nine*

L ate twentieth-century reproductive medicine offers both benefits and burdens. Its technologies are aimed at reducing maternal and infant mortality
and helping assure normal, healthy outcomes. At the same time, however, it controls conditions of pregnancy, birth, and parenting in ways that scientize our most
fundamental experiences. Being a woman, becoming a parent, experiencing birth,
and sometimes confronting death are processes increasingly organized by reproductive medicine rather than by individuals, families, and communities. Indeed,
many of the core experiences of sex, gender, and family formation are now culturally defined by medical science. The access people have to reproductive medicine, as well as its respected or coercive quality, in part defines their experience
of pregnancy.

Examining prenatal diagnosis, especially the use of amniocentesis, reveals a
great deal about the changing definitions and controls of pregnancy and birth.
On this frontier of reproductive technology, medical services are transforming the
experience of pregnancy, personhood, and parenthood for the women and their
families who use prenatal diagnosis. In offering a test for chromosome anomalies
and some other inherited disabilities, amniocentesis holds out the possibility of
choosing to carry or not to carry to term a pregnancy in which a fetus will become a child with a genetic disability. That choice is part of the medical definition of what constitutes an acceptable or an unacceptable child in American culture. The choices people make around amniocentesis also reveal the similarities
and differences between medical and maternal perceptions of what it means to
have a child with a disability.

Rayna Rapp, "The Power of 'Positive' Diagnosis: Medical and Maternal Discourses on
Amniocentesis," in Karen L. Michaelson, ed. *Childbirth in America: Anthropological Perspectives* (South Hadley, Mass.: Bergin & Garvey, 1988): 103–16. Reprinted by permission.

Amniocentesis: Technology and Risks

The technology of amniocentesis is easily described. Pregnant women who choose the test are screened between the sixteenth and nineteenth weeks of their pregnancies. To help prepare parents, genetic counselors provide information about the risks and benefits of the test. A team of doctors and nurses uses ultrasound visualization of the fetus and placenta to guide the insertion of a thin, hollow needle into the amniotic sac, through which about three tablespoons of fluid are extracted. The liquid is cultured in a genetics laboratory, and sufficient fetal cells are usually available in three to four weeks for a diagnosis to be made. At that time, chromosome numbers, shapes, sizes, and bands can easily be read. About 98 percent of the women who have amniocentesis will receive the good news that their fetuses are free of the conditions for which they have been tested. The other 2 percent will have to confront the distressing news that their fetus has a disability. These women must weigh the stress and stigma of choosing a late abortion against the choice of having a disabled child.

Three groups of people are usually recommended for amniocentesis. One includes pregnant women and their partners whose families include someone with an inherited condition for which prenatal screening is now available. The second includes couples from ethnically specific populations in which certain autosomal recessive genetic diseases (for example, Tay-Sachs among Ashkenazi Jews; sickle cell anemia among African-Americans) are relatively frequent and for which both partners are known carriers. The third is "older" women, who are considered to be at elevated risk for several chromosomal abnormalities, of which Down's syndrome is the best known and most significant one. "Older" is, however, a social, not simply a biological construct. Although the incidence of Down's syndrome live-born babies steadily rises as women progress from their twenties to their forties, the cutoff age for the test has varied considerably. It was first recommended for women who were forty years of age or older. Then the recommendation dropped to thirty-eight and then thirty-five, and it is now moving toward the lower thirties.

The procedures used in amniocentesis are themselves not without risk, and thus the recommended age is identified by the intersection of two epidemiological patterns: One is the safety of the technology itself, and the other is the incidence of Down's syndrome in live-born babies of women in different age groups. Amniocentesis adds a small additional risk of miscarriage to the pregnancies of older women. Three more women per thousand who have had amniocentesis will miscarry than will women who have not had the test. The incidence of miscarriage with amniocentesis is thus 1/333. This number approximates the incidence of fetuses with Down's syndrome born to pregnant women who are thirty-five, which is 1/360 (Hook, 1981; Hook, Cross, & Schreinemachers, 1983; PDL, n.d.). If the technology improved so that it caused one less miscarriage per thousand, then the recommended age for its use would drop to match the incidence of fetuses with Downs' syndrome in that lower age group. We are thus witnessing the intersection of an increasingly routinized technology with the social pattern of delayed pregnancy in some parts of the U.S. population and not any absolute epidemiological threshold of risk.

The Sociology of Amniocentesis

The sociology of amniocentesis is more complex to describe. Initially recommended for relatively small numbers of older pregnant women, the test is rapidly becoming a pregnancy ritual for certain sectors of the highly educated urban middle class. Each year scores of thousands of women use amniocentesis, but the test is very expensive and unevenly available.[1] Women living in major urban areas and/or near teaching hospitals and covered by comprehensive health insurance are most likely to use it. With the exception of a very few states that fund the procedure through Medicaid, amniocentesis remains the prerogative of the well-to-do. Several studies, however, indicate that low-income women would use the procedure if it were available to them for a minimal charge (Hsu, 1982; Joans, 1980; Marion et al., 1980; Sokal et al., 1980).

The discourse on amniocentesis is filled with the clamor of experts. Health economists tell us that it is cheaper to offer mass screening for Downs' syndrome than to support the services that disabled children require (Sadovnick & Baird, 1981). Geneticists assess the limits and future possibilities of their scientific field, hopeful of screening increased numbers of serious disabilities (Filkins & Russo, 1985; Harris, 1974; Lipkin & Rowley, 1974). Bioethicists comment on the eugenic implications of the technology (Hilton et al., 1973; Powledge & Fletcher, 1979). And feminists worry that the technique will be used for sex selection, discriminating against female fetuses (Corea, 1985; Hanmer, 1981). But when I entered the discourse as an anthropologist (and as a pregnant woman), the silence of the women and their families using or refusing the technology was deafening (Rothman, 1986). Yet it is precisely those voices that might describe the lived reality of a new reproductive technology that we must make audible if we are to understand its cultural and not simply its medical meaning, probing how the latter may be shaping the former.

A Pilot Study

This chapter reports on one aspect of the study of the social impact and cultural meaning of prenatal diagnosis: my initial pilot work with women and their families who received positive diagnoses—that is, the information that their fetuses had serious disabilities.[2] In interviews and letters, I asked people to recall the experience of getting a positive diagnosis, making a decision, and coping with its aftermath. My data come from forty women and their families, eleven of whom I interviewed in their homes, five of whom I interviewed by telephone and twenty-four of whom entered into extensive correspondence with me. All but two ultimately chose to abort affected fetuses.

My sample was developed using medical and personal networks and responses to an article I published on amniocentesis in a nationally circulated women's magazine (Rapp, 1984). All respondents were self-selected, and the quality of information varied considerably, the telephone interviews yielding the most perfunctory information. Although the letters were written by women from all sections of the United States (in addition to two that came from abroad) recalling experiences with amniocentesis up to a decade ago, the home interviews were conducted with women who came from the metropolitan New York area and had received a positive diagnosis within the past twelve months.

My interview schedule probed for images of fetuses, disabilities, pregnancy, and family life. It asked for information about religious, ethnic, educational, and occupational backgrounds and queried the knowledge people had about the disability diagnosed for their fetus prior to the time that they received their prenatal diagnosis. It contained questions concerning support and criticism from family and community members, experiences with the medical system, and steps toward resolution and recovery. It was sensitive to the use (or nonuse) of medical language in describing this perplexing experience and its aftermath. I include here many quotations from these interviews, changing only the names and ages to protect the women's privacy.

The Privatization of Experience

Although the pilot data are somewhat uneven, three themes appear consistently throughout. The first is the extreme privatization of the experience of reproductive choices—including abortions—which are considered to be personal matters in the contemporary United States, choices conventionally taken by an individual or a couple. Most of the women and their families told their immediate families about the positive diagnosis and, usually, about the subsequent abortion. Children of the family received age-appropriate information. Most also told a few close friends. But some told no one, because they lived in communities and in families where strong antiabortion sentiment was expressed. And virtually all referred to a "miscarriage" or "loss of a baby" in some contexts. The pain of reproductive loss is universal; the boundaries along which people fear they will incur judgment rather than support for a voluntary loss vary considerably. Privatization allows people some control over shaping that boundary between intimate friends who "deserved the truth" and public others who simply "needed some explanation." But privatization also reduces the quantity and quality of special support that an individual may receive for her grieving. No one with whom I spoke or corresponded had ever met another woman who had been through the same experience. This new form of intentional pregnancy loss occurs in unknown interpersonal territory. Technology here creates a traumatic experience that is so deeply medicalized and privatized that its social shape has yet to be excavated, and a cultural language to describe it is yet to be found.

The degree of isolation inherent in the experience of receiving a positive diagnosis is in part conditioned by the diagnosis itself. For the more than 80 percent of my respondents whose fetal diagnosis was Down's syndrome, some cultural knowledge was available. Everyone had an image of a child with Down's syndrome. Some had friends, family members, or community members whose children had the condition. Although their images of mentally retarded children, especially children with Down's syndrome, were often out of date, they still had a reference point for the diagnosis and felt competent to decide whether or not to end the affected pregnancy. In this pilot study, I had no cases of women continuing a pregnancy after a prenatal diagnosis of Down's syndrome. And medical statistics suggest an abortion rate of about 95 percent after this particular diagnosis (Hook, 1981).

Other, more arcane diagnoses were harder to understand and to judge. Two of my respondents received diagnoses of XYY syndrome, a sex-chromosome anomaly. The diagnosis of XYY includes possible mental retardation, anomalous sexual development, and putative aggressiveness. But the diagnosis is highly controversial and has sparked both technical and popular discussions of whether screening is appropriate or is an artifact of the abuse of minimal scientific information blown out of proportion (Hook, 1973). Both respondents who received this diagnosis spent whole days in a medical library trying to interpret the meaning of XYY syndrome before reaching their decisions. One family's fetus was identified as having a chromosomal tag so rare that a nationally known geneticist could point to just fifteen other reported cases and only vaguely predict its outcome. Another family received a diagnosis of organ damage and displacement so complete that they consulted with a battery of pediatric surgeons and neonatologists over the course of one month before they reached a decision. Two others didn't understand the language of the diagnosis and had to have it explained many times before they could make a choice. In such cases, unlike Down's syndrome, there is no collective fund of information available, and medical language necessarily dictates the shape of familial understanding.

The Language of Prenatal Diagnosis

The use of medical language in itself creates tensions in the discussion of prenatal diagnosis. This is the second theme that ran through all the interviews and letters. Medical language is not neutral; medical practices are often intentionally distancing, as the quotation that opens this chapter suggests. Some patients find this distance reassuring in its promise of rationality; others find it cold and denying of their experience. A war of words accompanied virtually all the stories I collected. Cells, embryos, and fetuses vied for center stage with babies. "Positive diagnoses" describe the medical discovery procedures, but they painfully reverse and mask the very negative experiences of parents who learn that their fetuses have disabilities. In some cases here, women literally assumed the burden of this impersonal language, speaking in total disconnection from their pregnant bodies: "So I was in labor for twenty-four hours and absolutely nothing happened. I mean nothing. A dead fetus, but it wouldn't come out. So I called Dr. X at eight A.M. and I guess I must have sounded crazy. 'Hello,' I said, 'I'm a demised fetus and a failed prostaglandin.' 'Oh no you're not, honey,' the nurse said. 'You're a lady that's losing a baby, and you'd better stop talking and start crying.'" (Sandra Larkin, age thirty-six).

Several families mentioned the struggles they had waged to see their dead fetuses or to retrieve them for burial. Usually fetuses were sent to pathology to confirm a diagnosis. Legal and hospital procedures dictate this practice, which brings the reality of family mourning into conflict with medical protocols. Denied access to dead fetuses, some chose to bury or frame the sonogram visualizations that they had been given during amniocentesis. One family pasted the image into the family Bible. They thus created the emotional personification, albeit through technology, that family life required and medical procedures could not grant.[3]

The use of medical language and its accompanying procedures are purposive. As one respondent put it, "This late-abortion business is no picnic for the doctors and nurses." Medical discourse protects medical staff from the sad and disorienting experiences of their patients, allowing the routinization of services. But each woman I interviewed had to perform a complex translation of the medical words she had been given into whatever her own experience of that pregnancy and its ending had been. Often only medical language seemed legitimate. Many women couldn't use the word *abortion*, yet hesitated over *termination*, the term used by medical professionals. Almost all switched from *fetus* to *baby* while describing their situations. Yet no one could recall the affected pregnancy without using medical descriptions of its length, dated from last menstrual period rather than by nausea, quickening, or some other intrabody sign. And, of course, the diagnosis itself was always discussed medically. Medical language here reinforces the privatization of the problem, for each woman is seen, and sees herself, as an individual patient rather than as a member of a larger group of women confronting a new technological possibility or coping with grief.

There is an awkward gap between medical and maternal discourses. Although some might argue that medical language neutralizes some of the anxiety associated with amniocentesis (Brewster, 1984), its function is actually more complex and powerful. Many scholars and activists have noted that medical discourses increasingly define pregnancy itself as a pathological (or potentially pathological) condition, thus justifying professional management and intervention (Rothman, 1982; Shaw, 1974; Wertz & Wertz, 1977). But pregnancy is also an embodied state and a time-framed activity about which a great deal of popular knowledge has been accumulated, often passed down from mothers to daughters, shared among friends, and held by ethnically specific communities (Oakley, 1979, 1980, 1981; Snow, Johnson, & Mayhew, 1978; Thompson, 1983). Thus, multiple discourses construct pregnancy as a whole, subdivided among specialists (for example, obstetricians and midwives may think and speak differently about their pregnant patients) and between specialists and pregnant women.

The same cannot be said for prenatal diagnosis, which is constructed as a specifically medical event. The experience itself exists only in relation to the technology, services, and personnel within which it is embedded. Unlike pregnancy, for which a woman has embodied experiences she can and does articulate and share with others (both pregnant and nonpregnant), the event of receiving a positive diagnosis bears no relation to either internal body cues or collective popular knowledge. There is no tradition to call upon in coping with the diagnosis. Acceptance of the test and its results implies a belief in epidemiological statistics, an acknowledgement of risk factors, population parameters, and laboratory procedures all far removed from the individual or the collective sense of pregnancy itself. Those for whom a positive diagnosis is given are thus operating on an unknown terrain, far removed from pregnancy as they have experienced or learned about it. The stumbling words, the gaps of language, the silences surrounding this experience, are testimony to its totally medical construction. It is an experience removed from the maternal discourses by which pregnant women gradually become mothers, not simply medical cases.

The Ethics of Decision Making

A third generalization that emerged from these interviews is the ethical complexity and social embeddedness of the decision to abort (or in two cases, to keep) an affected pregnancy. Five respondents discussed their cases with religious advisers, and six saw psychological counselors in the course of making their decisions. But the majority did not seek nonmedical professional help. They retrospectively identified their decision as having been made at one of two times: it was made "on the day I decided to go for amniocentesis" (that is, with an almost-conscious knowledge that a diagnosis of any fetal genetic disability would be reason enough to choose abortion), or the decision was made "the minute we got the news" (in which case the couple, not the pregnant woman, was recalled as the decision-making unit, and their conversations were recalled verbatim). In the five cases for which anomalous diagnoses were given, decision making was protracted, involving several rounds of medical consultation and sometimes library research or home visits with families whose living children had the diagnosed condition. Yet even those couples who conducted research before making a decision reported strong leanings toward an abortion as soon as they knew that something was wrong.[4]

Reasons for the abortion decision were often phrased in terms of other family members:

> Some people say that abortion is hate. I say my abortion was an act of love. I've got three kids. I was forty-three when we accidentally got pregnant again. We decided there was enough love in our family to handle it, even though finances would be tight. But we also decided to have the test. A kid with a serious problem was more than we could handle. And when we got the bad news, I knew immediately what I had to do. At forty-three, you think about your own death. It would have been tough now, but think what would have happened to my other kids, especially my daughter. Oh, the boys, Tommy and Alex, would have done okay. But Laura would have been the one who got stuck. It's always the girls. It would have been me, and then after I'm gone it would have been the big sister who took care of that child. Saving Laura from that burden was an act of love. (Mary Fruticci, age forty-four)

Many families with other children expressed similar concerns, citing the effects of a disabled sibling on prior children as the reason for choosing abortion. But over 60 percent of the respondents made an abortion decision during a first planned pregnancy. They had to take responsibility for the decision on the basis of their own needs, not adopt an altruistic stance toward dependent children. In these cases, ambivalence about parenting skills was sometimes expressed:

> So he would have had this sex chromosome thing; he might have been slow, and he was going to be aggressive. I didn't know how to handle a kid like that. When he got rowdy and difficult, could I be a committed parent, or would I have thrown up my hands, thinking "It's in his genes"? [Q: What if you hadn't known through pre-natal diagnosis?] I'm sure if it had just happened, we would have handled it. But once you know, you're forced to make a decision. (David Kass, age thirty-five)

Concern for the marriage rather than the children was often identified as a reason for an abortion decision:

> I talked with this couple who had a kid with Down's, and I thought they were terrific. The kid was nice, and they seemed like a fine family. But they'd been married almost twenty years when it happened, had raised three other kids, and were confident of their commitments. Stu and I have only been together for two years, and it's our first baby, and what if the strain were too great? What if we never got the chance to have a normal kid? What if we broke up over it? (Jane Butler, age thirty-five)

Altruism toward other household members was central to these descriptions. Yet two other themes were conspicuous in their absence. One was the fear of disability, a salient cultural theme for many Americans. The other was the limits of altruism, the admission that there are specific kinds of children that individual women would choose not to mother, given a choice. Both absent themes suggest a wealth of cultural attitudes concerning disability and maternity that medicalization of the experience masks. Of course, the standards for acceptable and unacceptable children and the meaning of specific disabilities are always culturally constructed. Some societies prescribe infanticide for those conditions they label socially inadmissible. In contemporary America, it is a medical procedure that appears to have become the cutting edge in defining the cultural construction of disability.[5]

To some degree the decision was diagnosis-specific: "When I heard my obstetrician's voice on the phone, I went numb. He told me it was Down's and said 'I think we should talk about it.' "What's there to talk about?' I said. 'The decision comes with the disease'" (Leah Rubinstein, age thirty-nine).

Others had a harder time, depending on what they knew or could find out about their fetal diagnosis. Ultimately, however, all had to take responsibility for ending a pregnancy to which they had already felt a commitment: "The whole time I was getting ready, the tests, the visits, the hospital procedure, I kept thinking, 'this is awful, this is the most terrible thing.' I never, ever wanted to be here. But I am here, and it's my choice, and I'm the one who's making it. No one can explain this to me, not why it happened. No one. I have to stop looking for answers out there and trust myself" (Michelle Kansky, age thirty-eight). Like David Kass, who doubted his ability to parent a child with a sex chromosome anomaly once he had that information, Michelle Kansky was also expressing the burdens of individual choice. Informed consent is thought to lead to optimal individual decision making, which is deemed an absolute good in American legal and medical culture. Yet this commitment to individual decision making, while culturally appropriate, increases the burdens of privatization as well. It pushes people to rely on their own information and feelings rather than on any larger social grouping, as they confront the problems and possibilities a new reproductive technology offers.

All respondents described their painful decisions in terms of themselves, their marriages, their other children—in terms of individuals in nuclear families. Yet when we stepped back from these self-descriptions, it became apparent that other sociological facts weighed heavily in the decision to use amniocentesis and the responses to positive diagnosis. One was the role of occupation. In a small and totally self-selected sample, it is striking to find such a large number of helping professionals. Nine of the forty respondents were teachers, four were social workers, and nine out of the two groups worked with retarded children, retarded adults, or their families. How did their commitment to education and to working with disabled people and families shape their responses to parenting a potentially disabled child?

Even more striking is the importance of religious background in descriptions of the abortion decision. Nationally, women using abortion services are as likely to be Catholic as non-Catholic (Henshaw & Martire, 1982; Petchesky, 1984). But because we do not yet have a general picture of amniocentesis users, we cannot know if Catholic women and their families are as likely to use these prenatal services as non-Catholics. Nor do we know if they are as likely to abort if they receive a positive diagnosis. Yet six respondents identified themselves as Roman Catholics, four currently practicing and two reared as Catholics. For them, the choice was very hard and involved a personal exegesis on the meaning of abortion:

> I was raised to take what you get in life, any life you get. If I had stayed at home in Granville, if I hadn't gone to college, if I hadn't married Joe [who is Jewish] I'd still feel that way. I do feel that way. But even though I was brought up Catholic to believe abortion is murder, I also believe in a woman's right to choose. In people's right to choose. And that choice is a big part of me now, just as big as my religion. (Terry Hanz, age thirty-four)
>
> I think the hardest problem I faced was confession. I needed to have that abortion, but I also needed to confess, and I couldn't go to our parish priest, even though my mother and my mother-in-law knew. I just couldn't go to him. So I finally went to St. X, across town, where criminals and celebrities go to confess. And that helped a lot. Later, I was talking with the father of an old friend; he's an old man, very conservative, very Catholic. But he was saying how much he admired Geraldine Ferraro for her stand on abortion. "What does the pope know about these things? Let the women decide on this one, not old men, like me." That helped me, that really helped me, even though he didn't know my situation. Now I say, "Let anyone who'll judge me stand in my shoes first." I'm still a Catholic, but I say Catholics who judge women for having an abortion haven't lived through hard times. Only when you're going to live with the consequences do you get to judge the act. (Marie Mancini, age thirty-eight)

For the more than 30 percent of respondents who identified themselves as Jewish, the choice of abortion was philosophically simpler, if still personally painful. Many gave some variant of this account: "You ask why we chose to have amniocentesis and follow through with the abortion. I'll tell you this: If the technology is there, it's better to use it. Better to live with the benefits of modern science, cry over your losses, but use every means science gives you to have a better life" (Michelle Kansky, age thirty-eight).

And whatever their religious orientation, almost all felt the need to respond to the abortion controversy, which is currently central in American political and cultural life:

> I share a lot of the feelings of the right-to-life movement. I've always been shocked by the number of abortion clinics, the number of abortions in this city. But when it was my turn I was grateful to find the right doctor. I sent him and his staff roses after it was all over. They helped me to protect my own life, and that's a life, too. (Mary Fruticci, age forty-four)

> We baptized our little son [aborted after a diagnosis of trisomy 18]; we put the sonogram picture in the family Bible. No one can tell us we did the wrong thing, no matter how much they don't believe in abortion. He's gone now. But he was real. And abortion is real, and sometimes necessary. (Lena Jarowlski, age thirty-six)

> There was no morally correct choice available. Abortion is a terrible choice. But so is the choice to bring a deeply damaged child into this world. People who are antiabortion can't imagine what this is like. (Carey Morgan, age thirty-six)

Amniocentesis and the Perception of Disability

The choice to abort after a positive diagnosis is made, in large part, because of the family's perception of what the child's disability will mean to them. The disability rights movement, however, has made a powerful case for the social rather than the biological nature of the problems that disabled people face. Whatever their individual medical problems and diagnoses, disabled children and adults—like pregnant women—are more than medical cases. They are people whose access to a high quality of life is limited by the social stigma and institutional barriers they confront. Prenatal diagnosis raises a complex of thorny issues about those prejudices. It is neither appropriate nor realistic to expect individual families to reexamine their attitudes toward disability at the moment that they are being informed that their fetus will have one. But as a society, we need to undertake that reexamination so that informed consent will include the social realities and not just the medical diagnosis of raising a child with a particular condition.

Many genetic counselors (especially if they work in pediatric, not only prenatal, service units) have information on services and support groups for children with genetic disabilities and their families. This information is rarely requested or volunteered during the crisis and decision making surrounding a positive diagnosis. Only two of the forty families requested visits with families whose liveborn children had the conditions that had been diagnosed in their fetuses. In both cases the visit engendered more knowledge about the disability, lessening its mythic terror. Both couples went on to make an abortion decision. In the 80 percent of diagnoses involving Down's syndrome, all respondents could recall seeing children with the condition in their communities and most had, somewhere in their network, friends, neighbors, or relatives with a child who had Down's syndrome. Some families were accepting, in principle, of children who are mentally retarded, but were grateful to avoid the reality in their own cases. Others expressed more shock, even revulsion, at the idea that their child would be retarded.

In almost all cases, the families' knowledge was outdated and did not usually include information about the accessibility of infant stimulation programs or the high level of function that many children with Down's syndrome now achieve (Garland et al., 1981; Pueschel, 1978). Nor did it include a realistic picture of what the emotional or financial costs of raising a child with both physical and mental disabilities were likely to be. This is not to suggest that the decisions were necessarily wrong ones or incorrectly made. I am only suggesting that at the present time, informed consent is a concept that focuses on individual medical knowledge, and that social knowledge about the real consequences of disabilities is often underdeveloped.

As long as disabled children (and adults) and their families remain segregated and stigmatized, the knowledge that potential parents might use to decide whether or not to abort a fetus with a diagnosis of disability will also remain unavailable. An individual rights focus is legally and medically appropriate to prenatal diagnosis and is consonant with deeply held American cultural beliefs. But it also masks the larger social attitudes on which knowledge, images, and insufficient services for disabled people are based. To enlarge the scope of informed consent, we must look beyond individual choice toward the sources of community knowledge and prejudice. And here, as with prenatal diagnosis, it is the voices and traditions of the disabled themselves, rather than only the medical and educational professionals, from which we need to learn.

Amniocentesis and the Language of Feminism

The language of individualism and prochoice feminism that was often used in describing the abortion decision after a positive diagnosis grows out of the transformation of work, gender relations, family life, and cultural politics that a generation of women in the United States has recently experienced.

> I've been a woman's movement activist for a million years; I've counseled abortions; I've helped to set up crisis hot lines for women. And this experience brought me as close to the right-to-life movement as I'll ever come. I'd felt the baby moving; it wasn't a fetus in my mind, it was our baby. Still I'm grateful to have had the choice. This was devastating; it permanently changed our lives, but then, so would the birth of a kid with Down's. I don't want the right-to-life movement changing my life. I have to do it myself. (Pat Cordon, age thirty-seven)

One informant cited Carol Gilligan's (1982) work to me: "Women are responsible for giving life, not for taking it. Women do have their own morality. Still, I've got to be responsible to myself, Stu, to our future kids, and those responsibilities come first" (Jane Butler, age thirty-five). These women (and their male partners) were wrapped in the discourses of prolife-prochoice politics and mainstream feminism. This language of individual, even feminist, morality seems comfortable to middle-class women, unlike the awkwardness of the medical language, which constructs and constrains their experiences of positive diagnosis. The "second nature" of this discourse is no accident. Mainstream feminism now infuses large sectors of American culture despite its sometimes embattled oppositional stance. The discourse of maternalism (even medicalized maternalism) is becoming more feminist, if by that we mean centered on the expansion of individual women's choices, whether we speak of choices in amniocentesis or styles of birthing babies.

But to examine the cultural imagery surrounding motherhood, it is necessary to shift our focus from the individual woman and her family to the larger community. Because the experience of prenatal diagnosis is so deeply privatized and medicalized, it is easy to miss the gender fault lines on which this new reproductive technology sits. The deeply internalized and socially pervasive imagery of motherhood in American culture is surely shifting. Women who have a choice, including the choice to abort genetically disabled fetuses, are less likely to see themselves or to be seen by others as "Madonnas"—long-suffering mothers whose nurturance is unconditional and ever-present. Although I would personally argue that freedom from such religiously referential, selfless images of maternity is, on the whole, liberating for women, I would also suggest that we cast a critical eye on the cultural imagery that may replace it—particularly if that imagery is defined in medical terms. The "new woman" of prenatal diagnosis may feel like an agent of quality control on the reproductive production line:

> I was hoping I'd never have to make this choice, to become responsible for choosing the kind of baby I'd get, the kind of baby we'd accept. But everyone—my doctor, my parents, my friends—everyone urged me to come for genetic counseling and have amniocentesis. Now I guess I am having a modern baby. And they all told me I'd feel more in control. But in many ways, I feel less in control. It's still my baby, but only if it's good enough to be our baby, if you see what I mean. (Nancy Smithers, age thirty-six)

Neither image—the selfless Madonna or the agent of quality control—is constructed by or for women's interests. Both are deeply embedded in patriarchal cultural discourses, the one traditional and religious, the other modern and medically technocratic. The future cultural conceptualization we hold of women as mothers in part depends on turning down the volume of expert voices so that the voices of women themselves may become part of the discourse of prenatal diagnosis.

Notes

1. Exact numbers of women using amniocentesis each year are unknown but seem to be growing rapidly. The President's Commission on Bioethics estimated 40,000 tests (1983) at the same time that the Center for Disease Control informally estimated 80,000, and the National Survey on Natality suggested 120,000. The lack of a "ballpark" estimate

among government health-policy experts should alert us to the unregulated nature of a service that is available as part of the free-market economy of health care.

2. I am currently doing fieldwork among scientists and support staff of a major genetics laboratory, observing genetic counselors at work with their patients, conducting home interviews with women and their families awaiting the results of amniocentesis, eliciting retrospective interviews with those who received positive diagnoses indicating serious genetic disabilities in their fetuses, participating in support groups for families whose children have the conditions (Down's syndrome, spina bifida) now diagnosable prenatally, and interviewing pregnant women who refused to use the new technology. This research is particularly concerned with differences of class, race, ethnicity, and religion in people's cultural construction of pregnancy and childhood disability. I hope it will result in a more complete picture of the social impact of amniocentesis than is given in this brief report of my pilot study.

3. Such technological personifications may be viewed as examples of cyborgs, science fiction chimeras interfacing people and machines, a late-twentieth-century cultural form insightfully analyzed by Haraway (1985).

4. Anomalous diagnoses are compounded by the newness of the technology and fears—both accurate and exaggerated—of human and technical error in using it. And, as Emily Martin pointed out to me, many more women are told that something may be wrong owing to technical errors that are later corrected (e.g., maternal/fetal cell confusion in an amniotic sample) than will actually confront a "truly positive" diagnosis.

5. Carole Browner and Shirley Lindenbaum both suggested that the cross-cultural evidence argues for universal constructions of acceptable and unacceptable disabilities. But our current cultural context is one of political struggle over the definition of disability and social responses.

References

Brewster, A. (1984). A patient's reaction to amniocentesis. *Obstetrics and Gynecology, 64*, 443-44.

Corea, G. (1985). *The mother machine*. New York: Harper and Row.

Filkins, K. & Russo, I. F. (1985). *Human prenatal diagnosis*. New York: Marcel Dekker.

Garland, C., et al. (1981). Early intervention for children with special needs and their families. WESTAR Series Paper no. 11. Chapel Hill: Frank Porter Graham Child Development Center, University of North Carolina.

Gilligan C. (1982). *In a different voice*. Cambridge, Mass.: Harvard University Press.

Hanmer, J. (1981). Sex predetermination, artificial insemination, and the maintenance of male-dominated culture. In H. Roberts (Ed.), *Women, health and reproduction*. London: Routledge and Kegan Paul.

Haraway, D. (1985). Science, technology, and socialist feminism in the 1980s. *Socialist Review 80*, 65–107.

Harris, H. (1974). *Prenatal diagnosis and selective abortion*. Cambridge, Mass.: Harvard University Press.

Henshaw, S., & Martire, G. (1982). Abortion and the public opinion polls *Family Planning Perspectives, 14*, 53–62.

Hilton, B., et al. (1973). *Ethical issues in human genetics*. New York: Plenum.

Hook, E. B.(1973). Behavior implications of the human XXY genotype. *Science, 179*, 139–49.

Hook, E. B. (1981). Rates of chromosome abnormalities at different maternal ages. *Obstetrics and Gynecology, 58*, 282–85.

Hook, E. B., Cross, P. K., & Schreinemachers, D. M. (1983). Chromosomal abnormality rates at amniocentesis and in live-born infants. *Journal of the American Medical Association*, 249 (April 15): 2034–38.

Hsu, L. (1982). *Keeping genetic service accessible*. Report from a conference on the continuing role of the Prenatal Diagnosis Laboratory of New York City, June.

Joans, B. (1980). *Dilemmas and decisions of prenatal diagnosis*. Symposium at the New York City Technical College, April.

Lipkin, M., and Rowley, P. (Eds.). (1974). *Genetic responsibility*. New York: Plenum.

Marion, J. P., et al. (1980). Acceptance of amniocentesis by low income patients in an urban hospital. *American Journal of Obstetrics and Gynecology*, 138, 11–15.

Oakley, A. (1979). A case of maternity: Paradigms of women as maternity cases. *Signs*, 4, 607–31.

Oakley, A. (1980). *Becoming a mother*. New York: Schocken.

Oakley, A. (1981). *Woman confined: Sociology of childbirth*. New York: Schocken.

Petchesky, R. (1984). *Abortion and women's choice*. New York: Longman.

Powledge, T., and Fletcher, J. (1979). Guidelines for the ethical, social and legal issues in prenatal diagnosis. *New England Journal of Medicine*, 300, 168–72.

Prenatal Diagnosis Laboratory of New York City. (n.d.). Counseling protocols, charts, and tables.

Pueschel, S. (1978). *Down syndrome: Growing and learning*. Kansas City: Sheed Andrews and McMeel.

Rapp, R. (1984). Amniocentesis: The ethics of choice. *Ms. Magazine*, April, 97–100.

Rothman, B. K. (1982). *In labor: Women and power in the birthplace*. New York: Norton. (Reprinted as *Giving birth: Alternatives in childbirth*. New York: Penguin, 1985.)

Rothman B. K. (1986). *The tentative pregnancy*. New York:Viking/Penguin.

Sadovnik, A. D., & Baird, P. (1981). A cost-benefit analysis of prenatal detection of Down syndrome and neural tube defects in older mothers. *American Journal of Medical Genetics*, 10, 367.

Shaw, N. S. (1974). *Forced labor: Maternity care in the United States*. New York: Pergamon.

Snow, L. F., Johnson, S. M., and Mayhew, H. (1978). The behavioral implications of some old wives tales. *Obstetrics and Gynecology*, 51(6), 727–32.

Sokal, D. C., et al. (1980). Prenatal chromosome analysis, racial and geographic variation for older women. *Journal of the American Medical Association*, 244, 1355–547.

Thompson, S. (1983). Felicia Garcia: I just came out pregnant! In A. Snitow, C. Stansell, & S. Thompson (Eds.), *The powers desire*. New York: Monthly Review Press.

Wertz, D., and Wertz, R. C. (1977). *Lying in: A history of childbirth in America*. New York: Free Press.

CHAPTER FOURTEEN

The Psychomorphology of the Clitoris

VALERIE TRAUB

> We have long realized that in women the development of sexu-
> ality is complicated by the task of renouncing that genital zone
> which was originally the principal one, namely, the clitoris, in
> favour of a new zone—the vagina.
>
> Sigmund Freud, "Female Sexuality"

Freud considered the clitoris a problem. From Anne Koedt's early feminist critique, "The Myth of the Vaginal Orgasm," to Thomas Laqueur's "Amor
Veneris, Vel Dulcedo Appeletur," critics have elucidated the strategies whereby
Freud attempted to reconcile women's physiology with a heterosexual imperative. His theory—that in the oedipal phase the female child must renounce clitoral stimulation in favor of vaginal penetration—secures phallic privilege by imposing a cultural solution on what he deemed a biological "problem." Such
psychosexual adaptation is enabled by Freud's equation between the clitoris and
the penis, an equivalence that simultaneously is physiological (the clitoris and penis are analogous in structure and function), psychological (both indicate an active masculine aim), and metaphorical (during the infantile "phallic" stage, "the
little girl is a little man": "Femininity" 104).

For Freud, the clitoris also is linked inextricably to "lesbianism." Female resistance to forgoing pleasure in the clitoris is associated with an inability to replace the first object of desire, the mother, with the more proper object, the
father. Just as vaginal satisfaction is the developmental sign of mature heterosexuality, clitoral attachment is the symptom of a recalcitrant, immature homoerotic desire. Retrospectively, every woman moves through a psychosexual stage
in which her clitoris threatens fixation on homoerotic objects; "lesbians" fail to
follow the dictates of culture, narcissistically remaining attached to "anatomy"
and "mother" and projecting their envy of the male organ onto their own "phallic" genitality. A system of equivalences, whereby the penis=the clitoris=
lesbianism=penis envy, sets up a smooth continuity among terms, the effect of
which is a transposition of bodily organs by psychic states. The enclosed circu-

Valerie Traub, "The Psychomorphology of the Clitoris," *GLQ: A Journal of Lesbian and
Gay Studies* 2 (1995):81–113. Reprinted by permission. *Editors' note*: The reference list for
this chapter was culled from the bibliography for the original volume of *GLQ*.

larity of this equation despecifies female erotic experience by referring body and desire back to the phallus. The formalization of two incommensurate object choices based on two separate genital "zones" moderates the more radical implications of Freud's theory of bisexuality and polymorphous perversity and resecures the direction of female desire toward men, reproductions and the reproduction of patriarchal culture.

Since the advent of psychoanalysis, then, the clitoris and the "lesbian" have been mutually implicated as sisters in shame: each is the disturbing sign that implies the existence of the other. Underlying the perversion of "lesbian" desire is not only the polymorphous perversity of the infantile body and the inherent bisexuality of all drives but an anatomical organ shared by the vast majority of females, regardless of age or gender identification. Joined through the imperative of repression, the clitoris and the "lesbian" together signify woman's erotic potential for a pleasure outside of masculine control. At the same time, Freud's binary model of incommensurate pleasures produces a bodily schema of "lesbian" eroticism that obscures the range of erotic activities, including vaginal penetration, historically performed by women with women.

Freud's views are credited with exerting enormous influence on modern understandings of "homosexuality." Indeed, most social constructionists attribute to psychoanalysis, sexology, and related epistemologies an originary, constitutive force in the construction of the "homosexual" subject.[1] However, neither Freud's association of clitoral pleasure with "lesbian" desire nor his equation of the clitoris and the penis were original to him or his culture. Sixteenth- and seventeenth-century European anatomists, physicians, and midwives regularly employed a penis-clitoris analogy as part of a system of representation that asserted the homologous yet hierarchical relation between male and female bodies. Likewise, the association between the clitoris and "tribadism" (an early modern antecedent to "lesbianism") has an equally long cultural history. The system of equivalences between the penis, the clitoris, and same-gender female desire predate Freud by several centuries, and is less an *effect* of the modern construction of female "homosexuality" than the cultural material out of which such a category was created.

This essay details the conjunction between the clitoris and the "tribade" during the period in which both were given their first (early) modern articulation as objects of anatomical inquiry. A circular, self-referential relation, whereby the clitoris and the "tribade" imply, necessitate, and support one another, structures the terms of intelligibility that have governed the cultural representation of "lesbian" desire. To put it another way, the structural link between the clitoris and the "tribade" has operated throughout modernity as a condition of intelligibility for same-gender female desire. Freud's recapitulation of this paradigm both reformulates and occludes this link; in his hands, what was previously conceptualized as a spatial, metonymic connection between body and body part becomes the symptomatic sign of a psychosexual phase.

Under the guise of explorer, Freud converted earlier paradigms of discovery, imposing a temporal narrative of psychosexual development onto a pre-existing map of the female body. Such maps derived from protocolonialist imperatives that instigated and invigorated the quests of early modern science. Freud's own exploration solicited not a new mapping but the authorizing power of a discourse that, in its replay of the "discovery" of the clitoris through the invention of clinical psychoanalysis (and the vaginal orgasm), materially transformed the (modern) body. At the same time, the conceptual paradigms to which Freud was indebted were obscured by the (institutional) power of psychoanalysis. Peter Hulme's assertion that "the gesture of 'discovery' is at the same time a ruse of concealment" (1) is true not only of Freud's reconstitution of earlier spatial metonymies but also of the concealments imposed *by those maps* upon other possible conceptualizations of the female body.

The terms of embodiment that govern the construction of the clitoris as the metonymic, material embodiment of same-gender female desire were engendered by a complex cultural interplay of psychic and material forces. The morphology of the clitoris is not merely a matter of empirical "knowledge"; rather, it is constituted by, and includes traces of, desires and anxieties about the meanings, possibilities and prohibitions of female sexuality. "Discovered" in the mid-sixteenth century and immediately subjected to cultural expectations, fantasies, fears, and warnings about its proper structure, size, function, and use, the clitoris and its attendant "psychomorphology" highlight the historicity of the terms by which Freud contributed to the modern consolidation of "lesbian" identity.

The point is not simply to historicize Freud. Rather, it is to demonstrate the extent to which current figurations of "lesbian" desire are implicated within the same "psychomorphology" that gave rise to Freud's pathology of the "lesbian" body. In the critique of Freud that pervades "lesbian" theory, a logic of reversal structures analytic resistance to the psychoanalytic narrative; rather than pathologize as Freud does the equation between the "lesbian" and the clitoris, theorists celebrate (and unwittingly reify) it as the enabling truth of "lesbian" sexuality. In rejecting the self-evident nature of this connection, I want to suggest that spatial metonymies that assume the commensurability of body parts to erotic desires and practices continue rather than challenge the history from which Freud's terms of female embodiment evolved.

The most historically detailed and analytically sophisticated account of the cultural representation of the clitoris is the work of Thomas Laqueur.[2] In *Making Sex: Body and Gender from the Greeks to Freud* and the essay "Amor Veneris, Vel Dulcedo Appeletur," Laqueur reconstructs a history of the female body that shows how anatomical knowledge is constructed through the coordinates of gender ideology.[3] Laqueur argues that the anatomical "discovery" of the clitoris in the sixteenth century drew from and reinforced the view of the two sexes as isomorphic: whereas the vagina visually resembled the penis, the clitoris *functioned* like the male organ, becoming erect when aroused and emitting seed during orgasm. The apparent conceptual contradiction involved in women having two penises (vagina and clitoris) while men possessed only one did not trouble medical conceptualizations, confined as they were within a one-sex model in which difference was inconceivable: "Thus, the elaboration in medical literature . . . of a 'new' female penis and specifically clitoral eroticism, was a re-presentation of the older homology of the vagina and penis, not its antithesis" ("Amor Veneris" 119).

However, the "Renaissance clitoris" is not entirely subsumed under the reproductive discourses that are Laqueur's primary concern. Although early modern anatomy treats clitoral orgasm as vital to reproductive success,[4] it not only concedes but emphasizes the clitoris's capacity to provide female pleasure: the clitoris is, according to its putative "founder," Realdo Columbo, "the seat of woman's delight." But pleasure per se is not Laqueur's concern; nor, ultimately, is the specificity of the female body. For in analytically "visibilizing" the female body *only in relation* to the male—either as homologous or as oppositional—Laqueur reiterates the same conceptual bias he purports to analyze.[5]

Laqueur's reliance on texts that inscribe the dominant ideology, which leads to his own (re)inscription of a hegemonic medical model, has already been noted by several feminist critics.[6] I want to suggest that a further methodological problem inheres in Laquer's acceptance of Foucault's contention that the appearance of the "homosexual" as a category of identity became available only after the rise of modern regimes of knowledge: "Lesbianism and homosexuality as categories were not possible before the creation of men and women as opposites," that is, before the two-sex model ("Amor Veneris" 119). References to "tribades" in Laqueur's account thus become merely gestural, as the focus is more on the social construction of an anatomical part (the clitoris) than the varied uses to which that part could be put. Resistance to examining the specificity of same-gender female eroticism prior to the instantiation of "homosexuality" allows Laqueur to describe and reaffirm a male-oriented paradigm in which the only erotic possibility is homoeroticism between men: "When among themselves, [these authors] seem to be saying, women rub *their* penises together. . . . Indeed, all sex becomes homoerotic" ("Amor Veneris" 118).[7]

Each of us makes interpretative choices. Laqueur has read the clitoris-as-penis analogy in terms of a putative masculine norm; by extension, he presents "tribades" as imitators of men and all sexual activity as male homoeroticism—thus reinscribing the hierarchy that his account ostensibly seeks to address.[8] I ask rather what is at stake in the cultural effort to disavow the gender specificity of the clitoris and erotic acts among women—culturally constructed though such specificity may be. The following discussion attempts to reassert such gender specificity, not in the interest of locating a pre-Enlightenment "lesbian" identity, but rather to demonstrate the conditions of emergence *for* such an identity. "Lesbians" did not arrive on the historical scene as fully formed social objects; nor did the ascendancy of a two-sex anatomical model ensure their arrival. The category of the "lesbian" was fashioned only after available rubrics for understanding and assimilating erotic variation failed to account for activities women had been pursuing—under widely divergent conceptual systems—at least since Sappho.[9]

Just as the "birth" of the "lesbian" is not a discrete social occurrence, the emergence of "anatomy" is not a singular scientific phenomenon. Rather, the consolidation of anatomy as a separate epistemology occurred in concert with the development of other domains of knowledge, and it was enabled by anatomy's ability to appropriate and reformulate the knowledges of other genres, including natural histories, herbals, and travel narratives. Early modern travel accounts, in particular, contribute significantly to the construction of the contours and meanings of the early modern body. Anatomies and travel narratives, generated at the same historical moment and governed by tropes of exploration and discovery,[10] share a common imperative to chart, catalog, and colonize the body.[11] Both genres synthesize received authority, observations and invention as they commit highly interpretative acts under the guise of disinterested description.[12] Their narrative strategies and cultural functions are allied closely: both are dedicated to rendering intelligible and distinct that which appears chaotic, primitive, or previously unknown, through strategies of description, nomination, and classification. Metaphorically, anatomical texts act as a discourse of travel, visually traversing the body in order to "touch" and reveal a cosmically ordained corporeal whole, while travel narratives observe and dissect peoples and countries, interrogating and reaffirming their place in the cosmic order. Together, their exploratory gazes create the possibility of looking "inward" and "outward" as they formulate the contours of bodily, social, and geographical boundaries.[13] Whereas anatomical dissection of the corpse and its textual reconstitution fashion a normative, abstracted body whose singularity encompasses and signifies all others, travel accounts create an exoticized body that reveals the antithesis of normativity. Locating the body (and bodies) within prevailing epistemic hierarchies by charting corporeal cartographies,[14] anatomies and travel narratives not only function as colonialist discourses but urge colonialism into being.

Whether primarily concerned with commerce or conquest, Western European travelers to foreign lands chart a cultural anthropology that functions similarly to a physical geography. Whether describing the New World, Africa, or the East, narrators obsessively remark upon those cultural practices that differentiate native inhabitants from Europeans, often employing rhetorics of gender and sexuality as explanatory tropes.[15] Marriage rituals, dowries, divorce, and polygamy excite Western curiosity and provide travelers to Africa and Arabia, in particular, with a means of deploying the sexual status of indigenous women as a primary marker of cultural definition and civility. The development of a spatial geography of erotic behavior constructs women (and thus their nation) as beautiful and chaste (for instance, Persians) or hideous and loose (Black Africans). The assumption of female lasciviousness gains the power of self-evidence through the structure of a cross-cultural polarity: whereas the partial nudity of women in various African nations authorizes readings of female incontinence, the practice of Muslim purdah constructs the woman whose body is hidden as a highly desirable (and thus desiring) object.[16] Although same-gender female eroticism is mentioned only rarely (and nowhere as often as male sodomy), its presence routinely is associated with certain locales. Travelers to Turkey, in particular, curious about Muslim attitudes toward cleanliness and intrigued by the segregation of women, typically relay rumors about women pleasuring one another—or themselves—within all-female spaces.

One such narrative is that of Robert Withers, published in 1625, which describes the architectural arrangements regulating the women inhabiting the Sultan's seraglio[17]:

> Now, in the Womens lodgings, they live just as the Nunnes doe in their great Monasteries; for, these Virgins have very large Roomes to live in, and their Bed-

chambers will hold almost a hundred of them a piece: they sleepe upon Sofaes, which are built long wise on both sides of the Roome, so that there is a large space in the midst for to walke in. Their Beds are very course and hard, and by every ten Virgins there lie an old woman: and all the night long there are many lights burning, so that one may see very plainely throughout the whole Roome; which doth both keepe the young Wenches from wantonnesse, and serve upon any occasion which may happen in the night. (1586–87)

Withers enumerates the precautions taken with the women's provisions:

Now it is not lawfull for any one to bring ought in unto them, with which they may commit the deeds of beastly uncleannesse; so that if they have a will to eate Cucumbers, Gourds, or such like meates, they are sent in unto them sliced, to deprive them of the meanes of playing the wantons; for, they being all young, lustie, and lascivious Wenches, and wanting the societie of Men (which would better instruct them) are doubtlesse of themselves inclined to that which is naught, and will be possest with unchast thoughts. (1590)

Whereas the Sultan's harem generated comparisons to Catholic monasteries (long reputed to be a haven for "unclean" behaviors), the public, yet segregated, Turkish baths occasioned even more comment. Nicholas de Nicholay's *Navigations into Turkie*, published in 1585, depicts typical procedures involved in visiting the baths, and concludes his description of female bathers in this way:

[They] do familiarly wash one another, whereby it commeth to passe that amongst the women of Levan, ther is very great amity preceding only through the frequentation & resort to the bathes: yea & sometimes become so fervently in love the one of the other as if it were with men, in such sort that perceiving some maiden or woman of excellent beauty they wil not ceasse until they have found means to bath with them, & to handle & grope them every where at their pleasures so ful they are of luxuriousnes & feminine wantonnes: Even as in times past were the Tribades, of the number whereof was Sapho the Lesbian. . . . (60)[18]

Other travelers confirm such rumors. Ogier Ghiselin de Busbecq, the Flemish ambassador to the Sultan in the late sixteenth century, penned four lengthy letters to a fellow ambassador; in the third letter he writes,

The great mass of women use the public baths for females, and assemble there in large numbers. Among them are found many girls of exquisite beauty, who have been brought together from different quarters of the globe by various chances of fortune; so cases occur of women falling in love with one another at these baths, in much the same fashion as young men fall in love with maidens in our country. Thus you see a Turk's precautions are sometimes of no avail, and when he has succeeded in keeping his wives from a male lover, he is still in danger from a female rival! The women become deeply attached to each other, and the baths supply them with opportunities of meeting. Some [men] therefore keep their women away from them as much as possible, but they cannot do so altogether, as the law allows them to go there. This evil affects only the common people; the richer classes bathe at home. (231)[19]

De Busbecq augments this description with an anecdote about an elderly woman who, having fallen in love with a young woman, crossdresses as a man, obtains permission to marry, and is foiled only upon being recognized by her beloved as someone she encountered at the baths.[20] If de Busbecq dilates on such possibilities, the more circumspect Thomas Glover concludes his description of Turkish baths with a terse condemnation: "Much unnaturall and filthie lust is said to bee committed daily in the remote closets of the darkesome Bannias: yea, women with women; a thing uncredible, if former times had not given thereunto both detection and punishment" (1298–99).[21]

In the third book of *The History and Description of Africa,* translated into English and published in 1600, Leo Africanus describes not the erotic activities occurring in public baths but the erotic practices of fortune-tellers in Fez:

> But the wiser and honester sort of people call these women *Sahacat,* which in Latin signifieth *Fricatrices,* because they have a damnable custome to commit unlawfull Venerie among themselves, which I cannot expresse in any modester termes. If faire women come unto them at any time, these abominable witches will burne in lust towardes them no otherwise then lustie yoonkers [young men] doe towardes yoong maides and will in the divels behalfe demaunde for a rewarde, that they may lie with them: and so by this meanes it often falleth out, that thinking thereby to fulfill the divels command they lie with the witches. Yea some there are, which being allured with the delight of this abominable vice, will desire the companie of these witches, and faining themselves to be sicke, will either call one of the witches home to them, or will send their husbands for the same purpose: and so the witches perceiving how the matter stands, will say that the woman is possessed with a divell and that she can no way be cured, unlesse she be admitted into their societie. With these words her silly husband being persuaded, doth not onely permit her so to doe, but makes also a sumptuous banket [banquet] unto the damned crew of witches: which being done, they use to daunce very strangely at the noice of drums: and so the poore man commits his false wife to their filthie disposition. (458–59)[22]

These exoticizing tales enable a number of observations about the figuration of same-gender female eroticism in the early modern period. First, notwithstanding assumptions about the nonexistence or invisibility of "lesbians," a vocabulary was available to Western writers with which to describe women's erotic desire for and contact with one another.[23] Whether perceived as the result of witchcraft, inherent "feminine wantonnes," or the unavailability of men, eroticism among women is assumed as a real threat that is made intelligible largely through signifiers of an ancient past. The Greek *"tribade"* and Latin *"fricatrice,"* etymologically referring to women who rub their genitals against other women's bodies, provide the historical lexicon and, in Glover's account, the authorizing lens through which to condemn the witches of Fez and the bathers of Turkey.[24] Second, an architectural logic seems to structure these accounts, as certain physical spaces (the harem, women's bath, and bazaar) enable "unnatural" female contact. In the case of the harem and the bath, spaces originally built to block male access and protect female chastity are imagined to enable the circulation of desire enclosed within. Third, such narratives assume not only that women willingly deceive their husbands or masters, but that same-gender erotic pleasures, once experienced, prove to be irresistible. The "burning lust" that de Nicholay and others figure as flowing indiscriminately through the waters of the Turkish bath is figured by all the narrators as undermining the patriarchal authority of the harem or household.[25] Fourth, despite their ostensible descriptive purpose, these travelers employ what seems to modern ears to be a vague, mystifying rhetoric—as in "commit unlawful Venerie," "burn in lust," "inclined to that which is naught," and "handle and grope them everywhere." Leaving the precise nature of erotic acts unspecified, these narratives both assume and occlude the reader's knowledge of "deeds of beastly uncleannesse."[26] In the absence of narratives about similar practices among Englishwomen, tales such as these imply that African and Muslim women are uniquely (if amorphously) amoral in their erotic desires and practices.

While the figural intertwining of the erotic with the exotic within an evolving racialized discourse of European colonialism is worthy of its own analysis, I want to focus here on the way the protocolonialist imperatives of these narratives ultimately contribute to the erotic representation of Englishwomen.[27] For near the end of the seventeenth century, Jane Sharp, the first Englishwoman to write her own midwifery,[28] alludes to such pseudoanthropological accounts in *The Midwives Book* as she describes women who make "unnatural" use of their genitals: "In the Indies, and Egypt," she says, such incidents "are frequent"; but she goes on to assert that "unnatural" contact among women occurs primarily beyond England's boundaries: "I have never heard but of one in this Country" (45). She concludes by saying that "if there be any they will do what they can for shame to keep it close" (45), a statement that, in its ambiguous syntax, could refer to keeping either genitals hidden or erotic practices secret.[29] In a later passage she writes,

> I told you the Clitoris is so long in some women that it is seen to hang forth at their Privities and not only the Clitoris that lyeth behind the wings [labia] but the Wings also. . . . In some Countries they grow so long that the Chirurgion cuts them off to avoid trouble and shame, chiefly in Egypt; they will bleed much when they are cut, and the blood is hardly stopt; wherefore maids have them cut off betimes, and before they marry, for it is a flux of humours to them, and much motion that makes them grow so long. Some Sea-mem [sic] say that they have seen Negro Women go stark naked, and these wings hanging out. (45–47)

Although Sharp does not marginally gloss these passages with citation of textual authorities, she does cite Leo Africanus elsewhere in her book. I want to suggest that her minimizing of the frequency of Englishwomen's same-gender contacts, and her displacement of "unnatural" erotic practices onto foreign women, is not simply a conventional English effort to refer the origin of unwelcome behaviors and diseases to other countries.[30] Nor is it merely an instance of the colonial imaginary that, as Jonathan Goldberg has shown, "is particularly throne to a desire to other its own desires" (*Queering* 13). Sharp's gesture is a strategy invited by the racialized travel literature that authorizes her account. At the same time, it registers (and attempts to dispel) the anxiety that erotic contact among Englishwomen was in fact occurring—a fear that may have had as much to do with the increased circulation of anatomical representations as with an increase in homoerotic practices.

Although medieval anatomies, primarily based on scholastic authority, did exist, Renaissance anatomies, generated out of "new" empirical methods of observation and dissection, gained currency with the publication of Andreas Vesalius's Latin *Fabrica* of 1543. Likewise, while a few ancient and medieval midwiferies were available,[31] the widespread distribution of anatomies in the latter half of the sixteenth century prompted an increase in midwiferies published in Latin and the vernacular throughout the next century. Sharp's *The Midwives Book* was, like most vernacular midwiferies, a synthesis of ancient and modern authority and contemporary practice, directing "Childbearing Women how to behave themselves" in the "Conception, Breeding, Bearing and Nursing" of children. As with almost every other seventeenth-century anatomy, her discussion of "tribadism" immediately follows the description of the clitoris and its possible enlargement. In the structural logic that informs these texts, the clitoris and the "tribade" invariably are positioned practically, as if the description of one would he incomplete without the other.

Supposedly discovered—or actually, rediscovered—in 1559 by two Italian anatomists, Realdo Columbo and Gabriele Falloppia, its existence disputed by Vesalius (the reigning authority on anatomy), the clitoris was, by the time of Sharp's publication in 1671, a thoroughly fetishized, if still controversial, object of inquiry.[32] Admittedly, it is difficult to take seriously the thrill of discovery accompanying the inclusion of the clitoris into anatomical discourse. The problem is succinctly addressed by Audrey Eccles, who asserts that "it would be naive to imagine [Columbo and Falloppia] actually discovered it, or that their statements that it was the chief seat of sexual pleasure in women came as a great revelation" (33–34). However, whereas Eccles's assertion of women's prior experience of their bodies is well taken—one's experience of erotic pleasure does not depend on the ability to articulate its source—her irony tends to elide the fact that it is only under the auspices of anatomy that the clitoris is given a name; and only with a name does the clitoris come into being as a location, a function, an *organ*. Despite the historical blindness to female embodiment retrospectively evinced by the anatomists' "rediscovery," and despite the intersection of knowledge, power, and misogyny manifested in the debate over the clitoris's existence, the incorporation of this organ within a specific domain of "modern" knowledge gave female erotic pleasure a new, albeit ambivalent, articulation.

With that articulation came a representational crisis. Not only was the existence of the clitoris disputed among anatomists, but the representation of the clitoris became a focal point for anxieties about the cultural meanings of the female body. As anatomical plates from Italy, France, Spain, and Germany made their way into England, as English physicians and midwives contributed their own methods of textually communicating the "new science" of anatomy, strategies of accommodation—of, quite literally, in-corporation—were developed. The trajectory of these strategies suggests that this clitoral "age of discovery" was a pivotal moment in the cultural history of women, embodiment, and eroticism. Over the next century, as information about this "new" anatomical part was incorporated into an old corporeal framework, a discourse evolved that increasingly fixated on the clitoris as the disturbing bodily emblem of female erotic power.

First depicted by Columbo in *De re anatomica* (1559) as "the seat of woman's delight," the clitoris entered anatomical discourse as the enabling source of female reproductive vitality. Columbo's influential treatise, repeated verbatim by medical writers for two centuries, reports that without sufficient attention paid to this organ, a woman neither conceives nor desires to conceive, for it alone governs the expulsion of female seed. By 1615 the existence of the clitoris was so well established that Helkiah Crooke's *Microcosmographia: A Description of the Body of Man*, the first English anatomy to discuss the form, function, and role of the clitoris, did so at some length:

> [The clitoris] commeth of an obscoene worde signifying contrectation but Properly it is called the womans yard. It is a small production in the upper, forward and middle fatty part of the share [genitals], in the top of the greater cleft where the Nymphes [labia] doe meet, and is answerable to the member of the man, from which it differs in length, the common passage and the want of one pair of muscles; but agrees in scituation, substance, and composition. For it consisteth of two nervous bodies (which Laurentius cals ligaments) round without, hard and thick; but within spongy and porous that when the spirits come into it, it may bee defended and grow loose when they dissipated[;] these bodies, as those of the mans yarde, are full of blacke, thicke, and sprightfull blood. . . . The head is properly cailed Tentigo by Juvenall, which is covered with a fine skin made of the conjunction of the Nymphae as it were with a foreskinne. It hath an entrance but no through passage; there are vesselles also running along the backe of it as in a mans yarde; and although for the most part it hath but a small production hidden under the Nymphes and hard to he felt but with curiosity. . . . (238)

It is with refreshing irony that Crooke follows Columbo in calling the clitoris "aestrum Veneris & dulcedo amoris [and] the especial seate of delight in [women's] veneral embracements, *as Columbus imagineth he first discovered*" (238; emphasis mine).

Two observations derive from the anatomies of Columbo and Crooke. First, the association of the clitoris with the penis—evident not only in the colloquial term "female yard"[33] but in the analogies drawn between male and female structures and functions—confirms Laqueur's observation that homologies informed the dominant anatomical view of female genitalia. The implications of conceiving of woman's morphology essentially as *imitation* extend beyond the descriptive realm of anatomy to authorize particular interpretations of erotic practice. The hegemony of these interpretations, however, is precisely what this essay seeks to contest. Second, in addition to being subsumed by the masculine model, representations of the female body were confined within the dominant ideology of reproduction. Crooke reiterates Columbo in stating that the clitoris "both stirs up lust and gives delight in copulation, for without this, the fair sex neither desire nuptial embraces nor have pleasure in them, nor conceive by them" (238).[34] In one concise statement desire, pleasure, and conception are conflated, all difference between them collapsed within the politics of reproduction.

On the one hand, a certain measure of female pleasure is authorized by reproductive politics, as prevailing Hippocratic/Galenic models legitimate an erotic ideology supporting the physiological mechanics of female arousal. Husbands thus were urged to spend time arousing their wives, as in Johnson's 1634 translation of the work of sixteenth-century French surgeon Ambroise Pare:

> When the husband commeth into his wives chamber hee must entertaine her with all kinde of dalliance, wanton behavior, and allurements to venery: but if he perceive

her to be slow, and more cold, he must cherish, embrace, and tickle her, and shall not abruptly, the nerves [penis] being suddenly distended, breake into the field of nature [vagina], but rather shall creepe in by little and little, intermixing more wanton kisses with wanton words and speeches, handling her secret parts and dugs, that she may take fire and bee enflamed to venery, for so at length the wombe will strive and waxe fervent with a desire of casting forth its owne seed. (889) So "enflamed to venery," a woman was believed to experience twice the physical pleasure of man: "For as the Delight of Men in Copulation, consists chiefly in the Emission of the Seed, so Women are delighted both in the Emission of their own, and the Reception of the Man's" (*Aristotle's Experienced Midwife* n.pag.).

On the other hand, female pleasure and its excessive potential could create reproductive and anatomical problems—signified by the clitoris that grows beyond "normal" bounds:

> [Y]et sometimes it [the clitoris] groweth to such a length that it hangeth without the cleft like a mans member, especially when it is fretted with the touch of the cloaths, and so strutteth and groweth to a rigiditie as doth the yarde of a man. And this part it is which those wicked women doe abuse called Tribades (often mentioned by many authors, and in some states worthily punished) to their mutuall and unnaturall lustes. (Crooke 238)[35]

That this early modern discourse confuses clitoral penetration (in which case the hypertrophy would needs be extreme), rubbing, and masturbation (for which a large clitoris might be useful but not necessary) does not diminish the fact that women's pleasure was both necessary and a potential threat to early modern patriarchal relations. This is not to imply that the meanings of these terms or the behaviors they signify were stable. Katherine Park, for instance, reserves the use of the term "tribadism" for the erotic activity of rubbing, and claims that "Renaissance legal and theological discussions of lesbian sex" used "exceedingly clear distinctions between rubbing and penetration" (22).[36] While I agree with Park that penetration—with enlarged clitoris, fingers, or dildo—signified the greatest usurpation of male prerogatives, and thus was the most readily recognized and most harshly punished,[37] the use of the term "penetration" bypasses the question of the nature of the "instrument" involved. I want to suggest that practices popularly conceived to be "tribadic" often did not, indeed could not, distinguish between clitoral penetration and rubbing. An enlarged clitoris could be an instrument of either friction or entry, and authors of anatomies and travel literature seem unconcerned with delineating the difference. Whereas the evolution of jurisprudence increasingly demanded, and thus created, ever more precise terms and delineations (as was also the case in the seventeenth-century formalization of legal definitions of "sodomy"), the artificiality of such pseudo-precision may have been evident to those whose bodies were most intimately involved.

Crooke's 1615 account of "tribadism" (which marginally cites Leo Africanus and Caelius Aurelianus [a fifth-century Latin translator of Soranus] under the heading "Tribades odiosae feminae") returns us to the racialized, "anthropological" images first put into play by travel writers only a few decades earlier. And yet something has changed in this intertextual transfer from one discursive domain to another. For none of the travel writers mention the "abuse" of a partic-

ular body part. Though cucumbers and public baths loom large, no enlarged clitoris haunts their accounts; rather, there is simply a boundless, deceitful desire of
which all foreign, non-Christian women presumably are suspected. With the publication of anatomical descriptions of the clitoris, however, imprecision gives way
to pseudoscientific accuracy, as the site of transgressive female eroticism shifts
away from the social excesses of Mediterranean climes to the excessive endowment of female bodies.

Paradoxically, the "modern" articulation of clitoral hypertrophy carries with
it lineages from medieval accounts of "marvels," a genre from which travel literature itself evolved.[38] Mary Campbell remarks, "The features of the organic marvels manifest characteristically grotesque principles: hyperbolic dimensions, mul-
tiplication of body parts, and fusions of species" (71). Likewise,

> The marvelous is marginal, biologically and culturally, although it may be used as
> a figure for central and interior desire. The marvelous is also, in start, a rhetorical phe-
> nomenon. A brief enough description, especially when communicated as a distortion
> of the familiar rather than as something *essentially* different, produces a marvel. (249)

Through the development and insertion of a "marvel" into anatomy the "tribade," as a phenomenon knowable to a specifically modern epistemology, is discursively born. By the early seventeenth century, under the auspices of anatomy,
a paradigm of desire is transmuted into a paradigm of bodily structure: it is not
the "tribade's" inconstant mind or sinful soul but her uniquely female yet masculinized *morphology* that propels her to engage in illicit hehavior.[39] If clitoral hypertrophy causes modern "tribadism," modern "tribadism" is inconceivable without clitoral hypertrophy.[40] Anatomy provides a map of this connection.

The mapping of the "tribadic" body produces and is produced by an anatomical essentialism that has haunted modern discourse ever since. Such essentialism
is the result not of natural, corporeal facts but of a strategy to organize and make
intelligible the plurality of bodily structures and behaviors within the conceptual
confines of Renaissance cosmological and earthly hierarchies. The seventeenth-
century production of anatomical essentialism is related to other historical shifts:
as the discourse of anatomy appropriates the tropes of travel narratives, the racialized "anthropology" born of a protocolonialist imperative momentarily is displaced in favor of an articulation and consolidation of normative bodily form.
This is not to suggest that cross-cultural comparisons are no longer relevant;
rather, a complex dynamic of articulation and disarticulation, knowing and un-
knowing, complicates such an exposition. Figuring "tribadism" as a "mutual lust"
that is "often mentioned by many authors" and "worthily punished," citing
Africanus but failing to locate such practices in any particular country, Crooke's
account either is unconcerned with, or deliberately elides, the possibility of "tribadism" in England.[41]

And yet, the unspoken assumption of "tribadism's" national otherness that
gives Crooke's account such an air of unflappability begins to break down by
mid-century. Thomas Bartholin's 1653 translation and expansion of his father's
Latin anatomy draws on Crooke for his entry "Of the Clitoris," and then proceeds
to recontextualize "tribadic" practices. After terming such women *Confricatrices*
or Rubsters, Bartholin introduces a reference to the "lascivious Practice" of Mar-

tial's Philaenis and Sappho. Then, after citing Romans 1.26 ("for this cause God gave them up unto vile affections: for even their women did change the natural use unto that which is against nature"), he asserts that such lascivious practices cause the clitoris to be called *Contemptus viorum* or "the Contempt of Mankind."[42] Bartholin continues in this vein as he discusses clitoral size:

> Its Size is commonly small; it lies hid for the most part under the Nymphs in its beginning, and afterward it sticks out a little. For in Lasses that begin to be amorous, the Clitoris does first discover it self. It is in several persons greater or lesser: in some it hangs out like a mans Yard, namely when young Wenches do frequently and continually handle and rub the same, as Examples testifie. But that it should grow as big, as a Gooses neck, as Platerus relates of one, is altogether praeternatural and monstrous. Tulpills hath a like Story of one that had it as long as half a mans finger, and as thick as a boys Prick, which made her willing to have to do with Women in a Carnal way. But the more this part encreases, the more does it hinder a man in his business. For in the time of Copulation it swells like a mans Yard, and being erected, provokes to Lust. (*Anatomical History* 77)

By morphologizing the "tribade," anatomy paradoxically moves her closer to home: the erotic excess that was attributed to foreign women now can be found on the Christian bodies of "Lasses" and "young Wenches" who handle themselves as well as each other. This "Englishing" of anatomical rhetoric suggests that it is not merely the clitoris's exaggerated size that might "hinder a man in his business," but women's erotic interest in their own and other women's bodies.[43]

The consistent linkage of what must have been proportionately insignificant physical aberrations to comparatively small social transgressions indicates an anxiety less about the body unnatural than the unnatural use to which any female body might be put. As the potential measure of *all* female bodies, clitoral hypertrophy metonymizes women's supposedly inordinate capacity for pleasure. As anatomies like Bartholin's begin to invoke cautionary references and biblical citation (assuming more and more frequently the function of conduct books), and as the anatomist's repudiation of women's pleasure grows more insistent, the specter of the enlarged clitoris looms larger: if not as big as a "Gooses neck," yet as big as a "Boys Prick."[44] And, in the pseudopornographic genre of marital advice books that developed out of the intersection of anatomy and conduct literature, discursive amplification and hyperbole insured excellent sales. Nicholas Venette's immensely popular *Conjugal Love, or, The Pleasures of the Marriage Bed* (aka *The Art of Conjugal Love*), for instance, asserts:

> This part lascivious women often abuse. The *lesbian Sappho* would never have acquired such indifferent reputation, if this part of her's had been less. I have seen a girl eight years of age, that had already the *clitoris* as long as one's little finger; and if this part grows with age, as it is probable it may, I am persuaded it is now as long as that of the woman mentioned by Platerus, who had one as big and long as the neck of a goose. (19)[45]

It is, I believe, the discursive amplification of the threat posed by this evergrowing "prick" that motivates Shari, in 1671, to resurrect the colonialist imperative, rise to the defense of Englishwomen, and exile the "tribade" from England.

As the observations of travel writers are harnessed to and appropriated by anatomy, the clitoris and the "tribade" are positioned paratactically as mutually constitutive forms of female matter. Not only does the "tribade" function as the abject other against which a normative female body is defined, but the clitoris comes into representation as the metonymic sign of the unnatural, transgressive "tribade." The anatomical representation of the female body's capacity for pleasure—which had the potential to benefit those women whose sexual practices colluded with reproductive exigencies—is oppositionally countered by the "tribade's" nonreproductive misuse of pleasure.

The seriousness with which anatomists took this misuse is evinced in the rhetorical linkages increasingly forged in their work between anatomy, eroticism, and surgery. If the narrative trajectory of these texts monotonously moves from a description of normative genitalia to a discussion of clitoral hypertrophy, and from there to excoriation of the "tribade," it perhaps comes as no surprise that the narrative often ends with a recommendation of genital amputation. Paré, who in his early discussion of "tribadism" confuses the clitoris with the labia, recommends labial amputation,[46] and Bartholin approvingly cites the practice of female circumcision adopted by ancient and Eastern nations. Nicholas Culpeper goes one step further in his *Fourth Book of Practical Physick* (published in 1684 with his best-selling *Directory for Midwives*), providing precise instructions for how to excise both the enlarged clitoris and the labia.[47] Despite their differences, a common logic structures these narratives: signifiable by the presence of genital hypertrophy, "tribadism" can be eradicated by surgical intervention.[48] Not only does anatomical enlargement cause "tribadism," but it is a physical sign and symptom that can and must be removed. Whether the clitoris or the labia are cut off, what is excised ideologically is a pleasure that grows beyond its own abjection.

The discursive appropriation by anatomy of travelers' descriptions and preoccupations demonstrates the emergence of a social *conflict* about the terms by which female desire, pleasure, and embodiment were to be represented. Such a conflict is the result of a "psychomorphology"—the fantasies that structure and the structures that fantasize—of "the clitoris" in the seventeenth century. I am not suggesting that such a conflict did not previously exist; the association of the clitoris with immoderate desire, and of clitoral hypertrophy with "tribadism," can be found in the medical works of medieval Arabic and classical authors and may in fact be one source of early modern accounts.[49] Indeed, by focusing on the interaction between sixteenth- and seventeenth-century discourses, I do not mean to occlude the prehistory of the "tribade" in the ancient and medieval periods. This prehistory, evident in both literature and science, situates the "tribade" primarily in Greece and Rome, not in Africa or Turkey. In discursive terms, however, the "tribade's" European presence was obscured by the political and linguistic revolutions of the late classical and medieval periods; it took the interaction between travel literature and anatomy to reposition her in Europe.

That is, under the auspices of emerging epistemologies and under pressure from new cultural exigencies, an ancient linguistic and social category was reborn and transfigured, giving rise in western Europe to new and, I want to argue, specifically modern significations. As the ancient binary logic which gave rise to the Greek "tribad" survived in early modern Galenic medicine, it interacted with new conceptual schemes for figuring gender, erotic, and cultural difference. The early modern category of the "tribade" is a product of the negotiation not only between modern and ancient modes of knowledge but between various epistemological domains that seek to map the early modern body. In this sense the early modern "tribade" is not a creature of exotic origins imported to Europe by travel writers, but rather is the discursive effect of (1) travel writers' transposition of ancient and medieval categories of intelligibility onto foreign "matters," and (2) anatomy's appropriation and refashioning of these "travel maps." In concentrating on two of the discourses involved in this mapping I do not mean to imply that they are the only genres relevant to the formation of early modern erotic categories.[50] At the same time, the convergence of these discourses in seventeenth-century England is a function not merely of the routes whereby knowledge was transmitted but of specific social processes that granted a renewed relevance to concerns about female erotic power.

In "Sappho in Early Modern England," which examines representations of Sappho in various texts including anatomies, Harriette Andreadis argues that "prurient Orient interest in the clitoris seems to be increasing" in the mid-seventeenth century, and she locates a discursive shift in English representations of "tribadism" "in or around 1650." While I would hesitate to pinpoint a decade in which such a transition might have occurred, I agree that by the end of the century anatomical discourses as well as the pseudopornography that evolved out of it, imparted to same-gender female eroticism not only a name and a morphology but an increasing opprobrium.[51]

The increased circulation of such discourses, I want to suggest, was in part a function of an intensifying social investment in the desire of the conjugal couple. Emphasis on the companionate relation of the conjugal pair, debated since the beginnings of the Reformation, gained hegemony within an increasingly private sphere of marital intimacy. Yet marital desire did not gain its new significance alone. The conjunction of pornography with anatomy suggests a growing cultural pressure to differentiate legitimate from illegitimate desire. Attempts to consolidate that distinction promoted a corresponding fetishization of the "tribade's" body—a body that metonymizes the threatening potential of every woman.

It is through women's common clitoral inheritance—an inheritance that is as much historical and psychological as biological—that the oppositional dyads of modernity develop.[52] If the clitoris comes into representation accompanied by the "tribade," if the "tribade" only enters England when endowed with an enlarged clitoris, and if the clitoris must be removed whenever the "tribade" rears her head, then these associations provide the raw material out of which the social categories of "lesbian" and "heterosexual" would begin to be constructed. The inauguration of "the heterosexual" as the original, normative essential mode of erotic behavior is haunted, from its first recognizably "modern" articulation, by an embodiment and practice that calls the analytical priority of "heterosexuality" into question. In historical terms, then, "lesbianism" is not, as Freud would have it, the preoedipal embryo of an adult "heterosexuality," but that which always accompanies and threatens to disrupt "heterosexuality." In the psychomorphology that our clitoral inheritance instantiates, "lesbianism" is less an alternative to female "heterosexuality" than its transgressive twin, "born" into modern discourse at the same ambivalent cultural moment.[53]

To make this assertion is to challenge the adequacy of two analytical models currently circulating in "lesbian" studies. On the one hand, my effort to produce a social constructionist account of erotic discourses prior to 1800 challenges the presentist bias of much recent work, particularly that which implies that little can be said of same-gender female eroticism before modern discourses of identity.[54] Although I do not wish to minimize the power of psychoanalysis and other late-nineteenth-century epistemologies to solidify modern erotic identities, I believe that subsuming erotic desire and practices under modern categories thwarts inquiry both into the *construction* of the homo/hetero divide and the regulatory function of identity. The erotic constructions of modernity are the product of a process rather than the signifiers of an event. The early modern construction of the "tribade" demonstrates that the anatomical essentialism that underpins modern formations of identity is not original to the regime of the subjects rather, it predates and helps to constitute such formations.[55]

At the same time, "tribades" were not "lesbians"; and if anatomy's mapping of the "tribadic" body provides a means of understanding the historical antecedents to modern identities, it does not reinscribe such identities as historically invariable or self-evidently knowable. My study thus contravenes the (re)essentializing account currently making a resurgence in "lesbian" studies, most persuasively in *The Apparitional Lesbian* by Terry Castle. In arguing that the lesbian (no scare quotes) "is not a recent invention" (8), Castle bypasses the more difficult issue of just when, and under what auspices, the "lesbian" was constructed. Her attempt to bring the "apparitional lesbian" into visibility prior to 1900 assumes rather than explores the cohesion of "lesbianism" with the Enlightenment; as a result, the "dark ages" from which she attempts to rescue the "lesbian" are simply pushed further back in time. If one of the pleasures of reading *The Apparitional Lesbian* is that it demonstrates the centrality of same-gender female desire to modern Western culture (much as Eve Sedgwick does for male homoeroticism), one of the disappointments is that Castle does so without formulating the historical terms of the "lesbian's" ghostly centrality. Furthermore, the assumption that one knows, in an "ordinary," "vernacular" sense, what a "lesbian" is (*Apparitional Lesbian* 15), and that on the basis of such stable knowledge one can forge connections across time and culture, obscures the recognition that such knowledge is less a position from which one can make autonomous claims than the result of normalizing discourses, the history of which I have been tracing.[56]

Under the auspices of protocolonialist discourses a new nexus of modern knowledge about female bodies was produced. Within the logics of this emerging epistemology are the primary terms by which, in subsequent centuries, certain female bodies would be pleasured as reproductive capital, while others would be condemned for their usurpation of masculine prerogatives and their pursuit of autonomous pleasures. If the regimes of Enlightenment knowledge inaugurated the category of the "subject" out of which a "lesbian identity" would be generated (by Freud et al.), such epistemologies inherited from seventeenth-century anatomies the bodily contours of that subject.

The disclosure of Freud's indebtedness to preexisting corporeal maps impels us to question the adequacy of spatial metonymies to organize our understanding of the relation between bodies, identities, and desires. If the psychomorphology of the clitoris demonstrates the extent to which the clitoris and the "lesbian" are mutually constituted by a colonialist dynamic (which represses as much as it reveals same-gender female desire), then perhaps we can recognize the impact of this history on our attempts to think beyond the pathologies inscribed by Freud. In particular, we can trace the lineages of history within current feminist strategies to displace the phallus by a female corporeal imaginary; as important as this displacement has been in refiguring female sexuality as something other than lack, the theoretical recourse to female genitals tends to reiterate the logic of metonymy through which same-gender female desire has been anatomized and colonized.

The problem extends beyond the inability to conceive of the pleasures of vaginal penetration (by fingers, penis or dildo) or the possibility of a non-phallocentric heterosexuality—although these are crucial issues as well.[57] Paula Bennett, for instance, recognizes that female sexuality is not limited to clitoral stimulation; and yet she concludes her essay on clitoral imagery in nineteenth century poetry by asserting that

> Without the clitoris, theorists have no physical site in which to locate an autonomous sense of female sexual agency. . . . With the clitoris, theorists can construct female sexuality in such a way that women become sexual subjects in their own right. . . . No longer married . . . to the penis or the law, they can become . . . by themselves, healthy and whole. (257)

Locating the possibilities of psychic health, wholeness, and agency on the clitoris seems a lot to ask of any one organ, particularly if the embodied experience of desire, pleasure, and orgasm are more fragmented and diffuse than unitary. But more is at issue here than the humanist basis of such claims: for the elevation of the clitoris (or labia) as the sine qua non of "lesbian" sexuality overvalues not only the genitals as a source of pleasure but the power of bodily metonymy to represent that pleasure.

The most analytically sophisticated redeployment of spatial metonymies occurs in the work of Luce Irigaray. By introducing a third term that displaces the equivalence of the clitoris and the penis, Irigaray challenges phallomorphic logic, with its emphasis on singularity, unity, and visibility, by mobilizing a labial logic characterized by multiplicity, movement, and tactility. Irigaray's invocation of vaginal and facial "lips" that "speak together" disperses the singularity of the signifier into a plurality of pleasures and erotic zones:

> [W]oman's pleasure does not have to choose between clitoral activity and vaginal passivity. . . . The pleasure of the vaginal caress does not have to be substituted for that of the clitoral caress. They each contribute, irreplaceably, to woman's pleasure. Among other caresses . . . Fondling the breasts, touching the vulva, spreading the lips, stroking the posterior wall of the vagina, brushing against the mouth of the uterus, and so on. . . . woman has sex organs more or less everywhere. (*This Sex* 28)

Supplementing the clitoris with the lips, Irigaray charts a new "geography of feminine pleasure" (*This Sex* 90) that would seem to bypass and subvert the history of equivalence I have been tracing.

Or does it?[58] Rather, does Irigaray's labial morphology reenact the anatomical essentialism that links body part(s) to erotic desire, and then enforces this link through the identification (and abjection or celebration) of a social type? I want to suggest that the metonymic association of female bodily organs (no matter how plural) with an erotic identity (no matter how "deviant") doesn't so much refigure "lesbian" desire as reproduce the contours of the colonialist geographies and anatomies out of which "lesbian" identity emerged.[59]

Irigaray's bodily aesthetic can be read as a *composition* rather than a *reflection* of the female body (see Gallop; Fuss). At the same time, however, this strategy of reading fails to take into account the extent to which the terms of that composition carry with them a particular history. The lineages of that history become accessible if one reads *This Sex Which Is Not One* as an effort to articulate not only a "feminine" voice and desire but a "lesbian" subject; this subject is brought into being by a textual progression of chapters that asserts the commensurability of body part(s) and erotic identity under the guiding auspices of metonymy.

It is metonymy that enables Irigaray's valorization of a tactile over a visual economy, that allows her to assert the possibility of a touch unmediated by culture and bodily difference. And it is metonymy that enables the supplanting of the category "woman" by the category "lesbian." In chapter 2, "This Sex Which Is Not One," the two lips that cannot be parted (except through phallic violence [24]) represent the inherent autoeroticism of the female body; in chapter 11, "When Our Lips Speak Together," they become the lips of (at least two) women erotically pleasuring one another. What began as an assertion of bodily self-sufficiency ("she touches herself in and of herself without any need of mediation" [24]) ends in a poetics of female merger: "You? I? That's still saying too much. Dividing too sharply between us: all" (218). Negating the difference between one and two (bodies, erotic practices), Irigaray collapses the labia, the female voice, and "lesbian(s)" into a unified expression of boundless feminine desire. Just as labial autoeroticism is positioned as antithetical to phallomorpism, "lesbianism" is positioned as antithetical to phallocentrism.

Where this correlation positions women who are not "lesbian," and the extent to which "lesbians" may not enact a transgressive politics, are questions left unanswered by Irigaray's bodily composition. But, more important to my argument, Irigaray's conflation of body part(s) and erotic identity maintains the psychomorphology of the clitoris by positing body part(s) as a sufficient sign of desire, and desire as adequately expressed through the rubric of (constructed) identity. Although the specific terms of embodiment have changed, the logic of metonymic equivalence still holds: if not penis=clitoris=lesbian, then labia= lesbian desire=lesbian identity. Despite the erasure of phallomorphism from the equations, the underlying structure of commensurability secured by the phallus remains: body part=embodied desire=erotic identity.

The phallus remains secure because it possesses the power of naming. Indeed, one reason the relational structure I've described is so resistant to alteration is that it functions as a metanarrative of legitimation.[60] Although the clitoris is no longer posited as an equivalent to the penis, female genitals are still invested with the power of the phallus: they serve as the authorizing sign of erotic desires, practices, and identities.

As long as the metonymic logic of legitimation holds steady, same-gender female desire is caught within the confines of history. And yet we seem stubbornly unaware of any history that extends beyond the past century. What finally is most troubling about the strategy to refigure the "lesbian" as a body composed of multiple lips is the extent to which it allows us to forget the material processes that have constructed as "lesbian" those psyches and bodies that desire other women. Indeed, it would seem that the metonymizing of the clitoris and the labia as signs of "lesbian" identity registers a longing to escape not only the logic of phallomorphism but an awareness of the embodied history through which such logic is lived. And yet "lesbianism" (the category of identity whose antecedents I have been tracing) is constituted by phallocentrism—or rather by the history that grants both phallocentrism and "lesbianism" their embodied meanings.

Our task now is not to revise or reject Freud's narrative of "lesbian" pathology; several critics already have done so brilliantly.[61] Rather, we must pry apart the terms—the equation of body part and embodied desire, of embodied desire and erotic identity—through which the metonymic logic of anatomical essentialism continues to delineate, define, and discipline erotic possibility. Only by disarticulating these links can we extend the meanings of same-gender erotic desires beyond the geographies and anatomies that would circumscribe them; only by articulating the incommensurability of desires, bodies, and identities can we move beyond the history from whence, inscribed, abjected and unintelligible to ourselves, "we" came.

Notes

1. This view, most influentially proposed by Foucault, has been refined by George Chauncey among others.
2. While what follows is a critique of Lacquer, any reader of his will recognize how much I owe to *Making Sex*, not least because of Lacquer's insistence on the effects of culture on biology. Like mine, Laquer's historicizing account also returns (in the end) to Freud, but his interest in Freud largely focuses on the psychoanalytic displacement of the clitoris by the "invention" of vaginal orgasm.
3. Lacquer argues that prior to the eighteenth century, and well after empiricist revelations of biologically distinct genders, medical science was dominated by the understanding of the female body as homologous (and yet inferior) to the male body. Anatomists, physicians, and midwives believed, for instance, that women, like men, expelled "seed" during orgasm and viewed the vagina as a structurally inverted penis.
4. Throughout this essay, I use the term "anatomy" to connote any self-evident structure of the body, but a discipline of knowledge that inscribes a bodily schema.
5. The term "visibilizing" is Barbara Maria Stafford's, and I use it here to suggest the activity involved in rendering an object visible.
6. According to *Making Sex*, all medical literature up to the eighteenth century speaks cohesively and insistently of gender isomorphism. Intent on demonstrating an epistemic shift from a one-sex to a two-sex body, Lacquer's macroscopic view tends to obscure differences and discontinuities among temporally proximate discourses. This method-

ological choice is indebted to and reproduces a history of sexuality heavily influenced by Michel Foucault. The existence of competing medical paradigms during the seventeenth century, including challenges to the anatomical basis of female inferiority, is proposed by Park and Nye, Dubrow, and Keller. Laquer's gender bias is analyzed in general terms by Paster. Most importantly for my purposes, Laquer's contention that the "discovery" of the clitoris had no impact on the one-sex model is challenged by Park and Nye, who argue that knowledge of the specificity of the clitoris pressured the paradigm of homology and helped to initiate, much earlier than Lacquer suggests, the shift to a model of two diametrically opposed genders.

7. Lacquer's approach is quickly becoming the dominant one in Renaissance studies, in part because of the use Stephen Greenblatt makes of it in "Fiction and Friction." In this essay, Greenblatt elides all possibility of female specificity by (re)privileging the dominant male homosocial/homoerotic milieu.

8. The language of imitation pervades Lacquer's account of "tribadism" and crossdressing. For a more detailed exposition of the way models of imitation obscure same-gender erotic practices, see my essay "The (In)Significance of 'Lesbian' Desire."

9. Mention of Sappho allows me the opportunity to clarify a number of issues that will become increasingly relevant as my discussion continues. As David Halperin writes in the forthcoming *Oxford Classical Dictionary*, Lesbos was originally associated with fellatio and Sappho with prostitution rather than "lesbian" desire; it was only after the second century A.D. that "Lesbos" was associated with Sappho's expression of desire for women. In fact, there was no established terminology in the ancient world specifically designating same-gender erotic acts between women. Rather, what the ancients found occasion to comment on were penetrative acts (with dildo or clitoris) that women might perform either with women or men. It is this preoccupation with penetration (and associated concerns about hypermasculinity) that gives rise to the Greek term "tribad," conventionally etymologized from "tribein," to rub (and hence the Latin "fricatrix"). It is not until late antiquity that the meaning of "tribad" begins to be conflated with male-female eroticism. The change in spelling from "tribad" to "tribade" reflects the French translation of the Greek; it is the form that most often makes its way into early modern English accounts.

10. Anthony Pagden provides a provocative account of the way in which tropes of discovery govern early modern science and, by implication, link anatomy to travel narratives: "The discoverer carries out with him his lexicon of names, his repertoire of classifications, his knowledge of the invisible isolates and parallels which link him to home. He returns with samples, exhibits, slaves. This itinerary, which is always invariable, is, as Descartes may have been the first to recognize, the same 'journey' which every scientist must make" (30–31).

11. In linking anatomies and travel narratives, I have been anticipated by Patricia Parker, who provocatively reads Renaissance discourses of the body through racialized discourse of colonialism. In addressing the relationship between these two discourses, Parker is most interested in their common imperative to reveal something monstrous or obscene; she is principally concerned with the Western visual orientation that constructs "the hunger to 'know' as a desire to 'see'" (87).

12. The instability of both kinds of text is worth underscoring. What Mary Campbell says of early travel literature is equally true of early anatomy: "Knowledge was scarce, reverenced, and largely inseparable from the particular texts that transmitted it. At the same time, text themselves were fluid; plagiarized, misquoted, mistranslated, interpolated upon, bowdlerized, epitomized, transformed, and transformable at every stage of their complex dissemination" (140).

13. In this respect Greenblatt's question, "What is the origin of boundaries that enable us to speak of 'within' and 'without'?" is crucial. See his mediation on the early modern construction of such boundaries (*Marvelous Possessions* 121).

14. My thinking about maps has been influenced by the "art historical" work of Barbara Maria Stafford, who historicizes the effort to spatialize the body, and the history of anthropology provided by Margaret Hogden. Hogden describes cosmographers and compilers of travel narratives thus: "they were all in some degree geographers, absorbed in the minutiae of the distribution of man and his cultures on every continent and island of the world. All were corners of maps, disposed to think of the array of strange rituals, creeds, and theologies in spatial terms; as associated with certain already located peoples; as distributed geographically" (218).

15. As Louis Montrose has noted, the identification of territory with the female virginal body provided explorers of the New World with powerful justifications for their determination to conquer and subjugate native inhabitants, while simultaneously providing an image of one's own nation as inviolable. Likewise, Jonathan Goldberg shows in *Sodometries* how the discourse of sodomy can be manipulated to rationalize European ascriptions of bestiality onto South American tribes, while occluding the very desires that constitute the colonial imaginary.

16. See, for instance, de Busbecq: "The Turks are the most careful people in the world of modesty of their wives, and therefore keep them shut up at home and hide them away, so that they scarce see the light of day. But if they have to go into the streets, they are sent out so covered and wrapt up in veils."

17. Because the following descriptions drawn from travel narratives and anatomies are not widely available in modern editions, I have reproduced them in full rather than summarized their contents.

18. De Nicholay's work was first brought to my attention by Mario Di Gangi, who generously shared his dissertation with me.

19. I am grateful for Doug Bruster for alerting me to the existence of this passage. The first of de Busbecq's "Turkish Letters" was published in Latin in 1581. The first edition of all four letters was printed in 1589. There were eleven further Latin editions in the seventeenth century, along with French, German, Bohemian, Flemish, and Spanish editions. The first "Englished" edition was printed in London in 1694. The quotation I cite is not from this first edition, but rather from the edition of 1881, which is faithful to the original.

20. Although the punishment this woman receives is harsh, her story serves both the authority who punishes her and de Busbecq as a source of amusement. As de Busbecq narrates it, the Aga of the Janissaries "tells her that an old woman like her ought to know better than to attempt so mad a freak, and asks, if she is not ashamed of herself? She replies, 'Tush! you know not the might of love, and God grant that you may never experience its power.' At this the Aga could not restrain his laughter; and ordered her to be carried off at once, and drowned in the sea. Thus the strange passion of this old woman brought her to a bad end. . . . I am afraid your hearts have been offended by my account of such an instance of wickedness; but, if I can, I will remove by a pleasanter story any disagreeable impression the former may have left, for I am sure you will have a good laugh over what I am going to tell you" (232).

21. Although the original date of publication of Glover's and Wither's narratives is ambiguous, both were included in Samuel Purchase's *Purchase His Pilgrims* of 1625. Purchase continued the work of the Elizabethan compiler Richard Hakluyt, collecting anecdotes, diaries, log books, letters, maps, and histories, as well as publishing many narratives that Hakluyt had collected but was not able to publish before his death in

1616. Together, the works published in Hakluyt and Purchase represent the greatest compendium of travel narratives from the sixteenth and early seventeenth centuries in English.

22. I am grateful to Kim Hall for alerting me both to the existence of this passage and to her analysis of it in her book.

23. With the exception of Africanus, a converted Moor who lived much of his adult life in Italy, all of the writers were born in Europe. Withers and Glover were English, de Nicholay was French, de Busbecq was Flemish. All traveled to the countries they describe. Each of their works was available either in the original English or in a seventeenth-century translation.

24. The use of this terminology registers the existence of what may be called a prehistory of the "tribade" in the ancient and medieval periods. I discuss this prehistory in fuller detail later in the essay.

25. In Africanus's story, the logical trajectory that transforms "objective" description into a cautionary tale is the shift in focus from the wicked witch to the silly husband. The OED defines "silly" in this time period as (1a) deserving of pity, compassion, or sympathy; (1b) helpless, defenseless; (2) weak, feeble, frail, etc.; (3) unlearned, unsophisticated, ignorant. The means by which the move is made from witch to husband is through the intermediary figure of the wife: the woman who, first assumed to be innocent and naive, is soon so "allured with delight" of an all-female erotic practice that she is sending her husband out to bring her consort home. If the diviner of Fez is initially represented as a woman who commits "unlawful Venerie" with others of her own kind, Africanus's primary interest seems to be less the unnaturalness or unlawfulness of her desires than the potential corrupting influence of her "burning lust," which effects an inversion of male triangular traffic in women.

26. Obscurity is not the normative rhetoric of travel narratives, as descriptions of clothing, planting methods, military operations, etc. are far more detailed. The vagueness here may be due partly to the lack of eyewitness authority, as men as foreigners would not have been allowed access to the harem or the women's bath. But I would suggest that such vagueness is also constitutive of the general discourse of sexuality in this period—contemporary assertions of sodomy are similarly ambiguous. It is precisely this vagueness that seventeenth-century anatomies (and legal discourse) will attempt to dispel.

27. What is at issue is less whether women actually engaged in the practices so described than the way in which cultural fantasies about their existence and cultural definitions of their meaning gain currency at particular historical moments. Greenblatt's remark on the truth value of European representations of the New World seems relevant to European representations of Asia and Africa: "We can be certain only that [such representations] tells us something about the European practice of representation" (*Marvelous Possessions* 7) Indeed, the question of facticity must be referred back to the genre of travel literature, born as it was at the intersection of the ancient and modern, the imagined and the encountered, the fabulous (or monstrous) and the domesticated. See also Campbell, Hodgen, and Friedman.

28. For a perceptive analysis of Jane Sharp's appropriation and subversion of dominant medical ideologies of the female body, see Keller.

29. Sharp's notion that women should "keep it close" may correlate with an increasing privatization of erotic behavior that accompanied its amplified discursivity, as I argue near the end of this essay.

30. Syphilis is a case in point. See my chapter on English discourses of syphilis in *Desire and Anxiety.*

31. Notably the work of Soranus, published as *Gynecology* by Owesei Temkin, and of Trotula of Salerno, published as *The Diseases of Women* by Elizabeth Mason- Huhl. See also the *Medieval Woman's Guide to Health: The First English Gynecological Handbook,* by Beryl Rowland.

32. Katherine Park makes clear that this "discovery" was in fact a "rediscovery" of knowledge that "had been lost to medieval Latin medical theorists. Misled by the linguistic imprecisions of the Arabic sources and the uncertain terminology employed by their Latin translators, they tended either to identify it [the clitoris] with the labia minora or, following Avicenna, to think of it as a pathological growth found in only a few women" (7). I draw heavily on Park's analysis of this modern "rediscovery" and the subsequent dispute about the clitoris's existence.

33. As William Engel notes, the colloquial term *yard* "comes from the Old English *gyrd*, meaning a stick, twig, or shoot; it also was used to designate a standard unit of English long measure. . . . But another origin and meaning is concealed in the word 'yard' as well. . . . [D]eriving from the Old English 'geard' the multiple implication is that of fence, dwelling, house—and it is the second element of the old English *outgeard*, meaning orchard. A yard, then, is that which is surrounded on all sides: it is an open space, enclosed for cultivation or productive activities; it signals a union of dwelling and earth."

34. This statement is reproduced verbatim in Nicholas Culpeper's enlarged edition of his 1641 *A Directory for Midwifes* (1684), and by the anonymous author of *Aristoteles Master-Piece* (1684).

35. Clitoral hypertrophy is linked to hermaphroditism by Culpeper: "Some are of opinion, and I could almost afford to side with them. That such kind of Creatures they call Hermaphrodites, which they say bear the Genitals both of men and women, are nothing else but such women in whom Clitoris hangs out externally, and so resembles the form of a Yard; leave the truth or falsehood of it to be judged by such who have seen them anatomized: however, this is agreeable both to reason and authority, that the bigger the Clitoris is in women, the more lustful they are" (*Directory* 23).

36. In addition to reading French medical literature, Park refers to a passage from *Apology of Herodotus* by French humanist Henri Stephen Estienne (I cite the 1607 English translation of the original Latin):

    By which examples [of two women marrying] we see that our Age may well boast, that (notwithstanding the vices of former times) it hath some proper and peculiar to it selfe. For this fact of hers [penetration with a dildo], hath nothing common with that which was practised by those famous strumpets, who in old times were called *Tribades*. (69)

    Estienne's desire to separate penetration with a dildo from "tribadism," I would argue, has more to do with his larger polemic about the moral degeneration of the modern age than with popular conceptions of "tribadism." It may also indicate a national difference, as the French seem far more preoccupied than the English with women's use of dildoes.

37. See my essay, "The (In)Significance of 'Lesbian' Desire."

38. Although medieval accounts of marvels regularly feature various monsters and amazons, none list "tribades" in their classifications.

39. During the early modern period, the deployment of concepts of "tribadism" and sodomy are disjunctive; the anatomical essentialism underlying the morphology of the "tribade" is not evident in the figure of the sodomite, whose actions were considered to be a measure of the sinful potential of all fallen beings.

40. This is not to suggest that all forms of same-gender female desire were subsumed by the discourse of "tribadism." See my essay, "The (In)Significance of 'Lesbian' Desire."

41. In this respect, it is interesting to note that references to the "tribade" (drawn from Leo Africanus) in the second edition of Paré's *Des Monstres et prodiges* (1573) were excised

from the third edition due to concern on the part of French authorities. Jean Céard, Paré's translator, notes that Paré was forced to replace his discussion of Leo Africanus with a much briefer citation about a recent French sodomy conviction of two women; eventually he removed the entire passage about female genitalia. This censorship is contextualized by Lacquer and Park. Park notes that Paré "had reassured his critics in the Faculty of Medecine that the deformity that allowed women to have sex with each other was extremely rare—so much so, he wrote, 'that for every woman that has it, there are ten thousands who don't.' His successors could fall back on no such reassurance" (9).

42. In French this was rendered as "le mespris des hommes" (Park 12).

43. Johnson's 1634 translation of Paré also invokes the specter of masturbation when detailing the etymology of "clitoris": "Columbus calls it Tentigo, Fallopius Cleitoris, whence proceeds that infamous word Cleitorizien, (which signifies imprudently to handle that part.) Because it is an obscene part, let those which desire to know more of it, read the Authors which I cited" (130).

44. Culpeper's *Complete Midwives Practice Enlarged* likewise states that the clitoris "hath been observed to grow out of the body, the breadth of four fingers."

45. Venette's book went through eight printings before his death in 1698; the 1750 English edition I quote is designated as the "twentieth edition." The other popular (and frequently republished) text in this genre, *Aristoteles Master-Piece*, passes over the clitoris rather quickly, stating merely that it "is the Seat of venerial Pleasure, being like a yard in Situation, Substance, Composition, and Erection, growing sometimes out of the Body two inches, but that rarely happens, unless thro' extreme lust or extraordinary accident" (105). First published in the mid-fifteenth century, subsequent editions of *Aristoteles Master-Piece* seem to have been unaffected by the discursive amplification of the seventeenth century.

46. Paré interprets Leo Africanus's description of female diviners as referring to the abuse of the labia minora. Likewise, Crooke (who did recognize a difference between the two) discusses labial (but not clitoral) amputation: "Sometimes, they grow to so great a length on one side, more rarely on both; and not so ordinarily in maidens as in women. . . . what through the affluence of humours, what through attrectation, that for the trouble and shame (being in many Countryes a notable argument of petulancie & immodesty) they neede the Chirurgions helpe to cut them off (although they bleed much and are hardly cicatrised) especially among the Egyptians, amongst whom this accident (as Galen saith) is very familiar. Wherefore in Maidens before they grow too long they cut them off, and before they marry" (237). This passage is printed with the marginal gloss: "The Egyptian women lascivious."

47. The entire passage from the *Fourth Book of Practical Physick* reads,

> The Aloe or Wings in the Privities of a woman, are soft spongy flesh like a Cockscomb in shape and colour; the part at the top is hard and nervous, and swells like a Yard in Venery, with much fruit. This part sometimes is as big as a mans Yard, and such women were thought to be turned into men.
>
> It is from too much nourishment of the part, from the looseness of it by often handling.
>
> It is not safe to cut it off presently: but fi[r]st use Driers and Discussers [?], with things that are little a stringe; then gentle Causticks without causing pain, as burat, Allum, Aegyptiacum.
>
> Take Aegyptiacum, Oyl of Mastick, Roses, wax, each half an ounce. If these will not do, then cut it off, or tie it with Ligature of Silk or Horse-hair, till it mortifie.
>
> Aetitus teacheth the way of Amputation he calls it the Nympha or Clitoris, between both the Wings: but take heed you cause not pain or inflammation. . . .
>
> Some Excrescenses grow like a tail, and fill the Privities: they differ from a Clitoris: for the

desire of Venery is encreased in that, and the rubbing of the Cloaths upon it, causes lust: but in an Excrescence of flesh, they cannot for pain endure Copulation, but you may cut off this better than a Clitoris, because it is all superfluous." (3–4)

48. Laquer argues that clitorectomy was neither advocated nor practiced in England until the eighteenth century. This view is contradicted at the level of advice, if not at the level of surgical practice, by Paré, Bartholin, and Culpeper; yet Culpeper's advice in particular suggests some knowledge based on actual practice. Whereas genital amputation in this Western context is not identical to culturally sanctioned ritual circumcision, it does effect some of the same ends: it forcefully imposes, and thereby affirms, cultural sameness, constancy, and homogeneity.

49. See Park for a discussion of classical and medieval anatomies. In addition, both Fallopia's 1562 edition and Laurentius's 1595 edition (both in Latin, both available in England) briefly mention "tribades." But, as Hariette Andreadis notes, seventeenth-century anatomies "tend to devote more space to their descriptions in order to add judgmental commentary." That representations of figures from Greek and Roman culture and mythology become important indices to changing cultural attitudes toward same-gender desire is clear in Adreadis's work on Sappho and Patricia Simon's work on the Italian Renaissance. It is the subject of my forthcoming essay, "'Let Us Kiss and Kiss Again (and Again)': Chaste Femme Love and the Perversion of 'Lesbian' Desire."

50. I would like to thank David Halpernin for helping me to see that the "tribade" is not so much invented or discovered in this period as refashioned according to modern cultural exigencies.

51. It would seem this discursive amplification was not isolated to anatomy. Poetry and drama began to speak in a more bifurcated rhetoric, as erotic expressions of "romantic friendship" seemed to require new protections from the charges of immorality that accompanied rumors about women at court. See, for instance, Antonia Fraser's discussion of Hortense Mancini, Duchesse de Mazarin, one of Charles II's mistresses.

52. Historicizing the production of anatomical essentialism provides a means of challenging modern regimes of identity formation that demand that people choose one of only two erotic "orientations" or seek to find the origin of such choices in biology. Indeed, the historical development of anatomical essentialism to render intelligible the "tribade's" behavior provides a perspective from which to view the current debate over genetic origins of homosexuality. That such debates do have a history seems to me to help dispel utopian visions of redemption through biology (whether expressed in a belief that an appeal to genetics will herald an end to homophobia or an end to homosexuals). Rather than authorizing modern quests for a "gay gene," early modern anatomies provide a cautionary tale: insofar as the "cure" of clitoral hypertrophy was genital mutilation, and the punishment for "tribadism" (at least in some countries) was burning at the stake, the discourse of anatomy sounds from the distance of centuries a warning about liberatory promises of biology.

53. In this sense my analysis confirms in historical terms the theoretical argument of Judith Butler in "Imitation and Gender Insubordination" and "The Lesbian Phallus and the Morphological Imaginary" in *Bodies That Matter*.

54. This bias, which was given theoretical grounding by Foucault, is less often articulated explicitly than assumed at the level of critical practice, where the vast majority of work on same-gender erotic desire concerns representations after 1850.

55. For sophisticated readings of this problem, see Jonathan Goldberg's introduction and Margaret Hunt's afterword to *Queering the Renaissance*. In addition, as Hunt points out, the definition of the "subject" itself has hardly been available to women on the same terms it was available to men.

56. The claims to such knowledge have been problematized searchingly by Eve Kosofsky Sedgwick in *Epistemology of the Closet* (see especially Axiom 5) and Judith Butler in "Imitation and Gender Insubordination" and *Bodies That Matter*. Judith Roof's study of representations of 'lesbians' in modern culture attempts to balance the problematics of identity and desire against the desire for identity, but she seems to retreat from her own insights when she asserts, "Even if I don't know precisely what lesbian is, I look for the lesbian in the text" (120). Her later essay, "Lesbians and Lyotard: Legitimation and the Politics of the Name," is more adamant in relinquishing "lesbian" as an identity, linking as it does the desire for such an identity with the desire for legitimation. For further reflections on the problematics of modern "lesbian" identity, see the essays anthologized in Doan, and my essay, "The Ambiguities of 'Lesbian' Viewing pleasure."

57. The need to reassert the pleasures of the vagina and penetration is made by Jane Gallop in *Thinking through the Body*. For analyses of the "lesbian" use of dildoes, see Lamos and Griggers.

58. Diana Fuss's reassessment of essentialism as a strategy that one risks in order to advance certain political claims as well as her analysis of the mutually implicated dynamic between essentialism and anti-essentialism are particularly helpful in reading Irigaray.

59. The problem with these bodily metonymies is the synecdochial presumption that a part can stand for a whole, and that there is in fact a whole to be represented. I do not mean to imply that bodily metonymy invariably is colonialist. As a local, strategic, performative strategy, metonymy may be as good a trope as any: one continually is in the process of narrativizing one's own body, and the more rhetorical figures at one's disposal the better. However, the particular metonymies at issue here have functioned hegemonically as a master narrative that occludes not only its own construction but the (anatomical) emergence of the body it purports to represent. Interestingly, Fuss praises Irigary's logic of metonymy because it displaces conventional linguistic hierarchies. While I agree that metonymy might, at certain historical moments, have some advantages over metaphor, it is not clear to me that this has been the case historically with the "lesbian" body.

60. My thinking about legitimization as a metanarrative has been enhanced by Judith Roof's "Lesbians and Lyotard."

61. The most helpful deconstructions of Freud's reading of the "lesbian" body are provided by Irigaray, Butler, and Roof.

References

Africanus, Leo. *The History and Description of Africa and of the Things Therein Contained.* Trans. John Pory. London, 1600. Ed. Robert Brown. Vol. 2. London: Hakluyt Society, 1896. 2 vols.

Andreadis, Harriete. "Sapphy in early Modern England." Lecture: "Attending to Women in Early Modern Culture." Baltimore, April 1994.

Aristoteles Master-Piece: or, The Secrets of Generation Displayed in All the Parts Thereof. London, 1684.

Aristoteles Experienced Midwife. London. c. 1700.

Bartholin, Casper. *Bartholini Anatomicae institutionis corporis humani.* Oxford, 1633.

Bartholin, Thomas. *The Anatomical History of Thomas Bartholin.* London, 1653.

Bennett, Paula. "Critical Clitoridectomy: Female Sexual Imagery and Feminist Psychoanalytic Theory." *Signs* 18 (1993): 235–259.

Butler, Judith. *Bodies That Matter: On the Discursive Limits of "Sex."* New York: Routledge, 1993.

———. "Imitation and Gender Insubordination." *Inside/Out: Lesbian Theories, Gay Theories.* Ed. Diana Fuss. New York: Routledge, 1991. 13–31.

Campbell, Mary. *The Witness and the Other World: Exotic European Travel Writing, 400–1600.* Ithaca: Cornell UP, 1988.

Castle, Terry. *The Apparational Lesbian: Female Homosexuality and Modern Culture.* New York: Columbia UP, 1993.

Chauncy, George. "From Sexual Inversion to Homosexuality: Medicine and the Changing Conceptualization of Female Deviance." Salmagundi 58/59 (1982/1983): 114–46.

Columbo, Realdo. *De re anatomica.* Venice, 1559.

Crooke, Helkiah. *Microcosmographia: A Description of the Body of Man.* London, 1615.

Culpeper, Nicholas. *The Complete Midwives Practice Enlarged* (aka *Culpeper's Midwife Enlarged*). 4th ed. London, 1684.

———. *A Directory of Midwives and The Fourth Book of Practical Physcik: Of Women's Diseases.* London, 1684.

de Busbecq, Ogier Ghiselin. *The Life and Letters of Ogier Ghiselin de Busbecq.* Ed. Charles Foster and F.H. Daniell. London: Kegan Paul, 1881.

de Nicholay, Nicholas. *The Navigations, Peregrinations, and Voyages, Made Into Turkey.* . . . 1585. Trans T. Washington. Rpt. *A Collection of Voyages and Travels* . . . Ed. Thomas Osborne. London: 1745.

Doan, Laura, ed. *The Lesbian Postmodern.* New York: Columbia UP, 1994.

Dubrow, Heather. "Naval Battles: Interpreting Renaissance Gynecological Manuals." Forthcoming.

Eccles, Audrey. *Obstretrics and Gynecology in Tudor and Stuary England.* Kent OH: Kent State UP, 1982.

Engel, William. *Mapping Mortality: The Persistence of Memory and Melancholy in Early Modern England.* Amherst: U of Massachusettes P, forthcoming.

Estienne, Henri Stephen. *A World of Wonders: Or, An Introduction to a Treatise . . . to a Apologie of Herodotus.* Ed. C.R. London, 1607.

Falloppoa, Gabriele. *Observations anatomicae.* Venice: Marco Antonio Olmo, 1561.

Foucault, Michel. *The History of Sexuality.* Vol. 1. Trans. Robert Hurley. New York: Random House, 1978–86. 3 vols.

Fraser, Antonia. *Royal Charles: Charles II and the Restoration.* New York: Knopf, 1979.

Freud, Sigmund. "Female Sexuality." 1931. *Sexuality and the Psychology of Love.* Ed. Phillip Rieff. New York: Macmillan, 1963. 194–211.

———. "Femininity." 1932. *New Introductory Lectures on Psychoanalysis.* Ed. and trans. James Strachey. New York: Norton, 1965. 99–119.

Friedman, John Block. *The Monstrous Races in Medieval Art and Thought.* Cambridge, MA: Harvard UP, 1981.

Fuss, Diana. *Essentially Speaking: Feminism, Nature and Difference.* New York: Rutledge, 1989.

Gallop, Jane. *Thinking Through the Body.* New York: Columbia UP, 1988.

Glover, Thomas. *The Muftie, Cadileschiers, Divans: Manners and Attire of the Turkes: The Sultan Described, and His Customes and Court. Purchase His Pilgrimes.* Ed. Samuel Purchase. Vol. 2. London, 1625. 2 vols.

Goldberg, Jonathan, ed. *Queering the Renaissance.* Durham: Duke UP, 1994.

———. Sodometries: Renaissance Texts, Modern Sexualities. Standford UP, 1992.

Greenblatt, Stephen. *Marvelous Possesions: The Wonder of the New World.* Chicago: U of Chicage P, 1991.

———. "Fiction and Friction," *Shakespearean Negotiationas: The Circulaion of Social Energy in Renaissance England.* Oxford: Claredon, 1988. 66–93.

Griggers, Cathy. "Lesbian Bodies in the Age of (Post) Mechanical Reproduction." Doan, 118–33.

Hall, Kim. *Acknowledging Things of Darkness: Economies of Race and Gender in Early Modern England.* Ithaca: Cornell UP, 1995.

Halperin, David M. "Homosexuality." Oxford Classical Dictionary. 3rd ed. Oxford: Oxford UP, forthcoming.

Hodgen, Margaret. *Early Anthropology in the Sixteenth and Seventeenth Centuries.* Philadelphia: U of Pennsylvania P, 1964.

Hulme, Peter. *Colonial Encounters: Europe and the Native Caribbean, 1492–1797.* London: Methuen, 1986.

Hunt, Margaret. "Afterword." *Queering the Renaissance.* Ed. Jonathan Goldberg. Durham: Duke UP, 1994. 359–74.

Irigaray, Luce. *Speculum of the Other Woman.* Trans. Gillian Gill. Ithaca: Cornell UP, 1985.

———. *This Sex Which Is Not One.* Trans. Catherine Porter. Ithaca: Cornell UP, 1985.

Johnson, Th. *The Workes of That Famous Chiurgion: Ambrose Parey, Translated out of Latine and Compared with the French.* London, 1634.

Keller, Eve. "Mrs. Jane Sharp: Midwifery and the Critique of Medical Knowledge in Seventeenth-Century England." *Women's Writing.* Forthcoming.

Koedt, Anne. "The Myth of the Vaginal orgasm." Radical Feminism. Ed. Anne Koedt, Ellen Levine, and Anita Rapone. New York: Quadrangle, 1973. 198–207.

Lamos, Colleen. "The Postmodern Lesbian Position: On Our Backs." Doan, 85–103.

Laquer, Thomas. *Making Sex: Body and Gender from the Greeks to Freud.* Cambridge: Harvard UP, 1990.

———. "Amor Veneris, vel Dulcedo Appeletur." *Fragments for a History of the Human Body.* Ed. Michael Feher. Vol. 1. New York: Urzone, 1989. 90–131. 3 vols.

Laurentius, Andreas. *Historia anatomica humani corporis et singularum eius parium multis.* Paris, 1595.

Mason-Huhl, Elizabeth. *The Diseases of Women.* Los Angeles: Ward Ritchie, 1940.

Montrose, Louis. "The Work of Gender in the Discourse of Discovery." *Representations* 33 (1991): 1–41.

Pagden, Anthony. *European Encounters with the New World: From Renaissance to Romanticism.* New Haven: Yale UP, 1993.

Paré, Ambroise. *Des Montres et prodiges.* 1573. Trans. Jean Ceard. Geneva: Droz. 1971.

Park, Katherine. "Hermaphrodites and Lesbains: Sexual Anxiety and French Medicine, 1570–1620." Unpublished essay.

Park, Katherine, and Robert A. Nye. "Destiny Is Anatomy." Rev. of *Making Sex: Body and Gender from the Greeks to Freud,* by Thomas Laqueur. New Republic 18 Feb. 1991: 53–7.

Parker, Patricia. "Fantasies of 'Race' and 'Gender": Africa, *Othello,* and Bringing to Light." *Women, "Race" and Writing in the Early Modern Period.* Ed. Margo Hendricks and Patricia Parker. London: Routledge, 1994. 84–100.

Paster, Gail Kern. *The Body Embarrassed: Drama and the Disciplines of Shame in Early Modern England.* Ithaca: Cornell UP, 1993.

Roof, Judith. "Lesbians and Lyotard: Legitimation and the Politics of the Name." Doan 47–66.

———. *A Lure of Knowledge: Lesbian Sexuality and Theory.* New York: Columbia UP, 1991.

Rowland, Beryl. *Medieval Woman's Guide to Health: The First English Gynaecological Handbook.* Kent, OH: Kent State UP, 1981.

Sedgwick, Eve Kosofsky. *Epistemology of the Closet.* Berkeley: U of California P, 1990.

Sharp, Jane. *The Midwives Book.* London, 1671. New York: Garland, 1985.

Simons, Patricia. "Lesbian (In)Visibility in Italian Renaissance Culture: Diana and Other Cases of Donna con Donna." *Journal of Homosexuality*, forthcoming.

Stafford, Barbara Maria. *Body Criticism: Imaging the Unseen in Enlightenment Art and Medicine.* Cambridge: MIT P, 1991.

Temkin, Owesei. *Gynecology.* Baltimore: Johns Hopkins UP, 1956.

Traub, Valerie. "The (In)Significance of 'Lesbian' Desire in Early Modern England." *Erotic Politics: Desire on the Renaissance Stage.* Ed. Susan Zimmerman. New York: Routledge, 1992. 150–69.

———. *Desire and Anxiety: Circulations of Sexuality in Shakespearean Drama.* New York: Routledge, 1992.

———. "The Ambiguities of 'Lesbian' Viewing Pleasure: The (Dis)articulations of *Black Widow*." *Body Guards.* Ed. Julia Epstein and Kristina Straub. New York: Routledge, 1991. 305–28.

Venette, Nicholas. *Conjugal Love: Or, The Pleasures of the Marriage Bed.* New York: Garland, 1984.

Vesalius, Andreas. *De humani corporis fabrica.* Basel, 1564.

Withers, Robert. *The Grand Signiors Serraglio. Purchase His Pilgrimes.* Ed. Samuel Purchase. Vol. 2. London, 1625. 2 vols.

6

Social Policy and Female Agency

These three articles provide important theoretical and methodological insights and strategies in conducting interdisciplinary social policy research. In addition to alerting us to the tensions that may arise in balancing the use of quantitative and qualitative data in making an effective argument for social change, these authors examine the potential abuse of social science data when it is used to support ideological biases and to justify social control within the social policy arena. They urge us to consider the wider sociopolitical context within which research is conducted and the need to maintain the strategic use of some essentialist categories to promote social change. Roberta Spalter-Roth and Heidi Hartmann's article, "Small Happinesses: The Feminist Struggle to Integrate Social Research with Social Activism," argues for a " dualistic approach" to the study of social welfare policy which combines quantitative and qualitative research designs as a strategy to advance social policy and promote social change. They suggest that while it is vital for research to be grounded in women's " lived experience," social scientists should not dismiss the usefulness of quantitative " positivist " data. They argue their case by using their own "positivist research on work and welfare " to promote new policy initiatives for women. For example, they cite the need to provide "credible evidence" to show how current welfare policy hurts the efforts of single mothers to take charge of their lives. By taking on the role of " scientific expert" they utilize positivist methods to "gain credibility" within the policy sphere where their research was taken up by mainstream media as "hard facts." At the same time, they note the tensions that arise in integrating this dual perspective. The conflicts these researchers felt between their commitment to the open circulation of academic data and activists' insistence on a more politically strategic use of information dramatize the necessity to keep dialogue open and to work toward effective coalitions between feminists working for similar goals inside and outside the academy.

Cindy Patton's article, "From Nation to Family: Containing African AIDS," demonstrates how social policy is often embedded in dominant discourse and is used as a mechanism of social control by the elite. She traces the psychological fears (in the heterosexual West) that motivate biased assumptions about race, class, and sexuality both in dominant state policy and in " scientific" theory and practice. She examines how AIDS policy in developing nations of Africa grew out of the legacy of the colonial construction of an "idealized" nuclear family. Holding up the traditional Western family model as a symbol of progress and a structure they sought to impose on African societies, early colonizers were able to undermine traditional African family structure, to control the African economy, and to justify discrimination against Africans. The depiction of the traditional colonial family is now used by the state to control the perception of who gets AIDS and how the disease is perceived. This representation of African AIDS derives from the interests of a Western heterosexual viewpoint of those eager to define Western AIDS as homosexual and heterosexual AIDS as foreign and distant. This in turn shapes the policy imposed on Africans as well as the solutions and aid offered to ameliorate the AIDS crisis. Using an elaborate set of quantitative data and maps social scientists and the media depict African AIDS as epidemiologically" out of control." Patton notes that political and social control of the population is displaced onto the issue of Africans' sexuality: ". . . alternately described as traditional (polygamy) or condemned as modern (rural-urban social breakdown resulting in 'prostitution')." One suggested solution to the epidemic, which itself is questioned by Patton, requires rapid imposition of the colonial view of the "traditional family" as a check to the rampant growth of AIDS. Patton notes that there is a nostalgia for a return to "a less urban Africa in which 'traditional family values' once prevailed." She notes that the logical outcome of this ideological bias among policy makers is that those who "cannot be contained within this family will be simply left to die." What is lacking in the discussion of AIDS policy is a strategy for social advocacy that would place Africans at the center of the analysis and formulate research issues from their viewpoint. Instead, by relying only on positivist social science data—the demographic statistics on AIDS, and maps of AIDS-infected areas—those in power are able to impose from the outside a definition of the AIDS "problem" as evidence of internal moral weakness in African society. While Spalter-Roth and Hartmann see a place for quantitative data in social policy analysis as a means to gain credibility in the social policy arena, Patton cautions us against the use of these data and their potential for enforcing Western dominance.

In the 1950s and 1960s the field of "development theory" emerged from researchers concerned about the lack of economic progress of "Third World" nations and the problems of poverty affecting native populations. Based on Western notions of progress, "development" required that less industrialized countries should advance toward a Western model of modernity, focusing on social policies and programs introducing Western technology and capital. Development theories and policies left out the crucial contribution that women's nonmarket work made to the economic stability and potential growth of "third world" nations. It was not until Ester Boserup's far-reaching analysis in *Woman's Role in Economic Development* (1970) that policy initiatives rendering women invisible in development policy began to be challenged. While there is now a broad range of research on the impact of development planning on women's lives, the gender gap in knowledge and training widens as development policies continue to promote and preserve the interests of men. Chandra Talpade Mohanty's essay, "Women Workers and Capitalist Scripts: Ideologies of Domination, Common Interests, and the Politics of Solidarity," concerns the plight of third-world women within an increasingly global economic arena where developing countries become sources of inexpensive labor and raw materials for technologically advanced industrialized nations. Mohanty is concerned with " the limits as well as the possibilities of constructing feminist solidarities across national, racial, sexual and class divides." She argues for the "strategic use" of essentialism among third-world women by urging them to organize around their shared material interests and identity as "workers." Drawing on three case studies of the incorporation of third-world women into the global division of labor, she analyzes how ideologies of domesticity, femininity, and race are deployed by global capitalism in the construction of a "domesticated woman worker." She calls for a reconceptualization of third-world women as agents rather than victims and argues for political solidarity among women workers whose shared material conditions might be a "potentially revolutionary basis for struggles against capitalist recolonization."

References
Ester Boserup (l970). *Woman's Role in Economic Development.* New York: St. Martin's Press.

CHAPTER FIFTEEN

Small Happinesses

The Feminist Struggle to Integrate Social Research with Social Activism

ROBERTA SPALTER-ROTH AND HEIDI HARTMANN

T he struggle to balance social science inquiry with social activism has been central in the lives of two generations of women. The first generation of researcher/activists was also the first group of women to be trained as social scientists in the new research universities of the late nineteenth-century United States. During this period, academic social science was in the process of becoming specialized and professionalized but was still oriented toward the illumination and solution of social problems (Fitzpatrick 1990). As part of the first wave of the feminist movement, these women were confident that the positivist method of social science inquiry and the voice of the social science expert could be employed in the service of progressive reform. A second generation of women, schooled in both the social sciences and the social movements of the 1960s and 1970s, became researcher/activists during the second wave of the feminist movement. Like the first generation, these women also use academic social science to raise public consciousness, advance public recognition of social problems, mobilize political support to change public agendas, and encourage structural reform. But unlike the first generation, who was committed to scientific objectivity as the basis of social reform, the second generation is more critical of the power relations embedded in the positivist method of the social sciences and is more ambivalent about its ability to bring about social reform.

In this chapter we first contrast the methodological views of these two generations of women. We then situate ourselves and our current research on work and welfare within what we have labeled "the dual vision of feminist policy research." This vision is an attempt to synthesize the views of the two generations—to create research that meets both the standards of positivist social science and feminist goals of doing research "for" rather than "on" women. Ideally, the research that results from this vision should provide reliable evidence while main-

Roberta Spalter-Roth and Heidi Hartmann, "Small Happinesses: The Feminist-Struggle to Integrate Social Research with Social Activism," in Heidi Gottfried, ed. *Feminism and Social Change* (Urbana: University of Illinois Press, 1996): 206–24. Reprinted by permission.

taining the agency of the research subject. It should combine the standpoint of both the expert and the activist, the insider and the outsider. Attempting to achieve this synthesis results in occasional moments of triumph, when we feel we have succeeded, fairly frequent questioning of ourselves and the chances for successfully attaining the political goals of the women's movement, and, most often, the daily small happinesses of doing our work.

The First Generation

Women such as Sophonisba Breckenridge, Edith Abbott, Katherine Bement Davis, and Frances Kellor, described in Mary Jo Deegan's *Jane Addams and the Men of the Chicago School, 1892–1918* (1988) and Ellen Fitzpatrick's *Endless Crusade: Women Social Scientists and Progressive Reform* (1990), undertook advanced study in sociology, political economy, and political science at the University of Chicago. The University of Chicago became a leader in forging links between the social science experts it trained and political and economic elites. The university did this in order to obtain the massive resources required to institutionalize disciplinary-based social sciences within the higher education system (Silva and Slaughter 1984). Despite the university's efforts to educate professional social science experts rather than radical reformers, some professors urged their students to "get out into the streets" and observe social realities, to organize social movements, and to use scholarship to advance both knowledge and reform (Fitzpatrick 1990).

Unlike their male colleagues who became academicians, the women trained at the University of Chicago were more likely to work for government and private organizations, where they developed surveys and statistical data in the service of social reform. Fitzpatrick portrays these women's efforts to advance the social sciences (with their special claims to expertise resting on adherence to scientific methods and values), while increasing the public's recognition of the structural nature of social problems and promoting the creation of a social welfare state. Fitzpatrick describes them: "Enamored of scientific fact, [they] mounted social investigations at every turn, convinced that knowledge itself was the key to intelligent reform. Research often served as an engine for reform—powering legislative change and political alliances, drawing in philanthropists, and justifying more sweeping intervention by the state" (1990:xiii). For example, Frances Kellor was so enamored of the scientific methods of the day that she used the hotly contested scientific apparatus of the eugenics movement in her study of women prisoners. She set up experimental laboratories equipped with an instrument called a kymograph to take cranial measurements of women prisoners. Although she engaged in some of the more repellent aspects of social science methodology, she was among the first to view women's imprisonment as a social problem rather than a result of moral weakness.

Some of these women were attached to Hull-House, the Chicago settlement house that served as the center for a massive network of women reformers. Deegan (1988) describes them as a "community of women researchers and reformers" who lived together, did survey research together, and formed organizations and movements for social change together. Deegan labels these women "critical pragmatists" because they developed a theory of science that linked the gathering of empirical data with social action in order to advocate for public policy within a framework of progressive social values.

During the heady days of the progressive movement, these women used the surveys they conducted and the statistics they compiled to build considerable careers, to develop organizations and coalitions, to educate the public, and to develop laws, bureaus, and commissions around a series of progressive causes, such as the alleviation of poverty, unemployment, child labor, and dangerous working conditions. The reputation of these researcher/activists waned with the ebbing of the progressive movement, the coming of World War I, and, in Deegan's view, the maturation of masculinist, academic social sciences that were increasingly divorced from social action. Stripped of a supportive movement for social change and faced with decreased political support for progressive measures, some, such as Kellor, became increasingly probusiness in their orientation.

With the waning of their influence, the stories of these women were lost to generations of scholars, including those of a second feminist generation who attended graduate schools during the 1960s and 1970s. The members of this new generation found themselves in academic departments largely bereft of women scholars, research on gender inequalities, and women's experiences. The prevailing explanations of social phenomena appeared largely directed to other scholars or to administrators and managers rather than to advocates of progressive change. The stories of the Progressive Era scholar/activists were rescued from social science oblivion by the members of the second wave of feminist scholar/activists, who were in search of their disciplinary foremothers.

The Second Generation

In contrast to their foremothers, who believed that the scientific method distinguished their efforts from that of do-gooders and rabblerousers (with whom they often worked), the members of the second wave are much less at ease linking the positivist methodology of the social sciences and the detached standpoint of the social science expert with the goals of the women's movement. Like the members of the first wave, the members of the second wave of feminist researchers also have been involved in doing research to influence the formation and implementation of social policy. They have produced a body of policy-relevant research on topics such as comparable worth, spouse abuse, rape, divorce, displaced homemakers, family and medical leave, women's poverty, women's health, and employment discrimination. They, too, have formed or participated in organizations, written scholarly and popular articles, testified before Congress and state legislators, and attempted to gain a hearing for those who are usually voiceless in the policy process. In spite of, and in some cases because of, their experiences as researchers and activists (see, for example, Steinberg and Haignere 1991), the members of the second wave, unlike the first generation, are more critical of the relationship between quantitative data and women's lived experiences, between the researcher and the subject of the research, and between the scientific expert and the political activist.

Unlike the first generation of researcher/activists, the members of the second generation conceive of science as a social construct, its inquiries and methods shaped by relations of power, specific historical contexts, dominant ideologies, and the standpoint of the scientist (Keller 1984; Harding 1986; Kitzinger 1987; Collins 1991). In her review of feminist research practices, Shulamit Reinharz (1992) suggests that the response of feminist researchers to survey and other statistically based forms of research is particularly characterized by "a profound ambivalence." The debate is frequently argued in terms of quantitative versus qualitative research methods, with proponents of the former claiming that appropriate quantitative evidence can be used to put issues on the map, counter sexist (and racist) research, which continues to be generated in the social sciences, and identify differences among women and change over time (Jayaratne 1983; Reinharz 1992). In contrast, those who distrust quantitative methods criticize the failure of the questions, concepts, and categories used to reflect women's experiences (Collins 1991; Stanley and Wise 1991; Westkott 1990; Oakley 1981). They criticize the preoccupation with "hard facts" that break the "living connections" between the data and flesh and blood reality (Mies 1991), and they criticize the hierarchical relations between interviewer and respondent that permeate survey research (Oakley 1981).

Equally distasteful to second-generation feminist researcher/activists is the standpoint of the neutral social science observer/ expert, rooted in the positivist understanding of the relation between science and politics in which science is perceived as free of power and politics (Mies 1991). Rather than take the stance of the objective expert and engage in what Mies (1991) labels as "spectator knowledge," feminist researcher/activists feel bound to contribute to women's liberation by producing research that can be used by women themselves (Acker, Barry, and Esseveld 1991) and that "speaks out" against injustice rather than speaking for others (Klein 1983).

Both generations of researcher/activists can be described as passionate scholars, although the former distinguished between disinterested science and passionate politics (but did both), while the later generation criticizes the methodologies that emphasize their separation.

Our Story

The stories of these two generations are of particular interest to us as research director and director, respectively, of the Institute for Women's Policy Research (IWPR), a Washington, D.C., feminist think tank. IWPR was founded to meet the need for womencentered, policy-oriented research with a special concern for the complexity of policy needs of women as they vary by race, ethnicity, and class. Like the first generation of researcher/activists, we use statistical analyses of quantitative data, often written in the language of the neutral social scientist, in order to raise consciousness, redefine agendas, and promote progressive change in women's interests. Like both generations, we are schooled in both mainstream so-cial science and oppositional social movements and are committed to linking re-search with social movements for women's liberation. Like our second-genera-tion cohorts, we are more self-conscious about the role of the scientific method in privileging the word of the researcher rather than the researched and distancing the expert from the activist and more realistic about the limitations of feminist so-cial science to bring about progressive reform that undermines the capitalist-patriarchal system.

The research we produce reflects an attempt to synthesize the scientific and the political, the neutral and the oppositional. We refer to this methodological synthesis as the "dual vision of feminist policy research" (see Spalter-Roth and Hartmann 1991). We want our research to give credibility to the claims made by groups attempting to use the policy process to improve women's lives. The dual vision results from our efforts to conduct policy research that simultaneously puts women's claims at the center and meets the standards of mainstream social sci-ence research. Our research reflects both dominant methodological and critical oppositional views because we employ mainstream social science techniques but filter these techniques through a feminist prism that critically examines how these techniques are likely to reproduce and legitimate relations of domination and in-equality within genders, races, and classes.

Reinharz (1992) credits the dual vision of feminist policy research with pro-viding a "feminist way of seeing," a critical feminist perspective, and a positive way of resolving the ambivalence of feminists toward the practices and arrange-ments of survey and other statistically based research. Although Reinharz (1992) cites our attempts to deal with feminist ambivalence through the dual vision as a solution, we view *developing* a dual vision as an ongoing struggle to be faced in each study we do. In what follows we analyze how we applied the dual vision in one IWPR research project, *Combining Work and Welfare: An Alternative Anti-Poverty Strategy* (Spalter-Roth, Hartmann, and Andrews 1992). We emphasize our efforts to provide statistically valid social science evidence while maintaining the agency of research subjects and our efforts to maintain our credibility with both mainstream experts and feminist activists in order to contribute to redefining the welfare policy agenda from a feminist perspective.

Combining Work and Welfare: An Example of the Dual Vision of Feminist Policy Research

Combining Work and Welfare grew out of our concern with the furor to get single mothers "off the welfare rolls and into the workplace." During the reactionary eighties, under the Reagan and Bush administrations, Aid to Families with De-pendent Children (AFDC) was increasingly portrayed by policymakers and the media as a program that "allowed women to live without a husband or a job" (Amott 1990) and as a program that perpetuated the American underclass and re-inforced its "dependence on government handouts" (U.S. Library of Congress 1987). The rhetoric of dependency was used to promote a political and ideological consensus in which conservatives and liberals aligned to pass the Family Support Act (FSA) of 1988, legislation that strives to transfer responsibility for the support of poor minority children from the state (via AFDC) to the market (by requiring "able-bodied" mothers to find paid employment or to participate in the JOBS program) and to biological fathers (via increased child support enforcement).[1] The FSA assumed that women who participated in the AFDC program did not work at paid employment and that work and welfare are mutually exclusive alternatives for poor women. In previous research (IWPR 1989), we found that a substantial portion of single mothers employed in low-wage work participated in means-tested government programs (such as AFDC and food stamps) as a supplement to their wages.

Based on our previous research, and in the face of the increasingly vitriolic attacks on AFDC participants, we sought to conduct and disseminate additional research that would destigmatize these women, recast their use of welfare and their participation in work as successful survival strategies, and reshape the policy debate. John Lanigan, then of the Ford Foundation's Urban Poverty Program, funded a new IWPR study. This new study proposed to examine the survival strategies, including employment activities, participation in government programs, income sources, and poverty rates of a nationally representative sample of women who participated in the AFDC program for at least two months during a two-year period. The principal research questions to be answered were How do women participating in AFDC put together their families' income package? What portion obtain enough money to move their families out of poverty? and What factors increase their ability to combine paid employment and participation in AFDC and to use these income packages to move their families out of poverty?

The study is based on data from a nationally representative, longitudinal sample of 585 single mothers, drawn from the 1986 and 1987 panels of the U.S. Bureau of the Census Survey of Income and Program Participation (SIPP), a data set that provides detailed information on family composition, employment, participation in government programs, and income.[2]

The findings that resulted from the first phase of this study challenge the consensus that welfare perpetuates dependence and that paid employment is the ticket out of poverty for single mothers and their children. We found that approximately four out of ten women who participated in the AFDC program worked for a substantial number of hours over a two-year period (approximately 1,000 hours per year—about half-time employment, the average amount worked by mothers with young children). They either combined paid employment and AFDC participation simultaneously or cycled between them. These women, referred to as income packagers, *increased* their family income and *decreased* their burden on the taxpayer by combining work and welfare. Despite their substantial work effort, their average family income remained below the poverty threshold (at about 95 percent of the poverty threshold for families of their size). Their average hourly wages only slightly exceeded the minimum wage, despite the fact that they had an average of six years of work experience.

Those recipients we labeled as "more welfare reliant," because their income package was composed of an average of twenty-three out of twenty-four months of AFDC benefits and almost no paid employment, were more likely to be disabled, had slightly more children (2.2 as opposed to 1.8, on the average), and were less likely to be high school graduates. Despite stereotypes of a Black, never-married underclass, we found no significant differences between the "more reliant" and the "income packagers" in terms of their race or ethnicity and their previous marital history. Despite income supplements from other family members and miscellaneous sources, these women's families were the poorest.

We also found that high state-level unemployment rates have a negative effect on the probability of work/welfare packaging. For every one percentage point increase in state unemployment rates, the likelihood of including paid employment in the income packages declines by 9 percent. These findings indicate the importance of examining the economic context in which AFDC participants develop their survival strategies.

Based on these findings, we concluded that the current system of regulations does not enable AFDC participants who are doing paid work to move their families out of poverty. We recommended that the combining of work and welfare, along with income from other sources, be made legitimate because, at current levels, neither earnings nor means-tested benefits alone can provide a minimally sufficient income for single mothers and their families. We suggested additional policies that "make work pay," such as encouraging unionization, strengthening collective bargaining, increasing the minimum wage, and increasing available jobs through a full employment program. Finally, we concluded that not all single mothers can be expected to participate in paid employment. In particular, AFDC participants with an above average number of children, little work experience and education, disabling conditions, limited access to other income sources, and living in areas with high unemployment rates are less likely to be able to do so. Higher benefit levels are a necessary poverty-reduction strategy for these women.

Evidence and Agency

Combining Work and Welfare, like the majority of IWPR studies, is based on the manipulation and analysis of nationally representative sample survey data usually collected by government bureaus. We use survey and statistically based research methods to provide the numbers that document the conditions of women as they vary by race, ethnicity, and class and to analyze whether public policies maintain, increase, or decrease these inequalities. Because we use secondary data analysis, we can be accused of engaging in the power relations found in the social arrangements of most mainstream research studies. We, not the respondents, choose the problem, design the study, analyze the data, and write up the results. We meet the subjects of our research in the most alienated and anonymous fashion, after they have been stripped of their names (to protect their anonymity), their own words, their own definitions of the situation, and after the connections between their responses to the survey questions and the "flesh and blood" reality of their daily lives have been severed.

Nevertheless, we believe the methodology we used in *Combining Work and*

Welfare is appropriate for the goals of the dual vision. We used a large-scale data set to support claims about the representativeness of our findings.

We attempted to put these women at the center of our analysis. We portrayed them as active subjects engaged in survival strategies, albeit under structural and ideological conditions not of their choosing. To counterbalance the stripping process, we created "narrative diaries" from the data tape, allowing an individual woman's data record to tell her story. *Combining Work and Welfare* documents that women who participate in the AFDC program use welfare as a "cushion"— although an inadequate one—to support their families in the face of a low-wage, discriminatory job market. Rather than describing these women as passive victims, or as deviants enveloped in cultures of poverty or underclass behavior, we formulated measures of activities such as income packaging, combining work and welfare, and moving their families out of poverty.

Placing these women and their survival activities at the center of the analysis contrasts with the use by mainstream policy researchers of administrative counting units, such as the welfare "spell," and with the treatment of welfare recipients as subjects of experiments. In spell analysis the duration of the period of AFDC receipt is detached from the person receiving AFDC and the spell, not the person, becomes the unit of analysis. Spell analysis tends to focus on the numbers and length of spells, the reasons for entry and exit from spells, and the probability of spells lasting over time (see, for example, Bane and Ellwood 1994). Knowing how many spells occur in a given period, how long they are, and why they start or stop is useful for policy programming, planning, and budgeting purposes, but it is liable to displace women from the center of the analysis and to strip their behavior from its context and from its agency. Likewise, analysis of randomly assigned control group experiments, which compare the dollar amounts of AFDC receipt and earnings before and after a given treatment (usually participation in job training and other behavioral modification programs), can provide useful administrative data on program costs and benefits that can guide policy choices (see, for example, Gueron and Pauly 1991), but also generally treat AFDC recipients as objects of scrutiny rather than as subjects of their own lives.[3]

Like mainstream policy researchers, and like the first generation of feminist researcher/activists, our use of survey methods and statistical analysis in *Combining Work and Welfare* is an effort to provide reliable and generalizable evidence that can be used to inform public policy. In contrast to mainstream researchers, we are concerned with developing methodologies that reveal the agency of the women we study and the economic, ideological, and political context in which they make their lives. We believe this study reflects the critical standpoint of the dual vision of feminist policy research and combines the perspectives of first- and second-generation research/activists.

The use of secondary, anonymous data means, however, that we cannot directly ask the women whose lives we write about whether our perspective on their lives reflects their own. Nor can we directly organize them to bring about change in the conditions that negatively affect their lives. For our research to bring about progressive reform that liberates women we must not only seek to reform policy debate through research but must also work with social activists and policy advocates to ensure that the context in which the research is carried to the debate does benefit those who are its subjects.

Expert and Activist

We want our research to be used by policymakers, by both mainstream and feminist researchers, by activists, and by women affected by policies. To fulfill this goal of producing *feminist* policy-relevant research, we attempt to synthesize the standpoint of the objective scientific expert with that of the participant in the women's movement.

In the case of *Combining Work and Welfare,* the purpose of the research was twofold. First, we wanted to counter policy and public discourse that stigmatized AFDC recipients as lazy, irresponsible, and solely dependent on taxpayer monies. Second, we wanted to suggest alternative policies to overcome the structures and patterns of inequality that they face, especially their dire poverty and their degraded treatment. Toward these ends, we distributed these findings widely through sale and complimentary distribution of the report, fact sheets (in English and in Spanish), press briefings, media interviews, meetings with advocacy groups, and public presentations.

In our efforts to provide credible evidence to demonstrate that current welfare policy stigmatizes the survival efforts of single mothers, we take the stance of the scientific expert. We do so because, for feminist researchers, the quest to gain credibility is difficult. Simply by having the term *women* in the institute's name, our work can be written off as biased, bleeding heart, and not worthy of consideration. Much like the first generation of researcher/activists, we use our reliance on the "scientific method" to gain credibility for our work by rhetorically reinforcing the distinction between science and ideology and by placing our research on the side of science. We introduce *Combining Work and Welfare* by distinguishing between our own use of random samples, "hard information," and "studies of actual behaviors" with the "fresh furor to get single mothers off the welfare rolls" inspired by "politics and ideology" (Spalter-Roth, Hartmann, and Andrews 1992:iii).

Part of our self-characterization as scientists is a performance and a rhetorical strategy to gain credibility for our analysis in the face of attack. By taking this standpoint, our research is more likely to be cited in the press as "hard fact" rather than rejected as the "whining of advocacy groups" (to use the words of a *Washington Post* reporter). As objective policy researchers, we are invited to present the research findings in the form of congressional testimony, and we are more likely than advocates to be invited to meetings convened by mainstream policy research organizations and other areas where policy is formulated. We hope this constant exposure helps to reframe the policy debate.

Yet when we are "inside" among policymakers and mainstream policy researchers, we speak out on behalf of women's interests in undermining systemic domination. Speaking out leads to our marginalization. Moreover, because of the questions addressed and the methods used, our research itself speaks out on behalf of women. At a recent meeting of the Advisory Committee to phase 2 of the *Combining Work and Welfare* project, a group composed of policy experts, program administrators, advocates, and researchers who accepted our invitation to provide guidance on the continuation of our study, a member from the Department of Health and Human Services described our research as inductive and as being concerned with the ability of welfare recipients to move out of poverty rather than off the welfare rolls. These characteristics were seen as making our research unusual—even unique—and, we inferred, less likely to be easily ingested and used by policymakers and program administrators. The advisor urged us not to change our methods or goals but to make our theoretical model, and its assumptions and expectations, more explicit.[4]

Our advisor's analysis of our research questions and policy goals was correct. These questions and goals are less likely to grow out of the mainstream research literature or administrative concerns than they are to grow out of our interactions with policy-oriented and grass-roots women's groups and from our own internationalization of the aspirations of the women's liberation movement. We often develop our research questions with women's advocacy groups and our interpretations of our findings through presentations to and discussions with them. If our findings mirror what advocates know to be true of women's lives, we consider them likely to be true or valid.

We have followed this validating procedure with *Combining Work and Welfare,* presenting and discussing our findings with many advocates. In spite of this activity, we are sometimes perceived as outsiders by these groups. Most recently we have been participating in a pro-welfare, women's economic survival coalition including the National Organization for Women (NOW), the NOW Legal Defense and Education Fund, and welfare rights groups. Among the purposes of this coalition is to move the policy agenda, under a new administration, from blaming poor women and their children for the results of welfare policy to implementing an agenda for their economic survival. As participants of this coalition, we were warned against disseminating research findings on the income packages put together by AFDC recipients because this information could be used by the media to reinforce powerful stereotypes of welfare cheats. As it turned out, this warning was accurate: an article written by a *Washington Post* reporter that went out over its wire service was published in the Madison, Wisconsin, *Capital Times* under the headline "Welfare Moms Work on Sly." Despite our chagrin over this misrepresentation of our findings, we think that the thousands of fact sheets and reports we have distributed have had a positive effect in stressing that many "welfare mothers" are already working to improve the financial lot of their children. In any case, we are reluctant to accede to the demands of advocacy groups to suppress study findings, despite their potential misuse. As we have reported elsewhere (Spalter-Roth and Hartmann 1991), tensions such as these—resulting in sleepless nights, day-long negotiations, and occasional name calling—typically occur between researchers and advocates, since researchers generally wish to expose findings while, in our experience, advocates wish to do so only when they feel sure that the findings will have positive political outcomes.

Despite the tensions and the marginality that result from our efforts to maintain our dual standpoint as credible research experts and as participants in an active women's reform movement, we hope that, in the long run, this dual standpoint increases rather than decreases our influence in the policy process. In the short-run our findings on work and welfare are less likely to affect the policy process than those of well-funded, well-connected mainstream research organizations such as the Manpower Research Development Corporation (MDRC). As Stacey Oliker (1994) suggests, MDRC was able to become the primary technical expert on the issue of "welfare reform" by gaining legitimacy for the use of an experimental design methodology that randomly assigned welfare recipients to treatment groups, by demonstrating that existing welfare experiments were marginally successful at moving recipients off the welfare rolls, and by bombarding the media and Congress with its findings. In contrast, our welfare policy proposals, even when modest in scope, tend to be critical of what exists. Further, we lack the resources to invest in large-scale publicity and dissemination campaigns.

But, as Oliker (1994) also notes, even groups such as MDRC, while much more likely to be treated as technical experts than is IWPR, did not set the welfare reform policy agenda implemented in the FSA. Rather, MDRC's research was used to legitimate an already existing political consensus that welfare was perpetuating the underclass and that public policy needed to "encourage self-sufficiency" and "help the needy to emancipate themselves" while providing cost savings to states (at least in the long run) by reducing the welfare rolls. MDRC's research demonstrated that state programs could move toward this goal. It is less likely that MDRC's research would have been perceived as useful by policymakers at the time of the FSA consensus if it had concluded, as IWPR's did, that moving recipients off the welfare rolls was less important than helping them to move out of poverty. In the longer run, IWPR's research, designed to reframe the debate, may be just as influential.

Although policy debates are often carried out in a discourse permeated by references to data (Weiss 1990), as if evidence always swayed minds and changed opinions, it is organized movements (be they rightwing, moderate, or progressive) that set the stage for policy change. An activist women's movement that carries the findings of our research and supports policy changes consistent with those findings can encourage policymakers to listen, especially when this movement contributes to electing members of Congress and presidents. By working in coalitions with advocates, our numbers and our scientific stance can legitimate feminist perspectives, if not during the initial policy formulation stage, then during the second or third go-round as policymakers face the likely failure of current policies based on blaming the victim. Our research helps to mobilize both the top and the bottom toward progressive policy change. Without a connection to the oppositional standpoints of activist women's groups involved in policy reform, our work either would be even more marginalized, as was the research of the first generation of researcher/activists when the progressive movement declined in influence, or, in search of an audience, would become more administratively oriented.

Conclusions

The first generation of researcher/activists believed that the scientific method, carried out through survey and other statistically based research methods, would illuminate social problems and provide the basis for enlightened state reform. From our standpoint as secondwave feminist critics, this view appears disingenuous about the power relations embedded both in the arrangements of social science research and in the public policy-making process. Can the more ambivalent notion of the dual vision of feminist policy research help to speak out against injustice and contribute to women's liberation? Under the pressure of deadlines and fund-raising, we do not spend a great deal of time consciously thinking about this issue. Rather, it is more a taken-for-granted assumption in our daily work lives. As oldtime socialist-feminists, we believe that the capitalist patriarchal state, in general, defends the interests of those who control the means of production and reproduction. The result, in the case of welfare policy, is a system that stigmatizes single mothers, pressures them to take low-wage jobs, and treats them as social problems rather than as citizens and workers. But we also believe that strong countermovements and democratic coalitions among diverse groups of women (and men) can change state policy.

IWPR's research, such as *Combining Work and Welfare,* is not science for its own sake. Although we do not always have control over its use, we hope that it helps to heighten consciousness and to provide credible numbers that can help advocates to mobilize political support. Our research methodology, although it can perpetuate the distance between researchers and subjects, does place women at the center of the analysis, as subjects of their own lives rather than as subjects of experiments. Our dual standpoint as experts and advocates is a political strategy that calls for us to distance ourselves from "do-gooders" and "rabble rousers," as did first-generation research/activists, whenever this role seems strategically useful in the struggle for progressive change, and to work with advocates to formulate our research questions, validate our results, and disseminate our findings. The result can be uneasy relations with mainstream researchers, policymakers, funders, advocacy groups, and feminist activists. But, it can also result in exhilarating moments when we see the numbers that we have generated cited in newspaper articles or hear them spoken by members of Congress to support arguments for change. Between these occasional brief moments of triumph and the longer periods of questioning whether we are making a difference (when we feel marginalized by everyone—allies, opponents, and targets of influence alike), we persist day to day experiencing the small happinesses of doing work that we hope contributes to the liberation of women.

Notes

1. The AFDC program, implemented as part of the Social Security Act of 1935, was designed, in part, by the Progressive Era researcher/activists. Modeled on state-level and private mother's aid and mother's pension programs, it aimed to prevent the trans-

planting of children from their households to orphanages because their widowed mothers were too poor to support them. This program operated using a regulatory model with intensive casework—including the investigation and monitoring of the moral fitness of the mothers. AFDC is often given as an example of the social control aspects of the programs designed by Progressive Era reformers.

2. As with all Census Bureau surveys, the SIPP can be accused of having an androcentric bias because families are viewed as income-pooling units rather than the locus of struggle over the production and distribution of goods and services (Hartmann 1981) and definitions of employment do not include unpaid work. For an in-depth analysis of the androcentrism of U.S. Census Bureau surveys, see Anderson (1992).

3. While we believe it is possible to use these techniques in a woman-centered way, mainstream policy researchers generally do not. The questions they ask focus less on the structural conditions in which women try to put together their livelihoods and more on the outcomes of program interventions.

4. We were fascinated by the extent to which "theory-based," deductive models were clearly preferred—had higher status—in the committee discussion to experience-based, inductive models. Our study, which attempts to put what women actually do (combine work and welfare) at the center of the analysis was seen as experience-based or inductive. Especially in the field of economics, the latter approach is viewed as a "fishing" expedition. It is thought far superior to state one's expectations of how people will behave, based on theory, and then either confirm or fail to confirm one's expectations through empirical testing. With our usual ambivalence, we are currently considering whether we should restate our model so as to make our "expectations" clear. Stating one's theory-based expectation up front, common in much social science research, tends to place the objective, neutral researcher at the center of the analysis, rather than the experiences of subjects.

References

Acker, Joan, Kate Barry, and Joke Esseveld. 1991. "Objectivity and Truth: Problems in Doing Feminist Research. In *Beyond Methodology: Feminist Scholarship as Lived Research,* ed. Mary Margaret Fonow and Judith A. Cook. Bloomington: Indiana University Press. 133–53.

Amott, Teresa L. 1990. "Black Women and AFDC: Making Entitlement Out of Necessity." In *Women, the State, and Welfare,* ed. Linda Gordon. Madison: University of Wisconsin Press. 280–98.

Anderson, Margo. 1992. "The History of Women and the History of Statistics." *Journal of Women's History* 4 (I): 12–36.

Bane, Mary Jo, and David Ellwood. 1994. *Welfare Relations: From Rhetoric to Reform.* Cambridge: Harvard University Press.

Collins, Patricia Hill. 1991. "Learning from the Outsider Within." In *Beyond Methodology: Feminist Scholarship as Lived Research,* ed. Mary Margaret Fonow and Judith A. Cook Bloomington: Indiana University Press. 35–59.

Deegan, Mary Jo. 1988. *Jane Addams and the Men of the Chicago School, 1892–1918.* New Brunswick, N.J.: Transaction Books.

Fitzpatrick, Ellen. 1990. *Endless Crusade: Women Social Scientists and Progressive Reform.* New York: Oxford University Press.

Gueron, Judith, and Edward Pauly. 1991. *From Welfare to Work.* New York: Russell Sage Foundation.

Harding, Sandra. 1986. *The Science Question in Feminism.* Ithaca: Cornell University Press.

Hartmann, Heidi. 1981. "The Family as the Locus of Gender, Class, and Political Struggle: The Example of Housework." *Signs* 6 (3): 366–94.

Institute for Women's Policy Research. 1989. *Low-Wage Jobs and Workers: Trends and Options for Change.* Washington, D.C.: Institute for Women's Policy Research.

Jayaratne, Toby Epstein. 1983. "The Value of Quantitative Methodology for Feminist Research." In *Theories of Women's Studies,* ed. Gloria Bowles and Renate Duelli Klein. Boston: Routledge and Kegan Paul. 140–61.

Keller, Evelyn Fox. 1984. *Reflections on Gender and Science.* New Haven, Conn.: Yale University Press.

Kitzinger, Celia. 1987. *The Social Construction of Lesbianism.* Beverly Hills, Calif.: Sage.

Klein, Renate. 1983. "How to Do What We Want to Do: Thoughts about Feminist Methodology." In *Theories of Women's Studies,* ed. Gloria Bowles and Renate Duelli Klein. Boston: Routledge and Kegan Paul. 88–104.

Mies, Maria. 1991. "Women's Research or Feminist Research?: The Debate Surrounding Feminist Science and Methodology." In *Beyond Methodology: Feminist Scholarship as Lived Research,* ed. Mary Margaret Fonow and Judith A. Cook. Bloomington: Indiana University Press. 60–84.

Oakley, Anne. 1981. "Interviewing Women: A Contradiction in Terms." In *Doing Feminist Research,* ed. Helen Roberts. London: Routledge and Kegan Paul. 30–61.

Oliker, Stacey. 1994. "Does Workfare Work?: Evaluation Research and Workfare Policy." *Social Problems* 4 (2): 195–213.

Reinharz, Shulamit. 1992. *Feminist Methods in Social Research.* New York: Oxford University Press.

Silva, Edward, and Sheila Slaughter. 1984. *Serving Power: The Making of the Academic Social Science Expert.* Westport, Conn.: Greenwood Press.

Spalter-Roth, Roberta M., Heidi I. Hartmann, and Linda Andrews. 1992. *Combining Work and Welfare: An Alternative Anti-Poverty Strategy.* Washington, D.C.: Institute for Women's Policy Research.

Spalter-Roth, Robert M., and Heidi I. Hartmann. 1991. "Science and Politics and the 'Dual Vision' of Feminist Policy Research: The Example of Family and Medical Leave." In *Parental Leave and Child Care: Setting a Research and Policy Agenda,* ed. Janet Shibley Hyde and Marilyn J. Essex. Philadelphia: Temple University Press. 41–65.

Stacey, Judith. 1988. "Can There Be a Feminist Ethnography?" *Women's Studies International Forum* 11 (1): 21–27.

Stanley, Liz, and Sue Wise. 1991. "Feminist Research, Feminist Consciousness, and Experience of Sexism." In *Beyond Methodology: Feminist Scholarship as Lived Research,* ed. Mary Margaret Fonow and Judith A. Cook. Bloomington: Indiana University Press. 265–83.

Steinberg, Ronnie, and Lois Haignere. 1991. "Separate but Equivalent: Equal Pay for Work of Comparable Worth." In *Beyond Methodology: Feminist Scholarship as Lived Research,* ed. Mary Margaret Fonow and Judith A. Cook. Bloomington: Indiana University Press. 154–70.

U.S. Library of Congress. Congressional Research Service. 1987. "New Ideas on Welfare," *Albuquerque Journal,* Nov. 9, 1986, B2. In *Welfare Reform: National Consensus/National Debate Overviews [Newspaper Editorials and Public Opinion Polls.]* CRS Report no. 87-556-L, Saundra Shirley-Reynolds and Roger Walke. Washington, D.C.: Congressional Research Service.

Weiss, Carol H. 1990. "The Uneasy Partnership Endures: Social Science and Government." In *Social Scientists, Policy, and the State,* ed. Stephan Brooks and Alain-G. Gagnon. New York: Praeger. 97–111.

Westkott, Marcia. 1990. "Feminist Criticism of the Social Sciences." In *Feminist Research Methods: Exemplary Readings in the Social Sciences,* ed. Joyce McCarl Nielsen. Boulder: Westview Press. 58–68.

CHAPTER SIXTEEN

From Nation to Family

Containing African AIDS

CINDY PATTON

C urrent AIDS-control efforts have invented a heterosexual "African AIDS" that promotes a new kind of colonial domination by reconstructing Africa as an uncharted, supranational mass. Whatever the overt concerns of the international health workers for containing AIDS in (within?) the continent, their construal of "Africa" as the margin of economic/cultural "development" and as the "heart" of the AIDS epidemic helps to stabilize a Euro-America adrift in a postmodern condition of lost metanarratives and occluded origins. As a totalizing grand history of nations has given way to a transcendent account of chance intersections of germs and bodies, the map of the postcolonial world has now been redrawn as a graph of epidemiological strike rates. Because international AIDS policy has discouraged or overlooked serious attempts to prevent HIV transmission through health education, community organizing, and improved blood-banking, this new Africa- with-no-borders functions as a giant agar plate, etched by the "natural history" of the AIDS epidemic.[1]

The very labeling of "African AIDS" as a heterosexual disease quiets the Western fear that heterosexual men will need to alter their own sexual practices and identity. If the proximate (homosexual) AIDS allows such men to ignore their local complicity in "dangerous" practices that lead to the infection of ("their") women, then a distant "African AIDS," by correlating heterosexual danger with Otherness/thereness, performs the final expiative act for a Western heterosexual masculinity that refuses all containment. Erased in this process are the colonially inscribed borders of sub-Saharan countries, while new borders are drawn between the "African family" and a "modernizing society" populated by "single people" who have been dying at an appalling rate throughout the epidemic. The nation, once the colonial administrative unit *par excellence*, has been replaced in the minds of healthworkers with (an image of) the bourgeois family, thereby constituting

Cindy Patton, "From Nation to Family: Containing African AIDS," in Abelove, Barale, and Halperin, eds. *The Lesbian and Gay Studies Reader* (New York: Routledge, 1993): 127–38. Reprinted by permission.

what had never truly existed before in Africa as the only defense against modernization and its "diseases." In what follows, I explore some of the implications of this movement from nation to family as the preferred prophylaxis in the catastrophe of "African AIDS."

Mapping "African Aids"

Accompanying a *New York Times* article "AIDS in Africa: A Killer Rages On" (whose headline continues "AIDS Is Spreading Rapidly and Ominously Throughout Africa") is a nearly full-page chart, "AIDS in Africa An Atlas of Spreading Tragedy."[2] These headlines displace responsibility for the epidemic—who exactly is this killer? what is the tragedy?—and elide the disease's biological mechanics in exploiting its symbolic resonances. The article's spatialization of AIDS in its accompanying map of the continent simultaneously locates countries and underscores the irrelevance of their borders: in *this* Africa, disease transcends nation. Replacing what had been colonialism's heart of darkness is the calculated horror of a new interior density, represented on the map by dark-to-light shadings corresponding to HIV attack rates. The "AIDS belt" supposed to exist in central Africa is depicted here not only as the "heart" of the regional epidemic but as the imagined origin of the entire global pandemic. Yet the "evidence" employed by the map reveals the duplicities of Western discourse about AIDS in Africa: seroprevalence rates for the continent are concocted from sensationalist media accounts of specific locations and from the records of epidemiologists working from strictly limited samples (often as few as 100 people) of pregnant women, prostitutes, and clients with sexually transmitted diseases. When not enough AIDS is found, it needs to be imagined, as the key to the *Times's* map suggests:

> The shadings on this map indicate the percentage of sexually active adults believed to be infected with the AIDS virus in major urban areas. Rural rates tend to be much lower. The numbers are based on the latest available data, which may understate current rates. Blank spots do not necessarily mean an absence of AIDS.

Despite its disclaimers about "missing data," there are in fact no "blank spots" on the map; the *Times* fills in the *entire* surface, lumping together countries with "infection rates less than 5 percent" with those for which "data [is] not available." Although we are told that high attack rates (of HIV, which is consistently conflated here with AIDS) are characteristic only of urban areas, whole countries are shaded to indicate "At least 5 percent to 10 percent," "At least 10 percent to 20 percent," and "At least 20 percent." The curious use of the nonexclusive "at least" for the increasingly darker/denser shadings suggests that errors in data will always underestimate "AIDS" for a country. But the note on "sources" at the bottom of the map gives us a clearer indication of the accuracy of the epidemiologic data from which the map is derived:

> Surveys of subgroups are useful but must be interpreted with caution. Urban infection rates cannot be extrapolated to rural areas. Rates among prostitutes, soldiers,

hospital patients, and patients at clinics for sexually transmitted diseases tend to be far higher than in the population at large. Blood donor figures may overstate prevalence if donors are recruited among high-risk groups or understate it if efforts are made to avoid high-risk donors. Often surveys of pregnant women visiting prenatal clinics are considered the best indicator of infection among the adult population.

In this brief summary of data offered for the twenty-four countries that appear to have data (this leaves as "blank spots" another twenty-nine, which include some of the continent's largest),[3] the *Times* acknowledges that seroprevalence studies vary from nation to nation, but all of these studies have been used indiscriminately to present the worst case scenario within any given country.

While HIV is certainly an important African health concern, seroprevalence rates are rising *everywhere* and not just in African locales. The *Times,* however, suggests no reason for singling out Africa as exceptional and offers no comparative data on rates in Euro-America or other global regions (Asia, the Pacific Rim, Eastern Europe, Central and South America, and the Caribbean are the real "blank spots" on the *Times's* map). The article's one comparison to the U.S. serves to inscribe "their AIDS" as heterosexual in comparison with "our AIDS":

> In contrast with the pattern in the United States, AIDS in Africa is spreading mainly through heterosexual intercourse, propelled by long-neglected epidemics of venereal disease that facilitates viral transmission. . . . In the United States, gay men and residents of a few inner-city pockets face comparable devastation, but over all, fewer than 1 percent of adults are believed to be infected with the AIDS virus.

"Inner-city pockets" is of course a reference to poor people of color, the internal blank spot of the U.S. If the horror of the American crisis is the confrontation (of white heterosexuals) with both homosexuality and the feared black underclass, the tragedy in Africa seems rather more unthinkable: "Strange new issues are in the air. Where the disease spread earliest and large numbers have already died, as in Uganda, frightened young men and women are starting to realize that even marriage may be risky."

If AIDS has been thought to sail or jet[4] between the Euro-American countries, it is represented by the *Times* as traveling by truck throughout Africa. An insert showing trucks on a dusty road and entitled "Dangerous Traffic" tells us that:

> The highways of East and Central Africa, such as this one west of Kampala, Uganda, have been major conduits for AIDS. A study of Kenya of 317 truck drivers of varied nationalities found that three-fourths frequently visited prostitutes but that only 30 percent ever used condoms. One in four was infected with HIV. In 1986, 35 percent of drivers studied in Kampala were infected. Most prostitutes and barmaids along trucking routes are infected.

While the direction of infection is obscured here (truck drivers to prostitutes or prostitutes to truck drivers?), the conflation of truckers with their penises and of roads with vaginas is abundantly clear. If truck drivers "unloading" their "dangerous cargo" is a more compelling trope than the usual evocation of urban prostitutes spewing germs to hapless clients, this is because the spread of AIDS in Africa is itself hardly unrelated to the spread of "modernization."

Inventing African Aids

By 1986, Western media and scientists worldwide had created the linguistic distinction between "AIDS" and "African AIDS" that makes the *Times's* map readable. These designations are informal names for the more technical World Health Organization terms, Pattern One and Pattern Two. Pattern One describes epidemiologic scenarios where "homosexual behavior" and "drug injection" are considered the primary means of HIV transmission. Because Pattern One (or, as the unmarked category, simply "AIDS") is coded racially as "white," African American communities—where homosexuality is presumed to be absent—are now said to exhibit features of Pattern Two ("African AIDS"). Pattern Two indicates places where transmission is held to be "almost exclusively heterosexual."[5] Synonymous with "African AIDS," Pattern Two is a linguistic construction confusing an epidemiologic description (however unuseful) with an emerging "history" of the epidemic. The Caribbean has "African AIDS" but Latin America has "AIDS," an unprecedented if barely conscious recognition of indigenous homosexualities. A third category, Pattern Three, recognizes the emergence of "heterosexual" AIDS outside Euro- America and Africa in places where HIV arrived "late" and largely through postcolonial sex tourism and international bloodbanking.

The "history" of the epidemic reflected in these categories inverts the crucial epidemiologic issues. Rather than asking how HIV moved from the Pattern One countries (where AIDS was diagnosed first by epidemiologists' accounts) to the Pattern Two countries, the scientifically endorsed history of AIDS shows HIV originating in Africa and then moving to North America.[6] The scientific distinction between AIDS/gay/white/Euro-American and African AIDS/heterosexual/black/African/U.S.-inner-city neatly fails to inquire how HIV traveled from the bodies of U.S. homosexual men into the bodies of "Africans" a continent and ocean away, or how "African AIDS" then returned to diasporal African communities in the U.S. The blank spot within the Euro-American mind makes it far easier to imagine an alternative causal chain running from monkeys to Africans to queers than to recall the simple fact that the West exports huge quantities of unscreened blood to its Third World client states (much less acknowledge that black and white Americans have sex—gay as well as straight—and share needles with each other).

This difference between Patterns One and Two thus helps white, Euro-American heterosexuals evade the idea that they might themselves be vulnerable since African (and African American) heterosexuality is so evidently different than Euro-American. Euro-American heterosexuality is "not at risk" as long as local AIDS is identified as homosexual and heterosexual AIDS remains distant. The projected difference of African heterosexuality and the asserted absence of African homosexuality[7] continue to drive not only the forms of epidemiologic research (for example, researchers have been more interested in finding bizarre and distinctive "African" sexual practices[8] than in documenting transfusion-related cases) but also the forms of educational intervention whose focus in Africa is almost exclusively on promoting monogamy or, in more "sensitive" campaigns, "stable polygamy."

My earlier work on "African AIDS" investigated how Western scientific representations of the national and sexual cultures of postcolonial Africa direct the international AIDS research agenda. Reading conference documents and media reports on "AIDS in Africa," I marked the links between apparently innocuous or obviously fantastic assumptions made about Africa(ns) within Western discourse and the conduct and direction of Western science. In particular, I showed how the persistent Western description of Africa as a "catastrophe" and as "heterosexual" justified as altruistic the genocidal Western practices and policies toward their client-state "Others."

Because "African AIDS" is simultaneously "different" and "similar," conflicts in Western AIDS discourse, ethics, and medical research can be rationalized by drawing upon research undertaken throughout the continent. For example, while data from African clinics convinces Westerners that heterosexual transmission is possible (because all intercourse is the same), this same data is also read as suggesting that widespread transmission among heterosexuals is not likely enough to require the universal adoption of the condom (because Africans engage in other exotic sexual practices and polygamy).[9] Diagnosis of AIDS in Africa is said to be unreliable because medical facilities are alleged to be poor; this licenses demographers to multiply known cases by exorbitant factors in order to obtain a "true" (i.e., catastrophic) picture of AIDS in "Africa." But "African" diagnosis becomes a problem (and for epidemiologists rather than clinicians) only because the definition of AIDS is derived from the U.S. experience of largely well-cared-for, middle-class men who become inexplicably weak and unable to fight common illness. The fall from "previous health" is not a feasible diagnostic distinction in countries (or among U.S. women or those living in the inner city, for that matter) where people have received little health care or where infectious diseases and nutritional deficiencies make it difficult to distinguish between clinical AIDS and malaria, anaemia, tuberculosis, etc.

An important note on the terms I've employed here: in Western discourse, Africa, a continent of roughly eleven and a half million square miles and fifty-three countries, is treated as a homogeneous sociopolitical block. Yet this supposedly "unknown" continent—unknown, that is, to its pale neighbors to the north—is in fact far more culturally, linguistically, religiously, and socially diverse than North America and Europe. Collapsing the many cultures residing on the continent into "Africa" is an act of political and cultural violence. In order to complicate "Africa" as a Western construction, I employ the equivalent constructions "North American" and "Euro-American" to indicate the collection of relatively homogeneous northern administrative states as we appear to our southern neighbors. The resultant vagueness Euro-Americans will experience in this strategy should be read back from the "Other" point of view: "North Americans" in particular should consider their own discomfort at having their cultural space discursively reduced in this way.

But this is not the only critical reduction occurring in Western discourse about Africa: as a term, "Africa" can mean both the land mass and its people precisely because the people of Africa have been considered to be coextensive with the continent, a conflation I evoke through the shorthand "Africa(ns)." This conflation has been eloquently described by Frantz Fanon: what is done to the "African body," especially woman's body, is a metaphor for what is to be done to the continent, and vice versa.[10]

Imploding Borders

The flattening out of the racial, ethnic, and cultural diversity of non-European-descended Africans into a singular autochthonous people performed an important function during the era of colonialism. Carving up the land was not sufficient; a narrative reconstruction of Africa's "uncivilized" prehistory was necessary to justify the colonial presence. The colonial taxonomist's "racial" distributions— "Semites," "hamites," "negroes," "nilotes," "half-hamites," "bantus," "Khoisans," not to mention "Italians" and peoples of the Asian subcontinent ("Indian," another site of colonialist reduction through arbitrary racial taxonomic schemes)— mapped an Africa prior to colonial border construction in order to deny the social orders and political/cultural groups of *people* ("Zulus," "Sabaeans," "Berbers," "Ibos," etc.) who lived, intermarried, fought battles, and traded culture and religion with one another before the incursion of Europeans. These are peoples whose racial and sexual histories seemed always to defy the new administrative borders, but the Europeans still insisted that "natives" must be placed somewhere—spatialized—and organized properly through sexual and genealogical successions— temporalized.

Such a displacement of the political and social onto the sexual and racial has returned today, with similarly self-justifactory motives, as the narrative logic underwriting Western accounts of AIDS among the peoples of Africa. Again, spatial demarcation and temporal sequence organize historical narrative. In obvious ways ("AIDS began in Africa"), insidious ways ("AIDS 'jumped species' from green monkeys to 'African' humans"), and subtle ways (persistent descriptions of truck drivers, miners, "prostitutes," and soldiers traversing the continent), the Euro-American story of "African AIDS" concerns not only racial difference but also territory transected and borders gone out of control. But rather than continuing to adduce African "backwardness" as an excuse for colonial plunder, AIDS epidemiology offers "African sexuality" as a rationale for unethical experimentation and unwillingness to pursue education and community organizing projects that could decrease transmission of HIV. No longer content to carve up a massified Africa into "proper" nations, AIDS media reportage offers a view of African sexuality—alternately described as traditional (polygamy) or condemned as modern (rural-urban social breakdown resulting in "prostitution")—which now requires rapid reorganization into bourgeois families.

This is the side of "African AIDS" I wish to take up here: "containment" through the promotion of racist and heterophobic conceptions of "safe sex." Reading the *Times*'s map alongside the new pamphlet series "Strategies for Hope," collaboratively produced by British international relief organizations and two African national AIDS committees,[11] I want to show how "self-help" manuals for use in Anglophone communities in Africa recall previous border constructions in seeking to promote as "safe sex" a bourgeois "African family" that has never in fact existed.

Strategies for Hope

With an international recession under way, the only capital-intensive educational projects possible in poor countries are collaborative ones with (largely) European international relief organizations. The set of concepts underlying "African AIDS" have become so naturalized today that such projects must rewrite local experience to conform to the internationally adopted narrative. The Euro-American fascination with a "different" African sexuality can routinely be glimpsed in epidemiologic studies and newspaper accounts (witness this sidebar to the *Times* article discussed previously):

> Studies in the United States show that transmission of the AIDS virus during vaginal intercourse is usually quite difficult, especially from female to male. But research in Africa has revealed conditions that multiply the danger. . . . One is the rampant extent of sexually transmitted diseases . . . above all, chancroid, which causes festering ulcers. . . . A second major factor . . . is the lack of male circumcision in much of Africa. . . . Researchers are just now turning attention to little-known sexual practices that might also raise transmission odds. . . . In parts of Central Africa . . . women engage in a practice known as "dry sex." In variations of the practice, designed to increase friction during intercourse, women use herbs, chemical powders, stones, or cloth in the vagina to reduce lubrication and cause swelling. . . . Promiscuity helps drive the epidemic. While data do not exist for comparing sexual behavior on different continents, surveys do show that extramarital sex is commonplace in Africa.

The Western imaginary runs wild in these few lines: the easy slide between the gaping vagina and the gaping hole that, on the map, is the "heart" of African AIDS; the undisguised preoccupation with the shape and size of African penises; the assertion of a relative promiscuity, which even the author admits has no data to support it; the conflation of "extramarital" and "promiscuous"—all of these together form a shorthand litany of the "difference" of African sexuality. Such accounts, however, are not limited to the Western media but can be discovered in educational materials designed specifically for "African" use. The following is taken front the "Strategies for Hope" pamphlet series:

> HIV infection in Africa is spread primarily by *heterosexual intercourse*. It affects sexually active men and women in equal numbers, rather than subgroups of the population such as male homosexuals or intravenous drug users. (Homosexuality and intravenous drug use are rare in Africa.) High-risk sexual behavior therefore consists of sexual intercourse with more than one partner. (Pamphlet 1, 3)

The claim in the colonial voice-over to this ostensibly "local" pamphlet that "African" homosexuality is rare is extraordinarily duplicitous. Indeed, same-sex affective and domestic relations were not at all unusual in many precolonial cultures. When colonial and especially British administrators arrived, they were distressed by these relationships, which often played key roles in the distribution of goods and the maintenance of lineages. Colonial law grouped these disparate practices together under one name, "homosexuality," which it pronounced uncivilized and banned by law. Thus contemporary denials by African leaders of the category "homosexuality" are as often a refusal of the European notion of static homosexual identity as they are a denial of same-sex affective and domestic relations. Neocolonialists now can denigrate homosexuality as a Western import and thereby gain increased control over indigenous economic and social relations by tightening control over the remaining cross-sex relations.[12]

In the context of the reigning transnational distinctions between "AIDS" and "African AIDS," (bad) individuals are routinely figured against (good) families, a strategy that both denies the existence of Euro-American gay people's social networks and excommunicates them from their blood relatives. The language employed in the pamphlets—"HIV infection in Africa is primarily a *family disease*, rather than a disease affecting mainly single people" (Pamphlet 1, 3; emphasis in original)—begins to reveal what is at stake. The homophobic Section 28 in Britain (similar to the Helms Amendment in the U.S.) was not content to refuse government funding to projects that "promote homosexuality" but also derided "pretend families." The unit to be sanctioned and protected is thus the statistical minority, the bourgeois family—white, heterosexual, mother and father, small number of children. The logo for the 1987 International AIDS Conference in Stockholm proposed a similarly compacted description of the AIDS epidemic: here was a stylized (and nude) mother and father, each holding a hand of the small child who stood between them. To the Western mind, AIDS is most importantly a threat to the family, and a double one—not simply the threat of an entire family being infected, but also the threat of growing numbers of single people challenging the supremacy of the family unit.

Besides "African AIDS," the only other media image of a "family with AIDS" that has received wide attention focuses on the hemophiliac, the less celebrated Other whose "feminine" bleeding shores up heterosexual masculinity. The October 1988 *Scientific American*, a special issue entitled "What Science Knows About AIDS," presents a full-page picture of a white, North American Family (the Burkes, who were outspoken advocates for the rights of people with HIV). We are told that the father is a hemophiliac who "infected" his wife before he knew he was himself infected, and she in turn gave birth to an infected son. Even as the Burkes' membership in a community of blood-product users is completely elided in the magazine's account, this apparently isolated family encodes the story of the tragic innocence of those who lack knowledge, pitted against those who do or should have had it (gay men and drug users are said to infect "knowingly" or recklessly). Though the article's passive constructions describing how wife and son "became infected" minimize the heterosexual component of the "Burkes' AIDS," the fact of the matter is that, throughout this account, Mr. Burkes' hemophilia has itself been sufficient to undercut his masculine identity. We have a glimpse here of the power of heterosexual culture's own heterophobia: the horror of this North American "family with AIDS" is that the unit was actually engaging in the identity-bestowing activities of a small, well-disciplined family.

The African family's purported problem is its similar inability to construct itself properly as a small, well-disciplined unit. Oddly enough, the families (that is, everyone defined as "not an individual") in the "Strategies for Hope" pamphlets are comprised of multiple adults, not just "polygamous" units but "sisters" who "often visited the nearby rural bar, where they sold chicken . . . and sexual favors" (Pamphlet 1, 19). Like homosexuality, the Euro-American category of "the prostitute"—an individual with a professional identity as a sex worker—is seen as distinct from those who engage in the traditional practice of "selling favors." Located outside the confines of the family proper, "prostitutes" are singled out by the media to bolster support for "family values" and by epidemiologists to mark the historical progress of HIV through a country or city. Such "prostitutes" are said to have "Western" AIDS since they are constructed as "single people"; they are not as recuperable into families as are the women who seem to mimic traditional female roles by selling chicken and sexual favors. In the "Strategies for Hope" series, the various extramarital and nonmarital sexual relations that have resulted in "family AIDS" (as represented in the thirteen "true story" inserts in the pamphlets) are considered, in contrast, to form part of "family life." The issue, it becomes clear, is not sex per se but the failure to organize it within the disciplined borders of the bourgeois family.

The pamphlets invoke a nostalgia for a less urban Africa in which "traditional family values" once prevailed—and this despite the reality that polygamy and age-specific sexual experimentation were the dominant organizational strategies in the many different cultural strands of this "tradition." In a gesture remarkably like Thatcher's privatization and Reagan's New Altruism, the pamphlets posit the family as the idealized site for support, care, and education: "Even in urban communities the family retains much of its cohesive power, although weakened to some extent by the spread of 'modern' attitudes and values" (Pamphlet 3, 3). Instead of noticing how this conception of the family-as-primary-political-unit disempowers both women and the community, this odd *recto-verso* history of the rise of the bourgeois family in Africa secures as "traditional" the mother-father-child unit by conflating the image of the single urban person ("prostitute" and perhaps migrant workers and truck drivers) with the image of "the modern." But what, after all, could be more modern than the bourgeois family?

Legible throughout the pamphlets is the heterophobic dread of the condom. The litany that "Africans won't use condoms," which formed a crucial part of Western rationalizations for pursuing vaccine trials,[13] is repeated under the guise of "cultural sensitivity" in this Christian missionary/British neocolonial collaboration:

> *Sexual attitudes and habits* are different from those of industrialized countries. Resistance to the idea of using condoms is widespread, especially among men. Many years of intensive health education and attitude-forming would be required to achieve sustained attitudinal and behavioral change in this area.
>
> Condoms do have a significant—but limited—role in AIDS control in Africa, but promoting the use of condoms is a diversion from the central issue of *sexual behavior.* The practice of having multiple sexual partners is the main causal factor in the transmission of HIV in Africa. Promoting the use of condoms does not address this issue.

It advocates a technical solution to a problem which can be addressed only through fundamental changes in social attitudes, values, and behavior. (Pamphlet 3, 21)[14]

Such distinctions are of course completely ludicrous—Euro-American heterosexual men seem no less resistant to condom use than African men; condom use and sexual behavior are scarcely two separable matters; the spatial dispersions invoked in the image of HIV-infected truck drivers and wandering prostitutes are only slightly more imaginative than the idea of mobile yuppies with bicoastal life styles transporting HIV around the U.S. or, as Pattern Three implicitly suggests, around the world. The crucial point here is that bourgeois family units in Africa— understood, from the outset, to be free of infection—must not rely upon condom use to prevent infection, for how otherwise could they succeed in reproducing themselves? Conversely, since those outside the family must be prevented from reproducing, it is they alone who must be urged to use condoms. The already infected persons, especially women, in their haphazard, defamilialized units are thus to be "eliminated" in a kind of final prophylactic solution. Advocated only for "people already infected with HIV or those who engage in recognizably high-risk sexual behavior" (such as sex with "prostitutes"), condoms "reduce but *do not eliminate the risk of transmission*" (Pamphlet 3, 21). "Elimination" of transmission slides easily into elimination of persons: what is implicit here is a brave new world of monogamous or faithful polygamous relationships[15] that will rise from the ashes of the "modernization" that, in its destruction of "traditional values," becomes a "cause" of AIDS.

If any doubts remain about the nature of the pamphlet series, its descriptions of AIDS counseling make it clear that the "cure" for AIDS in Africa lies in the proliferation of bourgeois families. "Communication" is repeatedly proscribed for counselors and families. Although noting that other social support networks continue to exist (though always fractured by "modernization"), the pamphlets urge one-on-one, paraprofessional counseling to replace functioning social relations involving grandmothers, cousins, or jokesters who teach about sexuality. In the abstract, such programs seem desirable in a crisis setting, but their longer-term effect is to destroy existing social relations while promoting disciplining interventions from the local clinic.

The TASO project of Uganda (Pamphlet 2) follows precisely from this model of the reconstructed bourgeois family and describes how the transition "back" to the family and the "elimination" of the already infected will be managed. I do not want to undercut the important work of TASO, modeled on the grass-roots "self-help" (though largely gay male) people-living-with AIDS movement in the West.[16] Instead, I want to underline what is presented here as "appropriate" AIDS work. While this organization has been enormously helpful, it is crucial to realize that the conception of "self-help" as employed in its project is as culture bound as the idea of the bourgeois family. *Self*-help arises only in the context of already existing (or already denied) *state*-mediated services, hence the emphasis on "self-"rather than on community mobilization. Not surprisingly, most of the TASO clients whose stories appear in this pamphlet are men who are themselves both counselors and clients of the five-year-old organization. These stories suggest in effect that the organization has become a kind of surrogate family; indeed, a client named Gilbert has moved to a house near the TASO office, where he now works part-time, so that he "can see a lot more of his children. . . . As a father I feel much closer to my children" (Pamphlet 2, 24). These transitional family units, "victims" of the modernization that permitted the disease of Western single people to invade the African family, are presented as evidence for the "safeness" of bourgeois families to come. Though never specifically addressed in the pamphlet, the paradigmatic act that defines the bourgeois family—regulated heterosexual intercourse—is itself to be protected from the condom. In one sweep, the pamphlet's refusal to promote universal condom use paves the way for the virtual genocide of anyone outside the chastity-before-marriage-monogamous-couple and enables Euro-American epidemiologists to name the "difference" constitutive of "African AIDS." *If only they'd had proper families.*[17]

African social patterns once were deemed unnatural or hypernatural (uncivilized) by the West, but African sex is still considered profoundly natural, too close to the body and its supposedly prediscursive desires to be able to accommodate the inhibiting condom. Having failed to demonstrate anatomical, behavioral, or even sociomedical differences between Euro-American and African sex acts, international AIDS workers now conclude that intercourse itself must ultimately be declared safe, and that the "risk" be situated in its practice outside the legitimate borders of the bourgeois family. Those who cannot be contained within this family will be simply left to die, but such an outcome will be rapid because "African AIDS" seems inexplicably to move faster than "AIDS" (largely because the Western drug companies cannot make any money there). "Africa" is thus once more experiencing border constructions that mask state-sponsored genocide as indigenous social and cultural formations are elided in the interests of a brave new world of disease-free—and controllable—bourgeois family units.

Notes

1. "Natural history" is the term employed within epidemiology to describe the development of a disease, epidemic, or pandemic if left to run its course. The desire to learn the natural history of HIV/AIDS has resulted in debates, for example, about whether the few remaining long-time infected but asymptomatic men in a San Francisco "natural history" cohort should now "be allowed" to take prophylactic AZT or pentamidine, two of the most widely accepted life-prolonging drugs. Researchers in Africa have expressed a similar wish to allow existing conditions to continue to "see what happens." In one study of the effectiveness of contraceptive sponges for interrupting HIV transmission, researchers gave half of the targeted women (who were sex workers) placebos—in essence a wad of cotton. Despite early data suggesting that both groups in the study were becoming infected at a rapid rate, the experiment continued for three years until "statistically sound samplings" were obtained. Tragically, the same research data showed that sex workers in an adjoining district had been able to get many of their male clients to use condoms, thereby decreasing not only HIV trans-

mission in these women but other sexually transmitted diseases overall. For more on such experiments, see my *Inventing AIDS*.

2. *New York Times*, September 16, 1990, pp. 1, 14. The map and accompanying article, "What Makes the 2 Sexes So Vulnerable to Epidemic," appear on p. 15.

3. Specific information is given for: "Most Severely Affected"—Malawi, Rwanda, Uganda, Zambia; "Urban Rate 10 percent to 20 percent—Burundi, Ivory Coast, Tanzania, Zimbabwe, Central African Republic, Congo, Guinea Bissau, Kenya, and Zaire (Rwanda has the same percentages but is placed in the "Most Severely Affected" category apparently because of a single study showing a 30 percent rate of seroprevalence in a cohort of pregnant women in the capital city); and "Ominous Signs"—Angola, Burkina Faso, Mali, Ethiopia, Ghana, Namibia, Nigeria, Senegal, Sierra Leone, South Africa, and Sudan.

4. I am alluding here to the highly publicized accounts that suggest (based on fantasy) that either Tall Ships sailors who toured the world in 1976 or "Patient Zero," a steward on Air Canada in the early 1980s, brought AIDS to the U.S. See Randy Shilts, *And the Band Played On* (New York: St. Martin's Press, 1987).

5. This assumption of heterosexuality seems to be based only on the simple statistical fact that the male to female ratio in Africa as a whole is about 1:1. Scientists have been slow to recognize, however, that the number of women who receive transfusions (and thus the transfusion-related HIV infection) has been grossly underestimated. Since it is standard medical practice throughout much of Africa to give whole blood transfusions for malarial, nutritional, or maternal anemia, scientists have consistently conflated pregnancy with transfusions as "risk" factors. See Alan Fleming "Prevention of Transmission of HIV by Blood Transfusion in Developing Countries," Global Impact of AIDS Conference (London, March 8–11, 1988).

6. A scientist of the stature of Luc Montaigne has persistently maintained, despite contrary epidemiologic data, that "AIDS" started in "Africa." His claim is based on the genetic similarity of a simian immunodeficiency virus found in monkeys. This insistence is an updating of racist evolutionary theory, only in place of the old missing link between apes and homo sapiens, the new missing link connects monkeys with North Americans. By a clever sleight of hand, the AIDS-came-from-Africa theory first situates the virus as more or less dormant in Africa and then transports it to Europe and/or America where it rapidly disseminates. At the same time, so this theory runs, a variant of the virus suddenly proliferates in Africa (urbanization is cited as an explanation—but this process was already well underway before the onset of the epidemic).

7. I remain perplexed by Westerners' insistence that there is no homosexuality in Africa—after all, it would have been much simpler to lay AIDS at the door of a single "perversion." Yet Western homosexual panic works overtime in AIDS discourse: homosexuality is more controllable if it can be retained as a category of Western bourgeois culture. To acknowledge other homosexualities would implicitly challenge Western notions that homosexuality is a symptom of cultural decadence, even if "primitive" homosexualities can be written off on that basis. But such panic also enables the denial of miscegenation through the denial of cross-race homosexual congress. This is nowhere clearer than in South African AIDS discourse where both "white (homosexual)" AIDS and "black (heterosexual)" AIDS are said to exist. Well into the 1980s, South African commentators would wryly note that apartheid may have "saved" South African blacks from AIDS. Studies of male relations in the mines, conducted as gay history, were appropriated as "proof" of the effectiveness of sexual apartheid (perhaps the least violent but most fundamental aspect of racial separation): black miners, it was

argued, did not acquire AIDS while in the male-only dormitories since they had "intercourse" only with their female partners.

8. The persistent effort to establish an African heterosexual "difference" began with allegations that Africans favored anal intercourse because it is, as many media reports called it, "a primitive form of birth control." This assumed that HIV transmission was paradigmatically sodomitic; the handful of Army cases in which men alleged that they had been infected by prostitutes also rested on this idea since, as one researcher told me, "their wives wouldn't do it (permit anal intercourse)." Sadly, for the Western sexual imagination, epidemiologists failed to find higher rates of anal intercourse or any other exotic practice to explain differences between "African" and "Euro-American" heterosexual practice. But researchers and journalists are still searching, as can be seen in a passage from the *Times* on "dry sex" that I discuss below. Who knows what lurks in the Euro-American male imaginary here—"African" penises smaller than fantasized? "African" vaginas even larger than feared?

9. See, for example, Robert E. Gould, "Reassuring News About AIDS: A Doctor Tells Why You May Not Be at Risk, " *Cosmopolitan* (January 1988), p. 147: "The data I gathered concerning heterosexual intercourse in Africa show marked differences from the way it is usually practiced in the United States."

10. See especially Frantz Fanoll, "Unveiling Algeria," in *A Dying Colonialism* (New York: Monthly Review Press, 1965). I am also indebted here to Kirstin McDougall, whose unpublished manuscript on maternal metaphors in AIDS discourse confirms that such slippage occurs not only in Western but also in Anglophone African media.

11. The three "Strategies for Hope" pamphlets published jointly by ACTIONAID in London, the African Medical and Research Foundation in Nairobi, and World in Need in Colchester (U.K.) are now distributed widely by the World Health Organization Global Program on AIDS. The series includes two pamphlets about Zambia and one about Uganda; these have been reviewed respectively by the National AIDS Surveillance Committee of Zambia and the National AIDS Control Programme of Uganda. Pamphlet One is entitled *From Fear to Hope: AIDS Care and Prevention at Chikankata Hospital, Zambia,* authored by U.K.-based Glen Williams, who is also the series editor. Pamphlet Two, by U.K.-based Janie Hampton, is called *Living Positively with AIDS: The AIDS Support Organization (TASO), Uganda.* The third pamphlet is *AIDS Management: An Integrated Approach,* by Williams and Capt. (Dr.) Ian D. Campbell, Chief Medical Officer of the Salvation Army Hospital in Chikankata, Zambia.

12. For more general information on the inscription of sexual cultures as subaltern see especially T. Dunbar Moody, "Migrancy and Male Sexuality in South African Gold Mines," *Journal of South African Studies,* 14, 2 (January 1988), pp. 228–56: Lourdes Arguelles and B. Ruby Rich, "Homosexuality, Homophobia, and Revolution: Notes Toward an Understanding of the Cuban Lesbian and Gay Male Experience," in Martin Duberman, Martha Vicinus, and George Chauncey, Jr., eds. *Hidden from History* (New York: New American Library, 1989); Pat Caplan, ed., *The Cultural Construction of Sexuality* (New York: Tavistock, 1987); "Homecoming," *Black/Out,* 2, 1 (Fall 1986); and Alfred Machela, "The Work of the Rand Gay Organization," Conference on Homosexual Identity Before, During, and After HIV (Stockholm, June 1988).

13. For the longer argument on Western medical ethics anal proposed vaccine trials, see my *Inventing AIDS.*

14. To their credit, in Pamphlet 3, the authors emphasize that condoms are not currently being supplied to African countries in sufficient supply to meet potential demand (21). However, this can hardly be used as an excuse not to promote condom usage at all, since it is probably easier and quicker to increase condom supplies than it is to pro-

mote monogamy. Indeed, the ease with which the lack-of-supply argument becomes an excuse for not promoting condoms is rooted in the widespread notion that "in Africa, AIDS is a disease of poverty."

15. See Pamphlet 1, which invokes "traditional values and norms of sexual behavior, which have been lost in the recent wave of 'modernization,'" and which defines "stable polygamy" as a form of "safe sex" (20).

16. It is critical to recognize how limiting are the terms of the international health regime; many local strategies remain "unreadable" because they defy the standardizations favored by the World Health Organization.

17. I am indebted here to the brief sections on the construction of the "Algerian" family in Malek Alloula, *The Colonial Harem,* trans. Myrna Godzich and Wlad Godzich (Minneapolis: University of Minnesota Press, 1986). A similar pattern occurs in the media reportage about AIDS in Africa, where the existing "African" family is often implicitly denigrated for having, besides a surfeit of children, either too many parents or too few (usually the father died or has run off).

CHAPTER SEVENTEEN

Women Workers and Capitalist Scripts

Ideologies of Domination, Common Interests, and the Politics of Solidarity

CHANDRA TALPADE MOHANTY

> We dream that when we work hard, we'll be able to clothe our children decently, and still have a little time and money left for ourselves. And we dream that when we do as good as other people, we get treated the same, and that nobody puts us down because we are not like them. . . . Then we ask ourselves, "How could we make these things come true?" And so far we've come up with only two possible answers: win the lottery, or organize. What can I say, except I have never been lucky with numbers. So tell this in your book: tell them it may take time that people think they don't have, but they have to organize! . . . Because the only way to get a little measure of power over your own life is to do it collectively, with the support of other people who share your needs.
>
> *Irma, a Filipina worker in the Silicon Valley, California[1]*

I rma's dreams of a decent life for her children and herself, her desire for equal treatment and dignity on the basis of the quality and merit of her work, her conviction that collective struggle is the means to "get a little measure of power over your own life," succinctly capture the struggles of poor women workers in the global capitalist arena. In this essay I want to focus on the exploitation of poor Third-World women, on their agency as workers, on the common interests of women workers based on an understanding of shared location and needs, and on the strategies/practices of organizing that are anchored in and lead to the transformation of the daily lives of women workers.

This has been an especially difficult essay to write—perhaps because the almost-total saturation of the processes of capitalist domination makes it hard to envision forms of feminist resistance which would make a real difference in the daily lives of poor women workers. However, as I began to sort through the ac-

Chandra Talpade Mohanty, "Women Workers and Capitalist Scripts: Ideologies of Domination, Common Interests, and the Politics of Solidarity," in M. Jacqui Alexander and Chandra Talpade Mohanty, eds. *Feminist Genealogies, Colonial Legacies, Democratic Futures* (New York: Routledge, 1997): 3–29. Reprinted by permission.

tions, reflections, and analyses by and about women workers (or wage laborers) in the capitalist economy, I discovered the dignity of women workers' struggles in the face of overwhelming odds. From these struggles we can learn a great deal about processes of exploitation and domination as well as about autonomy and liberation.

A recent study tour to Tijuana, Mexico, organized by Mary Tong of the San Diego-based Support Committee for Maquiladora Workers, confirmed my belief in the radical possibilities of cross-border organizing, especially in the wake of NAFTA. Exchanging ideas, experiences, and strategies with Veronica Vasquez, a twenty-one-year-old Maquila worker fighting for her job, for better working conditions, and against sexual harassment, was as much of an inspiration as any in writing this essay. Veronica Vasquez, along with ninety-nine former employees of the Tijuana factory Exportadora Mano de Obra, S.A. de C.V., has filed an unprecedented lawsuit in Los Angeles, California, against the U.S. owner of Exportadora, National O-Ring of Downey, demanding that it be forced to follow Mexican labor laws and provide workers with three months' back pay after shutting down company operations in Tijuana in November 1994. The courage, determination, and analytical clarity of these young Mexican women workers in launching the first case to test the legality of NAFTA suggest that in spite of the global saturation of processes of capitalist domination, 1995 was a moment of great possibility for building cross-border feminist solidarity.[2]

Over the years, I have been preoccupied with the limits as well as the possibilities of constructing feminist solidarities across national, racial, sexual, and class divides. Women's lives as workers, consumers, and citizens have changed radically with the triumphal rise of capitalism in the global arena. The common interests of capital (e.g., profit, accumulation, exploitation, etc.) are somewhat clear at this point. But how do we talk about poor Third-World women workers' interests, their agency, and their (in)visibility in so-called democratic processes? What are the possibilities for democratic citizenship for Third-World women workers in the contemporary capitalist economy? These are some of the questions driving this essay. I hope to clarify and analyze the location of Third-World women workers and their collective struggles in an attempt to generate ways to think about mobilization, organizing, and conscientization transnationally.

This essay extends the arguments I have made elsewhere regarding the location of Third-World women as workers in a global economy.[3] I write now, as I did then, from my own discontinuous locations: as a South Asian anticapitalist feminist in the U.S. committed to working on a truly liberatory feminist practice which theorizes and enacts the potential for a crosscultural, international politics of solidarity; as a Third-World feminist teacher and activist for whom the psychic economy of "home" and of "work" has always been the space of contradiction and struggle; and as a woman whose middle-class struggles for self-definition and autonomy outside the definitions of daughter, wife, and mother mark an intellectual and political genealogy that led me to this particular analysis of Third-World women's work.

Here, I want to examine the analytical category of "women's work," and to look at the historically specific *naturalization* of gender and race hierarchies through this category. An international division of labor is central to the establishment, consolidation, and maintenance of the current world order: global assembly lines are as much about the production of people as they are about "providing jobs" or making profit. Thus, naturalized assumptions about *work* and *the worker* are crucial to understanding the sexual politics of global capitalism. I believe that the relation of local to global processes of colonization and exploitation, and the specification of a process of cultural and ideological homogenization across national borders, in part through the creation of the consumer as "the" citizen under advanced capitalism, must be crucial aspects of any comparative feminist project. This definition of the citizen-consumer depends to a large degree on the definition and disciplining of producers/workers on whose backs the citizen-consumer gains legitimacy. It is the worker/producer side of this equation that I will address. Who are the workers that make the citizen-consumer possible? What role do sexual politics play in the ideological creation of this worker? How does global capitalism, in search of ever-increasing profits, utilize gender and racialized ideologies in crafting forms of women's work? And, does the social location of particular women as workers suggest the basis for common interests and potential solidarities across national borders?

As global capitalism develops and wage labor becomes the hegemonic form of organizing production and reproduction, class relations within and across national borders have become more complex and less transparent.[4] Thus, issues of spatial economy—the manner by which capital utilizes particular spaces for differential production and the accumulation of capital and, in the process, transforms these spaces (and peoples)—gain fundamental importance for feminist analysis.[5] In the aftermath of feminist struggles around the right to work and the demand for equal pay, the boundaries between home/family and work are no longer seen as inviolable (of course these boundaries were always fluid for poor and working-class women). Women are (and have always been) in the workforce, and we are here to stay. In this essay, I offer an analysis of certain historical and ideological transformations of gender, capital, and work across the borders of nation-states,[6] and, in the process, develop a way of thinking about the common interests of Third-World women workers, and in particular about questions of agency and the transformation of consciousness.

Drawing specifically on case studies of the incorporation of Third-World women into a global division of labor at different geographical ends of the new world order, I argue for a historically delineated category of "women's work" as an example of a productive and necessary basis for feminist crosscultural analysis.[7] The idea I am interested in invoking here is not "the work that women do" or even the occupations that they/we happen to be concentrated in, but rather the ideological construction of jobs and tasks in terms of notions of appropriate femininity, domesticity, (hetero)sexuality, and racial and cultural stereotypes. I am interested in mapping these operations of capitalism across different divides, in tracing the naturalization of capitalist processes, ideologies, and values through the way women's work is *constitutively* defined—in this case, in terms of gender and racial parameters. One of the questions I explore pertains to the way gender identity (defined in domestic, heterosexual, familial terms) structures the nature of the work women are allowed to perform or precludes women from being "workers" altogether.

While I base the details of my analysis in geographically anchored case studies, I am suggesting a comparative methodology which moves beyond the case-study approach and illuminates global processes which inflect and draw upon indigenous hierarchies, ideologies, and forms of exploitation to consolidate new modes of colonization. The local and the global are indeed connected through parallel, contradictory, and sometimes converging relations of rule which position women in different and similar locations as workers.[8] I agree with feminists who argue that class struggle, narrowly defined, can no longer be the only basis for solidarity among women workers. The fact of being women with particular racial, ethnic, cultural, sexual, and geographical histories has everything to do with our definitions and identities as workers. A number of feminists have analyzed the division between production and reproduction, and the construction of ideologies of womanhood in terms of public/private spheres. Here, I want to highlight (a) the persistence of patriarchal definitions of womanhood in the arena of wage labor; (b) the versatility and specificity of capitalist exploitative processes providing the basis for thinking about potential common interests and solidarity between Third-World women workers; and (c) the challenges for collective organizing in a context where traditional union methods (based on the idea of the class interests of the male worker) are inadequate as strategies for empowerment.

If, as I suggest, the logic of a world order characterized by a transnational economy involves the active construction and dissemination of an image of the "Third World/racialized, or marginalized woman worker" that draws on indigenous histories of gender and race inequalities, and if this worker's identity is coded in patriarchal terms which define her in relation to men and the heterosexual, conjugal family unit, then the model of class conflict between capitalists and workers needs to be recrafted in terms of the interests (and perhaps identities) of Third-World women workers. Patriarchal ideologies, which sometimes pit women against men within and outside the home, infuse the material realities of the lives of Third-World women workers, making it imperative to reconceptualize the way we think about working-class interests and strategies for organizing. Thus, while this is not an argument for just recognizing the "common experiences" of Third-World women workers, it *is* an argument for recognizing (concrete, not abstract) "common interests" and the potential bases of cross-national solidarity—a common context of struggle. In addition, while I choose to focus on the "Third World" woman worker, my argument holds for white women workers who are also racialized in similar ways. The argument then is about a *process* of gender and race domination, rather than about the *content* of "Third World." Making Third-World women workers visible in this gender, race, class formation involves engaging a capitalist script of subordination and exploitation. But it also leads to thinking about the possibilities of emancipatory action on the basis of the reconceptualization of Third-World women as agents rather than victims.

But why even use "Third World," a somewhat problematic term which many now consider outdated? And why make an argument which privileges the social location, experiences, and identities of Third-World women workers, as opposed to any other group of workers, male or female? Certainly, there are problems with the term "Third World." It is inadequate in comprehensively characterizing the economic, political, racial, and cultural differences *within* the borders of Third-World nations. But in comparison with other similar formulations like "North/South" and "advanced/underdeveloped nations," "Third World" retains a certain heuristic value and explanatory specificity in relation to the inheritance of colonialism and contemporary neocolonial economic and geopolitical processes that the other formulations lack.[9]

In response to the second question, I would argue that at this time in the development and operation of a "new" world order, Third-World women workers (defined in this context as both women from the geographical Third World and immigrant and indigenous women of color in the U.S. and Western Europe) occupy a specific social location in the international division of labor which *illuminates* and *explains* crucial features of the capitalist processes of exploitation and domination. These are features of the social world that are usually obfuscated or mystified in discourses about the "progress" and "development" (e.g., the creation of jobs for poor, Third-World women as the marker of economic and social advancement) that is assumed to "naturally" accompany the triumphal rise of global capitalism. I do not claim to explain *all* the relevant features of the social world or to offer a *comprehensive* analysis of capitalist processes of recolonization. However, I am suggesting that Third-World women workers have a potential identity in common, an identity as *workers* in a particular division of labor at this historical moment. And I believe that exploring and analyzing this potential commonality across geographical and cultural divides provides both a way of reading and understanding the world and an explanation of the consolidation of inequities of gender, race, class, and (hetero)sexuality, which are necessary to envision and enact transnational feminist solidarity.[10]

The argument that multinationals position and exploit women workers in certain ways does not originate with me. I want to suggest, however, that in interconnecting and comparing some of these case studies, a larger theoretical argument can be made about the category of women's work, specifically about the Third-World woman as worker, at this particular historical moment. I think this intersection of gender and work, where the very definition of work draws upon and reconstructs notions of masculinity, femininity, and sexuality, offers a basis of cross-cultural comparison and analysis which is grounded in the concrete realities of women's lives. I am not suggesting that this basis for comparison exhausts the *totality* of women's experience cross-culturally. In other words, because similar ideological constructions of "women's work" make cross-cultural analysis possible, this does not automatically mean women's lives are the *same* but rather that they are *comparable.* I argue for a notion of political solidarity and common interests, defined as a community or collectivity among women workers across class, race, and national boundaries which is based on shared material interests and identity and common ways of reading the world. This idea of political solidarity in the context of the incorporation of Third-World women into a global economy offers a basis for cross-cultural comparison and analysis which is grounded in history and social location rather than in an ahistorical notion of culture or experience. I am making a choice here to focus on and analyze the *continuities* in the experiences, histories, and strategies of survival of these particular workers. But this does not mean that differences and discontinuities in experience do not exist or that they are insignificant. The focus on continuities is a *strategic* one—it makes possible a way of reading the operation of capital from a location (that of Third-World women workers) which, while forming the bedrock of a certain kind of global exploitation of labor, remains somewhat invisible and undertheorized.

Gender and Work: Historical and Ideological Transformations

"Work makes life sweet," says Lola Weixel, a working-class Jewish woman in Connie Field's film "The Life and Times of Rosie the Riveter." Weixel is reflecting on her experience of working in a welding factory during World War II, at a time when large numbers of U.S. women were incorporated into the labor force to replace men who were fighting the war. In one of the most moving moments in the film, she draws attention to what it meant to her and to other women to work side by side, to learn skills and craft products, and to be paid for the work they did, only to be told at the end of the war that they were no longer needed and should go back to being girlfriends, housewives, and mothers. While the U.S. state propaganda machine was especially explicit on matters of work for men and women, and the corresponding expectations of masculinity/femininity and domesticity in the late 1940s and 1950s, this is no longer the case in the 1990s. Shifting definitions of public and private, and of workers, consumers and citizens no longer define wage-work in visibly masculine terms. However, the dynamics of job competition, loss, and profit-making in the 1990s are still part of the dynamic process that spelled the decline of the mill towns of New England in the early 1900s and that now pits "American" against "immigrant" and "Third-World" workers along the U.S./Mexico border or in the Silicon Valley in California. Similarly, there are continuities between the women-led New York garment-workers strike of 1909, the Bread and Roses (Lawrence textile) strike of 1912, Lola Weixel's role in union organizing during WW II, and the frequent strikes in the 1980s and 1990s of Korean textile and electronic workers, most of whom are young, single women.[11] While the global division of labor in 1995 looks quite different from what it was in the 1950s, ideologies of women's work, the meaning and value of work for women, and women workers' struggles against exploitation remain central issues for feminists around the world. After all, women's labor has always been central to the development, consolidation, and reproduction of capitalism in the U.S.A. and elsewhere.

In the United States, histories of slavery, indentured servitude, contract labor, self-employment, and wage-work are also simultaneously histories of gender, race, and (hetero)sexuality, nested within the context of the development of capitalism. Thus, women of different races, ethnicities, and social classes had profoundly different, though interconnected, experiences of work in the economic development from nineteenth-century economic and social practices (slave agriculture in the South, emergent industrial capitalism in the Northeast, the hacienda system in the Southwest, independent family farms in the rural Midwest, Native American hunting/gathering and agriculture) to wage-labor and self-employment (including family businesses) in the late-twentieth century. In 1995, almost a century after the Lowell girls lost their jobs when textile mills moved South to attract nonunionized labor, feminists are faced with a number of profound analytical and organizational challenges in different regions of the world. The material, cultural, and political effects of the processes of domination and exploitation which sustain what is called the New World Order (NWO)[12] are devasting for the vast majority of people in the world—and most especially for impoverished and Third-World women. Maria Mies argues that the increasing division of the world into consumers and producers has a profound effect on Third-World women workers, who are drawn into the international division of labor as workers in agriculture; in large-scale manufacturing industries like textiles, electronics, garments, and toys; in small-scale manufacturing of consumer goods like handicrafts and food processing (the informal sector); and as workers in the sex and tourist industries.[13]

The values, power, and meanings attached to being either a consumer or a producer/worker vary enormously depending on where and who we happen to be in an unequal global system. In the 1990s, it is, after all, multinational corporations that are the hallmark of global capitalism. In an analysis of the effects of these corporations on the new world order, Richard Barnet and John Cavanagh characterize the global commercial arena in terms of four intersecting webs: the Global Cultural Bazaar (which creates and disseminates images and dreams through films, television, radio, music, and other media), the Global Shopping Mall (a planetary supermarket which sells things to eat, drink, wear, and enjoy through advertising, distribution, and marketing networks), the Global Workplace (a network of factories and workplaces where goods are produced, information processed, and services rendered), and, finally, the Global Financial Network (the international traffic in currency transactions, global securities, etc.).[14] In each of these webs, racialized ideologies of masculinity, femininity, and sexuality play a role in constructing the legitimate consumer, worker, and manager. Meanwhile, the psychic and social disenfranchisement and impoverishment of women continues. Women's bodies and labor are used to consolidate global dreams, desires, and ideologies of success and the good life in unprecedented ways.

Feminists have responded directly to the challenges of globalization and capitalist modes of recolonization by addressing the sexual politics and effects on women of (a) religious fundamentalist movements within and across the boundaries of the nation-state; (b) structural adjustment policies (SAPs); (c) militarism, demilitarization, and violence against women; (d) environmental degradation and land/sovereignty struggles of indigenous and native peoples; and (e) population control, health, and reproductive policies and practices.[15] In each of these cases, feminists have analyzed the effects on women as workers, sexual partners, mothers and caretakers, consumers, and transmitters and transformers of culture and tradition. Analysis of the ideologies of masculinity and femininity, of motherhood and (hetero)sexuality and the understanding and mapping of agency, access, and choice are central to this analysis and organizing. Thus, while my characterization of capitalist processes of domination and recolonization may appear somewhat overwhelming, I want to draw attention to the numerous forms of resistance and struggle that have also always been constitutive of the script of colonialism/capitalism. Capitalist patriarchies and racialized, class/caste-specific hierarchies are a key part of the long history of domination and exploitation of women, but struggles against these practices and vibrant, creative, collective forms of mobilization and organizing have also always been a part of our histories. In fact, like Jacqui Alexander and a number of other authors, I attempt to articulate an emancipatory discourse and knowledge, one that furthers the cause of feminist liberatory practice. After all, part of what needs to change within racialized capitalist patriarchies is the very concept of work/labor, as well as the naturalization of heterosexual masculinity in the definition of "the worker."

Teresa Amott and Julie Matthaei, in analyzing the U.S. labor market, argue that the intersection of gender, class, and racial-ethnic hierarchies of power has had two major effects:

> First, disempowered groups have been concentrated in jobs with lower pay, less job security, and more difficult working conditions. Second, workplaces have been places of extreme segregation, in which workers have worked in jobs only with members of their same racial-ethnic, gender, and class group, even though the particular racial-ethnic group and gender assigned to a job may have varied across firms and regions.[16]

While Amott and Matthaei draw attention to the sex-and-race typing of jobs, they do not *theorize* the relationship between this job typing and the social identity of the workers concentrated in these low-paying, segregated, often unsafe sectors of the labor market. While the economic history they chart is crucial to any understanding of the race-and-gender basis of U.S. capitalist processes, their analysis begs the question of whether there is a connection (other than the common history of domination of people of color) between *how* these jobs are defined and *who* is sought after for the jobs.

By examining two instances of the incorporation of women into the global economy (women lacemakers in Narsapur, India, and women in the electronics industry in the Silicon Valley) I want to delineate the interconnections between gender, race, and ethnicity, and the ideologies of work which locate women in particular exploitative contexts. The contradictory positioning of women along class, race, and ethnic lines in these two cases suggests that, in spite of the obvious geographical and sociocultural differences between the two contexts, the organization of the global economy by contemporary capital positions these workers in very similar ways, effectively reproducing and transforming locally specific hierarchies. There are also some significant continuities between homework and factory work in these contexts, in terms of both the inherent ideologies of work as well as the experiences and social identities of women as workers. This tendency can also be seen in the case studies of black women workers (of Afro-Caribbean, Asian, and African origin) in Britain, especially women engaged in homework, factory work, and family businesses.

Housewives and Homework: The Lacemakers of Narsapur

Maria Mies's 1982 study of the lacemakers of Narsapur, India, is a graphic illustration of how women bear the impact of development processes in countries where poor peasant and tribal societies are being "integrated" into an international division of labor under the dictates of capital accumulation. Mies's study illustrates how capitalist production relations are built upon the backs of women workers defined as *housewives*. Ideologies of gender and work and their historical transformation provide the necessary ground for the exploitation of the lacemakers. But the definition of women as housewives also suggests the heterosexualization of women's work—women are always defined in relation to men and conjugal marriage. Mies's account of the development of the lace industry and the corresponding relations of production illustrates fundamental transformations of gender, caste, and ethnic relations. The original caste distinctions between the feudal warrior castes (the landowners) and the Narsapur (poor Christians) and Serepalam (poor Kapus/Hindu agriculturalists) women are totally transformed through the development of the lace industry, and a new caste hierarchy is effected.

At the time of Mies's study, there were sixty lace manufacturers, with some 200,000 women in Narsapur and Serepalam constituting the work force. Lacemaking women worked six to eight hours a day, and ranged in age from six to eighty. Mies argues that the expansion of the lace industry between 1970 and 1978 and its integration into the world market led to class/caste differentiation within particular communities, with a masculinization of all nonproduction jobs (trade) and a total feminization of the production process. Thus, men sold women's products and lived on profits from women's labor. The polarization between men and women's work, where men actually defined themselves as exporters and businessmen who invested in women's labor, bolstered the social and ideological definition of women as housewives and their work as "leisure time activity." In other words, work, in this context, was grounded in sexual identity, in concrete definitions of femininity, masculinity, and heterosexuality.

Two particular indigenous hierarchies, those of caste and gender, interacted to produce normative definitions of "women's work." Where, at the onset of the lace industry, Kapu men and women were agricultural laborers and it was the lower-caste Harijan women who were lacemakers, with the development of capitalist relations of production and the possibility of caste/class mobility, it was the Harijan women who were agricultural laborers while the Kapu women undertook the "leisure time" activity of lacemaking. The caste-based ideology of seclusion and purdah was essential to the extraction of surplus value. Since purdah and the seclusion of women is a sign of higher caste status, the domestication of Kapu laborer women—where their lacemaking activity was tied to the concept of the "women sitting in the house"—was entirely within the logic of capital accumulation and profit. Now, Kapu women, not just the women of feudal, landowning castes, are in purdah as housewives producing for the world market.

Ideologies of seclusion and the domestication of women are clearly sexual, drawing as they do on masculine and feminine notions of protectionism and property. They are also heterosexual ideologies, based on the normative definition of women as wives, sisters, and mothers—always in relation to conjugal marriage and the "family." Thus, the caste transformation and separation of women along lines of domestication and nondomestication (Kapu housewives vs. Harijan laborers) effectively links the work that women do with their sexual and caste/class identities. Domestication works, in this case, because of the persistence and legitimacy of the ideology of the housewife, which defines women in terms of their place within the home, conjugal marriage, and heterosexuality. The opposition between definitions of the "laborer" and of the "housewife" anchors the invisibility (and caste-related status) of work; in effect, it defines women as *nonworkers*. By definition, housewives cannot be workers or laborers; housewives make male breadwinners and consumers possible. Clearly, ideologies of "women's place and work" have real material force in this instance, where spatial parameters construct and maintain gendered and caste-specific hierarchies. Thus, Mies's study illustrates the concrete effects of the social definition of women as housewives. Not only are the lacemakers invisible in census figures (after all, their work is leisure), but their definition as housewives makes possible the definition of men as "breadwinners." Here, class and gender proletarianization through the development of capitalist relations of production, and the integration of women into the world market is possible because of the history and transformation of indigenous caste and sexual ideologies.

Reading the operation of capitalist processes from the position of the housewife/worker who produces for the world market makes the specifically gendered and caste/class opposition between laborer and the nonworker (housewife) visible. Moreover, it makes it possible to acknowledge and account for the hidden costs of women's labor. And finally, it illuminates the fundamentally *masculine* definition of laborer/worker in a context where, as Mies says, men live off women who are the producers. Analyzing and transforming this masculine definition of labor, which is the mainstay of capitalist patriarchal cultures, is one of the most significant challenges we face. The effect of this definition of labor is not only that it makes women's labor and its costs invisible, but that it undercuts women's agency by defining them as victims of a process of pauperization or of "tradition" or "patriarchy," rather than as agents capable of making their own choices.

In fact, the contradictions raised by these choices are evident in the lacemakers' responses to characterizations of their own work as "leisure activity." While the fact that they did "work" was clear to them and while they had a sense of the history of their own pauperization (with a rise in prices for goods but no corresponding rise in wages), they were unable to explain how they came to be in the situation they found themselves. Thus, while some of the contradictions between their work and their roles as housewives and mothers were evident to them, they did not have access to an analysis of these contradictions which could lead to (a) seeing the complete picture in terms of their exploitation; (b) strategizing and organizing to transform their material situations; or (c) recognizing their common interests as women workers across caste/class lines. As a matter of fact, the Sere-pelam women defined their lacemaking in terms of "housework" rather than wage-work, and women who had managed to establish themselves as petty commodity producers saw what they did as entrepreneurial: they saw themselves as selling *products* rather than *labor*. Thus, in both cases, women internalized the ideologies that defined them as nonworkers. The isolation of the work context (work done in the house rather than in a public setting) as well as the internalization of caste and patriarchal ideologies thus militated against organizing as *workers*, or as *women*. However, Mies suggests that there were cracks in this ideology: the women expressed some envy toward agricultural laborers, whom the lacemakers saw as enjoying working together in the fields. What seems necessary in such a context, in terms of feminist mobilization, is a recognition of the fact that the identity of the housewife needs to be transformed into the identity of a "woman worker or working woman." Recognition of common interests as housewives is very different from recognition of common interests as women and as workers.

Immigrant Wives, Mothers, and Factory Work: Electronics Workers in the Silicon Valley

My discussion of the U.S. end of the global assembly line is based on studies by Naomi Katz and David Kemnitzer (1983) and Karen Hossfeld (1990) of electronics workers in the so-called Silicon Valley in California. An analysis of production strategies and processes indicates a significant ideological redefinition of normative ideas of factory work in terms of the Third-World, immigrant women who constitute the primary workforce. While the lacemakers of Narsapur were located as *housewives* and their work defined as *leisure time activity* in a very complex international world market, Third-World women in the electronics industry in the Silicon Valley are located as *mothers, wives,* and *supplementary* workers. Unlike the search for the "single" woman assembly worker in Third-World countries, it is in part the ideology of the "married woman" which defines job parameters in the Valley, according to Katz and Kemnitzer's data.

Hossfeld also documents how existing ideologies of femininity cement the exploitation of the immigrant women workers in the Valley, and how the women often use this patriarchal logic against management. Assumptions of "single" and "married" women as the ideal workforce at the two geographical ends of the electronics global assembly line (which includes South Korea, Hong Kong, China, Taiwan, Thailand, Malaysia, Japan, India, Pakistan, the Philippines, and the United States, Scotland, and Italy)[17] are anchored in normative understandings of femininity, womanhood, and sexual identity. The labels are predicated on sexual difference and the institution of heterosexual marriage and carry connotations of a "manageable" (docile?) labor force.[18]

Katz and Kemnitzer's data indicates a definition and transformation of women's work which relies on gender, race, and ethnic hierarchies already historically anchored in the U.S. Further, their data illustrates that the construction of "job labels" pertaining to Third-World women's work is closely allied with their sexual and racial identities. While Hossfeld's more recent study reinforces some of Katz and Kemnitzer's conclusions, she focuses more specifically on how "contradictory ideologies about sex, race, class, and nationality are used as forms of both labor control and labor resistance in the capitalist workplace today."[19] Her contribution lies in charting the operation of gendered ideologies in the structuring of the industry and in analyzing what she calls "refeminization strategies" in the workplace.

Although the primary workforce in the Valley consists of Third-World and newly immigrant women, substantial numbers of Third-World and immigrant men are also employed by the electronics industry. In the early 1980s, 70,000 women held 80 to 90 percent of the operative or laborer jobs on the shop floor. Of these, 45 to 50 percent were Third-World, especially Asian, immigrants. White men held either technican or supervisory jobs. Hossfeld's study was conducted between 1983 and 1986, at which time she estimates that up to 80 percent of the operative jobs were held by people of color, with women constituting up to 90 percent of the assembly workers. Katz and Kemnitzer maintain that the industry actively seeks sources of cheap labor by deskilling production and by using race, gender, and ethnic stereotypes to "attract" groups of workers who are "more suited" to perform tedious, unrewarding, poorly paid work. When interviewed, management personnel described the jobs as (a) unskilled (as easy as a recipe); (b) requiring tolerance for tedious work (Asian women are therefore more suited); and (c) supplementary activity for women whose main tasks were mothering and housework.

It may be instructive to unpack these job labels in relation to the immigrant and Third-World (married) women who perform these jobs. The job labels recorded by Katz and Kemnitzer need to be analyzed as definitions of *women's work*, specifically as definitions of *Third-World/immigrant women's work*. First, the notion of "unskilled" as easy (like following a recipe) and the idea of tolerance for tedious work both have racial and gendered dimensions. Both draw upon stereotypes which infantilize Third-World women and initiate a nativist discourse of "tedium" and "tolerance" as characteristics of non-Western, primarily agricultural, premodern (Asian) cultures. Secondly, defining jobs as supplementary activity for *mothers* and *housewives* adds a further dimension: sexual identity and appropriate notions of heterosexual femininity as marital domesticity. These are not part-time jobs, but they are defined as supplementary. Thus, in this particular context, (Third-World) women's work needs are defined as temporary.

While Hossfeld's analysis of management logic follows similar lines, she offers a much more nuanced understanding of how the gender and racial stereotypes prevalent in the larger culture infuse worker consciousness and resistance. For instance, she draws attention to the ways in which factory jobs are seen by the workers as "unfeminine" or not "ladylike." Management exploits and reinforces these ideologies by encouraging women to view femininity as contradictory to factory work, by defining their jobs as secondary and temporary, and by asking women to choose between defining themselves as women or as workers. Womanhood and femininity are thus defined along a domestic, familial model, with work seen as supplemental to this primary identity. Significantly, although 80 percent of the immigrant women in Hossfeld's study were the largest annual income producers in their families, they still considered men to be the bread-winners.

Thus, as with the exploitation of Indian lacemakers as "housewives," Third-World/immigrant women in the Silicon Valley are located as "mothers and home-makers" and only secondarily as workers. In both cases, men are seen as the real breadwinners. While (women's) work is usually defined as something that takes place in the "public" or production sphere, these ideologies clearly draw on stereo-types of women as home-bound. In addition, the *invisibility* of work in the Indian context can be compared to the *temporary/secondary* nature of work in the Valley. Like the Mies study, the data compiled by Hossfeld and Katz and Kemnitzer in-dicate the presence of local ideologies and hierarchies of gender and race as the basis for the exploitation of the electronics workers. The question that arises is: How do women understand their own positions and construct meanings in an exploitative job situation?

Interviews with electronics workers indicate that, contrary to the views of management, women do not see their jobs as temporary but as part of a lifetime strategy of upward mobility. Conscious of their racial, class, and gender status, they combat their devaluation as workers by increasing their income: by job-hopping, overtime, and moonlighting as pieceworkers. Note that, in effect, the "homework" that Silicon Valley workers do is performed under conditions very similar to the lacemaking of Narsapur women. Both kinds of work are done in the home, in isolation, with the worker paying her own overhead costs (like elec-tricity and cleaning), with no legally mandated protections (such as a minimum wage, paid leave, health benefits, etc.). However, clearly the meanings attached to the work differ in both contexts, as does the way we understand them.

For Katz and Kemnitzer the commitment of electronics workers to class mo-bility is an important assertion of self. Thus, unlike in Narsapur, in the Silicon Valley, homework has an entrepreneurial aspect for the women themselves. In fact, in Narsapur, women's work turns the men into entrepreneurs! In the Valley, women take advantage of the contradictions of the situations they face as *indi-vidual workers*. While in Narsapur, it is purdah and caste/class mobility which provides the necessary self-definition required to anchor women's work in the home as leisure activity, in the Silicon Valley, it is a specifically *American* notion of individual ambition and entrepreneurship which provides the necessary ideo-logical anchor for Third-World women.

Katz and Kemnitzer maintain that this underground economy produces an *ideological* redefinition of jobs, allowing them to be defined as *other than* the basis of support of the historically stable, "comfortable," white, metropolitan working class. In other words, there is a clear connection between low wages and the de-finition of the job as supplementary, and the fact that the lifestyles of people of color are defined as different and cheaper. Thus, according to Katz and Kem-nitzer, *women* and *people of color* continue to be "defined out" of the old industrial system and become targets and/or instruments of the ideological shift away from class towards national/ethnic/gender lines.[20] In this context, ideology and popular culture emphasize the *individual maximization* of options for personal success. Individual success is thus severed from union activity, political struggle, and collective relations. Similarly, Hossfeld suggests that it is the racist and sexist management logic of the needs of "immigrants" that allows the kind of exploitative labor processes that she documents.[21] However, in spite of Katz and Kemnitzer's complex analysis of the relationship of modes of production, social relations of production, culture, and ideology in the context of the Silicon Valley workers, they do not specify why it is *Third-World women* who constitute the primary labor force. Similarly, while Hossfeld provides a nuanced analysis of the gendering of the workplace and the use of racial and gendered logic to consolidate capitalist accumulation, she also sometimes separates "women" and "minority workers" (Hossfeld, p. 176), and does not specify why it is women of color who constitute the major labor force on the assembly lines in the Valley. In distinguishing between women and people of color, Katz and Kemnitzer tend to reproduce the old conceptual divisions of gender and race, where women are defined primarily in terms of their gender and people of color in terms of race. What is excluded is an *interactive* notion of gender and race, whereby women's gendered identity is grounded in race and people of color's racial identities are gendered.

I would argue that the data compiled by Katz and Kemnitzer and Hossfeld does, in fact, explain why Third-World women are targeted for jobs in electronics factories. The explanation lies in the redefinition of work as temporary, supplementary, and unskilled, in the construction of women as mothers and homemakers, and in the positioning of femininity as contradictory to factory work. In addition, the explanation also lies in the specific definition of ThirdWorld, immigrant women as docile, tolerant, and satisfied with substandard wages. It is the ideological redefinition of women's work that provides the necessary understanding of this phenomenon. Hossfeld describes some strategies of resistance in which the workers utilize against management the very gendered and racialized logic that management uses against them. However, while these tactics may provide some temporary relief on the job, they build on racial and gender stereotypes which, in the long run, can be and are used against Third-World women.

Daughters, Wives, and Mothers: Migrant Women Workers in Britain

> Family businesses have been able to access minority women's labor power through mediations of kinship and an appeal to ideologies which emphasize the role of women in the home as wives and mothers and as keepers of family honor.[22]

In a collection of essays exploring the working lives of black and minority women inside and outside the home, Sallie Westwood and Parminder Bhachu focus on the benefits afforded the British capitalist state by the racial and gendered aspects of migrant women's labor. They point to the fact that what has been called the "ethnic economy" (the way migrants draw on resources to survive in situations where the combined effects of a hostile, racist environment and economic decline serve to oppress them) is also fundamentally a gendered economy. Statistics indicate that Afro-Caribbean and non-Muslim Asian women have a higher full-time labor participation rate than white women in the U.K. Thus, while the perception that black women (defined, in this case, as women of Afro-Caribbean, Asian, and African origin) are mostly concentrated in part-time jobs is untrue, the *forms* and *patterns* of their work lives within the context of homework and family firms, businesses where the entire family is involved in earning a living, either inside or outside the home bears examination. Work by British feminist scholars (Phizacklea 1983, Westwood 1984, 1988, Josephides 1988, and others) suggests that familial ideologies of domesticity and heterosexual marriage cement the economic and social exploitation of black women's labor within family firms. Repressive patriarchal ideologies, which fix the woman's role in the family, are grounded in inherited systems of inequality and oppression in Black women's cultures of origin. And these very ideologies are reproduced and consolidated in order to provide the glue for profit-making in the context of the racialized British capitalist state.

For instance, Annie Phizacklea's work on Bangladeshi homeworkers in the clothing industry in the English West Midlands illuminates the extent to which family and community ties, maintained by women, are crucial in allowing this domestic subcontracting in the clothing industry to undercut the competition in terms of wages and long work-days and its cost to women workers. In addition, Sallie Westwood's work on Gujarati women factory workers in the East Midlands hosiery industry suggests that the power and creativity of the shop-floor culture—which draws on cultural norms of femininity, masculinity and domesticity, while simultaneously generating resistance and solidarity among the Indian and white women workers—is, in fact, anchored in Gujarati cultural inheritances. Discussing the contradictions in the lives of Gujarati women within the home and the perception that male family members have of their work as an extension of their family roles (not as a path to financial independence), Westwood elaborates on the continuities between the ideologies of domesticity within the household, which are the result of (often repressive) indigenous cultural values and practices, and the culture of the shopfloor. Celebrating each other as daughers, wives, and mothers is one form of generating solidarity on the shopfloor—but it is also a powerful refeminization strategy, in Hossfeld's terms.

Finally, family businesses, which depend on the cultural and ideological resources and loyalties within the family to transform ethnic "minority" women into workers committed to common familial goals, are also anchored in women's roles as daughters, wives, mothers, and keepers of family honor (Josephides 1988, Bhachu 1998). Women's work in family business is unpaid and produces dependencies that are similar to those of homeworkers whose labor, although paid, is invisible. Both are predicated on ideologies of domesticity and womanhood which infuse the spheres of production and reproduction. In discussing Cypriot women in family firms, Sasha Josephides cites the use of familial ideologies of "honor" and the construction of a "safe" environment outside the public sphere as the bases for a definition of femininity and womanhood (the perfect corollary to a paternal, protective definition of masculinity) that allows Cypriot women to see themselves as workers for their family, rather than as workers for themselves. All conflict around the question of work is thus accommodated within the context of the family. This is an important instance of the privatization of work, and of the redefinition of the identity of women workers in family firms as doing work that is a "natural extension" of their familial duties (not unlike the lacemakers). It is their identity as mothers, wives, and family members that stands in for their identity as workers. Parminder Bhachu's work with Punjabi Sikhs also illustrates this fact. Citing the growth of small-scale entrepreneurship among South Asians as a relatively new trend in the British economy, Bhachu states that women workers in family businesses often end up losing autonomy and reenter more traditional forms of patriarchal dominance where men control all or most of the economic resources within the family: "By giving up work, these women not only lose an independent source of income, and a large network of often female colleagues, but they also find themselves sucked back into the kinship system which emphasizes patrilaterality."[23] Women thus lose a "direct relationship with the productive process," thus raising the issue of the invisibility (even to themselves) of their identity as workers.

This analysis of migrant women's work in Britain illustrates the parallel trajectory of their exploitation as workers within a different metropolitan context than the U.S. To summarize, all these case studies indicate ways in which ideologies of domesticity, femininity, and race form the basis of the construction of the notion of "women's work" for Third-World women in the contemporary economy. In the case of the lacemakers, this is done through the definition of homework as leisure time activity and of the workers themselves as housewives. As discussed earlier, indigenous hierarchies of gender and caste/class make this definition possible. In the case of the electronics workers, women's work is defined as unskilled, tedious, and supplementary activity for mothers and homemakers. It is a specifically American ideology of individual success, as well as local histories of race and ethnicity that constitute this definition. We can thus contrast the *invisibility* of the lacemakers as workers to the *temporary* nature of the work of Third-World women in the Silicon Valley. In the case of migrant women workers in family firms in Britain, work becomes an extension of familial roles and loyalties, and draws upon cultural and ethnic/racial ideologies of womanhood, domesticity, and entrepreneurship to consolidate patriarchal dependencies. In all these cases, ideas of *flexibility, temporality, invisibility,* and *domesticity* in the naturalization of categories of work are crucial in the construction of Third-World women as an appropriate and cheap labor force. All of the above ideas rest on stereotypes about gender, race, and poverty, which, in turn, characterize Third-World women as workers in the contemporary global arena.

Eileen Boris and Cynthia Daniels claim that "homework belongs to the decentralization of production that seems to be a central strategy of some sectors and firms for coping with the international restructuring of production, consumption, and capital accumulation."[24] Homework assumes a significant role in the contemporary capitalist global economy. The discussion of homework performed by Third-World women in the three geographical spaces discussed above—India, U.S.A., and Britain—suggests something specific about capitalist strategies of recolonization at this historical juncture. Homework emerged at the same time as factory work in the early nineteenth century in the U.S., and, as a system, it has always reinforced the conjoining of capitalism and patriarchy. Analyzing the homeworker as a wage laborer (rather than an entrepreneur who controls both her labor and the market for it) dependent on the employer for work which is carried out usually in the "home" or domestic premises, makes it possible to understand the *systematic* invisibility of this form of work. What allows this work to be so fundamentally exploitative as to be invisible as a form of work are ideologies of domesticity, dependency, and (hetero)sexuality, which designate women—in this case, Third-World women—as primarily housewives/mothers and men as economic supporters/breadwinners. Homework capitalizes on the equation of home, family, and patriarchial and racial/cultural ideologies of femininity/masculinity with work. This is work done at home, in the midst of doing housework, childcare, and other tasks related to "homemaking," often work that never ceases. Characterizations of "housewives," "mothers," and "homemakers" make it impossible to see homeworkers as workers earning regular wages and entitled to the rights of workers. Thus, not just their *production,* but homeworkers' *exploitation* as workers, can, in fact, also remain invisible, contained within domestic, patriarchal relations in the family. This is a form of work that often falls outside accounts of wage labor, as well as accounts of household dynamics.[25]

Family firms in Britain represent a similar ideological pattern, within a different class dynamic. Black women imagine themselves as entrepreneurs (rather than as wage laborers) working for the prosperity of their families in a racist society. However, the work they do is still seen as an extension of their familial roles and often creates economic and social dependencies. This does not mean that women in family firms never attain a sense of autonomy, but that, as a system, the operation of family business exploits Third-World women's labor by drawing on and reinforcing indigenous hierarchies in the search for upward mobility in the (racist) British capitalist economy. What makes this form of work in the contemporary global capitalist arena so profoundly exploitative is that its invisibility (both to the market, and sometimes to the workers themselves) is premised on deeply ingrained sexist and racist relationships within and outside heterosexual kinship systems. This is also the reason why changing the gendered relationships that anchor homework, and organizing homeworkers becomes such a challenge for feminists.

The analysis of factory work and family business in Britain and of homework in all three geographical locations raises the question of whether homework and factory work would be defined in these particular ways if the workers were single women. In this case, the construct of the *worker* is dependent on gender ideologies. In fact, the idea of work or labor as necessary for the psychic, material, and spiritual survival and development of women workers is absent. Instead, it is the identity of women as housewives, wives, and mothers (identities also defined outside the parameters of work) that is assumed to provide the basis for women's survival and growth. These Third-World women are defined out of the labor/capital process as if work in their case isn't necessary for economic, social, psychic autonomy, independency and self-determination—a nonalienated relation to work is a conceptual and practical impossibility in this situation.

Common Interests/Different Needs:
Collective Struggles of Poor Women Workers

Thus far, this essay has charted the ideological commonalities of the exploitation of (mostly) poor Third-World women workers by global capitalist economic processes in different geographical locations. The analysis of the continuities between factory work and homework in objectifying and domesticating Third-World women workers such that their very identity as *workers* is secondary to familial roles and identities, and predicated on patriarchal and racial/ethnic hierarchies anchored in local/indigenous *and* transnational processes of exploitation exposes the profound challenges posed in organizing women workers on the basis of common interests. Clearly, these women are not merely victims of colonizing, exploitative processes—the analysis of the case studies indicates different levels of consciousness of their own exploitation, different modes of resistance, and different understandings of the contradictions they face, and of their own agency as workers. While the essay thus far lays the groundwork for conceptualizing the common interests of women workers based on an understanding of shared location and needs, the analysis foregrounds processes of *repression* rather than forms of *opposition*. How have poor Third-World women organized as workers? How do we conceptualize the question of "common interests" based in a "common context of struggle," such that women are agents who make choices and decisions that lead to the transformation of consciousness and of their daily lives as workers?

As discussed earlier, with the current domination in the global arena of the arbitary interests of the market and of transnational capital, older signposts and definitions of capital/labor or of "the worker" or even of "class struggle" are no longer totally accurate or viable conceptual or organizational categories. It is, in fact, the predicament of poor working women and their experiences of survival and resistance in the creation of new organizational forms to earn a living and improve their daily lives that offers new possibilities for struggle and action.[26] In this instance, then, the experiences of Third-World women workers are relevant for understanding and transforming the work experiences and daily lives of poor women everywhere. The rest of this essay explores these questions by suggesting a working definition of the question of the common interests of Third-World women workers in the contemporary global capitalist economy, drawing on the work of feminist political theorist Anna G. Jonasdottir.

Jonasdottir explores the concept of women's interests in participatory democratic political theory. She emphasizes both the formal and the content aspects of a theory of social and political interests that refers to "different layers of social existence: agency and the needs/desires that give strength and meaning to agency."[27] Adjudicating between political analysts who theorize common inter-

ests in formal terms (i.e., the claim to actively "be among," to choose to participate in defining the terms of one's own existence, or acquiring the conditions for
choice), and those who reject the concept of interests in favor of the concept of
(subjective) individualized, and group-based "needs and desires," (the consequences of choice), Jonasdottir formulates a concept of the common interests of
women that emphasizes the former, but is a combination of both perspectives.
She argues that the formal aspect of interest (an active "being among") is crucial:
"Understood historically, and seen as emerging from people's lived experiences,
interests about basic processes of social life are divided systematically between
groups of people in so far as their living conditions are systematically different.
Thus, historically and socially defined, interests can be characterized as 'objective.'"[28] In other words, there are systematic material and historical bases for
claiming Third-World women workers have common interests. However, Jonasdottir suggests that the second aspect of theorizing interest, the satisfaction of
needs and desires (she distinguishes between agency and the result of agency)
remains an open question. Thus, the *content* of needs and desires from the point
of view of interest remains open for subjective interpretation. According to Jonasdottir, feminists can acknowledge and fight on the basis of the (objective) common interests of women in terms of active representation and choices to participate in a democratic polity, while at the same time not reducing women's common
interests (based on subjective needs and desires) to this formal "being among"
aspect of the question of interest. This theorization allows us to acknowledge common interests and potential agency on the basis of systematic aspects of social location and experience, while keeping open what I see as the deeper, more fundamental question of understanding and organizing around the needs, desires,
and choices (the question of critical, transformative consciousness) in order to
transform the material and ideological conditions of daily life. The latter has a
pedagogical and transformative dimension which the former does not.

How does this theorization relate to conceptualizations of the common interests of Third-World women workers? Jonasdottir's distinction between agency
and the result of agency is a very useful one in this instance. The challenges for
feminists in this arena are (a) understanding Third-World women workers as having objective interests in common as workers (they are thus agents and make
choices as workers); and (b) recognizing the contradictions and dislocations in
women's own consciousness of themselves as workers, and thus of their needs
and desires—which sometimes militate *against* organizing on the basis of their
common interests (the results of agency). Thus, work has to be done here in analyzing the links between the social location and the historical and current experiences of domination of Third-World women workers on the one hand, and in
theorizing and enacting the common *social identity* of Third-World women workers on the other. Reviewing the forms of collective struggle of poor, Third-World
women workers in relation to the above theorization of common interests provides a map of where we are in this project.

In the case of women workers in the free-trade zones in a number of countries, trade unions have been the most visible forum for expressing the needs and
demands of poor women. The sexism of trade unions, however, has led women

to recognize the need for alternative, more democratic organizational structures, and to form women's unions (as in Korea, China, Italy, and Malaysia)[29] or to turn to community groups, church committees, or feminist organizations. In the U.S., Third-World immigrant women in electronics factories have often been hostile to unions which they recognize as clearly modeled in the image of the white, male, working-class American worker. Thus, church involvement in immigrant women workers struggles has been an important form of collective struggle in the U.S.[30]

Women workers have developed innovative strategies of struggle in women's unions. For instance, in 1989, the Korean Women Workers Association staged an occupation of the factory in Masan. They moved into the factory and lived there, cooked meals, guarded the machines and premises, and effectively stopped production.[31] In this form of occupation of the work premises, the processes of daily life become constitutive of resistance (also evident in the welfare rights struggles in the U.S.A.) and opposition is anchored in the systematic realities of the lives of poor women. It expresses not only their common interests as workers, but acknowledges their social circumstance as *women* for whom the artificial separation of work and home has little meaning. This "occupation" is a strategy of collective resistance that draws attention to poor women worker's *building community* as a form of survival.

Kumudhini Rosa makes a similar argument in her analysis of the "habits of resistance" of women workers in Free Trade Zones (FTZ) in Sri Lanka, Malaysia, and the Philippines.[32] The fact that women live and work together in these FTZs is crucial in analyzing the ways in which they build community life, share resources and dreams, provide mutual support and aid on the assembly line and in the street, and develop individual and collective habits of resistance. Rosa claims that these forms of resistance and mutual aid are anchored in a "culture of subversion" in which women living in patriarchal, authoritarian households where they are required to be obedient and disciplined, acquire practice in "concealed forms of rebelling" (86). Thus, women workers engage in "spontaneous" strikes in Sri Lanka, "wildcat" strikes in Malaysia, and "sympathy" strikes in the Philippines. They also support each other by systematically lowering the production target, or helping slow workers to meet the production targets on assembly lines. Rosa's analysis illustrates recognition of the common interests of women workers at a formal "being among" level. While women are conscious of the contradictions of their daily lives as women and as workers, and enact their resistance, they have not organized actively to identify their collective needs and to transform the conditions of their daily lives.

While the earlier section on the ideological construction of work in terms of gender and racial/ethnic hierarchies discussed homework as one of the most acute forms of exploitation of poor Third-World women, it is also the area in which some of the most creative and transformative collective organizing has occurred. The two most visibly successful organizational efforts in this arena are the Working Women's Forum (WWF) and SEWA (Self Employed Women's Association) in India, both registered as independent trade unions, and focusing on incorporating homeworkers, as well as petty traders, hawkers, and laborers in the informal economy into their membership.[33]

There has also been a long history of organizing homeworkers in Britain. Discussing the experience of the West Yorkshire Homeworking Group in the late 1980s, Jane Tate states that "a homework campaign has to work at a number of levels, in which the personal interconnects with the political, the family situation with work, lobbying Parliament with small local meetings. . . . In practical terms, the homeworking campaigns have adopted a way of organizing that reflects the practice of many women's groups, as well as being influenced by the theory and practice of community work. It aims to bring out the strength of women, more often in small groups with a less formal structure and organization than in a body such as a union."[34] Issues of race, ethnicity, and class are central in this effort since most of the homeworkers are of Asian or Third-World origin. Tate identifies a number of simultaneous strategies used by the West Yorkshire Group to organize homeworkers: pinpointing and making visible the "real" employer (or the real enemy), rather than directing organizational efforts only against local subsidiaries; consumer education and pressure, which links the buying of goods to homeworker struggles; fighting for a code of work practice for suppliers by forming alliances between trade unions, women's, and consumer groups; linking campaigns to the development of alternative trade organizations (for instance, SEWA); fighting for visibility in international bodies like the ILO; and, finally, developing transnational links between local grass-roots homeworker organizations—thus, sharing resources, strategies, and working toward empowerment. The common interests of homeworkers are acknowledged in terms of their daily lives as workers and as women—there is no artificial separation of the "worker" and the "homemaker" or the "housewife" in this context. While the West Yorkshire Homeworking Group has achieved some measure of success in organizing homeworkers, and there is a commitment to literacy, consciousness-raising, and empowerment of workers, this is still a feminist group that organizes women workers (rather than the impetus for organization emerging from the workers themselves—women workers organizing). It is in this regard that SEWA and WWF emerge as important models for poor women workers organizations.

Swasti Mitter discusses the success of SEWA and WWF in terms of: (a) their representing the potential for organizing powerful women workers' organizations (the membership of WWF is 85,000 and that of SEWA is 46,000 workers) when effective strategies are used; and (b) making these "hidden" workers visible as *workers* to national and international policy makers. Both WWF and SEWA address the demands of poor women workers, and both include a development plan for women which includes leadership training, child care, women's banks, and producer's cooperatives which offer alternative trading opportunities. Renana Jhabvala, SEWA's secretary, explains that, while SEWA was born in 1972 in the Indian labor movement and drew inspiration from the women's movement, it always saw itself as a part of the cooperative movement, as well. Thus, struggling for poor women workers' rights always went hand-in-hand with strategies to develop alternative economic systems. Jhabvala states, "SEWA accepts the cooperative principles and sees itself as part of the co-operative movement attempting to extend these principles to the poorest women. . . . SEWA sees the need to bring poor women into workers' cooperatives. The co-operative structure has to be revitalised if they are to become truely workers' organizations, and thereby mobilise the strength of the co-operative movement in the task of organizing and strengthening poor women."[35] This emphasis on the extension of co-operative (or democratic) principles to poor women, the focus on political and legal literacy, education for critical and collective consciousness, and developing strategies for collective (and sometimes militant) struggle *and* for economic, social, and psychic development makes SEWA's project a deeply feminist, democratic, and transformative one. Self-employed women are some of the most disenfranchised in Indian society—they are vulnerable economically, in caste terms, physically, sexually, and in terms of their health, and, of course, they are socially and politically invisible. Thus, they are also one of the most difficult constituencies to organize. The simultaneous focus on collective struggle for equal rights and justice (struggle against) coupled with economic development on the basis of cooperative, democratic principles of sharing, education, self-reliance, and autonomy (struggle for) is what is responsible for SEWA's success at organizing poor, home-based, women workers. Jhabvala summarizes this when she says, "The combination of trade union and co-operative power makes it possible not only to defend members but to present an ideological alternative. Poor women's co-operatives are a new phenomenon. SEWA has a vision of the co-operative as a form of society which will bring about more equal relationships and lead to a new type of society."[36]

SEWA appears to come closest to articulating the common interests and needs of Third-World women workers in the terms that Jonasdottir elaborates. SEWA organizes on the basis of the objective interests of poor women workers—both the trade union and cooperative development aspect of the organizational strategies illustrate this. The status of poor women workers as workers and as citizens entitled to rights and justice is primary. But SEWA also approaches the deeper level of the articulation of needs and desires based on recognition of subjective, collective interests. As discussed earlier, it is this level of the recognition and articulation of common interest that is the challenge for women workers globally. While the common interests of women workers as *workers* have been variously articulated in the forms of struggles and organization reviewed above, the transition to identifying common needs and desires (the *content* aspect of interest) of Third-World women workers, which leads potentially to the construction of the *identity* of Third-World women workers, is what remains a challenge—a challenge that perhaps SEWA comes closest to identifying and addressing.

I have argued that the particular location of Third-World women workers at this moment in the development of global capitalism provides a vantage point from which to (a) make particular practices of domination and recolonization visible and transparent, thus illuminating the minute and global processes of capitalist recolonization of women workers, and (b) understand the commonalities of experiences, histories, and identity as the basis for solidarity and in organizing Third-World women workers transnationally. My claim, here, is that the definition of the social identity of women as workers is not only class-based, but, in fact, in this case, must be grounded in understandings of race, gender, and caste histories and experiences of work. In effect, I suggest that homework is one of the most significant, and repressive forms of "women's work" in contemporary global capitalism. In pointing to the ideology of the "Third-World woman worker" created in the context of a global division of labor, I am articulating differences located in specific histories of inequality, i.e., histories of gender and caste/class in the Narsapur context, and histories of gender, race, and liberal individualism in the Silicon Valley and in Britain.

However, my argument does not suggest that these are *discrete* and *separate* histories. In focusing on women's work as a particular form of Third-World women's exploitation in the contemporary economy, I also want to foreground a particular history that third- and first-world women seem to have in common: the logic and operation of capital in the contemporary global arena. I maintain that the interests of contemporary transnational capital and the strategies employed enable it to draw upon indigenous social hierarchies and to construct, reproduce, and maintain ideologies of masculinity/femininity, technological superiority, appropriate development, skilled/unskilled labor, etc. Here I have argued this in terms of the category of "women's work," which I have shown to be grounded in an ideology of the Third-World woman worker. Thus, analysis of the location of Third-World women in the new international division of labor must draw upon the histories of colonialism and race, class and capitalism, gender and patriarchy, and sexual and familial figurations. The analysis of the ideological definition and redefinition of women's work thus indicates a political basis for common struggles and it is this particular forging of the political unity of Third-World women workers that I would like to endorse. This is in opposition to ahistorical notions of the common experience, exploitation, or strength of Third-World women or between third- and first-world women, which serve to naturalize normative Western feminist categories of self and other. If Third-World women are to be seen as the *subjects of theory and of struggle*, we must pay attention to the specificities of their/our common *and* different histories.

In summary, this essay highlights the following analytic and political issues pertaining to Third-World women workers in the global arena: (1) it writes a particular group of women workers into history and into the operation of contemporary capitalist hegemony; (2) it charts the links and potential for solidarity between women workers across the borders of nation-states based on demystifying the ideology of the masculinized worker; (3) it exposes a domesticated definition of Third-World women's work to be in actuality a strategy of global capitalist recolonization; (4) it suggests that women have common interests as workers, not just in transforming their work lives and environments, but in redefining home spaces so that homework is recognized as work to earn a living rather than as leisure of supplemental activity; (5) it foregrounds the need for feminist liberatory knowledge as the basis of feminist organizing and collective struggles for economic and political justice; (6) it provides a working definition of the common interests of Third-World women workers based on theorizing the common social identity of Third-World women as women/workers; and finally, (7) it reviews the habits of resistance, forms of collective struggle, and strategies of organizing of poor, Third-World women workers. Irma is right when she says that "the only way to get a little measure of power over your own life is to do it collectively, with the support of other people who share your needs." The question of defining common interests and needs such that the identity of Third-World women workers forms a potentially revolutionary basis for struggles against capitalist recolonization, and for feminist self-determination and autonomy, is a complex one. However, as maquiladora worker Veronica Vasquez and the women in SEWA demonstrate, women are already waging such struggles. The end of the twentieth century may be characterized by the exacerbation of the sexual politics of global capitalist domination and exploitation, but it is also suggestive of the dawning of a renewed politics of hope and solidarity.

Notes

1. See Karen Hossfeld, "United States: Why Aren't High-Tech Workers Organised?"—in Women Working Worldwide, eds., *Common Interests: Women Organising in Global Electronics* (London: Tavistock), pp. 33–52, esp. pp. 50–51.
2. See "Tijuanans Sue in L.A. after Their Maquiladora Is Closed," by Sandra DriShle, in *The San Diego Union-Tribune*, Friday, December 16, 1994. The Support Committee for Maquiladora Workers promotes cross-border organizing against corporate impunity. This is a San Diego-based volunteer effort of unionists, community activists, and others to assist workers in building autonomous organizations and facilitating ties between Mexican and U.S. workers. The Committee, which is coordinated by Mary Tong, also sees its task as educating U.S. citizens about the realities of life, work, and efforts for change among maquiladora workers. For more information write the Support Committee at 3909 Centre St., #210, San Diego, CA 92103.
3. See my essay, "Cartographies of Struggle: Third World Women and the Politics of Feminism," in Mohanty, Russo, and Torres, eds. *Third World Women and the Politics of Feminism* (Bloomington: Indiana University Press, 1991), especially p. 39, where I identified five provisional historical, political, and discursive junctures for understanding Third-World feminist politics: "decolonization and national liberation movements in the third world, the consolidation of white, liberal capitalist patriarchies in Euro-America, the operation of multinational capital within a global economy, . . . anthropology as an example of a discourse of dominance and self-reflexivity, . . . (and) storytelling or autobiography (the practice of writing) as a discourse of oppositional consciousness and agency." This essay represents a continuation of one part of this project: the operation of multinational capital and the location of poor Third-World women workers.
4. See the excellent analysis in Teresa L. Amott and Julie A. Matthaei, *Race, Gender and Work: A Multicultural Economic History of Women in the United States* (Boston: South End Press, 1991), esp. pp. 22–23.
5. See Bagguley, Mark-Lawson, Shapiro, Urry, Walby, and Warde, *Restructuring: Place, Class and Gender* (London: Sage Publications, 1990)
6. Joan Smith has argued, in a similar vein, for the usefulness of a world-systems-theory approach (seeing the various economic and social hierarchies and national divisions around the globe as part of a singular systematic division of labor, with multiple parts, rather than as plural and autonomous national systems) which incorporates the notion of the "household" as integral to understanding the profoundly gendered character of

this systemic division of labor. While her analysis is useful in historicizing and analyzing the idea of the household as the constellation of relationships that makes the transfer of wealth possible across age, gender, class, and national lines, the ideologies of masculinity, femininity, and heterosexuality that are internal to the concept of the household are left curiously intact in her analysis—as are differences in understandings of the household in different cultures. In addition, the impact of domesticating ideologies in the sphere of production, in constructions of "women's work" are also not addressed in Smith's analysis. While I find this version of the world-systems approach useful, my own analysis attempts a different series of connections and theorizations. See Joan Smith, "The Creation of the World We Know: The World Economy and the Re-creation of Gendered Identities," in V. Moghadam, ed., *Identity Politics and Women: Cultural Reassertions in International Perspective* (Boulder: Westview Press, 1994), pp. 27–41

7. The case studies I analyze are: Maria Mies, *The Lacemakers of Narsapur, Indian Housewives Produce for the World Market* (London: Zed Press, 1982); Naomi Katz and David Kemnitzer, "Fast Forward: the Internationalization of the Silicon Valley," in June Nash and M. P. Fernandez-Kelly, *Women, Men, and the International Division of Labor* (Albany: SUNY Press, 1983), pp. 273–331; Katz and Kemnitzer, "Women and Work in the Silicon Valley," in Karen Brodkin Sacks, *My Troubles Are Going to Have Trouble with Me: Everyday Trials and Triumphs of Women Workers* (New Brunswick, N.J.: Rutgers University Press, 1984), pp. 193–208; and Karen J. Hossfeld, "Their Logic Against Them": Contradictions in Sex, Race, and Class in the Silicon Valley," in Kathryn Ward, ed., *Women Workers and Global Restructuring* (Ithaca: Cornell University Press, 1990), pp. 149–178. I also draw on case studies of Black women workers in the British context in Sallie Westwood and Parminder Bhachu, eds., *Enterprising Women* (New York: Routledge, 1988).

8. See my discussion of "relations of rule" in "Cartographies." There has been an immense amount of excellent feminist scholarship on women and work and women and multinationals in the last decade. In fact, it is this scholarship which makes my argument possible. Without the analytic and political insights and analyses of scholars like Aihwa Ong, Maria Patricia Fernandez-Kelly, Lourdes Beneria and Martha Roldan, Maria Mies, Swasti Mitter, and Sallie Westwood, among others, my attempt to understand and stitch together the lives and struggles of women workers in different geographical spaces would be sharply limited. This essay builds on arguments offered by some of these scholars, while attempting to move beyond particular cases to an integrated analysis which is not the same as the world-systems model. See especially Nash and Fernandez-Kelly, *Women, Men and the International Division of Labor;* Ward, ed., *Women Workers and Global Restructuring; Review of Radical Political Economics vol. 23,* no. 3–4, (Fall/Winter 1991) special issue on "Women in the International Economy"; Harriet Bradley, *Men's Work Women's Work* (Minneapolis: University of Minnesota Press, 1989); Lynne Brydon and Sylvia Chant, *Women in the Third World: Gender Issues in Rural and Urban Areas* (New Brunswick, N.J.: Rutgers University Press, 1989).

9. See Ella Shohat and Robert Stam, *Unthinking Eurocentrism: Multiculturalism and the Media* (London and New York: Routledge, 1994), esp. pp. 25–27. In a discussion of the analytic and political problems involved in using terms like "Third World," Shohat and Stam draw attention to the adoption of "third world" at the 1955 Bandung Conference of "nonaligned" African and Asian nations, an adoption which was premised on the solidarity of these nations around the anticolonial struggles in Vietnam and Algeria. This is the genealogy of the term that I choose to invoke here.

10. My understanding and appreciation of the links between location, experience, and so-

cial identity in political and intellectual matters grows out of numerous discussions with Satya Mohanty See, especially his essay, "Colonial Legacies, Multicultural Futures: Relativism, Objectivity, and the Challenge of Otherness," in *PMLA* (January 1995), pp. 108–117. See also Paula Moya's essay in this collection for further discussion of these issues.

11. Karen Brodkin Sacks, "Introduction," in Karen Brodkin Sacks and D. Remy, eds., *My Troubles Are Going to Have Trouble with Me,* esp. pp. 10–11.

12. Jeremy Brecher, "The Hierarch's New World Order—and Ours," in Jeremy S. Brecher et al., eds., *Global Visions Beyond the New World Order* (Boston: South End Press, 1993), pp. 3–12.

13. See Maria Mies, *Patriarchy and Accumulation on a World Scale: Women in the International Division of Labor* (London: Zed Press, 1986), pp. 114–15.

14. Richard J. Barnet and John Cavanagh, *Global Dreams: Imperial Corporations and the New World Order* (New York: Simon and Shuster, 1994), esp. pp. 25–41.

15. For examples of cross-national feminist organizing around these issues, see the following texts: Gita Sahgal and Nira Yuval Davis, eds., *Refusing Holy Orders: Women and Fundamentalism in Britain* (London: Virago, 1992); Valentine M. Moghadam, *Identity Politics and Women: Cultural Reassertions and Feminisms in International Perspective* (Boulder: Westview Press, 1994); *Claiming Our Place: Working the Human Rights System to Women's Advantage* (Washington, D.C.: Institute for Women, Law and Development, 1993); Sheila Rowhotham and Swasti Mitter, eds., *Dignity and Daily Bread: New Forms of Economic Organizing Among Poor Women in the Third World and the First* (New York: Routledge, 1994); and Julie Peters and Andrea Wolper, eds., *Women's Rights Human Rights: International Feminist Perspectives* (New York: Routledge, 1995).

16. Amott and Matthaei, eds., *Race, Gender, and Work,* pp. 316–17.

17. Women Working Worldwide, *Common Interests,* ibid.

18. Aihwa Ong's discussion of the various modes of surveillance of young Malaysian factory women as a way of discursively producing and constructing notions of feminine sexuality is also applicable in this context, where "single" and "married" assume powerful connotations of sexual control. See Aihwa Ong, *Spirits of Resistance and Capitalist Discipline: Factory Women in Malaysia* (Albany: SUNY Press, 1987).

19. Hossfeld, "Their Logic Against Them," p. 149. Hossfeld states that she spoke to workers from at least thirty Third-World nations (including Mexico, Vietnam, the Philippines, Korea, China, Cambodia, Laos, Thailand, Malaysia, Indonesia, India, Pakistan, Iran, Ethiopia, Haiti, Cuba, El Salvador, Nicaragua, Guatemala, Venezuela, as well as southern Europe, especially Portugal and Greece). It may be instructive to pause and reflect on the implications of this level of racial and national diversity on the shop floor in the Silicon Valley. While all these workers are defined as "immigrants," a number of them as recent immigrants, the racial, ethnic, and gender logic of capitalist strategies of recolonization in this situation locate all the workers in similar relationships to the management, as well as to the U.S. state.

20. Assembly lines in the Silicon Valley are often divided along race, ethnic, and gender lines, with workers competing against each other for greater productivity. Individual worker choices, however imaginative or ambitious, do not transform the system. Often they merely undercut the historically won benefits of the metropolitan working class. Thus, while moonlighting, overtime, and job-hopping are indications of individual modes of resistance, and of an overall strategy of class mobility, it is these very aspects of worker's choices which supports an underground domestic economy which evades or circumvents legal, institutionalized, or contractual arrangements that add to the indirect wages of workers.

21. Hossfeld, "Their Logic Against Them," p. 149: "You're paid less because women are different than men" or "Immigrants need less to get by."

22. Westwood and Bhachu, "Introduction," *Enterprising Women*, p. 5. See also, in the same collection, Anilie Phizacklea, "Entrepreneurship, Ethnicity and Gender," pp. 20–33; Parminder Bhachu, "Apni Marzi Kardhi, Home and Work: Sikh Women in Britain," pp. 76–102; Sallie Westwood, "Workers and Wives: Continuities and Discontinuities in the Lives of Guiarati Women, pp. 103–.31; and Sasha Josephides, "Honor, Family, and Work: Greek Cypriot Women Before and After Migration," pp. 34–57.

23. P. Bhachu, "Apni Marzi Kardhi, Home and Work," p. 85

24. For a thorough discussion of the history and contemporary configurations of homework in thc U.S., see Eileen Boris and Cynthia R. Daniels, eds., *Homework, Historical and Contemporary Perspectives on Paid Labor at Home* (Urbana: University of Illinois Press, 1989). See especially the "Introduction," pp. 1–12; M. Patricia Fernandez-Kelly and Anna Garcia, "Hispanic Women and Homework: Women in the Informal Economy of Miami and Los Angeles," pp. 165–82; and Sheila Allen, "Locating Homework in an Analysis of the Ideological and Material Constraints on Women's Paid Work," pp. 272–91.

25. Allen, "Locating Homework."

26. See Rowbotham and Mitter, "Introduction," in Rowbotham and Mitter, eds., *Dignity and Daily Bread.*

27. Anna G. Jonasdottir, "On the Concept of Interest, Women's Interests, and the Limitations of Interest Theory," in Kathleen Jones and Anna G. Jonasdottir, eds., *The Poltical Interests of Gender* (London: Sage Publications, 1988), pp. 33–65, esp. p. 57.

28. Ibid., p. 41.

29. See Women Working Worldwide, eds., *Common Interests.*

30. Ibid., p. 38.

31. Ibid., p. 31.

32. Kumudhini Rosa, "The Conditions and Organizational Activities of Women in Free Trade Zones: Malaysia, Philippines and Sri Lanka, 1970–1990," in Rowbotham and Mitter, eds., *Dignity and Daily Bread,* pp. 73–99, esp. p. 86.

33. Swasti Mitter, "On Organizing Women in Causualized Work: A Global Overview," in Rowbotham and Mitter, eds., *Dignity and Daily Bread,* pp. 14–52, esp. p. 33.

34. Jane Tate, "Homework in West Yorkshire, " in Rowbotham and Mitter, eds., *Dignity and Daily Bread,* pp. 193–217, esp. p. 203.

35. Renana Jhabvala, "Self-employed Women's Associations: Organizing Women by Struggle and Development," in Rowbotham and Mitter, eds., *Dignity and Daily Bread,* pp. 114–38, esp. p. 116.

36. Ibid., p. 135.